PRINCIPLES OF ECONOMICS: AN IRISH TEXTBOOK

Gerard Turley

and

Maureen Maloney

---

with contributions from

Eithne Murphy

GILL & MACMILLAN

Gill & Macmillan Ltd
Goldenbridge
Dublin 8
with associated companies throughout the world

www.gillmacmillan.ie

© Gerard Turley, Maureen Maloney 1997
Chapter 7 and 15.3 © Eithne Murphy 1997

0 7171 2509 2

Index compiled by Helen Litton
Print origination by Carrigboy Typesetting Services, Co. Cork
Printed by ColourBooks Ltd, Dublin

A catalogue record is available for this book from the British Library.

To my mother and the memory of my father
G.T.

To my parents
M.M.

CONTENTS

PREFACE

'Normality is a fiction of economic textbooks.'

Joan Robinson (1903–1983)

In 1948 the first mass-produced 'modern' textbook in economics was published. Since then, Paul Samuelson's *Economics* has sold millions of copies, being translated into over forty languages with fifteen editions. Many others, on both sides of the Atlantic, have tried to follow Samuelson's success. By the 1990s over fifty major introductory textbooks were available. American textbooks were soon adapted in order to meet the particular demands of the European market (Parkin and King's *Economics*, for example). European texts have also become popular (Burda and Wyplosz's *Macroeconomics: A European Text*, for example).

An economics textbook for the Irish third-level market is not a new idea. In the 1920s the Educational Company of Ireland published *A Groundwork of Economics*, written by Joseph Johnston. Macmillan & Co. Ltd published an Irish edition of a well-established British textbook in 1963. It was called *Textbook of Economic Analysis* and was written by Edward Nevin. At a more advanced level, Desmond Norton wrote *Economic Analysis for an Open Economy: Ireland* which was published by the Irish Management Institute in 1980. A second textbook by Norton, entitled *Economics for an Open Economy: Ireland* was published in 1994. An intermediate macroeconomic textbook, *The Macroeconomy of Ireland* by Brendan Walsh and Anthony Leddin is in its third edition since 1990. Other introductory textbooks in economics by Irish authors include *Economics* by Noel Palmer, *Economics for Irish Students* by Murphy & Ryan and *Economics* by Seán Nagle.

Notwithstanding these welcome developments on the publishing front, we believe that there is a need for an introductory third-level economics textbook. We hope that this book fills that gap. It covers the basic theory of both microeconomics and macroeconomics in a user-friendly way. Students are introduced to economic terminology and concepts. We attempt to reinforce these ideas by applying them in 'case studies' drawn from a number of sources including journals, newspapers, policy documents and CSO publications. An Irish section is included in each of the macroeconomic chapters. Wherever possible, we have used current national data.

Additional case studies and a wide range of questions (and answers) conclude each chapter. It was our intention to provide a 'complete' text, not requiring supplements. We hope that readers will find this useful, challenging and a welcome addition to the existing stock of economic textbooks already on the market.

ACKNOWLEDGMENTS

This book was made possible because of the large number of people who assisted us at different stages. We want to thank the members of the Department of Economics in University College Galway. In particular, we owe a special thanks to Tom Boylan, Michael Cuddy, Aidan Kane, Michael Keane, Terry McDonough, Eithne Murphy, Diarmuid Ó Cearbhaill, Joan O'Connell and Eamon O'Shea. Your contributions were invaluable.

We want to thank the staff of the Shannon College of Hotel Management and especially Joe McDonnell and Phillip Smyth for all their help and guidance.

Thanks to Imelda and Claire for your patience, to Gráinne for your assistance and to Siobhán, Pat, Matthew and Anthony for your 'moral' support.

We wish to acknowledge the assistance provided by many of the staff members of the UCG library. We wish to say a special word of thanks to Maeve Doyle and Mary Guckian.

There are many people from other institutions who have provided us with valuable information. To the staff members of the Central Bank of Ireland and the Central Statistics Office who assisted us, we are very grateful.

We pay tribute to the staff of Gill & Macmillan and, in particular, Ailbhe and Gabrielle. You were more than helpful at all stages throughout the writing of this book.

We wish to thank all of the academic staff members from the different third level institutions who were involved in reviewing this book. Your comments and suggestions were instrumental in making those drafts 'publishable'. A special word of thanks must go to Dr Francis O'Toole from Trinity College, Dublin. Your combination of humour and critical insight provided us with a welcome source of guidance.

The students of UCG, Shannon College of Hotel Management and St Angela's College in Sligo inspired us to write this textbook. For this and much more we thank you, one and all. We send a special note of thanks to the first B.A. (Social and Community Studies) students of St Angela's College who used an early draft as their text. You contributed enormously to the revision of this book.

Finally, we owe a massive debt of gratitude to the people who 'suffered' most during the past three years – our families, and in particular, Monica and Ellie. You, more than anybody else, deserve credit for 'putting up' with us.

We bear full responsibility for all errors and omissions.

G.T. and M.M.

AN INTRODUCTION TO ECONOMICS

'Economics is the science of economising.'[1]

John E. Maher

'What is lacking [in economics] is any effective means of communication between abstract theory and concrete application.'[2]

Barbara Wootton

'If all economists were laid end to end, they would not reach a conclusion.'[3]

George Bernard Shaw

The origins of Economics

The word 'economics' is derived from the Greek word *oikonomeo* which literally means 'to manage a household'. It comes from Xenophon's treatise on management and leadership, the *Oeconomicus*. The study of economics in modern times dates back to 1776 with the publication of *An Inquiry into the Nature and Causes of the Wealth of Nations*. Its author, Adam Smith, is acknowledged to be the founding father of modern economic science. Although once taught in conjunction with philosophy, jurisprudence and politics, economics has developed into a separate discipline.

Economists like David Ricardo, Alfred Marshall, Karl Marx, John Maynard Keynes, Joseph Schumpeter, Milton Friedman, John Kenneth Galbraith and many others have contributed enormously to its development throughout the years. Economic issues affect our daily lives. As for the economics profession, it was J. M. Keynes who once said 'For the next twenty-five years in my belief, economists, at present the most incompetent, will be nevertheless the most important, group of scientists in the world. And it is to be hoped – if they are successful – that after that they will never be important again.'[4] How accurate was he? The rest of this textbook will hopefully provide you with some answers to this and many other questions.

Scarcity, choice and opportunity cost

Economics is concerned with making choices in the face of scarcity under conditions of uncertainty (see Information Box 1). By 'scarcity' we mean that the world's resources are finite. On the other hand, people's wants are unlimited. We are forced to choose between alternative uses. In choosing, a cost is incurred. We call this the opportunity cost. It is one of the most powerful ideas in economics.

Definition
● ● ● ● ● ●

The opportunity cost of an activity is measured in terms of the highest valued alternative forgone.

That is a rather laborious way of saying that if you spend £5 for a ticket to the cinema, you preferred that option to drinking a couple of pints at the pub, or buying a book, or going to the theatre – these are all alternative ways to spend your £5. If the choice on the day was between the cinema and the pub, the opportunity cost of your trip to the cinema was a visit to the pub.

INFORMATION BOX 1

A brief 'Quotations' guide to economics

James B. Ramsey once described economics as 'the academic discipline most discussed by the general public. It is also one of the least understood.'[1]
What exactly is meant by 'Economics'? How different a discipline is it compared to other social sciences? Why does it provoke so much debate and controversy? Is it really 'the dismal science'?[2] Or, is it simply 'the science of greed'?[3]
Alfred Marshall and Lionel Robbins (two distinguished economists) have supplied us with two of the better definitions of economics. They are as follows:

' . . . Economics is the study of mankind in the ordinary business of life; it examines that part of individual and social action which is most closely connected with the attainment and with the use of the material requisites of wellbeing.'[4]

'Economics is a science which studies human behaviour as a relationship between ends and scarce means which have alternative uses.'[5]

Other memorable quotations as they relate to economics, economists and the economy are reproduced below.

Economics
'Economics isn't fair.' Anonymous
'In economics, everything depends on everything else — and in more than one way.' Anonymous
'Who put the con in economics?' Anonymous

Economists
'Please find me a one-armed economist so we will not always hear "On the other hand . . . "' Herbert Hoover (attributed)
'Economists, indeed, seem never in danger of unemployment, because, while new problems are constantly arising, old ones are never settled.' Warren B. Catlin (The Progress of Economics)

'It takes a fully qualified economist, dripping with academic distinction and armed with enough computerised economic models to sink the Titanic (or, indeed, given the amount of compressed hot air involved, to raise it), to fail to recognise a mature elephant at 10 yards in broad daylight.' Peter Jay (The Times)

Economy

'Economy is the art of making the most of life.' George Bernard Shaw (Maxims for Revolutionists)

We finish this selection of quotations with some light humour.
　'Do you have anything on economics?', asked a colleague in his local bookshop. *'Over there,'* replied the assistant, *'beyond fiction.'* [6]
　Sure, wasn't it the economist who suggested that there is only need for two Nobel prizes, one for economics and the other for fiction?

1 James B. Ramsey, Economic Forecasting; Models or Markets?, *Institute of Economic Affairs*, 1977.
2 Thomas Carlyle, 'The Nigger Question' in Critical and Miscellaneous Essays, *Thomas Carlyle's Works, The Ashburton Editions; Chapman and Hall, 1885/88.* It was the title of a pamphlet written by Carlyle.
3 F. V. Meyer (attributed).
4 Alfred Marshall, Principles of Economics, 8th ed., *Macmillan*, 1920.
5 Lionel Robbins, An Essay on the Nature and Significance of Economic Science, *3rd edition, Macmillan*, 1984.
6 Anonymous. Quoted in 'Men and Matters', *Financial Times, 9 November 1981.*

Efficiency versus equity

Economists are not as interested in the choice itself (cinema vs pub) as they are in whether or not that choice is 'efficient'. There are different types of efficiency.

Allocative efficiency means that it is impossible to redistribute resources in a way which will make one person better off without making another person worse off.

Productive efficiency means that the goods are produced using the least costly technique.

Efficiency does not imply that the distribution of goods and services is equitable or fair. The aims of economic efficiency and social equity are sometimes perceived as incompatible. Some economists believe that their role deals exclusively with issues concerning efficiency; others are more concerned with equity and distribution. The tension between the contrasting views is a theme running consistently through the economic literature. It is our hope that the economist can help to strike a balance between society's objectives which are at times a source of competition and of conflict.

The production possibility frontier

The resource problem and the choices that accompany it can be illustrated by means of a production possibility frontier (PPF).

Definition
●●●●●●

The production possibility frontier (PPF) shows all possible combinations of two goods that can be produced using the available technology and all available resources.

As an example we will consider an economy where only bottles and bananas are produced. Table 1 records some of the possible combinations of the two goods that can be produced given the resources available and the technology applied.

Table 1: Production possibilities

Combination	bottles	bananas (in pounds)
a	9	0
b	8	5
c	6	10
d	3	13
e	0	15

Points a and e reflect the two extreme cases where production of only one good takes place; nine bottles are produced at point a, fifteen pounds of bananas are produced at point e. At all other points some combination of the two goods is produced. Eight bottles and five pounds of bananas are produced at point b. At point c six bottles and ten pounds of bananas are produced. The production of three bottles and thirteen pounds of bananas is shown at point d.

It is customary to measure the units of the two goods involved on the vertical and the horizontal axis. The quantity of bottles is measured on the vertical axis and the quantity of bananas per pound is measured on the horizontal axis. This is represented in Figure 1.

Figure 1: The production possibility frontier (PPF)

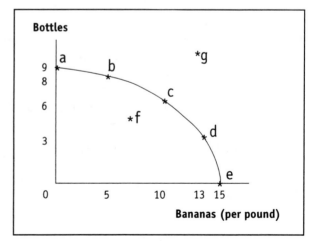

All points in the space represent different combinations of the two goods. A number of different possibilities exist. Combinations of the two goods which are found inside the curve are said to be attainable but inefficient. They are wasteful because resources are being used inefficiently or because some resources are lying idle. Point f, a combination of five bottles and seven pounds of bananas, is an example of an attainable but inefficient combination.

All points outside the curve are unattainable. Point g represents a combination of eleven bottles and twelve pounds of bananas. This combination of goods cannot be produced because the economy's resources and technology are limited.

Points along the curve represent attainable and efficient combinations. This locus of points forms the production possibility frontier. It shows the possible combinations of the two goods that can be produced when all the resources are fully and efficiently employed. Points a through to e are examples of productively efficient and attainable combinations. The PPF in Figure 1 is non-linear and concave.

Moving from one point on the PPF to another point involves an opportunity cost; units of one good (bananas) have to be given up in order to produce more of another good (bottles). For example, suppose that we move from point a to point b. At point a, only nine bottles are produced. At point b, the economy can produce five pounds of bananas and eight bottles. The opportunity cost of five pounds of bananas is one bottle. Alternatively, we gave up one bottle to produce five pounds of bananas.

It is evident from Table 1 above that the opportunity cost varies with the quantity of the goods produced. The first five pounds of bananas 'cost' one bottle. The second five pounds of bananas 'cost' two bottles. The next three pounds of bananas 'cost' three bottles. The last two pounds of bananas 'cost' three bottles. According to this table, the opportunity cost of producing additional units of bananas increases as we produce more bananas.

In fact, we believe that an increasing opportunity cost will generally be observed, regardless of the goods which we compare. Why? Although the factors of production are fully employed anywhere along the frontier, they are not equally productive. For example, if we move from point a to point b on the frontier, we will take the least suitable, and therefore the least productive resources away from the production of bottles and devote them to the production of bananas. As we move down the frontier, resources which were more productive in producing bottles are diverted to the production of bananas. The opportunity cost of producing additional units of bananas increases. Finally, at point e on the frontier, only bananas are produced, using all the resources of the economy, regardless of how poorly suited they are to this type of production.

Because the opportunity cost is increasing, the shape of the production possibility frontier is concave, or bowed out. Regardless of which good we consider, the opportunity cost of producing that good increases as we produce more of it.

The production possibility frontier is determined by resources and technology. If either of these change, so does the position of the PPF. For example, if an improved fertiliser is discovered, we can produce more bananas. We can show this by extending the PPF along the horizontal axis. With additional machines, we can produce more bottles. This extends the PPF along the vertical axis. An improvement in the education and training of our labour force could shift the PPF at both axis. Continuous outward shifts of the production possibility frontier is what economists refer to as economic growth. This is one useful application of the PPF.

In brief, the PPF is a diagrammatic representation of what an economy is capable of producing. At any point along the PPF, we can determine how resources are allocated between the two goods. However, we do not know which particular combination of the two goods will be produced in the economy.

Alternative economic systems

In order for the limited resources to be allocated, exchange occurs. Exchange links the activities of production and consumption. Exchange is possible through a 'market' system. We can think of a market as an arrangement whereby the consumer and the producer negotiate a price. In our two-good economy, negotiating prices will help us to determine the value that the residents in our economy place on these two goods. Once we have established the relative prices, we will be able to determine the level of production and allocate the amount of resources needed to produce each good. Allowing prices to allocate resources is a central feature of the market system. Private property rights and self-interested behaviour are other features of a market system.

Proponents of capitalism believe that the market system is generally efficient and relatively equitable. The state can intervene in the event of a market failure.

Alternatively, the state can be involved in all aspects of the production and the distribution process. This occurs in a planned economy, the opposite end of the economic spectrum. Public ownership of economic resources and industry is a common feature of the planned economy. The economy of the former Soviet Union featured extensive control by the state over labour, raw materials and technology. A centralised authority decided what was produced, how it was produced and who received it.

Most economies are mixed, combining elements of the market and the planned economy. In a mixed economy production is undertaken by the public sector and the private sector.

Three fundamental questions

There are three fundamental questions in economics which require explanations. They are

1. What? What goods are to be produced and in what quantities? This is an 'allocation' problem.
2. How? How should these goods and services be produced? Should production be labour-intensive or capital-intensive? This is a 'production' problem.
3. For whom? Who shall receive these goods and services? This is a problem of 'distribution'.

Most problems in economics can be reduced to these three areas. Moreover, an economy is a mechanism through which the decisions about What?, How? and For whom to produce? are made.

Microeconomics and macroeconomics

Since the 1930s it has become customary to divide the study of economics into micro-economics and macroeconomics.[5] Microeconomics and macroeconomics provide two perspectives from which the reader can view the economy. Microeconomics focuses on the individual decision-making units whereas macroeconomics concentrates on the economic system as a whole.[6]

Microeconomics deals with specific units and markets: a consumer, a firm, the market for beef, a state monopoly and so on. Macroeconomics is concerned with aggregates: national output, the general price level, total employment and so on. Microeconomics is a bottom-up view of the economy: macroeconomics is a top-down view of the economy. Yet microeconomics and macroeconomics can be viewed as two sides to the same coin. An analogy that is commonly used is that of the trees and the forest: the former is viewed as micro and the latter is viewed as macro. Another common analogy is that of the microscope and the telescope. It is left to the reader to work out this analogy!

The role of economic theory

A science is a classified body of knowledge. The social sciences study various aspects of human behaviour. Economics is considered to be a social science along with psychology, political science and sociology. One thing that distinguishes economics from the other social sciences is the way that the analysis is organised. Economic methodology is more akin to the natural sciences than the social sciences.

The main tool used by economists to understand economic events is a model. A model is a logical structure designed to determine the relationship between variables in order to explain the events that we observe. A model is a simplification of reality: it is not designed to fully explain a phenomenon, but hopefully it will identify the most important variables and the links between variables.

For example, we may observe that there are unusually high crime rates in places where there are large numbers of unemployed. There are a number of ways in which the unemployed and the crime rate may be related. First, the unemployed might commit the crimes. Second, the unemployed may be the victims of crime. Third, the unemployed might be more likely to use drugs than the rest of the population and the crime rate may be drug-related. Fourth, the simultaneous occurrence of both variables may be completely coincidental; they may be completely unrelated.

Figure 2 shows the procedure used to develop most economic theories.

Figure 2: Building an economic theory

First, the problem is identified. Next, certain assumptions are made. These are statements which are accepted as true, without proof. For example, when discussing the PPF, we assumed that neither the resources nor the technology were changing. While these assumptions make our model less realistic, they simplify the analysis. Assumptions allow us to proclaim that only the variables which we are considering are relevant. Next the economist develops the model and gathers data to test the model. If the data supports the model, the model is corroborated. If a model is validated, the researcher feels confident that he can use the model to predict the future. If the data does not support the theory, the researcher must re-examine the model. Perhaps he has used the wrong variables or the data may be of poor quality.

There are obvious criticisms to this approach. The models which we have described are called deductive models: we begin with the theory and then test it with data. Many are sceptical of this approach. One famous critic is Sir Arthur Conan Doyle who once said, 'It is a capital mistake to theorise before one has data. Insensibly one begins to twist facts to suit the theories, instead of theories to suit facts.'[7] He was obviously an advocate of inductive modelling where we begin with the data and attempt to explain the relationship between variables. This type of modelling is used by some economists, but it is not the norm.

Also, economic research is not conducted under laboratory conditions. The economic environment is constantly changing. An economist's response to this criticism is that a model does not have to mirror reality in order to be valid. The most important criterion for success in terms of modelling is the predictive power of a model. An economist who develops an 'elegant' economic model, one which predicts accurately using only a few variables, is the envy of his or her peers!

Why study economics in Ireland in the 1990s and beyond

Economics affects our daily lives in countless ways. It impinges on the numerous decisions that we make – buying a car or a house, saving, exercising, eating and so on. Important national issues like unemployment, taxation, poverty, crime and European Union have at least one feature in common – their connection to economics. Most of the big news stories of the past decade have had an economic dimension to them – the Gulf Crisis, the break-up of the Russian empire, the currency crisis, the prospect of peace in former Yugoslavia and the troubles in Northern Ireland.

An understanding of the principles of economics has never been more important. Economics is not, and should never be left to economists. Everyone has a vested interest in this discipline. In the words of Joan Robinson, 'The purpose of studying economics is not to acquire a set of ready-made answers to economic questions, but to learn how to avoid being deceived by economists.'[8]

Finally, we will end with the words of the great, yet humble economist Alfred Marshall. He describes the frustration that all of us encounter when we enter into the serious study of this discipline. In his own words, ' . . . the more I studied economic science, the smaller appeared the knowledge which I had of it, in proportion to the knowledge that I needed; and now, at the end of nearly half a century of almost exclusive study of it, I am conscious of more ignorance of it than I was at the beginning of the study.'[9]

Summary

1. Economics is the study of how individuals and society choose to allocate finite resources to satisfy unlimited wants. It is the science of scarcity. Economists are concerned with issues of economic efficiency and social equity.
2. The problems of scarcity and choice can be analysed by means of a production possibility frontier. It shows the maximum output that can be produced when all resources are fully utilised. Moving from one point on the production possibility frontier to another point involves an opportunity cost: less of one good in return for more of another good.
3. Economics teaches people to think in a particular way. Scholars of economics are trained to think in terms of choice, scarcity, resource allocation, exchange and opportunity cost. It is a particular view of how society operates.
4. There are three fundamental questions in economics. What goods are to be produced? How are they to be produced? For whom will these goods be produced? In short, these are the allocation, production and distribution problems in economics.
5. Economics is traditionally divided into microeconomics and macroeconomics. Microeconomics is the branch of economics that is concerned with the study of individual, economic decision-making units. Macroeconomics is the branch of economics that deals with the economy as a whole. It deals with aggregate variables.
6. Economics is a social science: it uses scientific methods to study people's behaviour. The purpose of an economic model is to study how certain aspects of the economy work. Although they can be quite abstract and can contain a lot of assumptions, most economists believe that a theory is best judged by its predictive powers.

Key terms

Choice
Scarcity
Resources
Opportunity cost
Allocative efficiency
Productive efficiency
Equity
Production possibility frontier
Exchange
Market system

Planned economy
Mixed economy
Production
Allocation
Distribution
Microeconomics
Macroeconomics
Social science
Economic model

PART I

MICROECONOMICS

INTRODUCTION TO MICROECONOMICS

Microeconomics studies individual decision-making units. These include consumers, and producers. Each is studied in isolation from one another before they interact in the market for a particular good or service. The purpose is to develop a full understanding of the behaviour and actions of individual agents in the economy.

We begin our analysis of microeconomics in the marketplace where voluntary exchange between consumers and producers takes place largely in the absence of government intervention. This voluntary interaction is the essence of the market system.

Chapter 1 deals with the behaviour of consumers and producers. The price mechanism, a central feature of the market system, is explained. A brief account of price controls is also given.

In Chapter 2 we examine the sensitivity of demand and supply to changes in price. This concept called the elasticity of demand and supply has important implications for the pricing strategy of firms in their quest for profit-maximisation.

Chapter 3 concentrates on the role of the consumer in the marketplace. The negative relationship between price and quantity demanded is explained. The demand curve for different types of goods is examined.

The behaviour of producers and their decisions to supply are examined in Chapter 4. In traditional neoclassical economics, firms are profit-maximisers. We will see that costs of production are an important element in a firm's decision to produce.

In Chapter 5, we examine different types of market structures. The environment within which the firm operates determines a firm's behaviour. The pricing and output decision of the firm is largely influenced by the degree of competition facing the firm.

These initial chapters deal with the market for final goods and services. In Chapter 6 we focus on the market for factor inputs. Land, labour, capital and enterprise are all part of the production process.

In the market system, market failures arise. Externalities or spillover effects are common. To combat these effects, more extensive government intervention may be required. This aspect of microeconomics is discussed in Chapter 7. The provision of public goods is also examined.

CHAPTER 1

DEMAND, SUPPLY AND THE MARKET

....

'The price of ability does not depend on merit, but on supply and demand.'[1]
George Bernard Shaw

'Economic life is an organisation of producers to satisfy the wants of consumers.'[2]
John R. Hicks (1904–89)

'When the demand price is equal to the supply price, the amount produced has no tendency either to be increased or to be diminished; it is in equilibrium.'[3]
Alfred Marshall (1842–1924)

....

Chapter objectives

Upon completing this chapter, the student should understand:

- demand and the demand curve;
- supply and the supply curve;
- factors influencing demand and supply;
- price mechanism and equilibrium;
- price controls.

Outline

1.1 **Demand and consumers**
1.2 **Supply and producers**
1.3 **Market equilibrium and the price mechanism**
1.4 **Price controls**

Introduction

Why do consumers pay 30p for a chocolate bar and £30 for a sweater? The answer lies in the analysis of demand and supply. We begin by considering consumers and their actions (what economists refer to as 'demand'). An examination of producers and their behaviour (what economists define as 'supply') follows. The interaction of these agents and their behaviour is then analysed to arrive at the selling price (what economists refer to as 'equilibrium' price). This analysis takes place within the framework of a market system.

1.1 Demand and consumers

Demand is the quantity of the good or service that consumers purchase at each conceivable price over a given period of time. The phrase 'over a given period of time' suggests that demand has a time dimension. It may be days, weeks, months or even longer.

In simple terms demand is related to wants. Economists distinguish between a desire to buy and an ability to buy. The former reflects unsupported desires whereas the latter reflects only those desires that are backed by income or what economists call 'purchasing power'. A consumer may want ten chocolate bars and eight sweaters but because of a limited income he demands only six chocolate bars and four sweaters.

Demand does not refer to a particular quantity, but to a whole range of quantities. The reason we associate a commodity with a particular price is because in a market system, price is determined by the interaction of the consumers and the suppliers. If we observe consumers in isolation, we are then faced with a range of prices, and subsequently, with a range of quantities.

What determines the level of demand? Why do we demand a small or large quantity? One of the key factors which determines demand is the price of the good. We can write this relationship in mathematical form:

$$\boxed{\textbf{Qd = f(P)}} \qquad [1.1]$$

where: Qd = Quantity demanded; P = Price.

This relationship can be expressed in a number of different ways. For example,

Quantity demanded is a function of price
or
Quantity demanded depends on price
or
Each level of quantity demanded is associated with its own price

Equation 1.1 is called the demand function. It involves two variables where a variable is defined as a symbol that can represent any unspecified number or value. Price is the explanatory variable in that it serves to explain the specific level of quantity demanded. It is autonomous or independent. Quantity demanded is the dependent variable. It is conditional on the level of price.

We can examine the relationship between price and quantity for a good by considering a demand schedule.

Definition
● ● ● ● ● ●

A demand schedule is a table which indicates the quantity of a particular good which consumers are willing to purchase at various prices during a specified time period.

In this definition, we implicitly assume that any other factors which could conceivably influence the quantity demanded are held constant. Among these factors are the prices of all related goods, consumers' income and their tastes. Using the terminology of the economist, we say that a demand schedule examines the relationship between price and quantity demanded, *ceteris paribus* (Latin phrase meaning 'other things being equal').

Table 1.1 shows the demand schedule for chocolate bars. For each price, there is a corresponding level of quantity demanded.

Table 1.1: The demand schedule for chocolate bars (per month)

Price, P (pence)	Quantity, Q (thousands)
0.10	100
0.15	90
0.20	80
0.25	70
0.30	60
0.35	50
0.40	40
0.45	30
0.50	20
0.55	10

We can see from this schedule that when price increases from 10p to 20p, the quantity demanded falls from 100,000 to 80,000 units. The quantity demanded falls to 60,000 when the price of the chocolate bar increases to 30p.

This demand schedule is a specific example of a general relationship. With few exceptions, as the price of a good falls, the quantity demanded of that good rises. This relationship is observed so frequently that we call it the law of demand.[4]

Definition
● ● ● ● ● ●

The law of demand refers to the inverse or negative relationship between price and quantity demanded, *ceteris paribus*.

Generally, we illustrate this relationship using a two dimensional graph. It is customary to represent price on the vertical axis and quantity on the horizontal axis. We plot the points from the demand schedule and join them together to form the demand curve.

Definition
● ● ● ● ● ●

A demand curve shows the quantity of a good demanded at each price, *ceteris paribus*.

Figure 1.1 illustrates the demand curve for chocolate bars described by the demand schedule. Because the relationship between price and quantity is negative, the demand curve is downward sloping.

Figure 1.1: The demand curve for chocolate bars

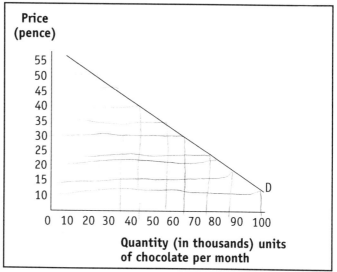

The demand curve cannot tell us the actual selling price or the quantity sold. This information is only determined when the consumers, represented by the demand curve interact with producers, represented by the supply curve to form a market.

At this stage we only offer an intuitive explanation as to why the demand curve is downward sloping. Recall that when we discussed the law of demand, we stated that other factors which affect demand are 'held constant'. Among those factors are the prices of related goods. A number of goods can be substituted for a chocolate bar, like biscuits, ice cream or fruit. As the price of the chocolate bar increases, some consumers will purchase substitute goods in place of chocolate bars. Therefore, as the price of the chocolate bar rises, the quantity demanded of chocolate bars falls. Alternatively, if the price of chocolate bars falls, they become cheaper relative to other goods. People will purchase more chocolate bars at a lower price instead of biscuits, ice cream or fruit. We offer a more detailed explanation of the downward sloping demand curve in Chapter 3.

When the demand curve is a straight line, it can be represented in a simple linear form, as follows:

$$Qd = a - bP$$ [1.2]

where: Qd = Quantity demanded; P = Price; a and b = constants.

Equation 1.2 shows the general form of a linear relationship between price and quantity. The negative relationship between the two variables is reflected in the minus

sign before price, the independent variable. The demand schedule for chocolate bars, which we have been discussing, is based on a linear demand relationship. The equation for this specific relationship is:

$$Qd = 120,000 - 200,000P$$

A demand curve is not always a straight line. A convex demand curve which is bowed towards the origin is shown in Figure 1.2.

Figure 1.2: A convex demand curve

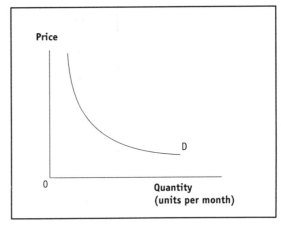

The exact shape of the demand curve depends on the nature of the relationship between the change in price and the subsequent change in quantity demanded. We will examine this in greater detail in Chapter 2.

Exceptions to the downward sloping demand curve

There are a few exceptional cases where the demand curve is not downward sloping. For a limited number of goods, the demand curve may be 'perverse' or upward sloping as shown in Figure 1.3.

Figure 1.3: A 'perverse' demand curve

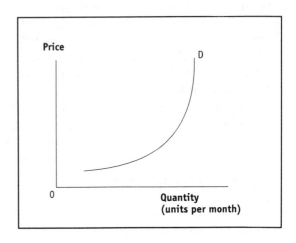

One exception is a snob or Veblen good. The demand curve of a Veblen good is upward sloping. The behaviour which underlies this demand curve was coined 'conspicuous consumption' by Thorstein Veblen (1857–1929), the American Institutional economist and author of *The Theory of the Leisure Class* (1899). He argued that certain parts of society, in particular the 'leisure' class, may not act like the consumers whom we have just described.

Veblen suggested that the ownership of goods which were expensive and frivolous conferred status on the owner because others realised that these 'ostentatious' goods could only be purchased by members of the upper economic class. Status increased when the price of the good increased. If the price of the good fell, the 'snob' value also fell, since it was now less expensive and more affordable to lower classes. In some circumstances the demand for the 'snob' good may actually fall when the price falls resulting in an upward sloping demand curve. Rolex watches and BMWs are usually cited as examples.

Another exception is the Giffen good. The 'Giffen paradox' was described by Sir Robert Giffen who, it is said, observed that an increase in the price of bread in nineteenth-century London, '. . . makes so large a drain on the resources of the poorer labouring families . . . that they are forced to curtail their consumption of meat and the more expensive farinaceous foods: and, bread being still the cheapest food which they can get and will take, they consume more, and not less of it'.[5]

This quotation suggests that the observation of a Giffen good requires a very specific set of circumstances. First, income levels must be low and the good must constitute a significant part of a consumer's purchases. Second, the good in question must have few affordable substitutes. Even so, an increase in demand in response to an increase in price will probably only occur over a very narrow range of prices. In Western economies, characterised by relatively high levels of income and numerous substitutes, most economists believe that the Giffen paradox is no longer relevant.

In short, although a perverse demand curve is theoretically possible, this relationship is seldom observed. In general, we can rely on the negative relationship between price and quantity demanded described by the law of demand.

Other factors influencing demand
....

In reality there is a wide range of factors which determine the level of quantity demanded. Here we focus on the more important determinants or, as they are sometimes referred to, the underlying conditions of demand. Until now, these determinants were 'held constant' according to our '*ceteris paribus*' condition.

1. The price of related goods (Prelated goods)

If two goods are related, they are either substitutes for, or complements to, each other.

● Definition
● ● ● ● ● ●

Two goods are substitutes if consumers consider one good as an alternative for the other good. If the price of one good falls, demand for the other good falls and vice versa.

Butter and margarine, tea and coffee, cassette tapes and CDs, bus and rail transport and umbrellas and raincoats might be considered as examples of substitute goods and services. If the price of a return ticket on a bus between Galway and Dublin falls, we would expect the demand for railway tickets for the same journey to fall. If we tested this and found that this relationship exists, we would consider these services to be substitutes.

• Definition
• • • • • •

Goods which are complements are bought and consumed together. This implies that if the price of one good falls, demand for the other good increases and vice versa.

Examples of complementary goods include CDs and CD players, personal computers and printers, paint and white spirits, and shoes and shoelaces. Consider CDs and CD players. When they first appeared on the market, CD players were reasonably priced but CDs were expensive. Subsequently, the demand for CD players increased dramatically when the price of CDs fell, indicating that these goods are complements.

2. Consumers' income (Y)

Income was also 'held constant' when we considered the demand schedule. However, it is another explanatory variable. This means that if income changes, it will usually have an effect on demand. Normal and inferior goods are defined in terms of income.

• Definition
• • • • • •

Demand for a normal good increases with income. If income falls, demand for the normal good falls.

In this case, there is a positive relationship between income and demand. Most goods, from a walkman to an automobile are considered to be examples of normal goods. We predict that demand for these goods will increase with income.

• Definition
• • • • • •

A good is classified as an inferior good, if demand for that good falls when income increases and vice versa.

For an inferior good, there is a negative relationship between income and demand. Minced beef, bus rides and 'yellow packs' are possible examples of inferior goods. Consider minced beef. If income increases, we would expect consumers to substitute a better grade of meat for the minced beef. If we can establish a negative relationship between demand for minced beef and income, we classify minced beef as an inferior good.

3. Consumers' tastes (T)

Tastes and preferences for the good also affect demand. Taste, in this context, is a broad concept. It is shaped by time, custom, tradition, fashion, location and social attitudes.

4. Other factors (O)

Customs, quality, habits, advertising, expectations about future market conditions, etc. are factors which can also lead to a change in the demand for a particular commodity.

Hence, the quantity of a good demanded is determined by the price of the good itself and by the price of related goods, by the consumers' income, by the consumers' tastes and by a range of other related factors. The complete mathematical representation for our demand function is in the form of:

$$Qd = f(P, Prelated\ goods, Y, T, O) \qquad [1.3]$$

where: Qd = Quantity demanded; P = Price; Y = Income; T = Tastes; O = Other factors.

We now examine the distinction between a movement along the demand curve and a shift of the demand curve.

A movement along the demand curve
....

A movement along the demand curve is caused by a change in price. Because of our *ceteris paribus* clause, all other factors influencing demand are held constant. For example, a move along the demand curve from A to B, as in Figure 1.4, is caused by a fall in price. As the price falls from 45p to 30p, the quantity demanded increases from 30,000 to 60,000 units. This increase in quantity demanded is represented by the movement along the demand curve. Similarly, a movement from B to A is caused by an increase in price.

Figure 1.4: A movement along the demand curve

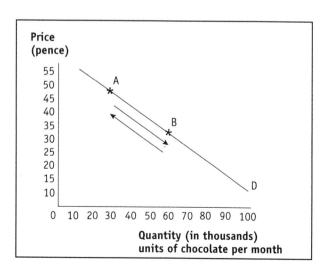

A shift of the demand curve
....

A rightward or leftward shift of the entire demand curve is caused by a change in one or more of the underlying factors. If one of these factors changes then each single point on the demand curve moves either out to the right or in to the left. Figure 1.5 provides an example. D is our original demand curve. Every single point on D represents a price level and a corresponding level of quantity demanded. The demand curve is drawn, holding constant the price of related goods, the level of income, consumers' preferences and other factors.

Figure 1.5: A rightward shift of the demand curve

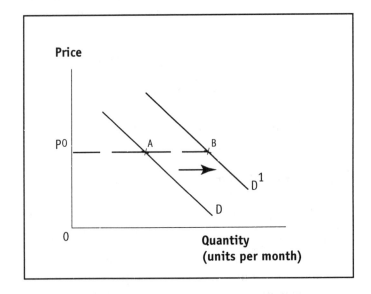

Assume income rises. If D represents a demand curve for a normal good then the result is an increase in demand. For every conceivable price we no longer demand the old set of quantities but a new and higher set of quantities. For example, if price is at P^0, the corresponding level of quantity demanded moves from A to B. This applies to every single price. The demand curve moves out to the right from D to D^1. This is known as a rightward shift of the demand curve.

If income had fallen for the normal good, the shift would have been to the left. This is known as a leftward shift of the demand curve and is shown in Figure 1.6.

Figure 1.6: A leftward shift of the demand curve

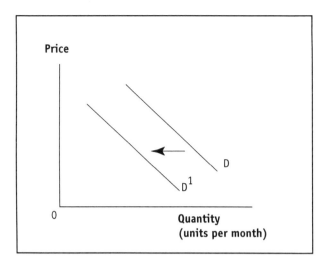

Table 1.2 contains a number of possible changes in underlying factors which would result in either a rightward or a leftward shift of the demand curve. Draw these for yourself.

Table 1.2: Changes in underlying factors that cause shifts of the demand curve

---

Changes in factors which result in a rightward shift of the demand curve
1. D represents the demand curve for a good which has a substitute. An increase in the price of its substitute good results in a rightward shift of D.
2. D represents the demand curve for a good which has a complement. A decrease in the price of its complementary good results in a rightward shift of D.
3. D represents the demand curve for a normal good. An increase in income results in a rightward shift of D.
4. D represents the demand curve for an inferior good. A decrease in income results in a rightward shift of D.
5. D represents the demand curve for a good. If tastes for the good improve (if the good becomes more fashionable, for example), this results in a rightward shift of D.

Changes in factors which result in a leftward shift of the demand curve
1. D represents the demand curve for a good which has a substitute. A decrease in the price of its substitute good results in a leftward shift of D.
2. D represents the demand curve for a good which has a complement. An increase in the price of its complementary good results in a leftward shift of D.
3. D represents the demand curve for a normal good. A decrease in income results in a leftward shift of D.
4. D represents the demand curve for an inferior good. An increase in income results in a leftward shift of D.
5. D represents the demand curve for a good. If tastes for the good deteriorate, this results in a leftward shift of D.

CASE STUDY

Extract from The Irish Times
House prices in the North rise by 10.7% in year
by Suzanne Breen

House prices in Northern Ireland have risen by 10.7% in the past year, according to a survey published yesterday by the University of Ulster. It is the largest recorded rise during the 11 years that the survey has been compiled and shows that the price differential between the North and Britain is narrowing. The report attributes the price increases to improving economic conditions, competitive mortgage interest rates and the 'feel good' factor following the IRA and loyalist ceasefires. The rise compares to average price increases of 7.8% for second-hand houses in Dublin last year. In the Republic as a whole prices rose by 4.7% in 1994.

. . .

Ms Beth Robinson of the Belfast estate agents Temple-Robinson, said her firm had been constantly surprised by the number of people moving back to the North. 'These are buyers not just from England, Scotland and Wales, but also from places like the United States, who want to move home because there is peace. We have had cases where rival bidders on property have both been from abroad', she said.

The authors of the report, Dr Alastair Adair and Dr Stanley McGreal, said 'The buoyant conditions here contrast with the situation in most other regions in the UK, where the housing market is still performing poorly.'

Source: The Irish Times, *16 August 1995.*

Questions
....

1. What market are we looking at? Is there a regional dimension to this market? What is the relevant time frame?
2. The article mentions a number of variables affecting demand which have changed. Discuss the variables and their impact on demand. Will the variables lead to a movement along the demand curve or will the variables cause the demand curve to shift?
3. Using a diagram, show the demand curves for 1993 and 1994.

Answers
....

1. The relevant market is the housing market for Northern Ireland. Yes, there is a regional dimension. The author notes that prices have increased more rapidly in the North than in the Republic or in Britain. The survey is taken annually. Therefore, we are comparing demand in one year with demand in another year.
2. The improvement in economic conditions suggests that incomes are rising. Since houses are a normal good, this affects demand in a positive way. The 'feel good'

factor may signal an improvement in consumers' preference for houses in the North. The queries from people who are currently living abroad may also indicate that the population in the North may increase as people move home. Finally, the competitive mortgage interest rate is another underlying variable which affects demand.

The demand curve looks at the relationship between price and quantity demanded, *ceteris paribus*. The variables discussed in the article refer to underlying variables. All of these factors signal a change in demand and will cause a shift of the demand curve.

3. Based on the changes in the underlying variables discussed above, we expect the demand curve for housing in Northern Ireland to shift out to the right.

Figure 1.7: Northern Ireland housing market

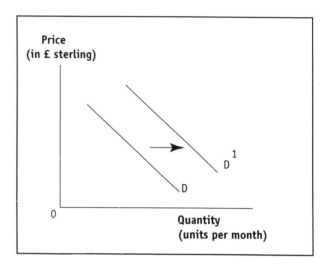

1.2 Supply and producers

Supply and the quantity supplied can be analysed in a similar fashion to that of demand and the quantity demanded. Supply is the quantity of the good that sellers offer at each conceivable price. It is not a particular quantity, but a whole set of quantities. Whereas demand is related to wants, supply is related to resources. As with demand, there is a specific time frame implied. It may be hours or it may be months.

Resources are 'inputs' which are used to produce goods and services, i.e. the 'output'. These inputs or factors of production are land (the natural resource), capital (the manufactured resource), labour and enterprise (the human resources). It is the cost of the factors of production which underlie the supply curve. This will be discussed in greater detail in Chapter 4.

Again, we begin with price as the main explanatory variable. Quantity supplied is the dependent variable. This relationship can be written in a mathematical form, as follows:

$$\boxed{Qs = f(P)}$$ [1.4]

where: Qs = Quantity supplied; P = Price.

This equation states that the quantity supplied depends on price. It is a function of price. There is a positive relationship between price and quantity supplied. We can examine the relationship between these two variables by looking at a supply schedule for chocolate bars.

Definition
● ● ● ● ● ●

A supply schedule is a table which indicates the quantity of a particular good which producers are willing to supply at various prices, over a particular period of time.

In this case, the factors which we are 'holding constant' include the wage of labour, the price of materials, the state of technology and government regulations. Table 1.3 shows the supply schedule for chocolate bars.

Table 1.3: The supply schedule for chocolate bars (per month)

Price, P (pence)	Quantity, Q (thousands)
0.10	0
0.15	10
0.20	20
0.25	30
0.30	40
0.35	50
0.40	60
0.45	70
0.50	80
0.55	90
0.60	100

From the table, we can see that there is a positive relationship between price and quantity supplied. At 10p, suppliers are unwilling to produce chocolate bars. At 15p per bar, 10,000 bars are produced. Production continues to increase with price.

Again, we illustrate this relationship by plotting a supply curve on a two dimensional graph.

Definition
● ● ● ● ● ●

A supply curve maps the relationship between price and quantity supplied over a particular period of time.

By plotting the range of prices on the vertical axis and the levels of quantity supplied on the horizontal axis, we can derive the upward sloping supply curve.[6] Figure 1.8 illustrates the positive relationship between the two variables.

Figure 1.8: The supply curve of chocolate bars

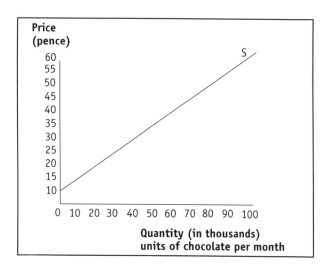

At this point, we will only offer an intuitive explanation about why the supply curve is upward sloping. A more rigorous explanation will be advanced in Chapter 5.

At a price which is less than 10p per unit, firms will not produce chocolate bars. This is because the manufacturers must pay for the inputs needed for the production process. At a price below 10p per unit, even the most efficient producer cannot cover the costs. Applying a concept which we discussed in An Introduction to Economics, the opportunity cost of producing chocolate bars is too high. Since we assume that all producers attempt to maximise profits, we expect them, whenever possible, to divert their resources to markets where they can do this.[7] Chocolate bar manufacturers may expand production of mints or ice creams and forgo the production of chocolate bars until market conditions improve.

At a price above 10p, chocolate bar manufacturers begin production. As price increases, production expands. In doing so, resources may have to be diverted from the production of other goods to produce chocolate bars.

The supply curve can be represented in a linear form, as follows:

$$Qs = c + dP$$ [1.5]

where: Qs = Quantity supplied; P = Price; c and d = constants.

Equation 1.5 is the general form of a linear relationship between price and quantity. The plus sign before the price variable reflects the positive relationship between the price and the quantity supplied. As price increases, so does the quantity supplied. The supply schedule for chocolate bars which we have been discussing is based on a linear relationship. The specific equation for this example is:

$$Qs = -20,000 + 200,000P$$

A supply curve may not be a straight line, depending on the nature of the manufacturers' costs. A non-linear upward sloping supply curve is shown in Figure 1.9.

Figure 1.9: A non-linear upward sloping supply curve

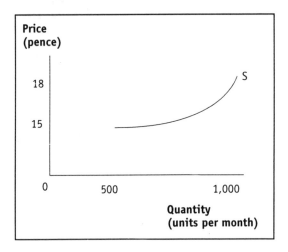

Exceptions to the upward sloping supply curve

The positive relationship between price and quantity supplied holds true for most goods produced in competitive markets.[8] There are, however, exceptions to this rule. One example is illustrated below.

Figure 1.10: An exception to the upward sloping supply curve

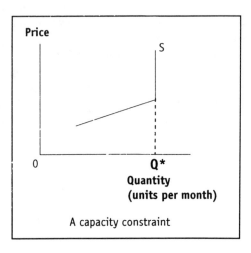

Figure 1.10 depicts a 'kinked' supply curve. The supply curve is upward sloping over a range of production. Then the supply curve changes and is vertical. Beyond Q*, firms operating in this market cannot respond to an increase in price because of plant size, access to raw materials or the availability of skilled labour. The vertical part of the supply curve reflects maximum production capacity. It is impossible to produce beyond output level Q* because of this capacity constraint.

Factors such as the level of technology, the price of inputs or raw materials and the extent of government regulations will affect the position and shape of the supply curve.

Other factors influencing supply
....

1. Technology (T)

A supply curve is drawn for a particular technological process. A technological improvement means that suppliers can use inputs more efficiently, and the cost of producing a unit of output falls.

2. Input prices (I)

Output is produced by using a certain combination of inputs, including labour, raw materials and machinery. A supply curve is drawn for a particular price level of these factors of production. A reduction in input prices (e.g. lower wages, lower fuel costs, lower rental prices for machinery) induces firms to supply more output at each price. Higher input prices, making production less profitable at each conceivable price, results in less output.

3. Government regulations (G)

Compliance with restrictions and regulations legislated by government can increase the costs of firms operating in a particular market. By adding to the cost of production, regulations may lead to lower levels of output at each price level. Similarly, a reduction in these restrictions or deregulation may induce higher levels of output if costs are reduced.

4. Taxes and/or Subsidies (T/S)

Taxes on wages, property, utilities or other inputs increase the costs of production. In contrast, government subsidies to producers usually decrease the cost per unit of output.

5. Other factors (O)

Other factors influencing the level of quantity supplied include the price of other commodities, expectations of the future, climatic conditions and other unpredictable events.

The extended supply function is of the form:

$$\boxed{Qs = f(P, Th, I, G, T/S, O)} \qquad \text{[1.6]}$$

where: Qs = Quantity supplied; P = Price; Th = Technology; I = Input costs;
G = Government regulations; T/S = Taxes/Subsidies; O = Other Factors.

We now examine the distinction between a movement along the supply curve and a shift of the supply curve.

A movement along the supply curve

A movement along the supply curve is caused by a change in price. This is illustrated in Figure 1.11 below. The move along the supply curve from A to B is caused by an increase in price. As price rises from 40p to 55p quantity supplied rises from 60,000 to 90,000 units. Similarly, a decrease in price from 55p to 40p results in a fall in the level of quantity supplied. This is represented by a movement from B to A.

Figure 1.11: A movement along the supply curve

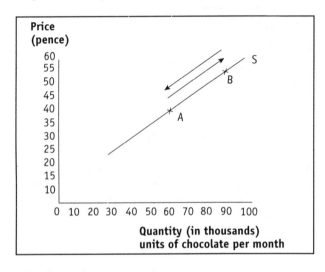

A shift of the supply curve

A shift of the entire supply curve is caused by a change in one or more of the underlying factors. Figure 1.12 illustrates a rightward shift of the supply curve.

Figure 1.12: A rightward shift of the supply curve

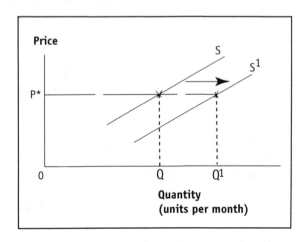

Suppose that a new technological process is developed and adopted by chocolate bar manufacturers. The process is labour-saving, so that it takes less labour input to produce each chocolate bar. Because the wage component per chocolate bar falls, manufacturers can produce each bar at a lower cost.

We can illustrate this improvement by a rightward shift of the supply curve. Because of the change in an underlying variable, the supply curve shifts from S to S^1. If we hold the quantity constant, we observe that Q chocolate bars can be produced at a lower cost per bar.

This rightward shift indicates an increase in supply. At every price, manufacturers produce a larger number of chocolate bars. For example, at price P*, the quantity of chocolate bars supplied increases from Q to Q^1.

Alternatively, suppose that the price of cocoa beans increases due to a partial crop failure. This resource is a necessary input for chocolate production. Figure 1.13 shows the original supply curve (S) which reflects the lower price of cocoa beans. Supply curve S^1 illustrates the new supply curve reflecting the new and higher price of cocoa beans.

Figure 1.13: A leftward shift of the supply curve

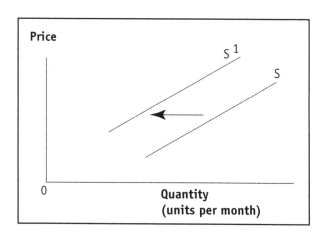

Table 1.4 contains a number of possible changes in the underlying factors which would result in either a rightward or a leftward shift of the supply curve. Draw the supply curves for yourself.

Table 1.4: Changes in underlying factors that cause shifts of the supply curve

---

Changes in factors which result in a rightward shift of the supply curve

1. A reduction in input prices results in a rightward shift of S.
2. A reduction in government regulations may result in a rightward shift of S.
3. An improvement in technology results in a rightward shift of S.

Changes in factors which result in a leftward shift of the supply curve

1. An increase in input prices results in a leftward shift of S.
2. An increase in government regulations may result in a leftward shift of S.

1.3 Market equilibrium and the price mechanism

● Definition
● ● ● ● ●

The market is any arrangement whereby consumers and suppliers of goods and services exchange goods for goods or goods for money.

A market can vary from the stock exchange to the corner shop. Its location and size are largely irrelevant. The important feature is its economic function: solving the What, How and For whom questions which were discussed in the Introduction to Economics.

In an economic context, we usually discuss the market for a particular good or service, like a chocolate bar or a potato. It is a theoretical concept or model. The demand curve, which represents the collective purchasing decisions of all consumers for a particular good, interacts with the supply curve which shows how much of the same good that firms produce. When consumers and firms interact, as reflected in the intersection of the demand curve and the supply curve, price is established as we will soon discover.

Market equilibrium
....

Alfred Marshall, the economist most noted for bringing demand and supply to the forefront of economic thinking, compared demand and supply to the blades of a pair of scissors (see Appendix 1.1).[9] The demand curve shows the negative relationship between price and quantity demanded. The supply curve shows the positive relationship between price and quantity supplied.

In a market economy, price is determined by both sides of the market.

● Definition
● ● ● ● ●

Price can be defined as that which is given in exchange for a good or service.

It is impossible to say whether it is demand or supply which determines the market price just as it is impossible to say which blade of Marshall's scissors does the actual cutting. Price is determined by the interactions of consumers and producers. Theoretically, the consumer and the producer are equally important participants in the market.

It is the interaction of the demand curve and the supply curve which determines the quantity which will be traded in the market and the price that will be charged. There is one price and one quantity where the actions of the buyers and sellers coincide. We call this point equilibrium, a concept used frequently by economists.

Definition
● ● ● ● ● ●

Equilibrium implies a state of balance, a position from which there is no tendency to change.

At equilibrium, the 'market clears' in the sense that the quantity demanded equals the quantity supplied. At all other prices, either quantity demanded is greater than quantity supplied (excess demand) or quantity supplied is greater than quantity demanded (excess supply).

The equilibrium price does not reflect equity or fairness or any other moral concept. It simply reflects the positions of the demand and supply curves which, in turn, represent the interaction of the two basic economic agents in the marketplace.

The role of price
· · · · · · · · · · · · · · · · ·

The role of price in a market economy is very important. Price can signal, allocate, and motivate. Think of how much information is conveyed by this single piece of information. In most cases, we do not have to conduct a market survey to see if consumers like a product or if they value it in comparison to other products. Similarly, we do not have to contact all possible producers to examine their production methods. Instead, price is the information link between buyers and sellers. Buyers indicate that a price is too high if they do not purchase a good, causing inventories to accumulate. Similarly, producers may deduce that a price is too low if inventories are depleted and consumers are left waiting for a product. Price is the signal used to communicate information between buyers and sellers.

Price also has an important role in allocating society's resources. Figure 1.14 illustrates the price mechanism at work in the market. By observing a change in consumer preferences from good X to good Y, we can clearly see the important role of price.

Figure 1.14: The role of price in the allocation of resources

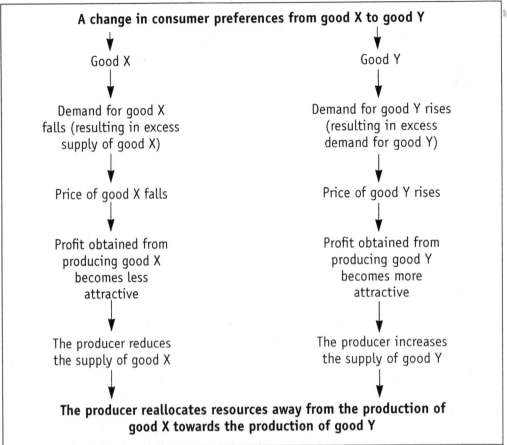

The falling price for good X and the higher price paid for good Y signals a change in the market which is communicated from the consumers to current and potential producers. The potential for higher profits causes a reallocation of resources away from the production of good X towards good Y. It is profit, in the absence of government intervention, which is assumed to act as the motivating force in a market economy. This means that more of the scarce resources of society are being allocated to the production of good Y, the good preferred by consumers.

In all economies, some form of mechanism must exist in order to allocate resources. In a market economy, it is the price mechanism which solves the three basic questions in economics: what is produced, how it is produced and for whom it is produced. The price mechanism is an automatic process. No central agency is required to signal, allocate or motivate. The market, through adjustments in prices, carries out these functions.

This does not mean that we can rely on the price mechanism to ensure that all of the goods and services which we value as a society are produced. Also, in some cases, the demand curve and the supply curve do not convey all of the important information needed to allocate society's resources. We will discuss the provision of public goods and market failures in Chapter 7. However, in most cases, the price mechanism is an effective way to convey information and to allocate society's resources.

Figure 1.15 illustrates a market for chocolate bars. The demand curve is represented by D and the supply curve is represented by S. It is the intersection of the consumers' demand curve D with the producers' supply curve S which determines the equilibrium price and the equilibrium quantity in this market. The intersection is at a price of 35p. This is the only price where quantity demanded (50,000 units) is equal to quantity supplied (50,000 units). In equilibrium, there is neither excess demand nor excess supply.

Figure 1.15: The market for chocolate bars

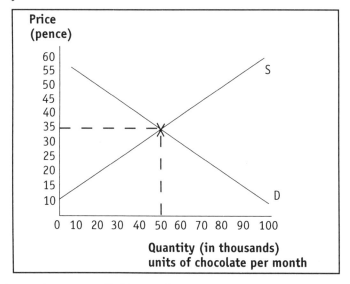

The equilibrium price and quantity (P,Q) can also be derived mathematically from a pair of linear equations. The general format of the two-variable demand and supply equations is as follows:

$$Qd = a - bP \qquad \text{[1.2]}$$

$$Qs = c + dP \qquad \text{[1.5]}$$

We can solve for price and quantity using these equations. In general, the equilibrium condition is as follows:

$$Qd = Qe = Qs \qquad \text{[1.7]}$$

where: Qe = equilibrium quantity.

The demand curve for chocolate bars was given by the equation Qd = 120,000 – 200,000P, whereas the supply curve was given by Qs = –20,000 + 200,000P. Solve for price and quantity using these simultaneous equations as follows:

$$120,000 - 200,000P = Qe = -20,000 + 200,000P$$

Solving for the unknown P, we get:

$$120,000 - 200,000P = -20,000 + 200,000P$$
$$140,000 = 400,000P$$
$$P = .35$$

If P = .35, then we can solve for the unknown Qe. This is solved by substituting P = .35 into either the demand or the supply equation since, in equilibrium, the quantity demanded equals the quantity supplied.

$$Qe = 120,000 - 200,000(.35) = 120,000 - 70,000 = 50,000$$

The equilibrium price and quantity is (.35, 50,000). This is the same equilibrium which is illustrated using the demand curve and the supply curve in Figure 1.15.

Tending towards market equilibrium
....

At all prices above the equilibrium price, quantity supplied is greater than quantity demanded. This is illustrated in Figure 1.16.

Figure 1.16: Excess supply in the market for chocolate bars

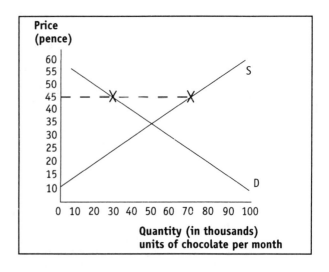

At 45p, suppliers are willing to supply 70,000 units, whereas consumers demand only 30,000 units. At this price there exists excess supply. We can actually estimate the amount of excess supply. At a price of 45p there is an excess supply of 40,000 bars of chocolate (70,000 – 30,000).

In order for the market to clear, quantity demanded must equal quantity supplied. In this particular case, suppliers cut price in order to eliminate the excess inventory or surplus. Price continues to fall. As price falls quantity supplied falls whereas quantity demanded rises. Thus, as price adjusts downwards, the excess is eliminated.

Remember, in a market economy, prices are allowed to adjust in order for markets to clear. Prices are continually cut until the excess is eliminated. In this particular market, price must fall to 35p before the excess is completely eliminated. At 35p the market returns to equilibrium.

At all prices below the equilibrium price, quantity demanded is greater than quantity supplied. This is illustrated in Figure 1.17.

Figure 1.17: Excess demand in the market for chocolate bars

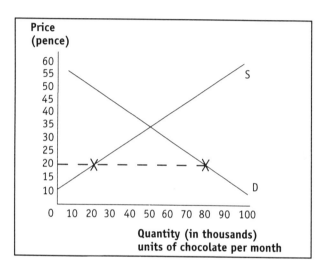

At 20p, consumers demand 80,000 units but suppliers are only willing to supply 20,000 units. In this example there exists excess demand. We can estimate the actual amount of excess demand. At a price of 20p there is excess demand of 60,000 bars of chocolate (80,000 – 20,000).

In order for the market to clear, quantity demanded must equal quantity supplied. Suppliers increase price, and by doing so the excess demand or shortage is eliminated. As price rises, quantity supplied rises and quantity demanded falls. Price continues to rise until quantity demanded is equal to quantity supplied. At 35p the market returns to equilibrium.

These two cases illustrate how market pressures or market forces, operating through the price mechanism, lead to equilibrium. The speed of the adjustment in prices depends on a number of factors. The level of transaction costs, the nature of the market and the availability of information can determine the speed of adjustment. The equilibrium level of price and quantity remains constant unless there is a change in either the conditions of demand or supply or a combination of both.

A change in the conditions of demand
....

Figure 1.18 illustrates an equilibrium position, E with quantity demanded equal to quantity supplied.

Figure 1.18: A change in the conditions of demand

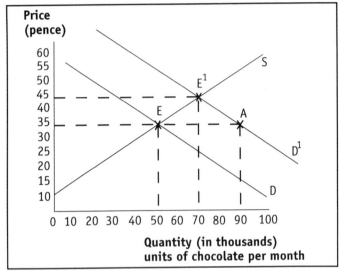

Suppose income rises. For a normal good, an increase in income shifts the demand curve out and to the right from D to D^1. Equilibrium is no longer at E. A new equilibrium is reached at E^1. The diagram indicates an increase in equilibrium price and an increase in equilibrium quantity. We need to explain the adjustment process by which we move from E to E^1.

At the old equilibrium price of 35p, quantity demanded is equal to quantity supplied. However, as income increases the quantity demanded increases at that particular price (and at all other price levels). At 35p, the new level of quantity demanded is 90,000 units. Quantity supplied is still at the old level of 50,000 units. At the old equilibrium price there exists excess demand. This is shown by the segment marked |EA| in Figure 1.18. The actual amount of excess demand is 90,000 – 50,000 = 40,000 units.

In a market economy, excess demand signals disequilibrium. Price adjusts in order for equilibrium to be restored. Suppliers respond to excess demand by increasing price. As price rises from 35p, quantity demanded falls and quantity supplied rises. Price continues to be pushed up until all the excess demand disappears. As price approaches 45p the excess demand is eliminated. At 45p the market clears. The new equilibrium quantity is 70,000 units. Due to an increase in income, both equilibrium price and equilibrium quantity increase.

A change in any factor which results in a rightward shift of the demand curve leads to an increase in the equilibrium price and quantity. Similarly, a change in any factor which results in a leftward shift of the demand curve leads to a decrease in both equilibrium price and quantity.

A change in the conditions of supply

Figure 1.19 illustrates an equilibrium position E.

Figure 1.19: A change in the conditions of supply

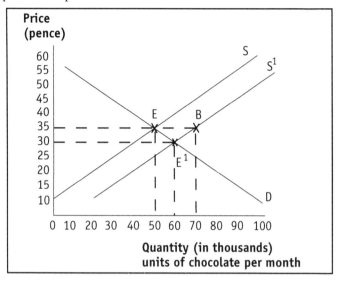

Suppose that technology improves. This means that, in theory, the same amount of inputs can now produce more output. In graphic terms an improvement in technology shifts our supply curve to the right. Equilibrium is no longer at E. A new equilibrium is reached at E^1. The diagram indicates a decrease in equilibrium price and an increase in equilibrium quantity. What is the adjustment process?

At the old equilibrium price of 35p, the equilibrium quantity is 50,000 units. However, due to the technological improvement the quantity supplied increases at that particular price (and at all other price levels). The new level of quantity supplied is 70,000 units. Quantity demanded is still at the old level of 50,000 units. At the old equilibrium price there exists excess supply. This is shown by the segment marked |EB| in Figure 1.19. The actual amount of excess supply is 70,000 – 50,000 = 20,000 units.

Price adjusts in order to restore equilibrium. Suppliers respond to excess supply by reducing prices. As price falls from 35p, the quantity demanded rises and the quantity supplied falls. Price continues to be pushed down until all the excess is eliminated. At 30p the market clears.

E^1 represents the new equilibrium. Equilibrium price is 30p and the equilibrium quantity is 60,000 units. Due to the improvement in technology, the equilibrium price falls and the equilibrium quantity rises. Any factor which results in a rightward shift of the supply curve leads to a decrease in the equilibrium price and an increase in equilibrium quantity. Similarly, any factor which causes a leftward shift of the supply curve results in an increase in equilibrium price and a decrease in equilibrium quantity.

A change in the conditions of demand and supply
....
We know that more than one change can occur at a time. Consider the market for chocolate bars. A recent report from the Minister of Health suggests that people should reduce the amount of fat which they eat. A change in consumer preferences, triggered by this report, could shift the demand curve for chocolate bars to the left.

Suppose at the same time, there is a crop failure for cocoa beans. The cost of an input will increase, causing the supply curve to shift to the left.

What can we deduce about the new equilibrium? We can say, unambiguously, that the equilibrium quantity will decrease. The shift of either curve to the left will lead to that result. But can we be as certain about price? Consider Figure 1.20.

Figure 1.20: Alternative scenarios for demand and supply curve shifts in the market for chocolate bars

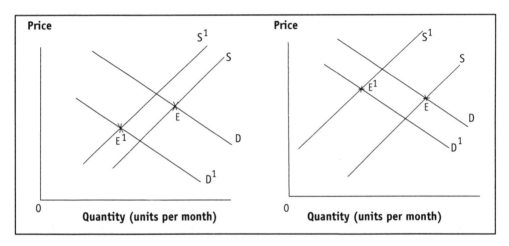

The left panel of Figure 1.20 is drawn to show a demand curve shift which is far greater than the supply curve shift. As a result, equilibrium price falls. The right panel of Figure 1.20 is drawn to show a relatively small demand curve shift and a relatively large supply curve shift. In this case, equilibrium price has risen.

We cannot predict the direction of change of the equilibrium price unless we have more information about the magnitude of the changes in both demand and supply.

This simple example exposes one of the serious limitations of this type of analysis. We can confidently predict the direction of change of the market equilibrium, if – and only if – one change occurs.

1.4 Price controls

In a market economy, price is determined by demand and supply. In a planned economy, this is not the case. It is government, through a particular department or pricing authority, that decides not only which goods to produce, but what price to charge.

Involvement by the state in the market is not restricted to planned economies. Authorities in the European Union and the United States have regularly intervened in agricultural markets with a variety of mechanisms designed to maintain domestic production levels and to supplement farm income. Tax incentives and grants are frequently used by the Irish government to promote certain kinds of activities (such as training and R&D) or to attract certain types of industry (such as multinational manufacturing subsidiaries). Many types of intervention are quite complex and at times it is difficult to disentangle their effects on the market for a particular good or service.

One of the easiest and most transparent forms of market intervention is price controls.

Definition
● ● ● ● ● ●

Price controls are government regulations which limit the ability of the market to determine price.

This price level may not equate demand with supply. An adjustment towards equilibrium will not result because prices are rigid.

Two common types of price controls are price ceilings and price floors.

Price ceilings
················

Definition
● ● ● ● ● ●

A price ceiling is a maximum price.

When implemented, the supplier cannot charge above this 'maximum' price. Its purpose is to help consumers. It is usually imposed in times of scarcity. Without the imposition of a price ceiling, scarce supply would usually result in a high equilibrium price. The government may regard this high price level as undesirable, particularly in a market for basic commodities such as food and fuel.

In order to make these products more affordable, the government sets a price below this high equilibrium price. It does so by imposing a price ceiling, which is legislated by the authorities at a price below the market clearing level. We know from the previous section that any price level below the equilibrium results in excess demand. However, prices will not adjust upwards in order for the market to clear. Prices are fixed at this level. It is illegal for suppliers to increase price in order to eliminate excess demand. This excess demand, or shortage, can be permanent.

Figure 1.21 provides us with an example of a price ceiling.

Figure 1.21: Imposition of a price ceiling

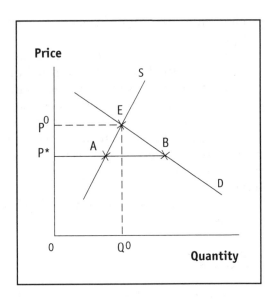

In the absence of price controls, the market price is at P^0. This equilibrium price is relatively high. Many consumers may not be able to afford the commodity at this market price. The government intervenes and imposes a price ceiling at P^*. The commodity is now priced at a lower and more affordable level. However, because of the lower price, quantity demanded increases whereas quantity supplied decreases. The net result is excess demand at this new price level. The shortage caused by the price ceiling is indicated on the diagram as the distance between point A and point B.

To alleviate the problems of excess demand and to ensure even distribution, the government may opt for a system of rationing. Rationing means that the government restricts the amount of a commodity that consumers are allowed to buy. Both price controls and rationing may result in the emergence of a black market. This exists if government's price controls are illegally broken and sellers attempt to sell at prices above the price ceiling. Consumers, unable to buy in the legal market because of restricted supply, choose to pay higher prices in the black market.

There are numerous examples of black market activities. During the Second World War, tea was rationed in Ireland. Every man, woman and child was entitled to purchase 1.5 ounces of tea per week from their grocer at a price of three shillings and sixpence per pound weight. This was approximately one-sixth of the pound before decimalisation. The black market price of tea was a 'pound for a pound'. Therefore, the black market price was approximately six times higher than the price ceiling which was imposed by government. At today's prices, a pound of tea on the black market would cost over £21!

An everyday example of a price ceiling is a rent ceiling. Rent controls are imposed on landlords in order to avoid excessive increases in the price of rental accommodation. Many landlords, however, respond to the imposition of these controls either by converting or selling rental property. This leads to a further shortage of, and a possible deterioration in, rental accommodation which only accentuates the original problem.

Price floors
· · · · · · · · · · · ·

Definition
● ● ● ● ● ● ●

A price floor is a minimum price.

When implemented, the consumer is not legally permitted to purchase the good or service below this price. The purpose of a price floor is to help producers. In order for the supplier to attain a price higher than the market price, the government can impose a price floor above the market level. Any price level above the market price results in excess supply. However, since prices are fixed they cannot adjust downwards in order for the market to clear. The resulting excess supply or surplus can become a permanent feature of the market. The surplus is purchased by a government agency or exported.

An example of a price floor is the intervention price within the Common Agricultural Policy (CAP). This price floor is imposed by the EU in agricultural markets. In theory, if price falls below a particular price, EU agencies 'intervene' and buy the surplus stocks of agricultural products.

Figure 1.22 illustrates the butter market and the imposition of intervention prices.

Figure 1.22: CAP and intervention prices

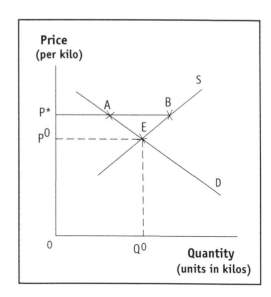

With no price controls the market price would be P^0. However, because of CAP, suppliers (farmers) are guaranteed fixed prices which are above the market price. This is operated by setting a price floor at P^*. This minimum price results in excess supply and is represented by the distance between points A and B. The surplus, however, is not eliminated through a downward adjustment of prices. The producers know that the surplus will be purchased by EU intervention agencies and put into storage. It is the imposition of price floors which explains the existence of the famous 'wine lakes' and 'butter mountains' and why up to 3.7 billion ECU-worth of food stocks were, at one time, in intervention.[10]

In the example above, we can see that the benefits received by the farmer impose a cost on other sectors of society. First, the consumers are paying P* for a product which is higher than the equilibrium price. Second, the intervention bureaucracy is expensive to operate. Various EU and national government agencies are involved in the inspection of produce and the payment of subsidies. Also, any surplus must be stored.

The higher price of food is absorbed by EU consumers. The cost of administering the programme is paid for by EU taxpayers. When we look at it this way, we can see that a price floor is really a method of income redistribution from one section of society to another.

Summary

1. Demand is a specific term used by economists to explain the consumers' desire for a commodity. This desire is supported by an ability to pay. The demand curve illustrates the negative relationship between price and quantity demanded. It is drawn on the assumption that all other factors are held constant. There is an important distinction between a change in quantity demanded (a movement along the demand curve) and a change in demand (a shift of the demand curve).
2. Supply is a specific term used by economists to explain the amount of a commodity produced and supplied to the market. The implicit assumption is that the motivating force behind production is profit. There is a positive relationship between price and quantity supplied and this is represented by an upward sloping supply curve. All other factors are assumed to be held constant. There is a distinction between a movement along the supply curve (change in quantity supplied) and a shift of the supply curve (change in supply).
3. Consumers and producers interact in the market and, in doing so, determine a market-clearing price. This market price, in graphic terms, occurs at the intersection of the demand curve and the supply curve. Adjustment to equilibrium is an automatic process in the market system. Any excess demand results in a price rise whereas excess supply leads to a price fall.
4. Central to the market economy is the price mechanism. Prices play many key roles: they allocate resources, provide incentives, signal changes and reward economic agents.
5. Demand and supply analysis is a very useful tool in the study of economics. Changes in demand and supply conditions and intervention by the state affect the market price and can be analysed using basic demand and supply diagrams.
6. Even in market economies, some prices are legislated by government in the form of price controls. Price ceilings (maximum) and price floors (minimum) are two types. Some examples of price controls can be found in market economies. Rent ceilings and price floors on certain agricultural commodities are two such examples.

Key terms

Demand
Purchasing power
Quantity demanded
Demand schedule
Ceteris paribus
Law of demand
Demand curve
Veblen good
Giffen good
Substitutes
Complements
Normal good
Inferior good
Supply

Factors of production
Quantity supplied
Supply schedule
Supply curve
Market
Price
Equilibrium
Price mechanism
Surplus
Shortage
Price controls
Price ceilings
Price floors

Review questions

1. Explain the law of demand. What are the exceptions to the downward sloping demand curve? Explain your answer.
2. Explain why the supply curve has a positive slope. Describe a possible exception to this norm.
3. What does the concept 'equilibrium' mean? How do markets which exhibit excess demand and excess supply 'clear' or return to equilibrium?
4. Explain the following economic terms:
   (a) substitute
   (b) complement
   (c) normal good
   (d) inferior good
   (e) Veblen good.
5. (a) Explain what effect an improvement in preferences would have on the equilibrium price and quantity of a good.
   (b) Explain what effect an increase in the price of inputs would have on the equilibrium price and quantity of a good.
6. How does the price mechanism within a market economy differ from that which would operate in a planned economy? In what way does a price ceiling or a price floor interfere with the price mechanism? Why are they imposed?

Working problems

1. The demand curve for milk is given by the equation $Qd = 79 - 3P$. The equation $Qs = 2P + 4$ represents the supply curve for milk. P denotes price per pint. Q denotes quantity of pints.

(a) Derive the equilibrium level of price and quantity of milk.
(b) Sketch this equilibrium on a two-dimensional graph.
(c) The government decides to set a price ceiling of 13p. What is the alternative name for this particular type of price control? Estimate the level of the excess.
(d) What excess would result, and by how much, if the government introduces a price floor of 16p?

2. A market is described by the following demand and supply equations:

$$Demand: Qd = 150 - P$$
$$Supply: Qs = -50 + P$$
where Q = quantity and P = daily price.

(a) What is the equilibrium price?
(b) What is the equilibrium quantity?
(c) Suppose the government opts for a minimum price of $P^* = 125$. Calculate the excess.

Multi-choice questions

1. On a number of occasions the Organisation of Petroleum Exporting Countries (OPEC) has succeeded in driving up the price of crude oil. It has been done by:
(a) increasing the demand for oil;
(b) increasing the supply of oil;
(c) restricting the supply of oil;
(d) restricting the demand for oil;
(e) none of the above.

2. $Qs = f(P)$. Thus:
(a) price is a function of quantity supplied;
(b) price is the dependent variable;
(c) this represents a negative relationship between the two variables;
(d) quantity supplied depends on price;
(e) none of the above.

3. Tapes and CDs are defined as substitutes for each other. An increase in the price of tapes would (holding all things equal):
(a) increase the demand for tapes;
(b) decrease the demand for CDs;
(c) increase the demand for CDs;
(d) both (a) and (b) above;
(e) both (a) and (c) above.

4. The price of video recorders is determined by demand and supply. Any decrease in input costs will:
(a) shift the demand curve out to the right;

(b) increase equilibrium price;
(c) shift the supply curve down and to the right;
(d) shift the supply curve up and to the left;
(e) none of the above.

5. A price floor is:
   (a) set above the equilibrium price;
   (b) set below the equilibrium price;
   (c) is commonly referred to as a minimum price;
   (d) both (a) and (c) above;
   (e) both (b) and (c) above.

6. Suppose the government, in response to representations from consumer interest groups, decides to introduce a price ceiling for bread. This may result in:
   (a) excess demand;
   (b) excess supply;
   (c) a surplus;
   (d) a price rise;
   (e) both (a) and (d) above.

True or false

1. The demand curve for a Veblen good slopes down from left to right. _____
2. Maximum revenue is the motivating force behind production and supply. _____
3. An increase in the costs of production reduces supply and, in turn, forces up the market price. _____
4. Excess demand in a market economy would force prices down towards the equilibrium level. _____
5. Rent controls are examples of price ceilings. _____
6. A minimum wage is an example of a price floor. _____

Fill in the blanks

_____ and their actions are represented by a negatively sloped _____ curve. It shows the quantity of the good demanded at each _____ . All other factors which influence demand are held _____ . _____ and their actions are reflected in an _____ sloped supply curve. This shows the _____ relationship between price and quantity supplied, holding all other _____ equal. It is the _____ of the demand curve and the supply curve which determines the _____ price and equilibrium _____ . In a _____ economy it is the price _____ rather than the _____ which allocates scarce _____ . Excess demand is choked off by a price _____ whereas excess _____ is eliminated by a price fall. In both _____ economies and market economies, governments sometimes impose price _____ . They can be in the form of price _____ or price _____ . Unintended and sometimes unfavourable results such as the need for _____ , in the case of a price ceiling, can follow. Butter mountains, which is an excess _____ of butter, resulted from price floors set through the CAP.

CASE STUDY

Extract from The Irish Times
B&Bs booked out as peace brings prosperity to Derry

Derry city has reaped a rich tourism dividend from the peace process, according to figures produced by the city council's marketing department. The figures show Derry had a record season, and council officers say that but for inadequate hotel and bed-and-breakfast accommodation visitor numbers would have been even higher.

Comparing January to August 1994 with the same period this year, money spent by tourists was up by 98% from £1.7 million to £3.3 million. Accommodation booking rose by 165% and there was an 80% increase in counter inquiries at the city's tourist information and an almost similar increase in television (*sic*) inquiries. Last month alone there were more than 17,000 visitor inquiries with 23,500 for the first eight months of last year.

Ms Catherine O'Connor, the council's tourist information development officer, said the record-breaking numbers were, if anything, even higher. 'I knew we had a great year, but these figures are absolutely incredible. Actually, the real figures are higher because staff at our visitor centre just did not have the time to record everything as they were so busy.

'Without question the peace process came across loud and clear from callers to our centre as the main reason for their visit . . .

'If we had more accommodation space the figures would have been higher, but we are working on improving our transit caravan facilities and at providing more hotel and bed-and-breakfast accommodation for next year', said Ms O'Connor.

Source: The Irish Times, *13 September 1995.*

Questions
....

1. What effect did the peace process have on the tourism market in Derry?
2. On a diagram, draw demand curve and a supply curve for the market for bed and breakfasts for 1994 (Jan.–Aug.). On the same diagram, show any changes to that market for 1995. (For this question, assume that there are no price controls.) Describe the original and the new equilibrium.
3. At equilibrium, supply equals demand. However, the article states that the bed and breakfast accommodation was inadequate. This implies that there was a shortage of accommodation. Suppose that bed and breakfast operators agreed with the Northern Ireland Tourist Board to hold the price of accommodation constant at £15 per bed per night for 1995. Could this possibly lead to a market shortage? Show this on a diagram.

Appendix 1.1: The history of demand and supply analysis

Most textbooks today explain the price mechanism with the aid of demand and supply analysis. Changes in the market price are explained by changes in the conditions of demand and supply. This analysis is simplified further by the use of the two-dimensional demand/supply diagram. However, this was not always the case.

At certain times throughout history different theories of price and value have been espoused. Some economists focused primarily on the demand side of the market. These include W. Stanley Jevons (1835–82) and Leon Walras (1834–1910) of the neoclassical school of economic thought. In contrast, the classical school led by David Ricardo (1772–1823) and John Stuart Mill (1806–73) concentrated on the supply side and the costs of production. The economist primarily responsible for bringing consumers and producers together, for studying the interaction of demand and supply and for, ultimately, pushing this analysis to the forefront of economic thinking was the Professor of Political Economy at the University of Cambridge, Alfred Marshall. The familiar demand and supply diagram appeared in Marshall's book *Principles of Economics* in 1890. The actual drawing is reproduced below in Figure 1.23.

Figure 1.23: Alfred Marshall's original demand and supply diagram

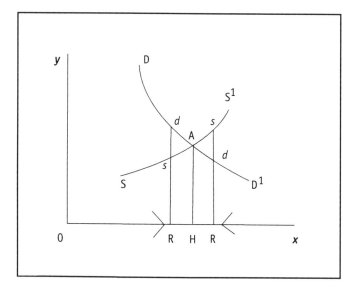

Source: *Principles of Economics*, 8th edition.

CHAPTER 2

ELASTICITY OF DEMAND AND SUPPLY

---

elastic: – *adj.* **1** able to resume its normal bulk or shape spontaneously after contraction, dilatation, or distortion. **2** springy. **3** (of a person or feelings) buoyant. **4** flexible, adaptable (*elastic conscience*). **5** *Econ.* (of demand) variable according to price. **6** *Physics* (of a collision) involving no decrease of kinetic energy.[1]

'The *elasticity* (or *responsiveness*) *of demand* in a market is great or small according as the amount demanded increases much or little for a given fall in price, and diminishes much or little for a given rise in price.'[2]

Alfred Marshall (1842–1924)

'It is clear that economics, if it is to be a science at all, must be a mathematical science.'[3]

W. Stanley Jevons (1835–82)

Chapter objectives

Upon completing this chapter, the student should understand:

- the concept of price elasticity of demand;
- determinants of price elasticity;
- the relationship between elasticity and total revenue;
- cross-price and income elasticity;
- price elasticity of supply.

Outline

2.1 Price elasticity of demand
2.2 Cross-price elasticity of demand
2.3 Income elasticity of demand
2.4 Elasticity of supply

Introduction

The demand curve illustrates the negative relationship between price and quantity demanded. Therefore, if price increases, we can confidently predict that the quantity demanded will fall, *ceteris paribus*. In Chapter 1, we described this relationship as the law of demand. Although the law is useful, from a producer's point of view, it is not enough. The producer would like to know the sensitivity or responsiveness of quantity demanded to changes in price. Why? Total revenue depends not only on price, but also on the quantity sold. The producer would like to know if the additional revenue generated from the price increase will more than offset the revenue lost arising out of the fall in sales.

The relevant economic concept is elasticity. This term was first used in an economic context by the British economist, Alfred Marshall.

Definition
● ● ● ● ● ●

Elasticity measures the change in one variable in response to a change in another variable.

A producer is interested in the change in quantity demanded which will result from a change in price. This is one of three forms of elasticity of demand. Specifically, they include:

- Price elasticity of demand, η, which measures the sensitivity of quantity demanded to changes in price.[4]
- Cross-price elasticity of demand, $\eta_{A,B}$, which measures the sensitivity of quantity demanded of good A to changes in the price of good B.
- Income elasticity of demand, η_Y, which measures the sensitivity of quantity demanded to changes in income.

The first three sections of this chapter examine the three elasticities of demand. The final section is a brief analysis of the price elasticity of supply. This considers the degree of responsiveness of quantity supplied to changes in price.

2.1 Price elasticity of demand

Definition
● ● ● ● ● ●

Price elasticity of demand measures the responsiveness of quantity demanded to changes in the price of the same good or service.

It is sometimes referred to as own-price elasticity. The additional term 'own' distinguishes it from cross-price elasticity. This concept expresses in numeric form what the demand curve illustrates in graphic form. However, it goes one step further. The demand curve illustrates the negative relationship between price and quantity demanded, *ceteris paribus*. Elasticity confirms this negative relationship but also indicates the strength of the relationship, i.e. whether the percentage change in quantity demanded is greater than, less than or equal to the percentage change in price.

The formula for calculating the price elasticity of demand is as follows[5]

$$\eta = \frac{\text{\% Change in Quantity Demanded}}{\text{\% Change in Price}} = \frac{\dfrac{Q_2 - Q_1}{Q_1} \times 100}{\dfrac{P_2 - P_1}{P_1} \times 100} = \frac{\dfrac{\Delta Q}{Q} \times 100}{\dfrac{\Delta P}{P} \times 100} \qquad [2.1]$$

where: ΔQ = change in quantity demanded; ΔP = change in price; Q_1 = original quantity demanded; Q_2 = new quantity demanded; P_1 = original price; P_2 = new price.

We can make sense of this formula by way of example.

The Cake Shoppe in Clifden is the only location in town which sells locally baked bread. The owner checks his records and notices that he sells 250 loaves per week at a price of £1. He increases the price to £1.10. The level of demand falls to 200 loaves. What is the price elasticity of demand, the single numeric value which describes the responsiveness of quantity demanded to changes in price for this particular example? It is explained in the following few steps:

Step 1

Find the percentage change in price which is calculated as follows:

$$\frac{P_2 - P_1}{P_1} \times 100 = \frac{1.10 - 1.00}{1.00} \times 100 = \frac{.10}{1.00} \times 100 = 10\%$$

There is a 10% change (increase) in price.

Step 2

Find the percentage change in quantity demanded which is calculated as follows:

$$\frac{Q_2 - Q_1}{Q_1} \times 100 = \frac{200 - 250}{250} \times 100 = \frac{-50}{250} \times 100 = -20\%$$

There is a 20% change (decrease) in quantity demanded.

Step 3

Compare the percentage change in price with the percentage change in quantity demanded, as follows:

$$\eta = \frac{\% \text{ Change in Quantity Demanded}}{\% \text{ Change in Price}} = \frac{\frac{\Delta Q}{Q} \times 100}{\frac{\Delta P}{P} \times 100} = \frac{-20\%}{10\%} = -2$$

A 10% increase in price results in a 20% decrease in quantity demanded. The percentage change in quantity demanded is twice as large as the percentage change in price. The single numeric value which explains the sensitivity of quantity demanded to a change in price in this example is –2 (or 2 if, for the sake of simplicity we omit the minus sign and work with absolute values).

Because we measure elasticity as a percentage divided by a percentage, we eliminate the problem of different units of measurement. For example, the demand for milk, at retail, is measured in terms of price (in pence) per litre. Fabric, on the other hand, is measured in terms of price (in pounds) per metre. If we calculate elasticities, we can directly compare the price elasticity of demand for milk with the price elasticity of demand for fabric. It is for this reason that we refer to elasticity as a 'unit free' measure of response. The numeric value, in this case –2, is called the coefficient of elasticity. Another example is illustrated below.

Table 2.1: The demand for FAI Cup final tickets

Price, P (pounds)	Quantity, Q (thousands)
15.00	0
12.00	15
9.00	30
6.00	45
3.00	60
0.00	75

Let us take two price levels and their respective quantity levels.

Price (pounds, £)	Quantity (thousands)
12.00	15
9.00	30

Let P_1 = £12.00, and Q_1 = 15,000

Suppose price falls from £12 to £9. As a result quantity demanded rises from 15,000 to 30,000 units. For calculation purposes, let

$P_2 = £9.00$, and $Q_2 = 30,000$

We now derive the coefficient of elasticity for this particular example.

$$\eta = \frac{\dfrac{Q_2 - Q_1}{Q_1} \times 100}{\dfrac{P_2 - P_1}{P_1} \times 100} = \frac{\dfrac{30,000 - 15,000}{15,000} \times 100}{\dfrac{9 - 12}{12} \times 100} = \frac{\dfrac{15,000}{15,000} \times 100}{\dfrac{-3}{12} \times 100} = \frac{100\%}{-25\%} = -4$$

In this example a 25% change in price results in a 100% change in quantity demanded. The percentage change in quantity demanded is four times greater than the percentage change in price. The elasticity coefficient is –4.

The six points which form the demand curve have their own respective measures of elasticity. Table 2.2 shows the various elasticity measures at each price.

Table 2.2: Elasticity measures

Price, P (pounds)	Quantity, Q (thousands)	Elasticity measures (numeric values)
15.00	0	–infinity
12.00	15	–4.0
9.00	30	–1.5
6.00	45	–0.67
3.00	60	–0.25
0.00	75	0.00

The demand curve, with the respective elasticity measures, is shown in Figure 2.1 below.

Figure 2.1: The demand curve for FAI Cup final tickets

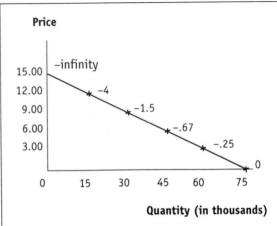

As we move down the demand curve the absolute values for the price elasticities decline. This applies in the specific case, as shown above, and in the general case, as shown below in Figure 2.2. Why so? Each successive fall in the price level, down along the vertical axis, represents a larger percentage fall in price. Therefore, the denominator in the formula for price elasticity of demand increases in size. Likewise, each successive rise in the quantity level, from left to right along the horizontal axis, represents a smaller percentage rise in quantity. The numerator in the formula for price elasticity of demand reduces in size. Hence, as we move down the demand curve the fractional measure of elasticity approaches zero.

Figure 2.2: Elasticity values and the demand curve

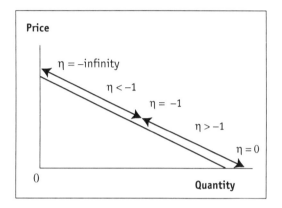

It is important to note that each point on the demand curve has its own unique elasticity measure.[6] It may appear odd that a straight line, with a constant slope in mathematical terms, can have a set of elasticity measures. The answer lies in the fact that we measure elasticity at different prices and subsequently examine the proportionate change in demand. This gives us a different elasticity measure at each price level on the demand curve (see Appendix 2.1 for an explanation of arc elasticity).

However, there are a small number of exceptions. Three of these exceptions are shown in Figure 2.3. In each of these cases, price elasticity is the same at each point along the demand curve.

Figure 2.3: Three special cases of price elasticity

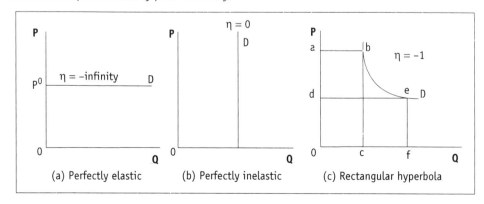

(a) A horizontal demand curve is perfectly (infinitely) elastic and has an elasticity coefficient equal to minus infinity. Demand is infinite at price P^0. The demand for an individual farmer's wheat in the US is an example of a perfectly elastic demand curve. If the farmer charges a price above P^0, there will be no demand for his product. Demand is perfectly responsive to a change in price. The market for agricultural commodities features perfectly elastic demand curves and is a good example of what economists call a 'perfectly competitive' market. We will discuss the different market structures in greater detail in Chapter 5.

(b) A vertical demand curve is perfectly inelastic and has an elasticity coefficient equal to zero. Price has no effect on the quantity demanded. For example, the demand for insulin by a diabetic is perfectly inelastic over a certain price range. A certain quantity is required regardless of the price. Demand is unresponsive to a change in price.

(c) A demand curve in the shape of a rectangular hyperbola has an elasticity coefficient equal to minus one. In this case, any percentage change in price is matched by an equal percentage change in quantity demanded. It is drawn so that the areas of all rectangles under the demand curve are equal. For example, the area of rectangle [ab0c] is equal to the area of rectangle [de0f]. We will see later that the area of any rectangle, at respective price and quantity levels, reflects total revenue.

Categories of price elasticity

There are three categories of price elasticity: elastic, inelastic and unit elastic.

Definition
● ● ● ● ● ●

The demand for a good is price elastic if the percentage change in quantity demanded is greater than the percentage change in price.

Numerically, the coefficient of elasticity is less than –1. The demand for a good with an elasticity coefficient equal to minus infinity is defined as perfectly elastic.

Definition
● ● ● ● ● ●

The demand for a good is price inelastic if the percentage change in quantity demanded is less than the percentage change in price.

The coefficient of elasticity falls between 0 and –1. The demand for a good with an elasticity coefficient equal to zero is defined as perfectly inelastic.

Definition
● ● ● ● ● ●

The demand for a good is unit elastic if the percentage change in quantity demanded is equal to the percentage change in price.

Numerically, the coefficient of elasticity is equal to –1.

A summary of the different categories of price elasticity is presented in Table 2.3 below.

Table 2.3: Summary of price elasticities

Category	ΔP compared to ΔQ (in percentage terms)	Elasticity Coefficient
Perfectly Elastic	ΔP < ΔQ	η = –infinity
Elastic	ΔP < ΔQ	η < –1
Unit Elastic	ΔP = ΔQ	η = –1
Inelastic	ΔP > ΔQ	η > –1
Perfectly Inelastic	ΔP > ΔQ	η = 0

The number line provides us with another opportunity to examine the different price elasticities. This is presented in Figure 2.4 below.

Figure 2.4: Using the number line to distinguish between the categories of price elasticities

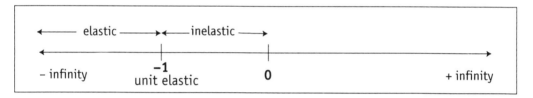

The determinants of price elasticity

The price elasticity of demand for any commodity is influenced by a number of different factors. The more common factors are examined below.

1. The number and availability of substitutes

The demand for commodities which have a large number of readily available and close substitutes is likely to be highly elastic. For example, the owner of the Cake Shoppe in Clifden found that the demand for his bread was elastic. Why? Numerous, acceptable substitutes are available from Allfresh, Pat the Baker, etc.

Similarly, if few substitutes are available for a good, demand is likely to be inelastic. For example, a commodity whose demand had, in the past, a low elasticity measure because of the scarcity of readily available substitutes was oil. OPEC, being aware that many consumers were heavily dependent on oil as their major energy source, took the opportunity to increase the price of oil by over 300% in 1973–74. The inelastic nature of the demand for oil meant that the fall-off in demand was not excessive.

2. The width of the definition

The narrower the definition of the good, the higher its elasticity measure. The broader the definition of the good, the lower its elasticity measure. For example, the demand for Guinness has a higher elasticity measure than the demand for alcohol whereas the demand for trousers has a lower elasticity measure than the demand for Levi 501s. In general, the demand for a particular brand of a commodity is more elastic than the demand for the commodity as a whole.

3. The time dimension

In certain circumstances, demand is inelastic over a short time period and is elastic over a long period of time. Sometimes it takes time for consumers to adjust their patterns of consumption to changes in price. Again, oil is a good example. The initial response to the increase in the price of oil was conservation. Consumers turned down the thermostat to use less oil. However, they could not immediately switch from oil to other fuels because that required a change in their heating systems. Over time, consumers did adapt or change their heating systems, often to combinations of oil, gas, electric and solid fuels. They were better able to switch from oil to other heating substitutes and their demand for oil became more price elastic.

Other factors influencing the price elasticity of demand include the proportion of income spent on the good, the durability of the good and the habit-forming or addictive nature of the good.

Although the measurement of price elasticity of demand seems to be quite straightforward, in reality it is not. Table 2.4 shows a sample of price elasticities for consumer goods in Ireland. These were calculated by different researchers over a seventeen-year period. Notice the variations in the estimations for each classification.

Table 2.4: Price elasticities in Ireland

Good	Price Elasticity estimation by		
	O'Riordan (1976)	Conniffe & Hegarty (1980)	Madden (1993)
Food	−0.43	−0.42	−0.57
Alcohol	−0.48	−0.56	−0.65
Tobacco	−	−	−0.35
Clothing and footwear	−1.01	−0.70	−0.69
Petrol	−	−	−0.19
Fuel and power	0.11	−0.06	−0.17
Durables	−0.48	−0.84	−1.05
Transport and equipment	−1.59	−1.02	−1.06
Other goods	−0.76	−0.35	−0.69
Services			−1.01

Source: 'A New Set of Consumer Demand Estimates for Ireland' by David Madden, *The Economic and Social Review*, 24, January 1993.

Although in certain classifications such as food and alcohol, the elasticity estimates are quite consistent, other classifications such as transport and equipment and durables show considerable variation. Part of this variation may be caused by actual changes in consumer behaviour over time.

However, most of the variation is probably due to differences in data and techniques. The earlier studies covered shorter estimation periods and the goods included in each classification have changed over time. Also, the mathematical techniques used to measure elasticity have changed with each new study. Madden, the author of the article, actually calculated fifteen different sets of estimates.

This shows us that we cannot simply accept that numbers, such as elasticities, are anything more than an estimate. If we want to use the elasticities for taxation policy or revenue projections, we must be quite certain that we understood the method by which the elasticities were calculated.

Elasticity and total revenue
······························

There is an important relationship between price elasticity and total revenue (TR). Total revenue is simply defined as price (P) multiplied by quantity (Q) and can be written as follows:

$$TR = P \times Q \qquad \text{[2.2]}$$

Total revenue is normally represented by a shaded area, as shown in Figure 2.5 below.[7] For example, quantity demanded is 45 when the price is £6. At this level of price and quantity total revenue is 45 x £6 = £270.

Figure 2.5: The demand curve and total revenue

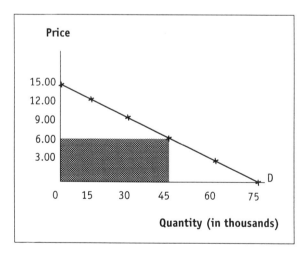

A change in price results in a change in quantity demanded which may result in a change in total revenue. The producer needs to know whether the price change will lead to an increase in total revenue?[8]

The price elasticity of the demand for the good determines the extent to which a change in price affects total revenue. This information could be used by the firm to decide if price should be changed. We can say pricing policy depends largely on the elasticity of demand. Two alternative cases are discussed below.

Case 1

A producer is considering an increase in the price of the commodity. The producer knows that if he increases price the consumer will respond by reducing the level of quantity demanded. However, it is the magnitude of the change in quantity which determines whether total revenue rises or falls. If the demand for the commodity is inelastic (or, at least inelastic between the two prices involved), the subsequent fall in demand in percentage terms is small relative to the price change in percentage terms. Consequently, the additional revenue received because of the increase in price outweighs the revenue lost due to the decrease in demand. The overall effect is an increase in total revenue.

If the demand for the commodity is elastic (or, at least elastic between these two particular prices), the subsequent drop in demand in percentage terms is large relative to the price change in percentage terms. Moreover, the revenue lost due to the fall in demand is greater than the additional revenue gained from the price increase. Thus, total revenue falls.

In brief, when revenue maximisation is the objective the producer will increase price if the demand for the commodity is price inelastic over the relevant price range, all other things being equal.

Figure 2.6 illustrates two possibilities for a price rise.

Figure 2.6: Case 1: A price rise

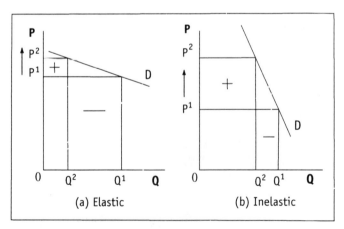

(a) Elastic   (b) Inelastic

In Figure 2.6(a), the demand curve is elastic between the two prices. The small box, denoted by +, represents the revenue gained from the increase in price. The large box, denoted by –, represents the revenue lost from the subsequent fall in demand. On account of the elastic demand over this price range, total revenue falls. The opposite is true for Figure 2.6(b). The revenue gained from the rise in price (represented by the large box and denoted by +) outweighs the revenue lost from the subsequent fall in demand (represented by the small box and denoted by –). The net change is positive.

Case 2

The producer considers a cut in price. If the producer reduces price, the consumer will respond by buying more of the product. However, it is the extent of the change in quantity which determines whether total revenue rises or falls. If demand for the commodity is inelastic (or, at least inelastic between the two specific prices), the subsequent rise in demand in percentage terms is small relative to the price change in percentage terms. Consequently, the loss in revenue due to the reduction in price outweighs the additional revenue gained from the increase in demand. The overall effect is a decrease in total revenue.

If the demand for the commodity is elastic (or, at least elastic between the two prices involved), the additional revenue received from the increase in demand out-weighs the revenue lost from the fall in price. By cutting price, the producer increases total revenue.

In brief, the producer will only cut price if the demand for the commodity is elastic, all other things being equal.

Figure 2.7 illustrates the case of a price fall.

Figure 2.7: Case 2: A price fall

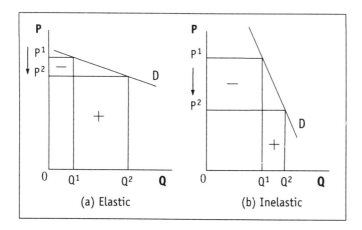

(a) Elastic   (b) Inelastic

A description similar to the one which accompanied Figure 2.6 applies here. The difference is the direction of the price change.

Table 2.5 presents the change in total revenue in response to price changes. Different demand elasticities are considered.

Table 2.5: Summary table of elasticity and total revenue

Price elasticity of demand	Price change	Total revenue change
Elastic	Increase	Fall
	Decrease	Rise
Inelastic	Increase	Rise
	Decrease	Fall

Price elasticity and maximum total revenue

Figure 2.2 indicates that elasticity coefficients (the fractional value) decline as we move down the demand curve. The top portion of the demand curve (the segment close to the vertical axis) reflects elastic demand whereas the bottom portion (the segment close to the horizontal axis) reflects inelastic demand. The point of unit elastic demand lies between the elastic and inelastic segments.

Figures 2.6 and 2.7 illustrate the changes in total revenue under different elasticity categories. As price falls total revenue increases if demand is elastic whereas total revenue decreases if the demand is inelastic. Taking these two observations together, we observe that total revenue reaches a maximum at the point of unit elastic demand. This is illustrated in Figure 2.8 below.

Figure 2.8: Price elasticity and maximum total revenue

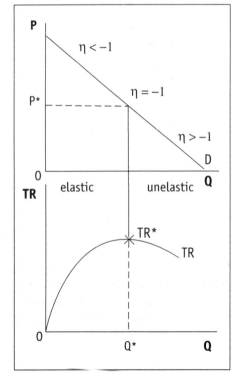

The top diagram is a reprint of Figure 2.2. The bottom diagram shows total revenue at different quantity levels. At the point of unit elastic demand, where $\eta = -1$, the total revenue curve is at its highest point. This indicates the specific price level, P* and corresponding quantity level, Q* where total revenue is maximised. If revenue maximisation is the producer's objective, (P*,Q*) is the desired price and output combination.

Government revenue and price elasticity

Governments as well as producers are interested in price elasticity of demand. Much government revenue is generated through Value Added Tax (VAT). This tax is levied as a percentage of the price of the good. This means that the amount of revenue which the government receives from VAT changes with the price per unit. For example, if the price of petrol is £1 per litre, and the VAT on petrol is 69%, the state will receive 69p for each litre of petrol sold. If the price of petrol increases to £1.10 per litre, the state receives approximately 76p per litre.

However, does an increase in price necessarily lead to an increase in tax revenue for the state? According to the Revenue Commissioners, the answer is 'No', at least in the situation described in the case study below.[9]

CASE STUDY

Extract from The Sunday Business Post
$.69PQ_1 = (.69P + .18dP)Q_2$
(or how the government says it will never get a windfall from the Gulf crisis)
by George Lee

Last week, The Sunday Business Post showed how, assuming Irish consumption of petrol does not fall below the level which prevailed in 1989, the government stand to benefit from a windfall gain of up to at least £36 million in a full year, on account of extra VAT on the higher world petrol prices generated by the Iraqi invasion of Kuwait.

But the Revenue Commissioners announced on Tuesday that when the price of petrol rises by 10% then consumption of petrol falls by 2.6%. This response factor is called 'the price elasticity of petrol'. If this response factor is applied to the petrol price changes experienced so far then it is the precise response factor which will generate the exact drop in petrol consumption required to wipe out completely any increase in VAT revenue from higher world petrol prices.

. . .

But the special response factor which the Revenue Commissioners say accurately measures the drop in petrol consumption in response to any increase in price is particularly worthy of comment. The Commissioners say that this response factor, or price elasticity as it is known to economists, is minus 0.26. What is mathematically unusual about this figure is that it suggests that government revenue from petrol sales will be broadly static over the next twelve months.

If this measure of the response factor is used then, regardless of petrol increases over the coming months, government revenue will always be broadly the same. It will not increase nor will it decrease.

This comes from the mathematical relationship between petrol sales and government revenue. Even if the world price of oil increased to $60 per barrel, total government revenue from petrol sales would be static.

. . .

Source: The Sunday Business Post, *21 October 1990.*

Questions

....

1. Why did the author of the original article in *The Sunday Business Post* assume that the government would benefit from a windfall gain of tax revenue as a result of the Iraqi invasion of Kuwait?
2. What is the author of this article initially assuming about the price elasticity of demand for petrol? Sketch the demand curve for petrol.
3. Why did the Revenue Commissioners disagree with the author's assessment of the petrol market?

Answers

....

1. The price of petrol on the world market increased as a result of the Gulf War. This led to a retail price rise in the Irish market. In other words, the price for a litre of petrol increased. This meant that the state was receiving more revenue per litre of petrol than it did before the Gulf War. The author assumed that Irish consumption of petrol would 'not fall below the level which prevailed in 1989'. If this was the case, the state would gain through higher tax revenues because the price that it received per unit increased while the quantity sold remained more or less the same.
2. If demand does not change, even though price changes, the demand curve must be perfectly inelastic. The vertical demand curve is shown in Figure 2.9.

Figure 2.9: The Irish market for petrol

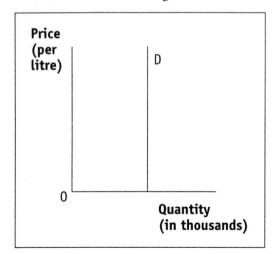

3. The Revenue Commissioners stated that the demand for petrol, although inelastic ($\eta = -0.26$), is not perfectly inelastic. Therefore, the extra tax revenue generated by the increase in the price will be offset, to some extent, by the decrease in revenue caused by falling demand. The author comments that the figure is 'mathematically unusual' because this particular magnitude of elasticity will ensure that 'government revenue from petrol sales will be broadly static over the next twelve months'.

The next section deals with cross-price elasticity of demand and the difference between substitutes and complements.

2.2 Cross-price elasticity of demand

Own-price elasticity measures the sensitivity of quantity demanded to a change in price of the same good or service.

Definition
● ● ● ● ● ●

Cross-price elasticity measures the sensitivity of quantity demanded of one good to a change in the price of another good.

If two goods are related, they are either substitutes for or complements to each other.
The formula for cross-price elasticity is very similar to the one used for own-price elasticity. It is the percentage change in quantity demanded of one good divided by the percentage change in price of the other related good. For two goods, A and B, cross-price elasticity $\eta_{A,B}$, can be expressed as follows:

[2.3]

$$\eta_{A, B} = \frac{\% \text{ Change in Quantity Demanded of Good A}}{\% \text{ Change in Price of Good B}}$$

$$\eta_{A, B} = \frac{\frac{\Delta Q}{Q} \times 100 \text{ of Good A}}{\frac{\Delta P}{P} \times 100 \text{ of Good B}}$$

If two goods are related to each other, the relationship is in either of two forms.
One possibility is for goods A and B to be substitutes for each other. Examples include beef and pork, apples and oranges, electricity and natural gas. Let us suppose the price of apples increases. The percentage change in the price of apples is positive. As apples and oranges can be used as substitutes for each other, consumers consequently consume less apples and more oranges. The percentage change in the quantity demanded of oranges is also positive. If both the numerator and the denominator are positive, then the quotient is also positive.[10]

A positive numeric value also results if the price of apples falls. In this situation, the percentage change in the price of apples and the percentage change in the quantity demanded of oranges are both negative. In brief, if goods are substitutes for each other, their cross-price elasticity is positive.

A second possibility is for goods A and B to be complements to each other. Examples include petrol and cars; pencils and erasers; cigarettes and lighters. Let us suppose the price of pencils increases. The percentage change in the price of pencils is positive. As pencils and erasers are consumed together, consumers subsequently demand fewer pencils and, in turn, fewer erasers. The percentage change in the quantity demanded of erasers is negative. If the numerator is negative and the denominator is positive then the quotient is negative.

A negative value also results if the price of pencils falls. In this situation, the percentage change in the price of pencils is negative but the percentage change in the quantity demanded of erasers is positive. In brief, if goods are complements to each other, their cross-price elasticity is negative.

The above analysis can be clearly illustrated by means of a number line, as Figure 2.10 shows below.

Figure 2.10: Using the number line to distinguish between different cross-price elasticities

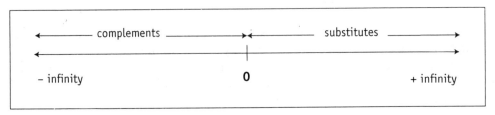

The magnitude of the change is reflected in the size of the numeric value. If the cross-price elasticity coefficient is relatively high, the percentage change in quantity demanded arising out of a percentage change in the price of a related good is relatively large. In contrast, a relatively low numeric value for the cross-price elasticity between two goods suggests that the percentage change in quantity demanded is small relative to the percentage change in the price of the related good.

If the cross-price elasticity is close to zero, the two goods are not related. An increase in the price of apples is unlikely to affect the demand for flowers, resulting in a zero cross-price elasticity between the two goods. We now consider income elasticity of demand.

2.3 Income elasticity of demand

Definition
● ● ● ● ● ●

Income elasticity of demand measures the responsiveness of quantity demanded to changes in income.

When discussing the role of the consumer and demand in Chapter 1 we distinguished between a normal and an inferior good. Both goods were defined, not in terms of price, but in terms of income.

The formula for income elasticity of demand is the percentage change in quantity demanded divided by the percentage change in income. The only difference between the formula of own-price elasticity and the formula of income elasticity is that income replaces price as the independent variable. Income elasticity of demand η_Y, is expressed as follows:

$$\eta_Y = \frac{\text{\% Change in Quantity Demanded}}{\text{\% Change in Income}} = \frac{\frac{\Delta Q}{Q} \times 100}{\frac{\Delta Y}{Y} \times 100} \qquad [2.4]$$

Consider the case of a normal good. Recall that as income changes the demand for a normal good changes in the same direction.

Let us suppose income increases. The percentage change in income is positive. As income increases the quantity demanded of the good increases. The percentage change in the quantity demanded is also positive. Since both the numerator and the denominator are positive, the quotient is also positive. If income falls the denominator is negative. However, less of the good is demanded as income falls so the numerator is also negative. The quotient is still a positive value. In brief, the income elasticity is a positive number for a normal good.

Consider the case of an inferior good. As income changes, the demand for the good changes in the opposite direction. Let us suppose income increases. The percentage change in income is positive. As income increases the demand for the inferior good decreases. The percentage change in the quantity demanded is negative. Since the numerator is negative and the denominator is positive, the quotient is negative. If income falls, the denominator is negative. However, more of the good is demanded as income falls so the numerator is positive. The quotient is still negative. In brief, the income elasticity is a negative number for an inferior good.

The relationship between income and quantity demanded can be shown diagramatically. It is called the Engel curve, after the German statistician Ernst Engel (1821–96) who carried out extensive research on the effect of changes in household budgets on household expenditures. Figure 2.11 illustrates the Engel curve for normal goods and inferior goods.

Figure 2.11: Engel curves

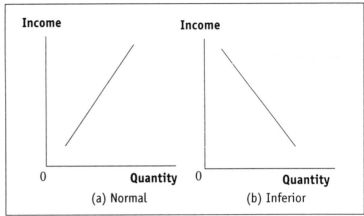

(a) Normal (b) Inferior

Figure 2.11(a) shows the positive relationship between income and quantity demanded which we associate with a normal good. By definition, as income increases, the demand for the normal good increases. The Engel curve for the normal good is upward sloping. Figure 2.11(b) illustrates the Engel curve for an inferior good. When income increases, we expect consumers to substitute goods of higher quality for the inferior good. The relationship between income and quantity demanded for the inferior good is negative. Hence, the Engel curve is downward sloping.

As with all elasticities, the above analysis can be illustrated by the use of the number line as shown in Figure 2.12 below.

Figure 2.12: Using the number line to distinguish between normal and inferior goods

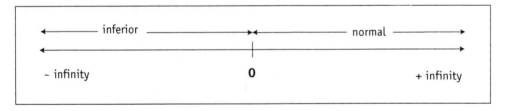

Positive income elasticities are observed for all normal goods. However, a further distinction can be made within this broad classification. If income rises, demand rises for a normal good. There is no restriction as to the actual magnitude of the increase in demand. It can be less than, equal to or greater than the increase in income. For a luxury good (sometimes referred to as a superior good) if income increases demand increases by a proportionately greater amount. In percentage terms the rise in demand is greater than the rise in income. It has an elasticity coefficient of greater than one. Examples include yachts, expensive cars and jewellery.

For a necessity (sometimes referred to as a basic or essential good) the increase in demand is proportionately less than the increase in income. In percentage terms the increase in demand is less than the increase in income. The elasticity coefficient is positive but less than one. Examples include soap and eggs.

The above examples apply to the domestic economy and to most Western countries. However, many of the commodities which are regarded as necessities in Ireland and other developed countries may be luxuries in less developed nations.[11]

Figure 2.13: Using the number line to distinguish between different income elasticities

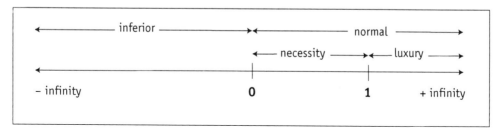

The number line in Figure 2.13 above illustrates the difference between a luxury and a necessity and how they compare to normal and inferior goods.[12]

A sample of income elasticities is listed in Table 2.6 below.

Table 2.6: Income elasticities in Ireland

| Good | Income elasticity estimation by | | |
	O'Riordan (1976)	Conniffe & Hegarty (1980)	Madden (1993)
Food	0.58	0.68	0.50
Alcohol	1.15	1.51	0.65
Tobacco	–	–	0.03
Clothing and footwear	1.75	1.37	1.74
Petrol	–	–	1.10
Fuel and power	1.61	1.66	0.29
Durables	1.67	1.72	1.95
Transport and equipment	2.12	3.52	2.31
Other goods	0.92	0.67	2.03
Services	–	–	0.90

Source: 'A New Set of Consumer Demand Estimates for Ireland' by David Madden, *The Economic and Social Review*, 24, January 1993.

Again, we observe considerable variation between the three sets of income elasticities. We notice that in looking at these broad classifications, there are no inferior goods. Only food and tobacco can be classified as necessities. According to the findings, clothing and footwear, durables, and transport and equipment are unambiguously luxuries. The other categories of goods vary between necessities and luxuries, depending on the study.

This reinforces the point that we made earlier. If anything, there is greater variation in the estimation of income elasticities than there was for price elasticities. This variation may be due to differences in consumer behaviour over time, differences in the data collection procedures and/or differences in technique.

2.4 Elasticity of supply

The analysis of the relationship between price and quantity applies equally as well to supply as it does to demand.

Definition

The price elasticity of supply measures the responsiveness of quantity supplied to changes in price.

The elasticity coefficient is positive, reflecting the conventional upward sloping supply curve of the firm. Terms such as elastic, unit elastic and inelastic are used to describe the degree of sensitivity between changes in price and the corresponding changes in quantity supplied.

Factors such as the costs of production, the level of technology, storage costs and the level of excess capacity affect the price elasticity of supply. Time is also an important factor in determining the price elasticity of supply. We can distinguish between three different periods of supply. They are shown in Figure 2.14.

Figure 2.14: Periods of supply

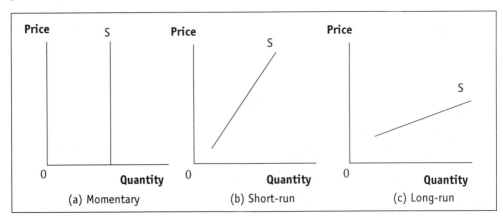

Momentary (market) supply

This period is so short that the firm does not have time to respond to price changes. In effect, the supply is fixed and this is reflected in a vertical supply curve. The momentary supply curve, shown in Figure 2.14(a) is perfectly inelastic with an elasticity coefficient equal to zero.

The term 'momentary' can be misleading. For example, the fish and fruit traders on Henry Street supply a certain amount to the market on any one day and are unable to vary the supply on that same day in response to a change in price. They can, however, vary their supply on the following day. In contrast, paper and timber suppliers may have to wait years for trees, the basic raw material for production, to grow. Momentary supply for the street trader may be a day whereas it may be a decade for the timber supplier.

Short-run supply
....
This period of time allows for some inputs to be varied while others remain unchanged.[13] The short-run supply curve, as represented in Figure 2.14(b), illustrates how quantity supplied responds to changes in price with the possibility that some alterations in the production process can be made. It has a positive elasticity coefficient.

Long-run supply
....
This period of time is long enough to allow for the full adjustment of the inputs involved in the production process. The long-run supply curve, as represented in Figure 2.14(c), shows how quantity supplied responds to price changes allowing for the possibility of adjustments of all inputs used in the production of the commodity. It also has a positive elasticity coefficient. The long-run supply curve is flatter than the short-run supply curve because more adjustments can be made in response to price changes in the long run.

A fourth possibility is the secular period.[14] This time period is very long and allows for changes in factors such as the education, training and skills of the workforce, the size of the population and the level of innovation and technology. These factors are generally ignored by mainstream, neoclassical economists and therefore do not feature in their theories and models.

The length of these periods varies from market to market. For example, the long run for a bakery may be a few weeks, a year perhaps for a furniture store, and possibly eight to ten years for an aircraft leasing company.

Only a brief discussion on the price elasticity of supply is given here. Supply and its price elasticity is largely influenced by costs and their responsiveness to output changes. This is analysed in greater detail in Chapter 4.

Summary

1. Elasticity explores the direction and the magnitude of changes in quantity arising out of changes in economic variables. Elasticity of demand is the most common measure. There are three elasticities of demand: price, cross-price and income.
2. Price elasticity of demand measures the responsiveness of quantity demanded to changes in price. This sensitivity can be expressed in the form of a numeric value. The coefficient of elasticity is usually negative. Each point on the demand curve

has an elasticity measure. There are three categories of price elasticity: elastic, inelastic or unit elastic. Factors which influence price elasticity include the time period, the number of substitutes available and the width of the definition.

3. The price elasticity of demand determines the extent to which a change in price affects total revenue where total revenue is simply price times quantity. In order to maximise total revenue, a producer will only increase price if demand is inelastic and, likewise, will only cut price if demand is elastic. Total revenue is maximised at the point of unit elastic demand.

4. Cross-price elasticity measures the sensitivity of quantity demanded of one good to changes in the price of another good. Substitute goods have a positive cross-price elasticity. Complementary goods have a negative cross-price elasticity.

5. Income elasticity of demand measures the sensitivity of quantity demanded to changes in income. A positive income elasticity reflects a normal good. An inferior good has a negative income elasticity. We also use income elasticities to classify goods as either necessities or luxuries, depending on the magnitude of the response to a change in income.

6. Price elasticity of supply measures the responsiveness of quantity supplied to changes in price. The elasticity coefficient is usually positive. Its magnitude depends on production costs and the time period.

Key terms

Elasticity
Elasticity of demand
Price elasticity
Cross-price elasticity
Income elasticity
Coefficient of elasticity
Elastic
Inelastic
Unit elastic
Perfectly inelastic
Perfectly elastic
Total revenue
Engel curve
Luxury
Necessity
Elasticity of supply

Review questions

1. Explain the term 'elasticity'. How is this term related to the theory of demand and supply?
2. What is the connection between the three different measures of elasticity of demand? What are the differences between each measure?

3. Explain the difference between point elasticity of demand and arc elasticity of demand.
4. What factors influence the price elasticity of demand for a good?
5. How is elasticity useful when analysing the effect of price changes on total revenue?
6. Explain why both cross-price elasticity and income elasticity can result in either positive or negative coefficient values whereas price elasticity is usually limited to negative values.

Working problems

1. The demand for cinema tickets is shown below.

Table 2.7

Price	Quantity
3	8
4	7
5	6
6	5
7	4

(a) Sketch the demand curve for cinema tickets.
(b) Estimate a measure of price elasticity at all five points on the demand curve.
(c) Explain why these values (in absolute terms) decline as the demand curve slopes down from left to right.

2. The set of data in Table 2.8 below was processed over a five-year period. It has been confirmed that there was no change in the preferences of the family in question. Also, there were no changes recorded in the price of any other good.

Table 2.8

Year	1	2	3	4	5
Price of A (£)	72	60	60	66	72
Price of B (£)	36	28	22	28	36
Family income (£000 per year)	170	250	250	250	265
Quantity of A demanded (per year)	60	75	85	70	65
Quantity of B demanded (per year)	130	150	180	170	160

From the above data, calculate:

(a) the price elasticity of demand for A;
(b) the price elasticity of demand for B;
(c) the income elasticity of demand for A;
(d) the cross-price elasticity of demand for B.

Interpret your answers.

Multi-choice questions

1. The price elasticity of demand for a commodity:
    (a) measures the sensitivity of price to changes in quantity demanded;
    (b) is always positive;
    (c) measures the degree of responsiveness of quantity demanded to changes in price;
    (d) can be positive or negative but never zero;
    (e) none of the above.

2. The price elasticity of demand for a good is –0.1. Thus:
    (a) a 10% increase in price increases demand by 1%;
    (b) a 10% decrease in price increases demand by 10%;
    (c) it is price inelastic;
    (d) both (a) and (c) above;
    (e) both (b) and (c) above.

3. If the price elasticity of demand is perfectly inelastic for the entire price range, then:
    (a) the elasticity coefficient is equal to minus infinity;
    (b) the elasticity coefficient is equal to zero;
    (c) the demand curve for the good is vertical;
    (d) both (b) and (c) above;
    (e) none of the above.

4. On the first day of the year the price of a daily newspaper is 25p. 200,000 copies are demanded. On the last day of the year price is 30p and quantity demanded is 150,000. The elasticity coefficient is equal to:
    (a) 0.80;
    (b) –1.25;
    (c) –0.80;
    (d) 1.25;
    (e) none of the above.

5. Cars and car tyres are complements. Thus:
    (a) as the price of cars increases the demand for car tyres declines;
    (b) the cross-price elasticity coefficient is positive;
    (c) the cross-price elasticity coefficient is negative;
    (d) both (a) and (b) above;
    (e) both (a) and (c) above.

6. Suppose income falls from £60 per week to £50 per week. As a result quantity demanded of good X falls from 300 units to 280 units. Thus:
    (a) X is a necessity;
    (b) X is a normal good;
    (c) the income elasticity measure is positive;
    (d) the income coefficient of elasticity is 0.4;
    (e) all of the above.

True or false

1. Price elasticity of demand measures the responsiveness of price to changes in quantity demanded. _____
2. A 15% rise in price with a subsequent 5% fall in quantity demanded results in a price elasticity coefficient of –3. _____
3. A good which has few or no substitutes is likely to have a relatively steep demand curve. _____
4. All necessities are normal goods but not all normal goods are necessities. _____
5. The longer the time period, the more elastic is supply and the flatter the supply curve. _____
6. A vertical supply curve is perfectly inelastic with a zero elasticity coefficient. _____

Fill in the blanks

In economic terms elasticity measures the _____ of one variable to changes in another variable. Economists are interested in both the elasticity of _____ and the elasticity of _____. There are _____ different elasticities of demand. _____ price elasticity measures the sensitivity of quantity _____ to changes in the _____ of the good. It is usually _____ which confirms the _____ of demand, *ceteris paribus*. Furthermore, there are three categories of price elasticity of demand: elastic, _____ and _____ elastic. _____-price elasticity measures the sensitivity between the price of one good and the quantity of _____ good. The relevant elasticity coefficient can be _____ or _____. The third is income elasticity of demand where the _____ variable is _____. Normal goods have a _____ income coefficient, _____ goods have a negative income coefficient. The elasticity _____ for price elasticity of supply is usually _____ reflecting the conventional _____ sloping _____ curve.

CASE STUDY

Extract from The Irish Times
Street price of drugs could soar with new Garda powers;
Drug project leader warns of effects of curbs on dealers
by Padraig O Morain

The street price of drugs could soar if the proposed legislation aimed at drug dealers is successful, one of Dublin's main drugs counselling services has warned. The new measures, which include Garda powers to detain suspected dealers for seven days for questioning, could make matters worse unless they are accompanied by more treatment facilities and more prevention programmes, according to Mr Tony Geoghegan, of the Merchant's Quay Project. The project counsels drug users and supports them in giving up drugs.

Mr Geoghegan said the project welcomes the tougher stance on drug dealers but warns that any success which the new policy enjoys 'will be gained at a price'.

→

'The curtailment in the supply of drugs will seriously inflate the price of drugs on the street and drug-related activity will, of necessity, become more clandestine, more organised and in some respects more criminally dangerous for the average drug user and the community as a whole', he said. 'Regardless of the changes in legislation, drug users will still seek drugs and, if the price is increased, they may resort to more serious crimes to secure money to finance their addiction', he said.

. . .

An effective campaign against the drugs problem would require a number of additional measures on top of those proposed by the government, he said. These included funding for prevention programmes, more facilities and a strong attack on poverty. Without such moves, the impact of the new measures will be minimal 'and will not make any significant difference to the life experiences of drug users', he said.

. . .

Source: The Irish Times, *22 July 1995.*

Questions

....

1. Why does Mr Geoghegan predict that the tougher stance on drug dealers will 'inflate the price of drugs on the street . . .'? Will it cause the demand curve or the supply curve to shift?
2. Do you think that the demand curve for drugs is elastic or inelastic? Draw a demand/supply diagram of the drug market. Arising from (a), show the change in the price of drugs.
3. Consider the revenue of the drug suppliers. What might happen to the total amount spent on drugs as more is seized?
4. Does Mr Geoghegan's subsequent discussion on an 'effective campaign against the drugs problem' appear to focus on the demand side or the supply side of the market? What problems might he face in introducing the new measures?

Appendix 2.1: Arc elasticity

The definition for price elasticity used in this chapter is often referred to as point elasticity. It measures the elasticity at every point along the demand curve. Each elasticity coefficient is calculated from an initial point or base. This base reflects the starting price and the corresponding quantity level. Consequently, the result varies as the initial price changes.

Arc elasticity measures the elasticity of demand over a price range using the midpoint or average price as the base. In graphic terms, it is the elasticity over the length of a segment or arc of the demand curve. Hence, it is called arc elasticity. The formula for arc elasticity is expressed as follows:

[2.5]

$$\frac{\dfrac{\Delta Q}{.5(Q_1 + Q_2)} \times 100}{\dfrac{\Delta P}{.5(P_1 + P_2)} \times 100} = \frac{\dfrac{\Delta Q}{Q_1 + Q_2} \times 100}{\dfrac{\Delta P}{P_1 + P_2} \times 100}$$

where: ΔQ = change in quantity demanded; ΔP = change in price; Q_1 = original quantity demanded; Q_2 = new quantity demanded; P_1 = original price; P_2 = new price.

An example is shown below using the same price levels and quantity levels as in the earlier example of FAI Cup final tickets.

Price (pounds)	Quantity (thousands)
12.00	15
9.00	30

Let P_1 = £12.00
$\quad$ Q_1 = 15,000
$\quad$ P_2 = £9.00
$\quad$ Q_2 = 30,000

Thus,

$$\frac{\dfrac{Q_2 - Q_1}{.5(Q_1 + Q_2)}}{\dfrac{P_2 - P_1}{.5(P_1 + P_2)}} = \frac{\dfrac{30{,}000 - 15{,}000}{.5(15{,}000 + 30{,}000)}}{\dfrac{9 - 12}{.5(12 + 9)}} = \frac{\dfrac{15{,}000}{22{,}500}}{\dfrac{-3}{10.5}} = -2.33$$

The elasticity coefficient using the arc formula is –2.33. As expected, it is between the coefficient of –4 (this is the point elasticity with a base of P_1 = £12.00 and Q_1 = 15,000) and the coefficient of –1.5 (this is the point elasticity with a base of P_1 = £9.00 and Q_1 = 30,000).

The arc elasticity method provides a measure at neither the start nor the end price but at an average price. Thus, the elasticity coefficient using the arc method lies between the two relevant point elasticity measures.

CHAPTER 3

THE CONSUMER AND DEMAND

'Value in use cannot be measured by any known standard; it is differently estimated by different persons.'[1]

David Ricardo (1772–1823)

'Value depends entirely on utility.'[2]

W. Stanley Jevons (1835–82)

'A person maximises his utility when he distributes his available money among the various goods so that he obtains the same amount of satisfaction from the last unit of money spent upon each commodity.'[3]

Hermann H. Gossen (1810–58)

Chapter objectives

Upon completing this chapter, the student should understand:

- marginal utility and the principle of diminishing marginal utility;
- the equi-marginal principle;
- indifference curves and budget lines;
- substitution and income effects;
- differences in the demand curves for normal, inferior and Giffen goods;
- the differences between the two main theories of demand.

Outline

3.1 **An historical perspective**
3.2 **The marginal utility analysis**
3.3 **The indifference-preference analysis**
3.4 **Consumer surplus**

Introduction

In Chapter 1 we gave an intuitive explanation as to why the demand curve slopes down from left to right. This chapter provides us with a more rigorous explanation of the theory of demand. It examines the behaviour of consumers in the market and how they react to price changes. Its purpose is to explain the downward sloping demand curve as described in Chapter 1.

We begin with an historical account of the theory of demand. This is followed by an analysis of the two main theories of consumer behaviour. The concept of consumer surplus is also explained.

3.1 An historical perspective

Marginal utility analysis
....

There are two main theories of demand. The first is the marginal utility or cardinalist analysis. Central to this approach is the assumption that utility can be measured in absolute terms like weight or height. It prescribes the measurement of satisfaction in absolute terms.

This approach was instrumental in elucidating the paradox of value which remained unresolved for many centuries and left scholars from Plato to Adam Smith baffled. The paradox of value means that some goods, for example, water and salt, have a high value in use but a low value in exchange while others, such as diamonds and gold, have a low value in use but a high value in exchange.

In the 1770s Adam Smith had asked the question, 'How is it that water, which is so essential to human life, has a low market value whereas diamonds, which are relatively trivial, have a high market value?'[4] This paradox remained unanswered until the marginal utility revolution of the 1870s. Economists including W. Stanley Jevons in England, Carl Menger (1840–1921) in Austria and Leon Walras (1834–1910) in Switzerland were independently responsible for bringing the marginal utility approach to the forefront of economic thinking.[5]

The 'marginalists', as they were later identified, claimed that the market value of a good is determined by its utility to the consumer. The marginalists' contribution was to distinguish between total utility and marginal utility. Total utility is the pleasure or satisfaction which an individual receives from consuming a particular good or service. Marginal utility is the additional utility which a person receives if she consumes one more unit of a particular good or service. While total utility increases with consumption, the addition to utility (or marginal utility) diminishes as more units are consumed.

The distinction between total and marginal utility was central to the solution to the water-diamond paradox. Water is essential. Therefore, the total utility that we receive from consuming it is high. But, the extra amount of satisfaction obtained by consuming an additional unit of water (or its marginal utility) is low because we consume such a large volume. On the other hand, because we consume such a small amount of diamonds, we obtain a high amount of satisfaction at the margin. The few units of diamonds which we do consume have a high marginal utility. The application of marginal utility was the first step in explaining the paradox of value.[6]

Indifference-preference analysis
....

The marginalists, particularly Jevons, believed that a method for measuring utility would ultimately be discovered. So far, we have not found an absolute measure of happiness and this deficiency limits the usefulness of this approach. A second approach, called the indifference-preference or ordinalist analysis relies on ranking or ordering preferences, rather than assigning absolute values to the level of utility gained from consumption. This approach entered the mainstream of economic theory through the efforts of John R. Hicks (1904–89) and Roy G. Allen (1906–83).[7]

Although the second approach dominates consumer theory, it is a modification rather than a replacement of the utility approach. Hence, we will begin our examination of consumer theory with the marginal utility analysis and then discuss the indifference-preference analysis.

3.2 The marginal utility analysis

An outline of utility theory
....

Classical economists, particularly David Ricardo, believed that the value of a good was determined by the wages paid to labour. This is called the labour theory of value. This explanation focuses on the supply side of the market. The marginalists, on the other hand, argued that utility was the basis of value. Their discussion focused on the consumer, or the demand side of the market. In terms of the theory of price determination as we know it today (and as explained in Chapter 1), each of the groups mentioned above was looking at only one half of the story. We will now look at the marginalists' contribution to our understanding of the demand side of the market. We begin by defining a few of the relevant terms.

● **Definition**
● ● ● ● ● ●

Utility is the economist's term for the satisfaction or pleasure that we derive from consuming a good or service.

● **Definition**
● ● ● ● ● ●

Total utility (TU) is the total satisfaction that a consumer gains from the consumption of a given quantity of a good.

● **Definition**
● ● ● ● ● ●

Marginal utility (MU) is the extra or additional satisfaction that the consumer gains from consuming one extra unit of the good.

The difficulty with this approach is in measuring utility which is both abstract and subjective. This problem can be overcome by defining a unit of measure called a 'util'. A util is an imaginary unit which measures satisfaction or utility. If a person consumes a particular commodity, the satisfaction which she receives is measured in utils.

Using the util as a unit of measure, we can examine the relationship between total utility and marginal utility. Table 3.1 shows the total utility and marginal utility derived by an individual from eating packets of crisps.

Table 3.1: Consumer's utility from consuming crisps

Quantity (packets)	TU (utils)	MU (utils)
0	0	
		7
1	7	
		4
2	11	
		2
3	13	
		1
4	14	
		0
5	14	
		–2
6	12	

To calculate total utility, we add the utilities for each unit consumed. Marginal utility is the utility gained from consuming one more unit.[8] The marginal utility gained from consuming the first unit is 7 utils. The marginal utility gained by consuming the second unit is 4 utils (11 utils – 7 utils), and so on.

This information is shown in Figure 3.1. Satisfaction, measured in utils, is the variable on the vertical axis. The number of packets of crisps consumed (Q) is the variable on the horizontal axis.

Figure 3.1: Total and marginal utility

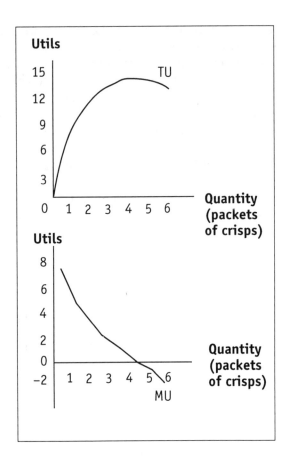

Typically, total utility curves are in the shape of a reverse U (our example only illustrates the first six units consumed). For the first few units total utility increases but at a decreasing rate. It is rising but at a slower and slower rate. Total utility then reaches a maximum. The level of satisfaction derived from consuming the particular commodity is at its highest. After this it declines and slopes down. The consumption of more units of the good would have a negative impact. In fact, these extra units would yield dissatisfaction or what economists call disutility.

The marginal utility curve slopes downwards. It reflects a very important concept in the theory of consumer choice, a concept which Marshall referred to as 'This familiar and fundamental tendency of human nature . . .'[9]

Definition
● ● ● ● ● ●

The principle of diminishing marginal utility states that the more of a commodity we consume, the less extra satisfaction we gain.

This extra satisfaction is the marginal utility. So the marginal utility for each additional unit decreases. In other words, the marginal utility curve declines as consumption increases.

Initially the total utility curve increases at a decreasing rate and the marginal utility curve slopes downwards but the values are still positive. The marginal utility curve intersects the quantity axis when total utility is at a maximum. Finally, as the total utility curve slopes downwards reflecting disutility, the marginal utility curve is below the quantity axis reflecting both negative and declining values. We now turn to the consumer's objective which economists assume to be utility maximisation.

Utility maximisation and consumer equilibrium
···

We begin with the assumption that the consumer aims to maximise utility subject to constraints. The two constraints which limit the choices of the consumer are income and prices.

The utility-maximisation equilibrium condition is best illustrated by way of an example.

The O'Farrell family travel to Dublin on All-Ireland Final day. On their arrival at Croke Park, they decide to dress in the colours of their team. However, they have a limited budget of £48 and can only choose between the following: flags, hats and scarves. Flags cost £2, hats cost £4 and scarves cost £6. Table 3.2 presents the total utilities of the three commodities.

Table 3.2: The O'Farrell family's three alternatives: flags, hats and scarves

Flags		Hats		Scarves	
Q	TU	Q	TU	Q	TU
0	0	0	0	0	0
1	24	1	48	1	60
2	46	2	92	2	114
3	66	3	132	3	162
4	84	4	168	4	204
5	100	5	200	5	240
6	114	6	228	6	270

The marginal utilities are presented in Table 3.3 below. They are constructed for differently priced goods. For the purpose of comparison we divide the marginal utility for a unit of good by its price to find the marginal utility per pound (MU/P).

Table 3.3: Maximising utility by equalising MUs per pound spent

Flags				Hats				Scarves			
Q	TU	MU	MU/P	Q	TU	MU	MU/P	Q	TU	MU	MU/P
0	0			0	0			0	0		
		24	12			48	12			60	10
1	24			1	48			1	60		
		22	11			44	11			54	9
2	46			2	92			2	114		
		20	10			40	10			48	8
3	66			3	132			3	162		
		18	9			36	9			42	7
4	84			4	168			4	204		
		16	8			32	8			36	6
5	100			5	200			5	240		
		14	7			28	7			30	5
6	114			6	228			6	270		

We will find the best bundle which the O'Farrell family can afford by applying the equi-marginal principle.

● Definition
● ● ● ● ● ●

The equi-marginal principle states that utility is maximised when the utility for the last pound spent on each good is the same.

Assuming that all of the consumer's income is spent, this principle ensures that the consumer will not find it possible to increase utility by switching a pound's worth of expenditure from one good to another.[10]

For two goods X and Y, the equi-marginal principle can be expressed in algebraic terms, as shown in Equation 3.1.

$$\frac{MU_X}{P_X} = \frac{MU_Y}{P_Y}$$ [3.1]

In the example above, the utility-maximising rule holds for four different combinations;

Combination 1 = (3 flags, 3 hats and 1 scarf)
Combination 2 = (4 flags, 4 hats and 2 scarves)
Combination 3 = (5 flags, 5 hats and 3 scarves)
Combination 4 = (6 flags, 6 hats and 4 scarves)

Total cost and total utility for these four combinations are calculated in Table 3.4.

Table 3.4: Four possible combinations

	Combination 1	*Combination 2*	*Combination 3*	*Combination 4*
Flags at £2 ea.	£ 6	£ 8	£10	£12
Hats at £4 ea.	£12	£16	£20	£24
Scarves at £6 ea.	£ 6	£12	£18	£24
Total cost	£24	£36	£48	£60
Total utility	258	366	462	546

Combinations 1 and 2 do not satisfy the condition that all income is used. Thus, the consumer is not maximising utility with either of these combinations. The income limit of £48 is exceeded in the choice of combination 4. The consumer maximises utility when he chooses combination 3. All income is spent and total utility is equal to 462 units.

The following is the utility-maximising combination subject to the £48 budget constraint,

$$\frac{16}{2} = \frac{32}{4} = \frac{48}{6}$$

Similarly, we can consider other combinations which will use all of the family's available income, but do not satisfy the principle that the utility for the last pound spent is equal for all available goods. We will compare combination 3 (the utility-maximising combination of flags, hats and scarves) with two other affordable combinations:

Combination 3 = (5 flags, 5 hats and 3 scarves)
Combination 5 = (4 flags, 4 hats and 4 scarves)
Combination 6 = (5 flags, 2 hats and 5 scarves)

Total cost and total utility for these three combinations are calculated in Table 3.5.

Table 3.5: Three affordable combinations

	Combination 3	*Combination 5*	*Combination 6*
Flags at £2 each	£10	£ 8	£10
Hats at £4 each	£20	£16	£ 8
Scarves at £6 each	£18	£24	£30
Total cost	£48	£48	£48
Total utility	462	456	432

All of these combinations are affordable, but only one, combination 3, maximises utility. This is the only one of the three combinations where marginal utility divided by price is equal for the last unit consumed.

Combination 3 is the best combination that the O'Farrell family can afford. They cannot increase utility by switching a pound's worth of expenditure from one good to another. Since there is no tendency to change, it is an equilibrium position.

This analysis can be used to explain why the demand curve is negatively sloped. For example, let us concentrate on the utility derived from the consumption of scarves. At the existing price level of £6 the utility-maximising rule indicates that the O'Farrell family will purchase three scarves. Suppose that the street hawkers cut their price. As a result the O'Farrells will switch consumption away from both flags and hats to the lower-priced scarves. The utility-maximising rule will yield a new combination in equilibrium. The new combination will include a higher quantity of scarves at the lower price. This suggests a negative relationship between the price and the quantity demanded which is reflected in a downward sloping demand curve for this commodity.

Synopsis of the marginal utility approach

The assumptions

1. The consumer can measure satisfaction by utils.
2. The consumer has a particular income, and prices are established in the market.
3. The principle of diminishing marginal utility.

The theory

The consumer wishes to maximise utility, given her income and price constraints.

The predictions

Consumer equilibrium is achieved with the combination of goods which satisfy the equi-marginal principle. In other words, the consumer will maximise utility where the utilities for the last pound spent are equal for all commodities, and all income is spent.

The weaknesses

1. There is no 'satisfactory' way of measuring utility.
2. Interpersonal utility comparisons are not possible.

We now turn to the second approach.

3.3 The indifference-preference analysis

The weaknesses in the marginal utility approach to consumer choice theory led to the development of the indifference-preference approach. This approach acknowledges the difficulties involved in attempting to measure utility. These difficulties can be overcome by an ordinal approach which merely requires that the consumer rank or order different alternatives according to preference. It does not depend on allocating specific numerical values to different levels of satisfaction.

For example, if the consumer is faced with a choice between food and drink the indifference-preference approach allows for three alternatives: either food is preferred to drink, or drink is preferred to food or, finally, the consumer is indifferent between various quantities of food and drink. Central to this approach is the importance of preferences.

A number of assumptions apply to the consumer's preferences.

1. The consumer ranks alternatives according to tastes and preferences which do not depend on income or prices.
2. Preferences must satisfy the law of transitivity, i.e. if a consumer chooses combination A over combination B and also chooses the same combination B over combination C then the consumer must be consistent by choosing combination A over combination C.
3. The consumer prefers more to less. This observation excludes what we call bads, e.g. pollution, garbage, where the consumer prefers less to more.
4. Any two consumption bundles can be compared. This is known as the axiom of completeness.

The first assumption makes reference to the two constraints, income and prices. These constraints are represented by a budget line which we will discuss later. We begin our analysis with a look at another new concept – an indifference curve.

The indifference curve
....

• Definition
● ● ● ● ● ●

An indifference curve shows all the bundles of two goods that give the same level of utility to the consumer.

Although these points represent different combinations of goods, the consumer is indifferent between the combinations. We say that utility is constant along any given indifference curve. Indifference curves reflect the consumer's tastes and preferences for the good.

There are a number of properties of indifference curves. These are listed here and discussed in greater detail in Appendix 3.1.

1. Indifference curves slope down from left to right.
2. The slope of the indifference curve is determined by tastes and preferences and is called the marginal rate of substitution (MRS).
3. Indifference curves are normally convex to the origin.
4. Indifference curves do not intersect.
5. There is a multiple set of indifference curves, called a preference map.
6. The higher the indifference curve, the higher the level of utility.

An indifference curve is illustrated in Figure 3.2.

Figure 3.2: An indifference curve

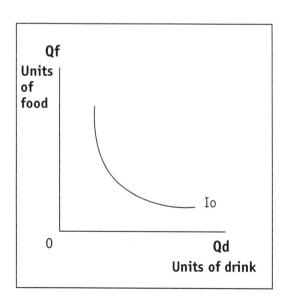

Indifference curves reflect individual tastes and preferences. For example, a consumer may consume both food and drink but prefer drink. This set of preferences is shown in Figure 3.3(a). The indifference curve is relatively steep. To gain an additional unit of drink, the consumer is willing to give up several units of food. Alternatively, Figure 3.3(b) shows a relatively flat indifference curve. In this case, the consumer is willing to give up several units of drink in order to gain an additional unit of food. This particular indifference curve indicates that the consumer prefers food to drink.

Figure 3.3: Indifference curves and preferences between two goods

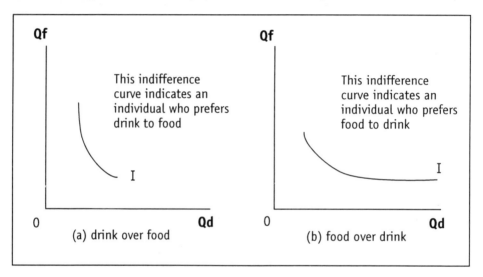

The income of the consumer and the prices of the goods, however, limit the endless wants of the consumer. These constraints are reflected in our second new concept, the budget line.

The budget line
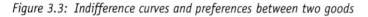

Definition
● ● ● ● ● ●

The budget line illustrates the maximum combination of two goods that the consumer can purchase, given her level of income and prices.

It constrains the consumer's choices. In effect, it splits the two-dimensional space into two parts, the affordable and the unaffordable. The feasible alternatives are located on or inside the budget line whereas the much larger range of infeasible alternatives is found outside the budget line. The two constraints, income and prices, determine the position and the slope of the budget line. A change in either or both of the constraints results in a new budget line.

The position of the budget line is determined by the level of income, as illustrated in Figure 3.4. As income increases, the budget line moves away from the origin and, as a result, the affordable space increases. If income falls, the budget line moves closer to the origin and the affordable space contracts.

Figure 3.4: The budget line and changes in income

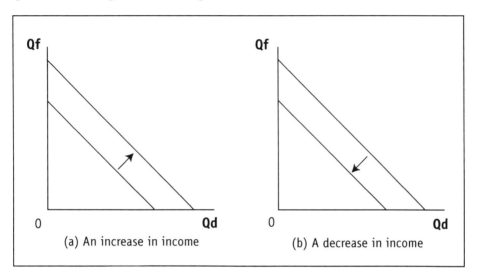

(a) An increase in income   (b) A decrease in income

The slope of the budget line is determined by the level of relative prices. The slope measures the opportunity cost of one good, food, in terms of another good, drink. For example, suppose that drink costs £2 per unit and food costs £1 per unit. In order to consume a unit of drink, the consumer must forgo two units of food. The opportunity cost of a drink is two units of food. To put this another way, the budget line indicates the trade-off between the two goods. Formally, the slope of the budget line is equal to the negative of the ratio of the two prices. Equation 3.2 states this in mathematical form.

$$\textbf{Slope of the budget line} = \frac{-\textbf{Pd}}{\textbf{Pf}} \qquad [3.2]$$

where: Pd = price of drink; Pf = price of food.

If the good on the vertical axis is expensive in relation to the good on the horizontal axis, the budget line is relatively flat. Conversely, if the good on the horizontal axis is expensive in relation to the good on the vertical axis the budget line is relatively steep. This is shown in Figure 3.5.

Figure 3.5: *Relative prices and the slope of the budget line*

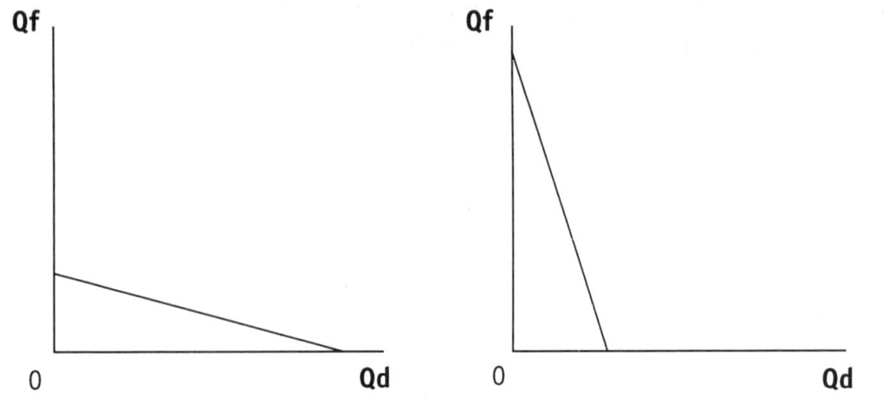

(a) The good on the vertical axis is relatively expensive. The result is a flat budget line.

(b) The good on the horizontal axis is relatively expensive. The result is a steep budget line.

We now consider the budget line of low-income families in Cork, where a ban on bituminous coal has been imposed.

CASE STUDY

Extract from The Irish Times
Use of bituminous coal to be prohibited in Cork city and suburbs from next year

Bituminous coal will be banned in Cork city from next year at a cost to the Exchequer of £1.2 million, it was announced yesterday by the Minister for the Environment, Mr Smith and the Minister of State for Environmental Protection, Mr John Browne.

The city, because of its basin-like geographical position, has suffered from twice the average level of smoke concentrations in other urban areas. The ban will cover the centre of the city and adjacent areas which have been covered since 1993 by other measures designed to reduce the use of bituminous coal, including the banning of slack. The restrictions will cover all of Cork city and the district electoral division of Ballicollig, Douglas, Inishkenny, Lehenagh, Rathcooney, Bishopstown and St Mary's.

The government has approved a £3-a-week supplement to the normal fuel allowance for lower-income households.

Mr Smith said that the decision to ban bituminous coal had been taken because smoke levels in Cork for the past few years had threatened to exceed the air quality limits fixed by national and EU legislation.

. . .

→

A health survey conducted by the Mahon Community Association in 1991 showed that 66% of the families had one or more members suffering from at least one respiratory illness . . .

Ms Harrington said that she and three of her four children suffered from asthma and on numerous occasions during winter could not go outside because of the smog.

Source: The Irish Times, *13 October 1994.*

Questions
....

1. Why has the state decided to ban bituminous coal? What hardship will this ban impose? How does the government propose to help the affected households?
2. Suppose that the Harrington family is receiving dole payments of £75 per week. Food and brown coal briquettes (a replacement fuel for bituminous coal) can both be purchased for £1 per unit. Draw the budget line of the family.
3. Suppose that the government pays a £3-a-week supplement which can only be used for brown coal briquettes. What effect does this have on the family's budget line?
4. Suppose that the state simply raised the dole payment by £3 per week. What would happen to the family's budget line? Do you think that the family would prefer a fuel subsidy or an increase of their dole payment? Why does the state subsidise fuel rather than income?

Answers
....

1. The state is banning the use of bituminous coal in Cork because smoke levels in the city 'had threatened to exceed' the limits fixed by the state itself and by the EU. Respiratory illness is, at worst caused by pollution and, at best aggravated by it. By banning bituminous coal, some of these health problems should be alleviated.

    On the other hand, bituminous coal is an inexpensive heating fuel. Low-income families will either have to reduce their consumption of dearer heating fuel or spend more of their weekly income on fuel. To assist these households, the 'government has approved a £3-a-week supplement to the normal fuel allowance for lower-income households'.

2. *Figure 3.6: The budget line for the Harrington family*

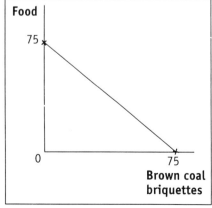

3. *Figure 3.7: The budget line for the Harrington family after the fuel subsidy*

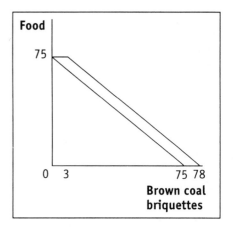

Relative prices have not changed. Therefore, the new budget line is parallel to the original budget line. The additional £3 can be used for fuel only. Therefore, the family can still only purchase a maximum of 75 units of food. If, however, they decide to purchase only fuel, they can afford 78 units.

For this reason, the budget line is 'kinked'. The first three units of fuel consumed will not affect the family's ability to consume food. Therefore, the first part of the budget line is flat. Beyond the three units, there is a trade-off between food and fuel. This is shown by the usual, downward sloping budget line.

4. If the state adds £3 to the dole payment, the budget line of the Harrington family will be parallel to the budget line shown in Figure 3.6. In the case of an increase in the dole payment, the family can afford more of either food or fuel.

Figure 3.8: The budget line for the Harrington family if dole payments are increased by £3 per week.

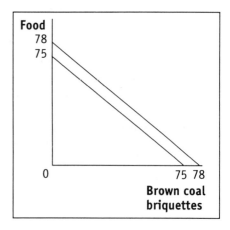

An increase in the dole payment increases the affordable space of the Harrington family by a greater amount than the fuel subsidy. Therefore, theoretically, they should prefer the higher dole payment. Practically, if they spend more than £3 per week on fuel, the type of subsidy (income vs fuel) may not make any difference to them.

The state may prefer the fuel subsidy for a couple of reasons. First, it is a direct response to the problem of paying for the increased cost of using alternative heating fuels. Second, it gives the state control over how the money is spent. An income subsidy can be used for alcohol or tobacco or any other type of good or service which may not be considered as beneficial to the family. This allowance can only be used for fuel, a good which is considered to be beneficial to the health and well-being of the family.

Consumer equilibrium
....

Consider a student who can choose between only two goods, food and drink. In Figure 3.9 the quantity of food, Qf, is depicted on the vertical axis and the quantity of drink, Qd, is depicted on the horizontal axis. A set of indifference curves and a budget line are drawn.

Figure 3.9: Maximising consumer utility constrained by income and prices

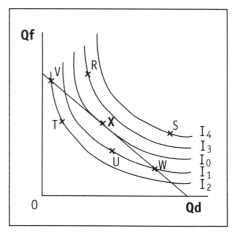

The student chooses the combination of food and drink that maximises her utility and uses all her income. Graphically, this is where the budget line, reflecting the budget constraint, is tangent to the highest possible indifference curve, reflecting the consumer's preferences. Alternatively, this is the point where the slope of the budget line is equal to the slope of the indifference curve.

Point X is the optimal consumption bundle. Recall that the slope of the indifference curve is the marginal rate of substitution (MRS) whereas the negative of the ratio of prices is the slope of the budget line. Equation 3.3 states that they are equal at X, the point of tangency, which is the optimum bundle which the consumer can afford.

$$MRS = \frac{-P_d}{P_f}$$ [3.3]

Let us examine other consumption bundles. Bundles R and S are desirable but unattainable. They are desirable because they are on higher indifference curves: they are unattainable because they are outside the budget line. In contrast, bundles T and U are attainable but undesirable. They are attainable because they are inside the budget line: they are undesirable because it is possible to reach higher indifference curves with the given amount of income. Neither V nor W is the optimal consumption bundle because it is possible to reach a higher indifference curve and still remain on the budget line.

Point X, and only point X, is the optimal consumption bundle. This point is called consumer equilibrium. Like any equilibrium, when the consumer is at this point, there is no tendency to change. She is at the highest level of satisfaction possible given her income and the prevailing prices. This is the best bundle that the consumer can afford.

Income change analysis
....

In the analysis above, income and prices were held constant. Now we will consider a change in equilibrium arising out of a change in income with prices held constant. We will observe that the changes in the equilibrium positions will differ, depending on whether the goods are normal or inferior.

Two scenarios are illustrated in Figure 3.10. In Figure 3.10(a) we continue to consider a budget line drawn for food (depicted on the vertical axis) and drink (depicted on the horizontal axis), where both goods are normal. Figure 3.10(b) shows a budget line drawn for food (a normal good) on the vertical axis but bus rides, an inferior good, is represented on the horizontal axis. In both cases income increases and the budget line shifts out and to the right. Since prices do not change, the new budget line is parallel to the original budget line.

Figure 3.10: A change in income

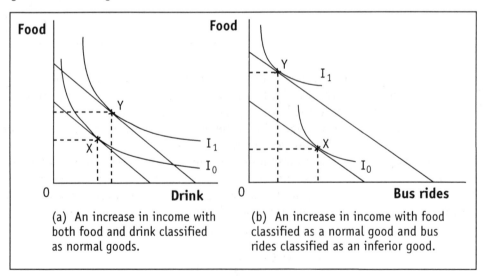

(a) An increase in income with both food and drink classified as normal goods.

(b) An increase in income with food classified as a normal good and bus rides classified as an inferior good.

Consider Figure 3.10(a). Before the income change, the consumer was in equilibrium at point X. The consumer is now in equilibrium at the optimal consumption bundle Y. This bundle contains more units of both food and drink. If both goods are classified as normal, an increase in income results in an increase in the consumption of both goods.

Now consider Figure 3.10(b). Again, the point of consumer equilibrium, after income increases, is represented by point Y. In this case, an increase in income results in the consumption of more of the normal good, food, but less of the inferior good, bus rides.

We can now see that an increase in income affects consumer equilibrium differently, depending on whether a good is normal or inferior. If a good is normal, more of that good will be consumed if income increases. On the other hand, if a good is inferior, less is consumed if income increases. We will now turn our attention to the effect of a change in price on consumer equilibrium.

Price change analysis and the demand curve

A change in price alters the equilibrium position. We begin by examining the effect of a change of price on the budget line. Different price adjustments are illustrated in Figure 3.11.

Figure 3.11: A change in price

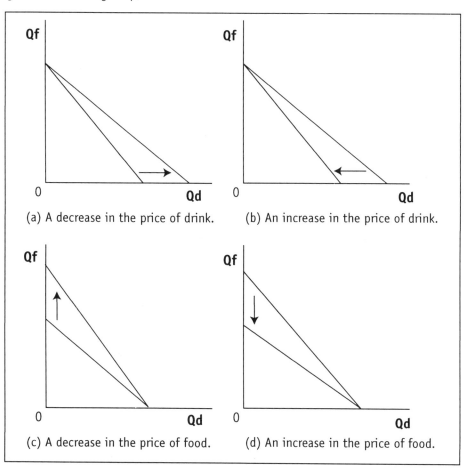

(a) A decrease in the price of drink.

(b) An increase in the price of drink.

(c) A decrease in the price of food.

(d) An increase in the price of food.

The slope of a budget line is equal to the negative of the ratio of prices. A change in the price of one commodity alters the slope of the budget line. When this happens the budget line pivots around one or other of the intercept points, outwards or inwards depending on whether there is a price decrease or price increase. All four possible cases are presented above.

Suppose the price of drink decreases. What happens to the consumption of drink? The change in the consumption of drink can be explained as follows. Any change in consumption arising out of a change in price can be split into two separate changes. The first is called the substitution effect, and the second, the income effect.

Definition
● ● ● ● ● ●

The substitution effect is the change in consumption that is caused by the change in the relative prices of the two goods, holding utility constant.

If the price of drink falls, food becomes relatively more expensive in comparison to drink. The consumer reacts to the change in relative prices by consuming more drink and less food.

Definition
● ● ● ● ● ●

The income effect is the adjustment of demand to the change in real income alone.

When price falls, the consumer is wealthier in the sense that the decrease in the price of drink has increased her real income. From Figure 3.11(a), we can see that the affordable space is larger as a result of the decrease in price. Using economic jargon, we say that the purchasing power of the consumer has increased.[11]

From the previous section, we know that the consumer does not respond uniformly to a change in income. The consumer's response depends on whether the good, as defined in economic terms, is normal or inferior.

Therefore, when price decreases, two separate effects are evident. The substitution effect results in an increase in quantity demanded. The consumer will purchase more of the good which is relatively cheaper. The income effect varies depending on whether the good is normal or inferior.

The addition of these two effects amounts to the total change in quantity and is called the total price effect. This is expressed in Equation 3.4 below.

$$\boxed{\textbf{Total price effect = substitution effect + income effect}} \qquad \textbf{[3.4]}$$

We first consider the case of a normal good.

A case of a normal good
....

Figure 3.12 shows the price change and its effect on the consumption of drink (and also food, the other good in this two-commodity model). Assume that drink is a normal good. X is the original equilibrium bundle. As the price of drink decreases the budget line rotates around the vertical intercept and moves out to the right along the horizontal axis. The new budget line reflects the change in price and, as a result, has a different slope. The new equilibrium is at bundle Z, the point of tangency between the new budget line and the highest possible indifference curve. More units of drink are consumed at bundle Z than at bundle X. This suggests that there is a negative relationship between price and quantity demanded.

Figure 3.12: The substitution and income effect for a normal good

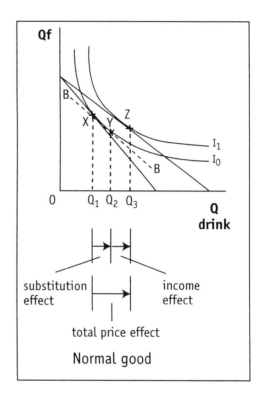

How do we know that bundle Z lies to the right of bundle X and thus reflects a higher level of quantity demanded? The move from X to Z can be divided into two separate parts. First, there is the substitution effect. This can be illustrated by drawing a hypothetical budget line, BB, which is parallel to the new budget line but is tangent to the original indifference curve, at point Y. Recall that the level of utility is constant along a particular indifference curve. The move from X to Y is the substitution effect. The consumer is changing her consumption bundle in response to the change in relative prices and at the same time keeping utility constant. Consumption of drink is higher at Y than at X.

Second, there is the income effect. As the price of drink decreases the purchasing power of the consumer increases. Since drink is a normal good, as income increases the consumer demands more drink. The income effect is the move from Y to the new bundle Z which must lie to the right of Y in order to reflect that drink is a normal good.

The total price effect is the move from X to Z with Z lying to the right and thus reflecting higher units of drink consumed. As price decreases, quantity demanded increases.

Figure 3.13 below shows how this analysis combined with a price consumption curve can help in the graphical derivation of a demand curve. Successive price changes result in a number of budget lines tangent to an equal number of indifference curves. In the diagram below three price levels are analysed. They are reflected in the three budget lines. Bundles X, Z and U are the optimal consumption bundles for alternative pairs of relative prices. The locus of optimal consumption bundles is called the price consumption curve.

Figure 3.13: The price consumption curve and the demand curve for a normal good

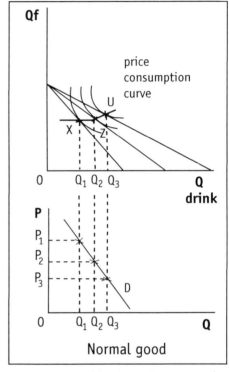

In the upper diagram of Figure 3.13 we observe the change in demand of both food and drink depending on relative prices and on the consumer's preference. The lower diagram depicts the relationship between the price of drink and the demand for drink. This is the price-consumption relationship which is commonly known as the demand schedule and in graphic terms called the demand curve. As we suspected, it is downward sloping from left to right.

The analysis above applies to a normal good. We now turn our discussion towards inferior goods and also to a third category of good, the Giffen good.

A case of an inferior good
....

Now we will consider a decrease in the price of an inferior good, bus rides. The substitution effect is always the same, regardless of whether a good is normal, inferior or Giffen; when the price of a good falls, the demand for that good increases. In this case, when the price of bus rides falls, we expect the consumer to react to the change in relative prices by using buses more often as a means of transport.

The income effect is the change in consumption which arises from a change in real income. For a normal good, as price decreases real income increases and, consequently, consumption increases. However, for an inferior good, as real income increases consumption decreases. In this case, as a response to the increase in real income, we expect that the consumer will demand fewer bus rides, an inferior good.

In total we now have an increase in consumption arising out of the substitution effect and a decrease in consumption arising out of the income effect. One appears to offset the other and since the total price effect is the addition of the two, it is unclear whether consumption increases or decreases.

In fact, the decrease in quantity due to the increase in income is relatively small so that it does not outweigh the increase in quantity which arises from the substitution effect. The substitution effect outweighs the income effect for an inferior good (with the exception of the Giffen good which is explained later). The increase in quantity arising from the substitution effect (reflected in the move from X to Y) is greater than the decrease in quantity arising from the income effect (reflected in the move from Y to Z). The total price effect (shown by the move from X to Z), which is the addition of the substitution and the income effect, is still an increase in quantity. This is shown in Figure 3.14 below.

Figure 3.14: The substitution and income effect for an inferior good

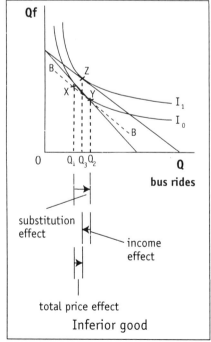

As price decreases for an inferior good the quantity consumed increases but not by as much as it would for a normal good. The demand curve for an inferior good is downward sloping but, on account of the smaller change in quantity consumed, the demand curve is relatively steep. The curve for the inferior good is shown in Figure 3.15 below.

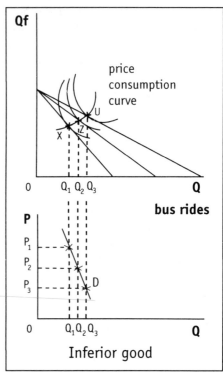

Figure 3.15: The price consumption curve and the demand curve for an inferior good

The difference between the normal good and the inferior good is reflected in the respective slopes of the demand curves. The demand curve for the inferior good is steeper than the demand curve for the normal good.

A case of a Giffen good
....

Definition
● ● ● ● ● ●

A Giffen good is a very inferior good with an upward sloping demand curve.

We need to consider the effect of a price change on a Giffen good. The Giffen good received its name from Sir Robert Giffen (1837–1910) who, it is believed, claimed that during the Irish famine of the 1840s, the consumption of potatoes increased even though the price increased.[12] Theoretically, this strange phenomenon can be explained using substitution and income effects.

The substitution effect is always the same. However, in the case of a strongly inferior or Giffen good, the income effect not only offsets the substitution effect, it actually outweighs it. In the case of a Giffen good a rise in the price results in a negative substitution effect, but a stronger, positive income effect. As price increases, demand increases. The demand curve for the Giffen good is upward sloping.

Figure 3.16 shows the substitution and income effects for a price fall of a Giffen good. The increase in quantity arising from the substitution effect (X to Y) is smaller than the decrease in quantity arising from the income effect (Y to Z). At the new consumer equilibrium, point Z, the consumer is consuming less of the Giffen good than before.

Figure 3.16: The substitution and income
  effect for a Giffen good

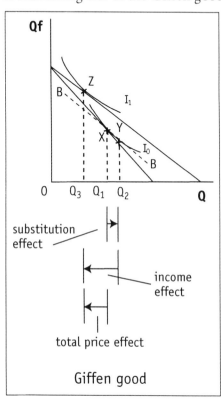

Figure 3.17: The price consumption curve and
  the demand curve for a Giffen good

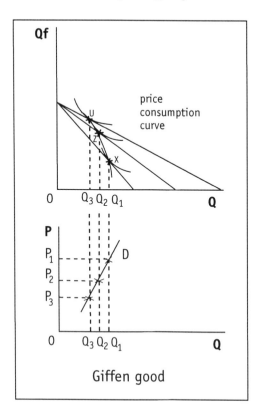

Figure 3.17 shows the backward bending price consumption curve. As price falls, the quantity consumed decreases. The price-quantity relationship is positive and this is reflected in an upward sloping demand curve.

A complete summary of the price changes and the subsequent quantity changes for all three categories of goods is presented in Table 3.6 below.

Table 3.6: Summary of price changes and quantity changes

Price change	Type of good	Substitution effect	Income effect	Total effect
Decrease	Normal	Qd increases	Qd increases	Qd increases
	Inferior	Qd increases	Qd decreases	Qd increases
	Giffen	Qd increases	Qd decreases	Qd decreases
Increase	Normal	Qd decreases	Qd decreases	Qd decreases
	Inferior	Qd decreases	Qd increases	Qd decreases
	Giffen	Qd decreases	Qd increases	Qd increases

Synopsis of the indifference-preference approach

The assumptions

1. The consumer ranks alternative combinations of goods according to her preferences.
2. The consumer's choices are limited by income and prices.

The theory

The consumer wishes to maximise her satisfaction subject to income and price constraints. She chooses the combination of goods from which she derives the highest level of satisfaction.

The predictions

The optimal consumption bundle is found where the budget line is tangent to the highest possible indifference curve. At this tangency point, the respective slopes are equal.

The weaknesses

1. Indifference curves are difficult, if not impossible, to derive in the real world.
2. The assumptions which underlie the theory are restrictive and ignore the effects of common practices e.g. advertising.

3.4 Consumer surplus

In the *Principles of Economics* Alfred Marshall defined consumer surplus as the ' . . . excess of the price which he would be willing to pay rather than go without the thing, over that which he actually does pay . . . '[13]

Definition
● ● ● ● ● ●

Consumer surplus is the excess of what a person is prepared to pay for a good over what the person actually pays.

Sometimes this concept is referred to as the social benefit accruing to the consumer who purchases the good. This term is used to describe the operation of the price mechanism which allows consumers to acquire goods at a lower price than they would be willing to pay.

Before we look at a market, consisting of many consumers, we will begin with the consumption decision of a single consumer. Consider Anthony, a hat lover. Figure 3.18 shows Anthony's demand curve for hats.

Figure 3.18: Anthony's demand curve for hats

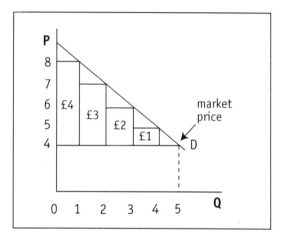

We can see that Anthony is willing to pay £8 for the first hat that he purchases. This is the hat from which he derives the highest marginal utility, therefore, he is willing to pay the most for it. However, the market price is only £4 per hat. Therefore, although Anthony is prepared to pay £8 for this hat, he only has to pay £4. His consumer surplus is £4 for the first unit. Because of diminishing marginal utility, Anthony is willing to pay only £7 for the second hat. For this unit, his consumer surplus is £3. Anthony continues to consume until the consumer surplus on the last unit purchased equals zero. In this example, the market price of £4 equals the price that Anthony is willing to pay for his fifth hat.

From Figure 3.18, we can see that Anthony is willing to pay £30 for five hats (=£8+£7+£6+£5+£4). To put this in another way, we can say that Anthony is gaining £30 worth of pleasure or benefit from his purchase of hats. Anthony's total expenditure is £20. Anthony's total consumer surplus for hats is the amount that he is willing to pay less the amount that he has to pay (the total expenditure). The consumer surplus in this example is £10 (the sum of £4+£3+£2+£1).

The market demand curve is derived by adding individual demand curves. We can think of the market demand curve for hats as representing the amount that consumers collectively are willing to pay for a particular quantity of that good. Consider Figure 3.19.

Figure 3.19: Market demand curve for hats

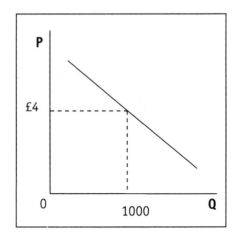

If 1000 hats are available for sale, consumers are willing to pay £4 per hat. This is the market price. However, there are some consumers who are willing to pay more for those hats. Since they only have to pay £4 per hat, some consumers pay less than they are willing to pay. In other words, just as with Anthony, we can identify consumer surplus for the market. It is the difference between the market price and the price that consumers are willing to pay.

Figure 3.20 shows consumer surplus for the market.

Figure 3.20: Consumer surplus

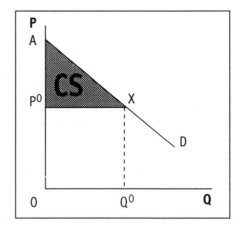

Suppose that the market price for hats is P^0 and at this price, the market demands Q^0 hats. The total benefit or satisfaction received by the market is represented by the area $[OAXQ^0]$. This is the total amount that consumers are willing to pay for Q^0 hats. The total expenditure on hats is represented by the area $[OP^0XQ^0]$. The difference between the total benefit and the total expenditure is represented by the shaded triangle P^0AX. This is the area of consumer surplus.

Consumer surplus is a very important concept in economics and has many worthwhile applications. These include cost-benefit analysis and the efficiency and distribution effects of tax changes and subsidies.

Summary

1. There are two main approaches to the theory of consumer behaviour and demand. The first is the marginal utility theory. It is based on the assumption that utility is measurable. A marginal utility curve is derived which slopes downward and reflects the principle of diminishing marginal utility. The consumer maximises utility if the utility for the pound spent on each good is the same. This is called the equi-marginal principle.

2. The second approach is the indifference-preference theory. It requires the ordering of different alternatives according to the consumer's preferences. The preferences of the consumer are reflected in indifference curves whereas the constraints are reflected in the budget line.

3. The consumer maximises utility where the budget line is tangent to the highest possible indifference curve. At this point, called consumer equilibrium, the negative of the ratio of prices is equal to the marginal rate of substitution.

4. The demand curve for a good can be derived by splitting the quantity change into two separate components. The substitution effect is the change in demand arising out of the change in relative prices. It is the same for all categories of goods. The income effect is the change in demand arising out of the change in real income. It varies depending on whether the good is normal or inferior.

5. The substitution and income effect analysis is useful when deriving the demand curve for the three categories of goods. The demand curve for a normal good conforms to the law of demand by sloping downwards from left to right. The demand curve for an inferior good also slopes down but it is steeper on account of an income effect which partially offsets the substitution effect. The exception is the Giffen good whose demand curve has a positive slope.

6. Consumer surplus arises from the difference between the price consumers pay for the good and the price they would be willing to pay. In effect, it is a benefit to consumers. It has many useful applications in economics.

Key terms

Marginalists
Utility
Total utility
Marginal utility
Util
Diminishing marginal utility
Equi-marginal principle
Preferences
Indifference curve
Marginal rate of substitution
Preference map

Budget line
Relative prices
Optimal consumption bundle
Substitution effect
Income effect
Nominal variable
Real variable
Price consumption curve
Giffen good
Consumer surplus

Review questions

1. Briefly explain the main differences between the marginal utility approach and the indifference-preference approach in the context of consumer choice theory.
2. Using the marginal utility approach explain how the consumer maximises utility. Show how this approach and, in particular, the concept of marginal utility is related to the law of demand and the conventional downward sloping demand curve.
3. List and briefly explain the assumptions of consumer's preferences and the properties of both the budget line and indifference curves.
4. Using the indifference-preference approach, explain how the optimal consumption bundle is derived.
5. Suppose we have a two-good model with both goods classified as normal. The price of the good, whose quantity is represented on the horizontal axis, increases. Use the substitution and income effect analysis to explain why consumption is likely to decrease in response to this price increase.
6. Suppose the good, whose quantity is represented on the horizontal axis, is a Giffen good. Consider a price increase. Derive the price consumption curve which is associated with this change in price. How does this vary from the price consumption curve for a normal or inferior good? Explain the reason for the difference.

Working problems

1. Monica spends a day on the beach. She has an income of £22 and can spend this budget on some combination of mineral water, ice cream and soft drinks. Mineral water sells for £4, ice cream for £2 and soft drinks for £1. The hypothetical marginal utility values are presented in Table 3.7 below.

Table 3.7: Monica's three alternatives: mineral water, ice cream and soft drinks

Mineral water		Ice cream		Soft drinks	
Q	MU	Q	MU	Q	MU
	36		30		32
1		1		1	
	24		22		28
2		2		2	
	20		16		20
3		3		3	
	18		12		14
4		4		4	
	16		10		8
5		5		5	
	10		4		6
6		6		6	
	6		2		4
7		7		7	

What combination yields Monica maximum utility?

2. Tom and Gerry are two students of economics. Both have £10 a week which they can spend on books (£2.50 per book) or beer (£1 per pint). Tom is the studious type and spends most of his time in the library. Gerry has not yet found the library but is frequently seen in the student bar. On two separate diagrams, draw the budget lines for Tom and Gerry. Draw an indifference curve on each diagram to show a combination of beer and books that Tom and Gerry might choose.

Multi-choice questions

1. According to the marginal utility approach:
   (a) the substitution effect and the income effect confirm that consumption responds negatively to price changes;
   (b) real income changes allow for the possibility of an upward sloping demand curve;
   (c) the consumer maximises utility where the utility for the last pound spent on each good is the same;
   (d) indifference curves slope downwards from left to right;
   (e) none of the above.

2. The difference between the price consumers pay for the good and the price they are willing to pay for the good is called:
   (a) substitution effect;
   (b) marginal utility;
   (c) marginal rate of substitution;
   (d) consumer surplus;
   (e) none of the above.

3. The substitution effect of a price change:
   (a) is the same for all goods;
   (b) is the change in demand due solely to the change in relative prices;
   (c) produces a downward sloping demand curve;
   (d) is the change in consumption holding utility constant;
   (e) all of the above.

4. Which of the following is <u>not</u> a property of indifference curves?
   (a) Combinations of goods on the one indifference curve yield the same level of satisfaction to the consumer.
   (b) Indifference curves reflect the income and price constraints.
   (c) The slope of an indifference curve is the marginal rate of substitution.
   (d) Indifference curves usually slope downwards from left to right.
   (e) Indifference curves do not intersect.

5. The budget line:
   (a) has a slope equal to the negative of the ratio of prices;
   (b) is drawn for a given set of prices and a given level of income;
   (c) reflects consumer's tastes and preferences;

(d) both (a) and (b) above;
(e) (a), (b) and (c) above.

6. The demand curve for an inferior good:
   (a) is steeper than the demand curve for a normal good;
   (b) is downward sloping because the income effect outweighs the substitution effect;
   (c) has a positive slope;
   (d) has the same slope as that of a Giffen good;
   (e) both (a) and (b) above.

True or false

1. The total utility derived from the consumption of water is less than the total utility derived from the acquisition of diamonds. It is this statement that was to resolve the water-diamond dilemma. _____
2. The marginal utility approach states that utility is maximised when utility for the last pound spent is equal on each good._____
3. The consumer surplus is the difference between the market price of a commodity and the price that suppliers are willing to supply the goods. _____
4. The optimal consumption bundle is the intersection point between the highest possible indifference curve and the given budget line. _____
5. The demand curve for an inferior good is positively sloped. _____
6. For an inferior good the income effect is stronger than the substitution effect and this produces an upward sloping demand curve. _____

Fill in the blanks

The theory of demand is concerned with consumer _____ in the face of income and price constraints. The _____ _____ approach assumes that utility is _____ whereas the indifference-preference approach requires only the _____ of different combinations. According to the former, the consumer maximises utility where the utility for the last ____ spent on each good is the _____ . In the latter case the _____ _____ bundle is where the _____ ____, which reflects the income and _____ constraints, cuts the highest possible_____ ____ at a point of _____ . A change in income _____ the budget line, out to the right for an _____ in income and in to the ____ for a decrease in income. The _____ of the new consumer equilibrium point will depend on the type of good – normal or ____ . A change in price causes a _____ of the budget line and with the help of the _____ and _____ effect analysis we can derive the downward sloping demand curve for a _____ good. A similar exercise results in a _____ sloping demand curve for an inferior good but, in contrast, an upward sloping demand curve for a _____ good.

CASE STUDY

Source: Guinness Ireland Group

Questions
....

(The student may want to read Appendix 3.1 which discusses the properties of the indifference curve, before attempting to answer these questions.)

1. Consider the Carlsberg advertising campaign. Why did the company engage in this kind of advertising?
2. Draw the indifference curve of an individual who initially preferred Heineken to Carlsberg. Now draw on the same diagram the indifference curve of the individual after the successful Carlsberg campaign.
3. Which property of indifference curves have we violated in 2 above?

Appendix 3.1: The properties of indifference curves

The properties of indifference curves were listed in Section 3.3. A more detailed explanation is provided below.

1. Indifference curves slope down from left to right.

Figure 3.21: Indifference curves slope down
from left to right

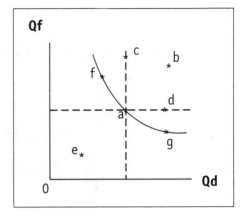

Consider bundle a in Figure 3.21. Now compare this bundle with other possible bundles. Let us begin with the quadrant to the northeast of a. Compared to bundle a, bundle b offers more of both goods, bundle c offers more food and the same amount of drink whereas bundle d offers more drink and the same amount of food. All of these bundles are preferred to bundle a because the consumer prefers more to less. Hence, these cannot form a locus of points with bundle a which reflect constant utility. This rules out all the possible bundles in the northeast quadrant.

A similar analysis can be applied to the southwest quadrant. All bundles in this quadrant contain less food and/or less drink than are included in bundle a. Since more is preferred to less, the consumer prefers bundle a to any bundle in the southwest quadrant. Bundle e and similar bundles do not lie on the same indifference curve as bundle a.

The only options left are areas to the northwest and southeast of bundle a. Bundles like f and g could possibly be on the same indifference curve. In comparison to bundle a, bundle f contains more food but less drink. Bundle g, on the other hand, contains more drink and less food. It is possible that the consumer is indifferent between bundles a, f, and g. Therefore, they form an indifference curve which slopes downwards from left to right.

2. The slope of the indifference curve is determined by tastes and preferences and is called the marginal rate of substitution (MRS).

The MRS indicates the willingness of the consumer to give up a certain amount of one good in order to obtain one unit of the other good without changing utility. If the two goods are food and drink then the MRS is given by the amount of food that the consumer is willing to sacrifice in order to gain an extra unit of drink. This is expressed in Equation 3.5.

$$MRS = \frac{-\Delta f}{\Delta d}$$

[3.5]

3. Indifference curves are normally convex to the origin.

Figure 3.22 indicates that as we move down and to the right along the indifference curve the MRS declines or diminishes. The indifference curve is said to exhibit a diminishing marginal rate of substitution. As we move down the indifference curve, less food and more drink is consumed. A rational consumer is now willing to give up less and less food in order to obtain an extra unit of drink. The MRS diminishes. In the example below, the MRS declines from 3 units to 1 unit.

Figure 3.22: The slope of the indifference curve and the marginal rate of substitution

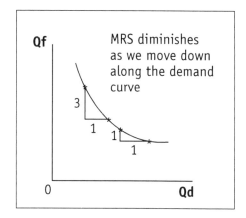

Diminishing marginal rate of substitution means that indifference curves are usually convex to the origin. However, there are many exceptions to the rule of convexity. Three exceptions are shown in Figure 3.23 below.

Figure 3.23: A sample of indifference curves

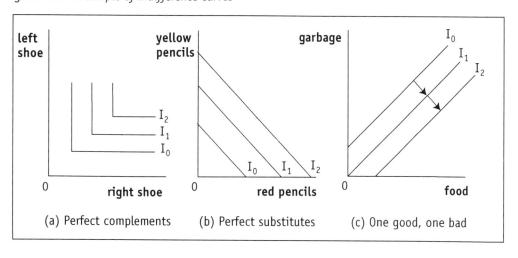

Case (a) represents perfect complements; two goods which are consumed together. The indifference curves for such goods are L-shaped. An example of perfect complements are left shoes and right shoes. An individual with one left shoe is no better off if she has two right shoes or three or four. Additional right shoes will leave her at the same level of utility (I_0) as the original pair. To move the consumer to a higher level of utility (I_1) she must have a second pair of shoes.

Perfect substitutes, such as red pencils and yellow pencils, are represented by case (b). Here the indifference curves are straight lines with negative slopes equal to –1. The consumer is willing to exchange one red pencil for one yellow pencil. In this case, the marginal rate of substitution is constant, rather than diminishing.

Case (c) shows the indifference curve for a good and a 'bad'. A 'bad' is a commodity that the consumer does not like. In order to accept more of the 'bad' which leads to increasing disutility, the consumer must be compensated with more of the 'good' which increases utility. Therefore, the indifference curve has a positive slope. Higher utility is achieved as the curves move from garbage towards food.

4. Indifference curves do not intersect

To establish the validity of this property we use the 'proof by contradiction' method which is used frequently in mathematics. In this particular case there are only two possible alternatives; the indifference curves either intersect or they do not intersect. These are mutually exclusive outcomes. Let us presuppose that they do intersect (the idea is to end up with a contradiction which then implies that the only other alternative must be true).

Figure 3.24: Indifference curves do not intersect

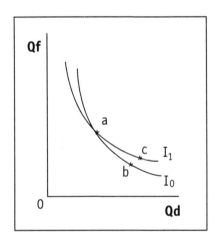

Two indifference curves are drawn, intersecting at point a, as in Figure 3.24. Consider I_0. The consumer is indifferent between bundle a and bundle b as both lie on I_0. Consider I_1. The consumer is also indifferent between bundle a and bundle c as both lie on I_1. If she is indifferent between bundles a and b, and also indifferent between bundles a and c then the law of transitivity implies that she is also indifferent between bundle b and bundle c. However, Figure 3.24 clearly shows that bundle c offers more of both goods than bundle b. The consumer is not indifferent between these two bundles and opts for bundle c over bundle b. Thus, we have a contradiction which implies that the original proposition was incorrect. The alternative must be true. Indifference curves do not intersect.

5. There is a multiple set of indifference curves, called a preference map.

Figure 3.25: A preference map

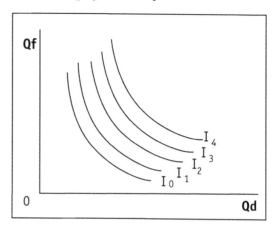

Every bundle represents some level of satisfaction to the consumer. Hence, every point is on an indifference curve. There is a set of indifference curves. This set is called a preference or indifference map and is drawn in Figure 3.25. For every two consumption bundles there is a third between them. Consequently, for every two indifference curves there is a third between them. Therefore, there is a multiple set of indifference curves.

6. The higher the indifference curve, the higher the level of utility.

Figure 3.26: A set of indifference curves, each reflecting a higher level of utility than the previous (lower) one

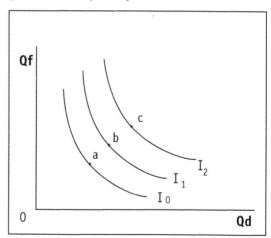

Figure 3.26 illustrates three indifference curves. Consider bundles a, b and c. Bundle c offers more of both goods compared to bundle b. Consequently, bundle c is preferred to bundle b. Likewise, bundle b is preferred to bundle a. The same applies to indifference curves. Indifference curves which are further from the origin are preferred to indifference curves which are closer to the origin. For example, I_2 is preferred to I_1 which, in turn, is preferred to I_0.

CHAPTER 4

THE FIRM AND PRODUCTION

'Whatever may be the abundance of the source of production, the producer will always stop when the increase in expense exceeds the increase in receipts.'[1]

Augustin Cournot (1801–77)

'If the choice lies between the production or purchase of two commodities, the value of one is measured by the sacrifice of going without the other.'[2]

H. J. Davenport (1862–1931)

'Normal profits are simply the supply price of entrepreneurship to a particular industry.'[3]

Joan Robinson (1903–83)

Chapter objectives

Upon completing this chapter, the student should understand:

- short-run production and the law of diminishing returns;
- long-run production and returns to scale;
- opportunity cost and normal profit;
- short-run and long-run costs; fixed and variable costs;
- the output decision for the profit-maximising firm.

Outline

4.1 **The objectives of the firm**
4.2 **Production**
4.3 **Costs**
4.4 **Profit-maximising output level**
4.5 **Economies of scale and implications for Ireland**

Introduction

Whereas the theory of demand is primarily concerned with the consumer and utility, the theory of supply is related to the producer and the costs of production. Costs are the main determinants used by producers to decide what amount of output is to be supplied at the different price levels. We begin the chapter by examining the traditional, neoclassical objective of profit maximisation. Other objectives are briefly mentioned. The theory of production and an analysis of costs follow. This is followed by a description of the output decision for profit-maximising firms. A brief discussion on economies of scale in the Irish context concludes the chapter.

4.1 The objectives of the firm

A firm's behaviour depends largely on its aims. By this we mean that the output produced and the price charged by the firm depend largely on the objective of the firm. For example, the price and output decision of a profit-maximising firm is likely to be different than that of a sales-maximising firm because of the different objectives. A few of these objectives and their associated models are discussed below.

The traditional, neoclassical theory is based on the assumption that the objective of the firm is to maximise profits. It differs from the 'managerial' model which emphasises the differences between ownership and control in modern corporations. Firms are owned by shareholders. Decisions on the operation of the firm are made by managers. Although the shareholders want to maximise profits, managers may choose to maximise other objectives such as sales revenue, market share or their own salaries.

Another alternative to the neoclassical model is the behavioural model developed by Simon (1955) and Cyert and March (1963). The behavioural model is based on the idea that a firm is comprised of groups or coalitions who have their own objectives. Workers demand better pay, job security and improved working conditions. Shareholders, seeking maximum return for their investment, demand higher profits. There are other demands made from outside the firm by the government, consumers' associations and other interest groups. This model is very different from the neoclassical model which sees the firm as an individual entity with only one objective, profit maximisation.

The managerial and behavioural models are important contributions to the theory of the firm. However, the neoclassical model, based on profit maximisation, continues to dominate microeconomic theory. We will explain this traditional model in detail.

4.2 Production

Any production process involves the transformation of inputs into units of output. Inputs, or factors of production, are usually classified into four categories: labour, land, capital and enterprise. The relationship between these inputs and the output which they generate can be presented in the form of a production function.

Definition
● ● ● ● ● ●

The production function shows the relationship between the amounts of inputs used and the subsequent maximum amount of output generated.

The production function can be expressed in algebraic form as follows:

$$Q = f(L, Land, K, Enterprise)$$

[4.1]

where: Q = output; L = number of workers employed; K = capital including plant and machinery.

Literally, this expression means that the amount of a good which a firm can produce, depends on the amount of inputs which are used in the production process. Land, labour, capital and enterprise are the independent variables and output is the dependent variable. In the examination of production which follows, we distinguish between the short run and the long run.

Production in the short run

To begin our discussion, we must explain a few relevant terms.

• Definition
• • • • • •

The short run is a period of time where there is at least one factor of production which is said to be 'fixed'.

The quantity of a fixed factor does not vary as the level of output varies. The fixed factor is generally land or machinery, the latter falling into the general classification of capital.

In order to discuss production, we will consider a business developed by Sean McHale, an entrepreneur from County Mayo. Sean owns a small firm called Key Chains Inc. He began producing key chains and selling them from the boot of his car. As his business expands, Sean finds that he cannot produce enough key chains to meet all of his orders. Therefore, he hires one employee, then a second and a third. We will consider how each additional worker affects Sean's output.

For this example, we will use a simple, short-run production function with only two inputs: capital and labour. To produce key chains, Sean uses two machines. These machines represent capital and this factor is fixed in the short-run. Labour is a variable input. Table 4.1 presents the changes in output which result from increasing the number of employees.

Table 4.1: Key chain production per week

(1) Number of workers	(2) K	(3) Total product (TP)	(4) Average product (AP)	(5) Marginal product (MP)
0	2	0	0	
				100
1	2	100	100	
				220
2	2	320	160	
				310
3	2	630	210	
				410
4	2	1040	260	
				360
5	2	1400	280	
				340
6	2	1740	290	
				220
7	2	1960	280	
				−120
8	2	1840	230	

We can see by looking at the total product column, that production begins with the addition of labour. In this case, Sean is the first labourer and, working on his own, he can produce 100 key chains per week. The total product continues to increase as Sean hires more staff. However, with the addition of the eighth worker, total product falls.

Figure 4.1: Production: total product, average product and marginal product

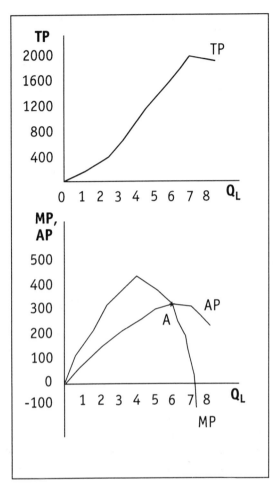

The same information is shown in Figure 4.1. The upper diagram shows the total product curve. It shows the relationship between the variable input, labour and output or total product. Labour is represented on the horizontal axis and total product is represented on the vertical axis. The total product curve shows the same relationship that we described above. Production begins with the addition of the first labourer. The upward sloping line indicates that output increases until we add the eighth worker. Then the total product curve slopes downward.

The total product curve separates space into attainable output and unattainable output. Levels of output which are above the curve are unattainable using the available labour. For example, three labourers could not produce 700 key chains. All output possibilities inside and on the curve are attainable. Those on the curve reflect the maximum attainable output levels. In this example, three labourers could produce 630 key chains (on the curve) or fewer (inside the curve).

It is more obvious from the diagram that the production level changes by a different amount with each additional worker because the total product curve is not a straight line. Variations in the total product curve are explained using the concept of marginal product.

Definition
● ● ● ● ● ●

The marginal product is the change in total output obtained from an additional unit of a variable input, holding other inputs constant.

In this example, the marginal product of labour is the extra output derived from the addition of one extra worker while capital is held constant. This relationship is described in Equation 4.2:

$$MP = \frac{\Delta TP}{\Delta Qv} \qquad [4.2]$$

where: Δ = change; MP = marginal product; TP = total product; Qv = quantity of variable input.

Column 5 of Table 4.1 presents the data for the marginal product of labour. Output begins with the addition of the first unit of labour. The marginal product of the first worker is 100 key chains, the number of units which Sean can produce if he works on his own. To find the marginal product of the second employee, we subtract the total product of two workers from the total product of one worker (320 – 100 = 220). Since the change in labour is one, we divide 220 by 1 which equals 220 key chains. This means that the addition of the second worker has increased total product by 220 key chains.

The bottom diagram of Figure 4.1 shows the marginal product of labour curve. We can see that the marginal product curve rises sharply with the addition of each labourer until four individuals are hired. In other words, each additional labourer is adding more to total output than the last. With the addition of the fifth worker, the marginal product of labour begins to fall. After the fourth worker, the marginal product curve is downward sloping.

To understand why the marginal product of labour rises and falls, we will return to Key Chains Inc. and look specifically at Sean's production process. Initially, Sean did everything himself. Before he hired his first employee, Sean made a list of all the tasks required to produce and sell key chains. He broke the process into seven stages:

1. order and receive materials;
2. cut design (machine 1);
3. laminate design (machine 2);
4. cut chain;
5. assemble ring, chain and laminated design;
6. inspect finished product;
7. sell.

Each of these tasks can possibly be completed by a different person who specialises at that task. The division of labour usually increases productivity. This is called increasing marginal returns.

Definition
● ● ● ● ● ●

Increasing marginal returns means that over a range of production, each additional worker adds more to total product than the previous worker.

Initially, Sean hires Maeve who worked as a machine operator in Dublin for a few years before returning home to Mayo. He trains her to use the machines, to cut the chain and to assemble the key chains. Sean continues to order materials, to inspect and to sell the key chains.

The addition of Maeve causes output per week to more than double, from 100 key chains to 320 key chains per week. The marginal product, caused by adding another worker, is 220 units. Maeve concentrates on the production of key chains while Sean specialises in ordering and selling.

A few months later, Sean decides to hire another person. Tom, a former assembly line worker, has recently been made redundant. Because of his previous experience, Sean divides the manufacturing process between Maeve and Tom. Maeve continues to work on the machines, while Tom cuts the chain and assembles the pieces. Total product almost doubles. The marginal product attributed to the addition of the third worker is 310 units.

Well pleased with the increases in output, Sean hires a fourth worker. Taragh assumes the tasks of ordering materials and inspecting the finished product. The addition of this worker results in an increase of 410 units per week.

Sean adds a fifth, sixth and seventh worker. He continues to divide the tasks. However, he finds that while total product continues to rise, the marginal product is falling. Increasing marginal returns ends with the addition of the fourth worker.

Perplexed by this development, Sean decides to take a day off from selling, to observe the operation. He notices that the two machine operators are constantly working. However, they do not produce enough of the laminated design to keep the other members of the staff constantly occupied. Sean can see that the problem is with the machines, not the operators. The odd breakdown of machinery suggests that the machines are being used to capacity.

The problem that Sean observes occurs so regularly, that it is called the law of diminishing returns.

Definition
● ● ● ● ● ●

The law of diminishing returns describes the phenomenon of extra units of the variable factor added to constant levels of the fixed factor leading to a decline in marginal output.

Sean decides that given the limitations imposed on the production process by the machinery, he will not hire any additional workers in the short-run. Indeed, we can see from Table 4.1 that the addition of the eighth worker would cause the total product to fall!

The 'law of diminishing returns' was identified by the classical economists. John Stuart Mill (1806–73), when describing agricultural production said, '. . . the state of the art being given, doubling the labour does not double the produce'.[4] The law of diminishing returns is widely observed in practice and characterises many production activities.

We can come to a further understanding of the total product curve by comparing it to the marginal product curve.[5] When the marginal product curve is rising, the total product curve is becoming steeper. This means that marginal returns are increasing; each worker is contributing more to total product than the last.

When the marginal product curve begins to fall, the total product curve becomes flatter. In other words, when the marginal product is falling, the total product curve is increasing at a decreasing rate. This means that marginal returns are decreasing; each worker is adding to total product, but by less than the previous labourer.

When the marginal product curve cuts the horizontal axis, the marginal product of labour becomes negative. The additional worker is causing the total product to fall. At this point, the total product curve begins to slope downward.

Next we will consider the average product and its relationship with the marginal product.

Definition
● ● ● ● ● ●

The average product is the total output divided by the number of units of the variable input employed.

For example, the average product of labour is the output per worker. Equation 4.3 states this relationship in algebraic form.

$$AP = \frac{TP}{Qv} \qquad [4.3]$$

where: AP = average product; TP = total product; Qv = quantity of variable input.

Column 4 of Table 4.1 presents the data for the average product of labour. If three workers produce 630 key chains, the average product of labour is 630/3 which equals 210. Notice that the average product of labour also rises and then falls. Both the average product of labour and the marginal product of labour are derived by looking at the relationship between total product and labour. But is there a particular relationship between the AP and the MP?

A simple example may clarify this relationship. Suppose that a footballer has an average score over three games of 1 goal per match. Consider two possibilities for the fourth match.

First, suppose that the footballer scores 2 goals in the fourth game. The 'marginal' score is 2. This is the amount of goals that he has added to his total by playing in the fourth game. The footballer's average has increased to 1.25 goals per game. We can think of the marginal goals as dragging up the average. Now consider the possibility that the footballer fails to score in the fourth game. The 'marginal' score is 0 which is below the average score of 1. This drags down the average to 0.75. If the marginal score is above the average score, the average score is dragged up. Conversely, if the marginal score is below the average score, the average score is dragged down.

We can see this same relationship in the bottom frame of Figure 4.1. When the marginal product of labour is above the average product of labour, the average product of labour is rising. However, when the additional labourer fails to add more to total product than the previous worker, the marginal product of labour falls. When the marginal product of labour is below the average, the average product of labour falls.

Hence, the marginal product curve must cut the average product curve at its highest point, labelled point A.

We will end this discussion with one final comment on the short run. The short run is not a particular length of time: it varies from market to market. For example, the short run may only last for a few months in the catering business. If Bewleys wants to expand, the management must find a new location, arrange for financing and prepare the site before they can open. This period of time will be far shorter than the time which it will take for Bord na Móna to open a new production site. Finding a suitable location, applying for planning permission, arranging for financing, and determining the technological processes might take years, rather than months.

Production in the long run
....

We observed that at Key Chains Inc., the level of output was limited by the machinery. In the short run, Sean's capital was fixed. In the long run, it is possible for Sean to increase the number of machines, the size of the plant and the production process. In the long run, all inputs can be varied.

Definition
● ● ● ● ● ●

The long run is a period of time when all the factors of production can be varied in quantity.

The long-run production function shows combinations of inputs and the quantities of output produced. There are three possible relationships between inputs and outputs. The long-run production function may exhibit all three relationships over the range of production.

1. Increasing returns to scale mean that the increase in output is proportionately greater than the increase in inputs. For example, if we double the amount of inputs, the level of output will more than double.
2. In the case of constant returns to scale, the increase in output matches the increase in inputs. In this situation, a doubling of inputs is matched by a doubling of output.
3. Decreasing returns to scale mean that the increase in output is proportionately smaller than the increase in inputs. Therefore, if inputs double, output will increase but by less than a factor of two.

These cases relate to the scale of production which requires further discussion.[6]

Increasing returns to scale are closely related to the concept of economies of scale where an increase in the scale of production leads to lower costs per unit produced. Where there are constant returns to scale, changing the level of output over a range of production does not affect the cost per unit. Decreasing returns to scale are closely related to the concept of diseconomies of scale where an increase in the scale of production results in higher unit costs.

There are a number of reasons why a firm experiences increasing returns to scale over a range of production. In the short run, as in the long run, the specialisation of labour will enable a producer to use inputs more efficiently. In the long run, since all inputs can be varied, more machinery can be added, the production process can change and labour can specialise in a particular stage of the production process.

Another source of increasing returns to scale is indivisibilities. A tractor or a furnace are included in this category. No benefit is gained from half of a tractor. The full benefit of this type of machinery is only experienced with high levels of output. Then, the cost of the machinery is spread over a large number of units. As the level of output rises, the cost per unit falls.

Overheads like advertising, marketing and research and development work in the same way. Generally, these activities are only undertaken by large firms who can spread the costs over a large number of units.

It is believed that firms experience decreasing returns to scale beyond a certain range of production. When a firm grows beyond a certain size, the cost of managing the firm may increase disproportionately. The decision-making process may become slower and more complex. Staff morale problems, which in turn lead to production problems, are more likely to occur. Firms may experience problems in co-ordinating production activities. All of these factors may cause the cost per unit of production to increase.

The relationship between the scale of production and the long-run cost of production will be discussed further in the next section.

4.3 Costs

Costs are payments for the use of factors of production. Labour receives wages. Rent is paid for the use of land. Interest is the cost of capital. Profit is the payment for enterprise.

At this point, a student of accounting as well as others may be confused. Why does the economist consider profit as a cost while the accountant considers profit as the difference between revenues and costs? The answer is that accountants and economists define costs differently.

Economists are interested in economic costs which include both the explicit costs like wages, rent and interest recognised by accountants and the opportunity cost discussed in an earlier part of the text. The opportunity cost is the economist's way of acknowledging that all factors of production, including enterprise, can be used in alternative ways.

Consider Sean, the owner of Key Chains Inc. Sean could use his talents in a number of different ways. He could produce something else besides key chains or he could work for another firm. Economists believe that Sean will continue to produce and sell key chains, if and only if he makes a 'normal' profit.

Definition
● ● ● ● ● ●

Normal profit is the level of profit, below which the entrepreneur will not supply his or her expertise.

It is the level of profit that the entrepreneur expects to earn in the next best alternative business. A normal profit is the opportunity cost of the entrepreneur. It is a cost to the firm in the sense that production will cease if the normal profit is not earned by the entrepreneur.

It is possible that the entrepreneur will earn more than a normal profit. Economists refer to this as economic profit or supernormal profit.

Definition
● ● ● ● ● ●

Economic or supernormal profit is the difference between revenue and economic costs.

An example showing the difference between accounting profit and economic profit is shown in Table 4.2.

Table 4.2: Accounting versus economic profit

The accountant's interpretation			
Total revenue			600,000
Total cost			380,000
Profit			220,000
The economist's interpretation			
Total revenue			600,000
Economic costs			570,000
of which:	Explicit costs	380,000	
	Opportunity cost	190,000	
Supernormal or economic profit			30,000

We will now consider costs in greater detail. As with inputs, we will distinguish between the short run and the long run.

Short-run costs
· · · · · · · · · · · · · · · · · ·

You will recall from our discussion of factor inputs that the short run is the length of time when some inputs are fixed and other inputs are variable. Factors of production must be paid. If the factor of production is fixed in the short run, we consider the cost to be fixed as well. Fixed costs are the payments to fixed factors of production. They remain constant as output varies.

We will return to the example of Key Chains Inc. Recall that Sean uses two machines to manufacture key chains, one to cut the design and the other to laminate it. The machines are Sean's fixed input. If we were considering a more complex production function, fixed costs might include rent, insurance premiums and the price of the phone connection.

You will also recall that other inputs, such as labour and raw materials, vary with the level of production. Variable costs are the payments to variable factors of production. They are incurred with the first unit of production and generally increase as production increases.

For Key Chains Inc., labour is the only variable input and therefore, wage is the variable cost. Other variable costs for Sean might include monies paid for the materials used to produce the key chains and the charge for telephone calls. Like wages, these costs will change with the level of production.

The short-run total cost is equal to the sum of the fixed costs and the variable costs. This relationship is expressed in the following equation:

$$\boxed{\textbf{STC = SFC + SVC}} \qquad \textbf{[4.4]}$$

where: STC = short-run total cost; SFC = short-run fixed cost; SVC = short-run variable cost.

Table 4.3 shows the details of the short-run costs for Key Chains Inc.

Table 4.3: Short-run costs (£ per week) for Key Chains Inc.

(1) Labour	(2) Q	(3) SFC	(4) SVC	(5) STC	(6) SMC	(7) SAFC	(8) SAVC	(9) SATC
0	0	100	0	100		–	–	–
					2.00			
1	100	100	200	300		1.00	2.00	3.00
					0.91			
2	320	100	400	500		0.31	1.25	1.56
					0.65			
3	630	100	600	700		0.16	0.95	1.11
					0.49			
4	1040	100	800	900		0.10	0.77	0.87
					0.56			
5	1400	100	1000	1100		0.07	0.71	0.79
					0.59			
6	1740	100	1200	1300		0.06	0.69	0.75
					0.91			
7	1960	100	1400	1500		0.05	0.71	0.76

Column 3 shows the fixed costs which remain the same regardless of the level of output. The variable costs, shown in column 4, increase with the level of production.

Column 5 shows the total costs. Since total costs include both fixed and variable costs, they increase as the quantity of output increases. The curves drawn in the left-hand panel of Figure 4.2 are based on the short-run fixed, variable and total costs.

Figure 4.2: Short-run cost curves for Key Chains Inc.

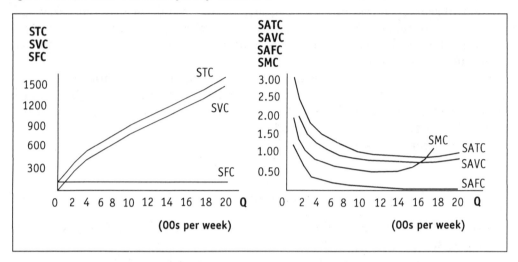

Fixed costs are independent of the level of production. These costs are incurred even if no output is produced. Therefore, the short-run fixed cost curve (SFC) is a horizontal line, at £100 (the cost of the machinery). Variable costs are incurred when production begins and increase as production increases. In this example the wage per worker equals £200. Therefore, the short-run variable cost curve (SVC) begins at the origin and is upward sloping.

The short-run total cost curve (STC) is the vertical summation of the other two curves: it begins at £100. The fixed costs are the only costs incurred before production begins. The STC curve is upward sloping and is always above the SVC curve by an amount equal to the value of the fixed costs. In the short run, fixed costs always separate the STC curve from the SVC curve.

We can examine other important economic concepts more conveniently by looking at the cost per unit. We will begin by defining the average cost and the marginal cost.

Definition
● ● ● ● ● ●

Average total cost is total cost divided by the number of units produced.

We can calculate average variable costs and average fixed costs. The addition of average fixed cost and average variable cost is average total cost.[7]

$$\text{SATC = SAFC + SAVC}$$

[4.5]

where: SATC = short-run average total cost; SAFC = short-run average fixed cost; SAVC = short-run average variable cost.

The key to understanding how much a firm will produce and sell is its marginal cost which is the most important of all cost concepts.

Definition
● ● ● ● ● ●

The marginal cost is the extra cost incurred from producing an additional unit of output.

In the short run it is expressed as follows:

$$SMC = \frac{\Delta STC}{\Delta Q}$$

[4.6]

where: Δ = change; SMC = short-run marginal cost; STC = short-run total cost; Q = level of output.

The marginal and average costs for this example are calculated in columns 6 through 9 of Table 4.3. We notice immediately that the short-run average fixed costs are falling as the costs are spread over more units. All of the other short-run costs fall initially and then rise again. These relationships can be examined more easily by looking at a diagram.

The right-sided frame of Figure 4.2 shows the short-run average fixed cost curve (SAFC), the short-run average variable cost curve (SAVC), the short-run average total cost curve (SATC) and finally the short-run marginal cost curve (SMC). Notice that the SAFC curve is downward sloping. As production expands, the average fixed costs fall. Both the SAVC and the SATC curves fall initially and then rise. The SMC curve also falls and rises again.

We can relate the changes in the marginal cost to our discussion about marginal productivity in Section 4.2. Remember that in the simplified production function for Key Chains Inc., labour is the only variable input. Therefore, wage is the only variable cost. With the addition of each of the first four workers, the marginal product increases. Assuming that all workers are employed at the same wage, if the marginal product of labour is increasing, the marginal cost to produce key chains falls. With the addition of the fifth worker at Key Chains Inc., labour is less productive. Therefore, the marginal cost of producing a unit of output increases.

To summarise this relationship, if the marginal product of labour is rising, its marginal cost is falling; if the marginal product of labour is falling, its marginal cost is rising.[8]

The relationship between 'average' and 'marginal' described in Section 4.2 also applies to costs. Both the short-run average total cost and variable cost 'follow' the marginal cost. When the marginal cost is below the average, the average costs fall. When the marginal cost is above the average, the average costs rise. In terms of the diagram, the SMC curve intersects both the SATC curve and the SAVC curve at their lowest points.

CASE STUDY

Extract from The Irish Times
Second furnace cuts costs as Ardagh profits rise 16%
by Bill Murdoch

The glass bottle manufacturer, Ardagh, has recorded a 16% increase in pre-tax profit from £4.46 million to £5.18 million in the year to June 27th last. The company is now getting the benefits from its new second furnace which has reduced energy costs and fattened its profit margins.

These margins have gone up from 13.8% to 15.27%. However, a breakdown of the figures shows margins of 16% in the second six months.

Group managing director Mr Eddie Kilty says the margins will 'ease up a bit'

this year. There has been a very heavy increase in cardboard prices, he adds. Cardboard accounts for about 7% of production costs so the price increases will have some impact.

Nevertheless, the new furnace uses between 15% and 20% less energy which accounts for 15% of production costs. So benefits will continue to come through.

Capacity utilisation is running at 100%. This, says Mr Kilty, just about meets demand.

. . .

Source: The Irish Times, *21 September 1995.*

Questions
....

1. How will the new furnace affect Ardagh's fixed costs? On a diagram, show fixed and average fixed costs before and after the furnace is installed.
2. How is the new furnace affecting Ardagh's marginal cost and variable cost? On a diagram, show Ardagh's marginal and average variable cost before and after the furnace is installed.
3. In this situation, which is more important, the fixed costs or the variable costs? Why?
4. An increase in the cost of cardboard threatens to 'squeeze' the profit margins of Ardagh. Do you think that this is a fixed cost or a variable cost?

Answers
....

1. The new furnace will probably increase the fixed costs, and therefore the average fixed costs of Ardagh. The change in fixed costs is shown in Figure 4.3(a) and the change in average fixed costs is shown in Figure 4.3(b) below.

Figure 4.3: Fixed costs and average fixed costs of Ardagh, before and after the installation of the new furnace

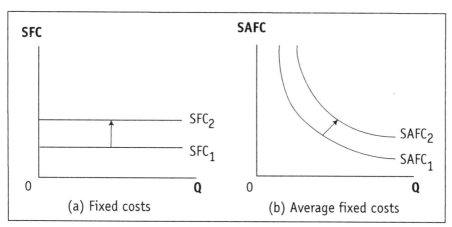

(a) Fixed costs   (b) Average fixed costs

2. In the article, it states that the new furnace has reduced energy costs. This means that the variable cost per unit is falling. This will cause the marginal and the variable cost curves to shift as shown in Figure 4.4 below.

Figure 4.4: Average variable cost and marginal cost of Ardagh before and after the installation of the new furnace

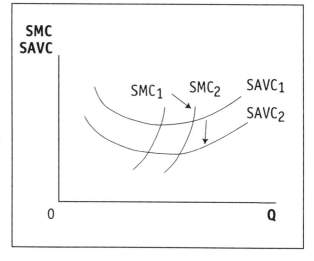

3. If many units are produced, the fixed costs are spread out and they are a small addition to the average total cost. In the article it states that energy costs account for 15% of production costs. This is a variable cost. In this situation, the decrease in variable costs appears to be more important to the firm than the increase in fixed costs.

4. Cardboard is probably used to pack the glass products. Therefore, cardboard is only used if there is production. Furthermore, the greater the production and sales of glass, the more packaging that is required. Hence, it is a variable cost.

Long-run costs
. . . .

The long run is a period of time which is long enough to vary all factors of production. Since inputs can be used with greater flexibility, we do not differentiate between variable and fixed costs. We will begin by discussing the shape of the long-run average cost curve (LAC).

The LAC curve shows the relationship between the lowest attainable average cost and output when all inputs are variable. In theory, the LAC curve can be in any of three forms or some combination of all three. A downward sloping LAC curve reflects declining unit costs as production increases. This is known as economies of scale. The straight line LAC curve reflects constant returns to scale. An upward sloping LAC curve reflects diseconomies of scale where the cost per unit of production increases as the level of output increases. Figure 4.5 below shows all three cases.

Figure 4.5: The slope of the long-run average cost curve

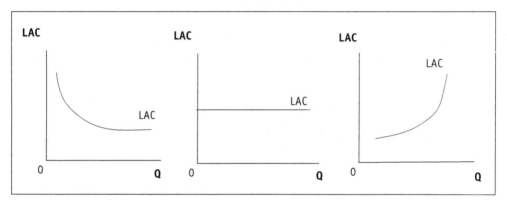

The typical long-run average cost curve is thought to be a combination of these three curves. The U-shaped LAC curve supposedly captures realistic trends in costs relative to output levels. It is shown in Figure 4.6.

Figure 4.6: The U-shaped long-run average cost curve

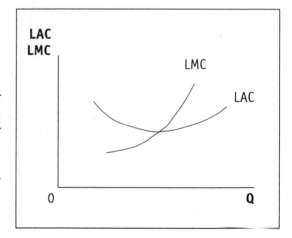

The LAC curve is downward sloping for relatively low levels of output. On this portion of the cost curve, the firm can take advantage of economies of scale if it can expand production. The LAC curve is relatively flat over a range of production. This means that the firm can expand production with little change in the cost per output. Over this range of production, the firm experiences constant returns to scale. Beyond a certain level of output, the LAC curve is upward sloping reflecting diseconomies of scale. The cost per unit of output is rising as output expands. The LMC curve is also shown in Figure 4.6.

At the bottom of the LAC curve, costs per unit of production are at their lowest. This level is called the minimum cost production level. It is of great significance and is explained in greater detail in the next chapter when we discuss different market structures.

The relationship between average costs and marginal costs also applies in the long run. In other words, when the marginal cost is below the average cost, the average costs fall. When the marginal cost is above the average cost, the average costs rise. As in the short run, the long-run marginal cost curve (LMC) cuts the LAC curve at the lowest point.

The envelope curve

The long-run average cost curve can be explained in terms of short-run average total cost curves. This is shown in Figure 4.7.

Figure 4.7: The envelope curve

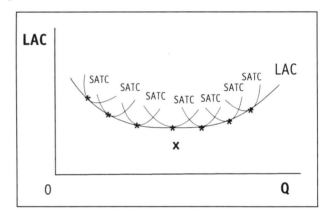

A set of SATC curves is reproduced in Figure 4.7 above. Each short-run average total cost curve is U-shaped because of the law of diminishing returns. The LAC curve is said to 'envelope' the SATC curves. Each point on the LAC curve is a point of tangency with respective points on corresponding SATC curves. There is a tendency to match the points on the LAC curve with minimum points on the SATC curves. This is incorrect.[9]

Point x is the minimum point of the LAC curve. Each point to the left is a tangency point with a point on the falling part of the respective SATC curves. Each point to the right is a tangency point with a point on the rising part of the respective SATC curves. Only at the minimum point x on the LAC curve is the corresponding SATC curve also at a minimum. This suggests that to the left of point x the plants are not working to full capacity whereas to the right of point x the plants are overworked. At point x the plant is optimally employed, in the sense that it is producing at the lowest possible cost per unit.

This completes the discussion of the derivation of short-run and long-run cost curves. We will now discuss the way that we use these cost curves to identify the firm's profit-maximising level of output.

4.4 Profit-maximising output level

The sole objective of the firm in the neoclassical model is profit maximisation. In this section we will derive the profit-maximising output level using two methods. These methods are essentially the same, though each looks at revenues and costs from a slightly different perspective.

The first approach requires values for total revenue (TR) and total cost (TC) for each level of production. The output level where the difference between total revenue and total cost is the largest is the profit-maximising output level. The second approach is based on marginal revenue (MR) and marginal cost (MC) values. By comparing marginal revenue and marginal cost we can derive the same profit-maximising output level as above.

We will use another example to illustrate the relevant concepts. Farmer Liam, from County Meath produces potatoes. Again, we will consider only two inputs for the short-run production function. Land is a fixed factor of production and rent is a fixed cost. Labour is the variable input and wage is the variable cost. Column 4 of Table 4.4 shows the total cost (fixed cost plus variable cost) associated with the different levels of output for potatoes.

Table 4.4: *Total revenue, total cost and profit for the production of potatoes*

(1) Q (tons)	(2) P (£00)	(3) TR (£00)	(4) TC (£00)	(5) Profit (£00)
0	–	0	36	−36
1	33.0	33	50	−17
2	31.5	63	62	1
3	30.0	90	73	17
4	28.5	114	82	32
5	27.0	135	92	43
6	25.5	153	105	48
7	24.0	168	119	49
8	22.5	180	144	36
9	21.0	189	171	18

Although Farmer Liam is always conscious of his costs, that is only half of the story. Over the years, he notices that to sell more potatoes, he must sell his potatoes at a lower price per ton. In other words, the demand curve for his product is downward sloping.

There is a particular price associated with each level of output. The price per ton of output is shown in column 2 of Table 4.4. Farmer Liam is interested in the total revenue which he will receive at each level of production. We know from Chapter 2 that total revenue is the price of the good times the quantity of output sold.

Total revenue is calculated in column 3 of Table 4.4.

Profit is the difference between total revenue and total cost. Recall that a normal profit is included in the calculations for cost. Therefore, if profit is zero, the firm (or in this case the farmer) is making a normal profit. Any profit which is greater than zero is called economic or supernormal profit. Profit is calculated in column 5 of Table 4.4.

In this example, the difference between total revenue and total cost is maximised when seven tons are produced. At this level of output, profit is £4,900.

As we mentioned earlier, this profit-maximising level of output can also be identified by comparing the marginal revenue and the marginal cost.

Definition
● ● ● ● ● ●

Marginal revenue is the change in total revenue resulting from a one unit change in output.

Algebraically, we can describe this relationship in the following way:

$$MR = \frac{\Delta TR}{\Delta Q}$$

[4.7]

where: Δ = change; MR = marginal revenue; TR = total revenue; Q = level of output.

Marginal revenue is calculated in column 3 of Table 4.5 below. Consider the additional revenue which Farmer Liam gains by producing and selling the seventh ton. When he produces and sells six tons, he earns £15,300 in revenue. For the production and sale of seven tons, Farmer Liam earns £16,800. The difference between the two is £1,500. Since one additional ton is produced, we divide this total by one. In this example, the marginal revenue gained from the production and sale of the seventh ton is £1,500.

We have already defined the marginal cost as the additional charge incurred from producing and selling one unit of output. The marginal cost is calculated in column 5 of Table 4.5.

The total cost of producing seven units is £11,900. However, producing the first six units costs the farmer £10,500. Therefore, the marginal cost of the seventh unit is (11,900 – 10,500)/1 which is £1,400.

Table 4.5: Total revenue, marginal revenue, total cost and marginal cost

(1) Q (tons)	(2) TR (£00)	(3) MR (£00)	(4) TC (£00)	(5) MC (£00)	(6) MR–MC (£00)	(7) Output decision
0	0		36			
		33		14	19	Increase
1	33		50			
		30		12	18	Increase
2	63		62			
		27		11	16	Increase
3	90		73			
		24		9	15	Increase
4	114		82			
		21		10	11	Increase
5	135		92			
		18		13	5	Increase
6	153		105			
		15		14	1	Increase
7	168		119			
		12		25	–13	Decrease
8	180		144			
		9		27	–18	Decrease
9	189		171			

The last two columns of Table 4.5 help us to determine the profit-maximising output level for Farmer Liam. Marginal revenue is greater than marginal cost from the first unit of production to the seventh unit of production. As output increases by one unit the additional revenue is greater than the additional cost incurred. This means that he can earn additional profits by increasing production. Since we assume that Farmer Liam wants to maximise profits, output should be increased.

Marginal revenue is less than marginal cost beyond the seventh unit of production. The extra revenue is not large enough to cover the extra cost incurred. Production should not be increased beyond seven units. A profit-maximising firm (farmer) will continue to produce as long as the difference between the marginal revenue and marginal cost is positive. The difference is calculated in column 6 above. In this example the difference is positive up to seven units of production.

In brief, when marginal revenue is greater than marginal cost, the level of output should be increased. When marginal revenue is less than marginal cost, output should be reduced. Consequently, a firm produces at the profit-maximising output level when marginal revenue is equal to marginal cost.

This is a necessary, but not sufficient condition for profit maximisation. An examination of the second condition will be covered after we compare the profit-maximising output level using total revenue and total cost with the level of output determined using marginal revenue and marginal cost. Figure 4.8 shows the relationship between the two approaches.

Figure 4.8: Profit maximisation with total
   revenue and total cost, marginal revenue
   and marginal cost

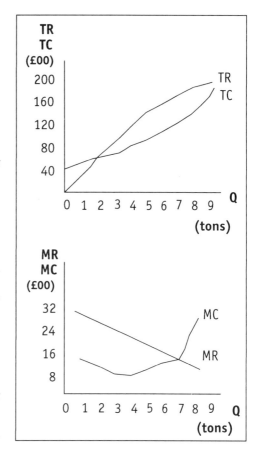

In the top frame of Figure 4.8, we have drawn the curves for total revenue (TR) and total cost (TC). When the gap between the TR and TC curves is the greatest, profits are maximised. As we saw in the table, this occurs at a production level of seven units.

In the bottom frame, we can see the relationship between marginal revenue (MR) and marginal cost (MC). Consider a production level of six units. From the diagram, we can clearly see that the MR curve is above the MC curve. Therefore, the firm can increase profits by producing and selling more units. Now consider the production level of eight units. On the diagram, we can see that the MC curve is above the MR curve. If the firm produces at this level, total profits will fall. Therefore, the profit-maximising level of production is between six and eight units of production. The profit-maximising firm will produce seven units. This is where the MR curve intersects the MC curve. Refer to Appendix 4.1 to see how this is related to cost minimisation and the least-cost production technique.

Using either approach, the profit-maximising level of output is the same.

In the example of the potato-producing farmer, the profit-maximising decision was to produce. This is not always the case. In some situations, firms operate at a loss, at least in the short run. The owner of the firm may decide that he can minimise his losses by producing where marginal revenue equals the marginal cost. Alternatively, he may decide that it is better to shut down, and pay only the fixed costs. In other words, it is costing him more to produce than it would to shut down. We will extend our analysis to show how the owner of a profit-maximising firm makes that choice both in the short run and in the long run.

The output decision of the firm in the short run

There are two conditions for short-run equilibrium. First, we have already discussed the marginal condition. A profit-maximising firm which is going to produce will choose a production level where marginal revenue equals short-run marginal cost (MR = SMC). However, there is a second condition which also must be met: it is the average condition. A firm will produce this level of output if, and only if, average revenue or price is no less than short-run average variable cost ($P \geq SAVC$).

● Definition
● ● ● ● ● ●

Average revenue is a firm's total revenue divided by the quantity sold.

It is simply the price of the good.[10]

This second condition implies that in order to produce the firm must at least cover its variable costs. This equilibrium position is illustrated in Figure 4.9.

Figure 4.9: Output decision in the short run

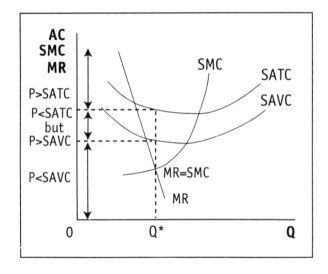

The marginal condition, where MR = SMC, is met at output level Q* in Figure 4.9. Given the present market conditions and the short-run costs the profit-maximising output level is Q*. However, this condition alone is not enough to determine the firm's production decision as it does not provide for the possibility of not producing at all. This requires the second condition. The average condition involves comparing average revenue with average cost, at Q*. Given the nature of costs in the short run, three distinct possibilities arise.

If average revenue or price exceeds the short-run average total cost resulting in an economic profit, the firm will continue to produce at this output level. If the price level falls between the SATC and the SAVC curves, the firm is operating at a loss. It is covering its variable costs and making some contribution to the fixed costs which must be paid even if production is temporarily halted. Under this condition, the firm will continue to produce because it will lose even more if it closes. Instead of maximising profits, the firm is minimising losses. A favourable change in market conditions could turn short-run losses into profits.

If price is lower than the short-run average variable cost the situation is more serious. In this case the firm is not covering its variable costs. The day-to-day expenses such as labour costs, tax bills, social insurance and so on are not met. At Q* the variable cost per unit of production exceeds the price received for each unit. The firm minimises losses by shutting down. A shutdown is preferred to continued production at Q*.

In brief, a firm that is not making profits will attempt to limit their short-run losses. The decision to produce in the short run requires that both the marginal and average conditions are met. Ultimately any profit-maximising firm produces in the short run as long as it covers its variable costs.

In the short run, we have seen that a firm may continue production, even if it is not making a normal profit. In the long run, the owner of the firm can make a number of choices, which include switching his resources to another form of enterprise where he can make at least a normal profit. We now explore the output decision for a profit-maximising firm in the long run.

The output decision of the firm in the long run
....

There are two conditions for long-run equilibrium. The first condition states that the profit-maximising firm will produce where marginal revenue equals the long-run marginal cost (MR = LMC). The marginal condition is met at the output level of Q* as illustrated in Figure 4.10 below.

Figure 4.10: Output decision in the long run

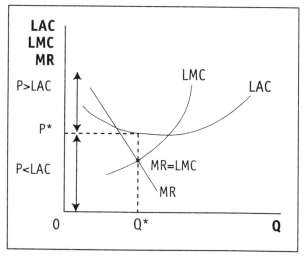

As before, this condition is not sufficient as it does not cover the alternative of not producing at all. The second condition states that a firm will produce in the long run if price is greater than or equal to the long-run average cost (P ≥ LAC). This condition implies that the firm will only produce in the long run if it can cover all of its costs. In the long run, two cases arise.

If price equals or exceeds the long-run average cost, the firm will continue to produce where marginal revenue equals marginal cost. If the price obtained for the product is P*, shown in Figure 4.10, the firm is covering its costs and making a normal profit. If price is greater than P*, the firm is making supernormal profits. In either situation, the firm will continue to produce in the long run.

Alternatively, if price is lower than P*, then losses result. Since a firm must cover all of its costs in the long run, it will have no choice but to stop production and close down. In this case, we would expect the factors of production to be released for use in activities which will earn at least a normal profit.

In brief, the long-run output decision requires that both the marginal and the average conditions are met. Ultimately all costs must be covered in the long run.

We will conclude this chapter by returning to economies of scale and discussing the important ramifications of this concept in the Irish context.

4.5 Economies of scale and implications for Ireland

Although economies of scale appears to be simply a technical relationship, its relevance for a small country like Ireland is quite profound.

When Fianna Fáil came into power in 1932, it attempted and succeeded in increasing industrial production by imposing tariffs on imports. This protected the domestic manufacturers since the tariffs made imported goods more expensive than goods which were manufactured in Ireland. One consequence of this protectionist policy was that it raised problems with our main trading partner, Britain, leading to the 'Economic War'.

What is more relevant to this discussion is that the small size of the domestic market meant that in most industries, production was not very efficient. Why? Although consumer products like clothing and shoes were being produced here, the inputs and machinery needed for production were largely imported. The domestic industries were not large enough to support the development of other domestic firms who could supply the inputs. Increasing returns to scale in the production process meant that inputs could be produced far more cheaply by foreign-based firms who were producing initially for larger domestic markets and then exporting.

Unfortunately, the cost of the foreign inputs made Irish products expensive relative to the goods produced in other countries. The small size of the Irish market meant that Irish manufacturers were producing at a high cost per unit and were unable to benefit from scale economies which would have lowered their costs and ultimately made the price of Irish goods more competitive in the international market.

For a number of reasons, the protectionist policies of the 1930s and 1940s were abandoned. One of the main reasons was the deterioration of the 'terms of trade'. This means that the price of imports increased faster than the price of exports. Ireland was importing more than she was exporting, a situation which cannot persist indefinitely for a small country. One of the main goals of policy-makers in the 1950s, a period of reorientation towards free trade, was to promote export growth. In 1965, Ireland joined Britain to sign the Anglo-Irish Free Trade Agreement (AIFTA) and began to dismantle trade barriers. In 1973, Ireland joined the European Economic Community (EEC) under an agreement that they would implement free-trade policies for all manufacturers by 1978.

By entering these trade agreements, Ireland was attempting to increase the size of potential markets. Only by expanding demand could Ireland hope to compete in the increasing number of markets that were characterised by 'scale' economies.

Ireland's concerns about producing for larger markets was mirrored by other member countries of the EEC. Because of different types of trade barriers, many industries were unable to produce at the lowest cost per unit. Some of these barriers were easily recognised, like the physical barriers at the entry of various European countries which delayed the movement of both goods and people. This added to the transportation cost of delivering goods to the market.

However, other non-tariff barriers are less transparent. To protect their domestic industries, governments often impose regulations and standards which favour indigenous firms. If foreign firms want to produce for the same market, they must comply with these regulations which are often different than the standards in their own country. Therefore, a firm must produce a different good for each market, and in doing so misses out on the economies of scale that would result from producing the same good for the two markets.

This problem was so pervasive that European policy-makers and firms felt that it was causing European firms to lose competitiveness to firms which were producing for larger markets. US and Japanese firms, many of whom produce for the US market, are able to manufacture goods for the entire market of over two hundred million people. Generally, regulations are established nationally. Goods move freely from New York to San Francisco. The situation in Europe was far different because regulations changed from country to country and goods were stopped at every national border.

This concern of the Commission to the European Council is clearly outlined in the White Paper entitled 'Completing the Internal Market', published in 1985. It states,

> 'Until such barriers are removed, Community manufacturers are forced to focus on national rather than continental markets and are unable to benefit from the economies of scale which a truly unified internal market offers. Failure to achieve a genuine industrial common market becomes increasingly serious since the research, development and commercialisation costs of the new technologies, in order to have a realistic prospect of being internationally competitive, require the background of a home market of continental proportions.'[11]

As we can see, economies of scale is far more than a technical relationship between the cost of production and the quantity produced. It is a concept which has helped to shape industrial policy, particularly since the 1950s, and has moved Ireland into closer relations with other European countries.

Summary

1. The production process involves the transformation of inputs into output. The production function shows the maximum possible output employing different amounts of inputs.
2. An analysis of the theory of production is divided into short run and long run. They reflect the ability of the firm to vary its behaviour within the market.
3. Opportunity cost is a measure of the best alternative forgone. Normal profit is a cost of production. Economic costs include explicit costs and the opportunity cost. Economic profit is the difference between total revenue and economic costs.
4. In the short run there is at least one fixed factor of production. The costs associated with these inputs are termed fixed costs. Other short-run costs are variable. In order for a firm to stay in business in the short run it must cover its variable costs. In the long run all factors of production are variable. As a result all costs are variable. A firm must cover all of its costs in the long run in order for it to stay in business.

5. The most important cost concept is marginal cost. It is the additional cost incurred as output is increased by one extra unit. It is central to the theory of supply.
6. Marginal revenue is the change in total revenue arising out of a one unit change in output. Marginal cost is the change in total cost arising out of a one unit change in output. A profit-maximising firm will produce where MR = MC. This is a necessary but not sufficient condition for profit maximisation.

Key terms

Profit maximisation
Factors of production
Production function
Short-run production
Fixed input
Variable input
Total product
Marginal product
Increasing marginal returns
Law of diminishing returns
Average product
Long-run production
Increasing returns to scale
Constant returns to scale
Decreasing returns to scale

Economies of scale
Diseconomies of scale
Specialisation of labour
Indivisibilities
Normal profit
Opportunity cost
Economic profit
Total cost
Fixed costs
Variable costs
Average cost
Marginal cost
Envelope curve
Marginal revenue
Average revenue

Review questions

1. What are the objectives of a firm? What is the objective of the firm in the traditional neoclassical theory?
2. Explain the difference between short-run production and long-run production. What is the difference between the 'law of diminishing returns' and 'returns to scale'?
3. List the three possibilities that production can exhibit in the long run. What are the sources of economies of scale?
4. How is the economist's interpretation of costs different from that of the accountant? What is the difference between accounting profit and economic profit?
5. What two conditions must be met in order for a profit-maximising firm to produce? How is the output decision in the short run different from the long run?
6. Explain the relationship between the diminishing returns of the variable factor and the short-run marginal cost curve. What does this suggest about the theory of production and the theory of costs?

Working problems

1. This is a weekly production schedule for mushrooms.

Table 4.6

Land	Labour	Output	Average	Marginal
20	0	0		
20	1	1		
20	2	3		
20	3	6		
20	4	10		
20	5	16		
20	6	20		
20	7	21		
20	8	20		
20	9	18		

(a) What are the inputs used in this production process?
(b) How do you know that this is a short-run production function? Which inputs are fixed and which are variable?
(c) Sketch the total product curve.
(d) Complete the table for the AP and MP of labour.
(e) Explain why the MP of labour declines.
(f) Where does the MP of labour curve cut the AP of labour curve? Explain why.

2. The cost of land is £50 per acre and the cost of labour is £100 per worker per week.

Table 4.7

Land	Labour	Output	SFC	SVC	STC	SMC	SAFC	SAVC	SATC
2	0	0							
2	1	1							
2	2	3							
2	3	6							
2	4	10							
2	5	16							
2	6	20							
2	7	23							
2	8	25							
2	9	26							
2	10	24							

(a) Complete the table.
(b) Draw the respective cost curves.
(c) Will the SATC curve and the SAVC curve ever intersect?
(d) Where will the SMC curve cut the SAVC and the SATC curves? Why?

Multi-choice questions

1. Diseconomies of scale:
   (a) arise due to indivisibilities and the division of labour;
   (b) exist when the cost per unit of production rises as the level of output rises;
   (c) exist when the LAC curve falls as output rises;
   (d) arise due to increasing layers of bureaucracy and problems with management-staff relations;
   (e) both (b) and (d) above.

2. The law of diminishing returns:
   (a) is reflected in the slope of the total product curve;
   (b) is a short-run concept;
   (c) sets in when the marginal product of the variable factor begins to decline;
   (d) occurs when production is constrained by fixed factors of production;
   (e) all of the above.

3. The short-run marginal cost curve:
   (a) reflects the law of diminishing returns;
   (b) cuts the SATC and SAVC curves at their lowest points;
   (c) is a mirror image of the marginal product curve;
   (d) both (a) and (c) above;
   (e) (a), (b) and (c) above.

4. The profit-maximising output level in the short run is given by:
   (a) $TR = TC$ and $AR = SAVC$;
   (b) $MR = SMC$ and $AR \geq SAVC$;
   (c) $TR > TC$ and $MR > SMC$;
   (d) $MR = SMC$ and $AR < SATC$;
   (e) none of the above.

5. Economic costs:
   (a) are no different than accounting costs;
   (b) include the opportunity cost of the entrepreneur;
   (c) are equal to the explicit costs of production;
   (d) guarantee that normal profit and economic profit are equal;
   (e) both (b) and (c) above.

6. The mainstream orthodox treatment of the firm is based on the assumption of:
   (a) sales maximisation;
   (b) revenue maximisation;
   (c) growth maximisation;
   (d) profit maximisation;
   (e) none of the above.

True or false

1. When the total product curve is upward sloping and increasing at a decreasing rate the marginal product of the variable input is declining. _____
2. Decreasing returns to scale arise out of indivisibilities and the division of labour. _____
3. The two conditions for a profit-maximising firm are the average and marginal conditions. _____
4. Normal profit is a cost of production. _____
5. A firm will only continue to produce in the long run if the market price covers both fixed and variable costs. _____
6. The LAC curve is formed by the minimum points of the SATC curves. _____

Fill in the blanks

Production involves the process of transforming _____ into output. Short-run production assumes that at least one input is_____ . _____ production involves a time period where all factors of production are variable. The relation between inputs and output is reflected in the short run by the ___ __ _____ _____ and in the long run by _____ __ ____ . This latter concept is closely linked to economies and _____ of scale. Any production involves the use of inputs which in turn involves _____. Short-run costs are associated with the inputs used in ____ __ production and can be either _____ or variable. In contrast, all long-run costs are variable. A firm will produce in the short run as long as it can cover its _____ costs and make some progress in covering its fixed costs. In the long run ____ costs must be covered. The above analysis is based on the traditional _____ model of the firm which assumes _____ maximisation. Economists are concerned primarily with _____ ____ which is a measure of the best _____ forgone. Any difference between total revenue and _____ _____, which incorporates opportunity cost, is termed pure or _____ profit.

CASE STUDY

Extract from The Irish Times
Small firms seek leeway on tax and labour laws
by Barry O'Keeffe

Small firms have appealed to the government to give them greater leeway on tax and labour legislation. They have submitted a seven-point plan aimed at curbing growth of such legislation, which they argue can be bad for business.

A delegation from the Irish Business and Employers Confederation (IBEC) told the Joint Committee on Business and Services yesterday that firms were being overburdened by legislation.

'We have an unsustainable amount of legislation to comply with,' said

———→

Mr Brendan Newsome, managing director Wire Ropes (sic). He said there were 40 statutes on labour law alone. 'There should be a two-year allowance period for small firms, before they must comply with new labour legislation.'

Mr Declan Madden, IBEC's director of social affairs and specialist services, said the legislature should impose restraint on itself. 'The decision to legislate is made much too easily,' he argued. 'Legislation is passed which deals with the worst possible scenario,' he said, adding that it hampered firms.

Mr Madden said other options should be tried before legislation. He suggested that in some cases agreed guidelines could be drawn up between the various parties, such as IBEC and ICTU (Irish Congress of Trade Unions), to deal with particular problems.

IBEC's seven-point plan urges that the cost to industry should be examined and that it should not have a disproportionate effect on different firms because of their size. It calls for particular attention to be given to companies employing fewer than twenty people.

The delegation also aired several other small firms' grievances. Mr Peter Malone, managing director of Jurys . . . called for employers' PRSI rates to be reassessed, arguing that it was a tax on employment. 'The first overhead an employer looks at is staff costs,' he said.

. . .

Source: The Irish Times, *14 June 1995.*

Questions
....

1. Why do politicians enact labour legislation? What is the opportunity cost of the legislation?
2. Why does Mr Madden suggest that legislation has a disproportionate effect on small firms? Does he seem to consider compliance with legislation a fixed cost or a variable cost?
3. Mr Malone suggests that PRSI (Pay Related Social Insurance) rates should be cut. Will this affect a variable cost or a fixed cost?

Appendix 4.1: Cost minimisation using isoquants and isocost lines

A more detailed analysis of the theory of production requires the use of concepts and techniques similar to those used in the theory of consumer choice. By the use and application of these new concepts, such as isoquants (equal quantity lines) and isocost lines (equal cost lines), we can derive the least-cost technique of producing a certain level of output.

An isoquant is a locus of points, showing the various combinations of two inputs that can be used to produce a given level of output. The most common combination of inputs discussed in neoclassical theory is labour and capital. Therefore, the isoquant is drawn on a diagram with capital on the vertical axis and labour on the horizontal axis. A single isoquant is shown in Figure 4.11 below.

Figure 4.11: An isoquant

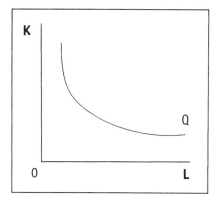

The slope of an isoquant is called the marginal rate of technical substitution (MRTS) which is equal to the amount of an input that can be replaced by one unit of another factor without changing the level of output. It measures the trade-off between two factors of production. Equation 4.8 states this in algebraic terms.

$$MRTS = -\frac{\Delta K}{\Delta L}$$ [4.8]

An isoquant has similar properties to an indifference curve. Isoquants slope down from left to right; they are usually drawn convex to the origin; there is an isoquant map with each isoquant representing a different level of output; the higher the isoquant, the higher the level of output. The slope is the MRTS. It diminishes as we move down the isoquant from left to right.

The isocost line reflects the cost of the inputs. The isocost line shows all the combinations of the two factors that can be employed for a certain amount of money. Figure 4.12 illustrates an example of an isocost line.

Figure 4.12: An isocost line

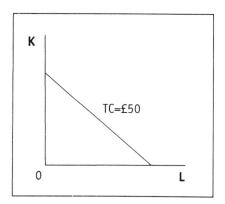

Higher isocost lines are associated with higher costs. Likewise, lower costs are reflected in isocost lines closer to the origin. The slope of an isocost line is equal to the negative of the factor price ratio, $-\frac{P_L}{P_K}$, the price of labour over the price of capital. A change in relative prices results in a change in the slope of the isocost line.

A profit-maximising firm chooses the particular combination of inputs that minimises cost. The least-cost technique of production is the combination of inputs that minimises the total cost of producing a given level of output. It is determined by superimposing a set of isocost lines onto a given isoquant. This is shown in Figure 4.13 below.

Figure 4.13: The least-cost input combination

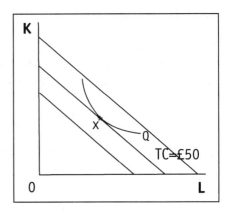

The optimal level, where the profit-maximising firm will minimise costs, is given by the tangency point between the isoquant and the lowest possible isocost line. At this point x the respective slopes are equal. This is expressed in algebraic form in Equation 4.9.

$$\text{slope of isoquant} = \text{MRTS} = \frac{-\Delta K}{\Delta L} = \frac{-P_L}{P_K} = \text{slope of isocost line} \qquad [4.9]$$

This approach is similar to the analysis used in consumer choice theory. The similarities are outlined in Table 4.8 below.

Table 4.8: Duality between consumer choice theory and production theory

Consumer theory	Production theory
Each indifference curve reflects a different level of utility.	Each isoquant represents a different level of output.
Constraints reflected by budget lines.	Costs reflected by isocost lines.
The consumer maximises utility subject to the price and income constraints.	The producer produces a certain level of output by using the least-costly combination of inputs available.
Utility maximisation occurs where $$\text{MRS} = -\frac{P_d}{P_f}$$	Cost minimisation occurs where $$\text{MRTS} = -\frac{P_L}{P_K}$$

CHAPTER 5

MARKET STRUCTURES

....

'By perfect competition I propose to mean a state of affairs in which the demand for the output of an individual seller is perfectly elastic.'[1]

Joan Robinson (1903–83)

'Opposition is the life of trade.'

An old Irish saying

'People of the same trade seldom meet together, even for merriment and diversion, but the conversation ends in a conspiracy against the public, or in some contrivance to raise prices.'[2]

Adam Smith (1723–90)

....

Chapter objectives

Upon completing this chapter, the student should understand:

- the supply curve of the perfectly competitive firm;
- efficiency;
- monopoly power;
- product differentiation and monopolistic competition;
- mutual interdependency between oligopolistic firms;
- the differences between the market structures.

Outline

5.1 **Perfect competition**
5.2 **Monopoly**
5.3 **Monopolistic competition**
5.4 **Oligopoly**
5.5 **Market structure spectrum**

Introduction

The theory of the firm was explained in Chapter 4. However, there are many aspects of a firm's behaviour which remain unanswered. Will the profits be high or low? Will the price charged to the consumer be high or low? Will the firm produce efficiently?

Will the level of output be small or large? Many of these questions depend on the environment within which the firm operates and, in particular, the degree of competition facing the firm. There may be only one firm in the market. If so, the firm will behave differently than a firm in a market where there are a large number of competitors.

It is traditional at this stage of our analysis to divide markets into categories according to the degree of competition and market power. Market power signifies the degree of control that a firm or a group of firms have over price. The market structure ultimately determines a firm's behaviour. There are four broad categories: perfect competition, monopolistic competition, oligopoly and monopoly. The differences between each case depend on a number of key characteristics. They are:

- the number of firms in the market;
- the freedom of entry and exit, depending largely on the existence of barriers to entry;
- the nature of the product, whether it is differentiated or undifferentiated;
- the availability of information.

Throughout the discussion of market structures, we assume that there are a large number of consumers whose actions are unco-ordinated, except through the market. In other words, consumers are not grouping together to exert pressure on firms in the market. Also, we assume that the objective of all firms is profit maximisation. The profit-maximising level of output for firms is explained in terms of the marginal condition and the average condition. These concepts were explained in the previous chapter.

We begin in Section 5.1 by explaining perfect competition. Monopoly, monopolistic competition, and oligopoly are discussed in Sections 5.2, 5.3 and 5.4 respectively. An overall summary of the complete market structure spectrum is explained in Section 5.5.

5.1 Perfect competition

Perfect competition lies at one end of the market spectrum.[3] The model of the perfectly competitive market is based on strict and unrealistic assumptions, which we will discuss below. This means that it is difficult to find examples of perfectly competitive markets. The markets for certain raw materials, agricultural products and the stock exchange are usually cited as examples of perfectly competitive markets.

With so few examples, a student might be forgiven for asking why she is required to spend so much time and energy in understanding this market structure. Perfect competition and monopoly are located at the two ends of the market spectrum. If we understand the extreme cases, we can use them as a basis of comparison for other commonly observable market structures which lie between the extremes. Also, at the end of this section, we will define and discuss efficiency. We examine perfect competition as the benchmark of efficiency and later discuss how other market structures compare.

Perfect competition is one form of market structure with a number of identifying characteristics:

1. There is a large number of firms and the output of any firm is small relative to the market output. Because its output is small, each firm is a price taker and cannot influence price.
2. There is complete freedom of entry to and exit from the market.
3. The market product is homogeneous. The commodity produced by one firm is identical to the product produced by any other firm in the market.
4. There is perfect information. Consumers are aware of market prices and firms are aware of the actions of their competitors.

The fact that the firm is a price taker has very important implications for the demand curve facing the firm.

Let us consider an example. Molly is a street trader on Moore Street. The price of apples is 25p each. Molly can sell as many apples as she likes at this market price; hence, there is no incentive to cut price. Likewise, there is no incentive to increase price. Her three sisters Margie, Annie and Bridie along with the other street traders are all selling apples for the same price. If Molly increases her price she will not be able to sell, as customers will go elsewhere. In summary, her individual actions will have no effect on the market price of apples which is determined by the total market demand and supply on any given day.

In terms of price, the demand for Molly's apples is perfectly elastic. The demand curve that Molly and other street traders face for their product is horizontal. This is illustrated in Figure 5.1.

Figure 5.1: The perfectly competitive market

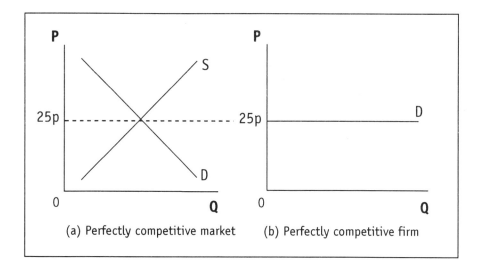

(a) Perfectly competitive market   (b) Perfectly competitive firm

The left-hand panel of Figure 5.1 illustrates the market for apples on any given day on Moore Street. The equilibrium price is 25p. It is determined by market demand and market supply. The market demand is the aggregate of all the individual consumers' demand curves whereas the supply curve is the sum of all the street traders' supply curves. Any change in market demand or market supply will affect the equilibrium price. For example, an influx of tourists into Dublin will increase the demand for apples. Hence, the market demand is pushed right resulting in an increase in the price.

The right-hand panel illustrates the demand curve of the perfectly competitive firm; in this case, Molly. Molly is a price taker. She sells her apples for 25p. On this day, all other things being equal, she will neither increase price nor cut price. The demand curve is horizontal. We say it is perfectly elastic at a price level of 25p.[4]

A horizontal demand curve has important implications for the relationship between price and marginal revenue. Before we consider a numerical example for a firm operating in a perfectly competitive market, we will briefly recall some of the definitions discussed in detail in Chapter 4.

Total revenue is the amount which a firm receives for selling its goods and services. It is calculated by multiplying price times quantity ($TR = P \times Q$). Marginal revenue is the change in revenue which a firm receives if it produces and sells one more unit ($MR = \dfrac{\Delta TR}{\Delta Q}$). Average revenue equals total revenue divided by the quantity sold ($AR = \dfrac{TR}{Q}$). If we multiply both sides of this equation by Q, we are left with another equation for total revenue ($TR = AR \times Q$). Comparing this with the first equation, we see that $P = AR$. This result will hold regardless of whether a firm's demand curve is horizontal or downward sloping.

However, if a firm is operating in a perfectly competitive market, marginal revenue is also equal to price and to average revenue. We will illustrate this with an example. Table 5.1 shows a firm's demand schedule.

Table 5.1: Price, marginal revenue and average revenue

Q	P	TR	MR	AR
0	10	–		
			10	
1	10	10		10
			10	
2	10	20		10
			10	
3	10	30		10
			10	
4	10	40		10

It is obvious from the table that this firm is operating in a perfectly competitive market because it does not have to lower its price in order to sell more output. Regardless of the quantity which the perfectly competitive firm chooses to sell, the last unit will be sold at the market price of P = 10. Hence, the marginal revenue received from selling additional output is equal to the price received, i.e. MR = P.

In terms of a diagram, the marginal revenue curve and the demand curve are one and the same for a firm in a perfectly competitive market. This is shown in Figure 5.2.

The output decision in the short run

How much will a perfectly competitive firm produce in the short run? From our discussion in Chapter 4, we know that if a firm is going to produce, the profit-maximising level of output is where marginal revenue equals marginal cost. This is also illustrated in Figure 5.2.

Figure 5.2: Marginal revenue and marginal cost

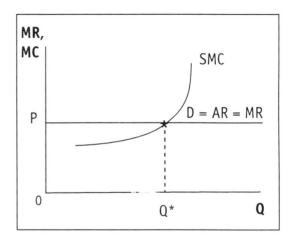

We can see from Figure 5.2 that the profit-maximising level of output is at Q* where MR = SMC. Moreover, at Q*, MR = SMC = P for a firm in a perfectly competitive market. We will see in the next sections that this result differs for firms which operate in other, less competitive market structures.

We know from Chapter 4 that MR = MC is a necessary but not sufficient condition for producing at the profit-maximising output level. The second condition relates to average revenue and average cost. The short-run cost curves which we derived in Chapter 4 are reproduced below. Four possible cases are presented in Figure 5.3.

Figure 5.3: Four scenarios for a perfectly competitive firm

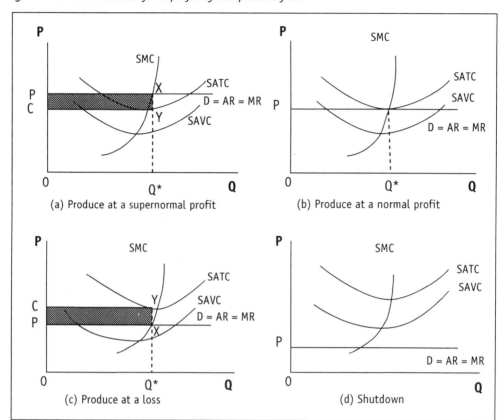

In panel (a), price is above the short-run average total cost. This is presented by drawing the demand curve above the short-run average total cost curve. The first condition is met at Q* where MR = SMC.

Secondly, at this output level, price is greater than average total cost. From our discussion in the previous chapter, we know that a 'normal' profit is included as a cost of production. Since the AR curve is above the SATC curve, at the profit-maximising level of production, this firm is making a supernormal profit. The supernormal profit per unit is measured by the distance between the SATC curve and the AR curve at Q*. This is shown on the diagram by line segment |XY|.

The shaded area on the diagram is the area of supernormal profits. We identify this area by subtracting the area of total cost from the area of total revenue. On the diagram, total revenue is defined by the area of the rectangle [PXQ*0]. Total cost is shown by the rectangle [CYQ*0]. The difference between the two areas is the shaded rectangle [PXYC] which represents the total supernormal profits received by the firm.

In panel (b), the AR curve is tangent to the SATC curve. In this situation, price equals average total cost. At this point, the firm is making a normal profit. The firm will produce Q* units of output, the level of output where marginal revenue equals short-run marginal cost.

In panel (c) price is below the average total cost but above the average variable cost. In this case, price is greater than SAVC but less than SATC. This is presented by drawing the AR curve above the SAVC curve but below the SATC curve. Because we assume that firms will maximise profits (or alternatively minimise losses), we conclude that a firm that faces this situation will produce at Q^*. The alternative is to cease production and pay all of the fixed costs. At Q^*, the firm is covering its variable costs and making some contribution to its fixed costs. The loss per unit is shown by the line segment |YX| which represents the difference between average total cost and price. The area of economic loss is shown by the shaded rectangle [CYXP]. This is the area which remains when total revenue, represented by the area [PXQ*0] is subtracted from total cost, represented by the rectangle [CYQ*0].

In panel (d) price is below the short-run average variable cost. This is presented by drawing the AR curve below the SAVC curve. The market price does not cover the variable costs of the firm. The firm in this situation minimises losses by discontinuing production.

Deriving the short-run supply curve
....

The above analysis can be used to derive the short-run supply curve for a firm in a perfectly competitive market. Let us begin with a market price of P_0. At P_0 the firm will produce at Q_0 where MR = SMC. Both the marginal condition and the average condition are met. This gives us point X, the first point on the supply curve.

Figure 5.4: Derivation of the short-run supply curve

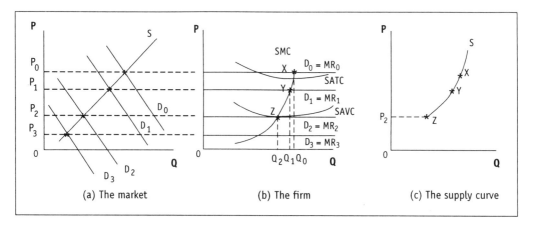

Suppose there is a change in market conditions. In panel (a) the demand curve shifts down to the left (from D_0 to D_1) due to a reduction in the number of tourists. The firm reacts to the lower price by cutting production to Q_1 where MR_1 = SMC. Point Y is another point on the supply curve. As price falls, less is produced.

Suppose the fall in demand reduces the market price to P_3. For the firm, this price level is below both the average total cost and the average variable cost. The firm minimises its losses by discontinuing production and paying its fixed costs. There is no corresponding output level for this price, or any price below P_2.

At P_2, price is equal to average variable cost. The AR curve is tangent to the SAVC curve. A price just below P_2 is the shutdown price.

• Definition
● ● ● ● ● ●

The shutdown price is less than the short-run average variable cost of producing a unit of output.

At P_2, the firm will produce Q_2 units of output, shown as point Z on Figure 5.4, panel (b). Below this price, the firm will not supply output.

We can see from panel (c) of Figure 5.4 that the SMC curve beginning at point Z is the supply curve for the firm in the short run. All profit-maximising firms produce where MR = SMC. For a firm in a perfectly competitive market, marginal revenue is equal to the price. Therefore, a firm in this market will produce where P = SMC, as long as the average variable costs are covered.

What can be implied from the above? Under perfect competition, the firm's supply curve in the short run is its marginal cost curve above the shutdown price. Hence, the amount the firm supplies to the market depends primarily on its costs of production.

The short-run supply curve for the competitive market is simply the horizontal sum of the supply curves of all individual firms. It shows the sum of all the quantities produced by all firms at each given price in the short run. This is the same supply curve which we discussed in Chapter 1.

The output decision in the long run
....

The analysis in the long run is a little different. It is based on the assumption that firms are free to enter and exit the market. Let us begin by looking at two possibilities: the long-run equilibrium following short-run losses and the long-run equilibrium following short-run supernormal profits.

Figure 5.5 below depicts the long-run position following short-run losses. Panel (a) illustrates the market demand and supply conditions whereas the firm's position is depicted in panel (b).

We assume that all firms maximise profits. However, we have seen that in the short run, a firm may operate at a loss, or shut down and pay its fixed costs. From our discussion in the last chapter, we know that in the short run, some inputs to the production process are fixed. In the long run, all inputs are variable. Therefore, a firm can exit a market in the long run, and channel its assets into another market where it can earn at least a normal profit. If losses are incurred by firms in a perfectly competitive market in the long run, we confidently predict, based on this model, that those firms will exit the market.

As the number of suppliers in the market falls, the supply curve shifts to the left. This is reflected in panel (a). As a result of this shift, price is driven up. The price continues to rise until market equilibrium is restored.

Panel (b) depicts the position for the individual firm. At P_0 losses result (the difference between AR and LAC). In a perfectly competitive market all individual firms are price takers. Hence, as price rises due to the change in market conditions, the price which the individual firm can charge also rises. The AR curve continues to shift upwards until it cuts the LAC curve at a tangency point, A. The firms which remain in the perfectly competitive market will earn a normal profit in the long run.

Figure 5.5: The long-run position following short-run losses

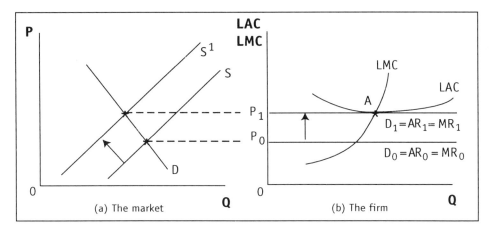

(a) The market   (b) The firm

Figure 5.6 below depicts the long-run position following short-run supernormal profits. Panel (a) illustrates the market demand and supply whereas the firm's equilibrium position is depicted in panel (b).

In the short run, firms in the perfectly competitive market can earn supernormal profits. However, because of the assumption of perfect information, other firms are aware of the supernormal profits in the market. Also, we assume that firms are free to enter the market. An increase in the number of firms shifts the market supply curve to the right from S to S^1, as shown in panel (a). Price falls until a new equilibrium is reached.

Figure 5.6: The long-run position following short-run profits

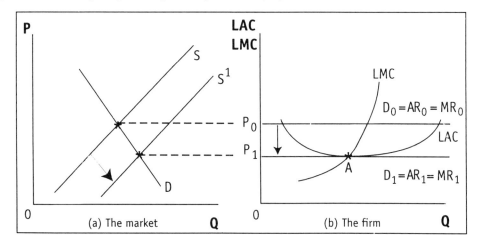

(a) The market   (b) The firm

Panel (b) depicts the position for the individual firm. Supernormal profits are made at P_0. As market price falls, the price which the individual firm can charge also falls. In this case, prices will continue to fall until all supernormal profits are 'competed' away. The AR curve continues to shift downwards until it cuts the LAC curve at a tangency point, A. The result is normal profit. The inflow of new firms stops as supernormal profits diminish.

Panel (b) in Figure 5.5 and Figure 5.6 illustrates the long-run equilibrium position for a perfectly competitive firm. At point A, the firm is producing at the minimum point of the long-run average cost curve. The firm is said to be making optimum use of its resources since it is producing at the least possible cost per unit. Also, at equilibrium, the firm is only making a normal profit.

This is very desirable from the point of view of the consumer and society as a whole. The firm is producing in its most efficient manner while at the same time the consumer is being charged no more than the marginal cost of production. This is an example of efficiency, a concept which requires further explanation.

Efficiency
....

When markets are perfectly competitive, the amount of a good produced will always be the socially optimal amount. In other words, perfectly competitive markets give us an efficient level of output. By efficient, we mean that no other level of activity could make some individuals better without adversely affecting the welfare of others.

In Figure 5.7, the market equilibrium level of output is Q^* and the market clearing price is P^*. If output was less than Q^* (for example Q^{**}), then there exists a potential supplier who is willing to supply more of the good at price P^*. Likewise, there exists a potential consumer who is willing to consume more of the good at price P^*. This is because at output level Q^{**}, a supplier is willing to supply the good at the price P_s but there are consumers who are willing to pay P_d. If more of the good were produced and sold at any price between the supply price and the demand price, then both the individuals producing the extra output and the individuals consuming the extra output are made better off. So output level Q^{**} is not an efficient level of output, since by increasing the level of output, at least two individuals are made better off.

Figure 5.7: Perfectly competitive markets and efficiency

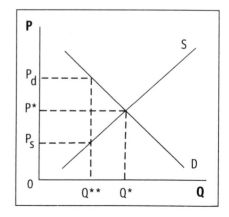

By contrast, at an output level greater than Q^*, the amount that someone is willing to pay for the extra output is always less than the amount required to get the good supplied. So there is no way to make a potential supplier and a potential consumer both better off by producing a level of output that exceeds Q^*. We therefore conclude that Q^* is the socially efficient level of output, since all the gains from trade have been exploited at that level of output.

CASE STUDY

Extract from The Sunday Business Post
Times are tough for small business
Special report ISME

The common misconception that all Irish companies are making fat profits was thrashed by a recent ISME survey on the profitability of Irish SMEs*. It shows that about half of those companies surveyed reported losses or returns on capital employed of under 10% per annum. 'This means that all these businesses would have been better off, and much better in many cases, investing their capital in government stock,' said Frank Mulcahy, director of ISME.

The survey of data extracted from thousands of accounts filed with the Companies Registration Office also showed that the majority of profitable businesses achieved pretax profits of under 5%. 'Contrary to public perceptions, the majority of Irish firms have paper-thin margins or they incur losses. This is particularly true in the case of smaller companies which lack any economies of scale.'

. . .

Almost half the firms analysed reported year-on-year declines in pre-tax profits or increases of under 10% – while one third experienced year-on-year reductions in shareholder funds. This proportion rose to 42% for the very small firms.

'The findings of this study are profound in their implications, particularly for small firms in which policy makers are placing so much of their faith for the resolution of our unemployment problems. As prac-

titioners, ISME members have always known that the profitability of their business determines their capacity to create future employment. They only recruit staff to handle increased sales when there is a profit or reward in prospect. Our report clearly illustrates why indigenous industry is not creating more jobs: because a significant portion of it is unprofitable and as PAYE taxpayers they are disproportionately penalised by the fiscal code.'

Mulcahy says that the report begs some basic questions about national policies for the future development of SMEs. To help achieve more profits Irish firms must be helped with their sales, to increase profitability and more capital must be made available.

. . .

On profitability, ISME wants the cost competitiveness of firms increased. This requires sustained increases in productivity and reductions in the cost of labour, bought-in-services and materials, whether they are imported or bought locally.

'More capital must be made available to firms in the form of long- and short-term loans and equity to help finance investment and working capital. This requires greater recognition by financial institutions of their partnership role in developing SMEs and a dramatic levelling of the investment playing-pitch to take account of risk-reward.'

Source: The Sunday Business Post, *12 November 1995.*

* Small and medium-sized enterprises

Questions
....

1. What is a 'normal profit'? Are the firms mentioned by Frank Mulcahy making a normal profit?
2. Assume that the firms discussed in the article are competing in perfectly competitive markets. Draw a diagram to show the profit position of a representative firm discussed in question 1.
3. To increase profitability, ISME recommends (a) increases in productivity, (b) labour cost reduction through taxation reform, (c) reduction in the price of inputs. How would these changes affect the diagram above? Why do they prefer these actions to the closure of firms?

Answers
....

1. Normal profit is the minimum amount of profit which is required in order to encourage businesses to remain in a market. Mr Mulcahy states that the profit for many small and medium enterprises was less than 10% per annum while many others were making losses. Had the owners invested the money in 'government stock', they would have been better off. We can conclude from this that these owners are not making a normal profit. The return on investment for an individual who is facing the risk of the business environment should be greater than on a relatively safe investment.
2. Since the firm is in a perfectly competitive market, the demand curve is perfectly elastic. Since the firm is not making normal profits, the demand curve must be below the average total cost curve. Since the firm is operating at a loss, the variable costs are covered. Figure 5.8 illustrates these observations.
   This firm is producing at a loss.

Figure 5.8: A perfectly competitive firm

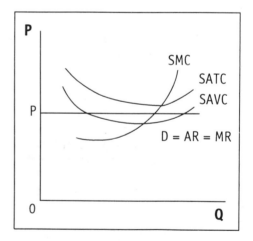

3. These measures are aimed at cutting variable costs. The SMC, SAVC and the SATC curves would shift downward which would mean that the firms could produce at a lower cost per unit and make a normal profit.

If firms continue to make less than a normal profit, we predict that the firms will close. In our theoretical model, we predict that labour released from unprofitable markets will move into profitable markets. The reality which we face is somewhat different. With a persistent unemployment problem, a person who loses her job is concerned that she will not find another. Therefore, ISME argues for policy changes to help existing firms to remain in business and to become profitable rather than allowing them to exit the market.

We will now examine alternative market structures. Having examined one end of the market structure, we will now move to the opposite end and discuss monopolies.

5.2 Monopoly

Monopoly is another form of market structure which is also identified by a number of characteristics:

1. There is only one firm in the market. In effect, the firm is the market.[5]
2. There are barriers to entry which preclude the possibility of new firms entering the market, even if the monopolist is making supernormal profits.
3. A unique product is sold. There are no close substitutes.

Barriers to entry are the main sources of monopoly power. They include government franchises and licences, patents and copyright laws, the high cost of entering a market, economies of scale and the exclusive control of scarce raw materials. Monopolies can emerge from one or a combination of these sources.

There are many examples of monopolies. In Ireland, for example, electricity, gas supply and rail transport are all monopolies. Monopolies can be state owned or privately owned. Up until the early 1990s Ireland, unlike other countries including the UK, had escaped the rush to privatise certain companies (see Section 13.4). Thus, most of Ireland's monopolies are state owned. This is likely to change in the future given the pressures of commercialisation and foreign competition.

Single-price monopolist
....

Since the monopolist is the only firm in the market, its demand curve is the downward sloping market demand curve. If the demand curve is downward sloping, marginal revenue is less than price. This point is best illustrated with an example. In this example, we are considering the behaviour of a 'single-price' monopolist. This monopolist does not practise price discrimination. All of the monopolist's customers are charged the same price. Table 5.2 is the demand schedule for the monopolist.

Table 5.2: Price, marginal revenue and average revenue

Q	P	TR	MR	AR
0	10	–		
			9	
1	9	9		9
			7	
2	8	16		8
			5	
3	7	21		7
			3	
4	6	24		6

In order to sell more of its product, the monopolist must lower price. In this example, to increase sales from two units to three units, the monopolist cuts its price from £8 to £7. Let us consider what happens to the marginal revenue. At P = £8, the monopolist sells two units, collecting total revenues of £16. The total revenue increases to £21 when the monopolist charges £7 per unit. However, the marginal revenue falls to £5 per unit. Why? Because to sell the extra unit, the single-price monopolist must cut the price for all units. The monopolist has gained revenue by selling more units, but has lost revenue because the price per unit is lower. For this reason, marginal revenue is always less than price, if the demand curve is downward sloping. Notice, however, that the average revenue equals price, for reasons which were explained in the previous section.

On a two-dimensional graph, the marginal revenue curve is drawn below the demand curve. Since price equals average revenue, the demand curve and the average revenue curve overlap. The revenue curves are illustrated in Figure 5.9.

Figure 5.9: The demand curve and the marginal revenue curve

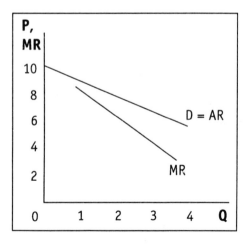

We will now examine the equilibrium for the monopolist.

Short-run equilibrium
....
Figure 5.10 below illustrates the equilibrium position for the monopolist.

Figure 5.10: Monopoly equilibrium

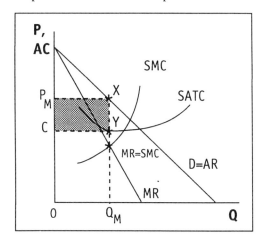

The demand curve, D is downward sloping with the marginal revenue curve drawn below it. The cost structure of the firm is given by the average total cost curve, SATC and the marginal cost curve, SMC. The two profit-maximising conditions are the marginal condition and the average condition. These two conditions must be met in order for the monopolist to produce in the short run.

The marginal condition is met at output level Q_M. At this level of production, marginal revenue is equal to marginal cost. The second condition requires that the average revenue is no less than the average variable cost at this output level.

In Figure 5.10 the difference between price and SATC is profit and is given by the vertical distance |XY|. The total profit made by the monopolist is the profit per unit multiplied by the total quantity sold. In Figure 5.10 it is given by the area [P_MXYC], the difference between the total revenue area [P_MXQ_M0] and the total cost area [CYQ_M0]. This shaded area represents supernormal profits.

The distinction between the long run and the short run is less important for the monopolist who is making supernormal profits. Unlike the perfectly competitive firm, competition will not drive down price and profit. Supernormal profits, as shown in Figure 5.10 can persist in the long run.

However, there is no guarantee that a monopolist will make supernormal profits. Profits depend on cost conditions and demand conditions, regardless of market structure. Panel (a) of Figure 5.11 shows a monopolist who is making normal profits. In panel (b), the monopolist is operating at a loss.

Figure 5.11: Monopolist earning a normal profit; sustaining a loss

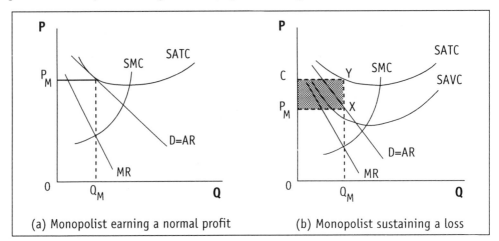

(a) Monopolist earning a normal profit   (b) Monopolist sustaining a loss

In panel (a) the marginal condition is fulfilled when Q_M units of output are produced. However, at this level of output, the average revenue curve is tangent to the average total cost curve. Therefore, the monopolist is making a normal profit.

The monopolist in panel (b) is sustaining a loss (maybe due to weak demand or high costs). The level of output is Q_M, determined by the intersection of the marginal revenue curve and the marginal cost curve. In this situation, the monopolist will produce at a loss because the price is greater than the average variable cost. In other words, the monopolist minimises her losses by producing, rather than closing down and paying her fixed costs. The loss per unit is shown by the segment |YX|. The total loss is shown by the shaded rectangle [$CYXP_M$].

If a monopolist is operating at a loss in the short run, we expect the owner to close if she is not covering her variable costs. In the long run, we expect a monopolist who cannot make a normal profit to exit. This 'loss minimising' strategy is the same as we observed for a firm in a perfectly competitive market.

It is evident from Figure 5.10 and Figure 5.11 that the monopolist does not produce at the lowest point of its average cost curve. In addition, price generally exceeds marginal cost. This is due to the existence of monopoly power which is reflected in the downward sloping demand curve. With price exceeding marginal cost, the consumer pays more for the good than the marginal cost to produce it.

Price discriminating monopolist

In the discussion above, the monopolist charged the same price to all consumers. Under some circumstances, a monopolist may charge different prices for the same product.

Definition

A price discriminating monopoly occurs when a monopolist charges different prices to different customers for the same product for reasons other than differences in costs.

There are two conditions necessary for price discrimination:

1. Submarkets featuring demand curves with different price elasticities must be identified. In other words, the producer must be able to classify consumers into separate groups.
2. The markets must be separated so that the products cannot be resold.

The separation may be physical. Generally, price discrimination occurs with commodities like electricity, or services like medical treatment which cannot be resold.

The monopolist is attempting to charge as close as possible to the maximum price which the consumer is willing to pay. A monopolist who can practise price discrimination can increase profits, beyond what is earned by a single-price monopolist.

There are different methods of price discrimination. The most common forms are called third degree and first degree price discrimination.

● **Definition**
● ● ● ● ● ●

Third degree price discrimination occurs when a market is divided into a number of submarkets.

Consumers in each sub-market are charged the same price.

Airlines that charge different fares for business customers and tourists are practising third degree price discrimination.

The supplier who practises first degree price discrimination must have detailed knowledge of the preferences of the consumer.

● **Definition**
● ● ● ● ● ●

First degree price discrimination occurs when every buyer is charged the maximum price that he or she is willing to pay.

Customised financial or legal services are examples where the seller of the service may be able to charge the maximum price. The consumer must believe that the good or service offered by the monopolist is unique in order to purchase under these circumstances. Either form of price discrimination results in higher profits because the monopolist is capturing all or part of the consumer surplus. (See Section 3.4 to revise consumer surplus.)

We will consider an example involving first degree price discrimination. Table 5.3 is a demand schedule for the price discriminating monopolist.

Table 5.3: Demand schedule for the price discriminating monopolist

Q	P	TR	MR
0	10	–	
			9
1	9	9	
			8
2	8	17	
			7
3	7	24	
			6
4	6	30	

This table is similar to the table which we used for the single-price monopolist with one important difference. To sell the second unit, the producer does not have to cut the price on the first unit. The monopolist sells the first unit for £9, the second unit for £8.

This leads to the collection of higher total revenue with the marginal revenue per unit sold higher for the price discriminating monopolist than it was for the single-price monopolist. In this case, the marginal revenue is equal to price. (Look back to Table 5.2 to see that the marginal revenue is lower than price for the single price monopolist.) Therefore, the demand curve and the marginal revenue curve overlap for the price discriminating monopolist. The marginal revenue curve was below the demand curve for the single-price monopolist.

Now, we will consider the difference in the quantity produced between the two types of monopolists. Consider Figure 5.12.

Figure 5.12: Profit-maximising levels of output for the single-price monopolist and the price discriminating monopolist

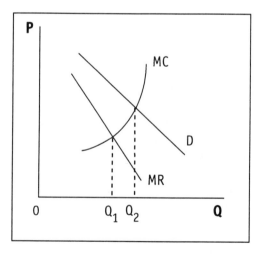

If the monopolist is charging a single price, its marginal revenue curve is below the demand curve. Profit maximisation requires that it produce where marginal revenue equals marginal cost. This is indicated by the level of output Q_1.

For the monopolist practising first degree price discrimination, the demand curve and the marginal revenue curve overlap. The profit-maximising level of output is Q_2. You can see from the diagram that the level of output increases if the monopolist practises price discrimination.

The absence of a supply curve
....

One important characteristic of a monopoly is the absence of a supply curve. For a perfectly competitive firm, the marginal cost curve is effectively its supply curve. For a monopoly, supply is affected by cost considerations and also by demand conditions. Hence, it is impossible to draw a supply curve which is determined independently of demand. This is illustrated in Figure 5.13.

Figure 5.13: The absence of a supply curve

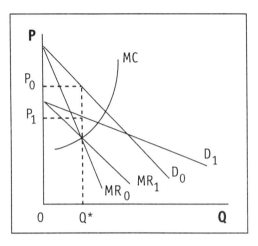

Figure 5.13 is similar to Figure 5.10 above. The demand curve, D_0 is drawn downward sloping with the marginal revenue curve, MR_0 drawn inside it. The marginal cost curve, MC, is upward sloping.

Let us now superimpose another set of demand and marginal revenue curves onto the diagram. The marginal cost curve cuts both sets of marginal revenue curves at the same point. At output level Q^*, price can either be P_0 or P_1 depending on the conditions of demand. Q^* is sold at P_0 when the demand curve is D_0, and at P_1 when the demand curve is D_1. Hence, for a given level of output different demand conditions give rise to different prices. There is no unique relationship between price and quantity supplied. In conclusion, there is no identifiable supply curve for the monopolist.

Students tend to think that a monopolist can charge any price and produce any quantity of output that she wants. In other words, she has an unlimited ability to extract supernormal profits. From the discussion above, we can see that this is not true. Like the perfectly competitive firm, the monopolist will maximise profit by producing where MR = MC. The maximum price which she can charge is limited by the demand curve which the monopolist faces for her product.

Comparing the perfectly competitive market with the monopoly
....

It is a useful exercise to compare the equilibrium position of the perfectly competitive market with that of the monopolist. To do this, we join all the firms in the perfectly competitive market together to form one single firm. Further, we assume that the demand and cost conditions remain the same although the market structure changes. We then compare the price and output decision of the perfectly competitive market with that of the monopoly. This is illustrated in Figure 5.14 below.

Figure 5.14: Perfect competition and monopoly compared

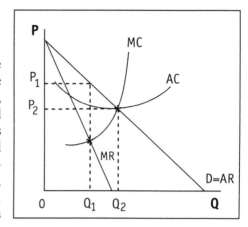

For the perfectly competitive market, the equilibrium in the long run is given by the equation MR = MC = AC = AR. In this case, the output level is Q_2 and the price charged is P_2. The single-price monopolist produces where MR = MC. The output level is Q_1 and the price is P_1. Since barriers to entry preclude the entry of new firms to the market, this equilibrium can persist into the long run. The single-price monopolist is producing less output and charging a higher price than the perfectly competitive market.

The monopolist practising first degree price discrimination will produce at Q_2, the same level of output as the perfectly competitive market. A unique price level is not shown because price changes with every unit of output. However, we do know that the price discriminating monopolist is charging the consumer more for every unit of output except for the last one.

With regard to efficiency, when the market structure is characterised by monopoly, the level of output produced in this market is not efficient. The level of output will be below its socially optimal level and the price charged for that output will be above the socially optimal level.

Figure 5.15 shows market equilibrium for a single-price monopolist. At market equilibrium, the additional cost of producing the last unit of output (MC_1) is less than what consumers are willing to pay (P_1). Since the price that consumers are willing to pay must reflect the utility to them of the good, then increasing output beyond Q_1 adds more to consumer utility than it adds to producers' cost. The monopolist does not want to increase output beyond Q_1 simply because he is a monopolist and he knows that if he does so, the price that he will get for all existing units sold will fall as a result.

So the potential gain to the monopolist from increasing output beyond Q_1 is wiped out by the loss in earnings on the existing level of output Q_1, as a result of the fall in market price.[6] This is still socially inefficient as the value of the gain to consumers exceeds the cost of producing the extra output. In fact, if it were possible for consumers to share some of their gains (from higher output and lower prices) with producers, both could be made potentially better off.

If the market structure were perfectly competitive, then output would be at its socially efficient level Q_2. The shaded area ABC represents the net gain to society from increasing output to the level that would occur in a perfectly competitive market.

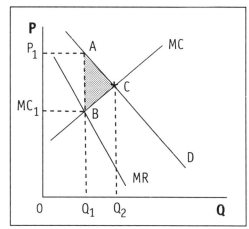

Figure 5.15: Monopoly equilibrium and efficiency

5.3 Monopolistic competition

The model of monopolistic competition was independently developed in the 1930s by the American economist Edward Chamberlin (1899–1967) and the English economist, Joan Robinson. Some credit must also go to Piero Sraffa (1898–1983) who was unhappy with the existing market set-up in the 1920s and who subsequently began the search for alternative market structures.[7]

Monopolistic competition incorporates features of both perfect competition and monopoly. It is similar to perfect competition in that there are a large number of firms in the market. There is also freedom to enter and exit. However, it differs from perfect competition in that the product is differentiated rather than homogeneous. Product differentiation means that in the short run, firms have a degree of market power resulting in supernormal profits.

Definition
● ● ● ● ● ●

Product differentiation means that the good produced by one firm is different from the good produced by the firm's competitor.

There are close, but not perfect substitutes available.

Differentiation is achieved through various strategies which include product design, customer service, packaging and advertising. Examples of monopolistically competitive markets include book publishers, filling stations, retail outlets and restaurants.

Product differentiation has implications for the demand curve which the firm faces. Recall that the demand curve for the firm in the perfectly competitive market is perfectly elastic because there are perfect substitutes. The demand curve for the monopolist is inelastic because there are no substitutes. A firm in a market classified as monopolistically competitive faces competitors who are producing similar, but not identical products. Therefore, the demand curve faced by this firm is downward sloping, but more elastic than the demand curve of the monopolist.

The short-run equilibrium position for the monopolistically competitive firm is illustrated in Figure 5.16 below.

Figure 5.16: A monopolistic competitor's short-run equilibrium

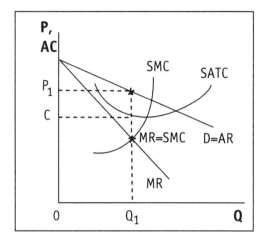

The firm's demand curve is downward sloping with the marginal revenue curve drawn below it. The average cost curve and the marginal cost curve are superimposed onto Figure 5.16. The profit-maximising firm in a monopolistically competitive market must meet the same conditions as firms in other markets.

The firm will produce at output level Q_1, where marginal revenue is equal to marginal cost, (MR = SMC). It will charge a price based on its demand or average revenue curve. In this case, the price is P_1. At this price, average revenue exceeds average cost. The difference, given by the distance between P_1 and C, is profit per unit. This profit per unit multiplied by the quantity sold gives us the total profit earned by the firm.

In the short run, the firm in the monopolistically competitive market can earn supernormal profits. However, it cannot maintain this equilibrium position or continue to earn supernormal profits in the long run.

The long-run equilibrium position is illustrated in Figure 5.17.

Figure 5.17: A monopolistic competitor's long-run equilibrium

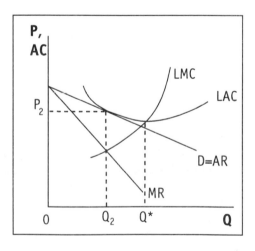

In the long run, because of the absence of entry barriers, new entrants will enter the market. The overall market supply rises, causing the market price to fall. The demand for the existing firm's product subsequently falls as it's share of the market demand declines. The existing firm's demand curve also becomes more elastic because new firms produce similar products.

Supernormal profits are 'competed away' with the influx of new firms. Equilibrium in the long run is achieved when participating firms are making normal profits only. There is no further incentive for potential firms to enter the market. In graphic terms, this occurs when the firm's average revenue curve is tangent to its average cost curve. Long-run equilibrium is achieved at point A in Figure 5.17. Hence, the monopolistic competitor is not producing at the point of full productive capacity. The difference between Q_2 and Q^* represents excess capacity.

The long-run equilibrium condition for a monopolistic competitor is $MR = MC$ and $AR = AC$. It is evident from Figure 5.17 that the firm under conditions of monopolistic competition does not produce at the lowest point on its average cost curve. In this regard, monopolistically competitive markets compare unfavourably to perfectly competitive markets. Furthermore, on account of product differentiation and the subsequent monopoly power that exists, price exceeds marginal cost. This market structure does not exhibit efficiency.

Part of the explanation for such inefficiencies lies in the fact that advertising, branding and other forms of product differentiation constitute additional costs to the firm. The positive aspect of monopolistic competition is the wider product choice it offers to the consumer. Benefits such as improved quality and service may also result from non-price competition. Unfortunately we gain variety at the expense of efficiency.

5.4 Oligopoly

Another commonly observed market structure is oligopoly.[8] It is another form of imperfect competition. An oligopolistic market consists of a small number of firms, each with some ability to affect the market price. The most important feature of this market structure is the recognition of interdependence between firms.

Firms in other market structures acted independently of each other when choosing market strategies. In oligopoly, the reaction of competitors to a change in price or some other market strategy is critical. Firms are said to be mutually dependent. If oligopolistic firms decide to compete with each other, they effectively act under conditions similar to perfect competition. In contrast, if they decide to collude, they act in the market as a monopolist. In either case, the level of price for this market structure is generally higher than the perfectly competitive market, and the level of output is lower.

Products are either homogeneous or differentiated. In some oligopolistic markets, products are identical. Examples include the oil market and basic commodity markets e.g. tin, copper, steel etc. In others, products are differentiated. The automobile, newspaper and the beer markets are examples.

The most common method of measuring the degree of market power is the use of concentration ratios, which are defined as the percentage of total output that is accounted for by the largest producers in the market. The most common concentration ratios are the four-firm and the eight-firm concentration ratios. The four-firm ratio, for example tells us the percentage of market output which is produced by the four largest firms. The larger the percentage, the more concentrated the market.

Table 5.4: Concentration ratios for two markets in Ireland

Motor fuel market CR4 in 1994 was 74%
Source: Statoil and Conoco
(In the 1996 *Report of Investigation* by The Competition Authority)

Tea market CR4 in 1995 was 83.7%
Source: Taylor Nelson AGB plc, supplied by Unilever
(In the 1996 *Report of Investigation* by The Competition Authority)

Note: CR4 = four-firm concentration ratio

Unlike the other market structures, there is no single theory of oligopolistic behaviour. This is because oligopolies exhibit a wide variety of behaviour. The most important models, however, are briefly explained below. They differ because of the assumptions made about a firm's behaviour and its reaction to its rivals' strategies.

The collusion model

One option available to firms in oligopoly is that of collusion. This occurs when firms get together and collude over price and output strategies. In such cases, the equilibrium position regarding price and output is similar to the monopoly. The equilibrium position is illustrated in Figure 5.18 below.

Figure 5.18: Collusive oligopoly

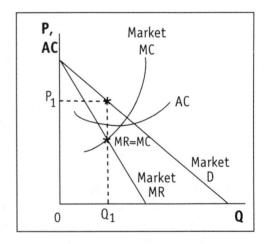

The market demand curve is drawn downward sloping with the market marginal revenue curve drawn below it. Profits are maximised at the output level where MR = MC. The total market output Q_1 is shared out in a number of different ways. For example, a quota system may be in place where each respective firm is allotted a sales quota. The results of collusion are higher prices, higher profits and lower output than would otherwise be the case. The name given to these formal groupings is a cartel.

Definition
● ● ● ● ● ●

A cartel is a group of firms in a particular market who collude on price and output decisions in an effort to earn monopoly profits.

Although very popular in the nineteenth century, they are now outlawed in many countries in order to protect the consumer and society. Examples of cartels include the Organisation of Petroleum Exporting Countries (OPEC) and the International Air Transport Association (IATA). See Information Box 5.1 below for more on OPEC.

INFORMATION BOX 5.1

The Organisation of Petroleum Exporting Countries

The Organisation of Petroleum Exporting Countries, or OPEC as it is commonly known was set up in 1960. There were five original member states: Saudi Arabia, Iran, Iraq, Kuwait and Venezuela. It emerged out of the growing conflict at the time between the oil-exporting countries and the major oil companies. Its impact on world markets was not felt until 1973 when oil production was curtailed after the Arab-Israeli Yom Kippur war. The price of oil rose from $2.91 per barrel in 1973 to over $11 per barrel in 1974. On account of the close co-operation between member states, among other factors, prices were steady during the 1970s.

All this changed in 1978 with the second oil crisis, triggered by the revolution in Iran. The result was an increase in the price of oil from $20 per barrel in 1979 to over $30 in 1980. A decline in demand in the early 1980s persuaded OPEC members to curtail production. A production ceiling of 16 million barrels per day was agreed in 1984. However, increasing production from non-member states and falling consumption led to gradually falling prices.

The 1990s brought with it an upturn in the world economy and the Gulf War of 1990. The effect of both these events was an increase in the price of oil. This was not to last, however. Divisions between members within the cartel, the growing number of substitute fuels on the market and competition from non-OPEC members resulted in the decline of OPEC's influence. This is partly reflected in the price of oil today – $20 per barrel. In real terms this is not very different to the price level that existed before the first oil crisis of 1973. Back to the future!

In general, once a cartel is formed, there is an incentive to cheat. The benefits of cheating on a collusive agreement as compared to adherence to the agreement (when joint profits are maximised) come in the form of higher output levels and higher profits for the cheating firm at the expense of rivals. Furthermore, cartels face competition from non-members who are not bound by any formal agreement.

The price leadership model

The price leadership model demonstrates a tacit form of collusion compared to the explicit collusion of the cartel. It is based on the existence of a dominant supplier. One producer sets price and others follow. Although other firms in the market are technically free to choose whether or not to 'follow the leader', their freedom is limited by the ability of the dominant firm to retaliate. Examples of dominant firms include Kellogg's (breakfast cereals), Goodyear (tyres), IBM (computers) and Coca Cola (soft drinks).

Figure 5.19 illustrates the equilibrium position for the price leadership model with a dominant firm.

Figure 5.19: The price leadership model with a dominant firm

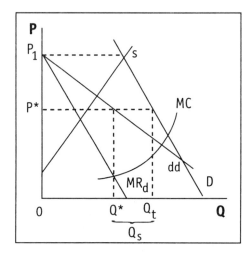

Market demand is represented by the demand curve, D. The quantity supplied by the smaller firms is given by the supply curve, s. The dominant firm's demand curve is the difference between these two curves. In graphic terms, we subtract the quantity supplied by the smaller firms at each price from the total quantity demanded in the market. The difference at each price is the dominant firm's demand curve and is labelled dd. Take, for example, the price P_1. At P_1 the smaller firms' supply curve intersects the market demand curve. This means that at this price the total market demand is met entirely by the smaller firms. As a result, the quantity demanded of the dominant firm is zero. Hence, at P_1 the dominant firm's demand curve intersects the price axis.

Knowing the demand curve for the dominant firm, we can now derive its marginal revenue curve. If a firm's demand curve is drawn downward sloping, its marginal revenue curve is drawn below it. The dominant firm's marginal revenue curve is labelled MR_d.

The profit-maximisation output level for the dominant firm is attained by producing where its marginal revenue is equal to its marginal cost. The output level is Q^* and the price charged is P^*. The total quantity demanded in the market at P^* is given by the output level Q_t. This comprises Q^* which is the amount supplied by the dominant firm, and Q_s, the amount supplied by the other smaller firms.

The dominance of the price leader depends on its costs, its financial assets and its excess capacity. If its marginal costs are substantially lower than its competitors, it can temporarily charge a price which is lower than the average variable costs of its competitors forcing them to temporarily shut down. Although the collusion is 'tacit', under certain circumstances, the dominant firm can be quite persuasive.

The kinked demand curve model
••••••••••••••••••••••••••••••••••

This model was developed by Paul Sweezy in the US and R. Hall and C. Hitch in the UK in the 1930s.[9] The model is used to explain why the price in an oligopolistic market, once established, tends to remain the same, even though demand and cost conditions change. It assumes asymmetrical reactions by competitors in a market to a change in price by one firm. For example, if one firm increases price, the others will not respond. The action of increasing price results in a sharp decrease in demand for the initiating firm. In contrast, if the firm cuts price, the others will follow. Only a small increase in the quantity demanded for its product will result for the firm who initiated the price cut. The kinked demand curve outlined in Figure 5.20 below results from the asymmetrical responses of market competitors.

Figure 5.20: The kinked demand curve

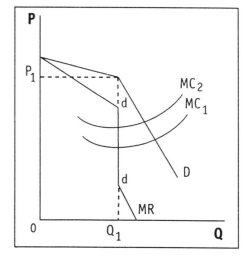

The oligopolistic firm's kinked demand curve is drawn in Figure 5.20. Suppose that the market price for the product supplied by the market is P_1. If one firm increases price above P_1, the other firms will not follow. As a result, the firm loses its market share. Consumers purchase the product at a lower price from the firm's competitors. The demand curve for the firm is elastic above the price of P_1.

Alternatively, suppose that the firm cuts price so that it is below P_1. Its competitors react by cutting their prices. The price change does not significantly increase demand for the firm's product. The demand curve for the firm is inelastic below the price of P_1.

Above P_1 the demand curve is relatively flat. Below P_1 the demand curve is relatively steep. At P_1, the demand curve is said to be 'kinked'. A kinked demand curve will result in a discontinuous marginal revenue curve. At Q_1, there is said to be a 'jump' in the marginal revenue curve.

This model of oligopoly is used to explain price rigidity and the absence of price wars in oligopolies even when there is no explicit collusion. In particular, the discontinuous part of the MR curve (the segment dd) provides a possible explanation for price rigidity. Along this segment, marginal cost could increase significantly without affecting the profit-maximising output or price level. In effect, the oligopolist absorbs the increase in costs and, by doing so, maintains the existing price level. This partly explains the price stickiness or inflexibility which is sometimes associated with oligopolies.

This model is based on the assumption made about the reactions of firms to changes in price by a competing firm. Although it is the most famous of all oligopolistic models, it omits a whole range of other possible reactions and consequently results in a rather restrictive model. It fails to explain how the initial price is reached. In explaining the reason behind price rigidity, it fails to account for other possible explanations such as the administrative expenses involved in changing prices. Finally, the model has not stood up well to empirical tests.

To address the criticisms directed at these models and their assumptions regarding firms' behaviour and pricing strategies, economists began to use a particular branch of mathematics called 'game theory' which focuses on the interdependent decision-making of firms in a market. It is applied to firms operating under conditions of oligopoly and in particular those firms which anticipate rivals' reactions. See Information Box 5.2 below for more on game theory.

INFORMATION BOX 5.2

Game theory

Game theory is a mathematical technique used to analyse strategic interaction. It was first developed in the 1940s by the mathematician and physicist John von Neumann and the economist Oskar Morgenstern to analyse the behaviour of firms in oligopolistic markets.[1]

A game consists of rules, players (decision-makers), strategies (actions) and pay-offs (scores). In any single game, the players are allowed to make certain moves, as defined by the rules of the game. The player tries to maximise his or her own payoff.

One of the most famous games in game theory is the prisoners' dilemma.

The prisoners' dilemma
Michael and Jean are charged for committing a lewd act in public. They are remanded in custody, each facing a possible sentence of up to one year in jail. On meeting the two prisoners, the sergeant immediately suspects them of involvement in another crime committed recently in the locality: the robbing of the local church funds.

He places the prisoners in separate rooms. Each prisoner is made aware of the sergeant's suspicion of their involvement in the more serious crime of robbery. They are told that if both confess to the crime, the jail sentence will be four years. Each is also told that if only one of them confesses to the crime, the confessor's sentence will be squashed while the accomplice will receive an eight-year jail sentence. If neither confesses, both prisoners will spend only one year in jail for the lesser offence.

This can be presented as a game with two players, each player having two strategies – to deny the charge or to confess to the crime. With two players and two strategies, there are four possible outcomes:

* *neither Michael nor Jean confess to the more serious crime;*
* *both Michael and Jean confess to the more serious crime;*
* *Michael confesses, Jean denies involvement;*
* *Jean confesses, Michael denies involvement.*

We use a payoff matrix to tabulate the possible alternative strategies of both players. Table 5.5 shows the payoff matrix for Michael and Jean.

Table 5.5: The prisoners' dilemma payoff matrix

		Michael's strategies	
		Confess	Deny
Jean's strategies	Confess	M. 4 years / J. 4 years	M. 8 years / J. Free
	Deny	M. Free / J. 8 years	M. 1 year / J. 1 year

Each square shows the payoffs for the two players (M for Michael and J for Jean) for each possible strategy. We begin with the top left-hand box. If both confess, they each get a four-year jail sentence. In contrast, if both deny the charge, they each get a one-year jail sentence. This strategy is recorded in the bottom right-hand box. The more interesting payoffs are to be found in the two remaining boxes. If Michael confesses and Jean denies, the court will free Michael but will hand down an eight-year jail sentence to Jean. This possibility is presented in the bottom left-hand box. The other possibility is for Jean to confess and for Michael to deny. This combination will involve freedom for Jean but the much longer sentence of eight years for Michael.

It is evident from the above analysis that the two players are faced with a dilemma. Neither player knows what the other's decision will be. Should Michael confess in the hope that Jean denies the charge? Likewise, should Jean confess hoping to minimise the amount of time she spends behind bars? The answers to these and other questions are to be found in the 'equilibrium' for the game. The equilibrium for this particular type of game is called the Nash equilibrium. This is the result of all participating players playing their best strategy given the actions of their competitors. It is named after John Nash, the American mathematician who introduced this concept in 1951.

In the case of the prisoners' dilemma, the equilibrium occurs when Michael makes his best choice given Jean's choice and, likewise, when Jean makes her best choice given Michael's choice. However, the Nash equilibrium for the prisoners' dilemma is a special case. No matter what Jean does, Michael's best choice is to confess. Likewise, no matter what Michael does, Jean's best choice is to confess. Hence, the equilibrium of the prisoners' dilemma is that both players confess. This equilibrium where there is a unique best action regardless of what the other player does is called the dominant strategy equilibrium.

From the prisoners' viewpoint, however, this is a bad outcome. If both denied the charges, they would receive only a one-year jail sentence. Unfortunately, they have no way of communicating to each other. Yet, they do know that despite the action of the other individual, their best choice is to confess. On confessing, a bad outcome is delivered.

Similar techniques can be applied to firms in oligopolistic markets. Such firms may decide to alter output levels or prices, depending on the actions of others. Assumptions are made about the behaviour of their rivals. All possible strategies can then be analysed in the same way as above.

The application of game theory to the study of a firm's behaviour in oligopolistic markets has been one of the most outstanding recent developments in the field of economics. In recognition of this, the 1994 Nobel Prize in Economics was awarded to three economists for their work in this field. The recipients were John Nash (of Nash equilibrium fame), John Harsanyi and Reinhard Selten who introduced time and uncertainty to game theory models.

1 J. von Neumann and O. Morgenstern, The Theory of Games and Economic Behaviour, *Princeton University Press, 1944.*

5.5 Market structure spectrum

We have now completed our analysis of the different market structures. One useful way of comparing one structure with another is by examining the market structure spectrum. The market structure spectrum is similar to any other spectrum such as the spectrum of light or colour. The different market structures are presented in a line from left to right. It is primarily the degree of competition which explains the differences between the market structures.

On one extreme of the spectrum we have 'perfect' competition. Monopoly is the other extreme where there is no competition. Most markets, in reality, lie somewhere in between these two extreme cases. It is monopolistic competition and oligopoly that lie between these two polar extremes, with the former being known as 'competition among the many' and the latter being referred to as 'competition among the few'. In these two cases there are varying degrees of competition between the respective firms.

Figure 5.21: The market structure spectrum

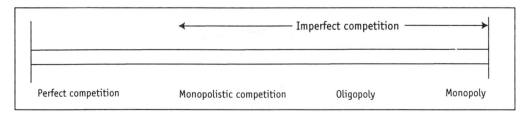

Figure 5.21 illustrates the market structure spectrum. The various market structures include perfect competition, monopolistic competition, oligopoly and monopoly. The last three structures are sometimes grouped together and referred to as 'imperfect competition' because in each of these structures, an individual firm has some ability

to control price. A summary of the different market structures and their characteristics are included in Table 5.6 below.

Table 5.6: The characteristic differences between market structures

	Perfect competition	Monopolistic competition	Oligopoly	Monopoly
No. of firms	Many	Many	Few	One
Type of product	Homogeneous	Differentiated	Identical or differentiated	Unique
Barriers to entry	None	None	Usually	Yes
Pricing strategy	Price taker	Price maker	Interdependent	Price maker
Long-run profits	Normal	Normal	Supernormal	Supernormal
Examples	Agricultural markets Capital markets	Service stations Restaurants	Oil/motor fuel Automobiles	Rail-transport Electricity

It is often difficult to classify firms into a specific market structure. Also, the framework which we have discussed is often criticised because the models are simple and static while the actual behaviour of firms is complex and dynamic. However, the more realistic and dynamic models developed by Joan Robinson, Herbert Simon, Michael Porter and others are reactions against these comparative static models. A thorough knowledge of these models is essential to understand and appreciate the models of the critics!

The next step in our analysis of microeconomics involves taking a closer look at the factors of production which are used in the production process. Chapter 6 examines, in detail, the four basic factors of production.

Summary

1. A firm's behaviour depends largely on the degree of competition and market power. We examined four market structures in detail: perfect competition, monopolistic competition, oligopoly and monopoly. They differ in relation to the number of firms in the market, the nature of the product sold, the entry to and exit from the market and, finally, the availability of information.
2. Perfect competition is a model which describes idealised economic conditions that are rarely met in practice. It consists of a large number of small firms with no single firm large enough to influence price. Each firm is a price taker. There is freedom of entry and exit on account of the absence of entry barriers. A standardised product is sold. Perfect knowledge exists with consumers and firms accurately informed

about prices, profits and quality. As a result, perfectly competitive firms cannot make supernormal profits in the long run.

3. A monopolist is the sole producer in the market. It is a price maker. There are barriers to entry. A unique product is sold with no close substitutes readily available. As a result, the monopolist can make supernormal profits. The monopolist charges a higher price, produces less output and earns supernormal profits compared to the perfectly competitive market. There is no well-defined supply curve for the monopolist. A monopolist can also practise price discrimination.

4. Monopolistic competition is similar to perfect competition, with one important exception: it assumes product differentiation. Goods are close rather than perfect substitutes for each other. This allows for some market power. The short-run equilibrium in monopolistic competition is similar to the monopoly equilibrium. A firm in this industry can earn supernormal profits in the short-run, but freedom of entry ensures that only normal profits are earned in the long-run. A firm in this industry does not produce at the lowest possible cost per unit. Its failure to exhibit efficiency is partly offset by the wider choice it offers to the consumer.

5. Oligopoly is another example of imperfect competition. In oligopoly, the actions of firms are interdependent. Each firm tries to anticipate the action and reactions of its competitors when formulating and implementing its own strategy. The models are broadly divided into two: those that assume collusion and those that assume competition. Collusion may be open or tacit.

6. The market structure spectrum highlights the differences between the market structures. The amount of competition varies from 'pure' in a perfectly competitive market to a complete absence of any competition in a monopoly. The other cases exhibit varying degrees of competition. Monopolistic competition, oligopoly and monopoly are sometimes called 'imperfect competition' to distinguish them from perfect competition. One characteristic common to all imperfectly competitive markets is the degree of market power, reflected in a downward sloping demand curve.

Key terms

Market power
Perfect competition
Monopolistic competition
Oligopoly
Monopoly
Price taker
Barriers to entry
Short-run supply curve
Shutdown price
Efficiency
Single-price monopolist
Price discriminating monopolist

Third degree price discrimination
First degree price discrimination
Product differentiation
Interdependency
Concentration ratios
Collusive oligopoly
Cartels
Dominant firm
Kinked demand curve
Game theory
Nash equilibrium
Imperfect competition

Review questions

1. Derive the short-run supply curve under conditions of perfect competition.
2. Explain why the perfectly competitive firm produces at the minimum point of the average cost curve in the long run. What does this suggest about perfect competition?
3. Outline the short-run equilibrium position for a monopoly. Why is it not possible to draw a well-defined supply curve for the monopolist?
4. (a) Outline the differences and the similarities between perfect competition and monopolistic competition.
   (b) Sketch the short-run and long-run equilibrium positions of the monopolistic competitor.
5. Using the kinked demand curve model, explain the rationale for price rigidity.
6. Explain the main differences between perfect and imperfect competition. Give examples of each.

Working problems

1. Examine Figure 5.22. Under conditions of perfect competition, complete Table 5.7.

Figure 5.22

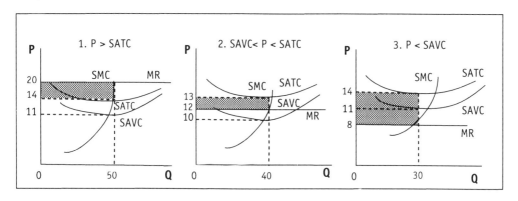

Table 5.7

TR = £	TR = £	TR = £ . . . .
TVC = £	TVC = £	TVC = £ . . . .
TFC = £	TFC = £	TFC = £ . . . .
TC = £	TC = £	TC = £ . . . .
Profit =	Profit =	Profit =
Production	Production	Production
Decision	Decision	Decision . . . .

2. Figure 5.23 shows two equilibrium positions in the long run. Which equilibrium is for a perfectly competitive firm and which is for a monopolistically competitive firm? Explain. What are the main differences between the two market structures at equilibrium? What are the similarities at equilibrium?

Figure 5.23: Long-run equilibrium

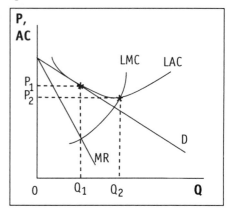

Multi-choice questions

1. Firms act independently of each other in the following market structures:
   - (a) perfect competition and imperfect competition;
   - (b) perfect competition, oligopoly and monopolistic competition;
   - (c) monopolistic competition and oligopoly;
   - (d) perfect competition and oligopoly;
   - (e) perfect competition and monopolistic competition.

2. Figure 5.24 illustrates a short-run equilibrium position for a perfectly competitive firm where price is less than average total cost.

Figure 5.24

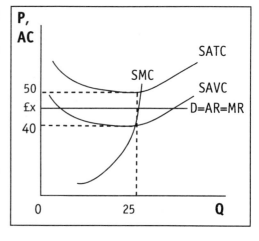

If the loss is equal to £75, the market price x must be equal to:
   - (a) 48;
   - (b) 46;
   - (c) 45;
   - (d) 47;
   - (e) none of the above.

3. The special identity for a perfectly competitive firm is:
   - (a) $MR = MC$;
   - (b) $AR = D$;
   - (c) $P = MC$;
   - (d) $ATC = AVC$;
   - (e) none of the above.

4. Assuming identical demand and cost conditions, a monopolist, compared to a perfectly competitive market, charges:
   (a) a higher price for a higher output;
   (b) a higher price for a lower output;
   (c) a lower price for a lower output;
   (d) a lower price for a higher output;
   (e) none of the above.

5. Figure 5.25 illustrates the equilibrium position for the profit-maximising single-price monopolist.

Figure 5.25

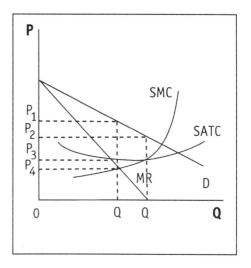

The single-price monopolist charges price equal to:
   (a) P_4;
   (b) P_3;
   (c) P_2;
   (d) P_1;
   (e) none of the above.

6. Which model in oligopoly is useful in explaining price rigidity?
   (a) price leadership model;
   (b) kinked demand curve model;
   (c) collusion model;
   (d) all of the above;
   (e) none of the above.

True or false

1. The market demand curve in perfect competition is downward sloping from left to right. _____
2. The supply curve for the perfectly competitive firm in the short run is its marginal cost curve above the shutdown price. _____
3. Price discrimination involves charging different prices for different goods to different consumers._____
4. The demand curve for the monopolistic competitor is more inelastic than the demand curve for the monopolist because of the absence of available substitutes. _____
5. At equilibrium in the long run, the firm under conditions of monopolistic competition produces at the output level where MR = MC = AR = AC. _____
6. Once a cartel is formed, there is no incentive to cheat. _____

Fill in the blanks

An important factor in determining a firm's _____ is the market structure to which it belongs. There are four main types of market structures: perfect competition, oligopoly, _____ competition and monopoly. The difference between all four categories hinges on the degree of market _____ and the extent of _____ facing the respective firm. _____ competition, although not very representative of the real world today, is a useful theoretical model. With the perfectly competitive firm facing a _____ demand curve for its product, its market power is zero. In the long run, perfectly competitive firms are _____ in the sense that they produce at the point of _____ average cost and they charge a price equal to the _____ cost of production. Any market structure which consists of firms that hold some degree of market power is defined as _____ _____. The extreme case is monopoly where the monopolist can earn _____ profits in the long run. In this case a _____ product is sold and the demand curve is downward sloping and _____. Most firms and industries do not subscribe to these extreme cases and are normally examples of either monopolistic competition or _____. Of vital importance to the monopolistic competitor is her ability to influence price because of product _____. This may take the form of branding, _____ or the use of promotional gimmicks. _____ between firms is a characteristic of an oligopoly. Oligopolists may or may not _____. This collusion may be formal or informal. If collusion takes place, there is an incentive to _____.

CASE STUDY

Extract from The Irish Times
Saudis concede to US on oil prices
by Eoin Belton

No amount of quasi-agreements hatched out in the corridors of Geneva's Intercontinental hotel can disguise the fact that the Organisation of Petroleum Exporting Countries has finally run aground.

Saudi Arabia is now determined to call the shots. And owing the Bush administration an immense debt of gratitude, it stands ready to settle up in the way it knows how – by keeping a lid on the price of crude.

. . .

Although set on fixing targets compatible with Washington's recently unveiled national energy strategy, the Saudis are fully capable of marshalling objective, face-saving arguments to support their case. At present these pivotally include higher world demand forecasts (and therefore higher production requirements) than those contemplated by the OPEC Secretariat. With the Gulf crisis far from over, Soviet oil production plummeting and the American economy about to turn around, what, the Saudis ask, is the point of cutting production targets to pre-war levels?

In addition to repaying their obligation to Washington, the Saudis demonstrate clearer foresight than their colleagues in

→

pressing for production levels at least commensurate with world demand.

While others want to cut output and raise prices in order to spur their economic development, Riyadh argues for price moderation in order to foster the western world's dependence on oil – making the point that petroleum demand shrank by over 5% in response to the price hikes of the past six months. Finally, the Saudis underline the perverse effect on OPEC of a higher barrel-age price that would simply retard the US recovery (every incremental $1 on a barrel sucks $2.5 billion out of US GNP) while slowing growth in Europe and Japan.

. . .

Source: The Irish Times, *13 March 1991.*

Questions

1. What type of market structure is inferred from the above article? Support your answer.
2. Which model within this market structure does the market for oil approximate to? Explain your answer.
3. If Saudi Arabia took control of the market for oil, what market structure would it then reflect? Is Saudi Arabia likely to achieve or maintain this market structure?

CHAPTER 6

FACTOR MARKETS

'*Wages* are determined by the bitter struggle between capitalist and worker.'[1]
Karl Marx (1818–83)

'Rent . . . is a symptom, but it is never a cause of wealth.'[2]
David Ricardo (1772–1823)

'Profit is the result of risks wisely selected.'[3]
Frederick B. Hawley (1843–1929)

Chapter objectives

Upon completing this chapter, the student should understand:

- derived demand;
- marginal productivity theory;
- wage determination;
- the capital market and the cost of capital;
- economic rent;
- the sources of profits.

Outline

6.1 **Labour and wages**
6.2 **Capital and interest**
6.3 **Land and rent**
6.4 **Entrepreneurship and profit**

Introduction

Until now, our analysis of markets focused on the final output of goods and services. We mentioned that land, labour, capital and entrepreneurship are combined in the production process. Further, rent, wages, interest and profit constitute the costs of the firm. However, when we mentioned the price of these factors, we assumed that they were held constant.

We will now look at each of the factor markets individually. We will attempt to explain how the rental rate, the wage rate, the interest rate and the profit rate are determined within their respective factor markets.

According to the traditional or neoclassical theory of distribution, factor prices can be explained in terms of demand and supply analysis. In the resource market, however, the roles of firms and households are reversed. The firms that supply the goods and services in the product markets are now the source of the demand for the factor inputs. The householders, who demand final goods and services are now the suppliers of the resources. In short, firms are the buyers of resources and households are the sellers of the same resources.[4] We will use marginal productivity theory to provide us with an understanding of the demand for the various factor inputs.

In this chapter we discuss each of the four factor markets. We begin with the labour market. Capital, land and enterprise and their respective factor prices are discussed in sections 6.2, 6.3 and 6.4 respectively. Although each market is explained separately, they are inter-related in practice; developments in one resource market can affect other resource markets.

6.1 Labour and wages

The labour market is comprised of a demand for and supply of labour. We begin by studying the demand for labour.

The demand for labour
....

A firm's demand for labour is a derived demand.[5]

Definition
● ● ● ● ● ●

> A derived demand is one which is not demanded for its own sake but for the use to which it can be put.

Labour is not wanted for itself but for what it can produce. A farmer requires labourers in order to produce foodstuffs; a car manufacturer requires workers to help on the production line; an insurance sales company requires staff to put together saleable products and to sell them to potential customers. The demand for this resource stems from what the employment of labour can produce.

In order to understand the demand for labour we need to return to production theory in general (Section 4.2) and to marginal productivity theory in particular. This was developed by several economists including E. von Bohm-Bawerk (1851–1914) and J. Bates Clark (1847–1938) in the late nineteenth century.[6] This theory postulates that wages, as well as other factor payments, depend largely on the productivity of the factor input. The existence of perfectly competitive markets is an underlying assumption of this theory.

Before we consider an example, recall a few of the terms which were defined in Chapter 4. We are considering the production function of a firm in the short run, which means that some inputs are fixed and some inputs are variable. Total product (TP) is the total output produced during a specified time period, using particular amounts of inputs. Marginal product (MP) is the additional units of output generated by the addition of a variable input. The declining productivity of labour reflects the law of diminishing marginal returns. The law states that in the short run, when capital is fixed, an additional worker will eventually produce less output than the previous worker.

We can also look at the contribution of an additional worker in monetary terms.

Definition
● ● ● ● ● ●

The marginal revenue product (MRP) of labour is the addition to revenue from the employment of an extra worker.

Equation 6.1 states this in algebraic form:

$$MRP = \frac{\Delta TR}{\Delta Q_L}$$ [6.1]

where: Δ = change; MRP = marginal revenue product; TR = total revenue;
Q_L = number of workers.

The MRP of labour measures the monetary value of the extra output generated from the employment of an additional worker. The MRP of labour can also be calculated by multiplying the marginal product by the price of the product.[7] In simple terms:

$$MRP = MP \times MR$$ [6.2]

where: MRP = marginal revenue product; MP = marginal product;
MR = marginal revenue.

We will now apply these concepts using an example in an effort to understand the hiring decision of the firm. Hibs (Ireland) Ltd is a manufacturing company. The relationship between the number of workers employed and the total output generated by the workforce is recorded in Table 6.1. Because Hibs is producing a good for a perfectly competitive market, MR = P.

Table 6.1: Production schedule for Hibs (Ireland) Ltd.

(1) Labour (wkrs)	(2) TP (units)	(3) MP (units)	(4) MR = P (£)	(5) MRP (£)	(6) Wage (£)	(7) Contribution (£)	(8) Wage (£)	(9) Contribution (£)
0	0							
		55	1	55	25	30	12	43
1	55							
		43	1	43	25	18	12	31
2	98							
		33	1	33	25	8	12	21
3	131							
		25	1	25	25	0	12	13
4	156							
		18	1	18	25	−7	12	6
5	174							
		12	1	12	25	−13	12	0
6	186							
		5	1	5	25	−20	12	−7
7	191							
		1	1	1	25	−24	12	−11
8	192							

How many workers will Hibs Ltd employ? Column 5 records the extra revenue that each additional worker contributes to the business. The cost to the firm of hiring each worker is recorded in column 6.[8] The difference (column 7) between the two is simply the net contribution that each additional worker makes to the firm. In other words, this is what the labourer produces, in excess of her or his wage.

For example, if the wage rate is £25 and the marginal revenue product of the first worker is £55, the net contribution of the first worker must be £30 (£55 – £25). The contribution from the second worker is £18 (£43 – £25) and so on. In this example the first four workers each make a positive net contribution, i.e. MRP ≥ W. The contributions from the employment of a fifth worker, a sixth worker, a seventh and so on are all negative (MRP < W). Hence, Hibs Ltd employs workers up to where MRP = W, i.e. marginal revenue product of labour equals the cost of employing her or him.[9] In this example, if the wage rate is £25, Hibs Ltd employs four workers.

If the wage rate falls from £25 to £12, will Hibs Ltd increase or decrease the size of its workforce? This scenario is shown in columns 8 and 9 of Table 6.1. For a wage rate of £12, the first six workers contribute positively to the firm. In this case, MRP = W when six workers are employed. Thus, if the wage rate falls, this model predicts that the profit-maximising firm will employ more workers. The opposite is true if the wage rate rises.

In general, the lower the wage rate the more workers will be employed.

Derivation of the demand curve for labour
....

Hibs Ltd employs workers up to the point where the MRP = W. In other words, the profit-maximising firm will employ an additional labourer if the amount that he produces is sufficient to pay his wage.

Figure 6.1 plots the relationship between the marginal revenue product of labour and the number of workers employed as described in columns 1 and 5 of Table 6.1.

Figure 6.1: Marginal revenue product curve for Hibs Ltd

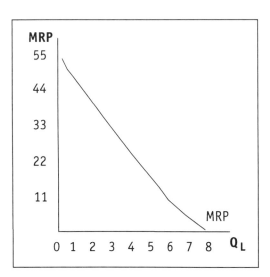

We can see from the figure that the MRP of the fourth worker is £25 while the MRP of the sixth worker falls to £12. However, we can interpret this diagram in another way. We can ask, 'If the wage is £25, how many employees will Hibs Ltd employ?' At a wage rate of £25, we would predict, using this model, that Hibs Ltd will hire four workers. All workers employed, including the fourth worker, are paid the same rate. If the wage rate falls to £12, the firm will hire six employees. At a lower wage rate, firms can hire additional workers.

For Hibs Ltd and for all other profit-maximising firms, workers will be employed up to the point where the marginal revenue product equals the wage paid to labour i.e. MRP=W. Therefore, the MRP curve is the firm's demand curve for labour.[10] Figure 6.2 depicts the same curve as Figure 6.1. However, we have substituted wage for the marginal revenue product on the vertical axis. The horizontal axis continues to represent the number of workers employed.

Figure 6.2: The demand curve for labour for Hibs Ltd

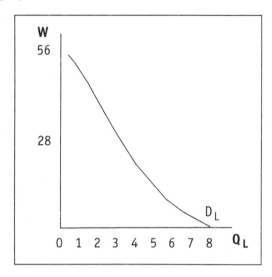

Figure 6.2 shows the amount of labour that Hibs Ltd will hire at each wage rate. It is downward sloping, depicting the negative relationship between the wage rate and the number of workers employed. It is drawn holding other variables constant, including the technological process and the training of the labour force. Also, because the demand for labour is 'derived', factors which affect the product market will also affect the labour demand curve. Any variable which changes the product's price will change the marginal revenue product. Any of these variables will cause the position and/or the slope of the demand curve to change.

In summary, we have used the marginal productivity theory to derive the marginal revenue product for labour. For profit-maximising firms, workers will be hired up to the point where W = MRP of labour. Hence, the marginal revenue product curve for labour is the demand curve for labour. It is derived from the productivity of labour, the wage paid to labour and the price of the final output.

Derivation of the market demand curve for labour
....

In order to obtain the market demand curve for labour we need to sum up all the individual firms' demand curves for labour. The market demand curve for labour shows the quantity of labour demanded at each wage rate by all firms in the market. In graphic terms this market demand curve can be derived by 'adding up' or aggregating the firms' individual demand curves. This exercise is illustrated in Figure 6.3.

Figure 6.3: Derivation of the market demand curve for labour

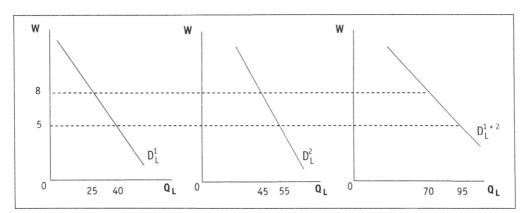

Two individual demand curves, D_L^1 and D_L^2, are drawn. The market demand curve, D_L^{1+2}, can be derived by summing up the separate levels of labour demanded at each wage rate. If, for example, the wage rate is £5, the total number of workers demanded would be 95 (40 + 55). At a wage level of £8, the total number demanded would be 70 (25 + 45). This exercise is repeated for each wage level. The result is a downward sloping market demand curve for labour.

We now turn our attention to the supply of labour.

The supply of labour
....

An individual's decision regarding the supply of labour is related to the wage rate. All other things being equal, an increase in the wage rate increases the incentive to work. As a result, the quantity of hours worked increases. Hence, the supply curve for labour for an individual is upward sloping. This is depicted in Figure 6.4.

Figure 6.4: The individual supply curve for labour

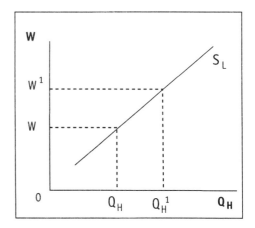

The individual supply curve for labour shows the number of hours offered for work at any given wage rate. At a wage rate of W, the quantity of hours worked is Q_H. At the higher wage rate of W^1, the number of hours worked increases to Q_H^1. As the wage rate increases, the number of hours worked increases.

An interesting aspect of an individual's labour supply is the possibility that the supply curve could be backward bending. This can be explained by examining the trade-off between work and leisure for an individual. According to this theory, individuals work to earn the money to purchase goods and services. At lower wage levels, any increase in the wage rate is likely to elicit an increase in the number of hours worked. At lower levels of wages, the labour supply curve is upward sloping.

However, the opportunity cost of labour is to forgo leisure activities. As wages continue to increase, individuals may resist a further increase in the number of hours worked, preferring leisure to labour. Hence, as wages increase, the number of hours worked declines. This is reflected in the backward-bending labour supply curve depicted in Figure 6.5.

Figure 6.5: A backward-bending labour supply curve

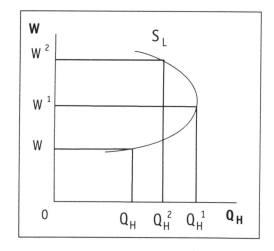

If the wage rate increases from W to W^1, the individual is prepared to increase the number of hours worked from Q_H to Q_H^1. Beyond this wage level, however, the individual is not prepared to work longer hours. If wage levels increase beyond W^1, the individual will sacrifice work in return for more leisure. For example, if wages increase from W^1 to W^2, the number of hours worked declines from Q_H^1 to Q_H^2.

The backward-bending supply curve can be explained using substitution and income effects. The substitution effect is caused by a change in the relative prices of work and leisure. At higher wages, more goods and services can be purchased. The opportunity cost of leisure time increases with the wage rate. The substitution effect suggests that labour will be substituted for leisure under these conditions.

The income of the worker increases with the wage rate. Leisure activities are considered to be 'normal' goods (or services). Therefore, the demand for these goods increases with income. More time allocated to leisure activities means that less time is available for work. The income effect suggests that more time will be allocated to leisure (and less to labour) as income increases.

Initially, the substitution effect outweighs the income effect and the first portion of the labour supply curve is upward sloping. However, beyond a certain wage, the income effect is stronger than the substitution effect. This part of the labour supply curve is backward bending.

In this instance, we cannot conclude that what is possibly true for an individual can be applied to the market. Empirical evidence suggests that the labour supply curve for the market is upward sloping, even over the wide range of incomes that we observe in modern, developed economies. As wages increase, the extra workers who enter the labour market more than offset the effects of the backward-bending individual supply curve.

Therefore, while admitting that the backward-bending supply curve of labour is a theoretical possibility which may one day be observed, we will assume that the market labour supply curve is upward sloping in line with the empirical evidence. This is drawn in Figure 6.6.

Figure 6.6: Market supply curve for labour

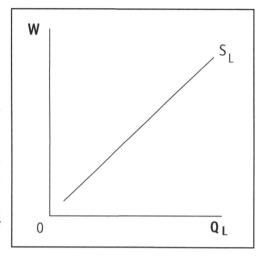

This positive relationship is depicted in an upward sloping market supply curve for labour. The supply curve for labour considers the relationship between wages and the number of people working, *ceteris paribus*. The variables which are held constant include the tax and social welfare system, educational policies, the degree of unionisation (see Information Box 6.1) and the size of the labour force. If any of these underlying variables change, the position and/or the slope of the labour supply curve will change.

INFORMATION BOX 6.1

The trade union movement in Ireland

The purpose of a trade union is to represent workers and to maximise their power in the workplace. They also play a wider role in the social and political arena. Trade union power is based largely on the solidarity between workers.

Although trade unions existed in Ireland in the eighteenth century, they were first legalised in 1871 when the first Trade Union Act was passed. Almost 25 years later, in April 1894 the Irish Trade Union Congress (ITUC) was founded.[1] 119 delegates from different labour organisations were present, representing 21,000 trade unionists directly and a further 39,000 indirectly through the trade councils. The first President of Congress was Thomas O'Connell. Other famous trade unionists included William O'Brien, James Larkin and Louie Bennett.

The Irish Transport and General Workers Union (ITGWU) was founded in 1909 by James Larkin. On his return from the US in 1910, James Connolly joined and worked as a full-time official in Belfast. The next few years were both eventful and traumatic for the labour movement in Ireland.

The Irish Labour party was formed in 1912. In its infancy, membership was restricted to trade unionists. Two years later, the great Dublin lock-out occurred. Even with the massive publicity which surrounded the lock-out, it had a detrimental impact on the union movement in the short term. Less than two years later, James Connolly was executed after the 1916 Easter Rising. Connolly had been the chief organiser of the ITGWU in Ulster as well as one of the founding members of the Irish Labour party. His loss to the trade union movement was immense.

Although membership of the ITGWU had increased to 100,000 in 1922, it subsequently fell to below 16,000 by the end of the decade. The ITUC membership also fell, falling from 189,000 in 1922 to 92,000 in 1929. The economic conditions during the Depression, in addition to government policy, were contributing factors to the decline in union membership.

The last sixty years have witnessed great changes in the trade union movement in Ireland. In 1959, the Irish Congress of Trade Unions (ICTU), the co-ordinating body for trade unions in Ireland, was established. In 1990, the country's two largest unions – the ITGWU and the FWUI (Federated Workers' Union of Ireland) – were amalgamated to form the Services, Industrial, Professional and Technical Union (SIPTU). In the same year, membership had reached circa 450,000.

The changes, however, were far from uniform. For example, whereas membership increased dramatically in the mid- to late 1940s, it virtually stagnated for most of the next decade. The employment density (trade union membership/civilian employees at work) increased from 20% in 1930 to almost 55% in 1990. It had peaked at over 60% by the early 1980s. The 1980s was a particularly difficult decade for the trade union movement in Ireland. In the 1990s, however, we observe a certain degree of consolidation of labour's position (due partly to the credibility gained from their participation in the centralised wage agreements of the early 1990s). In terms of unionisation, Ireland finds itself today in the middle of the range for European countries (see Section 15.2.4).

1   *The Irish Trade Union movement celebrated their centenary in 1994. As part of their celebrations, RTE broadcasted a series of Thomas Davis lectures, entitled 'Trade Union Century'. These lectures in addition to other material were published in book form, under the title* Trade Union Century *(Mercier Press, 1994). The editor was Donal Nevin, Congress Secretary 1982–89. For more on Irish trade unions read* Irish Industrial Relations in Practice *by T. Murphy & W. Roche, Oak Tree Press and Graduate School of Business UCD, 1994.*

Using the demand and the supply curve, we now consider the labour market.

Labour market equilibrium

Figure 6.7 below depicts the labour market with a downward sloping demand curve and an upward sloping supply curve. The intersection of the demand curve and the supply curve determines the equilibrium wage rate and the equilibrium quantity of labour. At W^*, the quantity demanded of labour is equal to the quantity supplied. W^* is the wage rate that clears the labour market.

Figure 6.7: Labour market equilibrium

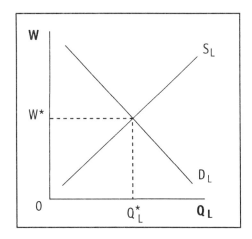

At all other wage levels, there is either a shortage or a surplus of labour. At wage rates above the equilibrium level, an excess supply of labour exists. This surplus labour results in downward pressure on wages. At wage rates below the equilibrium level, an excess demand for labour results. Such a shortage of workers puts upward pressure on wage levels. W^* is the equilibrium wage rate. At W^* the quantity demanded and quantity supplied of labour are equal.

As we discussed previously, the labour demand curve and supply curve are drawn holding other variables constant. A change in one of the underlying variables will cause the demand curve or the supply curve to shift. Any shift of the demand curve or the supply curve of labour results in a change in the equilibrium wage rate and the quantity of labour.

For example, suppose we examine demand and supply conditions for labour in the construction industry. In the winter months severe weather conditions can adversely affect the construction industry. In response to worsening weather conditions, construction companies reduce their demand for labourers. The effects of such a change are shown in Figure 6.8.

Figure 6.8: A change in labour demand

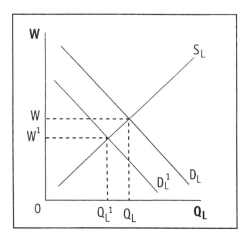

Equilibrium is initially at (W, Q_L). The adverse weather conditions force the construction companies to cut their workforce. Fewer labourers are required to work on the construction sites. This reduction in demand is illustrated in graphic terms as a leftward shift of the demand curve for labour. The excess supply of labour arising from the fall in demand forces wage levels downwards. As wage levels fall, fewer workers are willing to supply their services.

Equilibrium is restored at (W^1, Q_L^1), the intersection of the old supply curve, S_L and the new demand curve, D_L^1. The net result is a lower equilibrium wage level combined with a lower quantity of labour. An improvement in demand conditions will result in higher wages and a higher quantity of labour.

Conclusions and criticisms of the neoclassical model of the labour market
....

The neoclassical model of the labour market continues to influence the thinking of economists and policy-makers. The student, when reading this section, should recognise the similarities between the model of the product market and the model of the labour market. We have essentially adapted the 'tools of the trade' and used them to analyse a different market.

While one may question many of the assumptions of the product market, applying them to the labour market seems to be inappropriate. We speak of a labour market as if labour is homogeneous. We discuss workers as if they were interchangeable. While wheat may be homogeneous, labourers are not: workers differ in their training and their ability. There are huge differences in the education and training required for various occupations and professions. However, we lump everyone together to discuss the 'labour market'.

The labour demand curve is based on marginal productivity. Workers are not uniformly productive, either when compared to each other, or in comparison with themselves! Changes in health and personal circumstances cause the productivity of even the most stable workers to vary.

Also, although firms may be willing to vary their output decision fairly quickly, they are unlikely to change their employment levels, particularly if their workers are skilled. 'Derived demand' for labour suggests that if demand for a product increases, firms will demand more labour. Workers with sufficient skills may not be available. Similarly, if demand for a product falls, management may be reluctant to make labour redundant. Recognising the hardship caused by unemployment and the problems in reassembling a skilled group of employees, they may prefer to maintain their labour force in the hope that the demand for their product will increase. In other words, the labour market may not respond as quickly, or as predictably as the product market to a change in demand or supply.

In product markets, we expect a single price, except in cases of imperfect competition. Wage differentials in sectors of the labour market occur for many different reasons. These include working conditions in certain sectors, trade union power, workers' qualifications and skills, geographic immobility and discrimination. Even in a given industry, in a particular firm, one employee may be paid more than another to do the same job, simply because the employer values that employee more.

Alternative labour market models have been offered by Barbara Bergmann, Gary Becker, Victor Fuchs and others. Students who are interested in the criticisms above are encouraged to read more about this complex and important topic.

CASE STUDY

Extract from The Irish Times
Treating employees as long-term assets
by Cliff Taylor

Remember the advertisements for Toyota motor cars? The ones which boasted about the freedom any worker had to stop the production line to suggest a better way of doing things? In management jargon it's part of what is known as a 'lean production' system and it is held up by author Francis Fukuyama as an example of the way a modern industry should work.

. . .

Today Prof. Fukuyama will talk to the assembled business leaders about themes in his new book – *Trust* – which is a study of the link between culture and economics. And the key message to managers is that they must 'pay more attention to treating their workers not as short-term costs but as long-term assets'.

Prof. Fukuyama, a former deputy director in the US State Department's policy planning department, argues in *Trust* that the standard, neo-classical economic theory, based on rational consumers and producers acting in their own self-interest, does not tell the full story. Instead, the type of society and the way business is organised play a key role in economic development. Economics tells 80% of the story, 'but there is a missing 20% of human behaviour about which neoclassical economists can only give a poor account', the book says.

The message he would be bringing to the IBEC conference, he told *The Irish Times* was that the world of business was changing. Increasingly, organisations are

becoming 'flatter' – with fewer management layers – and employees are typically much better educated and able to take on more responsibility.

'Mastering that form of organisation will be a key to building an effective company moving into the next century', he says. Which brings us back to the Toyota production line – a long way from the old Ford motor company operation in the earlier part of this century.

Henry Ford made money through a mass-production, tightly-controlled production line, inspiring the leading management theorist of the time, Frederick Taylor, whose book *The Principle of Scientific Management* became the bible of the new industrial age. Taylorism emphasised the need for the greatest degree of specialisation on the production line, requiring no initiative from the individual workers.

The lean production system pioneered by Toyota is the exact opposite. As opposed to the lack of trust shown by the traditional system, the lean production method is an example of what Prof. Fukuyama calls a 'high trust' system, where responsibility is widely delegated and employees are encouraged to participate. He believes that managers who pay most attention to 'the sociable side of the human personality' may become the most efficient.

A tightly-regulated and hierarchical workplace 'is absolutely inappropriate for high technology sector, where

→

innovation is the key' and human capital is the key source of wealth creation. The key for management, he argues, may not be the networking and use of technology on which so much emphasis is placed, but rather whether it can create the necessary 'trust' in the organisation to get the best out of its employees.

. . .

Companies may also be tempted to go for short-term performance through cost-cutting. The management fad of laying off large numbers of employees in an attempt to boost short-term profits and push up the share price has a cost in destroying the trust of the remaining employees.

In looking for trust and participation from employees, 'managers often don't get the part that they have to give something in return'. This 'something' is usually some type of job security which, while not the guarantee of a job for life, will at least involve the employer showing loyalty through measures such as offering retraining and redeployment to employees whose old jobs are going.

Managers – particularly financial officers – tend to think that the stock market will reward them for being ruthless, he says. 'They only see employees as costs, not as assets, and cut into the bone rather than just trying to remove the fat.' This can leave the whole organisation damaged and, while delivering short-term savings, can limit its ability for long-term growth.

Source: The Irish Times, *5 May 1996.*

Questions
....

1. Why does Professor Fukuyama criticise the neoclassical interpretation of labour? Explain the neoclassical view of labour and Fukuyama's critique.
2. In what sense do the organisational changes described by Fukuyama reflect the 'new combinations' in production described by Schumpeter?
[See Information Box 6.2 on Schumpeter.]
3. Why does Fukuyama warn that trust, essential to the flatter organisational structure, will be destroyed if firms act in a neoclassical manner?

Answers
....

1. Professor Fukuyama points out that neoclassicals treat labour as short-term costs. We saw that the demand curve for labour is based on the marginal revenue product of labour. If there is a change in marginal revenue, we expect the profit-maximising firm to respond by increasing or decreasing the number of people employed. This treatment of the labour force is quite dehumanising. It does not recognise any responsibility by the firm to the individual worker. The only value placed on labour is their productivity. Workers are both interchangeable and disposable.

Professor Fukuyama is particularly critical of the treatment of labour by managers. In his own words, managers should 'pay more attention to treating their workers not as short-term costs but as long-term assets'. He also emphasises the importance of productivity but he points out that attention to 'the sociable side of the human personality' will increase efficiency.

2. One source of entrepreneurial innovation, according to Schumpeter, is the new organisation of industry. Fukuyama talks about the differences between the production lines developed by Ford and chronicled by Taylor and the 'flatter' organisational structure currently used by Toyota. Workers under Taylorism were controlled, not trusted. While it may have been appropriate at the time, the tightly-controlled production line of Ford did not allow for any creative thinking on the part of line workers.

   Today, workers are better educated and are able to assume responsibility. They are an important source of ideas to improve the product and to increase the efficiency of the process. The new organisational structure of firms, like Toyota, provides an environment which encourages participation and innovation.

3. Trust is essential to get the best out of employees. If firms demand the level of commitment by workers required for innovation, 'they have to give something in return'. This usually takes the form of job security for the employee.

   The goal of the neoclassical firm is to maximise profit or to minimise loss. Labour is a variable cost which can be cut in the short run to achieve this goal. Fukuyama warns that this behaviour by firms destroys trust. In reducing the workforce, a firm may deliver short-term profits to its shareholders, but it will be at the expense of long-term growth.

6.2 Capital and interest

We will now look at the market for capital. In this instance, we are looking at the relationship between the interest rate, the payment for capital and the amount of capital goods which are demanded and supplied by households and firms. We will begin by defining some relevant terms.

Definition
● ● ● ● ● ●

Capital goods are durable assets used during the production process.

Durable means that the assets are useful for longer than one time period. They include plant, machinery, tools and factories.[11]

Definition
● ● ● ● ● ●

The capital stock includes all of the capital goods controlled by a firm.

We measure the capital stock of a firm or of a country at a point in time.
   The capital stock of a firm loses value over time. This is called depreciation.

Definition
● ● ● ● ● ●

Depreciation refers to the decline in value of the capital stock due to its use in production or its age.

In order to maintain its capital stock, a firm must replace the machinery as it wears out. Investment changes the capital stock.

• Definition
• • • • • •

> Investment refers to additions to the capital stock purchased or leased over a particular time period.

Investment is a flow. Gross investment is the total increase to the capital stock over a period of time, including the additions necessary to replace depreciating assets. Net investment constitutes an increase over and above the replacements needed to maintain the capital stock.

Demand for capital goods
....

As in the labour market, the demand for capital goods is a derived demand. Firms invest in capital assets based on current demand and anticipated future demand for their product. Unlike the labour demand curve, the relevant time span for investment decisions may be considerably longer than a single period.

Marginal productivity theory can be used to derive the demand curve for capital goods.

• Definition
• • • • • •

> The marginal revenue product of capital is the extra revenue generated by additions to the capital stock.

In this case, if the size and training of the labour force is held constant and capital is added, additional units of capital are less productive than previous units.

For a profit-maximising firm, the addition to revenue which results from buying or leasing the capital asset must be greater than or equal to the cost of the asset. The process of determining when the two are equal is more difficult than in the labour market because a capital good is durable. The benefits accrue over a number of years. Therefore, we have to estimate the revenue stream generated over the life of the asset and compare that with the cost of the asset.

Present value and future value
....

We will try to clarify the process by looking at an example. We return to the owner of Hibs Ltd who is thinking of purchasing a new piece of machinery valued at £10,000. Ms Hibs anticipates that the asset will last for two years and will have no salvage value. She expects the asset to generate the following revenue stream:

Year	Revenue
1	6,000
2	7,000

She begins by estimating the present value of this revenue stream.

Definition
● ● ● ● ● ● ●

Present value is the estimate of what the revenue stream of a capital asset is worth today.

To grasp this concept, we can consider an alternative decision which Ms Hibs could make. Instead of purchasing a new piece of machinery, she could buy bonds which would earn a rate of interest of 10% per annum, compounded annually. In this case, we are considering the future value of the £10,000. If she invests this money today, what will it be worth in one year, in two years? We can use the future value formula to calculate the value of £10,000 in one year.

$$ FV = PV\,(1+ i) \qquad\qquad [6.3] $$

where PV represents the present value and FV represents the future value of this sum at the interest rate of i. In this example, with a 10% rate of interest, the future value of £10,000 at the end of the first year will be £11,000.

Since the interest is compounded annually, the interest from year one is added to the principal. In year two, Ms Hibs will earn 10% interest on £11,000. At the end of two periods, Ms Hibs would receive a sum of £12,100.

The general form if there is more than one period is:

$$ FV = PV(1+i)^t \qquad\qquad [6.4] $$

where t represents the number of time periods over which the sum is invested.

Suppose that Ms Hibs discovers that she will receive £12,100 in two years. She wants to know how much that sum is worth today, in other words, what is the present value of the £12,100? The general form of the equation used to solve this problem is derived from the future value formula. We simply solve for the present value.

$$ PV = \frac{FV}{(1 + i)^t} \qquad\qquad [6.5] $$

If the market rate of interest is 10%, the present value is $\dfrac{£12,100}{(1 + 0.1)^2}$ or £10,000. In this case we are discounting the future value.

Definition
● ● ● ● ● ● ●

Discounting is the process of reducing the future value of a sum of money or a flow of revenues to the present value.

The problem which confronts us with the revenue stream of the capital asset is slightly more complicated because the revenues for each year must be considered separately. To calculate the present value, we will use the following equation:

$$PV = \Sigma \ \frac{R_t}{(1 + i)^t}$$

[6.6]

where R represents the additional revenue earned by the asset in period t. The expression Σ means that we add together the discounted revenue for each of the t periods. We can use this equation to calculate the present value of the revenue stream which the new piece of machinery will generate.

$$PV = \frac{6,000}{(1 + 0.1)} + \frac{7,000}{(1 + 0.1)^2} = £11,240$$

Now, we compare this amount with the cost of the machinery. Obviously, £11,240 is significantly greater than £10,000. In this case, Ms Hibs will clearly benefit from purchasing this asset. However, she would still purchase the asset if the present value was £11,000 or £10,500. Indeed, we would expect Ms Hibs to invest in capital goods up to the point where the present value of the revenue generated by the asset is equal to the cost of buying the asset.

Rate of return on capital and the interest rate

We will now look at this problem from a slightly different perspective. We will try to determine the minimum rate of return which Ms Hibs must earn in order for her to decide to acquire an additional capital asset.

Definition
● ● ● ● ● ●

The rate of return on capital is a measure of the productivity of a particular capital asset.

We can calculate the rate of return using the following formula

$$C = \frac{R_1}{(1 + r)} + \frac{R_2}{(1 + r)^2}$$

[6.7]

where C is the cost of the asset, R_1 and R_2 are the revenues earned in periods 1 and 2 respectively and r is the rate of return on the asset. Substituting the figures from the asset purchased by Hibs Ltd and solving for r, we find that the rate of return equals approximately 0.19 or 19% for this asset.

$$10,000 = \frac{6,000}{(1 + r)} + \frac{7,000}{(1 + r)^2}$$

By comparing the cost of the asset to the present value of the anticipated revenue stream, we realised that Ms Hibs, as the owner of a profit-maximising firm, will purchase this asset. We reach the same conclusion by comparing the rate of return on capital to the interest rate. Using this form of analysis, we can see that Ms Hibs will buy or lease the asset because the rate of return on capital is greater than the 10% interest rate. Further, as long as the rate of return on capital is greater than the interest rate, we assume that a profit-maximising firm will continue to invest in capital assets.

Interest rates and the demand for capital goods

Finally, we can consider the relationship between the interest rate and the demand for capital goods. From our discussion above, we assume that capital becomes less productive as more capital is employed, *ceteris paribus*. We also know that a profit-maximising firm will acquire additional capital goods if the rate of return on capital is greater than or equal to the interest rate. What happens if the interest rate falls?

As interest rates fall, *ceteris paribus*, firms will acquire more capital goods. Although the new acquisitions are less productive than previous capital goods, the lower interest rate means that money invested in bonds will earn lower returns. Even less productive capital assets will earn more than the market rate of interest. The relationship between interest rates and the demand for capital goods is negative. As interest rates fall, the demand for capital goods increases.[12] Figure 6.9 shows a downward sloping demand curve for capital goods.

Figure 6.9: The demand curve for capital goods

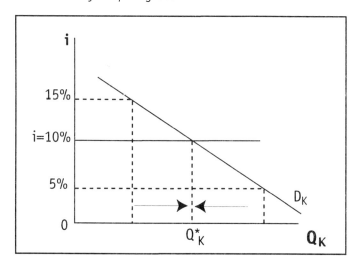

D_k represents the demand curve for capital goods. It is downward sloping: the lower the interest rate, the larger the number of capital goods demanded. We can think of this curve as representing, for any interest rate, the amount of capital goods demanded by profit-maximising firms, *ceteris paribus*. What variables are held constant? Among others, they include the size and training of the labour force, the taxation system and firms' expectations about the future.

The supply curve for capital goods

Funds are needed to finance capital goods. Whereas the labour supply curve is influenced by the labour/leisure trade-off, the supply curve for capital goods is influenced by the trade-off between consumption and savings. Households provide the funds for capital goods. As interest rates increase, the supply of capital increases. At higher rates of interest, households are willing to forgo present consumption in favour of future consumption. The supply curve for capital (S_K) is upward sloping as depicted in Figure 6.10.[13]

Figure 6.10: The supply curve for capital goods

At an interest rate of i^1, Q_K^1 is supplied. As interest rates rise, the supply of capital increases. With a higher interest rate of i^2, Q_K^2 is supplied.

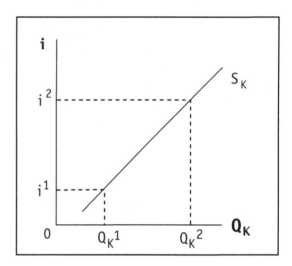

Equilibrium in the capital market

The demand curve D_K is derived from the demand for final output produced in the goods market. It is downward sloping. The supply curve shows the quantity of capital at any given interest rate. It is upward sloping. The equilibrium interest rate is determined by the demand for and supply of capital. In graphic terms, equilibrium occurs at the intersection of the demand curve D_K and the supply curve S_K. i^* is the return on capital that clears the market for capital goods. This is shown in Figure 6.11.

Figure 6.11: Capital market equilibrium

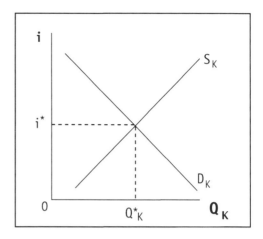

Adjustment to equilibrium is an automatic process in the market for capital goods. For example, suppose the market interest rate is above i*. At any rate above the equilibrium interest rate there exists an excess supply. The actions of savers and investors in the capital market will eventually push interest rates downwards. The interest rate continues to fall until it reaches i* where the market is in equilibrium. The inverse is true for interest rates below equilibrium where adjustments will occur upwards from positions of excess demand.

Conclusions and criticisms of the neoclassical model of the capital market

In this analysis, we assume that firms have perfect knowledge of their present and future revenue streams. This assumption is questionable in the short run. In the long run, over the lifetime of a durable asset, it is unrealistic. Today, all companies are concerned that new technologies will make capital goods obsolete before they are fully depreciated. Firms must begin the decision-making process concerning the acquisition of capital goods based on an estimate of the additional revenue that each asset will generate. Although firms face considerable uncertainty, economists rationalise this by saying that firms act 'as if' they have perfect knowledge.

Also, the analysis of the capital market presents a single interest rate established through market competition. In reality, interest rates offered to firms differ for a number of reasons. One of the main reasons why interest rates differ is risk. If the lender is concerned that the loan may not be repaid, he will charge a higher rate of interest as a premium against that risk. Interest rates also vary depending on the duration of the loan. Also, small loans generally pay higher rates of interest than large loans. The costs of administering the loan are high relative to the size of the loan and these costs are paid for by the borrower.

6.3 Land and rent

Rent is the return on land. The term 'rent' can be quite misleading as it means different things to different people.[14] In particular, it is often confused with another term frequently used by economists. The term is 'economic rent'.

Definition
● ● ● ● ● ●

Economic rent is a payment in excess of the opportunity cost.

It is a surplus payment to any factor in excess of the minimum payment needed to keep a factor in its present use (see Appendix 6.1). This minimum payment is known as transfer earnings because if earnings fall below this level, the factor input would be withdrawn, i.e. it would be transferred to some other activity.

Definition
● ● ● ● ● ●

> Transfer earnings is what a resource could earn in its best alternative use. It is the opportunity cost of employing a factor.

The essential feature of economic rent is that it is a surplus. Hence, its payment is not necessary to guarantee the supply of a particular factor.[15]

The terms 'economic rent' and 'transfer earnings' can be explained using demand and supply analysis. The demand for and supply of a factor resource is shown in Figure 6.12.

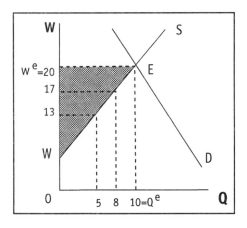

Figure 6.12: Economic rent and transfer earnings

Let us suppose that the actual market wage is £20. In the above market, the fifth worker is willing to work for a wage of £13. This amount is equal to her transfer earnings and her economic rent is the surplus, i.e. £7. If the eighth worker is willing to work only at the higher wage of £17, her economic rent is only £3 (£20 – £17). The tenth worker is the final addition to the workforce. Her transfer earnings amount to £20 with no surplus or economic rent.

In Figure 6.12 transfer earnings is given by the area under the supply curve [$0WEQ^e$]. The shaded area between the supply curve and the factor price [WW^eE], is equal to economic rent.

In reality, most factor earnings are a composite of transfer earnings and economic rent. It is the elasticity of supply of the factor input that determines the relative size of each component of total income. If the supply curve for a factor input is perfectly elastic, all of factor earnings will be transfer earnings. Continuing with the labour market, for example, each worker will earn exactly the amount necessary, to persuade them to remain in the industry. As the supply curve becomes increasingly inelastic, the area of economic rent increases. Many of the individuals working in the market would remain in their position for a wage which is far less than the equilibrium wage.

In terms of land, economic rent is specifically the price paid for the use of land and other fixed resources. It is this fixed supply which distinguishes rental payments from other factor payments.

As with all other economic resources, rent can be explained in terms of demand and supply analysis. The demand for fixed resources is a derived demand: it stems from the goods and services that the land is involved in producing. Figure 6.13 shows the market for land. In this market, we are looking at the relationship between rent, the price of land, and the quantity of land that is demanded and supplied.

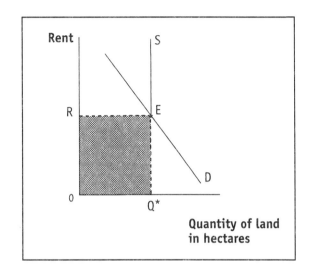

Figure 6.13: The market for land

The downward sloping demand curve for land is derived from the marginal revenue product of land.

In turn, the marginal revenue product of land is determined by the physical productivity of the land and the marginal revenue of the product produced on the land.

The demand curve is downward sloping because land exhibits diminishing marginal returns. The first units of land that are employed are the most productive.

Referring again to Figure 6.13, we observe that the supply curve for land is perfectly inelastic. This is because the supply of land is virtually fixed.[16]

The equilibrium rent R is determined by the intersection of the demand curve D and the supply curve S. With a fixed supply of land at Q*, the amount of economic rent is given by the shaded area [0REQ*].

In the market for land, the entire rental price is an economic rent. Why? Since land is a natural resource, fixed in supply and provided free by nature, the cost of production or supply cost is zero. Hence, the opportunity cost of supplying a fixed amount of this resource is zero. Since there are no transfer earnings, the entire price of land is an economic rent. If the economic rent is reduced or even removed, the supply of land remains the same.[17]

Given that the supply of land is fixed, demand becomes the sole 'active' determination of rent. A change in demand will cause a change in the rental price. For example, agricultural land along the west coast of Ireland is being bought by developers to build holiday homes. This constitutes a 'change in demand'. The marginal revenue product of land used for development is higher than the marginal revenue product of land devoted to agriculture. The demand curve for land shifts out to the right and rental prices increase. The subsequent higher rental prices do not induce landlords to increase supply. The only effect of the increase in demand is a rent increase.

The inverse is true for a decline in the demand for land. Changes in population, economic prosperity and property tax are examples of the factors which influence the demand for land and natural resources.

6.4 Entrepreneurship and profit

A fourth category of factor inputs is entrepreneurship. It is distinct from other resources in the economy in the sense that it is difficult to define and impossible to measure. The entrepreneur receives profit as a payment.[18]

Profit is different from other factor prices because it is a residual; it is paid out to the entrepreneur after all other factor payments are made. Also, profit is not guaranteed. In fact, it may be negative in the short run.

As we mentioned in Chapter 4, the use of the term 'profit' can be quite misleading (see Section 4.3 for a more complete discussion). In particular, accountants and economists define the word differently. Profit as defined by the accountant, is simply the difference between total revenue and total cost. The economist includes normal profit as an economic cost. A normal profit is the opportunity cost of the entrepreneur. Therefore, if total revenues equal total economic costs, the firm has made a 'normal' profit. For the economist, if total revenues exceed economic costs, the firm makes a 'supernormal' or economic profit. In terms of the difference between normal profit and supernormal profit, the former can be regarded as the entrepreneur's transfer earnings and the latter as the entrepreneur's economic rent.

There are several explanations for the existence of economic profits. We will consider three. Economic profits can be considered as:

1. a reward for uninsured risk;
2. a reward for innovation;
3. the result of a monopolistic market structure.

A brief explanation follows.

A reward for uninsured risk
....

For Frank Knight and other economists, profit is the reward entrepreneurs receive for taking risks in times of uncertainty.[19] Uncertainty arises from dynamic changes in the economy. Profit is the reward for a risk successfully taken. Knight distinguished between insurable and uninsurable risks. Insurable risk is covered by insurance premiums, he argued. Uninsurable risks are the source of profit. 'Business ability' was also a factor in the determination of profit.

A reward for innovation
....

For some, profit arises out of acts of innovation where innovation can be defined as the application of invention to industry. The great Austrian economist Joseph Schumpeter was the main exponent of this theory (see Information Box 6.2).[20] The act of innovation as described by Schumpeter was to be distinguished from the act of invention. Schumpeter's innovator, called the 'entrepreneur', was responsible for the dynamic characteristic of the capitalist system.

For Schumpeter, successful innovation depended on leadership rather than intelligence. The result of successful innovation was profit which was a central feature of the capitalist system.

INFORMATION BOX 6.2

Joseph Schumpeter (1883–1950)

Joseph Schumpeter was born and educated in Austria. While at the University of Vienna he studied under Bohm-Bawerk (refer back to Section 6.1 and marginal productivity theory). He began teaching Economics at the University of Czernowitz and later at the University of Graz. He was also the Austrian Minister of Finance for a brief period after World War 1. Between 1925 and 1932 he held the Chair of Public Finance at Bonn. After emigrating to the US in 1932 he became a Professor at Harvard University where he remained until his retirement in 1950.

One of Schumpeter's greatest contributions to economics was his economic character, the 'entrepreneur'. The entrepreneur played a central role in the capitalist system, argued Schumpeter. He was the agent largely responsible for change and for economic development. For Schumpeter, the entrepreneur's role was vastly different from that of the labourer, landowner, capitalist and so on. The entrepreneur was the person who innovates, the person who creates 'new combinations' in production.

Schumpeter identified several types of innovation. They include the creation of a new product, the creation of a new method of production, the opening of new markets, the discovery of a new source of supply and new organisations of industry. Schumpeter was a strong supporter of free enterprise, capitalism and the laissez-faire doctrine. Within a capitalist system, economic development is both a dynamic and erratic process, he argued. He openly acknowledged the dangers (arising not out of its weaknesses but rather out of its strengths) that inherently exist in a capitalist system. He discussed 'creative destruction', i.e. the implementation of new combinations that perpetuate economic change. He recognised that this has a disruptive process which required limited government intervention to reduce inequalities, control monopolies, smooth out the business cycle and so on. Continuous intervention by the state, however, would eventually undermine the role of the entrepreneur. The performance of the economy would begin to falter, he argued. In the long run, capitalism would decay and it would be replaced with socialism.

Schumpeter's major works include Theory of Economic Development *(1912) written when he was 28 years old.* Business Cycles *(1939) has been rediscovered in recent years, and recognised as an important work concerning an economic phenomenon which is constantly discussed but poorly understood. The entrepreneur plays a central role in Schumpeter's model of the business cycle.* History of Economic Analysis *(1954) was published posthumously. In it, Schumpeter critically reviews the work of economic scholars including Smith and Marshall.*

Schumpeter is not as widely known as Keynes nor did he hold Keynes in high esteem. His economic works are even further removed than Keynes' from the neoclassical tradition. Still, both economists are undoubtedly among the greatest economists of the twentieth century. Many current writers, particularly in the area of business economics, owe an intellectual debt to Schumpeter. He recognised that the individual contributed more than her marginal revenue product. The entrepreneur was the central figure in economic development.

A more recent account of innovation has been given by Michael Porter (see Information Box 6.3).

INFORMATION BOX 6.3

Michael Porter and Innovation

Michael Porter is regarded as the world's leading authority on competitive advantage. By competitive advantage, he is referring to the ability of certain firms to create and sustain a dominant position in particular industries for a significant period of time. Central to this theory is the importance of innovation.[1]

The factor conditions referred to by Porter move beyond the traditional endowments of land, labour and capital emphasised by the classical economists. Factors vital to economic growth are created, not inherited. The stock of factors is less important than the rate at which they are upgraded.

Porter groups factors into broad categories including human resources, physical resources, knowledge resources, capital resources and infrastructure. Competitive advantage is based on the efficient employment of factors which may be basic or advanced. Basic factors are internationally mobile and are attracted to where they are most efficiently employed. Advanced factors require sustained investment and are necessary to achieve higher-order competitive advantages which are difficult for other firms to duplicate.

For Porter, innovation is the key to achieving and maintaining competitive advantage. He defines innovation as 'improvements in technology and better methods or ways of doing things' that are 'commercialised'. He goes on to say that innovation can manifest itself in many different ways. They include product changes, process changes, new approaches to marketing, new forms of distribution, and new conceptions of scope (notice the similarity to Schumpeter's 'new combinations'). Innovation grows out of pressure, challenges and change. Whereas many view change as unwelcome, Porter sees it as both necessary and desirable. Innovation and change are inextricably linked together.[2]

Once innovation is achieved (more likely in a mundane manner rather than in any radical fashion), continuous improving must follow so that the advantage is not lost to competitors who attempt to imitate any improvement.

Finally, 'innovation is the result of unusual effort' which ultimately must lead to unnatural acts by firms if the advantage achieved from innovation is to be sustained. This behaviour is inherent in 'leaders', i.e. in firms or individuals that recognise the dynamics of an industry and the importance of embracing and institutionalising change rather than avoiding it. Of course, sixty years ago Schumpeter said the same thing!

1   *For a short summary of the book* (The Competitive Advantage of Nations), *read the article 'The Competitive Advantage of Nations' by M. Porter,* Harvard Business Review, Mar.–Apr. 1990.
2   *A leading guru on innovation and entrepreneurship is Peter Drucker. To understand why he views entrepreneurship as a practice which can be successfully managed, read his 1985 best-seller* Innovation and Entrepreneurship.

The result of a monopolistic market structure

Until now, we have discussed factor markets under conditions of perfect competition. Consider the case of a monopoly. A monopoly is a sole producer in an industry. Its ability to restrict output, control price and deter entry allow supernormal profits to persist. If the demand for the monopolist's product or service is high, profits will also remain high. Profits arising from a monopoly position are viewed as socially less desirable than profits sourced from risk and from innovation. And unlike the other two sources, government action may be taken in order to restrict monopoly profits.

Summary

1. The factors of production are the inputs used in the production process which ultimately result in final output. There are four factor inputs – labour, capital, land and entrepreneurship. The return on labour is the wage rate; interest is the reward to capital; rent is the return on land, and profit is the reward to entrepreneurship. According to the neoclassical theory of distribution, factor prices can be explained by demand and supply analysis.
2. The demand curve for labour is derived using marginal productivity theory. Profit-maximising firms will employ workers up to the point where MRP of labour = W. The MRP curve is the demand curve for labour, showing the number of workers employed at any given wage rate. It is downward sloping, showing the lower the wage rate, the larger the number of workers who will be employed.
3. The supply curve for labour shows the number of hours offered for work at given wage rates. It depends on the trade-off between work and leisure. It is normally upward sloping. The demand for and supply of labour simultaneously determine the equilibrium wage rate and quantity of labour.
4. The interest rate is the opportunity cost of capital. In deciding whether to purchase new capital, the firm must weigh the future benefits accruing from the investment

against the cost of the investment. The demand curve for capital goods is downward sloping. The supply curve for capital goods is influenced by the trade-off between consumption and savings. The equilibrium interest rate is the cost of capital that clears the market for capital goods.

5. Transfer earnings is the portion of total earnings that is required to keep a factor in its present use. Economic rent is the portion of earnings in excess of transfer payments. Economic rent is paid on any factor of production that is in fixed supply. In terms of land, rent is the price paid for the use of land and other fixed resources. It is this fixed supply which distinguishes rental payments from other factor payments. The entire rental price is an economic rent.

6. Entrepreneurship is difficult to define and to measure. The reward to enterprise is profit. Unlike other factor payments, profit is a residual. It is received after all other factor payments are made. There are several different sources of economic profit. One, it is the reward for uninsurable risk in the face of uncertainty. Two, it arises out of acts of innovation carried out by the entrepreneur. Three, monopoly profits arise from output restriction, high prices and barriers to entry.

Key terms

Labour	Investment
Wage rate	Present value
Derived demand	Discounting
Marginal productivity theory	Rate of return
Marginal revenue product	Interest rate
Demand curve for labour	Land
Supply curve of labour	Economic rent
Backward-bending supply curve	Transfer earnings
Wage differentials	Entrepreneurship
Capital goods	Profit
Capital stock	Uninsurable risk
Depreciation	Innovation
	Entrepreneur

Review questions

1. Explain the term 'the factors of production'. What are the rewards to each respective factor input?
2. Explain the derivation of the downward sloping labour demand curve.
3. What effect would an increase in labour supply have on the equilibrium price and quantity in the labour market?
4. (a) 'An investment is worthwhile if the present value of the future benefits exceeds the cost of the investment.' Explain.
   (b) 'The equilibrium interest rate clears the market for capital goods.' Explain.
5. Explain the term 'economic rent'. What is the difference between transfer earnings, opportunity cost and economic rent?

6. (a) Explain the three sources of economic profit.
   (b) Outline the contributions of Frank Knight and Joseph Schumpeter to the theory of profit.

Working problems

1. A number of entries in Table 6.2 have been deliberately omitted. Using marginal productivity theory, answer the questions below.

Table 6.2

Labour (wkrs)	TP (units)	MP (units)	P (£)	MRP (£)	Wage (£)
0	0				
		—	5	60	40
1	—				
		—	5	—	40
2	27				
		13	5	—	40
3	—				
		—	5	50	40
4	—				
		9	5	—	40
5	—				
		—	5	—	40
6	65				

(a) Complete the table.
(b) According to the marginal productivity theory, how many workers will be employed if the wage rate is £40?
(c) If the wage rate rises to £50, how many workers will be employed?

2. A hypothetical labour market is depicted in Figure 6.14 below.

Figure 6.14: The labour market

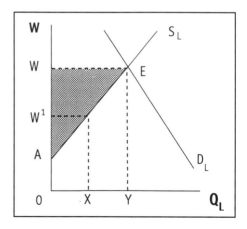

With respect to Figure 6.14 fill in the blanks below

(a) total earnings is given by the area [ ]
(b) transfer earnings is given by the area [ ]
(c) economic rent is given by the area [ ]
(d) transfer earnings for worker X is equal to _____
(e) economic rent for worker X is equal to _____

Multi-choice questions

1. Under conditions of perfect competition, the MRP of labour:
   (a) is equal to the MP of labour multiplied by the marginal revenue of the good;
   (b) is the additional revenue due to employing an extra unit of labour;
   (c) curve falls because of the short-run law of diminishing returns;
   (d) curve is the demand curve for labour;
   (e) all of the above.

2. A derived demand for labour:
   (a) can be explained using the marginal productivity theory;
   (b) is derived from the demand for the product which labour produces;
   (c) can be represented by a downward sloping demand curve;
   (d) all of the above;
   (e) none of the above.

3. The present value of £5,000 two years from now at an interest rate of 6% is:
   (a) £5,618;
   (b) £5,600;
   (c) £4,450;
   (d) higher than £5,000;
   (e) both (a) and (d) above.

4. Figure 6.15 shows the labour market for university postgraduates.

Figure 6.15: The labour market for university postgraduates

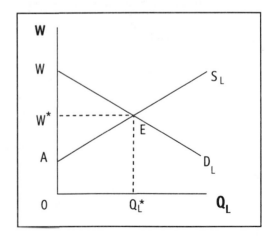

The economic rent is given by the area:

(a) $[AEQ_L^*0]$;
(b) $[W^*EQ_L^*0]$;
(c) $[W^*EA]$;
(d) $[WEQ_L^*0]$;
(e) none of the above.

5. The more inelastic the supply curve becomes:

(a) the more transfer earnings is paid;
(b) the more economic rent is paid;
(c) the less economic rent is paid;
(d) both (a) and (c) above;
(e) none of the above.

6. Profit is different from the other resource prices because:

(a) it is a residual;
(b) it can be negative;
(c) it is a category of factor income;
(d) both (a) and (b) above;
(e) both (a) and (c) above.

True or false

1. Resource prices serve as an allocative mechanism. _____
2. The declining MRP of labour reflects the law of diminishing returns: an additional labourer produces more output than the previous labourer. _____
3. The higher the interest rate, the lower is the present discounted value of the future MRPs and the smaller the number of capital goods demanded. _____
4. Transfer earnings is the opportunity cost of employing a factor. _____
5. A factor of production does not earn economic rent if its supply curve is perfectly elastic. _____
6. Profit is the return to the entrepreneur. _____

Fill in the blanks

Labour, capital, _____ and entrepreneurship are the four factors of production. The wage rate is the return on labour; _____ is the reward to capital; rent is the reward to land; profit is the return on _____. The demand for a factor input is a _____ demand. It can be explained using the _____ productivity theory which states that a factor input depends on its _____. For labour and land, the MRP curve is equal to the _____ curve. The supply curve of the respective factors varies; _____ supply is influenced by the trade-off between work and _____ ; the supply of capital is affected by the consumption-_____ trade-off; the supply of land is _____. A fixed resource results in the payment of _____. The _____ factor price clears the respective resource market; quantity demanded equals quantity _____. The fourth resource is entrepreneurship and its return is called _____. It is a _____. Risk, _____ and monopolies are the sources of profit.

CASE STUDY

Extract from The Irish Times
Craft workers' value highlighted by study
by Padraig Yeats

A high proportion of skilled craft and technical workers is more important to a country's productivity levels and wealth creation than a high proportion of graduates, a new internal report from FÁS, the state training agency, finds. It says the comparatively small proportion of craft workers in the Irish economy is a major inhibitor of growth and reflects 'undervaluing within business of the making function as opposed to the financing or the selling functions'.

'Ireland has almost the same proportions of graduates and technicians within its labour force as Germany. But while 56% of the German labour force were skilled craftsmen, only 18% were so skilled in Ireland.'

The report goes on: 'With Germany typically training 5% of its labour force as apprentices compared to 1% in Ireland, this skills deficit is increasing rather than diminishing. One of the major challenges facing the social partners in the 1990s will be to devise ways of substantially increasing the number of apprentices in training.'

The report compares the percentage of technicians and craft workers in the labour force of European countries with their capacity to generate wealth. In Switzerland, where 66% of the workforce fall into these skilled categories, the GDP per capita is $19,500 dollars (1990 figures). In Germany, where 63% of the labour force is skilled, the GDP per capita is $18,212. In the Netherlands, the respective figures are 57% and $15,376, and in France 40% and $17,376. In Ireland, where only 24% of the labour force are technicians and craft workers, the GDP per capita is $10,627.

The FÁS study also shows a remarkable recovery since 1990 in manufacturing productivity in established indigenous Irish companies. Before then, such firms lagged behind those owned by foreign transnational firms and the agribusiness sector. Between 1990 and 1994, productivity in foreign-owned companies rose 20%. It rose by 18.7% in the agribusiness sector which covers industries such as textiles.

FÁS compares its finding with earlier studies in other countries such as the 1990 study on 'Productivity, Education and Training' in the UK. This showed that the most significant factor in competitiveness of manufacturing industry was not the quality of the plant but that of the workforce.

. . .

Source: The Irish Times, *29 August 1995.*

Questions
....

1. How does the composition of the Irish labour force differ from the German labour force?
2. Consider the neoclassical model of the labour market. How does the type of training affect the GDP per capita?
3. Why do you think that more students are academically, rather than technically educated in Ireland?

Appendix 6.1: David Ricardo and economic rent

The theory of economic rent was developed in the nineteenth century by the British economist, stockbroker and MP David Ricardo (1772–1823) in his book *The Principles of Political Economy and Taxation* (1817). His theory arose out of the Napoleonic wars and the rising corn (grain) prices which occurred at the same time as the rise in land rents. It was argued at the time that the high corn prices were a direct result of the landlords' policy of high land rents. Ricardo disagreed strongly with such an analysis. He saw the cause and effect in reverse. High rents were an effect and not a cause of high corn prices, he argued. In his own words 'Corn is not high because a rent is paid, but a rent is paid because corn is high.'[21]

The Napoleonic wars were directly responsible for a shortage of corn. The subsequent rise in the price of corn, he argued, forced landlords to seek out more land in order to take advantage of profitable corn production. Subsequent high demand for land in turn forced up the land rents. For Ricardo, rent was price determined and not price determining.

The above analysis can be described in the context of the demand for and supply of land. The supply of land is fixed, with land having only one use: the growing of corn. The demand for land is a derived demand, stemming from the demand for corn. The payment to land is a surplus. This surplus payment is rent, according to Ricardo.

CHAPTER 7

MARKET FAILURE

by EITHNE MURPHY

'There are only two qualities in the world: efficiency and inefficiency, and only two sorts of people: the efficient and the inefficient.'[1]

George Bernard Shaw

'Good men are a publick good.'[2]

Proverb

'We have . . . to distinguish precisely between the two varieties of marginal net product which I have named respectively *social* and *private*.'[3]

Arthur C. Pigou (1877–1959)

Chapter objectives

Upon completing this chapter, the student should understand:

- perfectly competitive markets and efficiency;
- externalities, public goods and market inefficiency;
- educational, economic and legal remedies for market failures.

Outline

7.1 Markets and efficiency
7.2 Markets and inefficient outcomes
7.3 The market failure of externalities
7.4 Remedies for external effects
7.5 Public goods
7.6 Public good provision

7.1 Markets and efficiency

The principal, though not the only, ideological defence of the market system is that it represents a form of economic organisation that is efficient. By efficiency, we mean that the market system ensures that human wants and desires are satisfied without waste of resources. It is a system that validates self-interest. The efficiency outcome of the market system is predicated upon a number of behavioural, ethical and environmental assumptions.

The *behavioural assumptions* are that individuals know their own desires and wants, and that they attempt to satisfy these wants in a rational manner.

The *ethical assumptions* are that human want satisfaction adds to individual welfare, and that societal welfare is simply an aggregate of individual welfares.

The *environmental assumptions* are that markets are perfectly competitive in the sense of all economic agents being price takers, and that private benefit/cost is the same as social benefit/cost.

All market transactions are assumed to take place within a legal framework that recognises the right to private property and that provides for the enforcement of contracts.

The system ensures that not only are the right goods produced but that correct quantities of the goods are produced.[4] The correct quantity of a good is one that ensures that all mutually beneficial trades have been exhausted. Let us consider the market represented in Figure 7.1.

Figure 7.1: Equilibrium in a perfectly competitive market

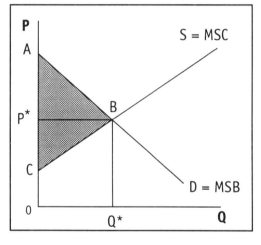

The market clearing price and output are P* and Q* respectively. The price P* is also the value of the utility that the last consumer received by consuming that good. Obviously, if she was willing to pay a price P*, she would not be rational unless the good yielded her a utility that was greater than or equal to the price that she paid. As long as there is net utility to be gained from consuming more of a good, it is rational for her to consume more of that good. By net utility we mean the monetary value of the satisfaction that she gets from consuming the good less the cost of the good.

The profit maximising level of output is one where marginal cost equals price. Any other level of output would not be profit maximising, which would not be rational behaviour for a self-interested producer. At price P* and output Q*, all mutually beneficial trades between the seller and the buyer of the good have been exhausted. If output sold on the market was less than Q*, then there is a potential buyer and a potential seller who can agree to trade at a price that would make both of them better off. Not to do so would be irrational if both are motivated by self-interest. Output will never exceed Q*, since there is no price for more output that will make a potential supplier and a potential buyer better off.

If we equate the private with the social, then the marginal cost to a producer of increasing output is the same as the marginal cost to society of increasing output. Likewise, the marginal benefit to a consumer of consuming extra output equals the marginal benefit to society of that extra consumption. In other words, the market supply curve, which is the private marginal cost curve (MC), is the same as the marginal social cost of production (MSC). Similarly, the demand curve, which is the private marginal benefit curve (MB), is the same as the marginal social benefit of consumption (MSB). Market equilibrium therefore occurs at Q*, where MSC of production equals MSB from consumption.

The shaded area ABC (in Figure 7.1) between the demand and supply curves represents the combined net gain (in monetary terms) to buyers and sellers from participating in the market. Equating the private and the social, we can say that the area ABC is the net value to society as a result of producing a quantity Q* of the good and selling it at a price P*.

7.2 Markets and inefficient outcomes

By pursuing his own interests in a rational way, the individual is assumed to maximise his own welfare and the social effects of such behaviour (when it occurs within the context of perfectly competitive markets) is an economic system without waste. As the eighteenth-century doctor and writer Bernard Mandeville claimed, 'Private vices are public virtues.'[5] Pushing this argument to its logical limit, one could in fact claim that if individuals did directly take the well-being of others into account in their behaviour, the social consequences would be less benign. Likewise, if individuals are not *rational* in the pursuit of their own interests, the market outcome will exhibit waste.

The efficiency of markets only holds if no economic agent has enough power to influence prices in the market and if markets actually exist for all goods and services. *Monopolistic competition*, *oligopoly* and *monopoly* are all forms of market structure where sellers have some power, which can be manifested in an ability to set prices. The market outcome in these instances is inefficient, usually because too little of the good is produced and the market price of the good is too high. When markets deviate from perfect competition in the ways just mentioned, the price at which the good is sold will exceed marginal cost. In other words, the marginal social benefit of the last unit sold exceeds the marginal social cost of production. There would be net utility gains to society if more of the good were produced.

There are goods and bads that are not traded in the market, yet they still affect human welfare. When these goods/bads are a by-product of production or consumption decisions – that is to say, when they are associated with private goods in some way – we call them *externalities*. These externalities have effects that are external to those effects captured by market exchange. These external effects may positively enhance human welfare or may reduce human welfare. Either way, the synonymity between individual private welfare and social welfare no longer exists. This results in either too much or too little production of certain goods.

An extreme form of externality are *public goods*. These goods have the characteristics that everybody must consume them in the same amount and that no one can be excluded from consumption. These are goods for which no private market exists, which is obviously inefficient if people derive utility from the existence of public goods.

7.3 The market failure of externalities

Externalities can be classified according to their causes and according to their effects. The general classification of causes are production activity and consumption activity. The general classification of effects are negative welfare effects and positive welfare effects. We will look at examples of each type of externality.

Negative production externalities
....

A negative production externality occurs when the act of producing a good or service has a side-effect that reduces the welfare of others not involved in that market.

   An example of a negative externality in an Irish context is the water polluting effect of agricultural practices. Farmers, in their rational pursuit of profits, responded to the incentives of the Common Agricultural Policy by intensifying their agricultural production. A common practice has been the use of animal manures (in particular slurry) as a fertiliser. A by-product of this activity has been the run-off of this highly toxic and polluting substance into waterways. The subsequent pollution and fish-kills have had repercussions for bathers, fishermen, those in the tourist trade (who depend on Ireland's pollution-free image) and for anyone who values the environment. We can say that the social costs of farmer behaviour exceed the private costs. Since farmers presumably only care about private costs, this results in too much of the polluting activity taking place.

   Figure 7.2 demonstrates how the market outcome differs from the socially efficient outcome. In the presence of a negative production externality, the private supply curve (which is the private marginal cost of production) is below the true marginal social cost of production (MSC), bearing in mind the negative external effects of that activity. The socially optimal level of output is where the demand schedule intersects with the MSC curve, which is the level of output Q_2. P_2 would be the market clearing price associated with this output level.

Figure 7.2: Market with negative production externality

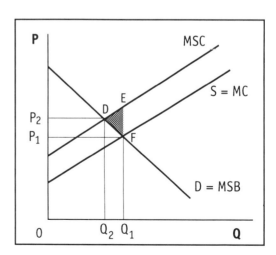

The actual market outcome is an output/price combination Q_1/P_1. P_1, which is also the marginal social benefit (MSB) from the last unit of output produced, is less than the MSC of producing that last unit. Increasing output from Q_2 to Q_1 adds more to social cost than it does to social benefit; that is to say it imposes a net loss on society. The area DEF is the net loss in societal welfare as a result of overproduction of the good which produces the negative externality.

It is interesting to note that the existence of negative externalities merely allows us to conclude that the level of an activity is too high. It does not necessarily imply that the optimal level of that activity is zero. For the latter to occur, there would have to be no intersection between the MSC and the MSB curves, as shown in Figure 7.3. It is possible that for an activity like nuclear power, which has the potential to impose devastatingly high costs on our environment, the socially optimal level of output is as depicted in Figure 7.3; that is to say, it is zero.

Figure 7.3: Market where no output is socially optimal

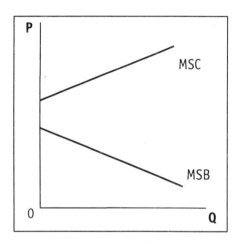

Positive production externalities

A positive production externality exists when the act of production improves the welfare of those not involved in that market. An example of a positive production externality in an Irish context is the effect of the decisions of firms to locate in a certain area, say for example Galway. The individual firm will weigh up the private benefits and costs of locating in an area and only if, on the basis of such calculations, the benefits exceed the costs, will they proceed with the location decision.

However when many firms locate in an area costs can fall. This is because their respective economic existences may be inter-dependent. A computer firm will prefer to locate where it has access to skilled labour, developed financial services and firms who produce inputs that it requires. Likewise, the decisions of related industries, who will be selling to or buying from the computer company, will be in part determined by whether or not the computer company locates in the area. These production externalities are also called *economies of agglomeration*. The net effect of each firm producing in a certain area is to reduce the cost of production to related firms.

Individual producers are not interested in the spillover effects of their decisions: their decisions are made on the basis of their own costs and benefits. As a result, the MC per unit which they calculate is above the MSC per unit which includes the positive production externalities.

As shown in Figure 7.4, when positive production externalities exist, the market level of output (Q_1), which occurs where MC equals price, is below the socially optimal level of output (Q_2), which occurs where MSC equals MSB. The area GHQ is the net loss in societal welfare which results from the underproduction of the good, whose production causes positive externalities.

Figure 7.4: Market with positive production externality

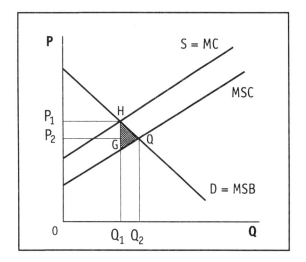

Negative consumption externalities

As a rational self-interested individual, I will purchase and consume a good if the value of the utility I derive from its consumption is greater than or equal to the cost of the good. For some goods, private consumption reduces the welfare of others as a by-product of the consumption activity. Notwithstanding the high cost of cars in Ireland, many Irish people drive cars or aspire to driving them as soon as their personal financial circumstances make driving a feasible option. A by-product of individuals' desire to drive is major traffic congestion, air pollution, noise pollution and increased danger to pedestrians, cyclists and other motorists. Undoubtedly, the marginal social benefit (MSB) of every additional car on the road is much less than the private benefit to its owner.

Since at each level of output the marginal social benefit is less than the marginal private benefit, the MSB curve is below the market demand curve. As shown in Figure 7.5, the market equilibrium results in too much consumption of that good. The market level of consumption (Q_1) is given by the intersection of the market demand and market supply curves. The socially efficient level of output is lower and occurs at Q_2, where the MSB and MSC curves intersect. The area MNO is the inefficiency (or the loss in net societal welfare) associated with overconsumption of goods that produce negative externalities.

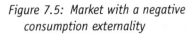

Figure 7.5: Market with a negative consumption externality

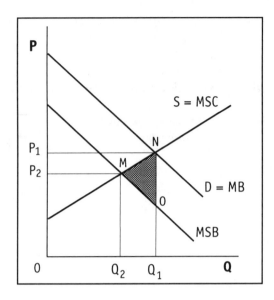

Positive consumption externalities

....

Some consumption activities confer utility, not just on those individuals who consume the good, but also on others as a by-product of their consumption. An example could be education. Individuals (and their families) make many sacrifices to ensure that they get a good education. Presumably, their motives are fairly self-interested. Education confers direct and indirect benefits on the individual: direct benefits in terms of the value of education in itself and indirect benefits in terms of its effect on one's prospects in the labour market.

However, it could be claimed that a highly educated population has positive social repercussions that are not confined to the individual. The marginal social benefit per unit of education which includes the positive externality, exceeds the marginal private benefit. Therefore, the MSB curve is above the market demand curve.

If left to the market, too little of the good will be consumed, since the market level of consumption (Q_1) (see Figure 7.6), is below the socially optimal level of consumption (Q_2), where MSB equals MSC. The efficiency loss, that is a consequence of the underconsumption of a good with positive external effects, is denoted by the area PQR in Figure 7.6.

Figure 7.6: Market with a positive consumption externality

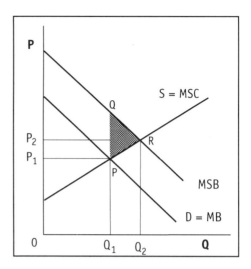

7.4 Remedies for external effects

Our use of language is very value laden. The fact that we refer to market imperfections or market failures seems to imply that perfection or success is achievable, if appropriate remedies are applied. Indeed the response of many economists to market failure is not to reject the market mechanism as an allocater of resources and wealth, but to identify the source of the market failure and to correct it with appropriate policy instruments.

Other economists are wary of any policies that entail government intervention, on the grounds that the remedy may be worse than the disease. Their thesis is that political failures will only compound market failures. The market system, notwithstanding its failings, is still the most efficient social and economic organisation for the allocation of goods and resources. In the rest of this section we are going to look at a variety of private and public responses to the market failures that are externalities.

Spontaneous market remedies
••••••••••••••••••••••••••••••••••

A socially inefficient level of production or consumption takes place precisely because those causing the external effect are only concerned with their individual welfare. External costs or benefits do not form part of their calculations and do not inform their decisions. If they did, then the market outcome would be efficient. Expansion of firms sometimes results in the internalisation of the externality.

For example, if a farmer is also in the tourist trade, then he will bear in mind the effect of his agricultural activities on his tourist business, since he is hoping to derive profit from both activities. He will weigh up the benefits of fertilising his land with animal slurry (in terms of its potential contribution to agricultural profits) with the potential costs to his tourist trade if water pollution occurs. If he can predict both accurately, then the level of animal fertiliser that he applies to his land will be efficient. (This does of course presuppose that nobody else is affected by his activity.)

Educational remedies
....

These are often recommended in the context of activities that create negative externalities. Can the farmer be persuaded to exercise better control over the dangerous animal wastes that his farming practices produce? Can the general public be persuaded to abandon their cars and use more environmentally friendly methods of locomotion? Can firms be persuaded to locate in certain areas because it will be good for the local economy and for the social fabric of the community where they locate?

The answer depends on how one perceives the individual. If one accepts that individuals are inherently self-interested, then the answer is negative, unless of course there is some way that doing the socially appropriate thing is in one's own private interest. Yet there are many educational initiatives that are designed to inform people of the negative social consequences of many of their activities and to persuade them to act differently.

Such initiatives (which are usually publicly funded) are either naïvely motivated and a waste of public finances or they have some effect because to say that individuals are only self-interested is an oversimplification of a more complex reality. To the extent that individuals are social beings and that their identity is also associated with something beyond themselves (for example their community, their class or their country), then education has a role to play in reducing activities that generate negative externalities and increasing activities that generate positive externalities.

Economic remedies
....

Economic remedies are those that operate through the market mechanism. The market environment is summarised in the prices that individual economic agents (be they consumers or producers) face. If prices change because of government policies, then economic agents will adjust their consumption and production behaviour in a rational way in response to the new set of price signals.

Recall the market with negative production externalities that was depicted in Figure 7.2. The market equilibrium output was too high and the market price was too low. The socially optimal level of output was output level Q_2, where the marginal benefit to society of the last unit of the good sold equals the marginal cost to society of producing that good. However at output level Q_2, the producer's actual private costs are less than price, so he has an incentive to produce more of the good.

The only way that the producer (who is a rational economic agent) can be persuaded not to produce more than Q_2, would be if it were not in his private interest to produce a higher level of output. This will only be the case if at output level Q_2 the private marginal cost to the producer is equal to the price P_2. The government can make this happen if it levies a unit tax equal to the difference between marginal social cost and marginal private cost; in other words a unit tax equal to the vertical distance |EF|. This is the same as increasing the marginal private cost of production; that is to say, it shifts the MC curve upwards. The socially efficient tax will shift the MC curve upwards until it is the same as the MSC curve.

The revenue from this tax could then be used to compensate those who are negatively affected by the production activity. There would be a net gain to society as the true social cost savings of lowering output from Q_1 to Q_2 would exceed the loss in consumer welfare caused by lowering output from Q_1 to Q_2.

Conversely, when a production activity yields positive production externalities, the optimal government strategy is to subsidise production of the good so as to increase production from Q_1 to Q_2 (see Figure 7.4). This can be achieved by offering a subsidy per unit of output equal to the difference between the higher private marginal costs and the lower social marginal costs of production. If the unit subsidy is equal to the vertical distance between the market supply curve and the marginal social cost curve; that is to say |GH| then the producer will rationally respond to this change in his economic environment by expanding production to its socially optimal level Q_2. The producer's MC of production is now the same as the MSC of production, thanks to the producer subsidy that they receive.

The revenue required to pay for the subsidy could be collected from those reaping the external benefit from the externality. There would be a net gain to society as the increase in social cost from increasing output from Q_1 to Q_2 is less than the increase in consumer welfare.

Where economic interventions are concerned, it does not matter whether the cause of the externality is production or consumption, since market clearing (equilibrium) means that production equals consumption in a closed economy. Hence, when there is a negative consumption externality, such as depicted in Figure 7.5, the appropriate economic strategy is to tax production (or consumption) of the good in order to reduce consumption to socially efficient levels. In terms of Figure 7.5, the appropriate unit production tax is the difference between marginal private benefit and marginal social benefit (the vertical distance |NO|), and the optimal level of output is where marginal social benefit equals marginal social cost; that is to say output level Q_2.

Conversely, when the consumption externality is positive, as shown in Figure 7.6, the appropriate policy is to subsidise production (or consumption) of the good in order to increase consumption of the good to its socially efficient level. The appropriate unit subsidy is the difference between marginal social benefit and marginal private benefit (the vertical distance |PQ|).

Government taxes and subsidies that are designed to indirectly influence the level of production and consumption are known as Pigouvian taxes/subsidies after the British economist Pigou.[6] The main drawback of this approach is information. When negative or positive externalities occur, it is very difficult to know the precise extent of the inflicted damage or conferred benefit. Thus such measures may adjust output in the correct direction (assuming that external effects from an activity are *either* positive *or* negative but not both) but it seems highly unlikely that the post tax/subsidy level of output will be exactly where marginal social benefit equals marginal social cost.

Legal remedies
....

There is a variety of legal possibilities. Where negative externalities occur, these remedies could incorporate any of the following:

1. a ban on the activity that is generating the negative externality;
2. legally compelling the creator of the externality to engage in activities that eliminate or reduce the external effects that arise from his/her activities;
3. legally defining property rights, either to engage in an activity or to prevent an activity taking place, and allowing that property right to be traded.

Banning an activity is beneficial to those suffering the negative externality from the activity in question but such measures hurt those whose livelihood may depend on the activity that inadvertently causes the externality. We all know that certain farming practices damage the environment, as do too many cars in our cities! Yet very few individuals suggest abandoning totally these agricultural practices or propose a care-free environment. Why is this? It is a recognition of competing rights and the complex interaction between certain activities and their external effects. Farmers have a right to make a livelihood. Banning certain practices outright may make it more difficult for them to carry on farming successfully. Cars represented an amazing technological advance over previous means of transportation. In many ways, possession of a private car can greatly enhance the quality of the owner's lifestyle.

Unless the marginal social cost of an activity exceeds the marginal social benefit for all positive levels of that activity, then a complete ban on the same activity is an inefficient response, since it inflicts a greater hurt than benefit. It is only an appropriate response to activities that are deemed to have very large (or potentially large) negative external effects such as, for example, nuclear energy.

The second legal response allows the creator of the negative externality to continue to engage in their original production or consumption activities but obliges him to modify these activities in some way in order to minimise the external effects. This response usually has negative financial repercussions for the individual subject to the new laws governing their activities. Farmers may be required to build better storage facilities for animal wastes or all cars may have to have catalytic converters.

For legal measures to have the desired effect, there has to be some degree of monitoring combined with sanctions in the event of breaches of the law. The appropriateness of financially penalising the creators of negative externalities by obliging them to modify their behaviour is an ethical question. All laws, just like all economic policies, inevitably have redistribution effects. Sometimes governments give financial assistance to parties to help them to comply with new standards and legal obligations.

A third potential legal response owes its origin to Ronald Coase, who wrote a paper entitled 'The Problem of Social Cost'.[7] This paper affected the way economists, lawyers, philosophers and others think about externalities. Returning to our farmer example, the farmer's activity is harming fishermen and those in the tourist trade. Should the farmer be restrained? If the farmer is banned from spreading animal wastes on his land, then water pollution will not occur and fishermen and those in the tourist industry will be better off. However the farmer will be worse off. *Either way some party is hurt.*

Traditionally, laws tended to penalise the creator of the negative externality. What Coase pointed out was that it was not the farmer's explicit intention to harm those engaged in other activities; the harm inflicted is merely a by-product of an activity, the purpose of which is to maximise farm income. For Coase, the optimal solution is one that maximises net welfare; that is to say it is an empirical issue. If the gain to the farmer from polluting the environment outweighs the losses to those who are harmed by the pollution, then it is socially more efficient if the pollution is allowed to take place. Conversely, if the gain to the farmer is less than the costs imposed on others, then it is socially efficient if the activity causing the pollution does not take place.

Coase went on to argue that, if property rights are clearly defined, then the parties affected by the externality will bargain their way to an efficient solution. (This does of course pre-suppose that bargaining is not a costly activity.)

Let us suppose that the gain to the farmer from his pollution activities outweighs the costs to others adversely affected by his pollution activities. In addition, let us suppose that the law gives precedence to fishermen and those in the tourist trade. In other words, they have the right to a clean environment, which is so important to their livelihoods. In this situation, it pays the farmer to compensate fishermen etc. in order to be allowed to continue the activity that is so profitable to him. The farmer is still better off than he would be if he did not engage in the polluting activity. Fishermen and those in the tourist trade are adequately compensated in order to allow this polluting activity. Otherwise, they would not have waived their rights to a clean environment. The outcome is an efficient one, since it maximises joint net welfare.

If the law gives precedence to the farmer's right to a livelihood, then the parties will bargain to the same socially efficient outcome. The fishermen etc. will have to pay the farmer to produce less, and therefore pollute less. The process continues until there is no compensation that the fisherman can offer the farmer that will leave them better off. That is because the value of the damage inflicted on them is less than the value of the gain to the farmer from inflicting that damage. So regardless of who has the property rights, if bargaining is possible the outcome will be socially efficient.

From an efficiency perspective, it is a matter of indifference how the legal regime allocates property rights (be it the right to a clean environment or the right to pursue one's livelihood). From a distribution point of view, the allocation of property rights is fundamental to the welfare of the parties whose interests are at stake. Whichever party is given the property right, they are in possession of a valuable asset that has a market value and that can be traded. Hence, if the property right is to a clean environment, then the law favours those who need and value a clean environment and the farmer will have to pay for the right to pollute it. The converse is the case if the law favours the farmer and gives him the legal protection to pursue his livelihood as he sees fit. He is then in possession of a valuable income-earning asset which he can trade.

Solving the efficiency problems of externalities is not as straightforward as it might appear in theory. Again, one of the biggest problems is information; information as to the source or sources of the externality, information as to the size of the external effects and information of the value to the various parties of the continuance or non-continuance of the externality inducing activity.

For example, in Ireland there have been many cases of water pollution and fish-kills as a result of slurry run-off from land. It is not always easy to identify the individuals responsible, just as it is very difficult to put a value on unpolluted waters.

An additional aspect to the problem is the number of individuals or parties affected. Unpolluted water is valued by anglers. It is valued by those in the tourist industry, who trade on Ireland's image as an unspoilt environment. It is valued by bathers. It is valued by all those who value the environment for its own sake. There are so many individuals involved that bargaining is no longer a costless activity (a necessary condition for the Coase theorem to hold).

An additional problem (and one that commonly afflicts groups) is the incentive(s) that individuals have to free ride on the efforts of others. I might value a clean environment but if others fight the battle for me, then I might achieve my objective at little personal cost in terms of time and effort. This tendency to free ride on the efforts of others makes it difficult for individuals, who are affected by the externality in different ways, to organise their efforts in order to bargain their way to an efficient solution.

Even when there are few parties involved, another barrier to the efficient resolution of the problem of externalities is the existence of asymmetric information. If the law guarantees the right to unpolluted waters and a farmer wishes to negotiate that right with me, then I have an incentive to overstate the value that I place on a clean environment, especially if that increases my compensation when I trade that right. There are many examples where it is possible that this form of overstatement is taking place.

Many companies when they are legally required to take measures to prevent pollution will overstate the cost to them of the new measures and the potential cost to the economy in terms of lost jobs. This is rational behaviour if it allows them to gain a waiver from the restrictive measures.

A very contentious, contemporary issue is the proposed new light rail (LUAS) development in Dublin. While everyone agrees that something needs to be done to alleviate traffic problems in the city, the LUAS appears to be arousing strong negative feelings as well as positive feelings. Among the groups opposed to the scheme are some traders, who feel that their businesses will be adversely affected by the development, as well as those who represent the motor car trade. Most of the arguments centre on the disruption that the development will cause during the construction phase and a suggestion that going underground is a better alternative. While not claiming to know the motivation of all the groups opposed to the scheme, it would be naïve not to presume that there is some degree of overstatement (on the part of the groups opposed to LUAS) of potential economic losses that will ensue if LUAS goes ahead, and of the expected disruption during the construction phase.

So far we have looked at legal remedies to negative externalities but the law also has a role to play where positive externalities are involved. Many firms, in their pursuit of profit, develop new products and processes. The development of new products and processes is never a costless process. The problem arises because information is an extreme form of positive externality. It is in fact a public good (a category of good that will be looked at in more detail in the next section). This is a problem because firms would obviously be reluctant to invest in research and development if the product of that investment could be costlessly copied by competitors. Yet the positive social benefits which result from the development of new products and processes make these activities very desirable from an efficiency perspective.

The legal response is usually to give a patent to the inventor for a specific but finite period of time, that allows him or her to internalise the external effects of the invention. Eventually, patent rights expire and others can exploit the knowledge that was previously protected by patent. The law is therefore designed to encourage activities that give rise to positive external activities in the first place and, eventually, to ensure that the external effect is widespread.

7.5 Public goods

The classic reference for the pure theory of public goods is Paul Samuelson (1954, 1955).[8] A characteristic of private goods is *rivalry* in consumption. If individual 1 consumes a good, then individual 2 cannot consume the same good: the good has finite properties. A public good, by contrast, is *non-rival* in consumption. Street lighting is a public good: its existence gives me utility by enabling me to see at night. However my consumption of street lighting does not reduce the amount of street lighting available for anybody else.

Another feature of private goods is their *excludability*. When a good is in my possession, I can exclude others from consuming that good. This capacity for exclusion is what enables me to sell my good for a positive price. If someone is not willing to pay me the price for the good that I demand, then I can prevent them from consuming the good in my possession.

By contrast many public goods have the characteristic of *non-excludability* or they are excludable at prohibitively high costs. It is not possible to prevent someone from consuming street lighting if they fail to pay for it. It is precisely this feature of non-excludability that renders the private market unsuitable for public good provision. No potential producer has any incentive to incur the costs necessary to provide public goods if a price cannot be charged for consuming the same goods. To the extent that public good consumption improves the utility of individuals and that the increase in aggregate utility for all concerned exceeds the cost of providing the public good, then on efficiency grounds it should be provided. If the market does not provide the good, then the market is not an efficient mechanism for maximising human welfare.

A feature of private goods is that individuals consume them in different quantities according to their preferences. A feature of public goods is that all individuals have to consume the public good in the same quantity regardless of their preferences. The marginal utility of the last unit consumed of a private good is the same for everyone, since all individuals face the same price and all maximise utility by consuming a good in such quantities that marginal utility equals price. By contrast, the marginal utility from consuming the last unit of a public good will differ among individuals. The market demand curve for a private good is derived by *horizontally* summing together individual demand curves. For each potential price, market demand is calculated from individual demands.

This procedure does not make sense for a public good since all individuals have to consume the same amount. Yet individuals value the public good differently. Some are willing to pay a high price as a reflection of the utility that they derive from it. Others are only willing to pay a low price for the good. In order to estimate the benefit that the public good yields to the public, we have to *vertically* sum together individual demand curves.

An individual demand curve can be interpreted in two ways. On the one hand, it shows us the quantity that a utility-maximising individual will consume at different prices. On the other hand, it shows us how much individuals are willing to pay for each successive unit of the good. Marginal willingness to pay must be a reflection of marginal utility from consumption, if individuals are rational utility maximisers. Vertically summing individual demand curves gives us group marginal willingness to pay for different levels of the public good. The efficient level of output of a public good is where the group marginal willingness to pay equals the marginal cost of providing the last unit of the public good.

Figure 7.7 illustrates how the market demand curve is derived when the market consists of only two individuals, individual 1 and individual 2, both of whom value the public good differently. When the marginal cost of providing the good is given by the supply curve S, then the optimal level of output of the public good is Q*, where marginal cost equals the combined marginal benefits to both individuals.

Many public goods have the characteristic that the marginal cost of provision is zero, since most of the cost of providing the good is a fixed cost. In this instance, the optimal level of output is Q** and the optimal price that should be charged at this level of output is zero, the same as marginal cost.

Figure 7.7: Constructing a demand curve for a public good

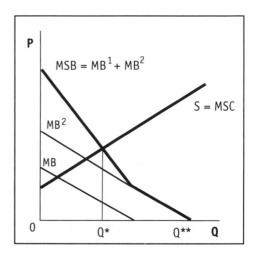

In reality, it is hard to find genuine examples of pure public goods. Coole National Park is an example of a public good; my enjoyment of what it has to offer should not diminish the enjoyment that others get from this unique environment. Yet if enough individuals decide that they want to experience Coole, this will affect my utility. Congestion will occur and consumption is no longer non-rival.

Likewise, there are ways and means of excluding individuals from consuming what is essentially a public good. The capacity to exclude depends on legal arrangements and on the state of technology. A law could be passed allowing Coole National Park to be fenced off and only those willing to pay would be permitted to enjoy what it has to offer.

Technological advances can also mean that the cost of excluding non-subscribers or non-payers is dramatically reduced. Excluding those who do not pay their television licences from watching RTE 1 and Network 2 is a difficult task, since all you need is an aerial to view these channels. Excluding non-subscribers to cable television from watching cable television is now a relatively inexpensive procedure, thanks to the technological advance that is cable.

Once exclusion is possible, then a price can be charged for use and private provision becomes a viable option. Private beaches and toll bridges are but two examples of public goods that have been made inaccessible to non-payers thanks to the possibility of exclusion.

7.6 Public good provision

The inability to exclude individuals from benefiting from a public good would appear to indicate that self-interested individuals would not be willing to pay for that good. The logic of self-interest implies that individuals would free-ride; that is to say they would hope to benefit from the provision of the good without having to pay for it. If all individuals behave in a rational self-interested fashion, then the good will not be provided, unless it is possible to finance provision in some compulsory fashion, such as taxation. Yet private provision of public goods does exist and not just where exclusion is possible.

Private donations
....

Many individuals give of their resources in order to provide public goods. For example, it is quite normal for individuals to donate money to support their local church, community centre, library etc. Money is not the only resource; many people give of their time in order to improve the quality of their local community. (Think of all the voluntary clubs or of the tidy towns competition.)

Why don't individuals free-ride and let others make the donations and let others put in the effort to provide goods from which all can benefit? Presumably some individuals do free-ride. However, it is interesting that many do not behave in what is deemed to be a rational, self-interested fashion.

Of course it may be that individuals perceive that their private contributions make a difference to the level of public-good provision and that the private utility that they get from the increase in the public good outweighs the value of their donation. This would be rational, utility-maximising behaviour. It may be that giving of one's time to the local community brings non-pecuniary rewards in the form of social approval. This could also be deemed rational utility-maximising behaviour.

This still does not explain why individuals make donations when the marginal effect of their donation is negligible and when, as is often the case, the donation is anonymous. Either their behaviour is not governed by narrow self-interest or they have a concept of rational behaviour that differs from that of narrowly self-interested man. If one's sense of identity is not completely individualistic, for example one may identify with their local community, then there is no conflict between what is in one's own interest and what is in the interest of the local community.

This could explain donations to help maintain the local community centre. But what about individuals who pay their TV licence or honestly declare all their income to the Revenue Commissioners (when they could get away with doing otherwise) or who make a contribution to help bone marrow research? Is this due to a broader sense of identity? It certainly could be (although one would expect the social identity to be stronger at local level) but it could also be due to a different concept of rationality. This individual could rationalise as follows: I could potentially derive utility from medical research, I would prefer if I did not have to pay but then if everybody reasoned in a like-minded fashion, there would be no research and no potential future benefits to me or to anyone else. Therefore in order to be consistent, I must behave as I would wish others to behave, which prompts me to ignore narrow self-interest and to contribute to the broader community.

Club membership is another example of a private market response to the demand for public goods. Usually the marginal cost of using the public good may be negligible but the cost of providing the good in the first place may be quite high. (Think of golf clubs.) The response is for a number of individuals to form a club and to make donations to the club in order to finance the provision of the good. Obviously a good such as a golf club is not a pure public good, in the sense that it is feasible to exclude non-members from benefiting from the good. The success or otherwise of private club provision of public goods usually depends on the size of their membership and on the size of the contribution necessary in order to provide the public good. Free-riding behaviour is more difficult, the smaller the club membership, as identification of the free-rider is more likely.

Government provision
....

Traditionally pure public goods such as national defence, street lighting, roads, clean water supply etc. were provided by central or local government and paid for by taxation. This is one way around the free-rider problem, to the extent that taxation is compulsory and universal. It does not, of course, ensure that the level of public good provision is optimal. As shown in Figure 7.7, the optimal level of that public good is Q^{**}, when the marginal cost of providing the good is zero. It is rational to provide that level of the good provided that the value of the utility to all individuals who consume the good exceeds the total cost of providing the good. Let us assume that this is the case.

How then should the tax burden be distributed among individuals? In an ideal world, taxation should be proportional to private benefit gained from the provision of that good. This does not work in reality because, firstly, it would involve a very complex taxation system; and, secondly, each individual would have an incentive to understate the value to them of the public good in order to minimise their tax burden. The net effect would be the under-provision of the public good.

An alternative approach is to decide in advance that, if a public project goes ahead, then everyone will have to pay a pre-determined amount towards its construction. Everyone is then asked the value they place on the public good, in order to determine whether the summation of individual benefits exceeds the cost of providing the good.

The problem with this approach is that everyone has an incentive to overstate the value to them of the good, if they value the good more highly than their pre-determined individual contribution. There is no cost to such behaviour and it could involve getting more of the good, which would be welfare enhancing to the individual concerned. Alternatively, if they value the good less than their pre-determined contribution, they have an incentive to state that the value they place on the good is zero, since that will increase the probability that the good will not be provided, which would be welfare-maximising for this individual. Either way, individuals do not have an incentive to truly reveal their preferences.

Demand revelation mechanisms
....

It is almost impossible to determine precisely the optimal level of public good provision. This is because of asymmetric information; only the individual knows the value he or she places on public goods such as, for example, a clean or a safe environment. This is information that they may not be willing to share with others, if dissemination of that knowledge reduces their consumer surplus by increasing their fee/donation/tax burden as a consequence. There are different mechanisms designed to extract this information from individuals.

Majority voting

There is a well-established literature on the efficiency of voting as a mechanism to determine the optimal mix of publicly provided goods and the optimal level of public good provision. It is also well established in the literature that such mechanisms do not work well. Crafty politicians are adept at manipulating the electoral agenda in order to get the outcomes that they most desire.

Also, when individuals are voting on the level of provision of a public good, the outcome will always be determined by the median voter. That is not necessarily efficient, since it does not guarantee an outcome where the optimal level of the public good is determined by the value of the good to the average individual (unless of course the median voter is also the average voter). If the value of the good to the median voter is less than the value of the good to the average voter, then the good will be under-provided. The converse is the case when the value of the good to the median voter is greater than the value of the good on average. This result occurs because each individual has one vote and each vote has equal weight, regardless of how strongly each individual feels about the provision or non-provision of the public good in question.

Revealed preference methods

One may not be able to get individuals to honestly declare their preferences, but in some instances the value they place on certain public goods can be inferred from their behaviour, if their consumption of that good is linked to private market behaviour.

For example, the time and cost that individuals spend in travelling to a national park or beach or nature reserve can give some indication of the value to them of that public good, so travel cost can be treated as a proxy for price.

Why do two identical houses located in different areas sell for different prices? Why do individuals pay a premium to live in a safe neighbourhood, in a neighbourhood with public amenities, near a park, or near the sea? The premium that they are willing to pay for an identical house must reflect the value to them of safety, public amenities, the park, and the sea.

Methods of indirectly inferring the value that individuals place on existing public goods are not without their flaws. These methods are dependent upon the existence of complementary markets for private goods. The cost that one is willing to incur to travel to a natural amenity or the premium that one pays to live in a certain location could very easily (and probably does) understate the value to the individual of the public good that they are consuming. Also, such methods are not suitable for all public goods, since not all public-good consumption has a related and complementary private-good consumption. The advantage of revealed preference methods is that they focus on what people actually do (as opposed to what people claim they do) and use behaviour to infer preferences.

Summary

1. Perfectly competitive markets ensure that there is no waste in the allocation of resources and goods. This presupposes that everyone is a price taker and that the private benefit/cost from an activity equals the social benefit/cost.
2. Externalities occur when the activities of a firm or individual inadvertently affect the welfare of others. Externalities are not transmitted through the market. When externalities are present, the market outcome is not efficient; that is to say, there is waste.
3. Positive externalities occur when the production or consumption of a good enhances the welfare of others. When externalities are positive, then the market outcome will result in either under-production or under-consumption of the good generating the externality. Negative externalities occur when the production or consumption of a good reduces the welfare of others. When externalities are negative, then the market outcome will result in either over-production or over-consumption of the good generating the externality. Inefficient levels of production or consumption occur when externalities are present because the firms or individuals causing the externality do not take into account the effect of their activities on other parties.
4. Government intervention can improve the efficiency of markets that generate externalities. The principal forms of intervention are the use of economic and/or legal instruments. Interfering with the price mechanism through indirect taxation or subsidisation is an economic response to the problem of externalities. The law can either defend the rights of those generating the externality, or defend the rights of those affected by the externality. If the law, as well as assigning property rights, also allows the parties involved to trade their legal rights, then the parties involved could bargain their way to an efficient solution. Parties will bargain their way to an efficient solution, provided that property rights are clearly assigned and that the transactions costs involved in bargaining are negligible. This result is known as the Coase theorem.

5. Public goods are an extreme form of externality. They are goods that are non-rival in consumption, in the sense that consumption by one individual does not reduce potential consumption by other individuals. They are also non-excludable, in the sense that it is impossible or prohibitively expensive to prevent someone from consuming a public good. Private markets will either not produce the public good or will under-produce the good. Either way, the private-market outcome is inefficient, which is why most public goods are provided by government and paid for via taxation.

6. A major difficulty in correcting market failures, such as externalities and public goods, is insufficient information about the effects of such market failures on the welfare of individuals. This problem is not easy to overcome since individuals often have an economic incentive not to be honest in such instances.

Key terms

Market efficiency
Marginal social benefit
Marginal social cost
Negative production externalities
Positive production externalities
Negative consumption externalities
Positive consumption externalities
Pigouvian taxes/subsidies
Coase theorem
Public goods
Non-rivalry
Non-excludability
Demand revelation mechanisms

Review questions

1. Explain what is meant by externalities and why it is that the market, if left to its own devices, will not be efficient when externalities are present.
2. Discuss and assess the different remedies designed to correct the market failure of externalities.
3. When the marginal cost of producing a public good is zero, why is it inefficient to exclude anyone from access to that good?

PART II

MACROECONOMICS

INTRODUCTION TO MACROECONOMICS

Macroeconomics is concerned with the operation of the economy as a whole. In this branch of economics, we deal with aggregate variables such as national output, the general price level and total employment. Arising out of our study of macroeconomics is an appreciation of policy issues.

Our starting point in macroeconomics is the measurement of economic activity. Chapter 8 examines the different ways of measuring economic activity. The problems associated with the National Accounts are also discussed.

The two main doctrines of economic thought are outlined in Chapter 9. The classical school of economics dates back to Adam Smith. The Keynesian revolution challenged the existing economic orthodoxy of the time.

In Chapter 10, the Keynesian model of income determination is explained. The policy implications arising out of the Keynesian model are also discussed. The chapter ends with an account of the Irish experience with Keynesian economics.

In a non-barter economy, transactions are facilitated by money. The money stock and interest rates are important variables in any modern economy. Monetary policy is a policy instrument used by government to achieve various economic objectives. Chapter 11 examines the role of money in the economy.

A model of the macroeconomy is presented in Chapter 12. The IS/LM model is a useful framework to explain fiscal and monetary policies and to examine the divergent views of Keynesians and monetarists.

A more complex model of the macroeconomy is examined in Chapter 13. Prices and output are determined in the AD/AS model. This framework can be used to analyse macroeconomic problems and policy options.

Chapter 14 introduces open economy macroeconomics. Our examination of macroeconomics until now has been largely within the confines of a closed economy. This chapter analyses the effect which factors such as external trade, foreign interest rates and flexible exchange rates have on the economy. It also examines Ireland's experience and performance within the European Monetary System. The wider issue of Economic and Monetary Union is also discussed.

Chapter 15 examines a number of important macroeconomic issues. Unemployment, inflation and international trade are discussed in the context of a small open economy. Some policy options are also examined.

CHAPTER 8

MEASURING THE MACROECONOMY

'Among the most effective measures of the economic performance of a nation is its total net product, or national income – the sum of all goods produced during a given period . . .'[1]

Simon Kuznets (1901–85)

'For, unlike many measurements in the physical sciences, there is no unique way of measuring either the size of an economy at a particular point in time, or its growth over time.'[2]

Paul Ormerod

'Several attempts have been made to devise new indices that rectify some of GNP's defects as a measure of economic welfare, although no one has got anywhere close to building one that measures human welfare as a whole.'[3]

Richard Douthwaite

Chapter objectives

Upon completing this chapter, the student should understand:

- the circular flow model of economic activity;
- the different ways of measuring economic activity;
- the meaning of gross domestic product (GDP) and other similar measures of economic activity;
- the shortcomings of GDP as a measure of economic activity;
- the Irish National Accounts.

Outline

8.1 The circular flow of economic activity
8.2 The three methods for measuring economic activity
8.3 The National Income Accounts
8.4 Limitations of GDP as a measure of economic activity
8.5 The Irish experience

Introduction

This chapter begins with the circular flow model of economic activity. Although it is a very simple model, it introduces all of the principal agents in the economy: households, firms, financial institutions, the state and foreign markets. The model also explains how these sectors interact.

We use this model to introduce the three ways by which economic activity is measured. Gross domestic product (GDP), the most common measure of economic activity, is explained in detail. GDP is often used as a measure of national economic activity and as a basis of international comparisons. Its defects as a measure of prosperity are also discussed.

The chapter ends with an analysis of the Irish National Accounts as published by the Central Statistics Office (CSO).

8.1 The circular flow of economic activity

The circular flow is a simplified model of the economy showing the movement of resources between consumers and producers. The French economist François Quesnay (1694–1774) is credited with its discovery.[4] It is believed that he modelled it on William Harvey's famous circulation of blood diagram.

A modern economy is very complex. There are many different sectors (households, firms, government, financial, foreign) with each sector comprised of many interacting individual units. In order to understand this sophisticated system we need to begin with a simple model.

We begin with a model of the private sector: households and firms. These are identifiable not by who they are but by what they do: households consume whereas firms produce. In a simple, closed economy the only transactions are between households and firms. The result is a model of the economy which shows the transactions between households and firms. This model is called the circular flow and is illustrated in Figure 8.1.

Figure 8.1: The circular flow between households and firms

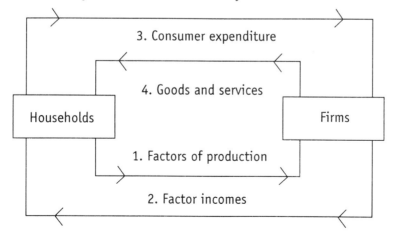

It is the households who own the basic factors of production. These inputs are supplied to the firms (1) in order to produce goods and services. The firms pay the households factor incomes for the use of these inputs (2). There is a special term given to each return on the different factors of production: wages are the return on labour, interest on capital, rent on land and profit on enterprise. Households receive the factor incomes and use them to buy goods and services from the firms (3). These goods and services are supplied by the firms to the households (4).

The transactions between households and firms are reflected in the loops drawn above. There is a distinction between the inner loop and the outer loop. Flows 1 and 4 (the inner loop) reflect the transfer of real or non-monetary resources. Flows 2 and 3 (the outer loop) reflect the transfer of money or monetary payments.

In this simple model all output is sold (output = expenditure) and all income is spent (income = expenditure). Thus, output must equal income (output = income). These equalities are discussed again in the next section of this chapter.

The transactions, in terms of the agent involved, are summarised in Table 8.1.

Table 8.1: Summary of transactions between households and firms

Households	Firms
Supply factors of production to firms.	Use factors of production to produce goods and services.
Receive factor income in return for inputs.	Pay households for use of inputs.
Spend income on goods and services.	Sell goods and services to households.

The simple circular flow can be modified to include the banking sector. In the above analysis, the households spend all of their factor incomes on goods and services. In Figure 8.2 below the households are faced with two options: to spend on goods and services or to save. One of the functions of the banking system in the circular flow is to facilitate savings. However, savings is a leakage or a withdrawal from the circular flow. A leakage is simply a movement of funds out of the circular flow. This can diminish the level of economic activity in the economy. A simple example is illustrated below.

Let us suppose income is equal to £10,000 and households save 20% of their income. Spending is now limited to £8,000 (80% of £10,000). In these circumstances there are no economic incentives for firms to continue producing £10,000 worth of goods since their sales on the domestic market (no foreign sector exists so there is no possibility of exporting goods to foreign markets) are limited to the £8,000 which households are prepared to spend. The value of output produced is limited to £8,000. Consequently the income generated is limited to £8,000. If we assume that households still save 20% of their income, spending in the next round is reduced to £6,400 (80% of £8,000). This process continues with the level of economic activity diminishing further with every round. This appears quite alarming and we might question whether there is any escape from this vicious circle. An escape exists in the form of 'investment expenditure' which is an injection into the circular flow. An injection is a movement of funds into the circular flow: it is an addition to economic activity. The term 'investment' was defined in Chapter 6. It is the corporate or business expenditure on machinery, fixtures and fittings, vehicles and buildings. It also includes inventory build-ups of raw materials, semi-finished and finished goods. Firms may finance investment expenditure by borrowing from the very same financial institutions which facilitated those households who had surplus funds and decided to save a percentage of their income. The borrowing facility is the other main function of the banking system. Financial institutions serve as intermediaries to bring together those who have excess funds (households) and those who are in need of funds (firms).

Figure 8.2: The circular flow, savings and investment

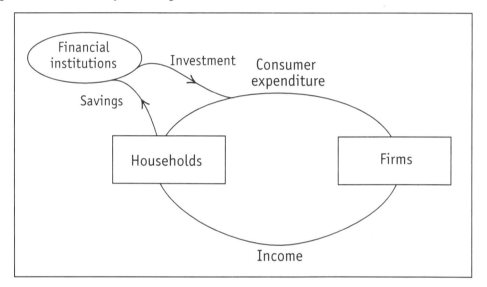

If savings are greater than investment in money terms the level of economic activity diminishes. However, if investment is greater than savings the level of economic activity increases. The level of economic activity remains unchanged if savings are matched by investment: the economy is said to be in equilibrium. See Appendix 8.1 for more material on this subject.

The circular flow with savings and investment is now adjusted to include the government or the public sector. The government is involved in spending large amounts of money on defence, security, education, health services and so on. It also spends money on transfer payments.

● Definition
● ● ● ● ● ●

Transfer payments redistribute wealth rather than provide a unique good or service. They include pensions, unemployment benefits, disability allowances and other payments.

All of these forms of expenditure are injections into the circular flow. However, these expenditures need to be financed. It is government revenue, primarily in the form of taxation, which finances such expenditure. Taxation, both direct and indirect, is a leakage from the circular flow.[5] The adjusted circular flow is illustrated in Figure 8.3 below.

Figure 8.3: The circular flow including the government

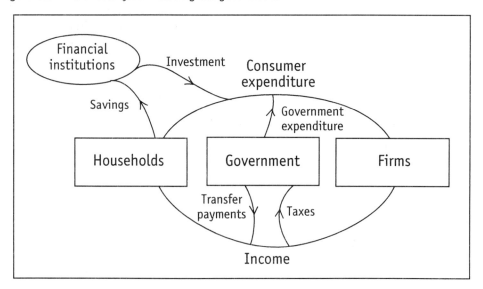

There is one final adjustment to be made to the circular flow model. International trade between countries is a very important part of total expenditure. The analysis to date, for the purposes of simplicity, was applied to a closed economy. We now adjust the model to include foreign markets. Exports and imports are included in the model. Export earnings are a monetary flow from the foreign market into the domestic market. Hence, it is an injection into the circular flow. Payment for imports is a monetary flow from the domestic market into the foreign market: it is a leakage out of the circular flow. The difference between exports and imports is referred to as net exports. Its value is positive if the value of exports exceeds the value of imports. It is negative if the value of imports exceeds the value of exports.

Figure 8.4: The complete circular flow

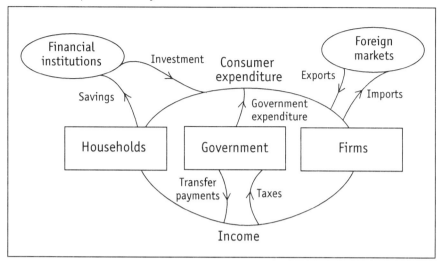

Figure 8.4 is the complete version of the circular flow diagram. All agents and their transactions with each other are included. A more complete explanation is now required.

On receipt of the factors of production from the households, the firms engage in the production of goods and services. The income which the firms pay out is reflected in the lower loop of the diagram.

In a simple model without government intervention or a banking sector, as represented in Figure 8.1, the households receive and, in turn, spend all of the national income. However, the introduction of the government sector ensures that the households do not receive all of the national income. The amount which the households actually receive is referred to as personal disposable income. This is national income supplemented by transfer payments but excluding personal taxes. On receipt of this income, the households allocate a certain amount to savings. The rest is allocated to consumer expenditure.

The upper loop shows that consumer expenditure is only one form of expenditure. Others include investment expenditure by the corporate sector, public expenditure by the government, expenditure on domestic goods and services by non-residents, and expenditure on foreign goods and services.

There were no leakages or injections in our simple model. The analysis is a little more complicated when we extend the model to include other sectors. In Figure 8.4 savings, taxation and imports constitute the leakages whereas investment, government expenditure, transfer payments and exports constitute the injections. Economic activity depends largely on the relative size of these injections and leakages.

National income is one measure of economic activity. An important difference between the leakages and the injections is their respective relationship with national income. Leakages are endogenous variables. This means that they vary with one of the other components of the model. In this particular case, the level of savings, the tax revenue collected and the amount of goods imported will all increase when national income increases. There is a functional relationship between these variables and national income.

In contrast, all four injections are independent of the income level. They are exogenous. They are part of the model in that they affect the level of national income. However, their values are determined by variables which are outside the model. For example, investment depends on expectations about the future and the interest rate. Government spending and transfer payments are determined within the political process. Exports increase or decrease with foreign income. These variables are not a function of national income. This subtle difference between leakages and injections is fundamental to the stability of the economy. This issue will be discussed in greater detail in Chapter 10.

In relation to the leakages and injections in the economy three possibilities arise and are summarised in Table 8.2.

Table 8.2: Injections, leakages and their effect on economic activity

Injections		Leakages	Effect on economic activity
Injections	<	leakages	decreases
Injections	>	leakages	increases
Injections	=	leakages	unchanged

If the leakages are greater than the injections, in money terms, the level of economic activity diminishes. If the injections are greater than the leakages the level of economic activity increases. The level of economic activity remains unchanged if the leakages and the injections are equal. The economy is said to be in equilibrium.

This completes our study of the circular flow model. We will now examine the ways in which economic activity is actually measured.

8.2 The three methods for measuring economic activity

There are three approaches to measuring the economic activity of a country. These are portrayed in Figure 8.5.

Figure 8.5: A simplified version of the circular flow

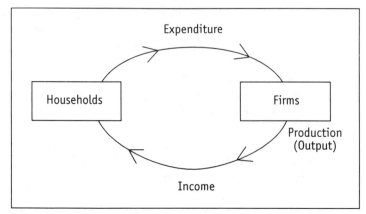

Figure 8.5 is a simplified version of the circular flow. It highlights the three approaches for measuring national economic activity. It indicates that the factors of production are combined to produce *output*. In turn, the factors of production are paid *income* which then becomes *expenditure*. These are the three methods for measuring a nation's economic activity. As we will see later they are defined in such a way that they should yield the same result. In practice they usually give slightly different results due to measurement errors which arise from the difficulty in collecting and tabulating all of the data involved.

Explanations for all three are provided below. All three approaches are published annually by the CSO in the report entitled *National Income and Expenditure*.[6] For our purpose the most important is the expenditure approach because many subsequent chapters in this textbook incorporate material which is largely based on this method of calculation.

Expenditure method
....

National expenditure is the sum of the expenditures of consumers, firms, government and the foreign sector on domestically produced goods and services. Given its importance and size, one may be surprised to find that the figure for consumer expenditure in Ireland is a residual.[7] Hence, revisions to investment, government spending or net exports impact largely on the estimate for consumer expenditure. To quote *National Income and Expenditure* 'This item . . . must bear the brunt of errors in the other constituents . . .'[8]

Table 8.3 shows the calculation of national income using the expenditure approach for the calendar year 1995. The numbers in the column on the left-hand side are the item numbers used by the CSO.[9]

Table 8.3: Measuring economic activity in Ireland using the expenditure method

	Description	£m
55	Personal consumption of goods and services	22,055
56	Net expenditure by public authorities on current goods and services	5,883
57	Gross domestic fixed capital formation	6,031
58	Value of physical changes in stocks	94
59	Exports of goods and services	30,016
60	less Imports of goods and services	–25,463
61	Gross domestic product at market prices	38,616
14	Net factor income from the rest of the world	–4,815
63	Gross national product at current market prices	33,801
24	less Provision for depreciation	–3,671
	Net national product at market prices	30,130
26	less Taxes on expenditure	–6,067
27	plus Subsidies	1,650
15	Net national product at factor cost = National income	25,713

Source: CSO, *National Income and Expenditure 1995*, July 1996.

Income method
··················

Alternately, national income is derived by adding the different incomes of the factors of production: wages and salaries, income from the self-employed, profit of companies and rent of dwellings (imputed in the case of owner-occupied). In Ireland it is based on data collected by the Revenue Commissioners for the purpose of income tax assessment. The calculation of national income for the year 1995 as published by the CSO is shown in Table 8.4.

Table 8.4: Measuring economic activity in Ireland using the income method

	Description	£m
	Income from agriculture, forestry and fishing:	
1	Agricultural profits etc.	2,246
2/3	Agricultural wages/contribution to social insurance	227
	Non-agricultural income:	
4/6	Company profits	10,607
7	Adjustment for stock appreciation	–399
8/9	Rent	1,501
10	Wages, salaries and pensions	16,740
11	Employers' contribution to social insurance	1,192
12	Adjustment for financial services	–1,588
13	Net domestic product at factor cost	30,528
14	Net factor income from the rest of the world	–4,815
15	Net national product at factor cost = National income	25,713

Source: CSO, *National Income and Expenditure 1995,* July 1996.

Output method
··················

To arrive at a figure for national output, the CSO adds together the money value of the output produced from the various sectors of the economy. The source of data is the annual *Census of Production.* There is the danger of double or multiple counting when adopting this approach.

● Definition
● ● ● ● ● ●

Double counting occurs if the expenditure on intermediate goods is included in the calculation of national output.

National output does not consist of the full value of every single item produced in the economy since the output of one good may be the input for another.

For example, a farmer may sell his cow at the market to a retail outlet for £800. The cow is slaughtered, packaged and sold for the retail value of £1,000. A straight summation of transactions suggests that national output has increased by £1,800. In this case, national output would be overstated because the value of the cow has been double counted. The cow is the input for the retail meat trade. The addition to national output is actually £1,000.

In order to avoid double counting one of two methods can be used. Firstly, we can sum the value added at each stage of production. Secondly, the final value of all finished goods can be calculated with the value of all intermediate goods excluded. Since the sum of all the value added at each stage of production must equal the value of the final output produced, these two methods yield the same figure. Table 8.5 consists of the national output calculations as published by the CSO for the year 1995.

Table 8.5: Measuring economic activity in Ireland using the output method

	Description	£m
16	Agriculture, forestry and fishing	2,475
17	Industry	11,904
18	Distribution, transport and communication	5,210
19	Public administration and defence	1,812
20	Other domestic	11,113
21	Adjustment for stock appreciation	−399
22	Adjustment for financial services	−1,588
23	Net domestic product at factor cost	30,528
29	Net factor income from the rest of the world	−4,815
15	Net national product at factor cost = National income	25,713

Source: CSO, *National Income and Expenditure 1995*, July 1996.

Figure 8.6 summarises graphically the three ways of measuring the level of national economic activity.

Figure 8.6: The three methods of measuring economic activity

INCOME	OUTPUT	EXPENDITURE
Self-employment	Others	Net exports
Profit		Government expenditure
Rent	Agriculture	Investment expenditure
	Pub. adm & def	
Wages and Salaries	Dist, tran & comm	Consumer expenditure
	Industry	

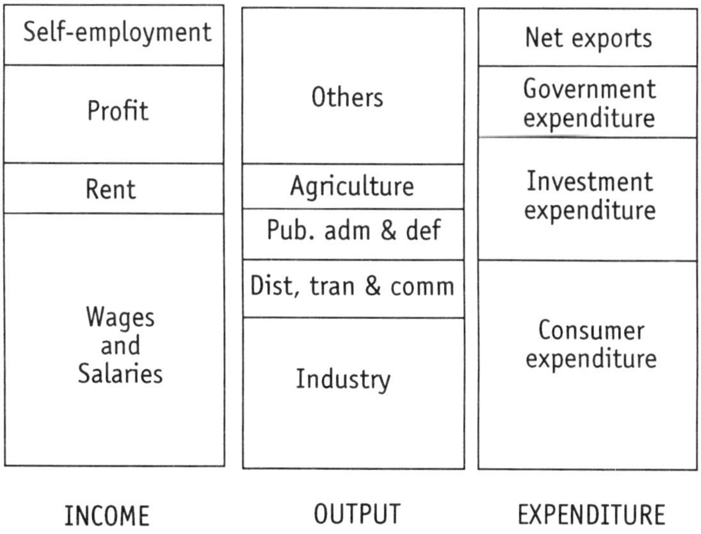

We will now define the various measures of economic activity which appear in the National Accounts.

8.3 The National Income Accounts

Simon Kuznets of Harvard University developed the national income accounting system which provided the first framework for measuring economic activity.[10] The key concept in the national income accounts and the most common measure of a country's economic performance is gross domestic product.

Definition
● ● ● ● ● ●

Gross domestic product (GDP) is the value of all goods and services produced domestically in the economy, regardless of the nationality of the owners of the factors of production.

GDP includes the value of output produced by subsidiaries of foreign multinationals operating in Ireland. The output of Irish multinationals operating outside the country is excluded. GDP is a flow concept i.e. it is the value of goods and services produced over a particular time period. In Ireland it is measured on a yearly basis. In 1995 the CSO estimate for GDP was £38.6bn.

There are many different variations to GDP, outlined in Figure 8.7. The figure also highlights the differences between the calculation of GDP and disposable income, another economic measure which is frequently used.

Figure 8.7: From GDP to disposable income

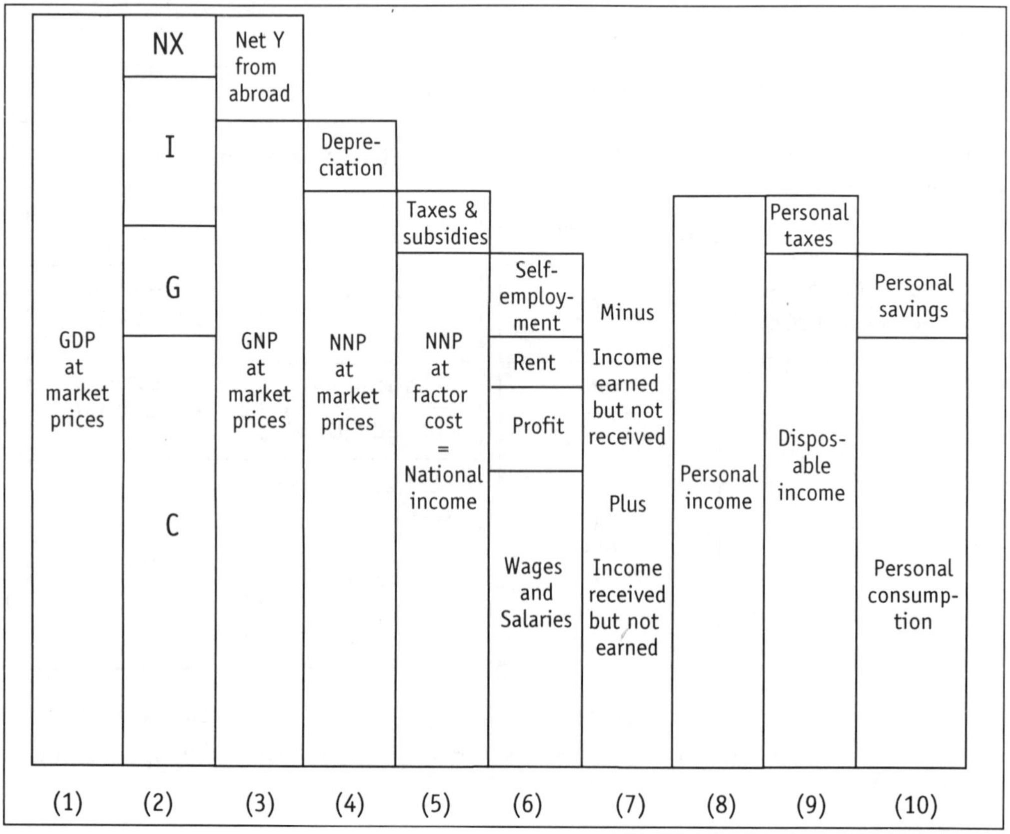

Composition of GDP
....

GDP is comprised of consumer expenditure, investment expenditure, government expenditure on goods and services and net exports (exports less imports), as shown in columns 1 and 2 in Figure 8.7.

• Consumer expenditure, or simply consumption (C) is spending by the household sector on durable and non-durable goods and services.[11] The CSO estimates that consumer expenditure for 1995 was £22bn, accounting for 57% of GDP. It is by far the largest component of GDP. However, in comparison to other western economies, the percentage of total expenditure devoted to consumption in Ireland is not high. Table 8.6 shows comparable percentages for other countries.

Table 8.6: Consumption as a percentage of GDP, 1992 (US$bn)

Country	GDP	Consumption/GDP
US	5,920	67
UK	903	64
Belgium	219	63
France	1,320	60
Japan	3,671	57
Ireland	43	56
Germany	1,789	54

Source: UNDP, *Human Development Report 1995.*

Research on this dominant component of GDP suggests that it is dependent on a range of factors including income, wealth, advertising, prices and expectations. These factors and their relationship with consumer expenditure are discussed in greater detail in Chapter 10.

• Investment expenditure (I), or to use its full title gross domestic fixed capital formation, is the total outlay on all capital goods. This category of goods includes machinery, factories, vehicles and so on. All new buildings and all construction work on roads, harbours, airports, forestry development and so on is included. It also includes new home spending. Although the contribution to a single year's GDP is small relative to consumption, investment expenditure is viewed as the key to long-run economic activity. In 1995 investment expenditure was over £6bn, accounting for almost 16% of GDP. This component of GDP is more volatile than any other and therefore more difficult to predict. Its volatility is primarily due to the factors which influence it. These include expectations and interest rates, two factors which are known to fluctuate wildly.

• Government expenditure, denoted by G, measures spending by the state on current goods and services. The CSO estimate for 1995 was £5.9bn. This accounts for over 15% of GDP. It is important to note that transfer payments are excluded from this component as they do not involve payment in exchange for production. Central government expenditure as a percentage of GDP varies significantly from economy to economy. In former centrally planned economies the ratio was normally high. Although the figures have fallen in recent years, the percentage of current government spending to GDP in 1992 for the Russian Federation and Kazakhstan were 23 and 30 respectively. In market economies the corresponding figures are somewhat smaller. Examples include Japan and the US where the percentages were 9 and 18 respectively for 1992.[12]

• Net exports, denoted by NX, is the difference between the exports and the imports of goods and services. Net exports can be positive, reflecting a trade surplus where the value of exports exceeds the value of imports; or negative, reflecting a trade deficit where the value of imports exceeds the value of exports. In Ireland the ratio of exports or imports to GDP is very high. In 1995 the ratio of exports to GDP was 78% whereas the ratio of imports to GDP was 66%. This reflects the extreme openness of the Irish economy. As a result, Ireland is an economy which is very susceptible to changes in the international economic climate. This component of GDP is determined by a wide range of factors including the level of domestic and foreign income, exchange rates and relative inflation rates.

GDP is the sum of consumer expenditure, investment expenditure, government expenditure and net exports and can be expressed as follows:[13]

$$\text{GDP} \equiv \text{C} + \text{I} + \text{G} + \text{NX} \qquad \text{[8.1]}$$

where the symbol $\equiv$ denotes an identity. An identity is something that is true by definition.

Variations of GDP
....

One variation of GDP is gross national product.

Definition
● ● ● ● ● ●

Gross national product (GNP) is the value of all goods and services produced by a country's citizens regardless of their geographical location.

In 1995, Ireland's GNP was valued at £33.8bn.

Values for GNP and for GDP in Ireland for the period 1970–95 are recorded in Appendix 8.2.

Although GDP is used for comparison with other EU countries, GNP is probably a better measure of Irish economic activity. GNP reflects only the part of economic activity that is produced and shared by Irish nationals.

Column 3 of Figure 8.7 indicates that the difference between gross domestic product and gross national product is net factor income from the rest of the world.

Definition
● ● ● ● ● ●

Net factor income from the rest of the world is the outflows of income earned by foreigners operating in Ireland minus the inflows of income earned by Irish companies with foreign subsidiaries.

There are more foreign multinationals operating in Ireland sending profits abroad than there are Irish multinationals sending profits home.[14] The net repatriation of profits and the interest payments on the national debt to non-residents are both outflows. This item in the National Accounts has been negative and rising for the past two decades. In 1995, net factor income from abroad amounted to an outflow of £4.8bn. Hence, GDP is consistently larger than GNP in Ireland. This was not always the case. Less than a quarter of a century ago, emigrants' remittances and interest on the country's external assets meant that the net factor income from abroad was positive. This resulted in GNP greater than GDP (see Appendix 8.2).

Gross national disposable income GNDI (not included in Figure 8.7) is GNP plus net current transfers from the rest of the world. These payments are not in exchange for goods or services and they include, among others, emigrants' remittances and net current transfers from the EU. These should be included in any accurate measure of Irish economic activity. In 1995, current transfers accounted for an inflow of over £1.1bn. Taking this into account, GNDI for 1995 was almost £35bn.

Columns 3 and 4 show that the difference between gross national product and net national product (NNP) is a provision for depreciation. We defined depreciation in Chapter 6 as the value of capital which has been used up during the production process. Whereas GNP does not account for the capital depleted in the production process, NNP does. The CSO estimated that depreciation for 1995 amounted to over £3.6bn.[15] Deducting depreciation from GNP meant that NNP at market prices was valued at just over £30bn in 1995.

Columns 4 and 5 illustrate the difference between NNP measured at market prices and NNP at factor cost. To calculate NNP at factor cost we deduct indirect taxes from and add subsidy payments to NNP at market prices. In 1995, £6bn of indirect taxes were deducted from NNP at market prices and £1.65bn of subsidies were added to arrive at a figure of £25.7bn which represents NNP at factor cost.

NNP at factor cost, or national income as it is commonly known, is represented in Columns 5 and 6. It is simply the addition of payments to the factors of production. These factor payments are wages, profits, interest and rent.

Column 7 of Figure 8.7 shows that the difference between national income and personal income is accounted for by what economists call 'income earned-but-not-received' and its counterpart 'income received-but-not-earned'. Examples of the former include retained earnings of companies, corporate tax on profits and social insurance contributions. Transfer payments are examples of the latter. In 1994 (latest figures available), personal income was £29.6bn.

The last term to be explained is disposable income which is sometimes referred to as take-home or after-tax income. Disposable income is defined as personal income minus direct taxes, as shown in columns 8 and 9 of Figure 8.7. An individual or household divides disposable income between personal consumption and personal savings. This is shown in column 10 of Figure 8.7. In 1994, disposable income was £23.3bn. Of this amount, over £20.8bn was spent on personal consumption while almost £2.5bn was reserved for personal savings.

The differences between national income and personal consumption for 1994 are shown in Table 8.7 below.

Table 8.7: From national income to personal consumption

	Description	£m
84	National income before adjustment for stock appreciation	24,456
85	less Government trading and investment income	−481
86	plus National debt interest	2,051
87	plus Transfer income	5,480
89	less Undistributed profits of companies before tax	−1,914
90	Personal income	29,593
92	less Personal taxes	−6,284
	Disposable income	23,308
	of which	
91	Personal consumption of goods and services	20,836
94	Personal savings	2,472

Source: CSO, *National Income and Expenditure 1995,* July 1996.

GDP can be measured in two ways.

Definition
● ● ● ● ● ●

Nominal GDP or GDP at current prices is a measure of economic activity based on the current prices of the goods and services produced.

Definition
● ● ● ● ● ●

Real GDP or GDP at constant prices measures economic activity in the prices of a fixed or base year.

This last measure is commonly referred to in the media as 'GDP corrected for inflation'.

Increases in nominal GDP can arise for two different reasons: an increase in the quantity of goods and services produced, or an increase in the price of these goods and services. Increases in real GDP arise from only one source: an increase in the quantity of goods and services produced. By measuring production in constant terms, we separate the actual changes in the quantity of goods and services produced from the change in the price level. In effect, we isolate the production change from the price change.

Two conclusions apply here. One, GDP at constant prices is a better measure of a country's economic performance. Two, in terms of the source of higher income and output levels, an increase in the quantity of goods and services produced is preferred to an increase in their price.

GDP at current prices can be converted to GDP at constant prices by means of a price index called the GDP deflator.

Definition
● ● ● ● ● ●

The GDP deflator is the ratio of nominal GDP to real GDP expressed as an index.

Price indices and their construction are discussed in Chapter 15.

Let us take an example to highlight the difference between the two measures. It is estimated that between 1979 and 1986 the Irish economy, measured in terms of increases in nominal GNP, grew by 130%. However, the increase over the same period measured in real GNP terms was 3%. This suggests that the increase recorded in nominal GNP during this period was due solely to changes in the price level with no significant increase in production recorded.

In order to take into account the size of or changes in the population of a country, GDP per capita is used. This measure is expressed in Equation 8.2.

$$\boxed{\textbf{GDP per capita = GDP/population}} \qquad [8.2]$$

This is a better measure of a country's standard of living than GDP itself. For example, two countries with similar values for GDP may have very different standards of living because of variations in the size of their respective populations. In this case, GDP per capita is a more suitable measure. Table 8.8 depicts GDP and GDP per capita for a small sample of countries. It is evident that GDP can be quite misleading at times, even when adjusted for the exchange rate. In Table 8.8, this is particularly true in the case of India whose GDP appears relatively high but because of its vast population its GDP per capita is relatively small.

Table 8.8: GDP, population and GDP per capita, 1992 (US$)

Country	GDP 1992 (bn)	Population Est. 1992 (m)	Real GDP per capita (PPP) 1992
Ethiopia	6.3	50.3	330
Bangladesh	23.8	112.7	1,230
India	214.6	884.1	1,230
China	506.1	1,183.6	1,950
Greece	67.3	10.3	8,310
Ireland	43.3	3.5	12,830
Switzerland	241.4	7.0	22,580
US	5,920.2	255.2	23,760

Source: UNDP, *Human Development Report 1995*.

Furthermore, any increase in GDP recorded may be offset by an increase in the size of the population. In this case, as above, GDP per capita is a more suitable measure.

We now consider the following case study in order to highlight some of the issues which we have already explained.

CASE STUDY

Extract from The Irish Times
Buoyant exports spur to record growth in economy
by Cliff Taylor

A strong export performance, a surge in investment spending and an end to the squeeze on government expenditure all contributed to record economic growth last year. The gross national product increase of 7.5% shown in the National Income and Expenditure accounts published today is the highest growth rate since 1968 (when it was also 7.5%). The figures for last year emphasise just how dramatically economic growth has slowed down over the past year, with the government estimating the increase of GNP this year at only 1.25% and many other forecasts expecting no growth at all. Last year's growth brought total GNP to £22.9 billion, with the overall roughly as recent forecasts had suggested, and was just 0.25 of a point above the latest estimate from the Department of Finance.

But some of the breakdown is surprising. In particular consumer spending rose by just 1.1% in real terms, well below the previous Department estimate of 2.75%. As total disposable income rose by 5.5%, the small rise in spending suggests that savings levels rose, particularly towards the end of the year when the outlook was getting worse. In other areas of the economy activity was much stronger. Investment spending rose by 10%, although this was below the rise in 1989. The trade performance was strong, with export volumes up 9% compared to a 6% increase in imports.

The figures also clearly show that the squeeze on overall government spending which started in 1987 ended last year. Net spending by the overall public sector rose by 3.5% in real terms after falls of 4.4% in 1987, 5.3% in 1988 and 2% in 1989. A more favourable flow of funds into and out of the country, possibly reflecting higher EC funding and lower profit repatriations also boosted growth.

The annual nature of GNP figures can give a misleading picture; the economy was not storming along until 31 December last year only to suddenly collapse moving into 1990. Growth began to slow in the second half of last year in tandem with the international slowdown. The official rate of GNP growth last year reflects the strong performance in the early part of the year after strong growth in 1989, now estimated by the Central Statistics Office at 5.7%. The strong growth in 1989 and early 1990 can be gauged by the fact that Gross National Product last year was 13.7% higher than two years earlier. Irish GNP growth in 1990 was five percentage points above the average of 2.6% across the international world, using figures from the latest Organisation for Economic Co-Operation and Development. Only Turkey, where growth was 9.2%, recorded a higher rate. Even adjusting to the drain on the Irish economy from profit repatriations still leaves the Irish economy at the top of

$\longrightarrow$

the international league. Growth over the two years 1989 and 1990 averaged 6.6%, compared to the OECD average of 3%.

Today's figures, the first CSO estimates of economic activity last year also show:

- National income per head last year was £5,049. This is 12% up on 1989, compared to an inflation rate of 3.4%. Total national income was £17.697 billion.
- Profits earned by companies and other businesses rose by 13.4%, after a 10.7%

rise in 1989. Employees' remuneration rose by 7.3% last year after a 6.3% increase the previous year.

- Income from agriculture fell by 1.5%, a fall of almost 5% after allowing for inflation.
- 1990 saw a slowing in industrial growth, with a 5.4% rise in the volume of output after 11.2% the previous year. Distribution, transport and communications saw a volume output rise of 10.4%.

. . .

Source: The Irish Times, *29 November 1991.*

Questions
....

1. What accounts for the strong growth rate of gross national product in 1990?
2. Suggest possible reasons why the investment increase in 1990 was lower than the investment increase in 1989. Why would policy-makers be concerned if this trend continued?
3. How does the Irish growth rate compare to other countries? Do you think that the Irish economy performed successfully in 1990?

Answers
....

1. Consumer spending increased by 1.1% in real terms. Investment spending rose by 10%. Net exports increased. Export volumes increased by 9% while imports increased by only 6%. Public sector spending also rose for the first time in three years. Growth may also have been fuelled by higher levels of EU funding and lower levels of profit repatriation by foreign multinationals. The combination of the improvements in these variables translated into a 7.5% increase in GNP over the previous year.
2. The decline in the growth of investment could be caused by high interest rates and/or poor expectations about the future. The article suggests that the slowdown of Irish economic activity mirrored the international slowdown. Consumers reacted by spending less and saving more. In this type of economic climate, investors are likely to put expansion plans on the 'long finger'.

   Policy-makers and economists are concerned about the rate of investment because it is the most important component affecting the long-run prosperity of the economy.
3. The Irish growth rate in 1989 and 1990 compared favourably with the OECD average. Only Turkey had a higher growth rate than Ireland. However, there are other issues mentioned in the article which indicate that all sectors did not benefit equally from the strong growth performance. Although per capita income increased by about 8% after inflation, farmers did not share in this growth. Farm incomes

fell by almost 5% during the same period. Unemployment is not mentioned in the article as it is not measured in the National Accounts. However, the economic growth rate was not matched by a decrease in the unemployment rate. This suggests that any evaluation of performance depends on the variables that we are considering.

In brief, the national income accounts do more than just describe the overall level of economic activity in the economy. Economists, policy-makers, interest groups and others are concerned with a whole range of issues such as the level of consumer spending, taxes, savings and other important components of the circular flow model. Notwithstanding the importance of these individual aspects of the national income accounts, its overall contribution to economics is in its ability to measure a country's economic performance, either from year to year or in comparison to other economies. The collection of this data has greatly facilitated research into macroeconomic issues.

Any measure of economic activity is subject to criticism for what it includes or what it fails to include. We will now examine some of the shortcomings of GDP.

8.4 Limitations of GDP as a measure of economic activity

GDP is not a perfect measure of a country's economic performance: it has many weaknesses. Listed below is a comprehensive, although not exhaustive, record of transactions which are omitted from GDP. In addition, GDP does not measure or account for many aspects of a modern economy. A list of these is also included below.

Omissions
. . . .

• *Transactions within the 'shadow' economy.* These include illegal activities such as drug-trafficking and prostitution and legal activities which are not reported to avoid tax payment. It is very difficult to estimate a value of such transactions (see Article 8.1). Estimates vary significantly from country to country. For example in the US, the value of unreported transactions is estimated at 10–15% of GNP while in Italy the figure is placed at 25%. In contrast, it is estimated that the underground economy only accounts for 3–5% of GNP for both Switzerland and UK. It is common for a large underground economy to exist in less developed countries. While this suggests that their national income statistics significantly underestimate the value of economic activity in these regions their standard of living is still far below the rest of the world.

ARTICLE 8.1

Extract from The Irish Times
'Black economy' may generate £2bn a year
by Cliff Taylor

Activity in the black economy could amount to around 8% of Gross National Product, or over £2bn a year, according to new estimates by Mr Gabriel Fagan, an Irish economist working at the Bank for International Settlements. His analysis estimates that the size of the black economy grew significantly from the 1960s to the mid-1980s, in line with an increase in the tax burden, before falling slightly since then. Mr Fagan, who is on secondment from the Central Bank to the committee of governors of EC central banks at the BIS, used a range of economic techniques to estimate the size of the black economy. Two of the main methods, using techniques based on the amount of money in circulation, concluded it equalled around 8% of recorded GNP last year, he told a meeting of the Statistical and Social Inquiry Society in Dublin last night. Other methods estimate it accounted for between 5% and 10% of GNP. The black economy is defined as activity not counted in the official statistics, although it does not include some areas such as household work which is also excluded from the national accounts. 'This level of the black economy is closely connected with tax-evaded income', the paper says, in other words non-taxed 'nixers' and other work hidden from the Revenue Commissioners.

. . .

International estimates of the size of the black economy vary widely. For the US, the estimates range as low as 4% of GNP and as high as 28%, while for Britain the range is 2.5% to 15%, and 5% to 12% for Germany. While the black economy has a significant influence on the level of GNP, Mr Fagan says it does not have a major impact on the recorded level of GNP growth. The paper computes a series of growth rates which included estimates of movements in activity in the black economy. The broad trend in growth rates is similar between the official estimates and those including the black economy, and the average growth rate from the early 1960s up to last year using the official estimates is 3.5%, compared with 3.8% including the most volatile measure of the black economy. 'These results provide some justification for the advice of the CSO, proffered annually in the National Income and Expenditure accounts, that greater reliance should be placed on year-to-year changes rather than actual levels of national accounts variables.' Mr Fagan rejects some earlier studies which said the size and growth of the black economy invalidated the use of official GNP growth rates for analysis and policy purposes.

Source: The Irish Times, *8 October 1993.*

- *Externalities.* These are side-effects generated in the production or consumption of commodities (see Chapter 7). They can either be positive, generating an external benefit, or negative, generating an external cost. Positive examples include education, inventions and attractive lawns. Pollution, congestion, waste disposal and the depletion of natural resources are examples of negative externalities. It is very difficult to calculate accurate values for these 'spillover' items. The omission of positive externalities from the National Accounts results in a GDP figure which underestimates the level of economic activity. The exclusion of negative externalities results in an overestimated value of GDP.

- *Non-monetary transactions.* These are activities which, although economically beneficial, are undertaken by individuals primarily for their own benefit and not sold to the market. They include household work, gardening and DIY. Another example is the work done by voluntary, community or charity organisations. The reason for the omission of such activities is the difficulty in obtaining accurate figures for the value of the product or service involved. The omission of these non-monetary transactions results in a value of GDP which underestimates the level of economic activity.
- *Non-marketable goods and services.* Examples include state education and health care, defence and justice. These contribute to economic activity but, by their very nature, are not priced by market forces. These economic activities are included in the calculations for GDP but are done so at cost price whereas if a private body undertook the same service it would be included at market price. These activities are particularly important when making international comparisons.

GDP is neither a measure of, nor accounts for, the following
· ·

- It is not a measure of economic well-being or welfare.[16] Arthur Pigou, an economist who wrote at the beginning of this century, argued that there is a close correlation between the level of national income and the level of economic welfare. In recent years, many would argue that the relationship is not very close. By definition, GDP measures only the value of goods and services produced. In preference to GDP, the United Nations (UN) uses a measure called the human development index (HDI). Its constituents are the purchasing power of an average income, adult literacy and life expectancy at birth (see Article 8.2). Table 8.9 below shows the HDI for a small sample of countries.

Table 8.9: The human development index, 1992

Country	HDI	HDI Rank	GDP Rank
Canada	.950	1	8
US	.938	2	1
Spain	.930	9	29
Switzerland	.925	13	2
UK	.916	18	23
Ireland	.916	19	30
Luxembourg	.893	27	5
Romania	.703	98	104
India	.439	134	141
Mozambique	.246	167	173
Guinea	.237	168	170

Source: UNDP, *Human Development Report 1995.*

ARTICLE 8.2

Extract from The Irish Times
Ireland's 'human development' ranking falls
by Peadar Kirby

Ireland's ranking on the Human Development Index (HDI) has fallen since 1990, according to the latest Human Development Report of the United Nations Development Programme (UNDP), published tomorrow. In 1990 it was number 17 on the index whereas this year it has fallen to number 21, overtaken by the US, Australia, Israel and Barbados. From Ireland's point of view, perhaps the most disturbing table in the report is the one which compares the difference between a country's HDI in 1970 and in 1990. In the table of 105 countries, Ireland ranks 55th, between Honduras and Pakistan and below every other OECD member.

Since being initiated in 1990, the UNDP's annual report has established itself as one of the major annual surveys of world development. This is mainly due to its elaboration of the HDI, the first comprehensive attempt to measure annually the comparative development of every country in the world based on a range of social indices rather than the purely economic measurement based on GNP which has been predominant. The HDI is based on three components – life expectancy at birth, knowledge as measured by adult literacy and years of schooling, and income.

Amid the wealth of information in the 100-page section of tables are some surprising findings for Ireland. We have the lowest life expectancy at age 60 of all the developed countries, 16 years for men and 20 for women. Yet our maternal mortality rate at three per 100,000 live births is the lowest in the world except for Iceland and Luxembourg.

Only Malta, among European countries, has a lower percentage of women in the labour force than Ireland (31% in Ireland's case, 25% in Malta's). Yet, Ireland has the third largest level in the world of female educational attainment as a percentage of male attainment, just behind New Zealand and the Netherlands. When adjusted for gender disparity, Ireland drops a place in the HDI ranking but the USA's is three lower, Germany's four, Canada's nine and Switzerland's ten lower. Ireland has the second highest percentage of single-parent homes in Europe (just behind Finland), the second-highest incidence of long-term unemployment (behind Italy), the third-highest level of central government expenditure as a percentage of GNP (behind Bulgaria and Czechoslovakia) and the second-lowest level of GNP per capita annual growth between 1980 and 1990 (above Greece and on a par with Romania).

. . .

Source: The Irish Times, *25 May 1993.*

- It is not a measure of the competitiveness of an economy or its workforce. More suitable measures are available, including average hourly earnings or unit wage costs relative to a country's major trading competitors.
- It does not (nor does it claim to!) take into account differences in the distribution of wealth. For example, it was estimated in 1980 that the top 20% of all households

in Ireland received 48% of all direct income whereas the bottom 20% received only one half of 1% of income.[17] According to the same source ' . . . Ireland's 1980 income distribution has a greater degree of income inequality than found in most of Western Europe.'[18] The welfare actions of the state, however, in the form of transfer payments, taxes and social insurance, reduce the extent of this income inequality. Although it is recognised that meaningful international comparisons of income inequalities are difficult to make, there is a measure which is sometimes used for this purpose. It is called the Gini coefficient.

The Gini coefficient is a measure of income inequality. Its range, as it is normally expressed, is between zero and one. Zero reflects no inequality. One reflects perfect inequality (all of the nation's income received by a single household). The source mentioned above notes a Gini coefficient for Ireland of 0.3667 in 1980 (using disposable income). The Gini coefficient was lower for most other European countries. In other words, income in those countries was more evenly distributed.[19]

- It does not take into account differences in the composition of GDP. A common example compares countries with similar values for GDP. One nation is engaged in the production of weapons while the other is involved in the production of food. There is a very large difference in terms of relative economic well-being yet the relative data for GDP would not detect this difference. Let us take one further example.

  Consider the relative importance of consumption and investment in terms of their respective contributions to the long-term prosperity of an economy. Some would argue that an increase in economic activity which arises out of greater expenditure on investment is more desirable than a similar increase in economic activity that arises out of greater expenditure on consumption. It is not coincidental that the countries which have achieved the fastest growth rates in recent years, the newly industrialised countries (NICs) for example, have proportionately more expenditure on investment relative to other countries. For example, investment expenditure accounted for 41% and 29% of GDP in 1992 in Singapore and Hong Kong respectively. This compares to 15% and 16% for the UK and Ireland respectively.[20]

  Unfortunately a straightforward comparison of the respective GDPs would not detect these and other subtle but important differences.

- It does not take into account the quality of the goods produced or improvements in quality over time. For example, a calculator purchased in 1970 was both more expensive and less sophisticated than a calculator purchased today.

Finally, there are two more shortcomings that do not fall into any of the above categories.

- The national income accounts are calculated from millions of different returns which the CSO gather and tabulate. Statistical errors and inaccuracies inevitably occur. A figure for a statistical discrepancy or residual error is included to account for these errors. Revisions are constantly made to reflect more accurate and up-to-date information.

- It does not facilitate worthwhile international comparisons. National income accounting conventions differ from country to country. Other more fundamental problems arise. These include, to name but a few, how we account for different currencies, differences in the size of the respective shadow economies and economies at different stages of the business cycle. Conclusions and subsequent policy recommendations arising out of such international comparisons can be quite misleading and must be treated with caution.

In response to the criticisms which the economics profession faced on account of these omissions a number of alternatives to GDP as a measure of a country's economic performance have emerged. For example, in 1972 Professors James Tobin (b. 1918) of Yale University and William Nordhaus (b. 1941) estimated a value of net economic welfare (NEW).[21] They argued from the outset that GNP, which measures production, is not the ideal measure and should be replaced with some measure of consumption. They adjusted the GNP figure by subtracting the following set of activities: health and educational spending which were considered capital expenditure, 'disamenities' and 'regrettable necessities'. A value of non-market activities and leisure were added to give us the NEW. Between 1929 and 1965 in the US it was estimated that the NEW grew at an annual rate of 1.1% per capita whereas an annual 1.7% per capita was recorded for the more conventional measure, NNP.

Notwithstanding the deficiencies listed above, GDP is still the most common measure used by the economics profession today. It is reasonably accurate given the complexities of a modern economy. Moreover, it is consistent from year to year and this facilitates yearly comparisons. It is likely to remain as the measure of economic activity for the foreseeable future.[22]

This chapter concludes with a brief account of certain aspects of the Irish National Accounts.

8.5 The Irish experience

Although the National Accounts appear to be quite technical and tedious, the controversies which arise from them are lively.

Most of the figures used in the tables in this section are taken from the annual CSO publication entitled *National Income and Expenditure*. Table 8.14 also includes figures from another CSO publication entitled *The Labour Force Survey*. Reports of this kind provide the 'raw materials' of economic research, and are the sources of data used in most studies. The annual editions of these publications are always reported by the media.

In this section, we want to show how an economist uses these reports to understand what is happening in the national economy. First, we examine in some detail the difference between GDP and GNP. We will then discuss why this is significant in terms of EU funding. Next we will look at the growth rates of GDP, and how this translates into jobs.

GDP vs GNP
··············

As we stated earlier, for Ireland, GDP is greater than GNP. The two figures are separated by net factor income from abroad. Table 8.10 is an extract from the report *National Income and Expenditure 1995*.

Table 8.10: Difference between GDP and GNP (at current market prices)

	1990	1991	1992	1993	1994	1995[P]
61. GDP at market prices	27,231	28,309	30,080	32,317	34,833	38,616
14. Net factor income from the rest of the world	–2,920	–2,796	–3,210	–3,521	–3,575	–4,815
63. GNP at current market prices	24,311	25,513	26,870	28,796	31,258	33,801

Source: CSO, *National Income and Expenditure 1995*, July 1996. P = Preliminary.

From this table we can see that net factor income from the rest of the world has increased in magnitude every year with the exception of 1991. Between 1990 and 1995, about 10% of GDP has left the country.

Table 8.11 shows the credit and debit items which combine to form net factor income from abroad.[23]

Table 8.11: Composition of net factor income from abroad

		1990	1991	1992	1993	1994	1995[1]
7. Remuneration of employees[2]	Cr	187	192	201	220	231	230
	Db	–41	–42	–44	–47	–48	–49
8. Investment income	Cr	1,845	1,889	1,781	1,726	2,171	2,950
	Db	–4,911	–4,835	–5,147	–5,419	–5,928	–7,946
Components of debit item:							
Direct investment income		–2,607	–2,538	–3,042	–3,355	–3,786	–5,435
National debt interest		–1,009	–1,031	–923	–1,021	–1,081	–1,015
Other[3]		–1,295	–1,266	–1,182	–1,043	–1,062	–1,496

Source: CSO, *National Income and Expenditure 1995*, July 1996.

1. Adjusted for balance of payments purposes (see note 2 in Table 8.17).
2. Revised on basis of new data.
3. Includes semi-state and bank interest flows and interest on EMCF borrowings.

We can see from Table 8.11 that over 50% of the debit results from the repatriation of profits. The National Accounts reflect the success of IDA (Ireland) in attracting foreign multinationals. The rest of the debit is split evenly between the interest payments on the national debt which is owed to foreigners and the 'other' category which also includes various types of interest payments.

Obviously, Irish nationals benefit more from the portion of GDP that remains in the country than from the portion that leaves. Therefore, GNP is generally considered to be a better measure of Irish economic activity than GDP. GNP is used as the basis of comparison for changes in national income by the Department of Finance, as well as by most Irish academic writers.

International comparisons
....

However, most international comparisons are based on GDP. More importantly, most comparisons within the EU are based on GDP. The reason is that for most developed countries, there is not much of a difference between GNP and GDP.

Table 8.12 shows the ratio of GNP to GDP. If the ratio is one, the two measures are essentially the same. This means that the outflows of interest and profits equal the inflows. A number greater than one indicates that the inflows are greater than the outflows. This could happen if a country is the home-base for many multinationals who are sending their profits home or if the country lends more to other countries than it borrows. These inflows are added to the income of the nation. If the ratio is less than one, then the outflows exceed the inflows.

Table 8.12:
Ratio of GNP/GDP
for 1991

Country	GNP/GDP
Belgium	.994
Denmark	.962
Germany	1.007
Greece	.996
Spain	.991
France	.994
Ireland	.900
Italy	.987
Luxembourg	1.355
Netherlands	.998
Portugal	1.000
UK	.993
EU 12	.995
US	1.005
Japan	1.007

Source: Eurostat, *National Accounts ESA 1970–91.*

Most of the countries exhibit a ratio which is very close to one with the exceptions of Luxembourg and Ireland. Ireland has the dubious distinction of exhibiting the most disproportionate outflows.

Ultimately, this means that while Ireland appears to be catching up to her European partners, in terms of GDP, the standard of living is probably not catching up as fast. The Irish performance may look better on paper than what is observed 'on the ground'.

This also has implications for EU funds. The last round of structural funds, which were intended to address the regional imbalances within the EU, focused on 'Objective 1' regions, where per capita income falls below 75% of the community average. The structural funds were directed towards specific regions, mainly on the periphery of Europe. Projects and programmes were designed to reduce costs and to raise productivity. In other words, these funds were not intended to subsidise income. Rather, they were aimed at enhancing the long-term growth prospects of the disadvantaged regions.

In 1989, Ireland qualified as an Objective 1 region. As a result, in 1994, almost one billion pounds of structural funds (partially offset by Irish government contributions) were transferred from the EU to Ireland to implement various projects and programmes. If 75% remains the benchmark, Ireland may no longer qualify as an Objective 1 region because the current Irish GDP per capita is, by some estimates, approaching 85% of the European average.[24] It is less clear if the living standard has improved substantially in Ireland, in comparison to other regions in Europe.

This is not an argument to change the measure of comparison to GNP so that Ireland can qualify for additional EU funds. Rather, it points out that no measure is perfect, particularly for international comparisons. In this particular case, reliance on this particular measure may have unfortunate consequences for Ireland.

It also points out that policies can unintentionally conflict. An industrial policy which successfully attracts foreign direct investments, causes a distortion in an important measure of national income (GDP per capita). That same measure is used to compare Ireland with her EU partners. She appears to be relatively wealthier, although a substantial portion of that income is actually leaving the country.

National income and employment

Finally, we will look at the relationship between national income and employment. Unfortunately, there is not a direct link between economic growth and employment growth. In fact, a comparison between the two for the period between 1960 and 1991 reveals that up to that point, Ireland experienced ' . . . little net growth in total employment, despite a substantial rise in national output'.[25]

The last time that this subject was comprehensively studied was by National Economic and Social Council (NESC) in 1992. Table 8.13 shows the relationship between the output growth and employment growth for Ireland and for the European Community.

Table 8.13: Output growth and employment growth for Ireland and the EC

Country	Ireland			EC		
Period	Output growth	Employ- ment growth	Employ- ment intensity	Output growth	Employ- ment growth	Employ- ment intensity
1973–79	3.4	1.2	0.35	2.5	0.2	0.08
1979–86	0.3	–0.8	N.A	1.6	–0.1	N.A
1985–90				3.1	1.4	0.44
1987–90	4.9	1.4	0.28			

Source: Combined from various tables in *The Association Between Economic Growth and Employment Growth in Ireland*, NESC No. 94, December 1992.

A few points are obvious from looking at this table. First, it takes strong, positive growth in output to generate an increase in employment. In the period between 1979 and 1986, the number of people employed fell in both Ireland and in the EC although there was weak output growth.

Second, Ireland's ability to generate employment from increases in income differs from the European average. We can make this comparison using the employment intensity ratio: this is the ratio of employment growth to output growth. In the period between 1987 and 1990, the ratio for Ireland was 0.28. We can interpret this figure as we would an elasticity measure. A 1% increase in national income results in an 0.28% increase in employment. If we look at other countries, we see large variations between their 'employment intensities'. During the period between 1985 and 1990, the ratio was 0.65 in the US and 0.78 in Canada.[26] In other words, these countries were able to generate more employment from smaller percentage increases in national income.

Third, and most disappointing, Ireland's output growth rate was far higher than the EC average for the last period, but the employment growth rate was exactly the same. It is taking larger increases in growth to generate the same percentage increase in jobs.

Fortunately, in the past few years, Ireland's employment growth performance has improved. Table 8.14 compares the change in national income with the change in the numbers employed for the years between 1991 and 1995.

Table 8.14: A comparison between the growth in output and the growth in employment for Ireland (1991–95)

Year	Output growth	Employment growth	Employment intensity
1991	2.8	0.0	–
1992	2.5	0.5	0.20
1993	3.1	0.6	0.19
1994	7.2	3.1	0.43
1995	7.7	4.4	0.57

Source: CSO, *National Income and Expenditure 1995*, July 1996 and *Labour Force Survey (1995)* May 1996.

We can see from this table that Ireland experienced high rates of growth in 1994 and 1995. These were matched by relatively large increases in the number of people employed.[27]

This brief discussion shows how economists use statistics in a descriptive way, but we have not addressed any of the issues that these statistics raise. For example, is the reliance on GDP as a measure of comparison detrimental to Ireland? Should this issue be addressed at the EU level? In this section, the important question is why do the employment intensity ratios vary from country to country and from period to period? Before we can engage in a discussion on these topics, we need to understand the parameters of the problems. The statistical reports help us to do just that.

Summary

1. The circular flow diagram depicts the workings of a modern economy where transactions between households, firms, government, the banking system and the foreign markets are described. These transactions are real or monetary.
2. The three methods for measuring a country's economic activity are the income, output and expenditure approaches. They are defined so that each yield the same result. In Ireland the data is published by the CSO in the annual *National Income and Expenditure* publication.
3. National income accounting is the system economists use to measure the economic activity of a country. The most common measure used is gross domestic product. All other terms used are simply a variation of this measure.
4. Nominal GDP is a measure of goods and services at current prices. Real GDP is measured at constant prices, by the use of a fixed or base year. Changes in GDP can come from two sources: price changes or production changes. Real GDP is a better measure because it isolates the production changes.
5. Although GDP is the most common measure of economic activity, it has a number of significant shortcomings. Both its omissions and its failure to capture changes in other economic variables have forced economists to look for alternative measures. The human development index (HDI) and the net economic welfare (NEW) are two of the more common alternatives.

6. The *National Income and Expenditure*, published by the CSO, is the main source of data for economists who are studying changes in national income. More importantly, it reports on GDP, the measure of national income which is used for international comparisons. We are concerned with the growth of national income because of its connection with employment growth. In Ireland, the connection between the two growth rates has been historically weak, but strengthening in recent years.

Key terms

Circular flow	Net national product
Leakages	Depreciation
Injections	Market prices
Investment	Factor cost
Transfer payments	National income
Personal disposable income	Personal income
Expenditure method	Disposable income
Income method	Nominal GDP
Output method	Real GDP
Double counting	GDP deflator
Value added	GDP per capita
National income accounting	Shadow economy
Gross domestic product	Externalities
Gross national product	Human development index
Net factor income from abroad	Gini coefficient
Gross national disposable income	Net economic welfare

Review questions

1. Explain, with the aid of a diagram, the complete circular flow model. List the injections and the leakages. Explain how these movements into and out of the circular flow can influence the level of economic activity.
2. Describe the transactions that occur between the following sets of agents: households and firms; households and government; firms and financial institutions; firms and government; firms and foreign markets.
3. List and briefly explain the three approaches to measuring economic activity. Explain, using the circular flow diagram, why they yield the same result.
4. Outline the differences between gross domestic product and national income. Explain all relevant terms used.
5. Do you think GDP is an underestimate or an overestimate of the level of economic activity in Ireland? Support your answer.
6. For Ireland, does GDP or GNP provide a more accurate measure of economic activity? Support your answer.

Working problems

1. On the basis of the data below determine national income using:

(a) income method;
(b) output method;
(c) expenditure method.

Table 8.15

Item	£bn
Rent	450
Interest	300
Agriculture	100
Investment	600
Indirect taxes	800
Net income from abroad	250
Exports	3,050
Public administration	650
Compensation of employees	4,200
Personal consumption	4,000
Transport and communication	1,500
Profits	300
Depreciation	300
Subsidies	400
Government expenditure	700
Industry	3,000
Imports	2,400

2. The following information has been gathered for an imaginary economy:

Table 8.16

Item	£bn
Consumer expenditure (C)	250
Government expenditure (G)	500
Investment (I)	150
Taxes (TX)	350
Transfer payments (TR)	200
Exports (X)	360
Imports (M)	340

Using the above data calculate the following:

(a) GDP;
(b) disposable income;
(c) savings;
(d) net exports;
(e) injections and leakages. Comment on their relative sizes.

Multi-choice questions

1. Within the circular flow model:
   - (a) transactions are either real or monetary;
   - (b) transfer payments are an injection and reflect current production;
   - (c) economic activity will increase if injections exceed withdrawals;
   - (d) both (a) and (c) above;
   - (e) (a), (b) and (c) above.

2. Which of the following set of variables is an injection into the circular flow diagram?
   - (a) exports, taxes and investment;
   - (b) government expenditure, exports and investment;
   - (c) investment, imports and subsidies;
   - (d) imports, savings and taxes;
   - (e) none of the above.

3. Which of the following is an example of a real flow from firms to households?
   - (a) factors of production;
   - (b) payments for goods and services;
   - (c) goods and services;
   - (d) payments for factors of production;
   - (e) none of the above.

4. The three broad methods of measuring economic activity are:
   - (a) GNP, GDP and NNP;
   - (b) income, expenditure and output;
   - (c) national income, personal income and disposable income;
   - (d) budget, balance of payments and expenditure estimates;
   - (e) none of the above.

5. The difference between gross national product and gross domestic product is accounted for by:
   - (a) depreciation;
   - (b) indirect taxes;
   - (c) transfer payments;
   - (d) net factor income from abroad;
   - (e) personal taxes.

6. Which of the following is a better measure of the standard of living?
   - (a) GDP per employee;
   - (b) consumer expenditure;
   - (c) GDP per capita;
   - (d) personal savings;
   - (e) GDP.

True or false

1. The circular flow model implies that the value of exports, a leakage, must be equal to the value of imports, an injection in order for economic activity to remain unchanged. _____
2. The four factors of production are wages, interest, rent and profit. Workers are paid rent, lenders earn profit, landowners earn wages and interest is the residual. _____
3. The values for GNP and national income would be equal if depreciation, indirect taxes and subsidies were all valued at zero. _____
4. If two countries have the same GNP, then the standard of living is the same in both countries. _____
5. If over some period of time prices have doubled and real GDP has doubled, then nominal GDP has doubled. _____
6. The Irish GDP figure exceeds the GNP figure because outflows of factor income exceed inflows of factor income. _____

Fill in the blanks

The simple _____ _____ model shows the transactions between _____ and _____. All flows are either _____ or _____. A more detailed version includes the _____, the _____ system and the _____ sector. Savings, taxes and imports are all described as _____ whereas ____ , ____ ____ , ____ ____ and _____ are defined as injections. _____ is achieved in the economy if these leakages and injections are equal. Such economic activity can be measured by three methods: _____ , _____ and _____. The most common measure used in the national income accounts is _____ or _____, the difference being a value of net factor income from abroad. In Ireland _____ exceeds _____. GDP or any of its variations is not a _____ measure of economic activity. It _____ a large number of substantial activities for one reason or another. These include, among others, transactions within the _____ economy, externalities and non-_____ activities. In addition, it does not account for changes in economic _____, a country's _____ or the distribution of _____. Possible alternatives include the United Nations' _____ or Tobin's _____. Notwithstanding these problems, GDP still remains the most universal measure of economic prosperity.

CASE STUDY

Extract from The Irish Times
Latest forecasts confirm optimism over economy
by Cliff Taylor

Strong recovery in consumer spending and business investment are expected to lead the economy to strong growth this year, according to the latest forecasts from the Department of Finance. Export growth is also predicted to remain buoyant, helping

→

the balance of payments to remain strongly in surplus to the tune of about 8.75% of Gross National Product. Last week, the Minister of Finance, Mr Ahern, announced that the Department had upgraded its growth forecasts for this year and the annual review and outlook confirms that the estimate for GNP growth this year has been increased to 5.25%, from 3.75% on Budget day. The breakdown on the figures shows that departmental forecasters have become more optimistic on almost every area of economic activity and, since the Budget, have increased their forecasts for exports, consumer spending, government spending and investment.

The forecast rise in consumer spending has been increased from 4% to 4.5%, with particular buoyancy noted in the demand for cars. The anticipated increase in investment is 5.5%, against 3.75% at Budget time, based largely on the upturn in the construction sector. The government is also now anticipating that its own spending will rise faster, increasing its estimated growth rate of public spending from 3% to 5.5%. The forecast for export growth has been increased from 5.75% to 7%, based particularly on an improvement in prospects in Continental European markets. In its figures for last year, the Department uses the recently published estimates from the Central Statistics Office, which have been criticised by private sector forecasters for showing too optimistic a picture. The CSO estimated that exports grew by 9.6% last year, propelling the economy to growth of 3.7%.

. . .

Source: The Irish Times, *27 July 1994.*

Questions

1. Which of the three methods of measuring economic growth is implied in the above article? Support your answer. What are the other two approaches? List their respective components.
2. What possible factors may be responsible for the 'Strong recovery in consumer spending' and the buoyant 'Export growth'?
3. Higher government expenditure contributes to the overall increase in GNP. Is this increase in public spending likely to result in any negative effects?

Additional case study questions based on Articles 8.1 and 8.2 from the text

Questions on Article 8.1: 'Black economy' may generate £2bn a year

1. Explain why the 'increase in the tax burden' might lead to an increase in the size of the underground economy.
2. 'International estimates of the size of the black economy vary widely.' Suggest possible reasons for these variations in estimates.
3. What can governments do to reduce the size of the underground economy?

Questions on Article 8.2: Ireland's 'human development' ranking falls

1. Do you think that the HDI is a better measure of human and social development than GNP?
2. Is GNP a perfect measure of economic development? Explain your answer.
3. How important is education expenditure in improving Ireland's human development ranking? Explain.

[The answers are not included.]

Appendix 8.1: Savings and investment

The classical doctrine of economics argued that the equality of savings and investment was an automatic process with the rate of interest playing the key role. This equality between savings and investment can be explained in mathematical form. Suppose there is no government and no foreign sector. The expenditure approach measures GDP as the sum of consumer expenditure and investment expenditure. This identity can be expressed as follows:

$$Y \equiv C + I \qquad [1]$$

However, we can also view GDP as national income which is equal, in the absence of government, to disposable income. Disposable income in turn is either spent on consumption or saved. This can be written as follows:

$$Y \equiv C + S \qquad [2]$$

Combine Identity 1 and 2

$$C + I \equiv Y \equiv C + S \qquad [3]$$

The left-hand side of [3] shows the components of expenditure whereas the right-hand side shows the allocation of income. Subtracting consumption from both sides yields:

$$I \equiv S \qquad [4]$$

Identity [4] shows that in a simple model of the economy investment and savings are equal. This was one of the basic tenets of the classical school which dominated economic thinking in the nineteenth century.

However, in the *Treatise on Money* Keynes argued that savings and investment were very different activities, carried out by two very different sets of people and, moreover, were not necessarily identical. In the next two chapters we will examine in greater detail Keynes' views on these activities.

Appendix 8.2: GNP and GDP for Ireland 1970–95

Table 8.17: GNP and GDP for Ireland 1970–95

Year	GNP Current (£m)	GDP Current (£m)
1970	1,658.2	1,629.9
1971	1,893.3	1,866.7
1972	2,296.9	2,267.3
1973	2,755.4	2,742.9
1974	3,058.7	3,039.5
1975	3,820.6	3,816.3
1976	4,644.8	4,680.8
1977	5,626.8	5,735.2
1978	6,572.7	6,800.9
1979	7,692.7	7,975.7
1980	9,074.6	9,432.7
1981	10,943.2	11,447.8
1982	12,561.6	13,489.3
1983	13,731.9	14,915.8
1984	14,916.9	16,555.7
1985[1]	16,003.2	17,968.9
1985	16,610.9	18,576.6
1986	17,686.1	19,702.7
1987	18,962.5	21,074.8
1988	20,056.1	22,717.9
1989	22,185.4	25,418.3
1990	24,310.8	27,231.4
1991	25,513.3	28,309.5
1992	26,870.4	30,079.8
1993	28,795.7	32,316.4
1994	31,258.0	34,833.0
1995[2]	33,801.0	38,616.0

Source: Central Statistics Office.

1. The discontinuity in 1985 is as a result of the revisions made by the CSO to their mini-data bank. The 1985 figures are approximate estimates.
2. When compiling the 1995 estimates, the CSO made some important changes. In particular, they relate to the treatment of international transfers, profits of multinationals and royalty payments. These arose from improvements in international standards. The changes have had minor effects on the levels of previously published GNP and GDP. The previously published growth rates of both GNP and GDP are 'largely unaltered'.

CHAPTER 9

THE KEYNESIAN REVOLUTION

'It is production which opens a demand for production . . . a product is no sooner created, than it, from that instant, affords a market for other products to the full extent of its own value . . . the only way of getting rid of money is in the purchase of some product or other.'[1]

Jean Baptiste Say (1767–1832)

'The General Theory of Employment is the Economics of Depression.'[2]

John R. Hicks (1904–89)

'Whenever I ask England's six leading economists a question, I get seven answers – two from Mr Keynes.'[3]

Winston Churchill (1874–1965)

Chapter objectives

Upon completing this chapter, the student should understand:

- the pre-Keynesian economic doctrine;
- the economic turbulence caused by the Great Depression;
- the contribution of Keynes to modern macroeconomics.

Outline

9.1 The classical doctrine of economics
9.2 The life and works of John Maynard Keynes
9.3 The Keynesian revolution

Introduction

This chapter deals with the background to Keynesian economics. We begin with a description of the classical doctrine of economics. This is followed by a discussion on Keynes and his life, his ideas and his contribution to macroeconomics. The last section deals with the Great Depression of the 1930s and the emergence of the economics of Keynes.

9.1 The classical doctrine of economics

Disagreement among economists is not new. In the seventeenth century, prior to the emergence of the classical doctrine, economics was not considered to be a distinct academic discipline. Even then, two groups, the mercantilists and the physiocrats, held radically different views about the way that the economy operates. Economic disagreements to this day, particularly about the appropriate role of government, date back to the mercantilist/physiocrat debate. These two groups helped to lay the groundwork for the discussion of economic issues.

The actual word 'mercantilism' had different meanings but was generally understood to mean 'the economics of nationalism'. According to followers of mercantilism the key to national economic prosperity was the accumulation of gold and silver. All policies were aimed towards building a positive balance of trade. Economic thinking was dominated by this policy concern.

Mercantilism was particularly strong in France. Jean Baptiste Colbert (1619–83) served as the Minister of Finance during the reign of Louis XIV. Under his guidance, every aspect of French production was state controlled. Manufactured products were promoted at the expense of agricultural products. All imports and exports were closely monitored.

Many of the writers of the day were merchant businessmen. Critics of mercantilism were quick to point out that the businessmen themselves were often the main beneficiaries of the policies which they advocated. At the time, many felt that the excessive regulations by government led to production inefficiencies. It is often said that the burden of taxation, unevenly spread, ultimately led to the French Revolution.

Not surprisingly, the main reaction against mercantilism also came from the French. While not advocating the overthrow of the monarchy, the physiocrats argued for a radical departure from the policy of state regulation. Physiocracy is derived from the French word 'Physiocrate' which means the 'rule of nature'. The physiocrats, and later the classical economists believed that there was natural order in the economic system which was analogous to the laws of nature. The massive state intervention of the mercantilists was at best ineffective, and at worst served as a deterrent to economic growth.

François Quesnay (1694–1774) was a prominent physiocrat. He attempted to explain and identify the general laws which govern economic behaviour. Quesnay and the physiocrats believed that the agricultural sector was the only productive sector of the economy. The export duties placed on grain by the mercantilists were both unnecessary and served as a disincentive to production. In this sense, the rule of government violated natural law. It is from the physiocrats that we inherit the ideological basis for *laissez-faire* which generally refers to an economic system which is characterised by free trade and low levels of state intervention.

Adam Smith (1723–90) is considered to be the father of economics and the founder of the classical school. His book, *An Enquiry into the Nature and Causes of the Wealth of Nations* was at one level a reaction against mercantilism. His thinking was obviously influenced by his acquaintance with François Quesnay. Like Quesnay, Smith attempted to understand the general principles which underlay economic growth.[4]

For Smith, the basis of wealth was the division of labour.[5] Production expands significantly as labour becomes more specialised. It is within this context that Smith adopted the free-trade doctrine of the physiocrats. A larger market expands the opportunities for specialised labour.

Smith also advanced the physiocrats' argument concerning 'deregulation'. He attempted to explain the economic forces which cause individuals, motivated by self-interest, to achieve objectives which are socially beneficial. The 'invisible hand' is often interpreted as the forces of competition. Consumers, acting independently of each other, nevertheless communicate their needs to producers. Producers, who are striving to make a living, attempt to satisfy consumer needs. This is the basis of the perfectly competitive market structure.

Smith observed that the mercantilist system promoted collusive agreements between merchants and politicians, often at the expense of the ordinary citizen. He argued that unregulated competition would ensure that goods were produced more efficiently and distributed more evenly among the population. Competition, in short, was a system that militated against a concentration of wealth and in favour of a more equitable distribution of resources.

Smith was one of a group of economists who came to be known as the classical school. Others include David Ricardo (1772–1823), Thomas Malthus (1766–1834) and John Stuart Mill (1806–73). They dominated economic thought in the hundred years following the publication of *The Wealth of Nations*.[6] They were academics, with the exception of David Ricardo, who was a stockbroker by profession. This raised the tenor of the economic debate since they could no longer be accused of advocating particular policies which advanced their self-interest.

Although they ultimately became known as economists, their writings span many of the classical subjects including history, politics, physics, philosophy and jurisprudence. Political economy was originally taught under the chair of moral philosophy by Smith at the University of Glasgow. Needless to say, Smith's economic perspective was influenced by his study of philosophy.

The classical economists focused on the issues of growth, value and distribution. Unlike their successors, the classical economists never saw growth as an automatic process. Discussions focused, not only on attempting to understand the conditions which promoted economic growth, but also on the type of policies which would foster these conditions. In this sense, *laissez-faire* should not be construed as the lack of government policy, but as a positive initiative to support competition.

The end of the nineteenth century was a period of transition. It was during this period that economics was firmly established as a distinct academic discipline. Many within the discipline attempted to align it with the natural sciences rather than with what were considered to be the less rigorous social sciences. A deductive methodology was adopted. Models were developed, based on restrictive assumptions, which are logical within their own framework. This approach may be traced back to Ricardo, but it is very different from the descriptive, historic approach which was more common to the other classical economists.

The 'Marginalists' were a group of economists who include W. Stanley Jevons (1835–82), Carl Menger (1840–1921) and Leon Walras (1834–1910). The work of these economists represented the transition between the classical and neoclassical schools. One of the unresolved issues of the classical school was the theory of value. This was partly because the classical economists concentrated on the supply side. They assumed that goods had some utility, otherwise nobody would want them. However, the value of goods was determined by the amount of labour which it took to produce them.

The contribution of the marginalists was to develop the downward sloping demand curve which was based on diminishing marginal utility. Goods had utility, as suggested by the classicals, but that marginal utility diminished as more of the good was consumed. Only falling prices could entice an individual to consume more of the same good.

This idea was later applied by neoclassical economists to the supply side. The upward sloping supply curve is based on the idea of diminishing marginal productivity which causes marginal costs to increase when more is produced. Part of the marginal cost curve is the supply curve for the perfectly competitive firm. The two curves combine to form a model of price determination. When price is set in the competitive market, based solely on the forces of demand and supply, it means that resources are efficiently diverted to the uses which achieve the highest possible utility for the consumer. The 'market' is the neoclassical model which conceptualises Adam Smith's 'invisible hand'.

In the decades which preceded the Great Depression, the neoclassical economists developed general equilibrium and partial equilibrium models which were mathematically difficult and aimed at a narrow range of consumption and production problems. They followed the thinking of the physiocrats and the classical economists, recommending a circumscribed range of government activity. Their emphasis on individual choice meant that they saw government as limiting the range of individual actions. Government spending meant that less money was available for private investment. It had to be paid for by taxation which limited the disposable income of consumers. Specific policy recommendations of the neoclassicals will be contrasted with Keynesian alternatives in section 9.3.

9.2 The life and works of John Maynard Keynes

Keynes is to economics what Freud is to psychoanalysis, Einstein is to Physics and Darwin is to biology.[7] Mark Blaug in his recent work *John Maynard Keynes: Life, Ideas, Legacy* referred to the three great revolutions in modern economics: Adam Smith's support for unregulated markets, the 'marginal revolution' and finally the emergence of a new orthodoxy – Keynesian economics.

John Maynard Keynes was born in Cambridge, England in 1883. His parents were middle-class intellectuals. His father John Neville was a well-respected philosopher and economist who worked with Alfred Marshall in Cambridge. Keynes, with the help of scholarships, was educated in Eton and then in King's College, Cambridge where he studied classics and mathematics, winning many college prizes in the process. At the time his other academic interests included philosophy and literature but noticeably, not economics.

He graduated in 1905 at the age of 22 and opted for a career in the civil service. In order to prepare himself for the entry examinations he attended economics lectures in Cambridge. His lecturer was Alfred Marshall who taught Keynes the basic tenets of neoclassical economics. Little did he know that this son of a former colleague would question the very essence of what he and his contemporaries represented.

After briefly studying economics Keynes disappointed Marshall and others by joining the civil service. On completing his exams, it is said that he remarked, 'I evidently knew more about Economics than my examiners.'[8] This was not the last time that Keynes expressed self-belief, verging on arrogance.

His two-year experience in the India Office was the inspiration behind his first book in economics, *Indian Currency and Finance*. While working for the civil service, Keynes made significant progress with his thesis on probability. On the basis of this work, Keynes was offered a Fellowship at King's in 1909. He began teaching economics and within two years had become the editor of *Economic Journal*, the most respected economics journal in the UK at the time. His *Treatise on Probability*, published in a revised form in 1921, was well received by his peers and particularly by philosophers.

Keynes' talents were also recognised outside academic circles. During World War I he had re-entered the civil service and by 1919 he had become the senior British Treasury representative at the Versailles Peace Conference. However, he became very disillusioned with the Allied treatment of the Germans and when the figure of £24bn in reparations was demanded, he resigned. On returning to England he wrote *The Economic Consequences of the Peace* for which he received international acclaim. In the book Keynes was highly critical of the harsh economic terms agreed by the Allies and he predicted serious consequences for the future including the possibility of 'vengeance' in the form of a 'final civil war . . . before which the horrors of the late German war will fade into nothing . . . '

Keynes spent the next few years teaching, writing and speculating in financial markets. This latest interest made Keynes a millionaire although he was to lose heavily during the Wall Street crash of 1929. By 1936 he had recovered his losses and was worth approximately half a million pounds.

In 1923 *A Tract on Monetary Reform* was published. This marked a change in Keynes' view on economics and, particularly, on the role of government. Prior to its publication Keynes was regarded as a supporter of the classical doctrine of economic liberalism. He had advocated the reliance on market forces in preference to active government intervention. He was also a strong supporter of international free trade which he saw as a necessary condition for economic prosperity.

In this publication Keynes advocated the active use of monetary policy in order to determine the price level. This was to be done within the context of a managed monetary system which was to replace the Gold Standard. This support for managing the economy, both in a positive and active fashion, was a shift away from the *laissez-faire* policies of the nineteenth century. However it was not until 1936, with the publication of *The General Theory*, that the economics profession acknowledged the beginning of a revolution.

The *A Tract on Monetary Reform* did make a significant impact but for a very different reason. In it Keynes argued against returning to the Gold Standard at the pre-war fixed exchange rate. He believed that price stability was more important than exchange rate stability with exchange rate policy ideally being subordinate to the needs of the domestic economy. In advocating this policy, Keynes argued against the conventional wisdom advocated by the economic and financial establishment of the day. The Treasury, bankers and business people, for various reasons supported the reinstitution of the Gold Standard. Unlike Keynes, they applauded the decision by the Chancellor of the Exchequer, Winston Churchill, to rejoin in 1925 at the pre-war exchange rate.

Keynes wrote a number of pamphlets prior to 1936 which indicated his growing mistrust of the market system and his belief in tackling unemployment with the aid of government policies. By this time he was involved with the Liberal Party and had the job of advising its leader, Lloyd George. It was widely known that Keynes supported public works programmes in order to provide employment. As usual Keynes presented his argument in a graphical and emotive way: 'If the Treasury were to fill old bottles with bank-notes, bury them at suitable depths in disused coalmines which are then filled up to the surface with town rubbish, and leave to private enterprise . . . to dig the notes up again . . . there need be no more unemployment . . .'[9]

Some of Keynes' early work was criticised within the economics profession because it was not grounded in theory. Whereas the *Tract* was written for a general audience, the *Treatise on Money* (1930) was pitched at a more professional level. Nonetheless, it was severely criticised. Friedrich von Hayek (1899–1992) and D. H. Robertson (1890–1963), two contemporaries of Keynes, wrote less than favourable reviews of the book.

Yet many elements of this book re-appeared in *The General Theory* which Keynes started shortly after the publication of the *Treatise* and took four years to complete. Valuable contributions were made by his Cambridge followers, including Richard Kahn (1905–89), Joan Robinson (1903–83), Piero Sraffa (1898–1983), Roy Harrod (1900–78) and James Meade (1907–95). His letter to George Bernard Shaw in 1935, in anticipation of the book's publication, is another example of Keynes' self-belief. He wrote ' . . . I believe myself to be writing a book on economic theory which will largely revolutionise – not, I suppose, at once but in the course of the next ten years – the way the world thinks about economic problems.'[10]

The General Theory of Employment, Interest and Money of 1936 is generally agreed to be a very difficult book to read and understand.[11] As the title suggests it is concerned almost exclusively with theory; this differentiates it from the *Treatise*. To this day, over sixty years later, economists and commentators argue over the precise meaning of many elements in the book. Essentially it is a book on unemployment, with the causes and solutions analysed in very abstruse language.[12] Terms such as the consumption function, the marginal propensity to consume and the multiplier confused many a reader. Yet most students of economics today are familiar with these and other Keynesian concepts. This partly illustrates the influence that *The General Theory* and more particularly Keynes has had on economics.

The pattern of his life was disturbed yet again by World War II. In 1939, he re-entered the Treasury as an adviser to the Chancellor of the Exchequer. *How to Pay for the War*, which was published in 1940, dealt not with the problems of deficiencies in demand as *The General Theory* did, but with the problems arising out of excess demand. His influence was evident in both the British budget of 1941 and the UK

White Paper on *Employment Policy* of 1944. The latter is of historical importance as it marks the first time in modern economic history that there was a government commitment to securing 'a high and stable level of employment'.[13]

In the same year Keynes was the head of the British delegation at the Bretton Woods Conference. Just prior to that, he put forward a plan, known as the Keynes Plan, which aimed to restore stability to the international economy and, in particular, to international trade which had been decimated by the break-up of the Gold Standard and the outbreak of World War II. The establishment once again rejected his ideas and opted instead for the less radical approach proposed by the American delegation. This led to the establishment of the International Monetary Fund (IMF).

On Easter Sunday, April 1946, at the age of 62, he died at his Sussex farmhouse in Tilton. After such a fulfilling life his only regret was the wish that he had drunk more champagne.

9.3 Tke Keynesian revolution

Though educated by neoclassical economists, Keynes diverged from them both theoretically and in terms of his policy prescriptions. The catalyst for this change was the Great Depression.

Thursday, 24 October 1929 will always be remembered as Black Thursday, the day that the stock market on Wall Street crashed.[14] Panic and confusion reigned. It was reported that eleven speculators committed suicide during the crash. Wall Street did not recover in the subsequent months or years. By November 1929, the average price of fifty leading stocks had fallen to 50% of their September levels. In July 1932, the Dow Jones index of industrial companies was 90% below its value of September 1929.[15]

The Great Depression followed the Wall Street crash in both the US and the UK. After a prosperous decade in the 1920s, aggregate economic activity in the US reached a peak in August 1929. Real GNP fell by nearly 30% between the 1929 peak and the 1933 trough. The unemployment rate rose from about 3% or 1.5 million people to close to 25% or 12 million people. Investment expenditure fell by 75% during this period while consumer expenditure dropped by 20%. The UK suffered a similar fate. Unemployment reached over 22% in the winter of 1932 which meant that 3 million people were out of work.

Economists, politicians and journalists could not agree on the cause of the crash or on the preferred policy response.[16] The classical school of economics advanced policies based on their belief in the ultimate stability of the market and its ability to return to full employment. Keynes argued against this non-interventionist approach and proposed radical changes in economic policy. He suggested an urgent need for active and extensive government intervention. To understand the differences between the policy recommendations, we must first consider some of the theoretical distinctions which separate the classical and Keynesian schools.

Often, when we discuss the upheaval in the study of economics which we attribute to Keynes, we call it the 'Keynesian revolution'. To understand why Keynes was revolutionary, we will look at how his point of view differed from the classical position.

We will begin with the theoretical differences and then discuss how these translated to differing policy recommendations.

Classical economists built on the foundation laid by the physiocrats. Their belief in the stability of the market led them to advocate minimum government intervention. Keynes, however, followed the mercantilists. He not only adopted some of their ideas, he advocated a much more prominent and active role for government. Keynes believed that the market was inherently unstable. Government policy could counter instability in the market.

Keynes began his theoretical attack by looking at the classical model of the labour market. For classical economists, this was the source of unemployment. Labour was demanded by firms and supplied by households. At the equilibrium wage rate, all labour that wanted to work could work: there was no involuntary unemployment. When confronted with the high unemployment which existed during the Great Depression, classical economists argued in favour of a cut in the wage rate to alleviate the excess supply of labour. Keynes had the advantage of learning from the US experience. In 1932–33, the wage rate fell but this did not lead to increased employment as classical theory would predict.

This led Keynes to look for a different explanation for unemployment. He thought that the cause of unemployment was a deficiency in the demand for goods. He argued that a cut in the wage rate would reduce consumer expenditure and lead to a deficiency in demand. This would create uncertainty among investors who would be less likely to undertake investment expenditure. As the demand for consumer and capital goods fell, so would the demand for labour. In short, the decrease of the wage rate actually exacerbated the problem of unemployment.

Moreover, there was little agreement between the classical school and Keynes on the flexibility of wages. Wage flexibility was an intrinsic part of the classical doctrine. In contrast, Keynes argued that wages may not respond quickly to changing market conditions. Institutional arrangements like labour contracts and unions keep wages rigid. In fact, he disputed the desirability of flexible wages. Since consumption is one source of demand, falling wages led to a decrease in consumer expenditure. Inflexible wages helped to maintain the level of demand in an economy.

Keynes continued his theoretical attack with a discussion of Say's Law which states that 'Supply brings forth its own demand.' This is an idea which is often depicted through the circular flow.[17] Households provide the factors of production which are used by firms to produce goods. The households are paid income by the firms which they use to purchase the goods which the firms produced. To take this one step further, households can either consume or save their income. However, in the classical model, based on Say's Law, savings will always re-enter the circular flow in the form of investment. In other words, savings, a leakage from the circular flow, always equals investment, an injection into the circular flow. The classical economists advocated thrift. A high savings rate released labour and capital from producing consumer goods to producing investment goods. This increased the productive capacity of the economy.

Keynes disagreed with the classical analysis of savings and investment. He argued that savings and investment were very different activities, carried out by different people and influenced by different factors. There was nothing automatic about the process. Savings might sit as idle balances if investors were not inclined to use them.

A high rate of savings reduced consumer expenditure which led to a reduction of national income. In this case, savings, the leakage from the circular flow, is greater than investment, the injection. The result is a slowdown of economic activity.

For classical economists, investment depends on the interest rate. The interest rate is determined in the market for loanable funds. The source of the supply of loanable funds is savings. Investors demand loanable funds for investment. The interest rate, which can be thought of as the price of borrowing money, adjusts to bring the demand and supply into equilibrium.

Keynes believed that interest rates were determined in the money market. Money supply was determined by the monetary authorities. Money demand depended on income and the households' preference for holding money rather than interest-bearing assets. The interest rate was determined by the interaction of the demand for and supply of money.

Keynes did not deny that interest rates influenced firms' investment decisions. However, he argued that investment decisions depended mainly on their expectations for future profits. Even at very low rates of interest, firms would not invest if they did not feel that their revenues would cover the cost of borrowing money. From Keynes' perspective, investment was not simply a mathematical decision based on anticipated costs and revenues. The revenue prediction depended on the investors' belief of future business conditions. In his own words, 'Thus if the animal spirits are dimmed and the spontaneous optimism falters, leaving us to depend on nothing but a mathematical expectation, enterprise will fade and die; – though fears of loss may have a basis no more reasonable than hopes of profit had before.'[18]

Differences in theory naturally led to differing policy recommendations. The policy recommendations of the British Committee on National Expenditure which was set up in 1931 to address the problems of the Great Depression offered policy prescriptions which were neoclassical. The preoccupation over the balanced budget led the Committee, under the chairmanship of Sir George May, to recommend cuts in government expenditure and increases in taxation. They were concerned that government spending would 'crowd out' private investment.

Keynes argued against this non-interventionist approach. Unemployment, according to Keynes, resulted from a failure of demand. The policy recommendations of the Committee would aggravate this situation in two ways. Increased taxation decreases disposable income. With less income, households will spend less and consumer expenditure falls. A decrease in government expenditure directly decreases the demand in the economy.

According to Keynes, government spending was not a diversion of funds from the private sector. The public sector compensated for deficient demand which originated in the private sector. Keynes advocated fiscal policy measures, primarily government spending on public works projects, in order to generate employment. He said, 'I expect to see the State . . . taking an even greater responsibility for directly organising investment.'[19] As a consequence of this higher expenditure, the neoclassical rule of balancing the budget each year was abandoned. Adam Smith's advice that 'The only good budget is a balanced budget' became redundant. Keynes' ideas were adopted by Lloyd George, leader of the Liberal party who proposed an increase in the amount spent on public works programmes.

In addition, Keynes advocated using monetary policy to stimulate demand. This would translate into low interest rates which would induce new investment expenditure. However, he was sceptical of relying solely on monetary policy because, as was mentioned earlier, reduced interest rates alone might not be enough to entice investment. The use of both fiscal and monetary policy to stimulate demand and increase employment, is in sharp contrast to the *laissez-faire* policies advocated by neoclassical economists.

Figure 9.1 illustrates the relationship between the economic variables which were mentioned in *The General Theory*.

Figure 9.1: *The relationship between the variables in the Keynesian model*

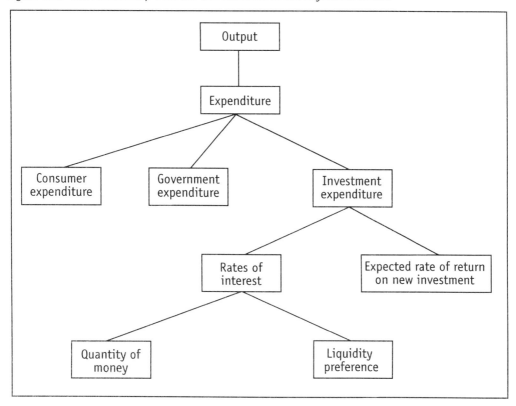

Output depends on total expenditure which is comprised of consumer, government and investment expenditure. Consumer expenditure is explained by the consumption function which is described in the next chapter. Investment expenditure depends on the rate of interest and the expected rate of return on new investment. Finally, the rate of interest is determined by the quantity of money and what Keynes called the liquidity preference, i.e. the demand for money.

The Keynesian model which is outlined in the next chapter and the policy recommendations which follow are ultimately short-term in duration. Keynes' dismissive nature of the long run explains the absence of any long-term analysis. Such a view is epitomised in his famous line '*In the long run* we are all dead.'[20]

Summary

1. The pre-Keynesian or classical school of economics believed that markets were inherently stable and would automatically tend towards a full-employment level. Unemployment arose out of imperfections in the market system which over time would disappear. Hence, government intervention was unnecessary and, in some cases, counterproductive.
2. Keynes' early grounding in economics was of a neoclassical origin. One of his first teachers in economics at Cambridge was Alfred Marshall. On returning to Cambridge, Keynes began to question the economic orthodoxy of the time. This was evident in many of his great works and, in particular *The General Theory*. Outside England, he is probably best remembered for his attack on the Versailles treaty and, later, for his contribution to the setting up of the international organisations after World War II.
3. The Keynesian revolution emerged out of the Great Depression of the 1930s and challenged the orthodox classical economic doctrine of the time. For Keynes, an economy could be at an equilibrium which is below the full-employment level. Insufficient demand was the primary cause of low output and high unemployment. There was a role for government in ensuring sufficient demand.

Key terms

Mercantilists
Physiocrats
Classical economics
Laissez-faire
Invisible hand
Marginalists
Keynesian revolution
Say's Law

Review questions

1. Briefly outline the main differences between the classical and the Keynesian schools of economic thought.
2. Assess J. M. Keynes' contribution to modern macroeconomics.
3. Why did the Keynesian revolution occur in the 1930s?

CHAPTER 10

THE DETERMINATION OF NATIONAL INCOME

'After several years of plunging production, followed by a sluggish recovery, his decision to examine the forces that determined output made sense, but after even more decades of regarding prices as the proper object of enquiry for economists, the shift was not easy.'[1]

Lorie Tarshis (b.1911)

'If the propensity to consume and the rate of new investment result in a deficient effective demand, the actual level of employment will fall short of the supply of labour potentially available . . .'[2]

John Maynard Keynes (1883–1946)

'. . . if I were an Irishman, I should find much to attract me in the economic outlook of your present government towards greater self-sufficiency'.[3]

John Maynard Keynes

Chapter objectives

Upon completing this chapter, the student should understand:

- the assumptions of the Keynesian income determination model;
- aggregate expenditure and the equilibrium level of national income;
- the expenditure multiplier;
- the policy implications arising out of the Keynesian model;
- the experience with Keynesian economics.

Outline

10.1 The model of income determination
10.2 The policy implications
10.3 The Irish experience

Introduction

Sixty years on from its inception, the Keynesian model of income determination is still considered to be the core of modern macroeconomics. This chapter deals with the Keynesian model. We begin with the income determination model for a closed economy. The framework is then extended to an open economy model. The last two sections deal with the major policy implications arising out of the Keynesian model and the Irish experience.

10.1 The model of income determination

We begin our analysis by constructing a simple model of the economy. We work with a two-sector economy with two primary sources of demand – households and firms. Households are engaged in consumption, denoted as C whereas firms are engaged in investment, denoted as I. Initially, there is no government or foreign trade sector. Furthermore, we ignore the differences between the different measures of national income. Henceforth, we use national income, total output and GNP interchangeably.

A number of basic assumptions concerning the Keynesian income determination model are made. First, wages and prices are inflexible. Second, since price does not adjust to changes in demand, all of the adjustment is made by the quantity produced. In other words, suppliers produce what is demanded at the going price. Third, the economy is generally operating at less than full capacity: this means that there are unemployed resources. Because of this excess capacity, an increase in demand will increase output and employment but it will have no effect on price. Fourth, the monetary system is omitted from the model.

In order to fully understand the workings of the model we need to examine both consumer and investment expenditure in detail. We do so by introducing two new concepts – the consumption function and the investment function.

Consumption and the consumption function
....

Consumption is defined as household spending on consumer goods and services which include food, clothes, videos, washing machines and so on. In the pre-Keynesian era, the predominant view was that the interest rate determined savings and, in turn, consumption. In contrast, Keynes believed that the level of income was the main explanatory variable. The relationship between consumption and income is described by the consumption function.

Definition
● ● ● ● ● ●

The consumption function shows consumer expenditure at different levels of income.

It can be written as an equation in the following form:

$$C = f(Y_d)$$ [10.1]

where C is planned household consumption and Yd is aggregate disposable income. Disposable income was defined in Chapter 8 as national income plus transfer payments minus personal taxes. In terms of explaining changes in consumer expenditure, it is a better explanatory variable than national income. Equation 10.1 simply states that consumption depends on disposable income. It is a positive relationship.

Keynes argued this was a stable relationship and as current income increased, expenditure on consumer goods increased. However, the increase in consumer spending is not as great as the increase in income because some of the extra income is saved. Keynes explained this tendency to consume in the following way: 'Our normal psychological law that, when the real income of the community increases or decreases, its consumption will increase or decrease but not so fast . . .'.[4] He called this the marginal propensity to consume.

Definition
● ● ● ● ● ●

The marginal propensity to consume (MPC) is the fraction of each additional pound of disposable income that is spent on consumer goods and services.

The consumption function can now be defined more specifically:

$$C = bY_d \qquad\qquad [10.2]$$

where

$$b = \frac{\Delta C}{\Delta Y_d} = MPC$$

Furthermore,

$$0 < b < 1$$

b is less than one because only a portion of disposable income is spent on goods and services. The remainder is saved.

Let us consider an example. Table 10.1 provides a set of disposable income and consumption levels.

Table 10.1: The consumption function

Disposable income, Y_d	Consumption, C
0	0
100	75
200	150
300	225
400	300
500	375
600	450
700	525
800	600

As disposable income rises in increments of £100 consumption rises in increments of £75. The MPC is equal to the change in consumption divided by the corresponding change in disposable income. Hence, in this example,

$$b = \frac{\Delta C}{\Delta Y_d} = \frac{75}{100} = 0.75$$

If disposable income increases, households will plan additional consumption equal to three-quarters of any increase in disposable income.

This particular consumption function is represented by the following equation,

$$C = .75Y_d$$

For example, if disposable income increases by £100, planned consumption increases by the b x £100 which in this example is equal to 0.75 x £100 = £75.

This consumption function is represented in Figure 10.1.

Figure 10.1: The consumption function, $C = .75Y_d$

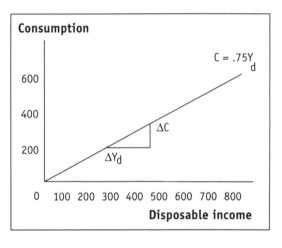

Figure 10.1 shows the specific consumption function $C = .75Y_d$ in diagrammatic form.[5] By convention consumption, the dependent variable is positioned on the vertical axis. Disposable income, the independent variable, is on the horizontal axis. The line shows the positive relationship between consumption and disposable income; as disposable income increases, so does consumption. The slope of any line shows how the variable on the vertical axis changes in response to a change in the variable on the horizontal axis. In this particular case, the slope of the consumption function relates the change in consumption to the change in disposable income which is the marginal propensity to consume.

The difference between disposable income and consumption is accounted for by savings. For example, at an income level of £100 consumption amounts to £75. The difference of £25 is accounted for by savings. As we will see, in every sense, the savings function is directly related to the consumption function.

Savings and the savings function
....

At a given level of income the household has two choices: either consume or save. This can be represented by the following identity:

$$Y_d \equiv C + S \qquad \text{[10.3]}$$

Rearranging the variables we can see that savings is, by definition the difference between disposable income and consumption,

$$S \equiv Y_d - C \qquad \text{[10.4]}$$

The savings function, defined below, is usually written in the following format:

$$S = (1-b)Y_d \qquad \text{[10.5]}$$

The derivation of the savings function is in Appendix 10.1.

Definition
● ● ● ● ● ●

The savings function shows the relationship between savings and disposable income.

The relationship between the change in savings and the change in disposable income has a special name. It is called the marginal propensity to save.

Definition
● ● ● ● ● ●

The marginal propensity to save (MPS) is the proportion of a change in disposable income that is saved.

Since b represents the amount of additional disposable income that is spent on consumption, $1-b$ shows the amount of additional disposable income that is devoted to savings. Hence $1-b$ is the marginal propensity to save.

The consumption function reconsidered
....

In Table 10.1 and Figure 10.1 we assumed that consumption depended only on disposable income. Excluding all other factors is unrealistic as there are many others which affect the level of consumption. Expectations, availability of credit and aggregate wealth are examples of such factors. Thus, we must adjust our consumption function to allow for these other factors. An adjusted consumption function can be written in the following manner:

$$C = \overline{C} + bY_d \qquad \text{[10.6]}$$

This new consumption function has two separate parts.

$\overline{C}$ is called the autonomous component. This is the part of consumption which is independent of income levels: it changes as other factors vary.

bY_d is called the income-induced component. This is the part of consumption which is solely determined by the level of disposable income. It changes as disposable income varies. It corresponds to our simple consumption function which was described above.

Let us take an example. Table 10.2 provides a set of disposable income and consumption levels.

Table 10.2: The consumption function

Y_d	$\overline{C}$	bY_d	$C = \overline{C} + bY_d$
0	50	0	50
100	50	75	125
200	50	150	200
300	50	225	275
400	50	300	350
500	50	375	425
600	50	450	500
700	50	525	575
800	50	600	650

This particular consumption function is represented by the following equation:

$$C = 50 + .75Y_d$$

where £50 is the autonomous component and .75 is the marginal propensity to consume. We can use this equation to find the level of consumption at any level of disposable income.

For example, if the income level is £100, planned consumption is £50 + b x £100 which is equal to £50 + 0.75 x £100 = £125.

This particular consumption function is graphically represented in Figure 10.2.

Figure 10.2: The consumption function, $C = 50 + .75Y_d$

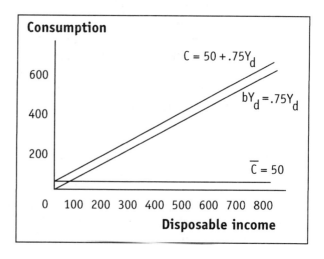

The position of the consumption function relative to the vertical axis depends on the value of $\overline{C}$. A change in the value of autonomous consumption will cause the consumption function to shift upwards or downwards. The slope of the consumption function depends on the value of b, the MPC. A small b results in a relatively flat consumption function whereas a large b results in a relatively steep consumption function.[6]

Investment and the investment function

Investment expenditure is planned spending by firms on capital or producer goods such as tools and machinery, vehicles, premises, factories and so on. In simple terms it is the addition to the capital stock of the economy. This component of total spending, denoted as I, is far more volatile and unstable than consumer expenditure. This is predominantly because of the role of expectations, or what Keynes referred to as 'animal spirits', in determining the level of investment expenditure.[7]

In the simple Keynesian model we treat investment as autonomous.[8] It is independent of the current level of income, and can be represented by the following equation,

$$I = \overline{I}$$ [10.7]

The case where investment expenditure is equal to £100 is illustrated in Table 10.3.

Table 10.3: The investment function

The equation for this particular investment function is as follows:

$$\overline{I} = 100$$

The corresponding diagram for investment expenditure is below.

Income, Y	Investment, $\overline{I}$
0	100
100	100
200	100
300	100
400	100
500	100
600	100
700	100
800	100

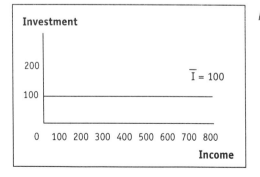

Figure 10.3: The investment function, $\overline{I} = 100$

Investment expenditure is constant relative to income levels. The diagram shows that investment is £100, regardless of the level of income. It changes, however, as other factors vary. One key factor which determines investment spending is the rate of interest, where the rate of interest is the cost of borrowed funds. This applies whether firms borrow funds to finance investment projects or forgo interest by financing investment with their own funds. Other factors include innovation and technical change, corporate taxes and, finally, expectations (of future earnings, inflation, interest rates and so on). Changes in any one or a combination of these factors cause the investment function to shift upwards or downwards.

Aggregate expenditure and the aggregate expenditure function

In our two-sector economy, total planned spending comprises planned consumer spending by households and planned investment spending by firms. In the Keynesian model total expenditure or total spending is termed aggregate expenditure, AE.

Definition
● ● ● ● ● ●

Aggregate expenditure is the amount that households and firms plan to spend on goods and services.

For a two-sector model, it is usually written in the following format:

$$AE \equiv C + \bar{I}$$ [10.8]

AE is simply the sum of planned consumer expenditure and investment expenditure. Table 10.4 shows a hypothetical example of an aggregate expenditure function which adds together the consumption and investment functions that were discussed above.[9]

Table 10.4: Aggregate expenditure

Y	C	$\bar{I}$	$AE \equiv C + \bar{I}$
0	50	100	150
100	125	100	225
200	200	100	300
300	275	100	375
400	350	100	450
500	425	100	525
600	500	100	600
700	575	100	675
800	650	100	750

In algebraic form,

$$AE \equiv C + \bar{I}$$

where: $C = 50 + .75Y$ and $\bar{I} = 100$

Thus,

$$AE = (50 + .75Y) + 100$$
$$AE = 150 + .75Y$$

Figure 10.4 illustrates this particular aggregate expenditure function.

Figure 10.4: Aggregate expenditure, AE = 150 + .75Y

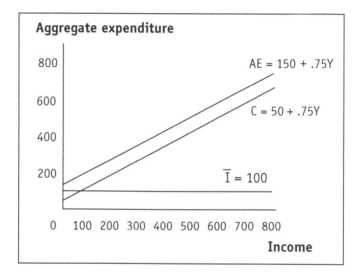

The diagram above clearly demonstrates that the AE function is simply the vertical summation of the consumption function and the investment function. It shows, at each level of income, the total planned expenditure by households and firms.

The equilibrium level of national income

Equilibrium is a state from which there is no tendency to change. In the context of the Keynesian model there is no tendency for income to either rise or fall at the equilibrium.

Keynes argued that the equilibrium level of income was determined by the planned level of expenditure in the economy.[10] At the equilibrium level of income, households and firms are spending what they had planned to spend. At this level, there is no unplanned change in the level of inventories.

Table 10.5 illustrates that equilibrium is achieved through changes in the inventories of firms.

Table 10.5: Determining the equilibrium income level

Y	C	$\bar{\text{I}}$	AE	Unplanned Δ in inventories	Change in Y
0	50	100	150	Falling	Increase
100	125	100	225	Falling	Increase
200	200	100	300	Falling	Increase
300	275	100	375	Falling	Increase
400	350	100	450	Falling	Increase
500	425	100	525	Falling	Increase
600	500	100	600	Constant	No change
700	575	100	675	Rising	Decrease
800	650	100	750	Rising	Decrease

The equilibrium level of income (column 1) is determined by the level of planned aggregate expenditure (column 4). In this example, the equilibrium level of income is £600. We explain why by using a trial and error approach.

Suppose Y = £400. When income is £400 planned expenditure is £450. Aggregate expenditure exceeds output. Firms will experience an unplanned fall in their stocks, and they will respond by increasing output. An income level of £400 cannot be the equilibrium level of income because of this tendency to change.

Suppose Y = £700. When income is £700 planned expenditure is only £675. Aggregate expenditure is less than output. Firms will experience an unplanned rise in their stocks. They will respond by reducing output. Hence, an income level of £700 cannot be the equilibrium level of income.

Suppose Y = £600. Planned expenditure is also £600. Aggregate expenditure equals output. This is the equilibrium level of income as there is no tendency to change. Equilibrium occurs when income is equal to aggregate expenditure. This is the equilibrium condition and it is expressed in the following equation:

$$\boxed{\text{Y} = \text{AE}}$$ [10.9]

There are ways of showing the equilibrium level of income other than by tabular form. It can be depicted graphically or derived algebraically. We first consider the graphical presentation. The algebraic derivation will follow.

The equilibrium level of income: a graphical presentation
....

The equilibrium level of income can be derived with the aid of a 45° line. A 45° line divides our two-dimensional space into two equal halves. All points on the 45° line are equidistant from both axes. Therefore, at any point on the 45° line, the value on the vertical axis equals the value on the horizontal axis.

In this example, the 45° line shows where expenditure and income are equal. In Figure 10.5, the 45° line is drawn with the aggregate expenditure line in order to derive the equilibrium level of income. The equilibrium point is where the 45° line intersects the AE line. Figure 10.5 is sometimes referred to as the Keynesian cross diagram.

Figure 10.5: The equilibrium level of income

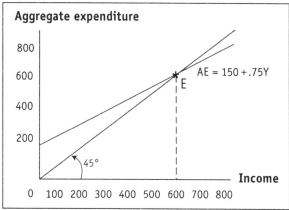

The 45° line and the AE line intersect at point E where Y = AE at an equilibrium level of £600. To the left of point E the AE line is above the 45° line. Aggregate expenditure exceeds output; excess demand results. There is an unplanned fall in inventories. As a result, the response of firms is to increase output.

The AE line is below the 45° line to the right of point E. Aggregate expenditure is less than output; excess supply exists. There is an unplanned rise in inventories. A decline in output is the response of firms.

At point E, aggregate expenditure is equal to output and an equilibrium state exists. At the level of output where Y = £600 there is no tendency for change to occur.

The equilibrium level of income: an algebraic derivation

The equilibrium level of income can be determined algebraically. Although the solution is the same as the one obtained using the above two methods, this method is faster and more accurate. As previously stated:

$$AE \equiv C + \bar{I}$$ [10.8]

where consumption is defined as:

$$C = \bar{C} + bY$$ [10.6]

Substituting Equation 10.6 into 10.8, we get:

$$AE = \bar{C} + \bar{I} + bY$$ [10.10]

Group the autonomous components of expenditure together and substitute into Equation 10.10 above:

$$\overline{A} = \overline{C} + \overline{I}$$ [10.11]

$$AE = \overline{A} + bY$$ [10.12]

In equilibrium, income equals planned expenditure:[11]

$$Y = AE$$ [10.9]

Substitute the right-hand side of Equation 10.12 for the right-hand side of Equation 10.9:

$$Y = \overline{A} + bY$$

Solve for Y:

$$Y = \overline{A} \times \frac{1}{1-b}$$ [10.13]

This is the equation for the equilibrium level of income. The equilibrium level of income can be calculated by substituting values for $\overline{A}$, the total level of autonomous spending, and for b, the MPC. In the example above,

$$\overline{A} = \overline{C} + \overline{I} = 50 + 100 = 150$$
$$b = .75$$

Thus,

$$Y = \overline{A} \times \frac{1}{1-b} = 150 \times \frac{1}{1-.75} = 150 \times 4 = 600.$$

£600 is the equilibrium level of income. This corresponds with the income level which we derived from both the tabular form and the graphical approach.

There is an alternative way of presenting the equilibrium level of income. Rather than focus on the income-expenditure approach as above, we can use the savings-investment approach. This is explained in Appendix 10.2.

The government sector
....

We now extend our model in order to include the government sector. Since this model is concerned essentially with the short run, we can assume that government spending is autonomous and is independent of national income.[12]

Thus

$$G = \overline{G}$$ [10.14]

Table 10.6 illustrates the equilibrium level of income (similar to Table 10.5) but incorporating government expenditure equal to £40.

Table 10.6: Determining the equilibrium income level with $\overline{G}$ = 40

Y	C	$\overline{\text{I}}$	$\overline{\text{G}}$	AE	Unplanned Δ in inventories	Change in Y
0	50	100	40	190	Falling	Increase
100	125	100	40	265	Falling	Increase
200	200	100	40	340	Falling	Increase
300	275	100	40	415	Falling	Increase
400	350	100	40	490	Falling	Increase
500	425	100	40	565	Falling	Increase
600	500	100	40	640	Falling	Increase
700	575	100	40	715	Falling	Increase
760	620	100	40	760	Constant	No change
800	650	100	40	790	Rising	Decrease

The corresponding diagram is represented in Figure 10.6.

With the inclusion of government, aggregate expenditure now incorporates expenditure by the government on goods and services.

In algebraic form:

$$\boxed{\text{AE} \equiv \text{C} + \overline{\text{I}} + \overline{\text{G}}}$$

[10.15]

where C = 50 + .75Y, $\overline{\text{I}}$ = 100 and $\overline{\text{G}}$ = 40.
Thus:

$$\text{AE} = (50 + .75\text{Y}) + 100 + 40$$
$$\text{AE} = 190 + .75\text{Y}$$

Figure 10.6 shows the new aggregate expenditure function. The addition of government means that the intercept changes from 150 to 190. However, since government spending is autonomous, the slope of the line does not change. It is the marginal propensity to consume and still equal to .75.

Figure 10.6: The equilibrium level of income with $\overline{G}$ = 40

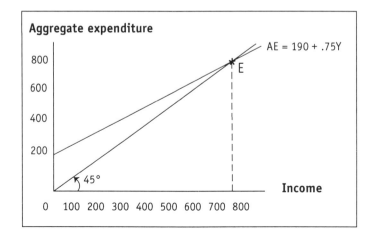

The inclusion of government expenditure has important implications. First, its inclusion results in a higher level of income. The equilibrium level of income was originally £600. Incorporating government expenditure into the model, where $\overline{G}$ = 40, increases the equilibrium level of national income to £760. This can be confirmed by applying the algebra formula which was derived earlier. In this case,

$$\overline{A} = \overline{C} + \overline{I} + \overline{G} = 50 + 100 + 40 = 190$$
$$b = .75$$

Thus,

$$Y = \overline{A} \times \frac{1}{1-b} = 190 \times \frac{1}{1-.75} = 190 \times 4 = 760.$$

Second, any fall-off in consumer or investment expenditure can be offset by an increase in government expenditure. Government expenditure can replace investment expenditure as a source of demand. Likewise, if the economy is below full employment (an assumption of the Keynesian model) an injection of government spending will increase output closer to the full-employment level.

We now consider changes in expenditure and analyse their effect on the equilibrium level of income.

Changes in aggregate expenditure: the multiplier effect
....
According to the Keynesian model, a change in aggregate expenditure results in a change in national income. Furthermore, the change in income is usually a multiple of the change in spending. Keynes described this concept stating that a '. . . definite ratio, to be called the *Multiplier*, can be established between income and investment . . .'[13]

The concept of the multiplier was first developed by Richard Kahn (later Lord Kahn) and Colin Clark (1905–89) in 1931.[14] Kahn was regarded as Keynes' 'favourite pupil' and later became a colleague. Clark was a lecturer in statistics in Cambridge at the same time as Keynes. The early theory dealt with an employment multiplier, which explained how a change in public investment brought about a multiple expansion of employment. In *The General Theory* of 1936 Keynes focused attention on an expenditure multiplier and explained how a change in spending causes a multiple change in income. This multiple is called the Keynesian expenditure multiplier.

Definition
● ● ● ● ● ●

The expenditure multiplier is the ratio of the change in income to the change in autonomous spending.

Any injection of spending causes a multiplier or domino effect. Why so? An initial increase in aggregate expenditure generates extra income. The increase in income induces an increase in consumption, according to our analysis of the consumption function. Next, the increase in consumption generates a further increase in income which, in turn, leads to a further increase in consumption. This process continues.

Let us take a simple example to illustrate a multiplier effect. Suppose a tourist spends £1,000 in a hotel. As a result of this additional income the hotel management upgrades the restaurant facilities by spending £750 on the purchase of tables and chairs. The furniture suppliers decide to hire an additional worker for the month on account of the extra business. They pay their new employee £562.50 a month. This new member of staff is from the locality and spends over £420 of his income on food and drink from the local supermarket. In turn, the supermarket decides to buy in more foodstuffs and beverages to meet the extra demand. They spend an additional £316. This process, with each person's expenditure becoming someone else's income, continues.

The initial injection of spending has led to a successive series with the increases becoming successively smaller:[15]

$$£1000 + £750 + £562.50 + £421.875 + £316.40625 + \ldots\ldots$$

This is illustrated in Figure 10.7.

Figure 10.7: The multiplier with successive increases in consumption

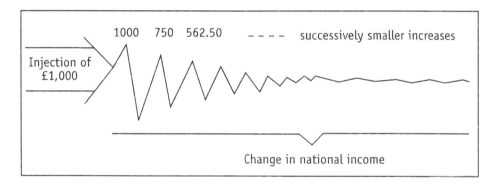

This is a convergent series which can be summed, in this case, to £4,000.[16] The initial £1,000 has now generated, in total, income of £4,000. The increase in income is four times greater than the increase in aggregate expenditure. The value of the multiplier is 4. This is an example of the Keynesian expenditure multiplier, or simply the multiplier, in action. This domino effect is illustrated in Figure 10.8.

Figure 10.8: The multiplier process

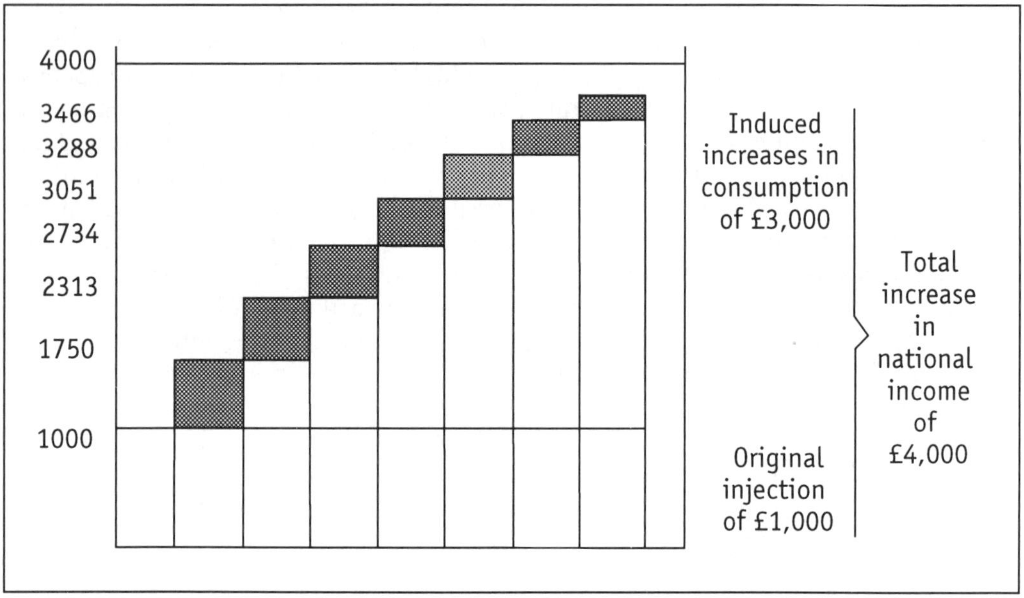

Figure 10.8 illustrates the effect of an initial injection of expenditure on both consumption and on national income. The increase in expenditure of £1,000 induces increases in consumer expenditure equal to £3,000. Thus, the final increase in total income is £4,000.

Example: Using the data from above

Continuing with the previous example, suppose that government expenditure increases by £50, from £40 to £90. Table 10.7 shows the effect on the equilibrium level of income.

Table 10.7: Determining the new equilibrium income level

Y	C	$\overline{I}$	$\overline{G}$	AE	Change in Y
0	50	100	90	240	Increase
100	125	100	90	315	Increase
200	200	100	90	390	Increase
300	275	100	90	465	Increase
400	350	100	90	540	Increase
500	425	100	90	615	Increase
600	500	100	90	690	Increase
700	575	100	90	765	Increase
800	650	100	90	840	Increase
900	725	100	90	915	Increase
960	770	100	90	960	No change
1000	800	100	90	990	Decrease

The table indicates that the increase of £50 in government expenditure, from £40 to £90, increases the equilibrium level of income by £200, from £760 to £960.[17] This increase of £200 suggests a multiplier of 4 ($\frac{200}{50} = 4$). This can be verified by tabular form, by the multiplier formula, and by means of a diagram.

By tabular form:
The example above is presented in Table 10.8.

Table 10.8: The multiplier process in action

Example: $\Delta\overline{G} = 50$ and b = .75

	$\overline{G}$	C	AE
Round 1	50		50
Round 2		50 x .75	50 x .75
Round 3		50 x .75^2	50 x .75^2
Round 4		50 x .75^3	50 x .75^3
,,		,,	,,
,,		,,	,,
,,		,,	,,
Totals	50	150	200

By the multiplier formula:
The multiplier formula is derived in Appendix 10.3. The multiplier is:

$$k = \frac{\Delta Y}{\Delta \overline{A}}$$

where $\overline{A}$ is autonomous spending. k is the symbol that Keynes used for the multiplier. k can also be calculated in the following manner:

$$k = \frac{1}{1 - b}$$

where b is the marginal propensity to consume. In terms of this example, the multiplier is:

$$k = \frac{\Delta Y}{\Delta \overline{A}} = \frac{200}{50} = 4, \text{ or:}$$

$$k = \frac{1}{1 - b} = \frac{1}{1 - .75} = 4$$

We can use the multiplier to directly calculate the change in income using the following formula:

$$\Delta Y = k \times \Delta \overline{A}$$

In this example, k = 4 and $\Delta \overline{A}$ is the change in autonomous spending of £50.

$$\Delta Y = 4 \times 50 = £200.$$

Our familiar cross diagram can also illustrate the multiplier effect. We use the same example as above where government expenditure increases by £50.

By diagram:

Figure 10.9: The new equilibrium level of income

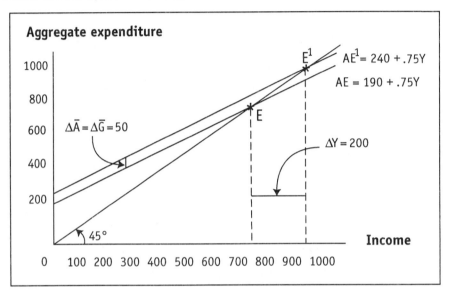

Figure 10.9 shows the multiplier effect on national income. The increase in government expenditure causes a shift of the aggregate expenditure line from AE to AE[1]. The equilibrium level of income, as reflected in the intersection point between the 45° line and the AE line, increases from E to E[1]. The vertical distance between the two AE lines, AE and AE[1], is equal to $\Delta \overline{A} = \Delta \overline{G} = 50$. The horizontal distance between the two income levels is equal to $\Delta Y = \Delta \overline{A} \times k = 50 \times 4 = 200$. In terms of length, the horizontal distance is four times the vertical distance. This reflects the multiplier which in this case is equal to 4.

The example above illustrates two important facts about the value of the multiplier. First, it depends on the size of the marginal propensity to consume. A large MPC results in a large multiplier; a small MPC results in a small multiplier. For example a MPC of .9 results in a multiplier of 10, a MPC of .75 results in a multiplier of 4 whereas a MPC of .6 results in a multiplier of 2.5.

Second, given that the MPC is less than one, the multiplier must be greater than one. This suggests than any increase in spending will lead to an increase in income of a greater amount. This has important implications for fiscal policy and its effectiveness in dealing with unemployment. This is discussed in greater detail in section 10.2.

Although most textbooks accredit Keynes with the discovery of the multiplier, they fail to give credit to one of Keynes' strongest supporters, Paul Samuelson (b. 1915), who was responsible for popularising the above diagram. Samuelson was the first American economist to win the Nobel prize in economics, in 1970. His book, first published in 1948, became the principal textbook in economics in the US in the 1950s and remained so for over thirty years. Moreover, the popularity of Keynesian economics in that era was in no small measure due to Samuelson and his book *Economics*.

It is important to note that the multiplier process is symmetric. Any decrease in expenditure causes a greater decline in national income because of the knock-on effect of lower induced expenditure. The failure of investment expenditure was the explanation given by Keynes to account for the Great Depression of the 1930s.[18]

Thus far, our analysis of the multiplier has been quite limited. First, the model has reflected a closed economy. Second, it has been expressed solely in terms of the MPC. We now redress these two shortcomings.

The foreign sector and a four-sector model
....

Our analysis so far has been almost entirely within the context of a closed economy. This is in line with Keynes' *The General Theory*. One reason for this was the major upheaval which was occurring in the international monetary system at the time *The General Theory* was written, after the collapse of the Gold Standard and before the Bretton Woods system was instituted. As a result, exchange rates floated freely on foreign exchange markets. Existing knowledge on flexible exchange rate regimes and how they influenced domestic economic variables was limited.

Another possible reason was the fact that foreign trade did not constitute a large percentage of GDP in either the US or the UK. Relative to the Irish situation, this position still remains. Moreover, given the open nature of the Irish economy (see Chapter 8 for a discussion on the relative openness of the Irish economy) the foreign sector is particularly vital to our analysis. We now adjust our model to incorporate the foreign sector.

The foreign sector is incorporated into the model by including a value for net exports, denoted by NX, the difference between exports, X and imports, M.

The level of exports from the domestic economy depends on a number of variables including foreign income, the competitiveness of domestic goods in relation to similar goods produced by firms in other countries and exchange rates. The most important variable is foreign income. Because exports are domestically produced goods and services purchased by foreigners, demand for these goods and services varies with the income of a country's main trading partners. Exports are not related to national income and thus exports are autonomous.

$$\boxed{X = \overline{X}}$$
[10.16]

In this example $\overline{X}$ = £90

The amount of goods and services which are imported into the domestic economy are affected by some of the same variables including the relative competitiveness of domestic goods and exchange rates. However, the ability of an economy to import goods depends on national income. Therefore, imports are a function of income. As income increases imports increase. The import function is of the form:

$$M = mY$$ [10.17]

where m represents the marginal propensity to import.

Definition
● ● ● ● ● ● ●

The marginal propensity to import (MPM) is the fraction of an increase in income that is spent on imports.

In this example, $M = .15Y$. This means that fifteen pence of each additional pound of national income is spent on imports. Table 10.9 shows hypothetical values for both exports and imports.

Table 10.9: Exports, imports and net exports

Y	$\overline{X}$	M	NX
0	90	0	90
100	90	15	75
200	90	30	60
300	90	45	45
400	90	60	30
500	90	75	15
600	90	90	0
700	90	105	−15
800	90	120	−30
900	90	135	−45
1000	90	150	−60

The net exports function is shown in Figure 10.10.

Figure 10.10: Net exports function

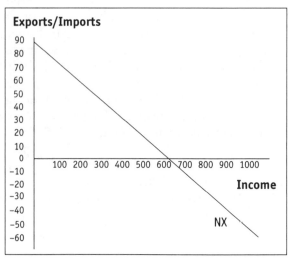

Table 10.10 illustrates the new equilibrium level of income with net exports varying as the level of income changes.

Table 10.10: Determining the equilibrium income level with net exports

Y	C	$\bar{\text{I}}$	$\bar{\text{G}}$	NX	AE	Unplanned Δ in inventories	Change in Y
0	50	100	40	90	280	Falling	Increase
100	125	100	40	75	340	Falling	Increase
200	200	100	40	60	400	Falling	Increase
300	275	100	40	45	460	Falling	Increase
400	350	100	40	30	520	Falling	Increase
500	425	100	40	15	580	Falling	Increase
600	500	100	40	0	640	Falling	Increase
700	575	100	40	−15	700	Constant	No change
800	650	100	40	−30	760	Rising	Decrease
900	725	100	40	−45	820	Rising	Decrease
1000	800	100	40	−60	880	Rising	Decrease

The corresponding diagram is represented in Figure 10.11.

Figure 10.11: The equilibrium level of income with net exports

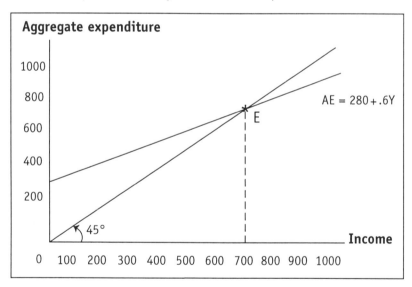

We can verify this equilibrium position algebraically. We begin with the expanded AE function, adding the foreign sector as follows:

$$AE \equiv C + \bar{I} + \bar{G} + \bar{X} - M \qquad [10.18]$$

where consumption and imports are defined as:

$$\boxed{C = \overline{C} + bY} \qquad \text{[10.6]}$$

$$\boxed{M = mY} \qquad \text{[10.17]}$$

Substitute Equations 10.6 and 10.17 into Equation 10.18 to get:

$$AE = \overline{C} + bY + \overline{I} + \overline{G} + \overline{X} - mY$$

Let $\overline{A} = \overline{C} + \overline{I} + \overline{G} + \overline{X}$, the autonomous components of AE, and substitute into the equation above:

$$AE = \overline{A} + bY - mY$$

Collect Y terms:

$$\boxed{AE = \overline{A} + (b - m)\ Y} \qquad \text{[10.19]}$$

In equilibrium:

$$\boxed{Y = AE} \qquad \text{[10.9]}$$

Substitute Y for AE in Equation 10.19 and solve for Y:

$$\text{[10.20]}$$

$$\boxed{Y = \overline{A} \times \frac{1}{1 - b + m}}$$

This is the equation for the equilibrium level of income for the four-sector model of the economy. We can now use this derivation to find (a) the AE function and (b) the equilibrium level of income for our example.

(a) Equation 10.19 states that:

$$AE = \overline{A} + (b - m)\ Y$$

For our particular example:

$\overline{C} = 50; \overline{I} = 100; \overline{G} = 40$ (before the change in government expenditure); $\overline{X} = 90$; $b = MPC = .75$; $m = MPM = .15$. Substitute these values into Equation 10.19 to find the AE function:

$$AE = (50 + 100 + 40 + 90) + (.75 - .15)Y = 280 + 0.6Y$$

(b) Equation 10.20 states that:

$$Y = \overline{A} \times \frac{1}{1 - b + m}$$

where: $\overline{A} = 280$; $b = .75$; $m = .15$.

$$Y = 280 \times \frac{1}{1 - .75 + .15} = 280 \times 2.5 = £700$$

At this stage we need to examine the multiplier in an alternative form.

The multiplier reconsidered
....

It is possible to express the multiplier in terms of marginal propensity to save MPS, rather than MPC. Since MPC = 1 – MPS, then the multiplier is the reciprocal of the MPS, or in equation form we can write it as follows:

$$\boxed{\frac{1}{1 - b} = \frac{1}{MPS}}$$
[10.21]

This allows us to express the multiplier in terms of leakages. In the simple model of the economy the only leakage is savings. The higher the leakage, the smaller the multiplier. This is not surprising: a tendency to save limits the extent of consumer expenditure which, in turn, limits the final change in income. This format can be very useful when we extend the model to four sectors and when assessing the effectiveness of fiscal policy.

The extension of our model to include the foreign sector complicates not only the derivation of the equilibrium level of income but also the multiplier. Using the leakages format, the multiplier is equal to:

$$\boxed{\frac{1}{MPS + MPM}}$$
[10.22]

where MPS is the marginal propensity to save and MPM is the marginal propensity to import. This multiplier is derived in Appendix 10.4.

If taxes are considered and treated as a function of income, a further complication arises in the form of the marginal propensity to tax.

● Definition
● ● ● ● ● ●

The marginal propensity to tax (MPT) is the proportion of any increment in income paid in taxes.

It is a leakage. Assuming consumer expenditure depends on disposable income, the multiplier is of the form:

$$\frac{1}{\textbf{MPS + MPM + MPT}}$$

[10.23]

The inclusion of the MPT, a leakage, further reduces the size of the multiplier.[19]

Approximations for these parameters in the Irish economy are MPS = 0.25, MPM = 0.6 and MPT = 0.3.[20] This gives us a multiplier of approximately unity which is relatively low by international standards.[21] This has important implications for the effectiveness of domestic fiscal policy. The Irish experience with Keynesian economics in general, and fiscal policy in particular, is discussed in Section 10.3.

One final concept which requires explanation is the paradox of thrift.

Thriftiness or savings is normally treated as desirable. The paradox of thrift suggests otherwise. How so? An increase in the planned level of savings results in a reduction in the equilibrium level of national income and because savings depends on income, the actual level of savings may even decline. This suggests that although savings can be viewed individually as a virtue it becomes a vice when the analysis is extended to society. It is, yet again, a fallacy of composition: the assumption that what is true for a part is true for the whole.

As a corollary to the above, the classical school and Keynes had very different views on the virtues of savings. The classical economists were in favour of high levels of savings which would lead to lower interest rates and higher investment levels. Keynes disagreed on the basis that too much savings had adverse effects on expenditure and output.

The Keynesian model, as presented above, is incomplete: it excludes money and interest rates, wages and prices, and finally, supply-side effects. These are dealt with in subsequent chapters. For the moment we turn our attention to the policy implications arising out of the Keynesian model and the Western economies' experience with Keynesian economics.

10.2 The policy implications

A number of important policy implications arise out of the Keynesian model. With the possibility that the economy may settle at an income level below the full-employment level, Keynesians argued in favour of government intervention in order to narrow this deflationary gap between actual output and full-employment output. In *The General Theory* he called for public works programmes to provide jobs and to increase national income. He strongly supported demand management and, in particular, the active use of fiscal policy. There remains some controversy over his support for counter-cyclical policy.

The terms demand management, fiscal policy and counter-cyclical policy require explanations.

Definition
● ● ● ● ● ●

Demand management is the collective term used to explain various government policies which influence the level of aggregate expenditure in the economy.

These include fiscal and monetary policy. We will discuss monetary policy in the next chapter. Fiscal policy is described below.[22]

Fiscal policy
···············

Definition
● ● ● ● ● ●

Fiscal policy refers to the use of government expenditure and taxation in order to influence aggregate expenditure and, in turn, national output.

Irish fiscal policy was inherited from the British model and in both countries it is synonymous with budgetary policy. This is because fiscal policy in the UK is implemented primarily through the budget.[23] The budget is a record of what the government pays out in the form of expenditure and what it receives, usually in the form of tax revenue. It is the responsibility of the Minister for Finance.

Each year's budget is divided into a current and a capital section. Current expenditure relates to spending on goods and services which are consumed during the fiscal year. For example, it includes wages and salaries of public servants and covers the operating expenses of public buildings. Current revenue is the income which accrues to the state from the day-to-day running of the economy. Examples include income tax, expenditure tax (e.g. VAT) and corporation tax. If expenditure exceeds revenue the budget is said to be in deficit. If revenue exceeds expenditure the budget is in surplus.

Capital expenditure refers to spending on items which are not completely consumed during the fiscal year. Examples include expenditure on infrastructure and investment projects. The details of the government's capital spending are published each year in the Public Capital Programme (PCP). Capital revenue normally consists of interest on stocks owned by government, loan repayments and capital grants received from the EU.[24]

Measures of fiscal policy
···························

An increase in expenditure or a decrease in taxation boosts demand and output and is termed expansionary fiscal policy. Similarly, a decrease in expenditure or an increase in taxation reduces demand and output and is termed contractionary fiscal policy. Both of these measures are used to indicate the stance of fiscal policy. For example, a large budget deficit is usually seen as expansionary whereas a similar-sized budget surplus is seen as contractionary. A budget which neither stimulates nor deflates the economy is said to be a neutral budget.

The addition of the current budget deficit and the capital budget deficit is called the Exchequer Borrowing Requirement.[25]

Definition
● ● ● ● ● ●

The Exchequer Borrowing Requirement (EBR) is the total amount of money that the central government must borrow in any one fiscal year in order to match revenue with expenditure.

It does not include borrowings of semi-state bodies and local authorities. The EBR is the most common indicator of the stance of fiscal policy. Commentators normally refer to changes in the EBR as being either expansionary if the EBR increases, or contractionary if the EBR decreases.

A broader measure of fiscal policy is the Public Sector Borrowing Requirement (PSBR). This includes borrowing by central and local government. Table 10.11 presents figures for these measures over the twenty-year period 1977–96.

Table 10.11: Measures of fiscal policy (£m)

Year	CuBD[1]	CaBD[2]	EBR[3]	PSBR
		(% of GNP)		
1977	201 (3.6%)	344 (6.1%)	545 (9.7%)	697 (12.4%)
1978	397 (6.0%)	413 (6.3%)	810 (12.3%)	973 (14.8%)
1979	522 (6.8%)	487 (6.3%)	1,009 (13.1%)	1,230 (16.0%)
1980	547 (6.0%)	671 (7.4%)	1,218 (13.4%)	1,559 (17.2%)
1981	802 (7.3%)	919 (8.4%)	1,721 (15.7%)	2,204 (20.1%)
1982	988 (7.9%)	957 (7.6%)	1,945 (15.5%)	2,466 (19.6%)
1983	960 (7.0%)	796 (5.8%)	1,756 (12.8%)	2,277 (16.6%)
1984	1,039 (7.0%)	786 (5.2%)	1,825 (12.2%)	2,375 (15.9%)
1985	1,284 (7.7%)	731 (4.4%)	2,015 (12.1%)	2,444 (14.7%)
1986	1,395 (7.9%)	750 (4.2%)	2,145 (12.1%)	2,506 (14.2%)
1987	1,180 (6.2%)	606 (3.2%)	1,786 (9.4%)	2,056 (10.8%)
1988[4]	317 (1.6%)	302 (1.5%)	619 (3.1%)	751 (3.7%)
1989	263 (1.2%)	216 (1.0%)	479 (2.2%)	667 (3.0%)
1990	152 (0.6%)	310 (1.3%)	462 (1.9%)	588 (2.4%)
1991	298 (1.2%)	201 (0.8%)	499 (2.0%)	762 (3.0%)
1992	446 (1.7%)	267 (1.0%)	713 (2.7%)	910 (3.4%)
1993	379 (1.3%)	311 (1.2%)	690 (2.5%)	862 (3.1%)
1994[5]	−15 (−0.1%)	687 (2.3%)	672 (2.2%)	782 (2.6%)
1995[6]	362 (1.1%)	265 (0.8%)	627 (1.9%)	826 (2.5%)
1996[7]	82 (0.2%)	647 (1.8%)	729 (2.0%)	836 (2.3%)

Source: Government Publications, *The 1996 Budget.*

1. CuBD is an abbreviation for current budget deficit.
2. CaBD is an abbreviation for capital budget deficit.
3. Since the ratification of the Maastricht treaty the General Government Deficit (GGD) has become a popular yardstick when measuring the stance of fiscal policy. The GGD includes the borrowing of the local authorities and the non-commercial semi-state bodies. It is particularly relevant in the context of the convergence criteria and quali-fication for EMU. Read the 1996 budget to see the Minister of Finance's thoughts (p. 12) on this measurement. To see the trend in the GGD since 1987 read Department of Finance, *Economic Review and Outlook*, July, 1996.
4. The figures for 1988 include receipts estimated at £500m from a tax amnesty.
5. The current budget balance of £15m in 1994 was a surplus.
6. The 1995 figures are provisional outturns.
7. The 1996 figures are post-budget estimates.

Using the EBR as an indicator of fiscal policy, we can see that the period up to 1981/82 was predominantly expansionary. The EBR was increasing both in size and as a percentage of GNP. The budgets between the years 1982–91 were largely contractionary. The EBR as a percentage of GNP fell steadily and then stabilised.

Although the EBR is often cited, it is a less than perfect indicator of changes in active fiscal policy. This is because the size of the EBR is influenced by automatic stabilisers which respond to changes in the economic environment. Examples include taxes and transfer payments. They are 'automatic' in the sense that they are built into the economy and do not require discretionary action by government. Their purpose is to reduce the impact of shocks that arise from cyclical fluctuations in the economy. If, for example, an economy is going into a recession, unemployment rises. Transfer payments increase because more people are receiving social welfare payments. The decline in national income means that tax receipts are likely to fall. The combination of higher expenditure and lower tax receipts results in a higher EBR. By the same logic, a lower EBR is likely to result during a boom period because of higher tax receipts and lower expenditures on transfer payments.

Therefore, changes in the EBR may reflect changes in the automatic stabilisers rather than deliberate action taken by the administration. Changes in the EBR which arise out of direct action taken by the government in order to move the economy in a given direction are called discretionary or structural changes. The budget deficit (or surplus) which results from these government decisions is called the structural or discretionary budget deficit (or surplus). An increase in the personal tax rate or an increase in the rate of old-age pensions are two such examples.

In brief, the structural or discretionary change in the EBR is a better measure of fiscal policy as it reflects active and deliberate changes by the government.

A second, more accurate measure of fiscal policy is the primary budget balance. Interest payments on the national debt are included as an expenditure item in the annual budget. However, the national debt and the subsequent interest payments do not reflect current policy but arise out of past government policy. Thus, in order to arrive at a correct measure for current fiscal policy it is necessary to exclude the debt service. This adjusted measure is known as the 'primary budget balance'.

Whereas the unadjusted-for-interest-payments current budget has been in deficit in every year since the early 1970s (1994 and 1996 being the only exceptions), the current primary budget has been in surplus continually since 1986. The difference is accounted for by the high level of interest payments on the national debt.[26] In 1996, for example, interest payments on the debt amounted to over £2.2bn. More importantly, it suggests that fiscal policy since the mid-1980s was even more contractionary than originally suspected.

Some economists argue that fiscal policy should be counter-cyclical. This is a restrictive use of fiscal policy. It means that the government should use the fiscal instruments available to it to boost the economy in times of recession and to deflate the economy in times of overheating. The government should increase spending and/or cut taxes to counter deficiencies in demand. This is the origin of the phrase 'spending your way out of recession'. During boom periods, when there is excess demand, the government cuts spending and/or increases taxes and thereby incurs a surplus. Over the lifetime of the business cycle the government budget would, in effect, be balanced, as the classical school endorsed, but with deliberate imbalances running countercyclically.[27] Terms such as 'pump-priming' and 'fine-tuning' the economy are also used to describe such a policy.

The question of whether domestic fiscal policy has been counter-cyclical has caused great debate among the economics profession.[28] Throughout the 1970s and the 1980s there are examples of periods when policies were strongly pro-cyclical, i.e. the fiscal changes implemented by the incumbent governments were either expansionary during the upturn or contractionary during the downturn of the business cycle.

One period was the mid-1970s. The world economy experienced an upturn in activity after 1976. On the back of this favourable international climate it was expected that the Irish economy would grow without any further stimulus from the state sector. Moreover, this was an opportunity to reduce borrowing and counterbalance the budget deficits of previous years. Yet domestic fiscal policy during these years was highly expansionary and pro-cyclical. This occurred partly because of the promises made during the general election of 1977 and partly because of deliberate action taken by the government on the advice of some economists. The expansionary fiscal policy of those years was justified on the basis of the 'self-financing' claim (see The Irish Experience in Section 10.3).

A second period was the early to mid-1980s when the international economic climate was unfavourable. Most Western economies were either in the depths of recession or else emerging from one with inflationary pressures looming. Financial markets were highly volatile with high interest rates and fluctuating exchange rates. As a result international trade suffered. Advocates of counter-cyclical fiscal policies would argue that such adverse economic conditions warrant expansionary fiscal policy at home in order to counter low demand and rising unemployment. Yet domestic fiscal policy during these years was highly contractionary and pro-cyclical.

The rationale behind this pro-cyclical policy was the attempt to restore order to the public finances. By 1982 the EBR was 15.5% of GNP. Borrowing to finance day-to-day spending was almost 8% of GNP. Fears grew both at home and abroad about the sustainability of the debt. A consensus was reached, among economists and politicians, to reduce borrowing and improve the national debt/GNP ratio. Other economic aims, including unemployment, were seen as subordinate to this primary objective (see The Irish Experience in Section 10.3).

Another aspect of fiscal policy which featured during this period is the concept of crowding out. Suppose the government increases expenditure. Furthermore, let us assume that it will be financed by borrowing rather than by tax increases. This induced borrowing creates a demand for funds in the financial markets, leaving less funds available for the private sector. This may lead to higher interest rates and in turn decreases in private sector spending.[29] In effect, the initial injection of public sector spending crowds out both consumer and investment expenditure. It is obvious from this simple explanation that crowding out has very important implications for the effectiveness of fiscal policy. Moreover, it appears from the above description that the expansionary fiscal policy adopted by the government may be far less effective than previously believed.

Opinions vary on the extent of crowding out. Supporters of fiscal policy, Keynesians included, argue that only partial crowding out occurs. Government spending is compensating for insufficient private investment. Critics of fiscal policy, monetarists for example, argue that full and complete crowding out is the norm. Government spending replaces private investment. The economy suffers as a result because private investment is more efficient than public investment, it is argued.

This discussion on fiscal policy has been limited to the confines of a closed economy. Little or no reference has been made to economic variables such as capital flows, foreign interest rates and output levels, fixed or flexible exchange rates. Changes in fiscal policy affect and are affected by these variables which play an important role in an open economy. Chapter 14 explains these international effects.

The Western economies' experience with Keynesian economics
....

The active use of public works programmes dates as far back as the 1930s when economies like Sweden, the US and even Germany, under Adolf Hitler, were using public investment to stimulate the economy. Hitler's Four-year Plan to abolish unemployment, announced in 1933, depended largely on demand-side measures including the Reinhardt Programme of public works.[30]

In the UK, both the Labour and Conservative governments of the 1950s and 1960s advocated and implemented Keynesian demand-management policies. The government policies of that period appear to have had their desired effects on unemployment. However, on account of their tendency to influence the level of imports, they also led to periodic balance of payments crises. In the UK, the subsequent mix of contractionary and expansionary policies that followed became known as stop-go policies. Many economists are highly critical of such short-term policies and advocate strongly against the use of similar policies in order to tackle present-day unemployment.

Nineteen sixty-three is the year most often cited in the US as the high point of Keynesian economics. The Kennedy administration advocated the use of Keynesian economic policies. Investment tax credits were introduced in 1962 in order to stimulate private sector spending and reduce unemployment. Many of the top economic advisers of the day, including J. K. Galbraith (b. 1908), James Tobin (b. 1918), the late Arthur Okun (1928–80), Robert Solow (b. 1924), the late Walter Heller (1915–87) and Paul Samuelson were advocates of Keynesian economics.[31]

Kennedy's successor, Lyndon Johnson, continued to adopt Keynesian-style policies early in his administration despite sufficient levels of demand and inflationary pressures arising from the US involvement in the Vietnam War. In 1964 Johnson persuaded Congress to enact personal tax cuts of 20% and a 10% cut for businesses. Notwithstanding the impact of the war, the results arising out of the Kennedy-Johnson experience with Keynesian economics were dramatic. Unemployment fell from 5.2% in 1962 to 4.8% in early 1965, and by 1966 it had fallen to 3.8%.

Support for Keynesian economics did not end with the Kennedy-Johnson administrations (1961–68). At the same time that the newly elected US President Richard Nixon was espousing the case for Keynesian economics with the infamous statement 'We are all Keynesians now', the UK Tory government under the leadership of Edward Heath was implementing similar Keynesian-style policies. The Chancellor, Anthony Barber, responding to the economic environment of the day which saw unemployment reach the one million figure for the first time in thirty years, increased public expenditure and cut taxes. What followed is commonly known as the 'Barber Boom' of the early 1970s. By the end of 1973 the unemployment figure was halved to 500,000. This dramatic improvement in the economy was attributed largely to the Keynesian-style policies adopted by the Chancellor.

However, things were to change in response to a number of factors. These included the economic environment of the time which was experiencing non-Keynesian trends of inflationary pressures in the face of deficient demand. Also, there was a growing dissatisfaction with Keynesian economics and the Phillips curve among the economics profession.[32] Finally, the ongoing economic research of the time focused less on the assumptions and conclusions of the Keynesian model and more on the microeconomic foundations of macroeconomics. Variables such as money, expectations and human capital were examined rather than the broad components of demand.

The economic environment of the 1970s was even more uncertain than the previous decade. The Bretton Woods system of regulating exchange rates broke down. There was an oil supply shock at the beginning and again at the end of the decade. There emerged a new phenomenon, called stagflation, which referred to rising unemployment accompanied by rising inflation. This phenomenon could not be explained within the framework of the basic Keynesian model.

In the UK, both the Tory government led by Edward Heath (in the later days of his administration) and, surprisingly, the Labour government of James Callaghan criticised the Keynesian economics of the past and adopted tough monetarist policies. Prime Minister Callaghan, addressing delegates at the 1976 Labour Party conference, said 'We used to think you could spend your way out of recession . . . I tell you in all candour that the option no longer exists and insofar as it did ever exist, it only worked by injecting demand into the economy.' However, it was the 1980s combination of Margaret Thatcher in the UK and Ronald Reagan in the US which was primarily responsible for the emergence of an alternative to Keynesian economics, i.e. supply-side policies. Supply-side economics and how it differs from demand management is explained in Chapter 13.

The revival of Keynesian economics in the 1990s was largely in response to the Anglo-American recession and the general dissatisfaction with the supply-side policies of the previous decade. This re-emergence is partly reflected in the election of a Democratic President in the US and the election of the Labour Party at home. Both parties in the past have supported and adopted Keynesian-style policies. It was believed that on the return to power they would re-introduce some demand-side policies.[33]

In brief, the adoption of Keynesian-style policies both in the US and in the UK in the 1960s and early 1970s coincided with a period of prosperity and low unemployment. This compared with the high unemployment rates of the inter-war period and likewise, the 1970s. Many attribute this success to the adoption of demand-management policies: this is open to debate. What is probably less contentious is the significant contribution of a number of events other than the implementation of Keynesian economics. These include the decline in protectionism in favour of free trade, the importance of innovation, R & D and the advance in technology and, finally, the stability of international financial markets.

Another contentious issue is the limits of Keynesian economics and the subsequent policy recommendations. Keynesian economics emerged out of the Great Depression, and the recommendations which followed were to apply to the economic environment of the time – one of mass unemployment, protectionism and floating exchange rates. The economic climate has changed dramatically over the past sixty years. Different periods with different problems require different solutions.[34] The adoption and success of Keynesian demand policies in the past does not necessarily require similar policies now or in the future.

This chapter concludes with a discussion on Keynesian economics within the context of Irish economic policy.

10.3 The Irish experience

Ireland was slow to adopt Keynesian economics. In the 1950s the authorities were more concerned with the substantial balance of payments deficits than with the unemployment trends. In the 1960s, policy was focused on attracting overseas industry and on building up the infrastructure in order to enhance the long-term development of the economy. Neither policy could be described as Keynesian which is in essence a short-term policy. However, if we lagged behind other European countries before the 1970s it is generally agreed that we have surpassed these same countries over the past twenty-five years in our adoption of Keynesian demand management. The debate now centres on whether Keynesian policies were effective considering, in particular, the openness of the Irish economy.

The Irish experience with active use of fiscal policy began in earnest in the early 1970s.[35] Prior to this the Minister of Finance would balance his current budget every year, in accordance with sound accounting principles and, to a lesser extent, the classical economic doctrine. Nineteen seventy-two marks a watershed in Irish government policy. This was the year of the first planned current budget deficit in modern times. The Minister of Finance, Mr George Colley, admitted to taking a 'calculated risk' in opting for expansion in preference to stability. He went on to acknowledge '. . . a risk that I may be fuelling the fire of inflation rather than the engine of growth'.[36]

Unfortunately such a radical change in policy was overshadowed by the events of the following year when the world economy suffered an oil crisis which induced inflationary pressures throughout the Western world, including Ireland. Inflation was exacerbated even beyond what the Minister had feared. The difference, however, was in the cause and the extent of the rise in prices.

By 1975 the current budget deficit had increased to 6.8% of GNP. This was viewed by the incumbent government as being too high. According to the then Minister of Finance, Mr Richie Ryan, 'Borrowing for capital purposes is justifiable in the context of our long-term economic aims' but 'Borrowing to meet current deficits is not, no matter how desirable it may be by reference to immediately pursuing requirements.'[37] Taxes were raised and expenditure was curtailed in order to reduce the borrowing.

The general election of 1977 brought an abrupt end to this contractionary fiscal policy. Political parties promised tax cuts and expenditure increases although there was evidence of an economic recovery worldwide. The new government acted on its promises by abolishing rates on private dwellings, reducing motor tax, increasing tax allowances and creating over 11,000 new public-sector posts.

These and similar measures introduced by the government were justified on the basis that a fiscal stimulus would ensure a stable standard of living and a reduction in unemployment. In economic terms the policy was rationalised by reference to a self-financing fiscal boost. The then Minister of Finance, Mr Colley, aided by his economic advisers, argued that such a fiscal boost would ensure an increase in national income which, in turn, would generate sufficient taxes to self-finance the initial expansion. On account of these additional tax receipts, no substantial increase in borrowing would be necessary, it was argued. Unfortunately the results were somewhat different than the forecast.

Policy continued to be highly expansionary during a period when the economy, without any fiscal stimulus, was growing satisfactorily in real terms. Although this policy did manage to keep unemployment down and at the same time maintain a relatively high standard of living, it was also responsible for transforming the country into a net debtor, characterised by high annual budget deficits, external borrowing and a looming balance of payments crisis. This situation was exacerbated by the second oil crisis in 1979 and the subsequent world recession.

By 1981 the Exchequer Borrowing Requirement was 15.7% of GNP with a national debt of over £10bn. Moreover, the government was borrowing over 7% of GNP to finance day-to-day expenditure. To make matters worse, the domestic political situation was far from stable with three elections within the space of eighteen months. Some commentators, unhappy with the domestic outlook, went so far as to call for assistance from the International Monetary Fund (IMF). This would have been a highly unusual and embarrassing move for a developed, Western economy.[38]

The first step towards restoring some stability in the domestic economy was achieved when a consensus on the need for order in the public finances was reached among the main political parties. Fiscal rectitude, as it became known, took precedence over all other objectives, including a reduction in unemployment. The Coalition government of 1982–86 set about tackling the problem primarily by increasing taxes and, to a lesser extent, curtailing capital expenditure.

Some commentators were very critical of such a policy mix. They argued that the higher tax rates acted as a disincentive to work and only succeeded in siphoning off legitimate work to the shadow economy. Capital expenditure, they argued, was a key element in the long-term development of the economy and did not warrant cutbacks. In addition, they postulated that cutting capital expenditure was an 'easy target' on the basis that it was politically more difficult to cut current expenditure and, secondly, a number of key investment projects were coming to an end at this time. Notwithstanding these criticisms, some credit must be given to the Coalition partners for attempting to tackle the problem.

The highly deflationary policies which followed appeared to have more of an impact on unemployment than on the public finances. By 1986 the current budget deficit was 7.9% of GNP, the national debt/GNP ratio was 128% and the unemployment rate had increased to 17% of the labour force. On the positive side, inflation fell from 20% in 1981 to 3.8% in 1986. This was due to a combination of the deflationary policies of the administration and the international trend of lower prices.

The general election of 1987 and the subsequent change in government, with the support of the Tallaght Strategy, brought about another turn in policy and with it a dramatic improvement in both the public finances and the economy as a whole.[39] The cuts in current expenditure, the return to centralised wage bargaining with the Programme for National Recovery and the favourable international economic background all contributed to an economic performance over the period which surpassed even the most optimistic of forecasts.

In terms of the public finances, the austere measures introduced by the Minister of Finance, Mr Ray MacSharry, resulted in significant reductions in budget deficits and national debt/GNP ratios. Government expenditure was cut by 3.7% per annum on average between 1987 and 1989. The EBR was reduced from 12.1% of GNP in 1986 to 2.2% in 1989. Such draconian measures earned MacSharry the nickname of 'Mac the Knife'. What was even more extraordinary was the recorded growth rates in GNP during the same period. The increase was close to 3.6% per year on average, the highest growth rate recorded for any three-year period since the mid-1960s. Unfortunately, as we already mentioned in the previous chapter, this did not translate into an equal growth in employment rates.

On reading the above account of the performance of the Irish economy during the period 1987–89 one might be led to believe that the remarkable transformation was due solely to the deflationary policies adopted by the government. However, the Keynesian model of income determination indicates that contractionary fiscal policy, as described above, deflates the economy and reduces national income. The Irish experience seems to suggest the opposite, that expenditure cuts led to increases in national income. This raises questions over the validity of the Keynesian model in the Irish context. It also gave rise to the phrase Expansionary Fiscal Contraction (EFC).[40] However, before we hastily disregard the work of Keynes, we need to look for possible explanations, other than the expenditure cuts, in order to explain the increases in GNP.

A detailed analysis of this period is beyond the scope of a basic textbook in economics. However, a number of possible, although not exhaustive, factors which contributed to the recovery are listed below. The occurrence of these raises doubts over this 'new, exotic and somewhat counter-intuitive concept' of EFC.[41]

- The tax amnesty of 1987 which raised over £500 million in unpaid taxes. This extra source of income contributed to the reduction in the budget deficit which otherwise would have required further cuts in expenditure and/or hikes in tax rates. Furthermore, the taxpayers who availed of the amnesty remained in the tax net and became an additional source of revenue in subsequent years.

- The 1980s was a boom period for the world economy. Higher income levels, lower inflation rates, stable exchange rates and lower interest rates all contributed to an environment which was conducive to external trade. Ireland, being a small open economy, availed of these conditions and recorded a strong export performance. The volume of Irish exports grew by 8.9% on average per annum between 1986 and 1989.
- An increase in private sector confidence and more optimistic expectations for the future resulted in an increase in both consumer expenditure and investment expenditure. This new-found confidence was due, in part, to the credible economic policy adopted by the government, typified by the relatively low wage agreements contained in the Programme for National Recovery. Furthermore, financial markets at home and abroad and, likewise, foreign investment both at home and abroad reacted positively to the change in policy.
- In 1986 the Irish pound was devalued by 8% within the EMS exchange rate mechanism. This benefited Irish exporters, particularly those doing business in the UK. Furthermore, interest rates declined as the domestic environment improved. The interest rate differential between Ireland and our UK and German counterparts narrowed significantly. For example, the three-month interest rate differential with the UK fell from –2.8% approximately at the end of 1986 to +4.8% approximately at the end of 1988. Likewise, the interest rate differential with Germany fell, from 9% approximately to 3% approximately over the same period.

The period between 1987 and 1990 was followed by the Anglo-American recession of the early 1990s which slowed economic activity both at home and, in particular, in the UK and the US. The subsequent decline in economic growth on the European continent and in the Far East was less severe. However, by 1993–94 both the UK and Ireland had clearly emerged from the recession and were recording very satisfactory growth rates. As a result, the Irish authorities were able to reduce borrowing, particularly for current purposes. In terms of GDP, they were recording one of the lowest budget deficits in the EU.

However, the one area of economic policy which concerned private-sector economists was the growth of public expenditure. It is estimated that between 1989 and 1993 current government spending increased by 31% whereas the inflation rate over the same four-year period was only 11.5%. At the time of writing this textbook, the same trends of higher tax revenue, higher expenditure and a low and stable budget deficit are the norm.

In brief, the consensus is that Keynesian-style policies were not very successful in Ireland in achieving their goals. Many commentators suggest that the legacy left behind is one of high unemployment and a massive public debt. However, on reflection, this is probably due more to the inappropriateness of fiscal policy in a small open economy like Ireland combined with the mismanagement by the authorities rather than the ineffectiveness of Keynesian economics in general.

CASE STUDY

Extract from The Sunday Business Post
'Like it or not, McAleese's theory of cutback-induced boom seems right'
by Damien Kiberd

. . . For this reason McAleese may have difficulty in driving home his argument. People do not want to believe that you can bring government spending down from 53.5% of GNP (in 1986) to 41.7% this year, without hurting various vulnerable groupings. Yet the facts as set out by McAleese show that you can promote such a fiscal contraction while improving profits, incomes and welfare payments if the international economic backdrop is favourable and if the productive economy has the capacity to grow rapidly.

The economy grew by 5.6% in 1987, by 1.2% in 1988 and by 4.3% in 1989. Price inflation in the same three-year period was cumulatively around 10%. At the end of 1989 those seeking to allocate national output were allocating one-fifth more in money terms than they were able to allocate at the end of 1985. The rising tide of economic growth paid for higher real disposable incomes, improved welfare payments (particularly for the long-term unemployed), higher farm profits and better returns on equity in business.

McAleese's view is that the rising tide of economic growth was made possible by the falling tide of public spending.

The debate over cause and effect will rage. But there can be few if any econ- omists who would suggest that what happened between 1981 and 1985 was in some sense preferable to what happened between 1986 and now. As McAleese points out, in 1986 Irish borrowers paid a premium of 9% for loans compared to what was paid by DM borrowers. Today that exchange rate premium has been brought below 4%. In the mid-1980s borrowers in Dublin paid 2.8% more for money than borrowers in London.

Today, the boot is on the other foot with Dublin rates 3% below those of the London market. Why have Irish money rates taken such a favourable trend? McAleese could point to the seriousness with which we have tackled the exchequer deficit (taking borrowing down from 13.8% of GDP to 2.1% in eight years) as the key factor underpinning confidence in the money markets.

Wage restraint on the part of public servants, who accepted general increases of 2.5% per annum under the Programme for National Recovery, has helped maintain inflation at very low levels (4% heading for 2% if you are to believe official estimates). According to McAleese, unit wage costs as expressed in a common currency, are now running at 63% of the 1980 level . . .

Source: The Sunday Business Post, *June 1990.*

Questions
....

1. What is the official term for the 'new, exotic . . . concept' which is described above? Explain its meaning.

2. How does it differ from the Keynesian interpretation? If it is true, what implications does it have for Keynesian economics?
3. In your own view, what brought about the improvement in 'profits, incomes and welfare payments'?

Answers
....

1. Expansionary Fiscal Contraction. A fiscal contraction (lower expenditure and/or higher taxes), given the right circumstances, can increase economic prosperity, measured by GNP.
2. This contrasts sharply with the views expressed by followers of Keynesian economics. For Keynesians, output is determined by the level of demand. Any increase (decrease) in spending will lead to an increase (decrease) in output. Furthermore, on account of the multiplier process, the change in output which is generated is larger than the initial change in spending. Thus, expansionary fiscal policy (some combination of higher expenditure and lower taxes) will tend to increase output while contractionary fiscal policy will tend to decrease output.

    EFC, if it is true, has serious implications for Keynesian economics and the active use of fiscal policy. During the period described above, government spending was curtailed in real terms. Yet, against the predictions of the Keynesian model, national output increased and did so dramatically. If one can prove cause and effect, it raises serious questions about the effectiveness, and more fundamentally, the validity of Keynesian economics and its policy recommendations.
3. There is no definitive answer. However, two important issues need to be raised – first, the occurrence of EFC, given the right circumstances; and second, the debate over cause and effect. The first suggests the possibility of EFC only under certain conditions. These necessary conditions include a favourable international economic environment and the capacity of the domestic economy to expand. The second is a more fundamental issue. It questions the cause and effect between the curtailment in government expenditure and the increase in national output. It appears that the author believes in cause and effect to some degree. This contrasts sharply with many other commentators who attribute the increase in output to factors other than the expenditure cutbacks. These other factors, as mentioned before, include the 1986 devaluation, the 1987 tax amnesty, the new credibility of the government's policy (which led to a positive response from financial markets, resulting in lower interest rates and a stable currency) and finally the change in expectations and confidence of the private sector.

Summary

1. There are a number of assumptions to the Keynesian model of income determination. It is a fixed price model. It assumes that the economy is below full employment and that any increase in demand will increase output but will have no effect on prices.

2. The model incorporates many new concepts such as the consumption function, aggregate expenditure, the marginal propensity to consume and the multiplier. Output is determined by aggregate expenditure which is simply equal to total spending in the economy. Equilibrium exists at a point where aggregate expenditure equals output.

3. Any change in aggregate expenditure results in a greater change in output. This is explained by the multiplier process where the multiplier is simply the amount by which income changes as a result of an initial change in spending. The value of the Keynesian multiplier depends on the size of the leakages.

4. The Keynesian model can be extended to include both government and foreign sectors. If so, public expenditure and exports augment total spending by the private sector. Also, the value of the multiplier is affected by the marginal propensity to tax and import. As a result of these leakages, the multiplier in an open economy is smaller than the simple multiplier in the closed economy model.

5. Demand management is the collective term used to describe policies which aim to influence the level of demand and in turn the level of output in the economy. One example is fiscal policy which depends on the active use of government expenditure and taxes to influence demand. In Ireland, it centres around Budget day and the Book of Estimates. Measures of active fiscal policy include the discretionary budget deficit and the primary budget deficit.

6. Keynesian economics was very popular among economists, policy-makers and politicians after World War II and particularly in the 1950s and the 1960s. However, Ireland was relatively slow, by international standards, to adopt short-term Keynesian-style policies. The success of such policy in Ireland, and in other countries has been limited.

Key terms

Consumption
Consumption function
Disposable income
Marginal propensity to consume
Savings function
Marginal propensity to save
Autonomous expenditure
Investment function
Aggregate expenditure
Equilibrium
Inventory changes
Keynesian cross diagram
Multiplier
Marginal propensity to import

Marginal propensity to tax
The paradox of thrift
Deflationary gap
Demand management
Fiscal policy
Exchequer Borrowing Requirement
Public Sector Borrowing Requirement
Automatic stabilisers
Structural budget deficit
Primary budget deficit
Counter-cyclical policy
Crowding out
Fiscal rectitude
Expansionary Fiscal Contraction

Review questions

1. Explain the significance of the consumption function in the Keynesian model of income determination.
2. What determines the equilibrium level of income in the Keynesian model? Explain, in words, how this position is reached.
3. What is the Keynesian multiplier? What factors influence its size? Explain how its value can vary. Explain how it is related to:
   (a) consumption function;
   (b) leakages;
   (c) fiscal policy.
4. Briefly explain the differences between the income determination model as applied to a closed economy and the model as applied to an open economy. How do the conclusions differ?
5. What policy recommendations arise out of the Keynesian model? When did support for Keynesian economics emerge? Why did it lapse in the 1970s?
6. Critically assess the success or failure of Keynesian economics in the context of the Irish economy.

Working problems

1. The following equations are from a simple model of the economy:

   $C = 110 + .8Y$

   $\bar{I} = 300$

   $\bar{G} = 150$

   $\bar{X} = 250$

   $M = .2Y$

   (a) Calculate the equilibrium level of income for this model.
   (b) Suppose the government decides to double its expenditure on goods and services. What is the new equilibrium income level?
   (c) Calculate, and interpret the size of, the multiplier for this particular model.
2. Prove, using algebra, that the sum of the marginal propensity to consume and the marginal propensity to save is equal to 1.

Multi-choice questions

1. The classical school of economics held the view that:
   (a) the economy was at or close to full-employment;
   (b) large-scale government intervention was unnecessary;
   (c) large-scale government intervention was necessary;
   (d) both (a) and (b) above;
   (e) both (a) and (c) above.

2. If the marginal propensity to save increases from .2 to .25, then:

   (a) the slope of the consumption function steepens;
   (b) the marginal propensity to consume increases by the same proportion;
   (c) the expenditure multiplier increases from 4 to 5;
   (d) the savings function shifts downwards;
   (e) none of the above.

3. In the Keynesian cross diagram for the two-sector model:

   (a) investment is dependent on income levels;
   (b) when savings is less than investment output tends to decrease;
   (c) equilibrium is where $AE > \bar{I}$;
   (d) income is determined by the level of expenditure;
   (e) unplanned increases in stocks lead to an increase in output.

4. Due to a change in the pattern of consumption, the consumption function has flattened. This implies that the value of the multiplier has:

   (a) decreased since the marginal propensity to consume has increased;
   (b) decreased since the marginal propensity to consume has decreased;
   (c) increased since the marginal propensity to consume has increased;
   (d) increased since the marginal propensity to consume has decreased;
   (e) none of the above.

5. Suppose a model of the economy is represented by the following equations:
   $C = 120 + .8Y$, $\bar{I} = 280$, $\bar{G} = 300$. The equilibrium level of income is:

   (a) £700;
   (b) £3,500;
   (c) £560;
   (d) £140;
   (e) £584.

6. The government wants to increase national output by £300 million. It's economic advisers provide it with the following information: $S = .2Y$, $\bar{I} = 200$, $\bar{G} = 300$, $\bar{X} = 100$, $M = .2Y$. By how much should the government increase its spending on goods and services?

   (a) £120;
   (b) £300;
   (c) £750;
   (d) £1,500;
   (e) none of the above.

True or false

1. The classical school of economic thought argued that the self-adjusting mechanism of the market ensured the absence of any involuntary unemployment. _____
2. The autonomous component of the consumption function varies as income varies. _____

3. Unplanned decreases in inventories are a signal to firms to increase production. _____

4. The Keynesian multiplier is always greater than zero but less than one. _____

5. Adjusting the income determination model to include a value for exports and government expenditure (both autonomous) increases the equilibrium level of income. _____

6. Counter-cyclical fiscal policy implies the adoption of a budget deficit during a recession and a budget surplus during a recovery. _____

Fill in the blanks

The pre-Keynesian or _____ school of economics believed that markets were inherently _____ and they tended _____ towards a full-employment equilibrium level. The mechanisms which guaranteed this were the _____ of wages, prices and _____ _____. The latter was responsible for equating _____ and investment. There was little role for _____ intervention. Keynesian economics viewed the market and its operations very differently. _____ believed that the economy could be at an equilibrium which was _____ the full-employment level. The level of output in the economy was determined largely by the level of _____ . Wages were _____ which prevented a clearing of the _____ market. Hence, _____, of an involuntary and long-term nature, was possible. In order to tackle the problem of unemployment government intervention in the form of higher _____ was required. Furthermore, a _____ effect was likely which would result in a _____ increase in income than the initial injection in autonomous spending. However, this multiplier is _____ by _____ such as high taxes and a high propensity to import. The simple Keynesian model, as described, is _____ and requires adjustments to include such variables as money and interest rates, wages, prices and _____ levels of GDP and interest rates.

CASE STUDY

Extract from The Sunday Independent
Galbraith urges jobs spend
by John Moore

Eminent US economist John Kenneth Galbraith is to tell the government to abandon its strict budgetary discipline in order to tackle record unemployment. The Professor of Economics at Harvard University lambasts as 'paranoid' those who insist on strict control of public spending, and advises that they be ignored.

'The Irish Government should increase the budget deficit to create jobs and stimulate growth', Professor Galbraith will tell listeners to RTE Radio 1's Thomas Davis lecture series on The Jobs Crisis tonight. He goes on: 'All countries, including Ireland, must have a disciplined will to adjust taxation and expenditure to the prevailing economic condition.

---->

'For now, deficits should be accepted and, by Government action and expenditure, put people to work. This in the short run will increase the public deficit and the public debt, attitudes on both of which have now reached paranoiac proportions. These attitudes, must for the time, be ignored, and when prosperity returns, the deficits should be reduced.'

He said Ireland, with a young, eager and well-educated labour force, had a head start in job creation over other nation states.

. . .

Source: The Sunday Independent, 28 March 1993.

Questions

1. What type of government policy is Galbraith advocating in the above article? How would the use of such a policy 'create jobs'?
2. What are the dangers of such a policy? In your view, do they explain the 'paranoiac' attitudes of some commentators?
3. What is Galbraith suggesting when he proposes 'budget deficit to create jobs' followed by 'and when prosperity returns, the deficits should be reduced'? How does this policy differ from the classical view?

Appendix 10.1: The savings function

The following is the derivation of the simple savings function:

$$Y_d \equiv C + S \qquad [10.3]$$

which can be rewritten as:

$$S \equiv Y_d - C \qquad [10.4]$$

The consumption function is defined as:[42]

$$C = bY_d \qquad [10.2]$$

Substitute bY_d for C in Equation 10.4:

$$S = Y_d - bY_d$$

Since Y_d is common to the two components, we can rewrite the right-hand side of the equation as follows:

$$S = (1-b)Y_d \qquad [10.5]$$

We know from the previous discussion about the consumption function that b, the marginal propensity to consume, is a positive number which is greater than zero but less than one. The marginal propensity to save (1–b) must therefore also be a positive number which is greater than zero but less than one. Equation 10.5 shows that there is a positive relationship between disposable income and savings. As disposable income increases, savings increases by a fraction of that amount.

Let us take an example. Table 10.12 provides a set of disposable income and savings levels.

Table 10.12: The savings function

Disposable income, Y_d	Savings, S
0	0
100	25
200	50
300	75
400	100
500	125
600	150
700	175
800	200

As disposable income increases by increments of £100, savings increase by increments of £25. The MPS is equal to the change in savings divided by the corresponding change in disposable income. Hence:

$$MPS = \frac{\Delta S}{\Delta Y_d} = \frac{25}{100} = 0.25$$

If disposable income increases households will plan additional savings equal to one-quarter of any increase in disposable income. This particular savings function is represented by the following equation:

$$S = .25Y_d$$

Proof:

If MPC = .75

then MPS = 1 – b = 1 – .75 = .25

If $C = .75Y_d$

then $S = (1 – b)Y_d = (1 – .75)Y_d = .25Y_d$

For example, an increase in disposable income of £100 leads to an increase in planned savings of (1 – b) x £100 which is equal to 0.25 x £100 = £25. This particular savings function is graphically represented in Figure 10.12.

Figure 10.12: The savings function,
  S = .25Y$_d$

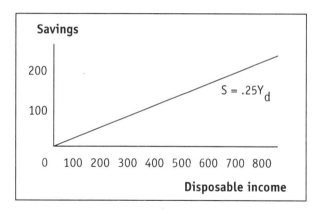

The upward sloping line shows that there is a positive relationship between savings and disposable income. The slope of the savings function is the marginal propensity to save.

The derivation for the more complicated savings function follows.

Beginning with Equation 10.4:

$$S \equiv Y_d - C$$

[10.4]

Recall that the consumption function is defined as:

$$C = \overline{C} + bY_d$$

[10.6]

Substitute into Equation 10.4:

$$S = Y_d - \overline{C} - bY_d$$

This can be written as:

$$S = -\overline{C} + Y_d - bY_d$$

Grouping the Y_d variables together, we obtain the equation of the savings function:

$$S = -\overline{C} + (1 - b)Y_d$$

[10.24]

The savings function, in the general case, with an intercept of $-\overline{C}$ and a slope equal to $(1 - b)$ is illustrated in Figure 10.13.

Figure 10.13: The savings function,
$$S = -\overline{C} + (1 - b)Y_d$$

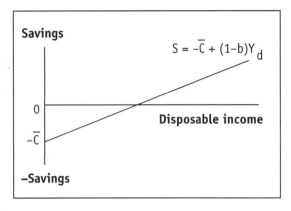

At low levels of disposable income savings are negative. This means that past savings are being used to finance expenditure. Dissavings is the reason why consumer expenditure can be larger than disposable income levels, as they are in Table 10.2. At the point where the savings function crosses the horizontal axis, savings is zero; all disposable income is spent. In the text the consumption function is $C = 50 + .75Y_d$. With a $\overline{C} = 50$ and a MPC $= .75$ the savings function is $S = -50 + .25\,Y_d$. This is drawn in the bottom frame of Figure 10.14 in Appendix 10.2.

Appendix 10.2: The savings-investment approach

In the income-expenditure approach, equilibrium occurs when income, Y, is equal to expenditure, AE. However, using the two-sector model we can also express equilibrium in terms of savings and investment.

Table 10.13 continues the example which we have been using throughout the chapter. The information from this table is depicted graphically in the bottom frame of Figure 10.14.

Table 10.13: The equilibrium level of income

Y	C	S	$\overline{I}$
0	50	−50	100
100	125	−25	100
200	200	0	100
300	275	25	100
400	350	50	100
500	425	75	100
600	500	100	100
700	575	125	100
800	650	150	100

By treating investment as autonomous, the investment function is drawn as a straight line. In our example it is equal to £100. The savings function is upward sloping. This reflects the positive relationship between savings and income. Savings equals £100 at an income level of £600. We can now compare the equilibrium levels of income from the income-expenditure approach and the savings-investment approach.

Figure 10.14 illustrates the equilibrium level of income. At £600, income equals expenditure (the top diagram) and savings equals investment (the bottom diagram).

Figure 10.14: Deriving the equilibrium level of income

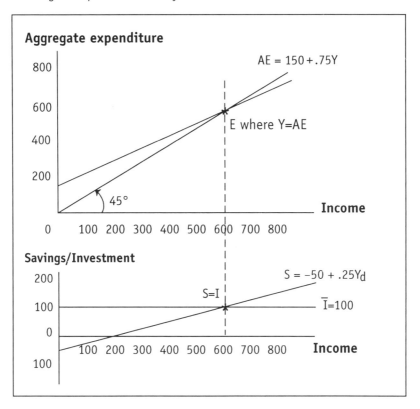

We confirm this as follows. Below £600 planned investment exceeds planned savings. Any excess of injections over leakages causes an unplanned reduction in inventories which leads to an increase in national income. Above £600 planned savings exceeds planned investment. The excess of leakages over injections causes unplanned increases in inventories which leads to a decrease in national income. National income is in equilibrium where planned savings equal planned investment.

Appendix 10.3: Algebraic derivation of the two-sector model

Keynesian multiplier

We begin with Equation 10.13 from the text:

$$Y = \overline{A} \times \frac{1}{1-b} \qquad\qquad [10.13]$$

where:

$$\frac{1}{1-b} = k \qquad\qquad [10.25]$$

Substitute Equation 10.25 into Equation 10.13 above:

$$Y = \overline{A} \times k \qquad [10.26]$$

If there is a change in the autonomous component of expenditure, we can adapt this equation to calculate the resulting change in income:

$$\Delta Y = \Delta \overline{A} \times k$$

Solve for k:

$$\frac{\Delta Y}{\Delta \overline{A}} = k \qquad [10.27]$$

Therefore k represents the multiplier. We can see that in this simple model, the magnitude of the multiplier is directly related to the marginal propensity to consume.

Appendix 10.4: Algebraic derivation of the Keynesian multiplier including the foreign sector

Begin with Equation 10.20 from the text:

$$Y = \overline{A} \times \frac{1}{1 - b + m} \qquad [10.20]$$

If there is a change in autonomous expenditure, what is the corresponding change in income?

$$\Delta Y = \Delta \overline{A} \times \frac{1}{1 - b + m}$$

Divide both sides by $\Delta \overline{A}$ to yield:

$$\frac{\Delta Y}{\Delta \overline{A}} = \frac{1}{1 - b + m} \qquad [10.28]$$

In this situation the multiplier is:

$$k = \frac{1}{1 - b + m} \qquad [10.29]$$

This multiplier is smaller than the simple multiplier $\frac{1}{1 - b}$. Imports are a leakage from the circular flow. The inclusion of the marginal propensity to import causes the multiplier to decrease in magnitude.

CHAPTER 11

MONEY, INTEREST RATES, THE CENTRAL BANK AND MONETARY POLICY

'Money is the most important thing in the world.'[1]

George Bernard Shaw

'How to have your cake and eat it too: lend it out at interest.'

Anonymous

'There have been three great inventions since the beginning of time: fire, the wheel and central banking.'

Will Rogers (1879–1935)

Chapter objectives

Upon completing this chapter, the student should understand:

- what money is, what money does;
- how the banking system creates money;
- the different theories of interest rate determination;
- the functions of the Central Bank;
- the implementation and effectiveness of monetary policy;
- the Irish experience of monetary policy.

Outline

11.1 **Money, money supply and money creation**
11.2 **Interest rate determination**
11.3 **The role of the Central Bank**
11.4 **Monetary policy in a closed economy**
11.5 **The Irish experience**

Introduction

In the words of the economist Milton Friedman, 'Money matters.' Money is indeed a very important feature of any modern state: it facilitates the workings of the economy. Its importance, however, is not confined to the day-to-day operations of an economy. Money and monetary policy play an important role in the macro-economic management of the country. It can influence such variables as expenditure, output, employment and prices.

We begin this chapter with a discussion on money: its definition, characteristics, functions and how it is created by the banking system. This is followed by the theory of interest rate determination. Two main theories are explained. A short history on the evolution of the Central Bank in Ireland follows. Monetary policy and its role in a closed economy is also discussed. The chapter finishes with a brief examination of monetary policy in Ireland.

11.1 Money, money supply and money creation

Over the centuries, money has taken many different forms. Examples include whales' teeth in Fiji, rats on Easter Island, dogs' teeth on the Admiralty Islands, silk and salt in China, sea-shells in Africa and cattle in ancient Ireland.

'Money', regardless of the form it takes, has a number of desirable attributes: it should be easily recognisable and acceptable, durable and divisible, convenient, uniform and relatively scarce.

Above all else, money is anything that is generally accepted as a means of payment. Any means of payment has a number of functions.

Functions of money
....

According to John R. Hicks, 'Money is as money does.'[2] This suggests that the functions of money are more important than its form (dollars vs pounds, gold vs silver). The real power of money is in what it does, rather than what it is. We will now explain the most important functions of money.

1. *A medium of exchange*. Money is used in a monetary economy in order to allow for exchange between buyers and sellers. A non-monetary or barter economy is one where there is no accepted medium of exchange. There is a direct exchange of one good for another good. Consequently, there must exist a 'double coincidence of wants', i.e. each person must possess what the other person requires. Each person involved in a transaction must be a buyer and a seller simultaneously.

For example, if you have apples but want chocolate ideally you must find somebody who has chocolate and is willing to exchange chocolate for apples. This 'coincidence of wants' involves a number of problems. They include, among others, the high level of transaction costs incurred if intermediate trades are necessary and the indivisibility and non-standardisation of some commodities.

Using money as a medium of exchange is more efficient. You can sell your apples to Roches Stores and buy chocolate bars at the corner shop.

2. *A measure of value*. Money is the common unit of measurement which allows for prices to be quoted. Hence, the exchange value of different commodities such as chickens, clothes and cars can be compared to one another. In Ireland, the prices of

these and other goods are expressed in Irish pounds or punts. The pound sterling is the unit of account in the UK, the dollar in the US, the franc in France and so on.

3. *A standard of deferred payment.* This is the same as the function above but with a time dimension added. Obligations for future payments like leases and contracts are denominated in money.

4. *A store of value.* Money, held rather than spent, can be used to make purchases in the future. Because of price inflation, money is not the best store of value. If it is not in an interest-bearing account, it is worth less in the future than it is worth today. Houses are the main store of value for most Irish families. In general, the value of a house appreciates with time.

In the modern world, there are many forms of money. Examples include coins, banknotes, cheques (drawn on current accounts), credit cards (plastic money) and balances in deposit accounts. There is, however, a need to define the money supply more strictly.

Definitions of money supply

In Section 11.3, we will discuss the functions of the Central Bank in detail. For now, we will briefly mention that the Central Bank is responsible for controlling the money supply. We continue the discussion of money by explaining the definitions of the money supply used by the Central Bank.

The 'narrow money supply' includes forms of money that can be spent directly.

Definition
● ● ● ● ● ●

The narrow money supply is defined as the notes and coins in circulation plus current (non-interest bearing) account balances.

It is labelled M1 by the Central Bank.

The broad money supply or M3 adds the narrow money supply to other forms of money that can be readily converted into cash.[3]

Definition
● ● ● ● ● ●

The broad money supply is defined as M1 plus deposit account balances.

Any definition of the money supply is somewhat arbitrary because it is very hard to draw a distinction between 'money' and 'non-money'. For example, although credit cards can be readily used to purchase things, they are not included in the definition of M3. Both M1 and M3 are graphed in Figure 11.1.

Figure 11.1: M1 and M3 in Ireland 1980–95

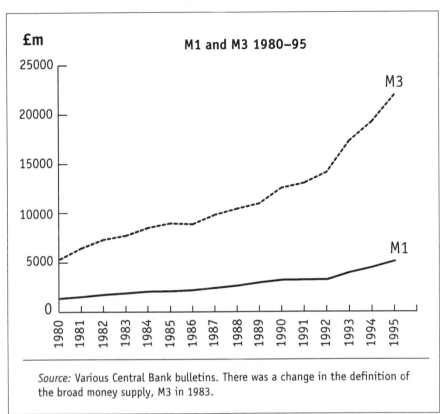

Source: Various Central Bank bulletins. There was a change in the definition of the broad money supply, M3 in 1983.

Values for M1 and M3 at end year 1994 and 1995 are included in Table 11.1.

Table 11.1: Monetary aggregates, end-December 1994 and 1995

	1994 (£m)	1995 (£m)	Year-to-year (change – %)
Currency	1,690.2	1,880.5	11.3
Current account balances	2,764.5	3,189.0	15.4
M1	4,454.7	5,069.5	13.8
Deposit account balances	14,754.3	16,841.0	14.1
M3	19,209.0	21,910.4	14.1

Source: Various Central Bank bulletins.

The annual percentage changes in M1 and M3 for the period between 1983 and 1994 are shown in Figure 11.2. The variability in both measures is striking.

Figure 11.2: Annual percentage changes in M1 and M3, 1983–94

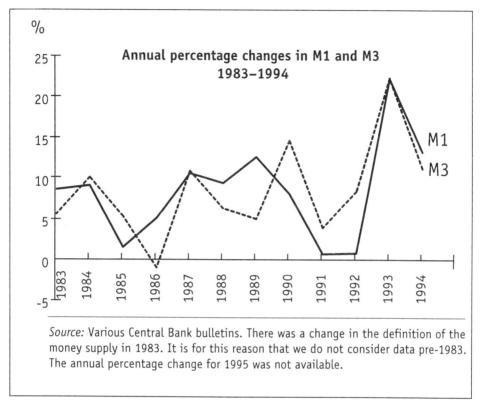

Source: Various Central Bank bulletins. There was a change in the definition of the money supply in 1983. It is for this reason that we do not consider data pre-1983. The annual percentage change for 1995 was not available.

Another term which requires an explanation is high-powered money or the monetary base.

Definition
● ● ● ● ● ●

High-powered money (H) is equal to currency plus reserves held by the Central Bank.

These reserves play an important role in the creation of money. We now explain 'money creation'.

Money creation
··················

We know from the discussion of the circular flow that banks are financial intermediaries; they facilitate the transfer of purchasing power from lenders to borrowers. They are, however, also involved in other activities. In particular, banks can 'create' money. They do so by taking deposits, keeping a certain amount in reserve and lending out the remainder. When they lend out these deposits, money is created. We will illustrate money creation with an example. In this particular example we assume that all the loans made by the bank are re-deposited.[4]

The Irish Bank (TIB) is the only financial institution on the island of Hibernia. A customer, Patricia O'Ireland deposits £1,000 in her local branch. The balance sheet of TIB Bank is presented in Table 11.2.

Table 11.2: The balance sheet of TIB Bank

	Assets	Liabilities	
Cash	1,000	Deposit	1,000

The deposit is a liability of the bank because it must return that money to Ms O'Ireland if requested. The bank manager, with many years of experience, knows that it is unlikely that Ms O'Ireland will withdraw all of her savings at once. Only a small percentage of this deposit is needed to meet the customer's demand for money. The remainder can be lent to other customers and firms who require funds.

The manager decides to keep 10% in reserves (£100) and lends out the residual (totalling in this case to £900) to another customer, Sean O'Shea.[5] The loan is an asset of the bank because it is owed to the bank by Mr O'Shea. The balance sheet reflects this transaction.

Table 11.3: The balance sheet of TIB Bank

	Assets	Liabilities	
Reserves	100	Deposit	1,000
Loan	900		
	1,000		1,000

A couple of days later, Patrick Murphy, the owner of the local furniture store, deposits the £900 which Sean O'Shea had spent on a suite of furniture. The bank manager proceeds to lend out 90% of this amount and retains 10% or £90. Mrs O'Brien, the local greengrocer, borrows the £810 in order to pay the builder for the extension to her shop. The builder, Niall Burke, who is also from the locality, decides to deposit this amount in order to guard against a 'rainy day'. With only one financial institution on the island the loan of £810 has found its way back to the bank. The bank holds £81 as reserves and advances the remaining £729 to another credible client. This process continues with the loan amount diminishing every time.

The final picture, in terms of the bank's assets and liabilities including all of the transactions described above is presented in Table 11.4.

Table 11.4: The balance sheet of TIB Bank

	Assets	Liabilities		Customer
Reserves	100	Deposit	1,000	O'Ireland
Loan	900			O'Shea
Reserves	90	Deposit	900	Murphy
Loan	810			O'Brien
Reserves	81	Deposit	810	Burke
Loan	729			
....				...
Total reserves	1,000	Total deposits	10,000	
Total loans	9,000			

At the end of the process the liabilities equal the assets. An initial deposit of £1,000 with a required reserve ratio of 10% results in the bank's total deposits amounting to £10,000. The money creation process is depicted in Figure 11.3 below.

Figure 11.3: Money creation

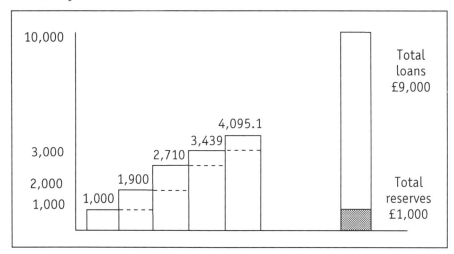

The deposits, loans and reserve amounts are recorded in Table 11.5.

Table 11.5: Money creation

Stages	Deposits (£)	Reserves (£)	Loans (£)
1	1,000	100	900
2	900	90	810
3	810	81	729
4	729	72.9	656.1
5	656.1	65.61	590.49
6 . . .			
7 . . .			
etc . . .			
Total	£ 10,000	£ 1,000	£ 9,000

In effect, there is a multiplier relationship at work. This multiplier is called the deposit multiplier.

Definition
• • • • • • •

The deposit multiplier is the multiple by which deposits will increase for every pound increase in reserves.

It can be expressed in equation form:[6]

$$\text{Deposit multiplier} = \frac{1}{r} \qquad\qquad [11.1]$$

where r equals the percentage of deposits which are held in reserve or the reserve ratio.

In this example, where 10% of deposits are held in reserve, the deposit multiplier is 1/0.1 and equals 10. Therefore, an increase in reserves will ultimately lead to a tenfold increase in deposits. The relationship between the change in reserves and the subsequent change in deposits can also be expressed in equation form:

$$\Delta D = \frac{1}{r}\,\Delta R \qquad\qquad [11.2]$$

where D represents deposits and R represents reserves.

For this example, we substitute 10 for the deposit multiplier and £1,000 for the change in reserves caused by Ms O'Ireland's initial deposit. Substituting these values into Equation [11.2], we find that the ultimate change in deposits is 10 x £1000 or £10,000. This is the same amount which we calculated by adding the total deposits in Table 11.5.

In summary, a change in reserves leads to a multiple change in bank deposits. The value of the multiplier depends on the reserve ratio. The larger the reserve ratio, the smaller the deposit multiplier; the smaller the reserve ratio, the larger the deposit multiplier. A more complicated version of this multiplier is derived in Appendix 11.1.

The money creation process is neatly summed up below.

Increase in reserves → increase in loans → increase in deposits → increase in money supply

The money creation process is also symmetric. Any withdrawal of money will lead to a decrease in reserves. As a result, banks reduce their lending, thus reducing the money supply. The reduction in the money supply will be a multiple of the fall in reserves.

This simplified analysis illustrates the power of a bank to create money. This analysis can also be extended to a two- or multi-bank system. Although the exercise is more difficult, the principle remains the same.[7]

11.2 Interest rate determination

Again, we must begin this section by defining two important concepts.

Definition
● ● ● ● ● ●

Interest is the amount that is paid on a loan or the amount that is received on a deposit.

For example, Tomas borrows £2,000 from the bank to buy a second-hand car. At the end of the year his repayments to the bank equal £2,200. The principal is £2,000 and the interest is £200.

Definition

●●●●●●

The rate of interest is the interest amount expressed as a percentage of the sum borrowed or lent.

In the example above, Tomas paid £200 in interest on a principal of £2,000. The interest rate is 10%.

In any economy there are many different rates of interest. They vary with time, risk, size and other factors.

There are two main theories of interest rate determination. The first is the classical approach where the interest rate is determined by the demand for and supply of funds. This is called the loanable funds theory. The second is the Keynesian approach where the interest rate is determined by the demand for and supply of money. This is called the liquidity preference theory.

The loanable funds theory

For classical economists, interest was the 'price' paid for borrowing funds. According to this theory, if a firm is considering the purchase of a capital good, the total cost of that good increases with the interest rate. As the interest rate increases, fewer and fewer investment projects are considered because the revenue which they generate is not sufficient to cover the price of the investment. Alternatively, as the interest rate falls, more projects are viable. In short, there is a negative relationship between interest rates and investment.

Firms often finance the purchase or lease of capital goods by borrowing funds.[8] The relationship between the interest rate and the demand for loanable funds is also negative. As interest rates rise, the price of capital goods rises and firms are less likely to borrow money to finance an investment project. Alternatively, as interest rates fall, the demand for loanable funds increases. Therefore, the demand curve for loanable funds, D is downward sloping as shown in Figure 11.4.

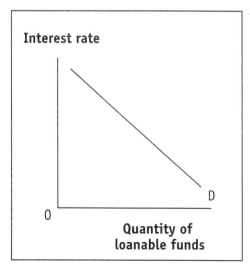

Figure 11.4: The demand curve for loanable funds

The supply of loanable funds is derived from the level of household savings. The classical economists argued that in order to persuade people to overcome the inclination to consume immediately, a reward in the form of interest had to be offered. The higher the rate of interest, the greater is the inducement to postpone current consumption, and so the greater is the supply of loanable funds. As the rate of interest rises, the supply of loanable funds increases.[9] Subsequently, the supply curve of loanable funds, S is upward sloping, as drawn in Figure 11.5.

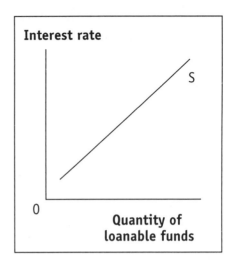

Figure 11.5: The supply curve of loanable funds

The rate of interest is determined by the demand for and supply of loanable funds. The function of the interest rate is to equate the demand for funds with the supply of funds in the same way that price adjusts to equate demand and supply in the goods market. The intersection of the demand and supply curves is the equilibrium rate of interest, i*. This is illustrated in Figure 11.6.

Figure 11.6: The market for loanable funds

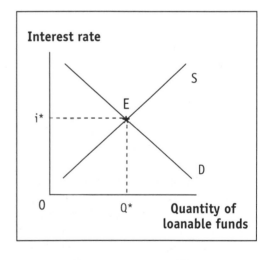

Changes in the demand for loanable funds occur for a number of reasons. Since firms carry out investment projects in anticipation of making a profit, it follows that anything which changes the expected profitability of investment projects will change the demand for loanable funds. An increase in demand causes a rightward shift of the demand curve whereas a decrease in demand causes a leftward shift of the demand curve.

Since the supply of funds is provided by household savings, any change in attitude towards savings will change the supply of loanable funds. An increase in supply causes a rightward shift of the supply curve whereas a decrease in supply causes a leftward shift of the supply curve.

In conclusion, the decision to save, or to hold cash balances, depends on one variable in the classical model: the interest rate. The decision of firms to invest depends on the same variable. The combination of the demand for and the supply of loanable funds determines the market rate of interest.

The liquidity preference theory
....

Keynes and his followers argued that the rate of interest was not determined by the demand for and supply of loanable funds but by the demand for money and the existing money supply.

The demand for money
....

The demand for money in the Keynesian model is more complex than in the classical model. We begin by defining liquidity preference.

● Definition
● ● ● ● ● ●

Liquidity preference is the desire by households to hold assets in liquid form.

According to Keynes, it is based on three motives which we will now explain. We will discover that the demand for money depends, not only on the interest rate, but also on the income of the household. In other words, the demand for money depends on two variables, rather than just one as we discussed in the classical model.

1. *Transactions demand.* A certain amount of money is required as a medium of exchange so that people can undertake day-to-day transactions such as the purchase of groceries, public transport and entertainment. The level of transactions demand depends on a number of factors. They include institutional factors such as the length of time between pay-days, the price level and, more importantly, the income level. The rate of interest has little or no effect on the transactions demand for money.[10]

2. *Precautionary demand.* A certain amount of money is held as a precaution against unforeseen contingencies such as illness or accidents. This desire to hold cash balances is related primarily to income. Other factors include the availability of overdraft facilities and the age of the economic agent involved.

The transactions and precautionary motives are often combined. The addition of the two is sometimes referred to as the demand for 'active balances'; 'active' in the sense that these funds will be actively used to purchase goods and services. These two motives are directly related to the medium of exchange function of money.

The demand for 'active balances' is drawn as a vertical line. This is shown in Figure 11.7.

*Figure 11.7: The demand for active
    balances curve*

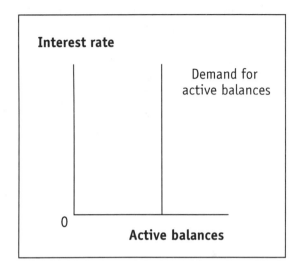

This means that it is interest rate
inelastic; the demand for money
balances does not change with the
interest rate. Instead, the demand
for money balances will change with
income. An increase in income will
shift the demand for active balances
curve to the right. At higher income
levels, more money is demanded for
transactions and as a precaution
against an uncertain future. If
income levels fall, the demand curve
will shift to the left.

3. *Speculative demand.* The final motive for holding money is to avoid losses from
holding interest-bearing assets. For example, if investors had foreseen the Wall Street
crash of 1987 they would have sold their interest-bearing assets and put the proceeds
into bank accounts. This form of demand is sometimes called the demand for idle
balances. It is related to the store of value function of money.

Suppose an individual holds a portfolio of assets. Assume there are only two types
of assets – money and bonds.[11] Money has the advantage of instant spending power
or complete liquidity. However, it earns little or no interest. In contrast, bonds earn
a rate of interest but suffer from being relatively illiquid.

The individual must choose between holding money or holding bonds. The higher
the rate of interest the more attractive it becomes to store wealth in bonds rather than
money and with this the speculative demand for money declines. Hence, the
speculative demand for money is inversely related to the rate of interest. If interest
rates are high, the demand for bonds is relatively high whereas the demand for money
is relatively low. A demand for 'idle balances' curve is drawn downward sloping,
reflecting the inverse relationship between the speculative demand for money and
the interest rate.

Figure 11.8: The demand for idle balances curve

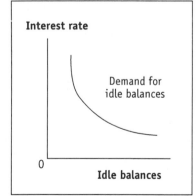

We can combine the demand for active balances
curve with the demand for idle balances curve to
yield the total demand for money curve. Keynes
referred to this as the liquidity preference curve,
denoted as L. It is the sum of the transactions
demand, the precautionary demand and the speculative demand for money. The liquidity preference
curve is downward sloping, reflecting the negative

relationship between the total demand for money and the rate of interest. This inverse relationship arises largely from the speculative demand for money.

The liquidity preference curve, L is drawn in Figure 11.9 below.

Figure 11.9: The liquidity preference curve

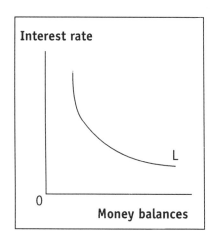

Money demand also depends on the level of income. As income increases, the demand for money increases; as income decreases, the demand for money decreases. A change in the level of income causes a shift of the demand for money curve. An increase in income shifts the money demand curve to the right. The opposite is true for a fall in the income level.

The supply of money
....

In the liquidity preference theory of interest rate determination, the money supply is assumed to be controlled by the Central Bank. Remember, because of the nature of the banking system, commercial banks have the power not just to transfer purchasing power but also to create it. In turn, if the Central Bank can regulate the amount that the commercial banks hold on reserve, it can regulate the amount of money which they can create, thus controlling the money supply. Hence, the money supply curve is vertical, independent of the rate of interest. We say it is interest rate inelastic, at least in the short run. The money supply curve, Ms is drawn in Figure 11.10 below.

Figure 11.10: The money supply curve

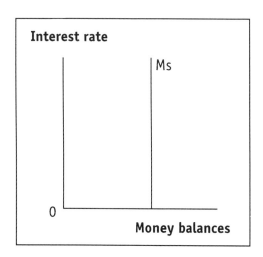

Money market equilibrium
....

Figure 11.11 shows a demand for money curve combined with a money supply curve. The interaction of the demand for and supply of money determines the interest rate. The rate of interest is the price of money and, like other prices it is determined by the forces of demand and supply. In the words of J. M. Keynes it is 'the reward for parting with liquidity for a specified period'.[12]

Figure 11.11: Money market equilibrium

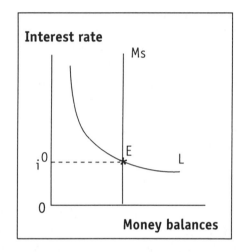

In Figure 11.11 the equilibrium rate of interest is i^0. At an interest rate above the equilibrium there exists an excess supply of money which leads to a downward movement of the interest rate. At an interest rate below the equilibrium there exists an excess demand for money which results in an upward movement of the interest rate.

Figure 11.12 illustrates the effect of an increase in the money supply. The money supply curve shifts to the right, from M_S to $M_S{}^1$. This results in an excess supply at the old rate of interest, i^0. Interest rates fall and continue to do so until the excess supply is eliminated. This adjustment process ends when the demand equals supply at a new and lower equilibrium rate of interest, i^1. Alternatively, a decrease in the money supply results in a higher equilibrium rate of interest.

Figure 11.12: An increase in the money supply

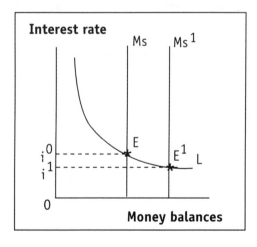

Figure 11.13 illustrates the effect of an increase in the demand for money (arising from an increase in income). The money demand curve shifts rightwards, resulting in excess demand at the old interest rate. Interest rates begin to rise and continue to do so until the excess demand is eliminated. Equilibrium returns to the money market at a higher interest rate, i^1, than before. Alternatively, a decrease in the demand for money results in a lower equilibrium rate of interest.

Figure 11.13: An increase in the demand for money

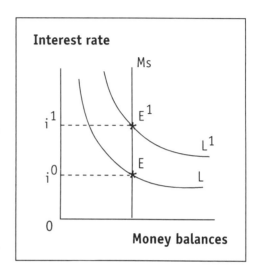

Finally, if interest rates are below 'normal', all market participants will expect a rise in interest rates. When explaining his liquidity preference theory, Keynes referred to the normal rate of interest, i.e. the rate of interest that is consistent with normal market conditions. If interest rates are low relative to the normal rate of interest, the market will expect an increase in the interest rate some time in the future. Due to the negative relationship that exists between interest rates and the price of bonds, we would expect a fall in the price of bonds.[13] In this case, investors would prefer to hold money to bonds because the holders of bonds will realise a capital loss.

Hence, at these 'low' interest rate levels, the demand for money may be perfectly elastic. This is illustrated by the horizontal part of the liquidity preference curve in Figure 11.9 above. Keynes referred to this as the liquidity trap. There is more discussion on the liquidity trap in the next chapter.

The two models suggest that the interest rate is determined in very different ways. In the loanable funds model, both the supply of funds and the demand for funds vary with the interest rate. In the liquidity preference theory, the interest rate is determined in the money market.

A more fundamental difference is that in the classical loanable funds theory, interest rate determination appears to be an automatic process. Funds become available from households as interest rates rise. Funds are demanded by firms as the interest rate falls. An adjustable interest rate clears the market. Keynes' speculative demand for money suggests that money is a 'safe' asset, preferred by investors, particularly in times of uncertainty. Equilibrium in the money market may be at very low rates of interest. Even at low rates of interest, firms are not enticed to put money to a productive use.

Finally, by introducing the money supply as the 'supply side' of the money market, Keynes suggests that in certain situations, it can be used to affect the interest rate. Since the money supply is controlled by the government, policy-makers are able to adjust it to affect the interest rate and ultimately, private investment.

We finish this section with a brief explanation of the term structure of interest rates.

The term structure of interest rates relates the yield or interest rate on a security to the length of time until the security matures. It is reflected in the yield curve.

Definition
● ● ● ● ● ●

The yield curve shows the way in which the yield on a security varies according to its maturity or expiry date.

It is customary to represent yields (interest rates on security) on the vertical axis and maturities (time period) on the horizontal axis. The slope of the yield curve can vary. Among other factors, inflation expectations can account for the differences in yield curve patterns.

The 'normal' yield curve slopes up from left to right, as shown in Figure 11.14(a). This reflects the case where long-term interest rates are above short-term interest rates. This is viewed as the norm because the expectation of higher inflation over the long run will result in long-term securities offering higher yields than short-term securities.

Others types of yield curves are also shown below.

In Figure 11.14(b) the yield curve is drawn as a straight line. A flat yield curve results when long-term and short-term interest rates are equal. When long-term interest rates are below short-term interest rates, a downward sloping yield curve is drawn, as in Figure 11.14(c).

Figure 11.14: Different yield curves

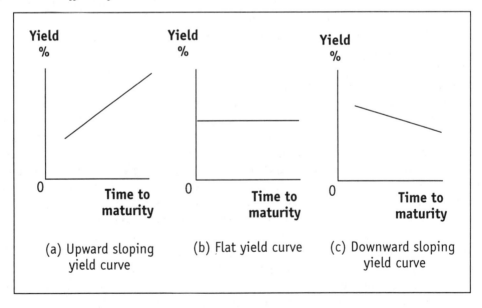

Analysing the behaviour of the yield curve is quite common in financial markets. In particular, yield curves are used as a prediction tool. Market predictions about movements of short-term interest rates in the future are reflected in the slope of the yield curve. For example, a steep upward sloping yield curve means that short-term interest rates are expected to rise. In contrast, a flat or downward sloping yield curve means that short-term interest rates are expected to fall. Either way, yield curves reflect the prevailing expectations in the financial markets.[14]

11.3 The role of the Central Bank

The Central Bank is a very important component of any banking system. Yet, while some central banks are centuries old, others have been established quite recently.[15]

The first tentative step towards the establishment of a central bank in Ireland was taken in 1783 when Parliament established the Bank of Ireland. Its primary role was to issue banknotes. To a lesser extent, it acted as a bankers' bank and a lender of last resort.

The Bank of Ireland's role as central bank diminished following the Act of Union in 1801 when the Bank of England began to take on central bank activities in Ireland. However, the Bank of Ireland's role as a central bank effectively ended with the passage of the Bankers' Act of 1845. This Act promoted competition and relaxed restrictions concerning the issuing of banknotes. From this date on, the Bank of Ireland concentrated on commercial banking.

The most important financial event following political independence was the establishment of the Banking Commission called the Parker-Willis Commission, after its chairman Professor Henry Parker-Willis. It was established in 1926, in an environment which was hostile to the emergence of a central bank. In the following year, the Currency Act of 1927 introduced the Saorstat pound which was later renamed the Irish pound.[16] The Commission was also responsible for the regulation of the newly designed Irish notes and coins.

The Central Bank of Ireland as we know it today was formally established in 1943. It received its powers from the Central Bank Act of 1942. It is responsible for safeguarding the integrity of the currency and for controlling the amount of credit in the economy. New techniques and instruments for the purpose of implementing monetary policy were developed in the intervening decades. Notwithstanding these developments, the continuation of the sterling link confined the Central Bank of Ireland to a secondary role. All this changed in the 1970s.

In 1971 the Central Bank Act was passed. It was primarily concerned with the licensing and supervision of banks in the domestic market. This was to meet the structural changes which had occurred throughout the banking industry. Powers were further increased in 1989 when, among other things, building societies and all financial institutions in the International Financial Services Centre were placed under the regulation of the Central Bank. By 1993, the activities of the ICC Bank and the ACC Bank had also been brought under the supervision of the Central Bank.[17]

Functions of the Central Bank
....

A central bank fulfils a number of functions.[18] It issues and controls the currency, sometimes referred to as 'legal tender'. It acts as banker to the state.

The Central Bank is also the banker's bank. Reserves, required by law, are held for the commercial banking sector by the Central Bank. Since commercial banks operate with only a fraction of their deposits, the Central Bank ensures that they can obtain cash to meet any unexpected withdrawal of funds. Because of this role, the Central Bank is sometimes referred to as 'the lender of last resort'.

The Central Bank formulates and implements monetary policy which we will discuss in the next section. Adjusting the interest rate is the aspect of monetary policy which is most widely reported in the news. It also implements the exchange rate policy as formulated by the Department of Finance.

Another function of the Central Bank is to manage the country's monetary system. It is responsible for the regulation and the supervision of all financial institutions.

All of these activities are important. However, each function forms only a part of the primary role of the Central Bank which is to safeguard the integrity of the currency.

One issue of concern is the degree of independence of the Central Bank from the political system. This can vary from country to country. For example, the Bundesbank has complete autonomy from the German government. Another example is the US Fed which operates independently from the US administration. In contrast, the Bank of England has relatively little independence from Westminster. Many monetary decisions in the UK are made by the Treasury or the Chancellor of the Exchequer, a member of the government in power. At home, the Central Bank of Ireland has some degree of independence but is also likely to be influenced by political circumstances.[19]

The functions of the central banks of all European countries are changing as the European Union moves closer to the adoption of a single currency. The European Monetary Institute (EMI), based in Frankfurt, is already operating to facilitate the transition from independent national monetary policies to a common European monetary policy. The EMI is the forerunner of the European System of Central Banks (ESCB) which will ultimately formulate and implement monetary policy for the European Union.

The role of the national Central Banks is uncertain. However, by the end of the century, they will certainly relinquish many of their current responsibilities. Many of the functions which we have described will be administered by the ESCB.

We now examine one of its functions in more detail – the formulation and implementation of monetary policy.

11.4 Monetary policy in a closed economy

Definition
● ● ● ● ● ●

Monetary policy refers to the use of money supply, credit and interest rates to achieve economic objectives.

We will discuss the use of credit guidelines and interest rates later. We begin, however, by looking at the supply of money in the economy.

In a closed economy, the supply of money can be controlled by the Central Bank which has a number of different options available. Three such options are described below. They are sometimes referred to as the tools or instruments of monetary policy.[20]

1. *Reserve requirements*. All financial institutions are required to hold a certain amount of their deposits on reserve.

● Definition
● ● ● ● ● ●

The reserve requirement is the percentage of deposits which banks are legally obligated to lodge at the Central Bank.

The primary reserve requirement is 3% for all Irish banks and building societies.

Changes in the rules that specify the amount of reserves a bank must hold to back up deposits can influence the money supply. For example, the higher the reserve requirement, the lower the deposit multiplier and subsequently the smaller the change in the money supply. Conversely, a decrease in the reserve requirement increases the amount of deposits that can be supported by a given level of reserves and will lead to an increase in the money supply.

2. *Open market operations*. This involves the buying and selling of government securities or bonds. When the Central Bank buys securities, a cheque is drawn on the Central Bank as payment in favour of the client's commercial bank. When the cheque is presented for payment, bank deposits are transferred from the Central Bank to the commercial bank. Hence, the reserves of the commercial bank are increased. Moreover, its ability to create more deposits via the money multiplier process also increases. The end result is an increase in the money supply. In brief, an open market purchase expands the money supply; an open market sale reduces the money supply.

3. *Discount/bank rate*. As we discussed above, commercial banks must hold a percentage of their deposits as reserves. If their reserves fall below the legal limit, commercial banks borrow money from other banks, if possible, or from the Central Bank to make up the shortfall. The interest rate charged is called the discount or bank rate.

● Definition
● ● ● ● ● ●

The discount or bank rate is the rate which the Central Bank charges financial institutions that borrow from it for purposes of maintaining the reserve requirement.

The term used to identify this rate varies from country to country. In Ireland it is called the Short-term Facility (STF) rate. In the UK it used to be called the Bank Rate and then after 1971 it became known as the Minimum Lending Rate. In the US it is referred to as the Discount Rate whereas in Germany it is called the Lombard Rate.

The lower the STF rate, the lower the cost of borrowing for reserves, the higher the amount of borrowing. As banks increase their borrowing from the Central Bank, the subsequent increase in bank reserves can support an increase in loans. We know from the money multiplier process that an increase in the money supply results. The opposite is true for a relatively high STF rate.

The STF rate is generally used as the base of all other interest rates. When the STF rate increases, all other interest rates on loans for firms and consumers generally follow. That is why announcements from the Central Bank concerning the STF rate are awaited with such interest by the financial markets. Read Appendix 11.2 to see where the STF rate fits into the interest rate structure in Ireland.

One further possibility is for the Central Bank to make a formal request to the commercial banks to meet certain credit guidelines or to maintain a required reserve ratio. The request is sometimes accompanied with constraints. This practice of discouraging banks and other financial institutions is called moral suasion.

In conclusion, an increase in the money supply results from an open market purchase, a reduction in the discount rate and a reduction in the required reserve ratio. A sale of securities, an increase in the discount rate and a higher required reserve ratio lead to a reduction in the money supply.

This completes the operational aspect of monetary policy. We now examine the effects that monetary policy have on the macroeconomic variables of output and employment.

The effects of monetary policy
....
We will begin with an example which illustrates the relationship between the money supply, interest rates and national income.

Suppose the monetary authorities conduct an open market purchase. We know from our earlier discussion on the tools of monetary policy that the purchase of securities increases the money supply. This creates a disequilibrium (excess supply) in the money market which drives down the interest rate. The fall in the interest rate induces an increase in investment expenditure (and possibly consumer expenditure, particularly consumer goods bought on credit).[21] Investment expenditure is one component of aggregate expenditure. The increase in aggregate expenditure will lead to an increase in national output, measured by GDP. If the link between economic growth and employment/unemployment is strong, such increases in output will increase employment and reduce unemployment. In short,

> Increase in Ms → decreases i → increases I → increases AE → increases GDP → decreases U

The effects of monetary policy are illustrated in Figure 11.15.

Figure 11.15: Monetary policy changes

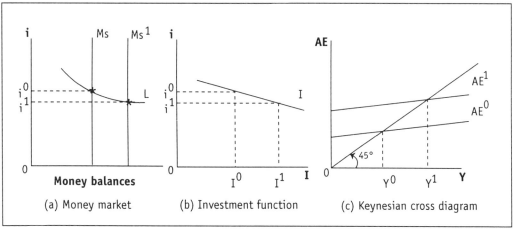

(a) Money market	(b) Investment function	(c) Keynesian cross diagram

The money market is represented in panel (a), the investment function in panel (b) and the Keynesian cross diagram in panel (c).[22] The increase in money supply shifts the money supply curve to the right. The equilibrium rate of interest falls from i^0 to i^1. Lower interest rates induce greater investment expenditure and this causes a movement down along the investment function (from I^0 to I^1). An increase in investment, one of the components of aggregate expenditure, shifts the AE curve upwards from AE^0 to AE^1, increasing the equilibrium income level.

We have shown that using a Keynesian model, an increase in the money supply expands national income. Conversely, a reduction in the money supply contracts national income. Using the IS/LM framework, changes in monetary policy are discussed in more detail in the next chapter.

This short discussion on monetary policy illustrates its effects on economic variables and its importance in the context of achieving macroeconomic objectives. A discussion on inflation and how changes in the money supply affect the general price level are omitted; these are explained in Chapter 15.

Monetary policy as a policy instrument
....

The use of monetary policy became fashionable in the 1970s because economists and governments were concerned that government spending was not having the desired effect on unemployment. Rather, it was increasing the percentage of national income which was controlled by the public sector. Further, high levels of government spending combined with interest payments led to spiralling government debts.

The main attraction of monetary policy is that it affects the spending patterns of the private sector. A change in the money supply affects the interest rate. Changes in the interest rate lead to changes in both investment and consumer spending. Therefore, everyone in the private sector can potentially benefit from the change in the price of capital funds. The economy is stimulated or deflated by lowering or raising the interest rate. The emphasis of this policy is on the private sector; it does not directly affect public sector spending or the national debt.

Monetary policy became the preferred macroeconomic policy in the US and the UK by the early 1980s. However, from the outset, the use of monetary policy to stabilise the economy was criticised by a group of economists called the 'monetarists'.[23] Milton Friedman and Edmund Phelps were both early contributors to the debate.[24]

They argued that the primary role of monetary policy is to maintain the price level which creates confidence in a national currency and ultimately in a national economy. They conceded that adjustments to the money supply might cause fluctuations in national output in the short run. However, they cautioned that the use of monetary policy to stabilise the economy leads to inflation and a weakening of the currency. Therefore, the use of monetary policy to stabilise the economy in the short run hinders the long-term growth of the economy.

We sometimes make the mistake of thinking that Keynesians advocate the use of fiscal policy, and monetarists advocate the use of monetary policy. In reality, particularly in the 1970s, Keynesians accepted and embraced the use of monetary policy.

In contrast, monetarists always believed in the importance of monetary policy but not in its use to stabilise the economy. Careful monitoring of the money supply ensures that inflation does not become entrenched in the national economy. For the monetarists, the role of monetary policy is to ensure price stability. This is much more limited than the role envisioned by the Keynesians.

Having discussed the two extreme positions on monetary policy, we will end with the observations of David Romer, who appears to be seeking the middle ground. He states that, 'The lesson I draw is that conducting monetary policy has always been difficult. The environment has been changing continually, the lags have been long, the uncertainty has been great. Thus, I would conclude that monetary policy should be conducted the way it always has been – using a mix of formal models, rules of thumb, shrewd observation, instinct, guesswork, and prayer.'[25]

11.5 The Irish experience

From the comments above, we can see that for a closed economy, the role of monetary policy is debatable and even contentious. We will find that the scope of policy effectiveness is even narrower in a small open economy (SOE) such as Ireland.

● Definition
● ● ● ● ● ●

A small open economy (SOE) is so small relative to the world economy that domestic economic events have no effect on the rest of the world. The domestic economy is a price taker: it accepts world prices. Also, external trade (exports and imports) represents a high proportion of the country's GDP.

Ireland's economy exhibits both of these characteristics. Further, we find that Ireland, in common with other small open economies, exhibits particular behaviours which limit its ability to effectively use monetary policy. We will list these and then discuss their relevance in detail.

1. A SOE whose currency belongs to a fixed or semi-fixed exchange rate system (operating with free mobility of capital) does not control its money supply.[26]
2. Domestic interest rates in the long term are determined primarily by external forces.
3. It may have some ability to manage the liquidity in the money market in the short term.

1. *Money supply*. The monetary authorities of a SOE cannot control its money supply to the same degree as other central banks.[27] Hence, there is little scope for an independent monetary policy. An example follows.

Independent of other central banks, suppose the Central Bank of Ireland decides to increase the money supply in order to boost domestic spending. As the domestic money supply increases, interest rates fall. Because domestic interest rates are now lower than world interest rates, an outflow of capital results. In order to invest in other economies where interest rates are now relatively higher, the Irish pound is exchanged for foreign currencies. An excess supply of the Irish pound leads to a weakening of the Irish currency against foreign currencies which should cause a depreciation of the Irish pound. Because Ireland is a member of a semi-fixed exchange rate system, the Central Bank is obliged to maintain the value of the Irish pound between certain limits. The Central Bank intervenes by buying up and, in the process, eliminating the excess supply. On the purchase of the domestic currency, the money supply decreases and effectively reverts to its original level. An independent monetary policy appears ineffective.[28]

2. *Interest rates*. Central banks in closed economies can 'set' their interest rate and adjust their money supply to support that interest rate. Interest rates in a SOE are determined largely by external factors, the most important of which is the level of foreign interest rates. As we explained above, investors will move capital to take advantage of higher interest rates in other economies. As a result, domestic interest rates cannot differ substantially from foreign interest rates if capital is mobile. Other external factors which affect the domestic interest rate work through the exchange rate. They include speculation and expectations concerning realignments of exchange rates. This dependency on foreign interest rates is illustrated in the following example.

If the Bundesbank increases German interest rates, the Irish Central Bank is likely to follow.[29] If it does not, an interest rate differential (a gap between German and Irish interest rates) results. Given the absence of exchange controls, capital is likely to flow from Ireland to Germany where the return is now higher. As a consequence, the Irish pound weakens against the German mark. This depreciation of the Irish pound will continue until the interest rate differential disappears. This will happen only when the Irish Central Bank increases domestic interest rates or in the unlikely event of the Bundesbank rescinding its earlier decision (see Article 11.1).

ARTICLE 11.1

Extract from The Irish Times
Interest rates set to rise in New Year
by Mary Canniffe

Irish interest rates now look likely to rise following the surprise decision by the German Central Bank to raise key interest rates by half of a percentage point. Bank borrowers and mortgage holders are likely to see their repayments rise in the new year as a result of the German move, which is aimed at controlling rising German inflation. The German Bundesbank announced a half-point increase in its two key interest rates yesterday after its normal fortnightly meeting. The increase in the German Lombard rate to 9.75% and in the discount rate to 8% was followed by central banks in Holland, Denmark, Belgium and Austria, all of which raised their key interest rates by a half point.

In Dublin interest rates on the wholesale money market, where the banks lend and borrow funds, rose after the German announcement. The interest rate on three-month money rose from 10.3% to 10.6% as the market traded nervously anticipating an announcement. With money market interest rates now well above the short-term facility rate of 10.25% at which the Central Bank lends emergency funds to the banks, an increase in the STF rate is expected. That increase may be announced today by the Central Bank after the meeting of its monetary policy committee in the morning.

. . .

The strength of the Irish pound in the EMS band, the fact that Irish money market rates are about 85 basis points higher than German rates and the 'comfortable' Irish external reserves give the Central Bank some room to manoeuvre.

Source: The Irish Times, *20 December 1991.*

3. *Liquidity.* The above analysis seems to suggest the absence of any role for the Irish monetary authorities.[30] This is not completely true. In the short term the Central Bank can influence liquidity levels by providing funds or withdrawing funds whenever necessary.[31] Liquidity can be added to or drained from the domestic financial system by a number of different instruments. These are called liquidity management instruments. They include the following:

- *The short-term facility.* The STF is an overdraft facility which the Central Bank provides to those financial institutions that are short of reserves. Funds are drawn down on a quota basis overnight and this facility is available for up to seven days. Frequent use of the STF reflects a shortage of liquidity. As we discussed before, the STF rate is frequently used to send a 'signal' to financial institutions to adjust their interest rates in accordance with the STF rate.
- *Secured advances.* The Central Bank provides a facility for banks to borrow funds against the security of government bonds. It is an extension of the STF and is normally only used when a bank's quota is filled. This seldom happens and, hence, this instrument is rarely used.
- *Foreign exchange (FX) swaps.* A foreign exchange swap is a financial instrument whereby one party lends foreign currency to another party in exchange for domestic currency.[32] If the Central Bank wishes to add liquidity it can do so by swapping

Irish pounds for foreign currency. Conversely, liquidity can be removed by swapping foreign currency for Irish pounds. This is called a negative swap. This particular instrument can provide liquidity for periods of up to four weeks.

- *Sale and repurchase agreements (REPOs)*. REPOs are financial instruments whereby one party agrees to buy a security on the condition that it will resell it to the other party at some future date. The Central Bank is often involved in buying securities from other financial institutions on the understanding that it will resell them back to the same banks on an agreed future date. Like swaps, REPOs can provide liquidity for periods of up to one month.
- *Term deposits*. At times of temporary surplus liquidity, the Central Bank quotes rates for overnight and term deposits. Although the Central Bank cannot add liquidity through this method, it can discourage banks from holding surplus liquidity by quoting unattractive rates for term deposits.
- *Changes in the reserve ratio*. Variations in the reserve ratio can be used to add or withdraw liquidity. A reduction in the ratio allows for greater liquidity; an increase permits less liquidity. Variations in the reserve ratio are usually confined to periods where seasonal changes occur, e.g. Christmas.

The level of support by the Central Bank to the domestic money market varies from year to year. Table 11.6 provides a summary of Central Bank supports during the period between 1979 and 1995. Three instruments are examined: the short-term facility, sale and repurchase agreements and foreign exchange swaps.

Table 11.6: Central Bank support 1979–95

End-year	STF	Repos	FX Swaps	Total
1979	56.8	–	62.7	119.5
1980	46.2	–	–85.6	–39.4
1981	28.4	–	60.0	88.4
1982	103.3	–	195.0	298.3
1983	68.6	–	50.0	118.6
1984	121.7	20.0	50.0	191.7
1985	32.4	54.2	105.0	191.6
1986	58.7	310.2	577.0	945.9
1987	64.8	273.2	40.0	378.0
1988	69.0	171.2	–	240.2
1989	161.3	1141.0	–	1302.3
1990	94.4	789.7	–	884.1
1991	18.3	798.8	–	817.1
1992	95.4	1979.1	800.0	2874.5
1993[1]	9.3	588.4	–	571.9
1994	0.9	284.9	–	283.9
1995	7.4	29.8	–	–264.8

Source: John Kelly, 'The Development of Money and Foreign-Exchange Markets in Ireland' *Central Bank Annual Report 1992*, Summer 1993.

1. The totals for the years 1993–95 include figures for overnight and term deposits.

A close examination of Table 11.6 reveals remarkable annual fluctuations in the level of Central Bank support. Four years in particular stand out. 1980 and 1995 were the only years when the Bank had to absorb liquidity by end-year. 1989 and 1992 were remarkable for the degree of Bank support. The relaxation in exchange controls largely explains the increase in 1989 whereas the EMS currency crisis explains the increase in 1992.

In general, changes in one or more of these instruments allow the Central Bank to add or remove liquidity from the domestic money market. In other words, they are increasing or decreasing the money supply. Such action by the Central Bank aims to avoid reductions in interest rates which would otherwise stem from excess market liquidity and, likewise, avoid increases in interest rates arising from shortages in liquidity in the market. In effect, the Central Bank attempts to smooth out changes in liquidity in order to prevent sharp movements in domestic interest rates.[33]

CASE STUDY

Extract from The Sunday Business Post
More scope for rates
by George Lee

The major focus for domestic markets last week was undoubtedly the release on Thursday of the Central Bank monthly statistics for April which cast further light on the reasoning behind the 0.5% reduction in the Central Bank's key STF rate. The monthly statistics show quite clearly that the changes in exchange control regulations from April 1 were of major significance and precipitated a massive capital inflow into Ireland in April.

The other factors supporting lower interest rates included a further reduction in the pace of private-sector credit creation down from 14.4% in March to only 11.1% in April. This is a major achievement indeed since annual private sector credit growth was over double this amount at 22.6% only eleven months ago. Foreign uptake of gilts was also of significance in April with non-residents increasing their holdings of Irish government securities by over £180 million.

. . .

Sterling had weakened sharply very early in March. The fact that reserve outflows were still responding in their traditional manner to this factor throughout April but that overall the level of reserves actually increased supports the view that the ground has shifted just as commentators had finally become unanimous that Irish interest rates were determined by two factors, German interest rates and the Sterling exchange rate. The upshot is that the simplicity of the two-variable model of interest rate determination is now a thing of the past. It was good while it lasted but it is now time for commentators to reconsider their understanding of Irish interest rate determination. Inevitably there will be disagreement.

The Central Bank influenced domestic money market conditions this week and suggested to the market that they should

→

not get carried away with enthusiasm for lower interest rates. The one-month interest rate climbed smartly up from last

week's close of 10.9% to 11.19% on Friday morning.

. . .

Source: The Sunday Business Post, *June 1990.*

Questions
....

1. What role do monetary statistics and, in particular, changes in private-sector credit, play in the context of Irish monetary policy? What two events, evident in the April statistics, were instrumental in the easing of Irish interest rates by the Central Bank?
2. What economic variables, other than 'German interest rates' and the 'Sterling exchange rate' would be influential in the determination of Irish interest rates?
3. What is meant by 'The Central Bank influenced domestic money market conditions . . . '? Explain your answer.

Answers
....

1. The Central Bank is responsible for the formulation and implementation of monetary policy in Ireland. The primary objective of monetary policy is price stability. The general price level is influenced by many different factors. One of these factors is the level of spending which in turn is partly influenced by the stock of money in circulation and the availability of credit in the economy. Hence, the Central Bank monitors the monthly changes in the money supply and private sector credit. Tough sanctions are normally taken (e.g. an increase in interest rates, penalties imposed on the banks which do not meet the credit guidelines) if excessive increases are recorded.
   The two events which occurred in April and which were responsible for the Central Bank's decision to reduce rates were the further relaxation of exchange controls and the reduction in the private-sector credit growth rate.
2. There is no definite list of variables which influence Irish interest rates. However, here is a comprehensive, although not exhaustive, list of economic variables: exchange rate expectations; interest rates of other member states of the EMS; uncertainty; speculation; government spending; inflation; capital mobility; GDP growth rates; the business cycle.
3. This sentence is concerned with Central Bank support to the market. The Central Bank can add or remove liquidity whenever necessary. The reference to 'they should not get carried away with enthusiasm for lower interest rates' suggests that the Central Bank may be involved in dampening down the possibility of lower interest rates. If so, there are a number of ways in which the Central Bank can withdraw liquidity. These include a foreign exchange swap, a REPO or a quote for term deposits.

The objective of monetary policy in Ireland
....

Monetary policy in Ireland has been described in many different ways.[34] Here is a small sample '. . . the poor relation of economic policy in Ireland'; '. . . an unutilised instrument of public policy';[35] '. . . always there, exerting an influence, behind the scenes' and finally, the 'Hidden Stabiliser'.[36] The objective of Irish monetary policy is price stability, i.e. low inflation.[37]

The mechanism through which the Central Bank achieves this aim is the exchange rate. By maintaining the value of the Irish pound within the Exchange Rate Mechanism (ERM), the Central Bank is able to sustain a low inflation rate. In order to maintain the exchange rate link with the German mark, it is sometimes necessary for the Central Bank to change interest rates. For example, a fall in the value of the Irish pound against the German mark would require a hike in interest rates, regardless of domestic economic conditions.[38]

The 1992 Central Bank statement on monetary policy summarises the aim of monetary policy, 'The basic objective of monetary policy is to keep inflation as low as possible through the maintenance of a firm exchange rate for the Irish pound within the narrow band of the EMS.'[39] To put this another way, the inflation rate is the ultimate objective; the 'intermediate target' is the exchange rate; the instrument used is the interest rate (see Appendix 11.3).

The monetary policy experience in Ireland
....

An Irish financial system, independent from the UK, was established in the mid-1960s. In 1969 the Central Bank started a market for government securities. In the following year, a foreign exchange market was established. Assets which were owned by Irish commercial institutions but held in London were re-routed back to Ireland. The most significant change in the Irish monetary system occurred in 1979 when Ireland broke with sterling and joined the newly-formed ERM of the European Monetary System. Prior to this, Irish interest rates were determined by factors such as UK interest rates, the value of sterling and the UK Treasury.

The close relationship between Irish and UK interest rates in the period up to 1979 is highlighted in Figure 11.16 below.

Figure 11.16: Irish and UK interest rates 1971–79

After 1979, UK interest rates and the value of sterling were no longer the dominant factors in the determination of Irish interest rates. This is not to suggest that the Irish monetary authorities were suddenly in charge of Irish interest rates: there was simply a change in the factors which determined Irish interest rates. Exchange rate and interest rate levels within the ERM became the most important factors in determining Irish monetary policy and, in particular, Irish interest rates. Moreover, it was the value of the German mark combined with German interest

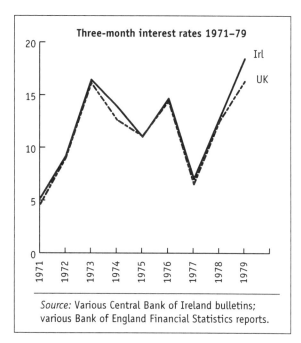

rates which became the dominant factor. This is because of the central role which Germany occupies within the exchange rate system. Irish, UK and German interest rates in the period 1980–95 are shown in Figure 11.17.

Figure 11.17: Irish, UK and German interest rates 1980–95

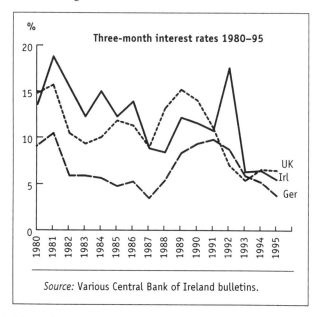

The large differential between Irish and German interest rates during the first few years of the EMS was unexpected and unwelcome. Fortunately in the later period of membership the differential has narrowed substantially.

The future of monetary policy in Ireland
....

The future of the operation of monetary policy in Ireland and throughout other member states of the EMS is uncertain. It has already experienced one change in recent times: the change in the operating procedures of the ERM (resulting from the widening of the fluctuation bands).[40] Adjustments to financial innovation and deregulation are ongoing. Although these changes have had an effect on the operation of monetary policy, the objective has not changed, i.e. the achievement of a low inflationary environment. The next change is likely to come from the move towards Economic and Monetary Union. Monetary union entails a single currency, a common monetary policy and one European Central Bank. In Section 11.3 we suggested that the role of the Irish Central Bank is likely to diminish in the future. This is likely to further diminish the scope and the effectiveness of monetary policy in Ireland.

We leave the last few words on monetary policy in Ireland to a former Governor of the Central Bank, Maurice Doyle:

> 'The [Central] Bank's policy is to underwrite a level of interest rates that is considered to be sustainable and justified on the basis of the economic fundamentals, having regard to the implications for the external reserves and the exchange rate. There are many techniques which the Bank can use to influence interest rates in the interbank market and these, in turn, influence the retail rates offered and charged to customers. However, I must emphasise that what we can do is limited by market forces, by the effects of Government fiscal policy and, in an era of increasingly free financial markets, most especially by the configuration of exchange rates and interest rates abroad.'[41]

Summary

1. Money is anything that is accepted as a medium of exchange. It is also a unit of measurement, a standard of deferred payment and a store of value. The two monetary aggregates used in Ireland are M1 and M3. M1 is the narrow money supply and is defined as notes and coins and balances on current accounts. M3 is the broad money supply, defined as M1 plus balances on deposit accounts.
2. The banking system can create money. This phenomenon can be explained by the multiplier process. The deposit multiplier relates a change in reserves to the change in deposits. It depends inversely on the reserve ratio.
3. The classical loanable funds theory and the Keynesian liquidity preference theory are the two main models of interest rate determination. In the former, the interest rate is derived from the demand for and supply of funds. In the latter, it is the demand for and supply of money which determine the interest rate. For Keynes, the demand for money depends on the interest rate and the level of income.
4. The functions of the Central Bank are many and diverse. It is the government and the banker's bank. It issues notes and coins. It regulates the financial institutions. It formulates monetary policy and is also responsible for the implementation of exchange rate policy. The latter is achieved by maintaining the value of the Irish

pound within the ERM. The Central Bank of Ireland was formally established in 1943. Its powers were increased in 1971 and again in the late 1980s.

5. There are a number of ways by which the Central Bank can control the level of reserves and, in turn, the money supply. They include open market operations, changes in the discount rate and changes in the reserve requirements. Changes in these instruments affect the money supply and, in turn, other macroeconomic variables such as interest rates, output and employment.

6. The operation and effectiveness of monetary policy is different in a SOE compared to a closed economy. Ireland is a SOE. Consequently, money supply is beyond the control of the monetary authorities. Irish interest rates are largely determined by interest rate levels among other member states of the EMS. Exchange rate expectations are also an important factor. The role of the Irish Central Bank is to manage liquidity in order to prevent sharp movements in interest rates. To achieve this, there are a number of liquidity instruments available to the Central Bank.

Key terms

Money	Speculative demand for money
Medium of exchange	Liquidity trap
Double coincidence of wants	Yield curve
Measure of value	Lender of last resort
Standard of deferred payment	Monetary policy
Store of value	Reserve requirements
Narrow money supply	Open market operations
Broad money supply	Discount rate
High-powered money	Short-term facility rate
Money creation	Moral suasion
Deposit multiplier	Monetarists
Interest	Small open economy
Interest rate	Liquidity
Loanable funds theory	Secured advances
Liquidity preference	Foreign exchange swaps
Transactions demand for money	Sale and repurchase agreements
Precautionary demand for money	Term deposits
Active and idle balances	Price stability
	Interest rate differential

Review questions

1. What is 'money'? What are its functions? What are the different definitions of money supply in Ireland?
2. Explain how the banking system creates money.
3. Explain Keynes' three motives for holding money.

4. What are the functions of a central bank? How can a central bank influence the money supply?
5. Explain what effect an increase in the money supply has on the rate of interest and the level of output.
6. How does the operation of monetary policy in Ireland differ from other countries such as the US or the UK? What role, if any, does the Central Bank of Ireland play?

Working problems

1. Patrick O'Ireland deposits £5,000 with ABC Bank. The reserve requirement is 20%.
   (a) What is the value of the deposit multiplier?
   (b) What will be the increase in the money supply?
   (c) Fill in the blanks in Table 11.7 below.

Table 11.7: Money creation

Stages	Deposits (£)	Reserves (£)	Loans (£)
1	5,000	_____	_____
2	4,000	800	_____
3	_____	_____	2,560
4	2,560	_____	_____
5			
6 . . .			
etc. . . .			
Total	£ _____	£ _____	£ _____

2. Suppose £400 falls from Milton Friedman's helicopter into the hands of Maria, a student. What is the minimum increase in the money supply that can result? What is the maximum increase that can result? (Assume the reserve ratio is 5%).

Multi-choice questions

1. Money:
   (a) is broadly defined as coins in circulation;
   (b) can be created by the banking system;
   (c) is equal to income;
   (d) both (a) and (c) above;
   (e) (a), (b) and (c) above.

2. A customer deposits £800 in AOB Bank. The required reserve ratio is 12.5%. What is the potential increase in the money supply?

(a) £ 6,400;
(b) £ 5,600;
(c) £10,000;
(d) £ 8,750;
(e) none of the above.

3. In the liquidity preference theory of money:
   (a) there are three motives for holding money;
   (b) the money supply is interest rate inelastic;
   (c) the interest rate is the price of money;
   (d) the demand for money is positively related to income;
   (e) all of the above.

4. An increase in the money supply results from:
   (a) an open market sale and a reduction in the reserve ratio;
   (b) a reduction in the discount rate and an increase in the reserve ratio;
   (c) an open market purchase and an increase in the reserve ratio;
   (d) an open market purchase and a reduction in the discount rate;
   (e) none of the above.

5. In a SOE:
   (a) interest rates are largely influenced by external factors;
   (b) an independent monetary policy is ineffective;
   (c) the monetary authorities control the money stock;
   (d) both (a) and (b) above;
   (e) both (b) and (c) above.

6. The short-term facility rate:
   (a) is used to add or withdraw liquidity whenever necessary;
   (b) is set by the money market;
   (c) is the rate at which financial institutions borrow and lend from each other;
   (d) both (a) and (c) above;
   (e) both (b) and (c) above.

True or false

1. There is no generally accepted means of payment in a barter economy. _____
2. M3 is defined as notes and coins and current account balances. _____
3. The higher the reserve ratio, the greater the bank's ability to create money. _____
4. The liquidity preference is positively related to income and negatively related to interest rates. _____
5. A lowering of the discount rate increases the money supply. _____
6. In a SOE, the Central Bank determines interest rates in the long term by using the liquidity instruments. _____

Fill in the blanks

_____ is anything that is generally accepted as a means of payment. Its other functions are as a unit of _____, as a store of _____ and as a standard of _____ _____. Money is created within the _____ system. It is the _____ of the commercial banks which support the creation of _____. In the _____ model of interest rate determination, the demand for capital funds depends solely on the _____ _____. In contrast, the demand for money in Keynes' _____ _____ theory depends on the interest rate and the level of _____. The _____ of loanable funds is determined from the level of household savings. Keynes' supply of money is interest rate _____ ; it is controlled by the _____ _____. It can be changed by an _____ _____ operation, a change in the _____ ratio or a change in the _____ rate. In a _____ , the Central Bank has less control over monetary policy and interest rates. _____ factors are more influential. The Central Bank does attempt to control _____ in the domestic _____ market. Nevertheless, monetary policy is an important policy option available to the authorities in achieving _____ objectives.

CASE STUDY

Extract from The Irish Times
Pressure on interest rates to continue
by Mary Canniffe

International currency and money markets are expected to remain volatile this week, increasing upward pressure on bank and building society interest rates. Adverse reaction to a number of key economic figures to be released in Britain and the US this week could intensify the flight from sterling and dollars and drive the German mark higher. This could put pressure on central banks in Europe to raise interest rates again to defend the value of their currencies.

. . .

In the Dublin market, two increases over the last ten days in the Central Bank's official lending rate failed to stem the fall of the Irish pound against the German mark. With the cost of one-month money on the Dublin interbank market now just over 7%, an increase in mortgage and deposit rates of at least one percentage point looks inevitable in coming weeks unless market rates fall.

. . .

While the other banks and building societies have adopted a 'wait and see' policy in the hope that market rates will come back down, most commentators consider it unlikely that the key one-month interbank rate could drop below 7% in the short term.

. . .

After two increases of a half of a percentage point the Central Bank short-term facility rate – for loans to the banks – is now 7.25%. The cost of one month's money on wholesale markets closed at 7.1% on Friday. While the one-month rate eased on Friday, most dealers do not expect the rate to fall below 7% because of the volatility in currency markets. If market rates stay above 7%, mortgage and deposit rates are likely to rise at least one percentage point.

Source: The Irish Times, *13 March 1995.*

Questions
....

1. In terms of exposure to higher interest rates, are banks or building societies more vulnerable? Explain your answer.   [The student should refer to Appendix 11.2]
2. What is the difference between the STF rate and the 'one-month rate'? How does one determine the other?
3. How does 'volatility in currency markets' influence interest rate levels?

Additional case study questions based on Article 11.1 from the text

Questions on Article 11.1: Interest rates set to rise in New Year

1. Explain why an increase in German interest rates arising out of higher German inflation is likely to lead to higher interest rates in Ireland.
2. What is likely to happen if the Central Bank of Ireland increased interest rates by two percentage points? What is the more likely scenario?
3. In the context of the Irish money market how are the 'mortgage' rates, 'money market interest rates' and the 'STF rate' related?

[The answers are not included.]

Appendix 11.1: Derivation of money multiplier

In Section 11.1 we explained the deposit multiplier. The analysis was based on the assumption that there were no leakages, i.e. no cash held by the public and no excess reserves held by banks. We now adjust our analysis to account for such leakages. The result is a money multiplier which relates a change in the money supply to a change in high-powered money.

The broad money supply, M, is defined as currency, C plus current and deposit account balances, D.

$$M = D + C$$ [1]

High-powered money, H is defined as currency, C plus bank reserves, R.

$$H = C + R$$ [2]

Dividing Equation [1] by Equation [2], we get the ratio of money supply to high-powered money:

$$\frac{M}{H} = \frac{D + C}{C + R}$$ [3]

Dividing the numerator and the denominator by D, we get:

$$\frac{M}{H} = \frac{1 + \dfrac{C}{D}}{\dfrac{C}{D} + \dfrac{R}{D}}$$ [4]

Multiplying both sides by H results in:

[5]

$$M = \frac{1 + \frac{C}{D}}{\frac{C}{D} + \frac{R}{D}} H$$

If there is a change in the reserves component of H, we can adopt this equation to calculate the resulting change in money supply:

[6]

$$\Delta M = \frac{1 + \frac{C}{D}}{\frac{C}{D} + \frac{R}{D}} \Delta H$$

Divide both sides by ΔH to get:

[11.3]

$$\frac{\Delta M}{\Delta H} = \frac{1 + \frac{C}{D}}{\frac{C}{D} + \frac{R}{D}}$$

The left-hand side of Equation 11.3 is the change in money supply arising out of a given change in the reserves component of high-powered money. The right-hand side of Equation 11.3 is the money multiplier. Any change in the reserves leads to a multiple change in the money supply. Its value depends on the currency deposit ratio, $\frac{C}{D}$ and the reserve deposit ratio $\frac{R}{D}$. If $\frac{C}{D} = 0$, the money multiplier is equal to the simple deposit multiplier defined in the text.

Table 11.8: *Central bank balance sheet December 1995*

	Assets		Liabilities
External reserves	5,472.5	Currency	2,092.3
Loans	219.8	Bank deposits	1,187.6
Others	417.8	Government deposits	1,080.0
		Others	1,750.2
	6,110.1		6,110.1

Source: Central Bank Annual Report 1995, Summer 1996.

By using the data presented in Table 11.1 and Table 11.8, we can calculate the value for the money multiplier in Ireland for December 1995 as follows:

$$\frac{C}{D} = \frac{1,880.5}{20,030} = 0.094$$

and

$$\frac{R}{D} = \frac{1,187.6}{20,030} = 0.059$$

Hence,

$$\frac{\Delta M}{\Delta H} = \frac{1 + \dfrac{C}{D}}{\dfrac{C}{D} + \dfrac{R}{D}} = \frac{1 + 0.094}{0.094 + 0.059} = \frac{1.094}{0.153} = 7.15$$

In December 1995, the money multiplier in Ireland was 7.15 approximately. Hence, a £100 increase in high-powered money would lead to an increase in the money supply of £715.

Appendix 11.2: The interest rate structure in Ireland

We begin with the interbank market, also called the Dublin wholesale market. This is where financial institutions borrow money from and lend money to each other for periods ranging from one day to a year. The most important rates are the one-month and three-month Dublin interbank offer rate, called the DIBOR which are the benchmark lending rates of the banks participating in the wholesale money market. The forces of demand and supply (which in turn are primarily determined by outside forces but in the short run can be influenced by central bank action) in this market determine these interbank rates. The Central Bank's STF rate is usually kept in line with the one-month interbank rate. If this interbank rate moves significantly out of line with the STF rate for whatever reason and continues to do so the Central Bank responds by publicly announcing a change in the STF rate. This is usually followed by changes in the lending and borrowing rates of financial institutions. The associated banks classify their customers into three categories. These classifications are presented in Table 11.9.

Table 11.9: Classification of customers

Category	Classification	Interest rate
Prime	Large commercial customers	Close to the STF rate
AA	Borrowers in the primary and construction, manufacturing and services sectors	Up to 4.25% above the STF rate
A	Personal and related retail borrowings	Up to 4.75% above the STF rate[1]

1. As of July 1996.

There may be differences between the non-associated banks, associated banks and building societies in terms of the time and the magnitude of the interest rate changes.[42] For example, non-associated banks are normally more dependent on the interbank market for funds than the associated banks. Hence, any change in interbank rates is likely to affect the non-associated banks immediately. The same holds true for building societies whose main business is the housing market. If interbank rates change, they quickly respond by changing their lending and deposit rates.

Appendix 11.3: Monetary policy implementation

A number of articles on the implementation of domestic monetary policy have been published. Among others, they include D. McGettigan, 'The Monetary Transmission Mechanism and the Operation of Monetary Policy in a Changing Environment: A Review of the Issues', *Central Bank Report*, Winter 1994; and P. McGowan, 'The Operation of Monetary Policy in Ireland', Presidential Address to the Statistical and Social Inquiry Society of Ireland, 29 October 1992.

Two tables describing monetary policy as operated in Ireland have been reproduced below.

Table 11.10: Monetary policy implementation as outlined by McGettigan

(A) Policy instruments ↓	(Open market operations, required reserve ratios, Central Bank lending rate)
(B) Operating targets ↓	(Short-term interest rate)
(C) Intermediate targets/indicators ↓	(Monetary targets, exchange rate targets, various inflation indicators)
(D) Ultimate target	(Price stability and/or output growth)

Source: Figure 3, 'The Monetary Transmission Mechanism and the Operation of Monetary Policy in a Changing Environment: A Review of the Issues' in the *Central Bank Report*, Winter 1994.

Table 11.11: Monetary policy implementation as outlined by McGowan

Ultimate objective	1 Stable domestic prices including strong exchange rate.
	2 Level of the exchange rate.
Intermediate	3 Level of the official external reserves.
	4 Level of the money market interest rates.

Source: 'The Operation of Monetary Policy in Ireland', Presidential Address to the Statistical and Social Inquiry Society of Ireland, October 1992.

CHAPTER 12

A BASIC FRAMEWORK FOR MACROECONOMIC ANALYSIS – THE IS/LM MODEL

'[The IS/LM diagram is] to macroeconomic textbooks what the benzene ring diagram is to textbooks of organic chemistry.'[1]

Christopher Bliss

'The IS-LM diagram . . . is widely . . . accepted as a convenient synopsis of Keynesian theory.'[2]

John R. Hicks (1904–89)

'A basic version of that model [IS/LM] remains the core of many introductory textbooks, which use it throughout to analyse the effects of changes in some exogenous macroeconomic variables and, in particular, the impact of alternative monetary and fiscal policies.'[3]

Jordi Gali

Chapter objectives

Upon completing this chapter, the student should understand:

* the purpose, derivation, position and slope of the IS curve;
* the purpose, derivation, position and slope of the LM curve;
* how interest rates and national income are determined in the IS/LM model;
* fiscal and monetary policy in the context of the IS/LM model;
* the policy differences between Keynesians and monetarists.

Outline

Introduction

Sir John R. Hicks, the 1972 Nobel prize winner in economics, is credited with bringing the IS/LM model to the forefront of economic thinking. His famous article 'Mr Keynes and the Classics: a suggested interpretation', which first described a SI-LL (now commonly referred to as the IS-LM) framework, was published in the journal *Econometrica* in 1937. With the help of refinements from economists such as Hansen (1887–1975), Klein (b. 1920), Modigliani (b. 1918) and Patinkin (b. 1922), the IS/LM model became the accepted framework for analysing macroeconomic concepts and policies.[4] It was the model which popularised many Keynesian ideas and, moreover, dominated macroeconomic theory until the 1970s. Notwithstanding the achievements of others, it was Hicks who converted many of his contemporaries to the Keynesian doctrine – a doctrine which many had failed to comprehend given the revolutionary nature of the ideas and the obscurity of the language used.

The IS/LM framework is an extension of the Keynesian income determination model which we introduced in Chapter 10. Many assumptions underlie both models. First, both are demand-side models with aggregate expenditure determining output and employment. Linked to this is the assumption that the economy is operating at less than full capacity, i.e. equilibrium is at less than full employment in both models. Second, prices are assumed to be exogenous, i.e. they are assumed 'fixed'.[5] Third, both models are developed for a closed economy.

These assumptions can also be viewed as inherent weaknesses of the model. Others include the absence of any reference to expectations and the supply-side of the economy where supply bottlenecks may exist. Notwithstanding these omissions, the IS/LM model has been described as the most successful textbook model in the history of macroeconomics.

The IS/LM framework differs in a number of ways from the simple Keynesian model. First, investment is now treated as a function of interest rates. Second, the money market is included. Moreover, it analyses the interaction between two markets: the goods market and the money market. Because both markets are included, the effects of fiscal and monetary policy on interest rates and income can be examined.

The outline to this chapter is as follows. We begin by analysing the goods market. A goods market equilibrium curve is derived. An analysis of the money market follows. Central to this is the derivation of a money market equilibrium curve. Following this, both markets and their respective curves are brought together to analyse the effects of fiscal and monetary policy changes on both interest rates and income levels. Finally, the differences in policy between Keynesians and monetarists are briefly discussed.

12.1 The goods market and the IS curve

The IS curve is the goods market equilibrium curve. The IS curve depicts the negative relationship between interest rates and income that exists in the goods market.[6] It can be derived from the Keynesian income determination model. However, we must first examine investment and its determinants in greater detail before we can derive the IS curve. In Chapter 10 we assumed that investment was independent of the explanatory variable, income. Investment was exogenous: it was determined by variables outside the model. We now adjust this in order to incorporate interest rates as an explanatory variable. With this adjustment to the model, investment is now a function of the interest rate. Figure 12.1 shows the relationship between interest rates and the level of investment when all other factors including expectations are held constant.

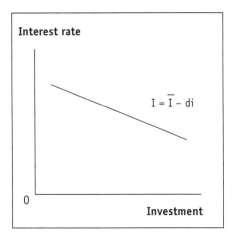

Figure 12.1: The investment function

The level of investment expenditure is related to the cost of borrowing investment funds. The investment function is downward sloping, depicting a negative relationship between interest rates and investment.[7] Lower interest rates induce higher investment expenditure. Likewise, high interest rates induce businesses to defer or postpone investment decisions. A change in expectations for future corporate earnings causes the entire curve to shift.

Another possibility is for a firm to use its own funds to finance capital projects. However, if the market rate of return on these funds is high, there is an opportunity cost involved. The firm can place the funds into an interest-bearing account rather than undertake the investment project. The higher the rate of return, the less likely the investment project is to be financed from these funds. The negative relationship still holds.

The equation for the investment function is as follows:

$$I = \bar{I} - di$$

[12.1]

where: I = total investment expenditure; $\bar{I}$ = autonomous investment expenditure; d = the investment sensitivity to interest rates; i = interest rates.

The position of the investment function is determined by the level of autonomous investment whereas the slope is given by the sensitivity of investment to interest rate changes, measured by d. This sensitivity measure plays an important role in the slope of the IS curve and the subsequent effectiveness of both fiscal and monetary policy.

Investment decisions must include interest rates as an explanatory variable in order to derive the IS curve. We begin with the Keynesian income determination model. Changes in interest rates will cause investment and ultimately income to change.

The IS curve: derivation, position and slope
....

The IS curve is derived from the Keynesian cross diagram as shown in Figure 12.2.

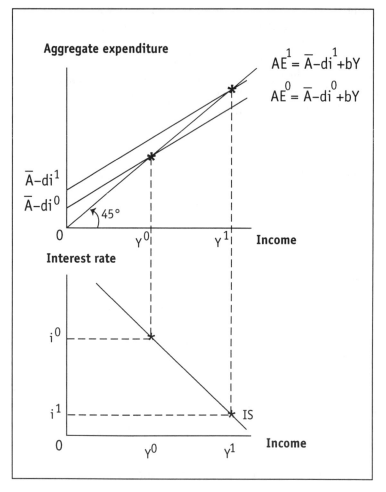

In the top diagram the AE curve, AE^0 is drawn for a particular level of interest rate, i^0.[8] This corresponds to an equilibrium level of income, Y^0. In equilibrium, expenditure is equal to income, $AE = Y$. This, in turn, gives us our first point in (i, Y) space.

Let us suppose interest rates decline, from i^0 to i^1. Lower interest rates increase the level of investment expenditure and, subsequently, aggregate expenditure. The higher AE function results in a new and higher equilibrium level of income, Y^1. This lower interest rate and higher income level gives us the second point in (i, Y) space. We could continue to change the interest rate and find corresponding levels of income. The locus of points would result in a downward sloping curve, illustrating the inverse relationship between interest rates and income.

We know that when the aggregate expenditure curve crosses the 45° line, the goods market is in equilibrium. Therefore, since every point on the IS curve is derived from these equilibrium points, the goods market is in equilibrium at every point along the IS curve. In other words, this locus of points reflects equilibrium in the goods market.

Definition
• • • • • •

> The IS curve depicts the combination of interest rates and income levels that is consistent with equilibrium in the goods market.

The equation for the IS curve is derived algebraically in Appendix 12.1.

The position of any given IS curve is determined by the level of autonomous spending. $\overline{A}$, consisting of autonomous consumer, investment and government expenditure, remained constant throughout the derivation of the IS curve. Any deliberate change in $\overline{A}$ will result in a shift of the IS curve. An increase in $\overline{A}$ results in a rightward shift whereas a decrease in $\overline{A}$ results in a leftward shift. In terms of broad macroeconomic policies any change in fiscal policy, either expansionary or contractionary, results in a change in the position of the IS curve. This, in turn, helps us to analyse the effect of fiscal policy changes on the equilibrium level of interest rates and income. This is discussed in Section 12.4 below.

The two factors which largely determine the slope of the IS curve are the interest rate sensitivity of investment and the expenditure multiplier. For example, the IS curve is relatively steep when investment is insensitive to changes in interest rates and the multiplier is relatively small. The opposite is true for a relatively flat IS curve. The slope of the IS curve has important implications for the effectiveness of fiscal and monetary policy.[9]

As an exercise, draw the relevant IS curves when the multiplier is low/high and for low/high interest rate-investment sensitivity measures.

We will now turn to the money market to derive the LM curve.

12.2 The money market and the LM curve

The LM curve is the money market equilibrium curve. It depicts the positive relationship between interest rates and income that exists in the money market.

The LM curve: derivation, position and slope
....

The LM curve is derived from equilibrium points in the money market as shown in Figure 12.3. Keynes suggested that the demand for money is inversely related to the interest rate. Therefore, the demand curve is downward sloping: as interest rates rise, the demand for money falls. The money supply is determined by the monetary authorities and is therefore independent of the rate of interest. Hence, the supply curve for money ($\frac{M}{P}$) is vertical (denoted by M_S in Chapter 11). At the intersection between the demand curve and the supply curve, the money market is in equilibrium. At this particular rate of interest, the demand for real balances equals the supply of real balances.[10] This is shown in the right-hand panel of Figure 12.3 and is identical to the money market as illustrated in Figure 11.11.

Figure 12.3: Derivation of the LM curve

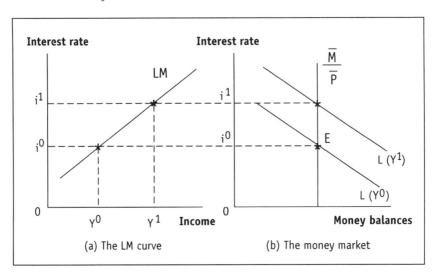

(a) The LM curve   (b) The money market

The interest rate and the level of income at point E in the money market gives us our first point in (i,Y) space (i^0,Y^0). The demand for money curve is drawn for a particular level of income.

Suppose that the level of income increases to Y^1. As a result, the demand for money increases. This is shown by a rightward shift of the money demand curve. If the supply of money is held constant, the subsequent excess demand of money pushes up equilibrium interest rates. Thus, as income increases, interest rates increase.

If we plot interest rates against income, we get the second point in (i,Y) space, (i^1,Y^1). We could continue to change the income level and find corresponding rates of interest. The locus of points would result in an upward sloping curve illustrating a positive relationship between income and interest rates in the money market. This is the LM curve.[11]

Definition
● ● ● ● ● ●

The LM curve depicts the combination of interest rates and income levels that is consistent with equilibrium in the money market.

The equation for the LM curve is derived algebraically in Appendix 12.1.

The position of the LM curve is determined by the real money supply. When we derived the LM curve, the real money supply was held constant. Any deliberate change in the real money supply, $\frac{\overline{M}}{P}$ will result in a shift of the LM curve.[12] For example, an increase in $\frac{\overline{M}}{P}$ results in a rightward shift of the LM curve. Similarly, a decrease in $\frac{\overline{M}}{P}$ results in a leftward shift of the LM curve. Monetary policy aimed at changing the real money supply will cause the position of the LM curve to change. This, in turn, affects the equilibrium level of interest rates and income. Section 12.4 below deals with these matters in greater detail.

The slope of the LM curve is largely determined by the income and the interest rate elasticities of money demand. A large income elasticity of money demand combined with a small interest rate elasticity of money demand results in a relatively steep LM curve. A relatively flat LM curve results from a combination of a small income sensitivity and a large interest rate sensitivity of money demand. The slope of the LM curve has important implications for the effectiveness of fiscal and monetary policy. Refer to Section 12.5 to see how this relates to the Keynesian-monetarist debate.

As an exercise draw the relevant LM curves for different combinations of income elasticities of money demand and interest rate elasticities of money demand.

12.3 Equilibrium in the IS/LM model

The IS curve depicts the negative relationship that exists in the goods market between interest rates and income. At all points along the IS curve, the goods market is in equilibrium. The LM curve shows the combinations of interest rates and income at which the money market is in equilibrium. All points on the LM curve are points where money demand equals the stock of money. The IS and LM curves together determine the equilibrium interest rate and the equilibrium income level. We know from Chapter 10 that the equilibrium income level may not coincide with the full-employment output level: it is independent of the labour market. The market clearing position is illustrated in Figure 12.4.

Figure 12.4: Equilibrium in the IS/LM model

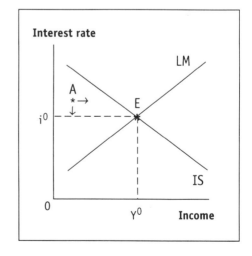

In this diagram the IS and LM curves intersect at (i^0, Y^0). This point E represents the equilibrium interest rate, i^0, and equilibrium income level, Y^0. At this point, the goods market and the money market are in equilibrium simultaneously. The forces of excess demand and excess supply act together to move the economy towards this equilibrium position. Let us take an example.

Consider point A in Figure 12.4. Point A is to the left of the IS curve. It is a point of excess demand in the goods market.[13] This excess demand will result in unplanned inventory depletions, and eventually to an increase in output. There is a subsequent move to the right, towards the IS curve.

In addition, point A is above the LM curve. It is a point of excess supply in the money market.[14] This excess supply of money will result in a downward movement of interest rates. There is a move towards the LM curve. Taken together, the economy moves from a point of disequilibrium to the one point where the goods market and the money market are in equilibrium simultaneously.

The separate analysis of the goods market (Section 12.1) and the money market (Section 12.2) is a deliberate exercise in understanding the framework to this model. In the real world, however, the goods market and the money market are dependent on each other. The interdependency between these two markets is explained in two examples below.

Example 1
·············

The demand for money (a money market concept) is influenced by the level of income which is determined in the goods market.

Example 2
·············

The level of investment expenditure (a goods market concept) is influenced by the rate of interest which is determined in the money market.

This interdependency has important consequences for government policy. For example, a policy which is targeted exclusively at the goods market may have implications for the money market. The inverse is also true.

Finally, any change in fiscal and/or monetary policy will change the position of the respective IS or LM curves and, in turn, affect the equilibrium interest rate and income level. A more detailed analysis follows.

12.4 Fiscal and monetary policy

Fiscal policy is concerned with government expenditure and taxation and how they affect national output. Monetary policy refers to the use of money supply, credit and interest rates to influence national output. Changes in these policies and in particular their effect on interest rates and national income can be explained by using the IS/LM framework. Let us begin with a fiscal policy change.

Fiscal policy
···············

Suppose the government decides to increase expenditure. We know from the Keynesian income determination model that an increase in expenditure will increase national income and do so by a multiple of itself. The increase in income may be quite large, depending on the size of the multiplier. However, this is a very simple model where interest rates are assumed to be fixed. The analysis is a little more complicated when interest rates are allowed to vary.

Figure 12.5 illustrates the effect of a change in government expenditure. The original equilibrium point reflects the old level of government expenditure. We know from our analysis of the IS curve that an increase in expenditure shifts the IS curve out and to the right. Interest rates rise, from i^0 to i^1. There is also an increase in the level of equilibrium income. A more detailed explanation is required.

Figure 12.5: Expansionary fiscal policy –
an increase in $\overline{G}$

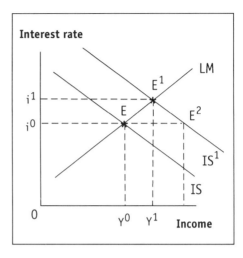

The Keynesian model predicts an increase in income arising out of an increase in government expenditure. Higher income levels increase money demand. The subsequent excess demand for money forces up interest rates. Higher interest rates have a negative effect on investment expenditure. The decline in investment expenditure causes a reduction in national income. As a result the overall increase in national income is not as large as originally predicted. This knock-on effect is known as crowding out. The extent of the crowding out can be measured by the move from E^2 to E^1, in Figure 12.5. In summary, higher public expenditure and its subsequent effect on national income is crowded out by higher interest rates and lower private spending.[15]

Expansionary fiscal policy and its effect on economic variables is shown below.[16]

Increase in $\overline{G}$ → increases Y → increases L → increases
i → reduces I → reduces Y

In this example, the initial increase in government spending does increase national income, but by less than it would if the interest rate was fixed (as in the Keynesian model of income determination).

Belief in the effectiveness of fiscal policy has changed over the years. Fiscal policy was in the ascendancy after World War II and in particular (as we saw in Chapter 10) during the 1960s. Changes in public expenditure or taxes were believed to have a large influence on the level of aggregate expenditure and, in turn, on national output. The belief in the active use of fiscal policy was particularly strong in the US and in the UK.

In the 1970s most governments, with few exceptions (Ireland being one), abandoned fiscal policy as a method of increasing national output and employment. In the 1990s, the use of fiscal policy has re-emerged as an alternative policy to the supply-side measures advocated by the followers of Reaganomics and Thatcherism. One of its strongest contemporary supporters is J. K. Galbraith (b. 1908) who has strongly advocated the use of fiscal policy. Recently, Galbraith suggested counter-cyclical fiscal policy for Ireland (see Case Study in Chapter 10 'Galbraith urges jobs spend').

Monetary policy
....

A change in monetary policy is now considered. Suppose the monetary authorities decide to increase the supply of money in the economy. The effect of a change in the stock of money is shown in Figure 12.6. The original equilibrium point, E reflects the old level of money stock. We know from our discussion in a previous section that an increase in the real money supply shifts the LM curve to the right. Interest rates fall, from i^0 to i^1. A higher level of equilibrium income also results. The relevant diagram below depicts the new equilibrium position. A more comprehensive explanation follows.

Figure 12.6: Expansionary monetary policy – an increase in $\frac{\overline{M}}{P}$

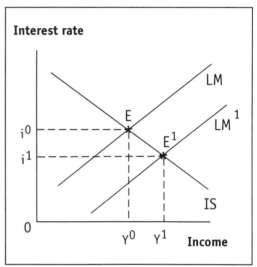

Lower interest rates induce higher investment expenditure. The increase in expenditure will contribute to an increase in national income. Higher income levels increase the demand for money which puts upward pressure on interest rates. As a result the initial easing of interest rates may be partly offset by this subsequent increase.

Definition
●●●●●●

The process where a change in monetary policy affects aggregate expenditure and national output is called the monetary transmission mechanism.

Expansionary monetary policy and its effect on economic variables is shown below.[17]

> Increase in $\frac{\overline{M}}{P}$ → reduces i → increases I → increases Y → increases L → increases i

Monetary policy became popular once again in the early 1970s with the advent of monetarism and the downfall of Keynesian economics. Controlling money supply and interest rate levels was paramount in attempting to stem the increase in the level of inflation which had become the primary objective of policy-makers in the Western world.

A policy mix
··············

A policy mix is the simultaneous use of fiscal and monetary policy. One example which is quite common among policy-makers is a monetary accommodation of a fiscal expansion. This is where the adverse effects of fiscal expansion, namely higher interest rates, are lessened by deliberate increases in the money supply.[18] National output increases but there is no corresponding rise in interest rates. This is illustrated in Figure 12.7.

Figure 12.7: A policy mix – a monetary accommodation of a fiscal expansion

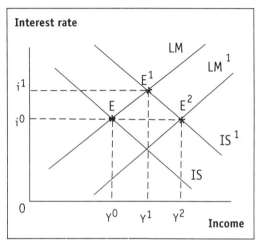

Expansionary fiscal policy shifts the IS curve rightwards, from IS to IS^1. As a result, income and interest rates rise, from Y^0 to Y^1 and from i^0 to i^1 respectively. To counteract the rise in interest rates, the Central Bank increases the money stock. This shifts the LM curve to the right, from LM to LM^1. This expansion of the money supply causes a further increase in income from Y^1 to Y^2 and a fall in interest rates from i^1 to i^0. The net effect of this particular policy mix is a relatively large increase in income from Y^0 to Y^2 combined with no change in the interest rate level. The monetary accommodation of the fiscal expansion keeps interest rates at the original level, i^0.

Monetary accommodation of fiscal expansion was used by the US authorities during the recessionary period 1974–75 and again in 1981–82.

CASE STUDY

Extract from The Sunday Press
Marking the route to mayhem
by Gerry Byrne

. . .
The Berlin Wall has fallen and Germany is reunified. Generous reconstruction subsidies by the Bonn government to the former East German government boosted spending and pushed German inflation to 4.5%. For a nation whose elders still recall with horror the runaway inflation of the 1920s, this rate, commonplace in Ireland or Britain, was clearly unacceptable.

Germany's central bank, the Bundesbank, is one of the world's most powerful financial institutions. It makes decisions without reference to the Bonn government, which has no

→

direct authority over it. The Bundesbank acted by pushing up interest rates to control inflation. By making money more expensive, the German Central Bank hoped to curb spending and thus cool the economy. Attracted by the high interest rates, money flowed into German banks from other EC economies.

After failing to persuade the Germans to drop theirs, other European central banks, Ireland's and Britain's included, responded with correspondingly high rates to stop their nation's money flowing into Germany.

In a weak British economy, the higher interest rates pushed the country further into recession. Burdened by high mortgage repay-ments, homeowners stopped spending on the High Street and small businesses with high borrowings went under, adding to unemployment.

Across the Atlantic, the American central bank, the Federal Reserve or Fed, embarked on a deliberate policy of encouraging low interest rates to encourage economic activity. US investors shifted cash to Germany and other strong European economies to avail of the higher deposit interest rates. The deutschmark had become the world's strongest currency.

. . .

Source: The Sunday Press, 20 September 1992.

Questions
....

1. Use the IS/LM framework to explain the link between the 'boosted spending' by the German government and the 'high interest rates' in Germany.
2. What sections of the article are not covered by the simple IS/LM model?
3. What concept within the IS/LM framework is useful in explaining the following sentence 'the higher interest rates pushed the country further into recession'?

Answers
....

1. The German government, as part of the reunification programme, gave subsidies to the former East Germany. This is an increase in government spending which causes a rightward shift of the IS curve.

Figure12.8: Higher spending and higher interest rates

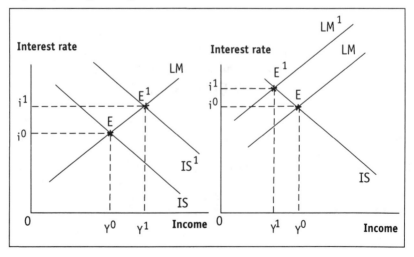

To finance the increase in spending, the German government could either increase taxes or borrow to finance the debt. It chose the latter.

The Bundesbank is run independently and is primarily concerned with inflation. The Bundesbank sets the interest rate, then adjusts the money supply to maintain that rate of interest. Rather than accommodating the Bonn government, the Bundesbank raised interest rates. It reinforced this by limiting the money supply. This can be shown by a leftward shift of the LM curve. By raising interest rates, the Bundesbank hoped to stem inflationary pressures.

2. First, the article states that German inflation was pushed to 4.5%. This increase in the general price level cannot be analysed or predicted by this IS/LM model on account of the assumption of fixed prices. Second, it refers to capital flows, currencies and exchange rates, and foreign interest rates. The simple IS/LM analysis is based on a closed economy model. The aforementioned variables are all outside the framework of the model.

3. The investment function or what Keynes called the marginal efficiency of capital. It starts from the premise that investment expenditure is affected by the level of interest rates. High interest rates deter investment decisions whereas low interest rates are conducive to undertaking investment projects. In this particular case the high interest rates in Germany have led to a similar policy in Britain. At high rates of interest, firms will not undertake investment projects and this component of aggregate expenditure is weak. Households also contribute to the recessionary problems. Households with variable mortgage payments have less money to spend on consumer goods. Consequently, consumers have 'stopped spending on the High Street'. Small businesses, facing lower demand for their goods and higher costs due to the higher interest rates, cannot survive. The result is a recession.

12.5 The Keynesian-monetarist debate

It is the slopes of the IS and LM curves which determine the effectiveness of fiscal and monetary policy. The slopes in turn are determined largely by a range of sensitivity measures which were outlined in Sections 12.1 and 12.2 above.

Fiscal policy is more effective when the LM curve is flat and the IS curve is steep. We know from our discussion of the IS curve that a steep IS curve results from investment expenditure which is insensitive to interest rate changes. Likewise, it is the particular combination of a demand for money which is insensitive to income and highly sensitive to interest rates which results in a flat LM curve. The inverse is true for the case of ineffective fiscal policy.

Monetary policy, in contrast, is relatively effective when there is a flat IS curve and a steep LM curve. When the sensitivity of investment to changes in interest rates is high, the subsequent IS curve is relatively flat. A steep LM curve results from a demand for money which is sensitive to income and insensitive to interest rates. The opposite is true for ineffective monetary policy.

This rather technical discussion prepares us for the debate between the Keynesian view and the monetarist view of either policy.

Keynesians argue that the IS curve is relatively steep, and is so because investment is insensitive to changes in interest rates. A steep IS curve results from investment pessimism. A change in interest rates does not entice investors to undertake new projects which would lead to an increase in economic activity. Of greater importance is their belief in a relatively flat or, in the extreme case, a horizontal LM curve.

This hypothetical situation is known as the liquidity trap which, in theory, could exist at very low interest rates where the demand for money may be infinitely large. In effect, people are willing to hold any amount of money at this given interest rate. However, even Keynes himself doubted the very existence of such a case. Nonetheless, since it was felt that the IS curve was relatively steep and the LM curve relatively flat, fiscal policy was preferred to monetary policy.

In contrast, monetarists argued that the IS curve is relatively flat, reflecting investment expenditure which is highly responsive to changes in interest rates. Their belief in a relatively steep LM curve, and vertical in the extreme, is a return to the classical doctrine. The vertical LM curve arises from an absence of any speculative demand for money. The demand for money does not change in response to changes in interest rates. Any increase in output which results directly from a rise in public expenditure is offset by subsequent increases in interest rates which have an adverse effect on private spending. This possibility is known as crowding out. In these circumstances, fiscal policy is largely ineffective.

The Keynesian/monetarist controversy is illustrated in Figure 12.9 below. In Figure 12.9 (a) the IS curve is relatively steep, reflecting the Keynesian position. The monetarist position of a vertical LM curve is depicted in Figure 12.9 (b).

Figure 12.9: The Keynesian and monetarist debate

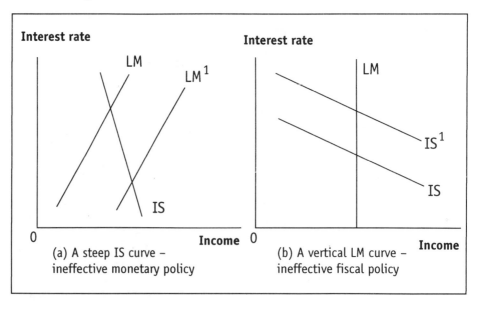

(a) A steep IS curve – ineffective monetary policy

(b) A vertical LM curve – ineffective fiscal policy

Both the liquidity trap and crowding out are extreme cases and are unlikely to exist in reality. Notwithstanding this fact, the above analysis is worthwhile in that it provides us with a brief account of some of the differences between two of the main schools of economic thought. It is also important to acknowledge that both these alternatives, as represented above, ignore supply-side considerations and changes in the price level. These must be included in a more comprehensive discussion of the Keynesian/monetarist controversy.

Summary

1. The IS/LM model is a static, short-run model which integrates the goods market with the money market. It is similar to the Keynesian model of income determination in that prices are fixed and demand determines output and employment. It is a model for a closed economy. It differs to the extent that interest rates are endogenous and the money market matters.
2. The IS curve illustrates the combinations of interest rates and income levels for which the goods market is in equilibrium. It is negatively sloped. Lower interest rates increase the level of investment which, in turn, increases national income. Its position is determined by the level of autonomous spending. The interest rate elasticity of investment and the multiplier determine its slope.
3. The LM curve shows the combinations of interest rates and income levels where the demand for and supply of money are equal. It is positively sloped. Higher income levels increase the demand for money which, in turn, increases interest rates. The stock of money determines the position of the LM curve. Its slope is determined by the interest rate and income elasticities of money demand.
4. The goods market and the money market do not operate independently. The intersection of the IS curve and the LM curve is the equilibrium point. Both markets are in equilibrium simultaneously at this point. A change in fiscal policy shifts the IS curve whereas a change in monetary policy shifts the LM curve. Changes in equilibrium interest rates and income levels will result.
5. Expansionary fiscal policy results in higher interest rates and higher income levels. Crowding out limits the increase in national income. Expansionary monetary policy results in lower interest rates and higher income levels. An example of a policy mix is a monetary accommodation of a fiscal expansion.
6. The IS/LM framework is very useful in explaining the divergent views of Keynesians and monetarists. The liquidity trap is the extreme Keynesian case. The classical case of full crowding out is supported by the monetarists.

Key terms

IS curve
Marginal efficiency of capital
Interest rate elasticity of investment
LM curve

Income elasticity of money demand
Interest rate elasticity of money demand
Fiscal policy
Monetary policy
Transmission mechanism
Monetarists
Policy mix
Liquidity trap
Crowding out

Review questions

1. What are the differences between the Keynesian model of income determination and the IS/LM model? What are the limitations to the IS/LM model?
2. Explain why the IS curve slopes down from left to right. What factors determine the position and the slope of the IS curve?
3. Why is the money market equilibrium curve upward sloping? What factors determine its slope?
4. Explain what effect a contractionary monetary policy would have on the equilibrium level of interest rates and national income.
5. What effect would a contractionary fiscal policy have on (a) the IS curve; (b) equilibrium income and, finally (c) equilibrium interest rates.
6. Explain 'crowding out'. What action can the Central Bank take to avoid the rise in interest rates which is usually associated with crowding out?

Working problems

1. The following equations describe an economy:

$C = .85Y$

$I = 700 - 25i$

$\overline{G} = 540$

$L = .5Y - 70i$

$\dfrac{\overline{M}}{P} = 400$

    (a) Derive the IS equation.
    (b) Derive the LM equation.
    (c) Calculate the equilibrium levels of interest rates and income.
    (d) Sketch the equilibrium position.   [Calculations to two decimal places]

2. If investment is insensitive to changes in the interest rate, is monetary or fiscal policy more effective? Explain your answer.

Multi-choice questions

1. The IS/LM model is an extension of the Keynesian income determination model with an adjustment for:

   (a) wages;
   (b) income levels;
   (c) exchange rates;
   (d) interest rates;
   (e) none of the above.

2. The IS curve:

   (a) is derived from the goods market;
   (b) shows combinations of interest rates and income such that expenditure equals income;
   (c) is the goods market equilibrium curve;
   (d) is drawn for a given level of autonomous spending;
   (e) all of the above.

3. The slope of the LM curve:

   (a) is determined by the interest rate elasticity of investment;
   (b) is relatively flat given a small income elasticity of money demand;
   (c) is relatively steep given a high interest rate elasticity of money demand;
   (d) both (a) and (b) above;
   (e) both (a) and (c) above.

4. Suppose investment becomes less responsive to changes in interest rates. As a result the:

   (a) IS curve will shift to the left;
   (b) IS curve will shift to the right;
   (c) IS curve will become flatter;
   (d) IS curve will become steeper;
   (e) none of the above.

5. Suppose the government decreases public expenditure. All other things equal, the likely result will be:

   (a) an increase in interest rates;
   (b) a decrease in national income;
   (c) a decrease in interest rates;
   (d) both (a) and (b) above;
   (e) both (b) and (c) above.

6. The extreme case of crowding out:

   (a) occurs when the LM curve is horizontal;
   (b) is caused by a large interest rate elasticity of money demand;
   (c) leads to ineffective fiscal policy;
   (d) is supported by Keynesians;
   (e) none of the above.

True or false

1. The IS/LM model is largely a demand-side model. _____
2. Equilibrium prices and income can be determined by the IS/LM model. _____
3. The position of the IS curve is determined by the size of the multiplier and the interest rate sensitivity of investment. _____
4. The real money supply is constant along any given money market equilibrium curve. _____
5. A cut in taxes is an example of contractionary fiscal policy and is likely to result in lower income and interest rate levels. _____
6. The liquidity trap means that there is little or no role for monetary policy. _____

Fill in the blanks

The IS/LM model is a Keynesian, _____-side, closed economy model where _____ are assumed to be held constant. It is comprised of _____ markets, each with their respective curves. Equilibrium in the _____ market, where expenditure equals _____ is represented by the IS curve. The _____ curve reflects equilibrium between the _____ for and the stock of money. _____ spending is constant along the IS curve whereas the real _____ _____ is constant along the LM curve. The _____ and different _____ measures are the factors which determine the _____ of both curves. The model is useful in many different ways. Firstly, it can be used to determine the equilibrium level of _____ _____ and _____ _____. Secondly, the effects of fiscal and _____ policy can be determined. Thirdly, the Keynesian-_____ debate, with both crowding out and the _____ _____ explained, can be analysed using such a model. However, it does have its limitations. It is a static model where prices are assumed to be _____. _____ variables such as foreign interest rates and income levels are excluded. The _____ -side of the economy is absent.

CASE STUDY

Extract from The Irish Times
Full circle back to recession
by Cliff Taylor

. . . Mrs Thatcher's ideas caught the mood of the times. Her economic policies were based on the newly fashionable tenet of monetarism, which was that governments should concentrate on controlling the growth of the supply of money in the economy. The doctrine was that, beyond this, governments had little power to manage economic growth successfully and should not try to do so. Mrs Thatcher's views on 'rolling back the frontiers of the state' through wide-range privatisation thus sat well with the monetarist doctrine, as did her policy of curbing trade union power and cutting taxes to encourage enterprise.

→

This agenda was carried through with vigour. In the 1980 budget, the then Chancellor, Sir Geoffrey Howe, doubled VAT and slashed public spending when the economy was already slowing. It devastated the economy, with national output falling by over 2% in 1980 and by 1.5% in 1981. Manufacturing output fell by 15%, hit by a high sterling rate. But calls for a 'U-turn' were met by the famous rejoinder: 'The lady is not for turning.'

. . .

The loosening of monetary policy in response to the 1987 stock market crash, and tax cuts in the 1988 budget by Mr Nigel Lawson, contributed to this unsustainable expansion. Mr Lawson held that inflation would have been much lower if sterling had become a full member of the European Monetary System (EMS) in the mid-1980s. He resigned over the issue last year.

Source: The Irish Times, *23 November 1990.*

Questions
....

1. Use the IS/LM model to explain how a doubling of VAT and a slashing of public spending 'devastated the economy'.
2. With regard to the policies adopted above, can you suggest a possible rationale for such a policy?
3. Use the IS/LM model to show how a 'loosening of monetary policy' combined with 'tax cuts' could lead to 'expansion'.

Appendix 12.1: Algebraic derivation of the IS and LM curves

To derive the equation for the IS curve we begin with the aggregate expenditure function:

$$AE \equiv C + I + G \qquad [12.2]$$

In the Keynesian aggregate expenditure model, investment was autonomous. In the IS/LM model, it depends on the interest rate. Therefore, we will define the components of aggregate expenditure in the following way:

$$C = \overline{C} + bY \qquad [12.3]$$

$$I = \overline{I} - di \qquad [12.1]$$

$$G = \overline{G} \qquad [10.14]$$

Substitute these equations into Equation 12.2:

$$AE = \overline{C} + bY + \overline{I} - di + \overline{G} \qquad [12.4]$$

Let $\overline{A} = \overline{C} + \overline{I} + \overline{G}$ the autonomous components of aggregate expenditure.

Substitute $\overline{A}$ into Equation 12.4:

$$AE = \overline{A} - di + bY \qquad [12.5]$$

Equilibrium in the goods market is where:

$$Y = AE \qquad [10.9]$$

Substitute Y for AE in Equation 12.5 and solve for Y:

$$Y = \frac{1}{1-b}(\overline{A} - di) \qquad [12.6]$$

Let $k = \frac{1}{1-b}$ as in Chapter 10. Substituting this expression into Equation 12.6 yields

$$Y = k(\overline{A} - di) \qquad [12.7]$$

Equation 12.7 shows that the relationship between the interest rate and income in the goods market is negative. Therefore, the IS curve is downward sloping. The strength of the relationship will be reflected in the slope of the line. This is determined by the expenditure multiplier, k and the interest rate elasticity of investment, d.

To derive the equation for the LM curve, we begin with the money market. The demand for money equation is

$$L = jY - hi \qquad [12.8]$$

where j is the sensitivity of money demand to changes in income and h is the sensitivity of money demand to changes in the interest rate.

In equilibrium in the money market, money demand equals real money supply ($\frac{\overline{M}}{P}$). Hence,

$$jY - hi = \frac{\overline{M}}{P} \qquad [12.9]$$

Solve for Y:

$$Y = \frac{1}{j}\left(hi + \frac{\overline{M}}{P}\right) \qquad [12.10]$$

In terms of i:

$$i = \frac{1}{h}\left(jY - \frac{\overline{M}}{P}\right) \qquad [12.11]$$

We can see that the relationship between the interest rate and income in the money market is positive. The LM curve is upward sloping. The strength of the relationship is reflected in the slope of the line. The variables which affect the slope of the LM curve are the two elasticity measures, j and h.

CHAPTER 13

EXPLAINING THE MACROECONOMY – THE AD/AS MODEL

'MACRO-ECONOMICS: a laudable attempt to explain how large parts (or the whole) of an economy work, without pretending to know how the component parts work.'[1]

Ralph Harris

'Although economists can tell the government much about how to influence aggregate demand, they can tell it precious little about how to influence aggregate supply.'[2]

Alan S. Blinder

'To many economists this [supply-side economics] has the potential to be the greatest single breakthrough in economic thinking since the Keynesian revolution.'[3]

Mark Brownrigg

Chapter objectives

Upon completing this chapter, the student should understand:

- aggregate demand;
- aggregate supply and potential output;
- short-run and long-run aggregate supply;
- macroeconomic equilibrium;
- demand-management policies;
- supply-side policies.

Outline

Introduction

Until now our analysis of macroeconomics has been quite limited. Our model of the economy is incomplete. For one, the focus has been exclusively on the demand side of the economy. We have been concerned with planned expenditure or spending. We have assumed that the supply side of the economy has been passive, reacting largely to changes in aggregate demand.[4] Policy considerations were limited to demand-side policies, i.e. fiscal or monetary policy. In addition, prices were assumed to be fixed throughout the model. Therefore, we could not explore inflation, a possible side-effect of government demand-side policies.

A complete model of the economy is inherently complex with many different variables. In this chapter, we discuss a model called the aggregate demand/aggregate supply (AD/AS) model. Both the demand and the supply sides of the economy are considered. Price is a variable. The purpose of the AD/AS model is to provide the student with a complete framework which can be used to analyse macroeconomic principles and policy options. The only constraint lies in the assumption that we are analysing a closed economy. The international aspects of macroeconomics are dealt with in the next chapter.

13.1 Aggregate demand

In the Keynesian model of income determination we defined aggregate expenditure as the total spending in the economy by all economic agents. It is comprised of consumer expenditure, investment expenditure, government expenditure and net exports. With the help of the income determination model, we examined the level of expenditure at each level of income. We now examine the level of expenditure at each price level.

Definition
● ● ● ● ● ●

Aggregate demand is the total output which is demanded at each price level holding all other variables constant.

The curve which shows the relationship between the level of demand and the aggregate price level is called the aggregate demand curve, or simply the AD curve.

The AD curve is normally downward sloping, showing that the lower the price level, the greater will be the aggregate quantity of goods and services demanded in the economy. The demand for national output is inversely related to the price level.

This negative relationship between price and the aggregate quantity of goods and services demanded exists for a number of reasons. First, as the price level falls, the purchasing power of money balances increases. This results in an increase in people's wealth. This so-called real balance effect or wealth effect leads to a rise in consumption.[5] As consumption increases, aggregate demand increases. This effect may be small on account of the weak link between prices, wealth and consumption.

Second, the increase in purchasing power arising out of lower prices may induce a separate effect. Less money is required to carry out a fixed level of transactions. As the excess money is saved, there is an increase in the supply of money. This, in turn, forces interest rates downwards. The lower cost of borrowing induces greater investment expenditure by firms and possibly greater spending by households. As investment increases, aggregate demand increases. This is called the interest rate effect and it may also be weak.

A third reason for why the AD curve slopes downwards is called the international trade effect. As the price level falls (or, to be more accurate, as the domestic price level falls relative to the foreign price level) domestic firms become more competitive. Accordingly, the level of domestically produced goods sold in foreign markets increases, i.e. exports increase. As exports increase, aggregate demand increases.

Derivation of the AD curve
....

In order to derive the AD curve we return to the income determination model of Chapter 10 and, in particular, the Keynesian cross diagram. The top panel of Figure 13.1 is similar to Figure 10.11. Aggregate expenditure is measured on the vertical axis and income is measured on the horizontal axis. The AE curve shows total spending for each level of income at a particular price level. As income increases, aggregate expenditure increases.

Figure 13.1: Deriving the AD curve

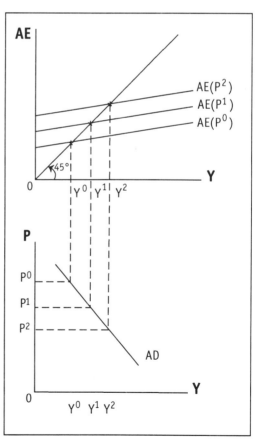

We now examine the relationship between aggregate expenditure and price. The AE curve is drawn for a price level, P^0. The equilibrium level of income is Y^0. Suppose prices fall. We know from our previous discussion that as prices fall aggregate expenditure rises. This is reflected in the higher AE curve, AE (P^1). The higher AE level results in a higher level of equilibrium income, in this case, Y^1. As price continues to fall, to P^2, AE rises further leading to, yet again, a higher level of income, Y^2. The result in (P,Y) space is a locus of points which form a downward sloping AD curve.

Definition
● ● ● ● ● ●

The aggregate demand (AD) curve traces the relationship between the aggregate price level and the equilibrium quantity of goods and services demanded.

As the aggregate price level rises, the quantity of output demanded falls. An alternative way of deriving the AD curve is depicted in Appendix 13.1.[6]

We have already stated that the real balance and interest rate effects may be quite small. Hence, the increase in aggregate expenditure arising out of the fall in prices is small. In graphic terms, the upward shift of the AE curve is quite modest. As a result, the subsequent AD curve is likely to be relatively inelastic or steep.

The AD curve depicts the relationship between price and total output demanded, *ceteris paribus*. The variables which we are holding constant include government spending, taxes, and the money supply. A change in any of these factors will cause a shift of the aggregate demand curve. We will examine changes in the underlying variables in greater detail in Section 13.3.

13.2 Aggregate supply

The term 'aggregate supply' is a macroeconomic concept.

Definition
● ● ● ● ● ●

Aggregate supply describes the total quantity of national output supplied by all producers at each level of price.

It is closely associated with the capacity of the economy to produce. This is often referred to as potential output.

Definition
● ● ● ● ● ●

Potential output represents the maximum level of output that can be produced given a country's productive capacity.

It is determined by the amount of natural, capital and human resources available and the efficiency with which these resources can be put to use.

The aggregate supply curve or simply the AS curve is to macroeconomics what the supply curve (of Chapter 1) is to microeconomics. It is, however, much more complex than the individual or market supply curve.

Definition
● ● ● ● ● ●

The aggregate supply (AS) curve shows the output of GDP produced at different price levels.

There is a distinction between the short-run AS curve and the long-run AS curve. This distinction is largely based on the speed at which factor inputs, particularly labour, react to a change in economic conditions.

In the short run, the costs of all factors of production are assumed to be constant or at least to respond slowly to changes in the demand for the factor input. For example, wage rates may be constant in the short run because of contracts between employers and employees.

At low levels of production, the output of the economy is far below its potential; to put this another way, there is excess capacity. Factories are idle, machinery is not being used and labour is unemployed. If the price level increases and factor costs are constant, firms will make more profit if they increase production.

Similarly, if prices fall and factor prices remain constant, there will be less profit and less incentive to produce goods. Firms respond to lower prices by producing less goods and services.

This positive relationship between output and prices in the short run is depicted in an upward sloping AS curve. It is drawn in Figure 13.2 below.

Figure 13.2: The conventional short-run AS curve

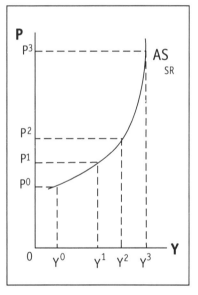

The AS curve, as drawn in Figure 13.2, becomes steeper as the level of national income increases. Why?

Initially, the AS curve is elastic. At low levels of output, there is excess capacity in the economy. Thus, a small increase in the price level, from P^0 to P^1, elicits a large increase in output, from Y^0 to Y^1.

The next portion of the AS curve is steeper. From our discussion in Chapter 4, we know that in the short run, some inputs are fixed and others are variable. As production levels increase, some firms reach full capacity. Further, as all firms demand more labour and other variable inputs, the cost of those inputs may increase. If prices continue to rise, output increases, but only by small increments. An increase in the price level from P^1 to P^2, similar in magnitude to the last price increase, leads to a much smaller increase in output, from Y^1 to Y^2.

The final section of the short-run AS curve is inelastic. We can think of Y^3 as the limit of what this economy can produce if all of its factors of production are fully employed. Even if the price level increases above P^3, the level of national output will not expand.

The AS curve is drawn to show the relationship between national output and price, *ceteris paribus*. The variables which are held constant include technology, the capital stock and the skills of the labour force. Any change in these determinants will alter the position of the AS curve. We will examine changes that shift the AS curve in greater detail in the next section.

This version of the AS curve combines the extreme classical and Keynesian views which are based on different assumptions about the labour market (see Section 9.3 for a more complete discussion on the differences between the classical and Keynesian interpretations of the labour market). We will look briefly at the two perspectives.[7]

The classical view
....

According to classical economists, the output of the economy is based on the labour market. As long as wages and prices are flexible, the labour market returns to full-employment equilibrium. Labour is combined with the economy's other inputs to produce goods and services. Therefore, in the classical view, the real output of the economy is the same as the potential output because all factors of production are fully employed. The short-run AS curve is vertical at the full-employment output level, as shown in panel (a) of Figure 13.3.[8]

Figure 13.3: The extreme classical and Keynesian short-run AS curves

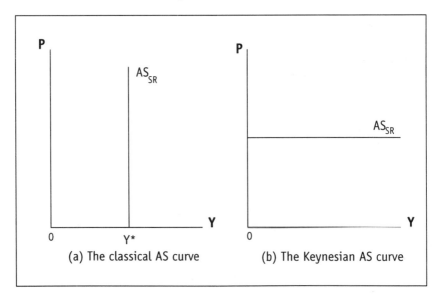

(a) The classical AS curve (b) The Keynesian AS curve

The inelastic AS curve means that output is unresponsive to changes in the price level. Any change in output occurs because of a shift of the aggregate supply curve.

The Keynesian view
....

Recall from our discussion in Chapter 9, that from the Keynesian perspective, demand for labour depends on the demand for output. In other words, causation is reversed. In the classical model, national output is determined by the number of people employed when the labour market is at equilibrium. From the Keynesian perspective, the number of people employed is derived from the demand for goods.

Also, recall that Keynes believed that there are institutional factors which cause wages to be rigid in the short run. In other words, firms can hire additional workers at the same wage that they are paying their current labour force. If firms are producing at less than full capacity, they can increase their variable inputs and increase production at a constant cost per unit.

This means that as demand increases, the level of output will increase, even though the price level has not changed. In other words, the short-run AS curve is perfectly elastic as shown in panel (b) of Figure 13.3.

As stated previously, the upward sloping AS curve is a compromise between the extreme views of the classicals and the Keynesians.

The elastic portion of the AS curve as shown in Figure 13.2 is Keynesian. At low levels of output, where there is excess capacity, changes in output can occur without increasing the price level. This means that over a range of production, the cost of variable inputs, particularly labour, is not changing. The upward sloping portion of the AS curve means that, as the price level rises, the level of production increases. The vertical section of the AS curve reflects the classical view that the maximum output of an economy is constrained at the level where all factors of production are fully employed.

In the long run, changes to factor prices and, in particular, wages are incorporated into the model. Input prices adjust fully to changes in the price level in the long run. There is no dispute between Keynesians and classical economists concerning the aggregate supply curve in the long run. The vertical long-run AS curve is drawn in Figure 13.4, at the potential level of national output, Y*. It shows the maximum output that the economy is able to produce at different price levels, assuming that input prices fully adjust to changing economic conditions.

Figure 13.4: The long-run AS curve

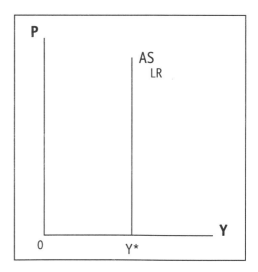

13.3 The policy debate

The AD/AS model is the centrepiece of modern macroeconomics. Both the demand and supply aspects of the economy are considered. Price changes are also incorporated in the analysis. Short-run equilibrium in the AD/AS model is shown in Figure 13.5.

Figure 13.5: Equilibrium in (P,Y) space

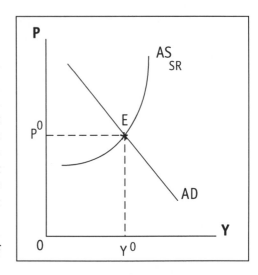

The downward sloping AD curve depicts the relationship between total spending and different price levels. The upward sloping, short-run AS curve shows the level of output which the economy produces at different price levels. Macroeconomic equilibrium occurs at (P^0, Y^0), the inter-section of the AD and the AS curves. At this point the output which households and firms demand is equal to the output which firms are willing to supply. Hence, equilibrium price and output are simulta-neously determined by the interaction of aggregate demand and supply.

If the price level is above equilibrium, aggregate supply exceeds aggregate demand resulting in a rise of unplanned stocks. For equilibrium to be restored, price must adjust downwards. Similarly, if the price level is below equilibrium, aggregate demand exceeds aggregate supply resulting in an excess demand of goods and services. In order for equilibrium to be restored, price adjusts upwards. At P^0, aggregate demand equals aggregate supply.

With a more complete model of the economy than before, we can analyse the full effects of both demand-management policies and supply-side policies. The analysis is divided into short-run and long-run effects.

We begin, however, with a brief explanation of both types of policies. We previously defined demand-management policies as the collective term used to explain various government policies which target the level of aggregate demand in the economy.

Examples of demand-management policies include changes in government spending, the tax rate, the money supply or the interest rate. Any of these policies will shift the AD curve.

Definition
● ● ● ● ● ●

Supply-side policies are targeted at increasing the productive capacity of the economy.

Measures include improving the infrastructure, adopting training programmes to reduce the costs of production and developing new technologies.

Any of these policies will shift the AS curve.

Short-run analysis
....
Demand-management policies

We will use the AD/AS model to assess the effect of discretionary fiscal policy on the aggregate price level and national income.

● Definition
● ● ● ● ● ●

Discretionary fiscal policy refers to deliberate, as opposed to automatic, changes in government expenditure or tax rates in order to influence national income.

Expansionary fiscal policy involves increasing government spending or cutting the tax rate in an effort to increase national income. Contractionary fiscal policy is initiated by decreasing government spending or raising the tax rate.

The AD curve is initially drawn for one set of fiscal policy variables, i.e. a particular level of government spending and a particular tax rate. Any change in a fiscal policy variable causes the AD curve to shift. Figure 13.6 illustrates the effect that an increase in government spending has on the aggregate demand curve.

Figure 13.6: An increase in government expenditure and the AD curve

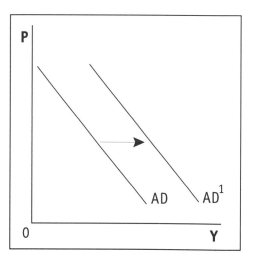

In effect, the increase in government expenditure shifts the original AD curve to the right. Along AD^1, there is a higher level of output demanded for each given price level. Alternatively, contractionary fiscal policy, initiated by a decrease in government spending, shifts the AD curve to the left.

The analysis is incomplete without the supply side of the economy. The overall effect in the short run is illustrated in Figure 13.7 below (assuming factor prices are not completely flexible).

Figure 13.7: Expansionary fiscal policy in the short run

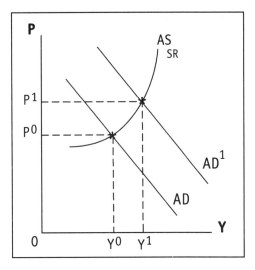

The conventional short-run AS curve is depicted in Figure 13.7. The economy is initially in equilibrium at the intersection of the AD curve and the AS curve: at the point (P^0,Y^0). We know from our previous analysis that an increase in government expenditure shifts the AD curve to the right, from AD to AD^1. At the original price level, P^0, there is excess demand caused by the increase in government expenditure. In order to re-establish equilibrium, the price level must rise. At the new equilibrium (P^1,Y^1), both price and output have increased. The extent of the output increase and the price rise will depend on the potential output of the economy and in particular the sensitivity of output changes to price changes. This is reflected in the slope of the AS curve.

In this model, the increase in aggregate demand causes the price level to rise, which partly offsets any subsequent change in output. The final result is a combination of higher prices and higher output but with a smaller change in output than in the Keynesian model of income determination (see below).

We have illustrated demand management using the example of an increase in government spending. However, a tax cut or an increase in the money supply would result in a similar rightward shift of the AD curve. Contractionary monetary or fiscal policy results in a leftward shift of the AD curve.

Keynes and the classicals

The increase in output from Y^0 to Y^1 in Figure 13.7 is less than the increase which arose out of the simple Keynesian model. The difference is accounted for by the price change. In the Keynesian income model, prices are fixed. We assume that firms expand their output without increasing the price. In terms of the economy production can expand without increasing the price level. Hence, any change in autonomous spending results, via the multiplier process, in a change in equilibrium output.

The Keynesian AS curve is depicted in panel (a) of Figure 13.8. We can see that a change in demand, caused by an increase in government spending, has a different result than what emerged from the conventional short-run AS curve.

Because the aggregate supply curve is perfectly elastic, an increase in government expenditure leads to a change in national income without changing the price level. For Keynes, excess capacity meant that idle factors of production could be put to work without fuelling inflationary pressures. If the AS curve is horizontal, the expansionary fiscal policies which Keynes advocated are rational and advisable.

Figure 13.8: Expansionary fiscal policy: the Keynesian and classical cases

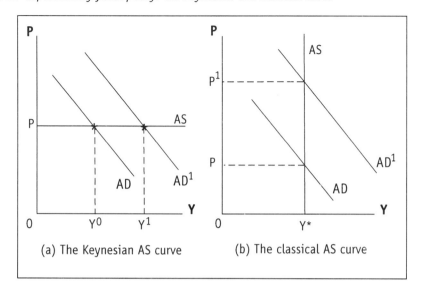

(a) The Keynesian AS curve   (b) The classical AS curve

The classical aggregate supply curve is depicted in panel (b) of Figure 13.8. From the classical perspective, expansionary fiscal policy is indefensible. With a vertical AS curve, an increase in government expenditure results only in higher prices. There is no change in the level of national output. Again, this reflects the classical assumption that output is determined by real factors such as technology and the training of human capital. From the classical perspective, demand-management measures can only lead to changes in price.

Supply-side policies

Aggregate supply is determined by a number of factors, including technology, population size, factor costs and expectations. Supply-side policies generally promote private enterprise within the market system by cutting costs or increasing incentives in order to stimulate output.[9] These policies found favour with both the US President Ronald Reagan and the UK Prime Minister Margaret Thatcher during their time in office (see Information Box 13.1). Examples of supply-side policies are included below.

The functioning of the market is enhanced by:

- reducing government controls;
- promoting competition;
- privatisation and deregulation;[10]
- restricting trade union power;
- legislating against monopolies.

Costs are reduced by:

- cutting tax on labour (reductions in marginal tax rates and PRSI rates);[11]
- cutting benefits and reforming the welfare state.

The incentive system is improved by:

- lowering capital gains tax and corporation tax;
- encouraging profit-related pay and wider share ownership.

The short-run AS curve describes the relationship between price and national output, *ceteris paribus*. Among the variables which are held constant are the level of technology, the skills of the labour force and the availability of natural resources. Any change in these factors causes a shift of the AS curve. An example is illustrated in Figure 13.9.

Figure 13.9: A rightward shift of the AS curve

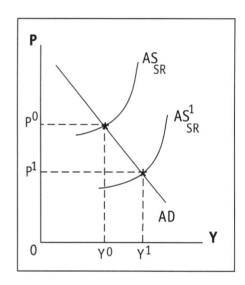

Equilibrium is initially at the point (P^0, Y^0). Let us suppose that the discovery of a new national source of oil allows for an expansion of the productive base of the economy in the short run. As production costs are lowered, the AS curve shifts rightwards; firms are willing to produce more output at any given price level. The lower costs increase the likelihood of profits which, in turn, induces greater production. A new equilibrium is reached at a higher output level and a lower price level. This new equilibrium is at point (P^1, Y^1). The extent of these changes will depend on the shape of the AD curve.

INFORMATION BOX 13.1

The supply-side policies of the 1980s

The disillusionment with Keynesian economics set in well before Reagan became the President of the United States in January 1981. The emergence of stagflation in the early 1970s left the economics profession asking many questions about the usefulness of Keynesian policies. A decade earlier, Milton Friedman criticised the active demand-management policies of previous administrations and advocated non-interventionist policies. With the 1980 election of Ronald Reagan, this economic philosophy found a political advocate. The emergence of supply-side economics is associated with the Reagan administration between 1981 and 1982.[12]

The background to 'Reaganomics' dates back to a December evening in 1974.[13] In the Two Continents restaurant in Washington DC, three individuals were discussing the state of the US economy: Arthur Laffer, a young economist; Richard Cheney, a White House aide under President Ford; and Jude Wanniski, an editorial writer for the Wall Street Journal. Laffer convinced his colleagues that the fundamental problem with the economy was the high marginal tax rates. This is the rate paid on each additional dollar earned. Laffer was discussing the relationship between the tax rate and the total tax revenue collected by the government. At low tax rates, he claimed, when tax rates rise, tax revenue increases. There was nothing sensational about this assertion.

It was his additional proposition that beyond a certain point, a cut in taxes may also increase tax revenue which surprised his colleagues. In support of his proposition, he argued that high taxes act as a disincentive. Work, savings and investment are discouraged. By cutting taxes, the supply side of the economy is stimulated. Lower taxes increase the attractiveness of work relative to leisure. Tax avoidance declines. In addition, investment and production increase. Encouraged by lower tax rates, new workers and firms broaden the tax base. Theoretically, these new sources of tax revenue meant that the total tax revenue collected by the state would increase.

The relationship, which is known as the Laffer curve, is illustrated in Figure 13.10.[14]

Figure 13.10: The Laffer curve

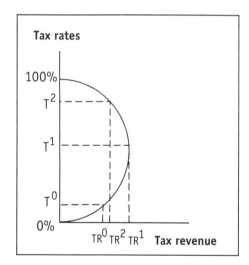

The tax rate is measured on the vertical axis and tax revenue is measured on the horizontal axis. If taxes are zero, total revenue amounts to zero. As tax rates increase, first from 0 to T^0 and then from T^0 to T^1, tax revenue increases from 0 to TR^0 and then to TR^1. Tax revenue is maximised when the tax rate is T^1. Any subsequent increase in the tax rate, from T^1 to T^2 for example, will only reduce tax revenue, in this instance from TR^1 to TR^2. Finally, if taxes are raised to 100%, nobody will work, resulting in zero tax revenue.

This diagram illustrates the essence of Laffer's argument. According to Laffer, marginal tax rates in the US had risen during the 1970s to levels beyond T^1. A tax cut would increase the incentive to work and to invest and possibly lead to an increase in tax revenue. On that basis, cuts in personal and business taxes were justified, even though there was a national debt which the state was trying to reduce.

While many people were sceptical of these proposals, they had the support of Ronald Reagan, the Republican candidate in the 1980 presidential election. Reagan was influenced heavily by Jack Kemp, the New York Congressman who three years earlier, together with Senator William Roth of Delaware, had introduced a bill to Congress proposing a 30% cut in personal income tax over a three-year period.

On taking office, Reagan appointed Murray Weidenbaum as his first chairman of the Council of Economic Advisers. Their economic plan centred around 'the four pillars of wisdom' which were:[15]

- *steady growth of the money supply;*
- *regulatory reform;*
- *cutting personal and business taxes;*
- *reducing federal spending.*

The Kemp-Roth tax cuts (1981–83), enacted by the Economic Recovery Tax Act of 1981, were the centrepiece of Reaganomics – cited by President Reagan as a 'second American Revolution'.[16] *The proposal was designed to cut marginal tax rates by 10% per year over a three-year period.*

Supply-side economists were criticised by their peers within the neoclassical school and by Keynesian economists.[17] *Their critics included J. K. Galbraith (see Article 13.1), Walter Heller (President Kennedy's chief economist) and Herbert Stein (President Nixon's chief economic adviser). All of these economists questioned the wisdom of the supply-side policies of the Reagan administration. In the words of Heller 'Only an ostrich could have missed the contradictions in Reaganomics.' In criticising supply siders, they highlight the record of supply-side policies – a large and rising federal debt, a failure to curtail government spending and sluggish output. They also assert that the so-called 'supply-side' Reagan recovery of the mid-1980s was largely attributable to the demand-side expansionary effects of the Reagan tax cuts rather than the supply-side effects.*

Even Reagan's successor and fellow Republican George Bush was not convinced, once describing his predecessor's policies as 'voodoo economics'.[18] *Although the influence of the supply siders subsided after the early 1980s, there was a reluctance to return to the interventionist policies of previous governments. While supply-side policies may have been discredited they did manage to raise some 'justifiable' doubts about the effectiveness of demand-management policies. That is their legacy.*

At the same time that Reagan was espousing the virtues of supply-side policies, Margaret Thatcher and others in the UK were embracing free-market economics.[19] *Like Reagan, Thatcher was sceptical of discretionary monetary and fiscal policies. During her three periods in office, she adopted many of the policies advocated by supply siders. Lower taxes, reforming the welfare state, reducing the power of trade unions and the privatisation programme were all examples of policies aimed at increasing competition, reducing costs and increasing productivity. Similar to the US experience, the record is one of many disappointments combined with limited successes.*

Like all the other theories that went before it, supply-side policies have their shortcomings. For one, supply siders failed to produce a coherent and rigorous model of the economy. Also, the assertion that a tax cut could possibly increase tax revenue was proven incorrect by the significant increase in the US budget deficit in the early 1980s. More critically, the evidence asserting a link between tax cuts and work incentive is conflicting. Moreover, a cut in the rate of personal taxation may have demand-side as well as supply-side implications. In the long run, the output of the economy might increase. However, in the short run, if income increases in excess of output, excess demand can lead to inflationary pressures.

On a broader level, welfare 'reform', even if it is combined with lower taxes, can often lead to greater hardship for the poor in society. The removal of statutory restrictions can often lead to a return of the abuses, to the environment for example, which were responsible for the imposition of the regulations in the first place. Many of these side-effects are the 'unacceptable face of capitalism', as described by former UK Prime Minister Ted Heath.

We leave the last few words on supply-side economics to Martin Feldstein. 'Experience has shown that the notion "supply-side economics" is a malleable one, easily misused by its supporters, maligned by its opponents, and misinterpreted by the public at large.'[20]

A supply-side shock

Definition

A supply-side shock or a supply disturbance refers to sudden changes in the conditions of productivity or costs which in turn impacts on aggregate supply.

Supply-side shocks were uncommon prior to the 1970s. In 1973, however, the world economy suffered a sudden supply-side shock in the form of higher oil prices. For more on the oil crisis see Section 5.4.

The effects of such a supply-side shock in the short run are illustrated in Figure 13.11.

Figure 13.11: A supply-side shock

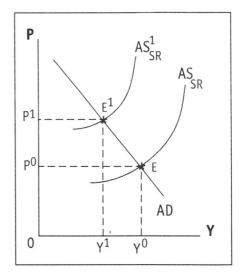

The economy is initially in equilibrium at (P^0, Y^0), the intersection of the AD curve and the AS curve. The increase in costs arising out of the rise in the price of oil causes a leftward shift of the AS curve. In the short run, the excess demand gives rise to an increase in the price level. Equilibrium in the short run is restored at the intersection of AD and the new AS curve, AS^1 at the point (P^1, Y^1).[21] This rather unusual combination of higher prices and sluggish output became known as stagflation. Another period of stagflation occurred at the end of the 1970s.

Long-run analysis
·····················

In the long run, factor costs adjust to changing economic conditions. In particular, wages will respond to changes in prices.

We know from our discussion in Section 13.2 that the long-run AS curve is vertical at the full-employment level of output. We now examine the effectiveness of demand-management policies and supply-side policies in the context of a vertical AS curve.

Demand-management policies

Consider an increase in government expenditure. We have already discovered that an increase in government expenditure shifts the AD curve to the right. In the short run, output and prices adjust upwards. In the long run, the only effect is an increase in prices: there is no change in output. This is illustrated in Figure 13.12.

Figure 13.12: Expansionary fiscal policy in the long run

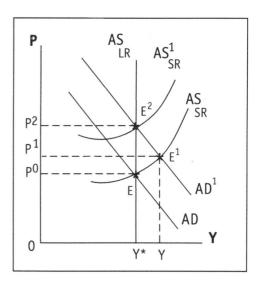

We begin at the full-employment equilibrium in the short run with the AD curve intersecting the short-run AS curve, AS_{SR} at point E. Y^*, the actual output of the economy equals the potential output. The increase in government expenditure shifts the AD curve out to the right, from AD to AD^1. The new point of intersection occurs at E^1, with prices at P^1 and output temporarily raised beyond the potential level, to Y. As a result many firms begin to experience supply bottlenecks; they want to increase production but limited resources do not permit such an increase.

The higher price level induces wage increases. The rising costs of production shift the short-run AS curve leftwards, to AS^1. The long-run equilibrium is shown by the intersection of AD^1 and AS_{LR} which is point E^2 and combination (Y^*, P^2). We can see that demand-management policies led to an increase in price from P^0 to P^2, but that output does not increase beyond the full-employment level in the long run.

To summarise, in the long run, this model predicts that a change in aggregate demand cannot affect output. The only change is a change in the level of prices. A decrease in government expenditure has similar but opposite effects to those that we have just studied.

Supply-side policies

Consider a supply-side policy directed at increasing potential output in the long run.[22] It is illustrated in Figure 13.13.

Figure 13.13: Supply-side policies in the long run

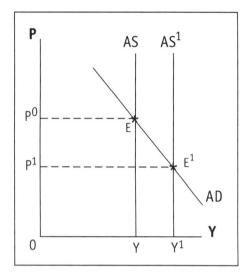

The long-run AS curve is vertical. A supply-side policy intended to increase potential output results in a rightward shift of the AS curve, from AS to AS¹. The net effect is an increase in output combined with a lower price level. This occurs because the quantity of the factor inputs increase or because existing resources are employed more efficiently. An example that will shift the supply curve is an improvement in the education or training of the labour force.

Keynes and the classicals

Keynesians and classical economists disagree about the effectiveness of supply-side policies. Essentially, the classical case is depicted above. The economy is always moving towards full-employment equilibrium. Technology, and the magnitude and quality of capital and labour constrain the level of output in the economy. An economy may be able to move beyond the full-employment level of output in the short run by working overtime, but ultimately, technology or the factors of production must change to expand national output in the long run. Therefore, if the state wishes to facilitate an increase in output, policies which shift the AS curve are the only ones which will achieve this goal.

Keynes did not agree that the economy moved toward full-employment equilibrium in the short run. If people are unemployed, labour is available for employment at the market wage. It is only if the short-run equilibrium of the AD curve and AS curve is at full employment, that demand-side polices put pressure on wages and ultimately on prices. Otherwise, demand management can be used to move the economy to full employment.

Supply-side policies, on the other hand, are completely ineffective. When Keynes wrote during the Great Depression, there was excess capacity and labour was idle. Supply-side policies have the effect of increasing capacity. This scenario is illustrated in Figure 13.14.

Figure 13.14: The Keynesian view of supply-side policies

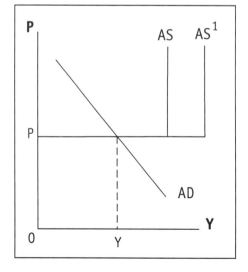

In Figure 13.14 the AS curve is drawn with a 'kink' at a point where the factors of production are fully utilised. An increase in the aggregate supply, in this case from AS to AS^1 will have no effect on the actual output level, according to Keynesians. Output can only be increased by boosting aggregate demand.

In terms of the long run, it is not clear what Keynes thought. In effect, he saw the economy moving from short run to short run. So the question of whether an economy ever reached its long-run capacity was not an issue. This view appears to be shared by one of his successors, J. K. Galbraith, whose opinions are discussed in the article below.

ARTICLE 13.1

Extract from The Sunday Independent
Galbraith still sparkling
by Kyran Fitzgerald

He may be 83, he may be an economist, but John Kenneth Galbraith, one-time US Ambassador to India and disciple of Keynes, Roosevelt and Kennedy, Harvard Professor and media guru, is still one of the world's great communicators, writes Kyran Fitzgerald.

He is only slightly stooped these days and he has lost none of his droll wit and cutting edge. Last week, a large gathering at Trinity College were treated to a gourmet mix of analysis and anecdote, heavily sauced with humour.

. . .

Galbraith proceeded to launch into a strong defence of the idea of free movement of both goods and people, although making an exception in the case of agriculture. Economic change for Galbraith comes in great waves, with new technologies continually emerging and industries continually decamping to new regions.

. . .

The free movement of people, too, is welcome in his eyes, sometimes representing a transfusion of new blood into enervated societies. Japan, which restricts immigration, could face industrial problems over the next ten years, he argues. At a time when Europe has millions of the downtrodden knocking on its well-appointed doorstep, this view is a healthy antidote to the poisons being spewed out by the Jean Marie Le Pens of this world.

But Galbraith still saves his sharpest opinions for his foes in General Motors and the Chicago School of Economics where the 80-year-old Milton Friedman still reigns. The men in grey suits who would carve up consumer markets, and economists who worship monetary targets he dislikes in equal measure. The 1980s to him was the era of Friedman, during which the gap between rich and poor widened, leading to a world of Trumps and tramps. Pavements cracked while private fortunes swelled.

Galbraith's mission now is to sell Keynes, who taught that governments should intervene to dampen demand in boom times, boost it during lean days. But now he faces a new battle, as the corporations mobilise opinion behind a new market carve-up and the ghost of economic protectionism stalks the land.

Source: The Sunday Independent, 2 February 1992.

A summary of policy effectiveness
....

At this stage, there is a need to sum up the policy conclusions. In the short run where there are unemployed resources, there appears to be a role for demand management. Wage and price rigidities allow output to respond to changes in aggregate demand over a short period of time. In the long run, however, fiscal and monetary policies have no effect on output. Output can only be expanded in the long run by supply-side policies.[23]

Finally, one way of explaining the differences between demand-management policies and supply-side policies is by focusing on the business cycle. Figure 13.15 illustrates the business cycle.

Figure 13.15: The business cycle

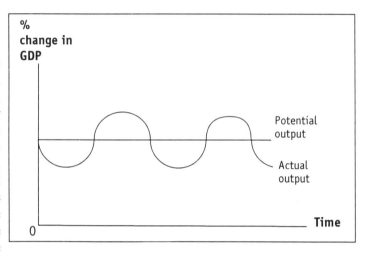

The actual output line depicts the annual increase in national output, as measured by changes in GDP. The potential output line depicts the rate at which the economy would grow if all resources were fully utilised. The purpose of demand-side policies is to stabilise actual output close to its potential. In terms of Figure 13.15 this involves the convergence of the actual output and the potential output lines. This entails short-term fine-tuning of the economy through frequent changes in tax rates, money supply, interest rates and expenditure levels.

In contrast, the purpose of supply-side policies is to increase potential output beyond its present levels. In terms of Figure 13.15 an upward shift of the potential output line is sought. This involves a long-term strategy, enhancing the efficiencies of the market system and lowering production costs wherever possible.

We will end this section with a note by A. Protopapadakis which summarises the value of both demand-management and supply-side policies:

> 'supply-side policies should not be looked at to replace counter-cyclical demand-management policies. Demand management may be the appropriate policy response to recessions that periodically are brought about by special sequences of economic events. But these policies are ill-suited to improving long-term growth in productivity and output, because they don't necessarily increase incentives to produce, save, and invest. Supply-side policies do precisely that, but they are likely to work slowly and therefore can't be used to combat recessions'.[24]

13.4 The Irish experience

Ireland's experience of demand-management policies has been well documented. Extensive use of fiscal policy was the norm during the 1970s and 1980s. At different times, this was combined with a mix of monetary, exchange rate and incomes policies.[25]

Supply-side policies were not as prevalent in Ireland in the 1980s as they were in the UK or the US. This was due to a number of factors.

First, in other countries there was a deeper divide between the left and right political parties. This focused the economic debate between those who favoured state intervention and those who preferred a limited role for the state. The 'right', who initiated the supply-side policies, were represented by the Republicans in the US and by the Tories in the UK. Until the formation of the Progressive Democrats in 1985, the economic policies of the 'right' were not coherently presented by any political party in Ireland. This partly explains why Irish policy-makers were slow to adopt supply-side policies.

Second, given the state of the public finances in the early 1980s, the Irish authorities were concerned less with ideology and more with restoring order and confidence to the financial markets at home and abroad.

Third, the Irish political and administrative system is conservative by nature. New economic policies would not have met with immediate approval or enthusiasm.

Finally, Irish authorities have limited autonomy. Given the open nature of the Irish economy, their ability to adopt policies independent of other countries is restricted.

By the late 1980s there was some evidence of a change in policy. Two semi-state companies, Irish Life and Irish Sugar, were privatised. Other state bodies such as B&I and Irish Steel were sold to foreign companies. A plan to restructure Aer Lingus was agreed and implemented. The remaining semi-state companies were encouraged to cut costs with a view to competitiveness, commercialisation and future competition from foreign companies.

Taxes on labour were cut in order to increase the incentives for both employers and employees. Controls on public expenditure were also implemented.[26] Pump-priming the economy was frowned upon. The business sector was also targeted via a lowering of corporate taxes, an expansion of the Business Expansion Scheme (BES), an increase in profit-sharing schemes and tax reliefs relating to capital acquisition.[27]

By the 1990s, the Culliton report (see case study) had become the blueprint for job creation in Ireland.[28] Its many recommendations include a fundamental reform of the tax system, greater competition in air services, telecommunications and energy supply and an improvement in training in Ireland. These and many of the other sixty-plus recommendations are 'essentially supply-side in tone'.[29]

In conclusion, in contrast to the late 1970s and the early 1980s, Irish policy-makers appear to be concentrating on the supply side of the economy. Economic policies are aimed at the private sector. This is obvious in the privatisation of semi-state companies. A sustained effort to improve the incentive system through tax and welfare reform has broad support across the political spectrum and has featured prominently in the past three Budgets. Irish industrial policy encourages technological change and constant upgrading of the factors of production. All of these policies are aimed at increasing the potential national output.[30] In short, they are designed to shift the aggregate supply curve.

CASE STUDY

Extract from The Irish Independent
A welcome but selective grasp at economic nettles
by Moore McDowell

. . .

In a capitalist market economy growth depends fundamentally on rewarding work effort and decisions which result in the creation of net wealth for the community, regardless of who owns that wealth and regardless of the impact of rewarding hard work on relative incomes. Efforts to prevent the accumulation of wealth and to confiscate the rewards of hard work in the end result in lower growth, lower average income, lower employment and lower standards of social services.

If growth in output and employment are top priority targets, then redistributive goals by definition must take second place, and be limited by the requirements of maintaining political consent for the growth process. In Ireland, however, the lethal combination of high taxation to finance high levels of government spending and the use of tax breaks, subsidies and grants to encourage what the government of the day regards as being in the social interest (i.e., likely to help get it re-elected) has resulted in a system which has stunted economic development.

The IPRG* correctly observes that what attracts the highest rewards in Ireland are the avoidance and evasion of taxes, the redistributing of existing assets to profit through arbitrage, the arrangement of production plans so as to attract the maximum state handout and acting as a passive rentier rather than an active entrepreneur.

. . .

There are several areas of detail where the IPRG can be faulted directly. To go through them all would be impossible in this article. Two, however, strike me as being particularly important. The first is the omission of any analysis of the impact of the developments of labour and social welfare legislation on growth and employment over the last 25 years. I suspect that this is the price which was paid to obtain consensus in the report given the powerful presence of Peter Cassels (sic) on the committee. The second is its understanding of the development of the educational system and its role in development.

. . .

Source: The Irish Independent, *11 January 1992.*

* Industrial Policy Review Group (authors of the *Culliton report*)

Questions
....

1. What particular extracts of this article suggest that the 'IPRG' report [*Culliton report*] is supply-side in nature?
2. The author suggests that 'Efforts to prevent the accumulation of wealth and to confiscate the rewards of hard work in the end result in lower growth . . .' What obstacles do you think is he referring to?
3. According to supply siders, how can 'work effort' be rewarded? Use a short-run AD/AS model to illustrate the effect of this policy change on national output.

Answers

....

1. Supply-side economists, true to their classical roots, emphasise the central role of the individual who, while promoting his own self-interest, also benefits society by contributing to economic growth. In order to promote economic growth, the IPRG reminds us that hard work must be rewarded. If we attempt to alter or redistribute wealth, we negatively affect growth because the individual is not gaining from his productive efforts.

   Similarly, the IPRG also believes that successive governments used grants and subsidies to the detriment of economic growth. Again, the state skewed the incentive system. The goal of firms became focused on maximising state aid rather than maximising profits and improving their competitive advantage. The goal of the parties in power was to gain political advantage at the expense of economic development.

   Both of these issues highlighted by the IPRG show the importance which it places on the private sector and its supply-side bias.

2. Obstacles which may hinder wealth accumulation include, among others, high taxes (both personal and business), costly legislation, red tape and bureaucracy, statutory regulations and a culture which promotes dependency at the expense of 'a spirit of self-reliance'.[31]

3. In the broad sense, supply siders support the notion that individuals should be allowed to maximise their own self-interest. In doing so, society at large also benefits. More specifically, this translates into tax cuts which in turn induces greater incentives. Savings and investment are stimulated; output increases. This is illustrated in Figure 13.16.

Figure 13.16: Increasing output by using supply-side policies

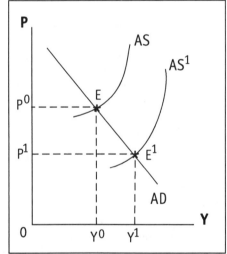

The original equilibrium is at (P^0, Y^0). By increasing work incentives and enhancing the return on work effort through a tax reduction, aggregate supply increases. The AS curve shifts from AS to AS^1. The new equilibrium is (P^1, Y^1). The net effect is lower prices and higher output.

Summary

1. Aggregate demand refers to the total quantity of output demanded at different price levels. There is a negative relationship between aggregate demand and price and this is represented by a downward sloping AD curve. The wealth effect, the interest rate effect and the international trade effect are the reasons for the negative

relationship. The AD curve is drawn for given levels of autonomous spending. Any change in autonomous spending or monetary variables results in a shift of the AD curve.

2. Aggregate supply is the total output supplied at different price levels. Potential output refers to the maximum output that a country can produce given the resources available and the efficiency to which they are put to use. The AS curve relates output levels to price levels. Factors such as technology, the level of human capital and expectations determine the position of the AS curve.

3. There is a distinction between the AS curve in the short run and the long-run AS curve. The assumption underlying the short-run AS curve is that factor costs are constant. Hence, higher prices are associated with higher output levels and result in an upward sloping AS curve. In the long run factor costs can vary; they adjust fully to price changes. With complete adjustments in the long run possible, the AS curve is vertical at the full-employment level of output. It is unresponsive to changes in the price level.

4. Demand-side policies include both fiscal and monetary policy. They are designed to influence the level of expenditure in the economy and, in turn, the level of output. In the short run, expansionary demand-side policies result in higher output levels and higher prices. Contractionary demand-side policies reduce both output levels and prices. In the long run a change in aggregate demand cannot affect output. The only change is in the level of prices.

5. Supply-side economics is concerned with changing the aggregate supply. Supply-side policies seek to influence production directly, by lowering production costs or by increasing incentives. A supply-side shock refers to changes in the conditions of productivity or costs which in turn affect aggregate supply. The adverse effects of a negative supply-side shock are twofold: higher prices and lower output.

6. The Irish authorities were slow to adopt demand-management policies. Active use of short-term fiscal policy only became the norm in the mid-1970s. Once tried, demand-side policies were extensively used thereafter. Supply-side policies were largely absent until the late 1980s. Possible reasons include the absence of a right-left political divide, the conservative nature of the Irish political system, the unsatisfactory state of the public finances and the lack of complete autonomy as regards the implementation of economic policy. There was some evidence of supply-side influences in economic policy by the 1990s.

Key terms

Aggregate demand
Real balance effect
AD curve
Aggregate supply
Potential output
Short-run AS curve
Long-run AS curve

Full-employment output level
Macroeconomic equilibrium
Demand-management policies
Supply-side policies
Discretionary fiscal policy
Reaganomics
Laffer curve
Supply-side shock
Business cycle

Review questions

1. Outline the reasons why the AD curve is downward sloping. What causes a shift of the AD curve?
2. Explain why the short-run AS curve slopes upwards. How is this different to the Keynesian and classical AS curves? What is the difference between the short-run and the long-run AS curves?
3. Using a short-run AD/AS model, explain what effect a contractionary fiscal policy would have on the equilibrium price and output.
4. What is a supply-side shock? Use the AD/AS model to illustrate the effect of an adverse supply side-shock on the equilibrium price and output.
5. Assess the use of supply-side policies both in the US and the UK since the early 1980s.
6. Comment on Ireland's use of both demand-management and supply-side policies.

Working problems

1. Data (expressed in billions of Irish pounds) for aggregate demand and aggregate supply curves is presented in Table 13.1. The price level is presented as an index number.

Table 13.1

Price level	100	110	120	130	140	150	160	170	180
Aggregate demand	7.0	6.7	6.4	6.1	5.8	5.5	5.2	4.9	4.6
Aggregate supply	1.4	2.4	3.4	4.3	5.0	5.5	5.8	5.8	5.8

    (a) Plot the aggregate demand and aggregate supply curves.
    (b) What do the portions of the AS curve reflect?
2. Sketch appropriate AD/AS diagrams (as they relate to Ireland) for the following:
    (a) the expansionary phase of fiscal policy during the 1970s;
    (b) the fall in oil prices since the early 1980s.

Multi-choice questions

1. The AD curve slopes down from left to right because of:
   (a) the international trade effect, the income effect and the substitution effect;
   (b) the price effect, the real balance effect and the substitution effect;
   (c) the income effect, the price effect and the interest rate effect;
   (d) the interest rate effect, the real balance effect and the international trade effect;
   (e) none of the above.

2. If the AD curve is relatively steep, which of the following is a likely source?
   (a) This is because the changes in AE arising out of price changes are relatively small.
   (b) A weak international trade effect.
   (c) The real balance effect is weak.
   (d) A weak interest rate effect.
   (e) All of the above.

3. Assuming spare capacity, constant inputs costs and a demand-constrained economy, the AS curve is:
   (a) vertical;
   (b) horizontal;
   (c) perfectly inelastic;
   (d) upward sloping;
   (e) both (b) and (c) above.

4. Under short-run conditions, contractionary demand-side policies are likely to:
   (a) reduce output and prices;
   (b) increase output, reduce prices;
   (c) increase prices, reduce output;
   (d) increase output and prices;
   (e) none of the above.

5. According to supply siders:
   (a) more government intervention is necessary;
   (b) high taxes are necessary to finance the welfare system;
   (c) discretionary fiscal policy is desirable;
   (d) tax rate cuts can cause total tax revenue to increase;
   (e) both (c) and (d) above.

6. In the long run, a change in which of the following is likely to cause a shift of the AS curve?
   (a) welfare expenditure;
   (b) money supply;
   (c) interest rates;
   (d) technology;
   (e) none of the above.

True or false

1. The AD curve shows total spending for each level of income at a fixed price level. _____

2. Underlying the upward sloping short-run AS curve is the assumption that all prices are constant. _____
3. The classical AS curve reflects supply constraints. _____
4. Both Keynesians and classical economists agree that the AD curve is downward sloping. _____
5. Supply siders perceive tax cuts as, among other things, disinflationary. _____
6. An adverse supply-side shock can lead to higher prices and lower output. _____

Fill in the blanks

_____ equilibrium occurs at the intersection of the AD and AS curves; the point at which the output which households and firms _____ is equal to the output which _____ are willing to supply. The aggregate demand curve shows the quantity of output demanded at different _____ levels. The aggregate _____ curve depicts the output produced by firms at different price levels. The AD curve is _____ sloping; as prices rise, fewer goods and services are demanded. The _____ of the AS curve varies. In the ____ ____ , the AS curve is _____ sloping; reflecting higher output levels at higher prices. In the _____-_____ when resource costs move in tandem with prices, the AS curve is _____ at the full-employment output level. If output is demand-determined, the AS curve is _____ ; if output is _____ or supply-determined, the AS curve is vertical. The former requires demand-management policies and receives support from _____. The latter requires _____-_____ policies which find favour with those who support the non-interventionist, _____ system doctrine.

CASE STUDY

Extract from **The Irish Times**
The taxing question of forming a government
by Cliff Taylor

The big political parties have shown us their manifestos, full of promises of lower taxes and higher government spending. But by now, with Fianna Fail looking most unlikely to win an overall majority, the top figures in each of the parties must be working out how they are willing to compromise in order to get a hand on the levers of power through participation in a coalition government. Of the possible coalition groupings after polling day, Fianna Fail and Labour would appear to agree on quite a lot. Crucially, both believe that the government should push up capital spending on key infrastructural projects in an attempt to boost the economy, a

→

potentially important shift in economic policy. They even agree broadly on what projects should be involved.

. . .

The two would find it simpler to agree on a tax programme, both emphasising the need to make reforms to benefit lower-paid workers. Labour might, however, oppose the Fianna Fail plan to reduce the top tax rate.

. . .

Overall Labour and Fianna Fail could agree on the economy, but only if they could overcome the key issue of how to fund the extra state spending. But as today's poll shows, there is public support for a coalition between Fine Gael and Labour and a slightly lower level of backing for a Fine Gael-Labour-Progressive Democrats government, the so-called rainbow coalition.

. . .

The obvious first hurdle to Labour agreeing a programme with the other two parties would be the opposition from Fine Gael and the Progressive Democrats to the idea of pushing up exchequer borrowing to boost public capital spending. This would be a crunch issue in any talks, with both Fine Gael and the PDs preferring to address the jobs crisis through taxation reform rather than higher government spending.

. . .

The other obvious area of difficulty would be in seeking agreement on the proper role of the state in industrial development. Could the PDs and Mr O'Malley, for example, agree to the Labour view of extra equity for state industry and an interventionist role in building up Irish industry. The differences in this area should not be overemphasised. Both parties agree that the economy should involve a mix between the private and public sectors. Labour's policies have moved considerably towards the centre over the last ten years. Likewise, Fine Gael and the PDs highlight the need to create the right climate for business, but neither calls for a withdrawal of state aids for business.

Where might the conflicts come? Probably they would surface on Labour's demands for extra state equity for companies like Aer Lingus and Bord na Mona and on that party's very interventionist approach to state assistance to industry.

. . .

On tax the three parties all see the need for reform. There would be disagreement on details; Labour would oppose the PD plan to cut the top tax rate to 40% and is also unhappy about Fine Gael's proposed big cut in employer PRSI. Here compromise would appear easier. All three also agree that the pound should be held at its current rate in the Exchange Rate Mechanism. There are, of course, other coalition possibilities. A Fianna Fail-PD link would face having to overcome not only bad feeling but also Mr O'Malley's opposition to the Fianna Fail plan to boost spending. If Democratic Left were to be involved in any talks, the right-of-centre parties would all oppose its plan for a new top 65% income tax rate and a wealth tax.

In terms of economic policy Fianna Fail and Labour would seem the most compatible bedfellows, although agreeing a programme would still be difficult. But the 'rainbow' option is also workable, if all are prepared to compromise. There are obvious grounds for tensions and disagreements among the three, but whether this is a bad thing or not in terms of economic management would depend on how cohesively the government worked and how the compromises were struck.

Source: The Irish Times, *20 November 1992.*

Questions
....

1. On the basis of the policies outlined above, which of the parties, do you think, is concerned with changing the level of aggregate demand (rather than aggregate supply) in the economy? Support your answer.
2. All parties are reported to support tax reform. Explain why. Does this suggest that there are no differences in the economic ideologies of the parties involved?
3. What particular extracts from this article might suggest that the PDs are the party that is closest to the supply-side ideology which has been outlined in the chapter?

Additional case study questions based on Article 13.1 from the text

Questions on Article 13.1: Galbraith still sparkling

1. In the article the author touches on many of Galbraith's main economic beliefs. What are they and how do they differ from his contemporaries?
2. Explain the sentence '. . . governments should intervene to dampen demand in boom times, boost it during lean days'. Illustrate by use of the AD/AS model.
3. How similar are these views to the ideas expressed in the Galbraith case study of Chapter 10 (p. 326)? Support your answer.   [The answers are not included.]

Appendix 13.1: Using the IS/LM model to derive the AD curve

An alternative way to derive the AD curve is by using the IS/LM model. The IS curve is drawn for a given level of autonomous spending. The LM curve is drawn for a given real money supply. At a given price level P^0 the IS and LM curves intersect, giving us our first equilibrium level of national income, Y^0. In turn, we have our first point in (P,Y) space.

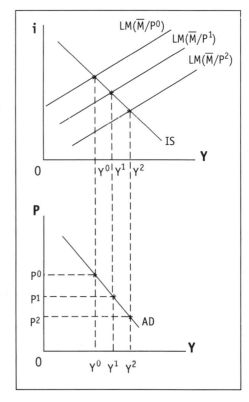

Figure 13.17: Deriving the AD curve

Suppose the price level falls. As price falls from P^0 to P^1, the real money supply increases from $\frac{\overline{M}}{P^0}$ to $\frac{\overline{M}}{P^1}$. The LM curve shifts rightwards, from LM $\left(\frac{\overline{M}}{P^0}\right)$ to LM $\left(\frac{\overline{M}}{P^1}\right)$. This results in a new and higher level of equilibrium income, Y^1 and our second point in (P,Y) space.

Assume the price level falls further. The fall in price from P^1 to P^2 results in a further increase in the real money supply, causing another rightward shift of the LM curve. This new equilibrium point results in another and yet again higher equilibrium level of income, Y^2. This is our third point in (P,Y) space.

A similar exercise can be carried out for all possible price levels. The subsequent income levels provide us with a relationship between the aggregate price level and national income. The relationship is depicted by a downward sloping AD curve. The goods market and the money market are both in equilibrium at every point on the AD curve.

CHAPTER 14

OPEN ECONOMY MACROECONOMICS

'There is no way in which one can buck the market.'[1]

Margaret Thatcher

'The States of Europe must form a federation or a "European entity", which will make them a single economic entity.'[2]

Jean Monnet (1888–1979)

'In short, there is *no* meaningful economic argument for a single currency in Europe – now or ever.'[3]

Bernard Connolly

Chapter objectives

Upon completing this chapter, the student should understand:

- the balance of payments;
- exchange rate determination;
- the operation of the European Monetary System;
- devaluation and the currency crisis;
- Ireland's record within the ERM;
- Economic and Monetary Union and the single currency.

Outline

14.1 **Balance of payments**
14.2 **Exchange rate determination**
14.3 **Exchange rate regimes and the balance of payments**
14.4 **The European Monetary System (EMS)**
14.5 **Economic and Monetary Union**
14.6 **The Irish experience**

Introduction

In Chapter 8 we examined the circular flow of economic activity. We began by studying the exchange between households and firms. We then adjusted this model to include the government and the foreign sector. A similar method of analysis was used for the income determination model. Variables such as prices, wages and interest rates were assumed to be fixed. Moreover, the government and the foreign sector were initially excluded before they were eventually incorporated into the model.

Even with these adjustments for the foreign sector, our examination of macro-economics until now has largely ignored the value of the domestic currency and its role in the economy. Foreign interest rates, exchange rate volatility, foreign markets and external trade were only briefly mentioned. In reality, these variables are very important and play a vital role in any modern economy. We now examine these variables in detail.

14.1 Balance of payments

We begin our investigation of the foreign sector by discussing the balance of payments.

Definition
● ● ● ● ● ●

The balance of payments is a set of accounts showing all economic transactions between residents of the home country and the rest of the world in any one year.

It is a 'flow' concept rather than a 'stock' concept. We are not measuring the debits and credits at a point in time. Rather, we are looking at outflows and inflows over a period of time, usually a year.

Receipts of foreign exchange from the rest of the world (e.g. arising from exports, sale of government bonds or 'gilts' etc.) are treated as a credit item and are denoted by a positive (+) sign in the balance of payments. Payments of foreign exchange to the rest of the world (e.g. arising from imports, purchase of French works of art etc.) are treated as a debit item and are denoted by a negative (–) sign.

At the end of the calendar year this statement must balance, i.e. receipts or inflows equals payments or outflows. It does so by following the principles of double-entry book-keeping.

The balance of payments consists of two subsections: the current account and the capital account. These are explained below.

Current account balance
. . . .

Definition
● ● ● ● ● ●

The current account in the balance of payments records all visible and invisible trade.

Merchandise trade is an example of visible trade. Invisible trade includes services such as tourism and travel.

This section of the Irish balance of payments is subdivided into four categories, including:

• merchandise trade, as explained below;
• services such as tourism, travel and freight;

- investment income. This includes the dividends, interest and profits paid and received by Irish residents. In this category the most significant amounts are repatriation of profits by multinational corporations and interest payments paid on foreign debt;
- current transfers such as remittances from emigrants, Irish aid to less developed countries and monies from EU funds.

The addition of all these plus a number of miscellaneous items is defined as the current account balance. If the value of receipts is greater than the value of payments, a surplus is recorded. If the value of receipts is less than the value of payments, a deficit is recorded. In 1995 there was a current account surplus of £850m; the value of inflows exceeded the value of outflows by almost £1 billion.[4]

Merchandise trade balance

The merchandise trade balance is the most publicly discussed component of the current account.[5]

Definition
● ● ● ● ● ●

The merchandise trade balance, or the balance of trade as it is sometimes called, is a record of transactions of merchandise exports (X) and imports (M) during a year.

If the value of exports exceeds the value of imports (X > M) a trade surplus results. A trade deficit results when the value of imports exceeds the value of exports (M > X). If the value of exports and imports is equal (X = M) we have a trade balance.
Figure 14.1 shows the record of the Irish trade balance between 1960 and 1995.[6]

Figure 14.1: The Irish trade balance 1960–95

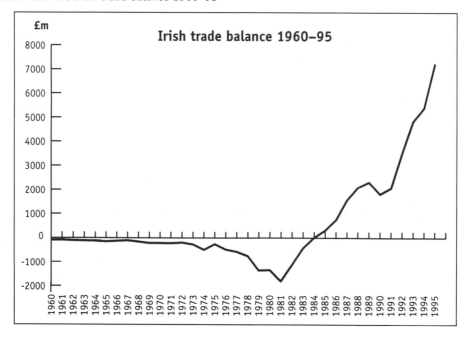

It is evident from the figure above that Ireland's first trade surplus in modern economic times was recorded in 1985. This 'favourable' trend has been repeated in each year, with a record surplus of £7,209m in 1995. It is widely believed that this improvement in the trade surplus is due, in no small part, to the activities of multinationals operating in Ireland.

The composition of trade by commodity and geographical location is shown in Tables 14.1 and 14.2 respectively.

Table 14.1: Trade by commodity, 1994

Category	Exports (%)	Imports (%)
Food and live animals	18.8	8.1
Beverages and tobacco	2.1	1.2
Raw materials, fuel and oil	2.8	6.5
Chemicals and related products	20.9	12.9
Manufactured goods	50.6	62.8
Others	4.7	8.5

Source: CSO, *Statistical Bulletin*, June 1996.

Table 14.2: Trade by geographical area, 1995

Destination	Exports (%)	Imports (%)
UK	25.4	35.6
Rest of EU	46.8	21.0
Other European countries	5.2	3.0
US, Canada and Mexico	9.3	18.5
Others	13.2	21.8

Source: CSO, *Trade Statistics*, February 1996.

This chapter deals with the monetary aspects of international trade. The gains from trade are discussed in detail in Section 15.3.

Capital account balance

·························

Definition
● ● ● ● ● ●

The capital account in the balance of payments is a record of a country's inflows and outflows of capital or assets.

Examples of these assets include government gilts, company shares and land.

Purchases of Irish financial stocks and loans to Irish residents by foreigners are capital inflows. Capital outflows include purchases of foreign financial securities and loans to foreigners by Irish residents. This particular section, now referred to as the capital and financial account, is subdivided into five categories, including:

- capital transfers, arising out of changes made by the CSO in July 1996;
- capital transactions carried out by the private sector;
- capital transactions carried out by the government;
- transactions of credit institutions;
- external reserves (see Section 14.3).

In 1995 there was a capital account deficit amounting to £1,329m; the value of payments was greater than the value of receipts by over £1.3 billion. In Section 14.3, we will discuss the relationship between the current and the capital account balance.

The Irish balance of payments for the calendar year 1995 is reprinted in Table 14.3.

Table 14.3: The Irish balance of payments 1995

Current account	
Merchandise trade	7,209
Services	–2,474
Investment income	–4,996
Current transfers	1,111
Balance on current account[1]	850
Capital account[2]	
Capital transfers	511
Private capital	–2,143
Official capital	24
Transactions of credit institutions	1,721
Change in the external reserves	–1,443
Balance on capital account	–1,329
Net residual (refer to Section 14.3)	480

Source: Central Bank Report, Autumn 1996. An alternative source for balance of payments data is the *Economic Review and Outlook Report* of the Department of Finance.

1. In July 1996, the CSO introduced significant changes in the definitions used in the official Balance of Payments statistics. As a result of these developments, surpluses for previous years were adjusted downwards. For 1995, the current account surplus was only £850m, or 2.5% of GNP. For more detail on these changes, read note 2, Table 8.17.
2. A more detailed breakdown of these categories is included in the balance of payments statement as recorded by the Central Bank bulletins.

Finally, once a balance of payments surplus or deficit exists, there are many different ways of correcting it. These measures include a revaluation or depreciation of the currency, the erection or dismantling of trade barriers, the introduction of exchange controls or simply the adoption of suitable fiscal and/or monetary policies. Many of these policies are explained later. We now examine the exchange rate and its determination.

14.2 Exchange rate determination

We will continue our discussion of the foreign sector by considering exchange rates.

• Definition
● ● ● ● ● ●

The exchange rate between two currencies is the price of one currency in terms of another.

Similar to interest rate determination, the equilibrium price can be explained in terms of demand and supply analysis. It is the equilibrium price that we call the exchange rate. The market in this case is the foreign exchange market.

There are many similarities between a market for a good and the foreign exchange market. However, there are a few important differences. We consider the market of a single good, like tea. When we discuss the foreign exchange market, we are considering two currencies, e.g. the US dollar (US$) and the Irish pound (IR£). For example, in the market for IR£/US$, a demand for IR£ implies a supply of US$ and a supply of IR£ implies a demand for US$. This is evident in our analysis of the IR£/US$ market below.

Another important difference which we will explain shortly is that the demand for and the supply of foreign exchange is derived. In spite of these differences, we will see that the foreign exchange market looks, and in many ways behaves, like the goods market.

The state often intervenes in the foreign exchange market and we will discuss that in the next section. However, we will begin our discussion of exchange rate determination by considering a foreign exchange market where the state does not intervene. We will see that the exchange rate is determined by the forces of demand and supply.

We will explain how the exchange rate is determined using a simplified example.[7]

Assume there are only two countries, Ireland and the US, with respective currencies, the Irish pound, IR£ and the American dollar, US$. In this case the price will be expressed as the number of dollars per one Irish pound.[8] We must examine both the demand for and the supply of the Irish pound in order to derive the market exchange rate.

The demand for Irish pounds
....

The demand for Irish pounds on the foreign exchange market is a derived demand. Holders of American dollars purchase Irish pounds in order to pay for:

- Irish goods and services including Kilkenny woollens, Bailey's Irish Cream, Waterford Crystal and tourism products;
- Irish assets including shares in AIB, government gilts and property.

When Americans buy Irish goods and assets, they supply dollars in exchange for Irish pounds. For example, if the rate of exchange is £1 = $1, £1m of Irish goods costs an American importer $1m.

Suppose the value of the pound increases or appreciates relative to the dollar. The new rate of exchange is £1 = $2. The same £1m of Irish goods now costs the American importer $2m. In other words, Irish goods are more expensive in the American market after the Irish pound appreciates. At this exchange rate, the demand for goods, and therefore the demand for pounds will be less than at the previous rate.

Alternatively, the pound could decrease in value or depreciate relative to the dollar. Suppose the new exchange rate is £1 = $0.5. The delighted importer can now purchase £1m of Irish goods for only $500,000. At this exchange rate, the demand for Irish goods will be higher and so will the demand for the Irish pound.

In summary, the higher the exchange rate of dollars for pounds, the lower the demand for Irish pounds. As the Irish pound depreciates, the demand for the Irish pound increases. Therefore, the demand curve for the Irish pound is downward sloping as drawn in Figure 14.2.

Figure 14.2: The demand curve for Irish pounds

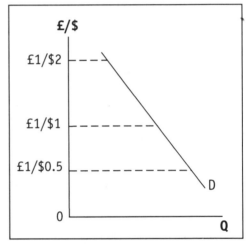

The supply of Irish pounds

The supply of Irish pounds on the foreign exchange market is also derived. Holders of Irish pounds wish to purchase dollars to pay for:

- American goods and services including Cadillacs, Harley Davidson motorcycles and Levis;
- American assets including IBM shares, US government bonds and real estate.

When Irish residents buy American goods and assets, they supply Irish pounds in exchange for dollars. For example, if the rate of exchange is £1 = $1, $1m of imports from the United States costs an Irish importer £1m.

Suppose the value of the Irish pound appreciates. At the new rate of £1 = $2, the same $1m of merchandise will cost the Irish importer only £500,000. In other words,

US goods are cheaper at this exchange rate. Irish importers may now be willing to supply more Irish pounds in exchange for US dollars.

Alternatively, the pound could depreciate relative to the dollar. Consider another exchange rate of £1 = $0.5. The Irish importer will have to exchange £2m in order to purchase the goods valued at $1m. At this exchange rate, US goods are more expensive in the Irish market. The demand for US goods will be less and so will the quantity of pounds supplied on the foreign exchange market.

In summary, the higher the exchange rate of dollars for pounds, the higher the supply of Irish pounds. As the Irish pound depreciates, the supply of the Irish pound decreases. Therefore, the supply curve is upward sloping as drawn in Figure 14.3.

Figure 14.3: The supply curve for Irish pounds

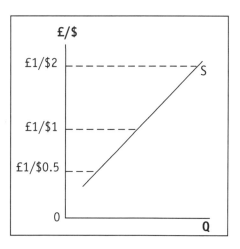

Equilibrium in the foreign exchange market

The demand for Irish pounds, represented by D, and the supply of Irish pounds, represented by S, determine the equilibrium rate of exchange in the IR£/US$ market.[9] This is illustrated in Figure 14.4.

Figure 14.4: The equilibrium exchange rate

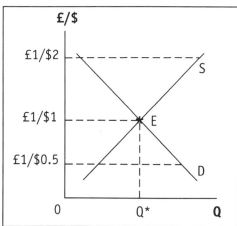

The demand curve for Irish pounds and the supply curve for Irish pounds intersect at point E, the equilibrium exchange rate. As in all markets there is an automatic process which moves the market towards equilibrium.

If the exchange rate is above equilibrium, the supply of Irish pounds exceeds the demand. At the exchange rate indicated by £1/$2 in Figure 14.4, American imports to the Irish market are relatively cheap and Irish importers are willing to trade pounds for dollars in order to buy them. However, Irish exports to the American market are relatively expensive. At this exchange rate, the American importer of Irish goods does not demand as many goods and therefore does not need Irish pounds to pay for them. In a market without restrictions, the exchange rate will fall. Equilibrium is restored when quantity demanded equals quantity supplied.

Similarly, if the exchange rate is below the equilibrium, at the rate indicated by £1/$0.5 in Figure 14.4, demand for Irish pounds exceeds the supply. American imports are relatively expensive and Irish importers are not willing to trade pounds for dollars in order to purchase them for the Irish market. However, Irish exports to the American market are relatively cheap and the American importers are willing to purchase Irish pounds in order to buy them for the American market. The shortage of Irish pounds will lead to an appreciation of the exchange rate. Equilibrium is restored when quantity demanded equals quantity supplied.

Factors which shift the demand curve or the supply curve

The foreign exchange market considers the relationship between the exchange rate and the quantity of pounds demanded and supplied, *ceteris paribus*. Other variables which influence the exchange rate between the two currencies are held constant. These include interest rate differentials, inflation differentials, income differentials and speculation. A change in any of these factors will cause the demand curve and/or the supply curve to shift. We will examine each of these factors briefly.

1. *Interest rate differentials.* Suppose Irish interest rates rise above US interest rates. American investors, seeking the highest rate of return, respond to this interest rate differential by investing in Irish assets. The change in demand for capital assets, caused by the interest rate differential, leads to a change in demand for the Irish pound. The demand curve for the Irish pound shifts out and to the right, as shown in Figure 14.5.

Figure 14.5: A shift of the demand curve and the supply curve caused by an interest rate differential

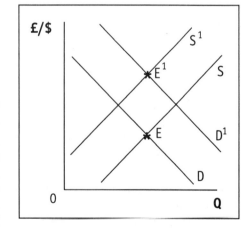

We can see that at every exchange rate, the demand for Irish pounds has increased.

In this situation, the supply curve may also shift. Irish investors are unwilling to purchase American assets since the return on Irish assets is higher. Fewer Irish pounds are supplied to the market. This change in the underlying variable causes the supply curve to shift to the left as shown in Figure 14.5. At each exchange rate, the supply of Irish pounds has decreased.

We can now compare the old equilibrium E with the new equilibrium E[1]. The combination of increased demand and decreased supply results in an increase in the IR£/US$ exchange rate. Hence, the higher interest rate in Ireland *vis-à-vis* the United States causes an increase in the value of the Irish pound against the dollar. Alternatively, lower interest rates in Ireland will cause a decrease in the exchange rate, all other things being equal.

2. *Inflation differentials.* Suppose the Irish inflation rate increases, resulting in an inflation differential with the United States. Irish goods are now relatively more expensive. This may lead to a decrease in demand for Irish goods in the US, depending on the elasticity of demand for Irish exports. This change in an underlying variable means that the demand curve for Irish pounds shifts to the left.

The supply curve for Irish pounds also changes because the relatively low inflation rate in the US causes the demand for US goods, which are relatively cheaper, to increase. These goods must be paid for by exchanging Irish pounds for US dollars. As the demand for US dollars increases, the supply of Irish pounds increases. The supply curve for Irish pounds shifts to the right.

As a result, the higher inflation rate in Ireland *vis-à-vis* the United States leads to a decline in the value of the Irish pound against the dollar. The relationship between exchange rates and inflation rates is expressed in terms of Purchasing Power Parity. For more on this subject, see Appendix 14.1 and Section 14.6 on the Irish Experience.

3. *Income differentials.* Suppose Irish GDP increases at a rate that is higher than her trading partners. As national income increases, domestic consumption increases. Part of this increase in consumption is met by purchasing more imports. As demand for imports increases, the supply of Irish pounds increases. As a result, the exchange rate falls. Hence, the higher income level in Ireland causes a decline in the value of the Irish pound against the US dollar, all other things being equal.

4. *Speculation.* This is a curious but powerful factor in the determination of the exchange rate. Suppose the demand for the Irish pound is expected to be weak. Expectations are for a fall in the value of the Irish pound. Market participants, in anticipation of making a capital gain, sell their Irish pound holdings.[10] As a result, the supply of Irish pounds in the foreign exchange market increases. This is represented by a rightward shift of the supply curve. If enough market participants act on this expectation, the value of the Irish pound will fall. Speculation, as is evident from this example, can be self-fulfilling if there are enough participants trading in the market. Although it is difficult to assess the level of speculation on the foreign exchange markets, it is estimated that less than one-fifth of daily foreign exchange transactions in London is trade/investment related, with speculation accounting for the remainder.

We now examine the relationship between the balance of payments and the exchange rate. Also, the different exchange rate regimes are explained.

14.3 Exchange rate regimes and the balance of payments

The composition of the balance of payments and how it actually balances depends on the ability of the domestic currency to adjust in value to other currencies. There are different types of exchange rate systems. The flexible and fixed exchange rate systems are polar opposites and do not reflect the exchange rate systems which operate in practice. However, we will begin by discussing the extremes and then explain the semi-fixed and managed exchange rate systems which we often observe. Figure 14.6 illustrates the range of exchange rate regimes.

Figure 14.6: Exchange rate systems

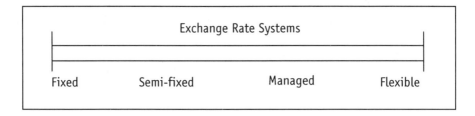

Flexible exchange rate systems
••••••••••••••••••••••••••••••••

Under this regime, the value of the domestic currency is allowed to change, *vis-à-vis* other currencies.

● Definition
● ● ● ● ● ●

A flexible exchange rate system operates on the basis of market forces whereby the exchange rate between two currencies is determined by demand and supply.

The Central Banks are not required to intervene on the foreign exchange market.

Under a flexible exchange rate regime there is an automatic adjustment process in operation. For example, a current account deficit is financed by an equal capital account surplus. How does this work?

If a country records a current account deficit, it means that it is importing more goods and services than it is exporting. The foreign exchange needed to pay for these imports must come from some source. It comes from either borrowing from foreigners or from the sale of domestic assets. When a country sells more assets than it buys, it runs a capital account surplus. This net inflow of foreign exchange is the source used to finance the deficit in the current account.[11] Likewise, a current account surplus is matched by an increase in the ownership of foreign assets.

A current account deficit may result in a change of the exchange rate. All other things being equal, a current account deficit causes the country's currency to depreciate. As a result, exports become cheaper whereas imports become more expensive. Likewise, a current account surplus is eliminated by an appreciation of the exchange rate.

In theory, flexible exchange rates will eliminate a current account surplus or deficit. Like any market system, it is the price mechanism that will eliminate any disequilibrium. If the foreign exchange market is at equilibrium, the balance of payments should balance. In practice there may be a discrepancy caused by book-keeping errors and omissions.

Fixed exchange rate systems
••••••••••••••••••••••••••••

Alternatively, governments often attempt to maintain the value of their currency *vis-à-vis* other currencies.

Definition
• • • • • •

Currencies that belong to a fixed exchange rate system are pegged to each other at rates which are usually agreed by their respective Central Banks.

In order to maintain the currencies at the fixed rates, intervention by the Central Banks is required.[12]

Under a fixed exchange rate regime, the balance of payments will balance with the external reserves playing a central role.

Definition
• • • • • •

The external reserves are the stock of foreign currency held by Central Bank for the purpose of intervention in the foreign exchange market.

To illustrate the operation of external reserves, we will consider the balance of payments for a fictitious state for the year 1996, as outlined in Table 14.4.

Table 14.4: Balance of payments, 1996

Current account	2,500	Change in external reserves	800
Capital account	−1,700		
	800		800

In Table 14.4, we observe a current account surplus of 2,500 units which is partially offset by a capital deficit of 1,700 units. Under these circumstances, there is excess demand for the domestic currency which should lead to a rise in its value. However, under a fixed exchange rate system, the Central Bank is obliged to intervene to maintain the value of the domestic currency *vis-à-vis* other currencies. To eliminate the shortage, the Central Bank purchases external reserves. In other words, foreign currencies are exchanged for the domestic currency. The stock of external reserves increases and with it, the foreign currency reserves of the Central Bank. In this example, the external reserves increase by 800 units.

In theory, any imbalance in the addition of the current and capital accounts is reflected by an equal and opposite change in external reserves. In practice, a discrepancy between the current and capital accounts and the external reserve figure often emerges. This discrepancy is referred to as the net residual. It reflects unrecorded transactions, illegal transfers of money into and out of the economy and errors and omissions in the current and capital accounts. The net residual can either be positive, reflecting hidden inflows or negative, reflecting hidden outflows.[13]

On the other hand, a negative balance in the current and capital accounts means that there is an excess supply of the domestic currency. In this situation, the Central Bank sells external reserves and purchases the domestic currency to eliminate the surplus. The balance of payments statement at the end of the year would show a decrease in the external reserves.

Appendix 14.2 outlines the arguments for and against the fixed and the flexible exchange rate systems.

Managed floating exchange rate systems

The managed floating exchange rate system closely resembles the flexible exchange rate system.

Definition

The managed floating exchange rate system is characterised by an exchange rate which changes with the market forces of demand and supply. However, the Central Bank intervenes periodically, particularly when the currency is very weak or very strong.

The danger of a weak currency is that inflationary pressures may arise. A strong currency may have a negative effect on the volume of exports. To avoid both of these threats to the domestic economy, the Central Bank may intervene.[14]

Semi-fixed exchange rate systems

The semi-fixed exchange rate system closely resembles the fixed exchange rate system but it is more 'flexible'.

Definition

Member states of a semi-fixed exchange rate system set the value of their currencies in relation to other participating currencies. However, currencies are permitted to fluctuate above and below these rates.

The 'fluctuation bands' are normally one or two percentage points above and below the established rate. If the domestic currency fluctuates within the band, the Central Bank does not normally intervene. If the domestic currency approaches the limit of the band, the Central Bank intervenes in the market to stabilise the exchange rate within the band.

Countries that participate in a semi-fixed exchange rate system must offset their interventions using external reserves.

One example of a semi-fixed exchange rate system is the European Monetary System, or the EMS. Since Ireland is a member of this system, we will discuss it in detail.

14.4 The European Monetary System (EMS)

The EMS came into operation on 13 March 1979.[15] Its aim was the 'creation of closer monetary co-operation leading to a zone of monetary stability in Europe'.[16] Until recently it was described as the most successful exchange rate system of all time. How does the EMS operate?

There are three separate components to the EMS. The first is the ECU, the European Currency Unit. It is a weighted basket of EU currencies, with the weightings changed every five years or when a new currency joins the system. The weights are based on a country's GNP and level of intra-EU trade. Although the ECU is not a currency in its own right, it is used as an international reserve currency and plays an important role in financial markets where trading in ECUs is very popular.

The second component is the EMCF, the European Monetary Co-operation Fund. On joining the system member states are obliged to submit 20% of their holdings of gold and foreign exchange reserves in return for ECUs. These funds are now used for settling accounts after foreign exchange intervention.

The third and most important part of the EMS is the Exchange Rate Mechanism (ERM). This is a semi-fixed system where members' currencies are allowed to fluctuate against each other's currencies within an agreed band.[17]

All currencies of the ERM are assigned a central rate against the ECU. Each member's currency is also committed to a central rate against other currencies, with bands of fluctuation.

When the ERM was first established, it was decided to operate two bands of fluctuation: a narrow band of 2.25% and a wide band of 6%.[18] The wider band was assigned to member states with volatile currencies. It was hoped that as their economies converged towards the European average their currencies would become more stable and they would eventually enter the narrow band.[19]

Table 14.5 is an example of a parity grid. It shows the central exchange rate between each member state and the respective upper and lower limits.

Table 14.5: European Monetary System parity grid

	Belg.	Denm.	Fran.	Germ.	Ire.	It.	Holl.	Port.	Spain	UK
				Central rate against ECU						
100BFr		18.0831	15.8990	4.7400	1.7695	3546.90	5.3415	396.98	296.80	1.54790
	<u>42.4032</u>	18.4938	16.2608	4.8484	1.8098	3627.64	5.4629	421.51	315.14	1.64352
		18.9143	16.6310	4.9590	1.8510	3710.20	5.5870	477.56	334.62	1.74510
1DKr	5.2870		0.8597	0.2563	0.0957	191.79	0.2888	21.4660	16.0490	0.08370
	5.4072	<u>7.84195</u>	0.8793	0.2622	0.0979	196.15	0.2954	22.7922	17.0405	0.08887
	5.5300		0.8993	0.2681	0.1001	200.62	0.3021	24.2010	18.0940	0.09436
1Frf	6.0130	1.1120		0.2915	0.1088	218.13	0.3285	24.4130	18.2530	0.09519
	6.1498	1.1373	<u>6.89509</u>	0.2982	0.1113	223.091	0.3360	25.9221	19.3806	0.10107
	6.2897	1.1632		0.3050	0.1138	228.17	0.3436	27.5240	20.5780	0.10732
1DM	20.1655	3.7300	3.2792		0.3650	731.57	1.1017	81.9000	61.2170	0.31928
	20.6255	3.8144	3.3539	<u>2.05586</u>	0.3733	748.22	1.1267	86.9393	65.0000	0.33898
	21.0950	3.9016	3.4305		0.3818	765.40	1.1524	92.3360	69.0170	0.35997
1IR£	54.0250	9.9913	8.7850	2.6190		1959.84	2.9510	219.35	163.997	0.85526
	55.2545	10.2186	8.9848	**2.6789**	<u>0.767417</u>	2004.43	3.0185	232.91	174.13	**0.90812**
	56.5115	10.4511	9.1890	2.7400		2050.03	3.0870	247.30	184.8920	0.96424
1000ITL	26.9530	4.9850	4.3830	1.3065	0.4878		1.4725	109.43	81.8200	0.42669
	27.5661	5.0980	4.4825	1.3365	0.4989	<u>1538.24</u>	1.5059	116.19	86.8727	0.45305
	28.1930	5.2140	4.5844	1.3669	0.5102		1.5400	123.38	92.2400	0.48105
1NLG	17.8985	3.3102	2.9104	0.8678	0.3239	649.28		72.6700	54.3310	0.28334
	18.3054	3.3854	2.9766	0.8875	0.3313	664.06	<u>2.31643</u>	77.1597	57.6883	0.30085
	18.7215	3.4624	3.0444	0.9077	0.3389	679.12		81.9000	61.2530	0.31945
100ESC	22.3435	4.1321	3.6332	1.0830	0.4044	810.50	1.2210		70.4130	0.36722
	23.7241	4.8870	3.8577	1.1502	0.4294	860.63	1.2960	<u>178.735</u>	74.7649	0.38991
	25.1900	4.6586	4.0961	1.2210	0.4559	913.80	1.3760		79.3850	0.41400
100ESP	29.8850	5.5260	4.8595	1.4490	0.5409	1084.10	1.6325	125.97		0.49116
	31.7316	5.8684	5.1598	1.5385	0.5743	1151.11	1.7334	133.75	<u>133.631</u>	0.52151
	33.6930	6.2310	5.4785	1.6335	0.6098	1222.30	1.8405	142.02		0.55374
1UK£	57.3033	10.5977	9.3179	2.7780	1.0371	2078.78	3.1304	241.55	180.5902	
	60.8450	11.2526	9.8939	2.9500	1.1012	2207.25	3.3299	256.47	191.7495	<u>0.696904</u>
	64.6037	11.9474	10.5055	3.1320	1.1692	2343.62	3.5293	272.32	203.5996	

Source: EMS Parity grid as at 6 April 1992, AIB Group Treasury.

We will explain how the ERM operates by discussing an example. Consider the relationship between the Irish pound and the German mark which is highlighted in Table 14.5.[20] Until January 1993, the central rate for the IR£/DM was IR£1 = 2.6789DM.[21] This means that one Irish pound was worth approximately 2.68 German marks. At that time, both the Irish pound and the German mark operated within the narrow band. The upper and lower limits, transcribed from Table 14.5 are shown in Figure 14.7.

Figure 14.7: IR£/DM trading range

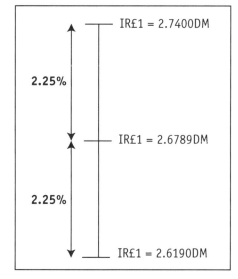

IR£1 = 2.7400DM

2.25%

IR£1 = 2.6789DM

2.25%

IR£1 = 2.6190DM

The Irish pound could move between the lower band of 2.6190DM and the upper band of 2.7400DM. These figures are 2.25% below and 2.25% above the central rate. In other words, if the value of the Irish pound fell below 2.6190DM or rose above 2.74DM, the Central Bank was obliged to intervene.

In a 'normal' day's trading, the IR£/DM will trade within these limits. The Central Bank uses a number of policies to ensure that its currency stays within these limits.

There are three policies available to any Central Bank involved in maintaining the value of its currency within the ERM fluctuation bands. A short-term measure is foreign exchange intervention which alters the external reserves. Central Banks can intervene on a daily basis. Domestic currency is bought and sold in exchange for foreign currency. According to the rules of the ERM, intervention is a joint responsibility, i.e. it involves the respective Central Banks of the strongest and weakest currencies. For example, if the IR£/DM rate is close to its intervention limits both the Central Bank of Ireland and the Bundesbank are required to act. There is a finite stock of external reserves. Hence, this is only used as a short-term measure.

A medium-term measure is an interest rate change. If a currency is continually weak and Central Bank intervention is unsuccessful, the monetary authorities may decide to increase domestic interest rates. For the Irish authorities, this is accomplished by increasing the short-term facility rate (see Section 11.4). We have already seen from Section 14.2 that there is a positive relationship between interest rates and the exchange rate. However, we know from our previous discussion that an increase in the STF rate will trigger an increase in rates for all other personal and commercial loans. Frequent changes in interest rates have a destabilising effect on the economy. In theory, this is not a long-term option. However, it has become a long-term practice for many countries.

The long-term measure is a realignment of a currency within the ERM. Both devaluation and revaluation involve a change in the central rate between two currencies.

Definition
● ● ● ● ● ●

Devaluation is a reduction in the value of a currency *vis-à-vis* other currencies. In terms of the ERM, the central rate is lowered by a certain percentage.

In a market without restrictions, the currency may depreciate due to the forces of demand and supply. The devaluation of a currency must be negotiated with other participating members of the exchange rate system. However, the reason for the devaluation is generally a disequilibrium in the market for the currency.

For example, suppose that the demand for the Irish pound is continually weak, indicating that Irish goods are not competitive on the international market. Foreign exchange intervention and interest rate changes fail to strengthen the pound. The only option left for the Central Bank is to negotiate a devaluation of the Irish pound.

Alternatively, increased demand for Irish goods and for the Irish pound could lead to a revaluation.

Definition
● ● ● ● ● ● ●

Revaluation increases the value of one currency *vis-à-vis* other participating currencies. In terms of the ERM, the central rate is raised by a certain percentage.

We now examine devaluation as a possible policy option within a semi-fixed exchange rate system.

Devaluation as a policy option
....

The end of the currency crisis in 1993 was the last major realignment of the European currencies. In order to understand the issues surrounding devaluation, we will explore the currency crisis in some detail. Information Box 14.1 explains the issues and the chronology.[22] (You may also benefit from reading Information Box 14.2.)

INFORMATION BOX 14.1

The currency crisis, the devaluation of the Irish pound and the demise of the ERM

For most people, the currency crisis began in the autumn of 1992 with the decline in the value of sterling and finished in the spring of 1993 with the devaluation of the Irish pound. In reality, events leading to the currency crisis date as far back as 1989 and only came to a conclusion in the autumn of 1993.

The reasons behind the currency crisis are many and varied. Possible contributing factors are categorised into long-term factors (dating back years) and medium-term factors (dating back months).

Long-term factors
1. Sterling's entry into the ERM. Sterling entered the ERM in October 1990. Many commentators viewed sterling's entry as a decision taken on the basis of political expediency rather than on economic fundamentals. In particular, one of the conditions that Mrs Thatcher stipulated prior to ERM entry was for the UK inflation rate to be close to the European average. However, it was then decided that entry into the ERM would aid the British effort to control inflation. When the UK entered

the ERM, the inflation rate differential between the UK and core EU member states was substantial. This differential was likely to cause tension within the system. Also, some felt that the central rate of UK£1 = 2.95DM was too high and therefore unsustainable. However, British authorities believed that they could maintain this rate within the wider 6% band.

2. German re-unification. *The re-unification of West and East Germany had some destabilising effects. First, prior to unification the old East German mark, the oestmark, was abolished. East Germans were allowed to convert a part of their savings into deutschmarks at the very favourable one-for-one exchange rate. This increased the purchasing power in the newly unified state and ultimately led to an increase in the inflation rate. Second, rejuvenating the East German economy led to substantial expenditure increases and ultimately to a large budget deficit. The Bonn administration was reluctant to completely finance this extra spending from higher taxes. Most of the expenditure was financed by borrowing which led to higher interest rates in Germany. This occurred at a time when the Bundesbank was trying to stem inflationary fears by operating a tight monetary policy. This caused the already high interest rates to increase even further. These high interest rates in Germany were the predominant factor behind the high interest rate regime prevalent throughout most of western Europe in the early 1990s.*

Medium-term factors

3. US-German interest rate differentials. *The loose monetary policy adopted by the US authorities (in order to thwart the American recession of the 1990s) combined with the high interest rate policy in Germany (in order to stem inflation) resulted in a significant interest rate differential between the two countries. This, alongside other factors, led to a large capital inflow to Europe, and particularly Germany. This increased demand for the mark caused it to increase in value and created tension and uncertainty within the ERM. In recent times, the value of sterling has followed the dollar, not the mark. Therefore, the combination of the weak dollar and strong mark added to the exchange rate pressure between sterling and the mark during the summer of 1992.*

4. The Scandinavian Connection. *Prior to the currency crisis all three Scandinavian currencies were shadowing the ECU. Shadowing is an informal arrangement. Currencies outside the ERM, particularly those with strong trading links to EU member states, attempt to maintain the value of their currency within the narrow or the wide band. Adherence to this policy in the Scandinavian countries became unpopular during the summer of 1992. Many felt that sustaining the value of the domestic currency against the currencies within the ERM was responsible for the depleted external reserves, high interest rates and high unemployment which were evident at the time.*

5. The Treaty on European Union. *The failure by the Danes to ratify the Maastricht treaty in June 1992 and the decision by the French to hold a referendum created further tension within the markets and the ERM. The European Monetary System without the Maastricht treaty was suddenly becoming a possibility that no one (with the exception of the Euro-sceptics) had imagined. The future existence of the EMS was now in doubt.*

Other events, including the removal of exchange controls and the perceived overvaluation of the French franc, were contributing factors.

Each of these factors individually placed the ERM under pressure. The combination of the factors made the entire system unstable. The instability quickly spread to the financial markets. A brief history of the events which preceded the devaluation of the Irish pound is outlined below.

8 September. *Finnish authorities break the unofficial link with the ECU and float the markka.*

13 September. *Italian lira is devalued by 7%.*

14 September. *Bundesbank cuts the discount rate (the rate which forms the floor for German interest rates) by 0.5% and the Lombard rate (the rate which sets the ceiling for German interest rates) by 0.25%.*

16 September. *Sterling collapses, falling below its lower limit within the ERM. UK Chancellor responds by raising the level of interest rates first by 2% and then by a further 3%. Sterling and the lira are both suspended from the ERM. Spanish peseta is devalued by 5%.*

20 September. *The French people ratify the Maastricht treaty, but by a very slim margin.*

28 September. *Irish Central Bank raises the STF rate by 3% from 10.75% to 13.75%.*

6 October. *A new £50m Market Development Fund is established for businesses that are being adversely affected by the currency crisis.*

16 October. *The emergency EC summit in Birmingham fails to discuss currency crisis.*

19 November. *Swedish Central Bank decides to float the krona.*

22 November. *Spanish peseta and Portuguese escudo are devalued by 6%.*

30 November. *Irish Central Bank raises its overnight lending rate from 30% to 100% in an attempt to limit capital outflows and to deter further speculative pressures on the Irish pound.*

10 December. *The Norwegian authorities break the link with the ECU and float the krone.*

12/13 December. *EU summit in Edinburgh. Ireland was promised £8 billion in structural and cohesion funds over a seven-year period.*

1 January. *The removal of exchange controls restricting the mobility of capital within the EU is completed.*

3 January. *John Major indicates that sterling will not rejoin the ERM for at least one year.*

7 January. *FF and Labour agree the Programme for a Partnership Government 1993–97.*

25 January. *John Bruton, the leader of the main opposition party, Fine Gael calls for 'unilateral realignment within the ERM'.*

26 January. *UK interest rates are cut from 7% to 6%.*

28 January. *President of the Bundesbank, Dr. Schlesinger defends Germany's high interest rate policy. He is not optimistic about the prospect of an early cut in rates.*

30 January. *EU Monetary Committee devalue the Irish pound by 10%.[1] The new IR£/DM central rate is IR£1 = 2.41105DM with an upper limit of IR£1 = 2.4660DM and a lower limit of IR£1 = 2.3570DM.*
4 February. *The Bundesbank cuts the discount rate by 0.25% and the Lombard rate by 0.5%.*

The uncertainty which was prevalent in the foreign exchange market for the previous six months subsided because of the devaluation of the Irish pound, further Central Bank intervention and the cut in German interest rates.
    The lull in the storm lasted until the summer of 1993 when speculators began to focus on the French franc and the Danish krone. Events came to a head in late July. Financial markets, certain that the ERM was about to collapse, were already discounting that event. However, their postmortem was premature. The ERM was saved by the decision taken on the first weekend of August to extend the fluctuation bands to 15%. Although the authorities did manage to save the ERM, it is debatable whether it can still be described as a 'semi-fixed exchange rate system'.[2]

1 *The EU Monetary Committee comprises the EU finance ministers and Central Bank officials.*
2 *In the run-up to the single currency, it has been agreed to set up an ERM Mark II. The relationship between the 'ins' and 'outs' is an issue of grave concern to many member states, including Ireland.*

The process involved in a devaluation of the Irish pound is described above. The controversy regarding devaluation relates to the possible benefits and drawbacks which may result from the decision. We will illustrate both the advantages and disadvantages involved by example.

On 30 January 1993 the Irish pound was devalued by 10%.[23] For several months prior to this, the Irish pound weakened against the core currencies of the ERM (German mark, Dutch guilder and Belgian franc). This problem was aggravated by a weak US dollar and an even weaker pound sterling.

Foreign exchange markets link sterling and the dollar. If the dollar weakens, this puts downward pressure on sterling. The dollar and the mark often move in opposite directions. Since sterling follows the dollar, during periods of deviation between the dollar and the mark, it is difficult for British officials to maintain their central rate with the mark.

Similarly, the Irish and the British currencies are linked in the foreign exchange markets. This is because of the strong trade links that persist between the two countries. Therefore, if the Irish pound gains in strength relative to the pound sterling, Irish exports become dearer in their main market. Under these conditions, the foreign exchange markets anticipate a devaluation of the Irish pound.

Between the months of July and September 1992, the IR£/UK£ exchange rate increased from IR£1 = UK£.93 to parity and then to IR£1 = UK£1.09. Irish firms exporting to the UK faced severe difficulties. Margins were squeezed.[24] In addition, interbank interest rates were extremely high, with the one month lending rate close to 50%. As speculators continued their domination of the foreign exchanges, the situation became unsustainable.

Arguments favouring devaluation

Some commentators called for a devaluation of the Irish pound. A devaluation, they argued, would improve Ireland's competitiveness by increasing the domestic price of imports and reducing the foreign price of the country's exports. Such a devaluation would probably return the IR£/UK£ exchange rate to its former trading rate. Prior to the currency crisis the IR£/UK£ exchange rate had traded at approximately IR£1 = UK£.93 for a period of over two years.

A weaker Irish exchange rate was particularly important for indigenous firms who rely, often exclusively, on the British market. Because the firms are often small, they cannot afford to 'hedge' against exchange risk.[25] This contrasts sharply with their Irish-based multinational competitors who are involved in either hedging or simply invoicing their Irish exports in US dollars. Either way, their exchange risk is lessened. Also, indigenous companies do not have the resources to maintain operations until the exchange rate becomes more favourable. Because the Irish firms are more labour intensive than foreign multinationals, the likely closure of indigenous firms added to an already serious unemployment problem.

Also, the Central Bank could lower interest rates if it did not have to defend the currency. High and rising interest rates were particularly devastating to mortgage holders, whose monthly payments increased. They had less income to spend which negatively affected consumer spending. Firms were unable to borrow money at the penalising rates of interest. The consequences of this lack of investment would be felt in the medium term and the long term.

In summary, those who favoured devaluation argued that a lower exchange rate and lower interest rates would save thousands of jobs. The opportunity cost of sustaining the exchange rate was becoming unacceptably high. The government's most important obligation was to lower unemployment.

Arguments opposing devaluation

Others, and in particular officials from the Department of Finance and the National Treasury Management Agency, a number of private sector economists and government spokespersons argued strongly against a devaluation of the Irish pound.

They argued that a devaluation is inflationary, particularly for a country that imports as much as Ireland. A devaluation has the effect of increasing the price of imports. If there are domestic substitutes, they become more competitive and so a devaluation can have a positive impact on indigenous industry. However, because the Irish economy is small, many goods are not produced here and many raw materials are not found here. Therefore, consumers and firms are forced to pay for higher priced imports which leads to inflation.

Devaluations can also lead to a vicious circle of inflation and devaluation which, once established, is difficult to break. For example, suppose a number of Irish firms lobby the government for a devaluation of the Irish pound. The government subsequently devalues the Irish pound. Irish firms gain a short-term competitive advantage over their trading partners. However, as import prices begin to rise, the Irish inflation rate increases. Consequently, the inflation rate differential with the UK worsens. Irish firms become even less competitive. As a short-term solution to the problem, Irish industry requests another devaluation. The government, facing a general election in the near future, devalue again. The inflation rate in Ireland increases, again. Another cycle begins. This is the devaluation-price inflation spiral which is sometimes used as an argument against devaluation.

Also, as we mentioned in Chapter 8, part of the national debt is denominated in foreign currency. If the Irish currency is devalued relative to these foreign currencies, the size of the foreign debt increases along with the debt service repayments. Therefore, the decision to devalue undermines the government's commitment to contain the national debt.

Short-term interest rates usually decline following a devaluation. However, the critics pointed out that the devaluation itself could lead investors to believe that the Irish pound is volatile and that investments denominated in Irish pounds are risky. Investors would demand a premium on Irish interest rates relative to, for example, German interest rates to compensate for the risk. Therefore, the benefit of lower interest rates might only last for a short time. Long-term interest rates may be higher as a result of the decision to devalue.

Finally, given the unstable market background of the time, it was argued that a single devaluation of the Irish pound would not suffice. Between September 1992 and May 1993, the Spanish peseta was devalued three times and the Portuguese escudo was devalued twice. The recent history of repeated devaluations within the ERM led many to believe that the Irish pound would not stabilise after the devaluation. In fact, the decision to devalue would show a lack of commitment on the part of the Irish government to maintain the value of the Irish pound. This could fuel future speculative pressure against the Irish pound.

To summarise, those who opposed the devaluation argued that the decision to devalue placed too much emphasis on the short-term goal of preserving employment. The long-term goals of the economy include maintaining low inflation rates, low interest rates and a stable exchange rate regime. Attaining these goals would encourage long-term growth and promote increased employment. The devaluation was a political expedient at the expense of the long-term national interest, it was argued.

The following article is an outsider's view of the dilemma which faced the Irish authorities.

ARTICLE 14.1

Extract from The Sunday Times
Irish battered by ERM crisis that Britain escaped
by Alan Ruddock

Britain's fare if the pound had not left the European exchange-rate mechanism (ERM) on White Wednesday (16 September) will be revealed tomorrow evening in Dublin's glittering National Concert Hall. Ireland's political and business leaders will gather there to celebrate the 50th anniversary of the country's Central Bank. The timing could not be worse. This weekend, battered by a five-month currency crisis, prime lending rates at 28%, unemployment already over 20% and rising, and no relief in sight, the Irish government has been forced to call an emergency meeting of the European Monetary Committee. There is only one item on the agenda: the devaluation of the Irish pound.

Since September, when Britain was forced out of the ERM, the Irish have been fighting a harrowing vanguard action to avoid a devaluation of their own. When Britain bowed to the inevitable, the Irish struggled on. Their determination to maintain the Irish pound's value within the system was fuelled, at the outset, by Ireland's commitment to the European ideal and by the fear that devaluation would undo all the hard-earned success of the Irish economy in the previous five years. The problem, the Irish government argued, was only a temporary one. If it refused to give in to the short-term pressure, then Ireland's reputation within Europe would only be enhanced. The Irish government decided that interest rates could be raised to whatever level was necessary to defend the currency. After all, it was argued, it would only be for a few weeks. The ERM would survive sterling's collapse and normality would return. It didn't, and interest rates in Ireland soared.

. . .

As the pain of high interest rates started to be felt throughout the economy, the tenor of the debate started to change. What had started as a logical, economic resistance to speculation became a nationalist determination to defend the currency against foreign speculators. Local banks which sold the currency short were branded traitors. Last week the Catholic bishops – traditionally a powerful force in Irish politics – joined the fray by labelling speculators as anti-Christian. The cost of resisting the speculators is coming home with a vengeance. Last week, Ireland's business leaders warned that 10,000 jobs were now at risk. For a country with over one in five already unemployed, that has become unacceptable.

. . .

The job losses and the unavoidable rise in mortgage rates have forced Albert Reynolds, the Taoiseach, to buckle. Devaluation is unavoidable, but there is no guarantee that it will work. The defence of the pound has wiped out the Central Bank's reserves and starved the banking system of cash. Reducing interest rates will be difficult until money flows back into the country from abroad.

. . .

Ireland is inextricably linked to the British economy. The Irish pound's problem within the ERM is that it is has been caught in the middle of a tug-of-war between the D-mark, to which it is bound by the ERM straitjacket, and sterling. It is a tension that has always caused problems for the currency, but was containable until Britain left the system. For the Irish to follow suit is logical, but politically unthinkable.

Yesterday, the scapegoats were already being lined up by Ahern's advisers. Their number one target is Britain, but Europe's leaders and Jacques Delors in particular will be attacked for failing to provide leadership in a time of crisis for the whole European Community and for failing to come more readily to Ireland's aid. But domestic targets will also be highlighted – bankers and stockbrokers who advocated devaluation from the start will be blamed, as will the few politicians who put their heads above the parapet.

Source: The Sunday Times, *31 January 1993.*

In conclusion, it can be seen from the above analysis that the decision to devalue is a difficult one to make. There are many who favour devaluation as a credible policy option; others are not so supportive. For one, Harold Wilson, the former UK Prime Minister who, in 1963, said 'Devaluation, whether of sterling, or the dollar, or both, would be a lunatic, self-destroying operation.' Incidentally, four years later he had this to say: 'From now on the pound abroad is worth 14% or so less in terms of other currencies. It does not mean, of course, that the pound here in Britain in your pocket or purse, or in your bank has been devalued.' Not surprisingly, this statement followed the decision to devalue sterling, in 1967. It is left to the readers to decide for themselves the reason behind the change of opinion!

The ERM is one aspect of monetary union. Most of the members of the EU aspire to both economic and monetary union. We will now discuss the distinctive features of both.

14.5 Economic and Monetary Union

The origins of Economic and Monetary Union, or EMU, date back to 1957, the year that the European Economic Community (EEC) was established.

The main features of an economic union are:

- the free mobility of capital, labour, goods and services;
- a community-wide competition policy;
- co-ordination of macroeconomic policy;
- economic and social cohesion and regional development.

The main features of a monetary union are as follows:

- the abolition of all exchange controls culminating in the complete liberalisation of all capital transactions;
- the irrevocable fixing of exchange rates culminating in a single currency;
- a European Central Bank and a common monetary policy.

The Delors Report, published in 1989, established a three-stage process and a timetable to achieve these goals. These were slightly modified at the Intergovernmental Conference in 1991. They were published in the Treaty on European Union, more commonly known as the Maastricht treaty, in December 1991. Because of problems in achieving the objectives set out in the Delors Report, the timetable was amended by the European Council at a meeting in Madrid during December 1995. The three stages for achieving EMU and the amended timetable are outlined below.

Stage 1: Laying the foundation

This stage began in July 1990 and ended in December 1993. One of the goals of the stage was to complete the Internal Market, made possible by the passage of the Single European Act in 1987. Theoretically, within the Single European Market there is free movement of people, goods, services and capital. All barriers to entry between European Union member states were to be eliminated. In other words, it was to be a Europe without national frontiers. Although much has been achieved, work continues to harmonise tax systems, to standardise technical specifications across member states and to reduce national incentives to industries.

Another goal of this phase was to co-ordinate macroeconomic policies between member states. It was hoped that the exchange rates of member states could be maintained within their 'narrow bands'. Exchange rate stability and the discipline that it imposes on national governments was to pave the way to the single currency.

In order to reduce disparities in the living conditions between member states, structural funds were awarded, particularly to countries whose GDP per capita was significantly below the EU average.

Stage 2: Moving towards union

Stage 2 was designed as a transitional phase. The European Monetary Institute (EMI) was established in Frankfurt to begin the transition from independent national monetary policies to a common European monetary policy. The EMI itself is a 'transitional' institution. It will eventually be replaced by a European System of Central Banks (ESCB).

Under the terms of the Maastricht treaty, the EMI and the Commission were to report to the European Council at the end of 1996 on the progress made by member states in fulfilling the convergence criteria (discussed below). At the summit in Madrid, the Council extended this deadline. As it currently stands, an assessment will take place in early 1998 on the basis of 1997 data. At that time, the Council will decide which states will participate in the single currency.

Stage 3: Completing the union

Under the terms of the Maastricht treaty, Stage 3 was to begin between 1997 and 1999, at the latest. The Council in Madrid confirmed the starting date for the irrevocable fixing of the exchange rates for 1 January 1999. The changeover to the single currency, to be called the Euro, will begin no later than 1 January 2002 and will last for a maximum of 6 months. The EMI will be replaced by the European System of Central Banks. This institution will be responsible for the formulation and implementation of a common, EU monetary policy.[26]

The proposed road to EMU is highlighted in Figure 14.8.[27]

Figure 14.8: The proposed road to EMU

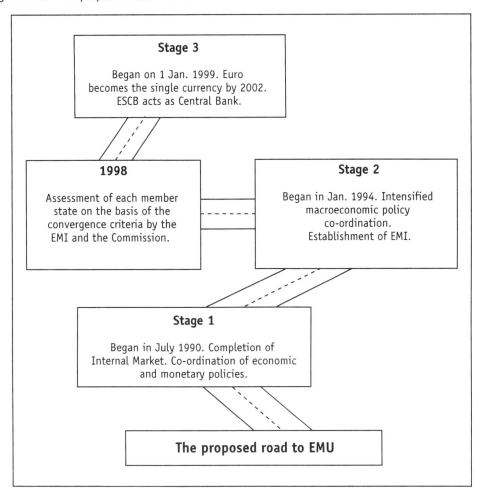

Convergence criteria to join the single currency

To prepare for the transition to a single currency, the Maastricht treaty established a set of targets called the convergence criteria. The treaty does not specify policies. The national governments of each member state determine how to achieve each criterion. The EMI and the Commission will report to the European Council on the ability of member states to meet these criteria using 1997 data. They are listed below (with the direct quote from the Treaty in quotation marks):[28]

- Inflation rates: 'an average rate of inflation . . . that does not exceed by more than 1.5 percentage points that of, at most, the three best performing Member States in terms of price stability';
- Interest rates: 'a Member State has had an average nominal long-term interest rate that does not exceed by more than two percentage points that of, at most, the three best performing Member States in terms of price stability';

- Exchange rates: 'the observance of the normal fluctuation margins provided for by the exchange-rate mechanism of the European Monetary System, for at least two years, without devaluing against the currency of any other Member State';
- 'the sustainability of the government financial position', as judged by the following two measures:

     Budget deficit: 'the ratio of the planned or actual government deficit to gross domestic product at market prices' cannot exceed '3%'.

     National debt: 'the ratio of government debt to gross domestic product at market prices' cannot exceed '60%'.

To date there has been much controversy surrounding these convergence criteria. The controversy relates to the absence of any social criterion, particularly the unemployment rate and the rigidity with which the criteria will be applied.[29]

Table 14.6 shows the ability of EU countries to fulfil the criteria in 1995.

Table 14.6: The convergence criteria in 1995

	Inflation rates	Interest rates	ERM	Budget deficit /GDP	Debt/GDP
Belgium	1.4	7.5	Yes	−4.5	134.4
Denmark	2.3	8.3	Yes	−2.0	73.6
France	1.7	7.5	Yes	−5.0	51.5
Germany	1.6	6.8	Yes	−2.9	58.8
Greece	9.0	17.3	No	−9.3	114.4
Ireland	2.4	8.3	Yes	−2.7	85.9
Italy[1]	5.4	12.2	No	−7.4	124.9
Luxembourg	1.9	7.6	Yes	0.4	6.3
Netherlands	1.1	6.9	Yes	−3.1	78.4
Portugal	3.8	11.5	Yes	−5.4	70.5
Spain	4.7	11.3	Yes	−5.9	64.8
United Kingdom	3.0	8.3	No	−5.1	52.5
New EU States					
Austria	2.0	7.1	Yes	−5.5	68.0
Finland[2]	1.0	8.8	No	−5.4	63.2
Sweden	2.9	10.2	No	−7.0	81.4
EU–15	3.0	8.9	–	−4.7	71.0

Source: European Monetary Institute, *Annual Report 1995*, April 1996.

1. Rejoined the ERM in Autumn 1996.
2. Joined the ERM in Winter 1996.

In 1995, only Germany and Luxembourg fulfilled all of the criteria. With reunification, however, it will be difficult for Germany to contain its budget deficit to 3% of GDP. The position of the French and British governments is also unclear. Many observers believe that if the criteria are strictly applied, the 1999 deadline for the transition to a single currency may not be met.[30]

A Stability and Growth Pact was agreed at the Dublin summit in December 1996. Member states of the single currency will be required to keep their budget deficits below 3% of GDP. Any deficit in excess of this limit will result in a fine imposed by Brussels. These limits can only be breached under 'exceptional circumstances' i.e. if the economy records a negative growth rate of 2% per annum. A decline in output of between 0.75% and 2% may result in a reduced fine imposed on overspending. The aim of such a pact is to achieve sustained financial stability by penalising national governments for overspending.

There is a genuine concern expressed about the effect that this pact will have on a country whose economic growth is 'negative'. Adherence to the stability pact will preclude governments from adopting counter-cyclical policies to offset fluctuations in economic activity. Some fear that the pact will only succeed in exacerbating cyclical fluctuations in the economy.

Finally, the agreement reached in Dublin on the relationships between the 'in' and 'out' countries from 1999 onwards is also unsatisfactory from an Irish perspective. The 'outs', likely to include the UK, will not be tied to the 'ins' in any formal binding way. This is likely to cause grave concern to future Irish administrations in general and, in particular, Irish companies doing business in the UK, our largest trading partner.

14.6 The Irish experience

The objective of Irish exchange rate policy

The primary objective of Irish exchange rate policy is to maintain price stability characterised by a low and stable inflation rate. One way to achieve this objective is by maintaining the value of the Irish pound within the bands provided for by the ERM. By maintaining a stable value for the Irish pound, the price of imports is kept stable. This policy, combined with wage restraint at home, results in price stability in the domestic economy.

The Central Bank is responsible for maintaining the value of the Irish pound within the ERM. We know from Section 14.4 above that the monetary authorities have three options available to them when implementing their policy: foreign exchange intervention, a change in interest rates and a realignment.

CASE STUDY

Extract from The Sunday Independent
Too cautious on currency
by Opinion (the Editorial)

Last week's move by the German central bank to cut interest rates has triggered a series of rate falls in Europe, with the Central Bank here following suit. But it has done so in a token fashion which has left many disappointed by its undue caution.

The Central Bank's minimalist response – a cut of 0.25% and half the Bundesbank's rate – has been just enough to ensure some small reduction in retail rates, but has achieved little else. Clearly mortgage holders will welcome any relief in their monthly repayments. However, for exporters to our main market, Britain, the latest move fails to address, or alleviate their problem. The pound, by trading above parity with sterling in recent months, has put both exporters to the UK and those facing the challenge of British imports in the home market, under huge competitive pressure. In particular, the combination of an overvalued currency and a higher cost base – given our distance from the British market and higher taxes – has hit low-margin exporters, such as the food sector, very hard.

So the challenge, not just for the Central Bank, but also the government, is a twofold one. Both must address the problem presented by a weak sterling which makes Irish exports less competitive in the UK. At the same time, both should decide how best to maintain the pound's position within the Exchange Rate Mechanism, so that we remain a credible candidate for a single currency by 1999. Unfortunately, at present the pound's over-valued position against sterling is combined with the currency's very weak position within the ERM. So, reading between the lines, the Central Bank's rationale for its own very modest interest rate reduction last week seems to be based on a number of considerations.

The Bank can argue that the stimulus of much lower interest rates for an economy growing at a record rate, could be infla-tionary. It can also claim that a small interest rate cut represents the best way of making up lost ground within the ERM. And it may also assume that sterling will strengthen in the coming months, thus relieving some of the pressures on our exporters. However, the reality is that the Central Bank is more concerned with protecting the value of the pound than with the competitiveness pro-blems a strong pound presents for Irish exporters to the British market.

The best way to address the competitive-ness difficulties created in part by an ambigu-ous exchange rate policy – where we are caught between a weak sterling and a strong D-mark – is for the government to help relieve the cost pressure on industry. And it should do so by a major re-direction of economic policy. For only determined gov-ernment efforts to cut spending, lower taxes and ensure greater de-regulation of industry will help offset the competitive disadvantage facing Irish exporters, handicapped by an overvalued currency, in the British market. The government should not wait for the next Budget to address this issue, but it should signal its future intentions right now.

Source: The Sunday Independent, *27 August 1995.*

Questions
....

1. Why did the Central Bank cut interest rates? What would happen to the Irish exchange rate if the Irish authorities did not cut interest rates? Explain your reasoning in terms of the foreign exchange market for IR£/DM.
2. Why were firms less than impressed with the magnitude of the interest rate cut? What problems were they facing at the time that this article was written?
3. The editorial suggests that the Central Bank 'is more concerned with protecting the value of the pound than with the competitiveness problems a strong pound presents for Irish exporters to the British market'. Why would the Central Bank place such emphasis on the relationship between the Irish pound and the German mark?

Answers
··········

1. The Irish Central Bank and the central banks in other European countries cut interest rates in response to a cut by the Bundesbank. If they did not cut interest rates, a differential between Irish and German interest rates would exist. This would cause a capital inflow into Ireland because investors want to earn the highest possible interest rate. To purchase Irish assets, foreign investors need Irish pounds.
    Figure 14.9 shows the foreign exchange market for IR£/DM.

Figure 14.9: The foreign exchange market for IR£/DM

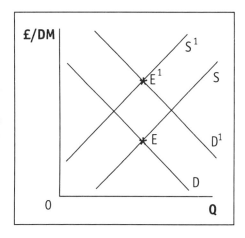

The demand curve D is drawn for the initial rate of interest. To purchase Irish assets, foreign investors need to exchange their currencies for Irish pounds. This pushes the demand curve out and to the right, shown by the demand curve D^1. The supply curve may also shift leftwards to S^1. With interest rates higher at home, investors may be unwilling to exchange Irish pounds for foreign currencies.
    The Irish pound increases in value *vis-à-vis* the German mark. This presents a problem if it forces the Irish pound outside the limits of the fluctuation band.

2. The article was written in 1995, after the pound sterling left the ERM. The pound sterling, in a free float, depreciated relative to the currencies within the ERM. This was beneficial to British producers because their goods became cheaper in foreign markets.
    At the same time, goods produced in other parts of Europe became dearer in the British market. While this causes problems for manufacturers in many countries, the situation in Ireland is more difficult because close to 30% of Irish exports are sent to Britain. Therefore, an increase in the value of the Irish currency means that Irish goods are not competitive in their main export market.
    Initially, firms may cope with the strong Irish pound by cutting the price of goods destined for the British market and accepting lower profits. The writer of the editorial notes that in many export sectors, like food, the profit margins are already low. Therefore, firms attempt to cut costs, another difficult option. It is in this regard that an interest rate cut is welcome. Since interest rates are a cost to firms who borrow, a cut in rates causes one important cost for firms to decrease. The interest rate cut initiated by the Central Bank was not substantial enough to offset the competitive loss caused by the strong pound. For that reason, firms were disappointed.

3. At present, the Central Bank's aim is to fulfil the convergence criteria so that Ireland can join the single currency. Therefore, it has to maintain the foreign exchange value of the pound with the other members of the ERM. In this context, the value of the pound *vis-à-vis* the mark is more important than the IR£/UK£ exchange rate.

The Central Bank is aware of the problems faced by indigenous firms exporting to the UK. However, it considers the exchange rate difficulties to be a short-term problem. By maintaining the value of the Irish pound within the ERM, the Irish authorities are trying to create an environment which is conducive to external trade beyond the UK. The policy of maintaining the 'strong' pound is designed to persuade their EU colleagues that Ireland is a serious contender for the single currency. This would benefit industry in the long run. In summary, they argue that Ireland will sacrifice long-run competitiveness if they pursue policies like devaluation which will make indigenous firms competitive with Britain in the short run.

This shows the very difficult decisions which face Irish policy-makers. In this case, current Irish jobs may be lost in an attempt to enhance the future long-term prospect of employment growth.

Ireland and the EMS
....

Ireland joined the EMS in 1979. It was a difficult decision to make for the Irish authorities. We will begin by discussing the arguments advanced by those who favoured membership in the EMS and then consider the arguments of the opponents.

Arguments favouring entry to the EMS

The main argument in favour of membership was the prospect of lower inflation. Until 1979, the pound was linked with sterling and its inflation rate mirrored the British rate. At the end of the 1960s and throughout the 1970s, both countries experienced persistently high inflation rates, peaking at almost 25% in the mid-1970s. The Irish monetary authorities believed that a link with a 'hard currency' which appreciates over time, like the German mark, was preferable to the British link with its inflationary tendency. They hoped that the link with the mark would result in a convergence of the Irish inflation rate to the German inflation rate which fluctuated between 3% and 4% per annum.

Also, the policy-makers believed that membership of the EMS would facilitate stronger trading links with other member states. This would diminish the reliance of indigenous industries on Britain as a destination for their products.

Finally, Irish authorities expected financial aid from the European Economic Community to assist Ireland to adjust to the new system.

Arguments opposing entry to the EMS

The main argument advanced by those who opposed EMS membership was that the UK decided not to enter. The UK authorities, under a Labour administration, were opposed to membership on the basis that it would result in a loss of autonomy, particularly in the area of monetary policy. They believed that Britain, as an exporter of oil, was subject to different, oil-related shocks than the other European currencies. They wanted to maintain control over their monetary policy to respond to these shocks. See Information Box 14.2 for a discussion of Britain's ambivalent relationship with the EMS.

INFORMATION BOX 14.2

The UK, the ERM and the IR£/UK£ exchange rate

Sterling's participation in the ERM and the broader issue of a single currency in Europe have been hotly debated in the UK. When the EMS was set up in 1979, the UK government decided to keep sterling out of its exchange rate mechanism. The UK authorities were insistent on allowing sterling to float freely on the foreign exchanges and on maintaining control over UK interest rates. There was little or no change in this policy until the mid-1980s when the UK Chancellor of the Exchequer, on recognising the benefits of the ERM, allowed sterling to shadow the German mark.

In October 1990, after much debate, sterling joined the wide band of the ERM at the central rate of UK£1 = 2.95DM. Although the decision to join was not surprising, some of the details took the market by surprise. In particular, many commentators believed that the central rate of UK£1 = 2.95DM was too high. The argument in favour of a high rate was its anti-inflationary bias. The argument against a high rate was its likely effect on UK industry and UK exports.

In Ireland, the authorities, not to mention the business community, were delighted with the decision. The IR£/UK£ exchange rate was now limited to a particular and favourable range. The central rate was IR£1 = UK£.908116 with an upper limit of IR£1 = UK£.96424 and a lower limit of IR£1 = UK£.85526. Unfortunately, this new trading environment did not last.

The critics were proven correct. During the currency crisis, Britain could not maintain its exchange rate with the mark within the 6% band. The British monetary authorities increased their interest rates and attempted to fight the speculators. Ultimately they decided that the damage to the domestic economy was too great. In September 1992, less than two years after joining, sterling's membership of the ERM was suspended. The IR£/UK£ exchange rate went above parity and traded close to IR£1 = UK£1.10. With sterling no longer tied to the mark, the IR£/UK£ exchange rate was once again exposed to conflicting forces.

Sterling remains outside the ERM with little or no likelihood of any change in UK policy. With the IR£/UK£ trading close to parity, Irish firms exporting to the UK remain vulnerable to any sterling weakness. Even with the changes that have taken place since Ireland's membership to the EMS, the UK remains Ireland's largest trading partner. In 1995 we delivered over 25% of all exports to the UK and 35.6% of all imports came from the UK.

On the broader issue of a single currency, the UK authorities negotiated an opt-out clause in the Maastricht treaty. If there is a move to a single currency, the UK Parliament will decide on the participation of sterling. Again, this is less than ideal for Irish firms. Given the importance of the UK market to Irish industry, Britain's opposition to a single currency causes Irish monetary authorities continuing pain and anguish.

Hence, the attraction to joining a fixed exchange rate system was dampened by the absence of Ireland's largest trading partner, the UK.[31] Although Irish exporters were promised a more favourable trading environment as members of the ERM, the prospect of a flexible, not to mention a volatile IR£/UK£ exchange rate, was chilling.

In the end, the Irish authorities were attracted more by the fixed exchange rate with the mark than by the old link with sterling. So, after much deliberation, Ireland decided in favour of the ERM. In 1979, the 153-year, one for one, no margins link with sterling was broken.

Next, we will attempt to evaluate Ireland's performance within the ERM.

Ireland's experience within the ERM
....

An assessment of Ireland's experience within the ERM is normally divided into two distinct periods, 1979–86 and 1987–92.[32] The first period was, in general, disappointing. Ireland's inflation rate remained high, as did Irish interest rates. Trade with member states of the ERM increased but not by a significant amount.

There are a number of reasons for the poor performance during these early years of membership. Possibly the most significant reason was the 'sterling' problem. Sterling was not a member of the ERM and subsequently the IR£/UK£ exchange rate was not subject to any fluctuation bands. Nonetheless, Irish authorities shadowed sterling and at the same time attempted to maintain the formal links with the member states of the ERM. The authorities were literally caught between a rock and a hard place because sterling and the mark often moved in opposite directions.

The financial markets, both at home and abroad, were aware of this dual policy (see Article 14.1). It caused the markets to question Ireland's commitment to the ERM. The market scepticism led to speculation whenever the Irish pound appreciated relative to sterling. The tendency for the Irish authorities to devalue in the face of uncertainty reinforced the market view of Ireland's relaxed attitude towards ERM membership.

The belief that Ireland's inflation rate would fall towards the German level on membership of the ERM was based on the theory of purchasing power parity (PPP). PPP is a theory of exchange rate determination. It states that changes in the exchange rate are accounted for by inflation differentials. In the context of Ireland's membership of the ERM, PPP implies that Ireland's inflation rate will be equal to the core member's (Germany) inflation rate, if the exchange rate between the Irish pound and the German mark is fixed. In this context, PPP is a theory of inflation. See Appendix 14.1 for more on the theory of PPP.

For PPP to hold, a sizeable amount of trade must exist between the two countries. A country cannot benefit from having a fixed exchange rate with another unless a sufficient amount of foreign trade is evident between the two states. Unfortunately, trade between Ireland and other ERM member states did not increase sufficiently during the early years of membership.

Finally, a precondition of entry to a semi-fixed exchange rate system is the agreement to sacrifice national autonomy over certain macroeconomic policies and to co-ordinate policies with other member states. A single member state cannot expect the benefits of a fixed exchange rate system unless its mix of demand-management policies is broadly in line with other member states. This did not happen in the early years of the ERM. Some member states, including Ireland, adopted short-term demand policies which sharply contrasted with the policies adopted by the core member states of the ERM. This is another reason for Ireland's poor performance from 1979 to 1986 (see Appendix 14.3 for a discussion on fiscal and monetary policy in the context of alternate exchange rate regimes).

The performance generally improved during the second period between 1987 and 1992. Unexpectedly, the Irish inflation rate fell below the EU average and the German rate. Interest rates also declined. The differential between Irish and German interest rates narrowed from 9% in 1986 to 3% in 1988. The trade account recorded a surplus, as did the current account. The IR£/DM exchange rate stabilised with the Irish pound reaching the top of the ERM band on a number of occasions.

The improvement in performance came from two sources, domestic and inter-national. The domestic source was the fiscal restraint exercised by the government beginning in 1987. The improvement in industrial relations and the moderate wage increases arising from the Programme for National Recovery also contributed to an Irish environment characterised by low inflation. The international economy, so important to the Irish domestic economy, was buoyant, contributing to the unusual combination of low inflation rates and strong demand for Irish products. The combination of internal discipline and external demand helped Irish policy-makers to maintain the value of the pound within the ERM while experiencing strong rates of economic growth.

Ireland and the single currency
....

From an Irish perspective there are arguments in favour of and against the adoption of a single currency.[33] We begin by examining the arguments favouring a single currency. For a broader view on Ireland's membership of the EU read Article 14.2.

ARTICLE 14.2

Extract from The Irish Independent
A question of options
by Joe Lee

Both champions and critics of Maastricht are agreed – or were agreed before the Danish verdict – that the decision to be taken on 18 June is one of the most impor-tant to ever confront the country. It can hardly be said that the quality of the debate reflects the importance of the issue.

. . .

But it is also true that it is difficult to debate Maastricht because so much depends on surmise and predictions. The short response to most predictions is that it is virtually impossible to make any predictions about the economic consequences of Maastricht. There will still be boom and slump in the international economy. Much will still depend on our own reactions to changing circumstances. The valuable survey of the likely impact of the structural funds by the ESRI comes to the moderately

→

optimistically conclusion that 55,000 new jobs could be created by the year 2000. But the authors scrupulously spell out the inevitable problematical nature of this type of prediction. Their qualifications naturally tend to get lost in the mouths of protagonists.

. . .

Critics are also correct to claim that a monetary union without a fiscal union – without internal redistributive mechanisms in the budget of the community – poses potential threats for Ireland. Yet, some of the critics also seem to oppose the idea of a closer political union, or even our continued EC membership at all. But a fiscal union is likely to bring a political union closer. The political power that the community would need to make a fiscal union work would require a giant step towards a genuine European union.

The needs of monetary integration will impose stricter limits on public spending. The targets for budget deficits, inflation rates, and interest rates, will limit our range of policy options. So will the requirement that significant progress be made in reducing the national debt towards 60% of GDP. But it is very much in the national interest to reduce the national debt quickly. The national debt situation makes significant tax reduction, or significant improvements in social policy, very difficult.

Any responsible government would identify reduction of the national debt as a priority for public policy, irrespective of EC requirements. There is a certain irony in Maastricht forcing self-interest on us.

. . .

Little attention has been devoted to the implications of the proposals for a European Central Bank for the domestic role of our Central Bank. Central Banks are intended to become more independent, and the European Central Bank, which is planned to evolve in a few years from the interim European Monetary Institute, will enjoy a large measure of power without responsibility. The bankers will have virtually no democratic accountability, despite soothing words to the contrary in the Treaty.

. . .

The Irish economy has recorded an uneven performance since entry to the EC. It is not true, however, that membership of the EC can be blamed for most of our economic ills. That is pure escapism.

. . .

It was not EC membership that obliged us to embark on the borrowing binge that has so damaged the economy. It was not EC membership that obliged us to follow incomes policies that have contributed to spiralling unemployment in the exposed sector. It was not EC membership that caused the baby-boom that has increased dependency ratios. It is not EC membership that leaves the linkages between multi-national and indigenous suppliers so weak. It is not EC membership that has inhibited the emergence of a genuine enterprise culture in Ireland.

The simple fact is that we entered the EC with no strategy for long-term national development. It took nearly twenty years for even an Institute of European Studies to be established to produce regular systematic appraisal of our performance. Many of our negotiators have given brilliant individual turns. But tactical skills cannot compensate for national strategic inadequacy.

. . .

There is no realistic alternative for Ireland outside the EC. But that does not mean there are no alternatives for Ireland within the EC, with or without Maastricht. There are. It is to these we should be turning our minds at this stage. Maastricht, if implemented, changes some of our options. It does not absolve us from responsibility for the quality of our own performance. It is still up to ourselves to raise our game to produce more consistently effective performance in the future than in the past.

Source: *The* Irish Independent, *11 June 1992.*

Arguments supporting Irish participation in the single currency

On completion of EMU, it is envisaged that all transactions will be carried out in a common currency. Compared to the present situation where each member state has its own national currency, a transformation to a single currency should result in lower transaction costs. One important transaction cost which will be eliminated is the cost of converting the domestic currency to foreign currencies when goods are imported and exported. Since most of Irish trade is conducted with other EU countries, this saving should be significant. At present, it is estimated that the elimination of transaction costs alone should increase Ireland's GDP by an additional 1%.

Also, exchange rate risk will be eliminated. Exchange rate risk occurs because exchange rates may change between the time when a sale is negotiated and when the goods and services are actually delivered. Large firms can eliminate this risk by purchasing foreign currencies in the forward exchange market to ensure that they pay in the future the price that they agree today. However, this is costly and requires a level of expertise, often lacking in small exporting/importing firms.

Many believe that a single currency will lead to increased competition and trade within the single currency area. Price discrepancies will be more obvious to firms. A higher price, charged in a market of a member state, should signal firms from other countries that opportunities exist in that market. Increased competition should lead to lower prices for consumers. Additionally, heightened competition should strengthen European firms and prepare them to compete in other markets like North America and the Far East.

Economic and social cohesion is an essential component of monetary union and the single currency. In practice, this involves the transfer of funds from the wealthy nations to the weaker nations. Ireland has benefited substantially from these EU funds. Currently it is the largest net beneficiary per head of EU funding. During the period 1989–93 Ireland received over £3 billion in funds which were used in the areas of human resources, agriculture, industry and physical infrastructure. Many worthwhile projects, beyond the means of the Irish state and the private sector, have been co-financed from the EU exchequer.

Another argument in favour of the move to a single currency area is the positive effects which have resulted from the convergence criteria. These requirements have acted as a constraint on the Irish authorities when dealing with the public finances in the recent past. Given the events of the late 1970s and the early 1980s when public expenditure was out of control, restrictions on the public finances is a welcome feature of Irish budgetary policy. In terms of its financial position, Ireland's ranking within the EU continues to improve.

Finally, a European Central bank, independent from national governments and political favouritism is likely to have as its aim price stability within the context of a stable economic environment. A country such as Ireland which relies heavily on foreign trade is likely to benefit from such an institution as the ESCB.

All of these changes are likely to impact favourably on Irish economic growth, as measured by GDP.

Arguments opposing Irish participation in the single currency

By far the most important economic argument of the opponents of the single currency is the future consequences for the Irish economy if Ireland enters and Britain 'opts out'. Although the level of trade with Britain has fallen in the past thirty years, it is still Ireland's most important trading partner and the outlet for most indigenous exports. Opponents of EMU argue that the scenario of Irish participation in the single currency without the UK is a non-starter. They are particularly concerned that the exchange rate links between EU countries inside the single currency area and those outside will not be strong enough. If the Euro appreciates against sterling, Irish manufacturers will become increasingly uncompetitive in their main export market. They argue that Ireland is sacrificing present employment in the hope that it will improve employment prospects in the future. This is considered to be an unacceptable risk for a country with such a high unemployment rate.

Another significant issue is the problem of peripherality and whether EMU can lead to economic convergence. A brief look at history would indicate that economic activity tends towards the centre, where the benefits of economies of scale are most evident. Although labour costs tend to be much lower in the peripheral regions compared to the more central regions, further economic integration may result only in a widening of the wealth gap between the core nations and the weaker nations of the EU.[34]

We have already mentioned the positive aspect to the convergence criteria. There is a downside, however, to these requirements. Given the present state of the Irish public finances, any attempt by the authorities to meet all five convergence criteria, and the debt/GDP criterion in particular, would only result in a severe contraction of the economy. In order for the authorities to meet the debt/GDP target of 60%, they would have to cut expenditure and increase taxes. A highly contractionary policy, as described here, would only reduce demand and, in turn, reduce employment. This option could prove to be politically unacceptable.

Another drawback is the absence of a fiscal union, which exists in other monetary unions like Australia and the United States. Member states of the EU do not share common tax and welfare systems. If there is a localised demand or supply shock in the US, the tax burden is reduced and social welfare payments increase, acting as 'automatic stabilisers' for the local economy. An adverse shock to an EU state is not followed by an automatic transfer of funds from the EU or a reduction of tax payments to the EU. Because of the convergence criteria, the national government is limited in its response to negative shocks. The government deficit/GDP ratio cannot exceed 3%. Given the UK's fierce resistance to a fiscal union, it is unlikely that it will be adopted by the EU in the near future.

Finally, devaluation as a policy option will no longer be available in a single currency market. In the past, public authorities have tackled unemployment by devaluing the domestic currency in order to boost foreign demand for Irish products. This will no longer be possible. Related to this is the issue of policy sovereignty. Membership in the EMU is likely to result in a loss of autonomy, and in particular control over monetary policy. This is an important issue in the UK and Germany where an independent monetary policy is a central part of their overall economic strategy. In

Ireland, it is not such an important issue because monetary policy is outside the control of the Irish authorities.

Summary

1. The balance of payments is an accounting record of all transactions between economic agents of one country and the rest of the world. It comprises a current and a capital account. The current account records the movement of all goods and services whereas the capital account is a statement of all capital transactions into and out of a country. The way in which the balance of payments actually balances depends largely on the exchange rate regime.
2. An exchange rate is the price of one currency in terms of another. Factors which influence the exchange rate include the level of foreign trade, interest rate differentials, inflation differentials, speculation and income differentials. There are a number of different exchange rate regimes. Under a fixed exchange rate system the Central Banks are obliged to maintain currencies at predetermined rates in terms of gold or of a 'hard' currency. Under a flexible exchange rate system, the exchange rate is determined by the forces of demand and supply. Semi-fixed exchange rate systems and managed floating systems are other examples of exchange rate regimes.
3. The European Monetary System is an example of a semi-fixed exchange rate system. Its aim is to create a zone of monetary stability. Central to the EMS is its exchange rate mechanism wherein member states are committed to a central rate and a band of fluctuation. Central Banks, in attempting to support the value of a currency, can intervene using external reserves or by changing interest rates or realigning the currency within the ERM.
4. A realignment within the ERM can be either in the form of a revaluation when the currency's relative value is increased or a devaluation when the currency's relative value is decreased. With a devaluation the level of exports is likely to increase, jobs in the exposed sector may be saved and the pressure on interest rates may be reduced. The drawbacks include higher import prices, the possibility of higher interest rates in the long term, an increase in the size of the foreign debt and larger debt service repayments. Devaluation will no longer be a policy option if a single currency is adopted in the EU.
5. Economic and Monetary Union has been an aim of the EU since its foundation. Central to the economic union is the creation of a single market where the flow of goods, services, labour and capital is unrestricted. Monetary union involves the creation of a single currency and one Central Bank. Co-ordination of economic policies is another feature of EMU. The three stages towards EMU are laid out in the Maastricht treaty. In order for member states to prepare themselves for the transition to a single currency, a set of macroeconomic targets has to be met. These convergence criteria relate to inflation rates, interest rates, exchange rates and a country's fiscal position.
6. The aim of Irish exchange rate policy is price stability. This is best achieved, according to the monetary authorities, by fixing the Irish pound to other member states' currencies within the ERM. Ireland's experience within the ERM has been

mixed. Sterling's absence from the exchange rate mechanism of the EMS causes policy problems for the Irish authorities, and trading problems for Irish businesses. Notwithstanding this dilemma, Ireland is fully committed to EMU. Being a small open economy, Ireland is likely to benefit from a market of 345 million people where the adoption of a single currency is likely to eliminate exchange rate volatility and reduce both transaction costs and interest rates. However, the dangers of EMU and in particular the issues of peripherality and the participation of the UK, cannot be ignored.

Key terms

Balance of payments
Current account
Merchandise trade balance
Capital account
Exchange rate
Flexible exchange rate system
Fixed exchange rate system
External reserves
Net residual
Managed floating
Semi-fixed exchange rate system
European Monetary System
European currency unit
European monetary co-operation fund
Exchange rate mechanism

Fluctuation bands
Foreign exchange intervention
Realignment
Devaluation
Revaluation
Economic and monetary union
The Maastricht treaty
Internal market
European Monetary Institute
European system of central banks
Convergence criteria
Purchasing power parity
Economic and social cohesion
Peripherality
Fiscal union

Review questions

1. Explain the term 'balance of payments'. Distinguish between the trade balance, the current account balance and the capital account balance.
2. Imagine that the only two currencies traded on the foreign exchange market are the UK pound sterling and the Irish pound. Explain how the IR£/UK£ exchange rate is determined. What factors influence this exchange rate? Explain.
3. Explain the link between the balance of payments and the different exchange rate systems.
4. Explain how the EMS operates. Briefly outline the background to and the details of the 1992–93 currency crisis.
5. (a) Outline the three stages to EMU as laid down in the Maastricht treaty.
   (b) How successful has Ireland been in meeting the convergence criteria? Support your answer.
6. (a) Critically assess Ireland's membership of the ERM.
   (b) What are the benefits and drawbacks to EMU as they relate specifically to Ireland?

Working problems

1. Items normally found in a balance of payments statement are randomly listed in Table 14.7. You are a Central Bank employee and it is your job to set up the balance of payments statement in its customary format, pre changes dated July 1996 (i.e. as it appears in the quarterly Central Bank bulletin which you can use as a source of information). You are also required to insert headings where appropriate.

Table 14.7: The balance of payments

Gross other interest outflows	−1,041	Imports	−12,114
Remuneration of employees	16	Government securities	1,320
National debt interest	−973	Net residual	801
Net balance on capital account	−453	Semi–State companies	83
Other Private capital	−1,953	Associated Banks	−493
Net balance on current account	−348	Other services	−863
External Reserves	640	Other transportation	265
Gross profits, dividends, royalties outflows	−2,564	Exports	14,358
Other public transactions	−307	International freight	77
Exchequer foreign borrowing	−50	Gross inflows	1,329
International transfers	1,108	Other licensed banks	146
Other financial institutions	115	Tourism and Travel	53
Counterpart to valuation changes	46		

2. The fifteen member states of the EU are as follows: Austria, Belgium, Denmark, Finland, France, Germany, Greece, Holland, Ireland, Italy, Luxembourg, Portugal, Spain, Sweden, United Kingdom. There has been some debate recently within the EU on the possibility of a multi-tier approach to the adoption of a single currency. Imagine you are a member of the EMI committee and you are proposing a three-tier system based on the performance of the economies in 1995 (see Table 14.6). It is your job to form three groups from the countries listed. Make your selection and defend your choice. What, do you think, will be the response to your proposal from the Irish delegation?

Multi-choice questions

1. An increase in imports from the UK will:
   (a) push the supply curve of Irish pounds to the left, leading to an increase in the IR£/UK£ exchange rate;
   (b) push the demand curve for Irish pounds to the right, leading to an increase in the IR£/UK£ exchange rate;
   (c) push the demand curve for Irish pounds to the left, leading to a reduction in the IR£/UK£ exchange rate;
   (d) push the supply curve of Irish pounds to the right, leading to a reduction in the IR£/UK£ exchange rate;
   (e) none of the above.

2. Suppose US national income increases. All other things being equal, the IR£/US$ exchange rate:

(a) increases on account of a rise in imports from the US;
(b) decreases on account of a rise in imports from the US;
(c) increases on account of a rise in exports to the US;
(d) decreases on account of a rise in exports to the US;
(e) none of the above.

3. There is a surplus in the current account of the balance of payments. Under a fixed exchange rate system this is reflected in:

(a) a rise in external reserves;
(b) a fall in the exchange rate;
(c) a fall in external reserves;
(d) both (a) and (b) above;
(e) both (b) and (c) above.

4. The central rate of the DM/Frf before August 1993 was DM1 = 3.3539Frf, with a 2.25% band of fluctuation. The upper limit (rounded off to two decimal points) was:

(a) 3.56;
(b) 3.41;
(c) 3.28;
(d) 3.43;
(e) none of the above.

5. The Treaty on European Union:

(a) is an amendment to the Treaty of Rome;
(b) arose out of the Intergovernmental Conference of 1991;
(c) sets out the path to EMU;
(d) is commonly known as the Maastricht treaty;
(e) all of the above.

6. If the convergence criteria were to be observed rigidly, Ireland would not meet the:

(a) deficit/GDP criterion;
(b) interest rate criterion;
(c) debt/GDP criterion;
(d) inflation rate criterion;
(e) exchange rate criterion.

True or false

1. The balance of payments statement always balances. _____
2. If sterling is the base currency and the Irish pound is the counter currency, then the exchange rate is expressed as the number of Irish pounds per one UK pound. _____

3. If the Irish pound strengthens and approaches its upper limit, the Central Bank can do one of three things: sell Irish pounds on the foreign exchange market, increase interest rates or devalue the Irish pound. _____

4. Devaluation is simply another term for depreciation. _____

5. The ultimate aim of Irish exchange rate policy is parity with sterling. _____

6. EMU involves a monetary and fiscal union. _____

Fill in the blanks

The balance of _____ is a record of all transactions between one country and the rest of the world. It is divided into a _____ account and a capital account. It is closely related to the exchange rate which is simply the _____ of one currency in terms of another. Under a flexible exchange rate regime, the exchange rate between the two currencies is determined in the _____ _____ market by the demand for and _____ of the respective currencies. In turn, these are determined by the level of _____ and imports and also by the level of _____ flows. The Irish pound belongs to a _____-_____ exchange rate system, called the _____. A member of the EMS exchange rate mechanism is committed to a _____ _____ against other member states' currencies and a _____ ___ _____. In keeping the currency within the limits, the Central Bank has three options available; foreign exchange _____ which involves the use of _____ _____, a change of interest rates or a _____ of the currency. The Irish pound has been devalued twice since it joined in _____ ; by _____% in 1986 and by 10% in _____ . The latter came at the end of the currency crisis of 1992/93 when the _____ and sterling left the system, the peseta, the _____ and the Irish pound were all devalued and the unofficial link which the _____ currencies had with the ECU was broken. The weakening of the _____ is a setback to EMU. The _____ treaty aims for a _____ currency by 1999 at the latest. Ireland is fully committed to EMU and, by meeting the _____ ___ , hopes to be in the 'fast track' to EMU.

CASE STUDY

Extract from **The Irish Times**
Humpty-Dumpty ERM not easily fixed
by Cliff Taylor

The EC finance ministers have recognised the obvious. The Humpty-Dumpty that was the old EC Exchange Rate Mechanism cannot easily be put back together again. Having sat back and watched the old ERM being torn apart in a year of turmoil, the finance ministers have now realised that there were fundamental problems with the old system. Suggestions immediately after last month's meeting which agreed the major ERM reform that currencies could quickly move back to the old 2.25% ERM bands have been quietly dropped. Now even the Minister for Finance, Mr Ahern, speaking at yesterday's meeting

→

of ministers, recognises that this would not be advisable.

For as long as the German economy remains affected by the aftermath of unification and German interest rates remain inappropriate for many of the other European states, trying to reform the old band would be only setting up many of the currencies for further attacks from the market. Along with his European colleagues, Mr Ahern yesterday emphasised that he remained committed to Economic and Monetary Union and a single currency. All are agreed that the European Monetary Institute, the institution proposed in the Maastricht Treaty as the forerunner to the EC central bank, should be established on schedule at the start of next year.

But the unspoken feeling at official level across Europe is that the treaty timetable for the move to a single currency over which the EMI was to preside is now unachievable. As things stand, the EMI is being set up in something of a vacuum. Europe's politicians obviously see the new institution as a crucial political signal that they will not abandon outright the plan to create an Economic and Monetary Union, whatever their doubts about the Maastricht plan. But even with the EMI in place, the obstacles to restarting the drive to monetary integration are obvious: all the European states are likely to go their own way to some extent on economic policy over the next year or so; there is strong political opposition in many of the member states to the Maastricht plan; and economic growth is likely to remain slow over the next year at least, keeping politicians focused on their home patches.

Against such a background, the attention of the EC is being increasingly drawn towards a strategy to try to combat unemployment and plans for monetary integration look set to take a back seat. One of the arguments for a single currency was that it would mean a genuine single market across Europe and boost the long-term job creation potential of the Community. But increasingly, the short-term costs were becoming too high, as the member-states clung to German-style interest rates and tried to keep government borrowing at a low level, in an attempt to meet the economic guidelines set down in the Maastricht treaty. The fundamental faultlines identified by Mr John Major a year ago have finally been recognised across the Community.

Source: The Irish Times, *September 1993.*

Questions
....

1. What are the new fluctuation bands within the ERM? What options do the Central Banks have available in order to keep the value of their currencies within these intervention limits?
2. When the EMI was set up in January 1994 Frankfurt was chosen in preference to London, one of the world's premier financial centres. Explain the rationale for such a choice.
3. What events have taken place since the Maastricht treaty of December 1991 which have put the three-stage EMU timetable for a single currency in jeopardy?

Additional case study questions based on Articles 14.1 and 14.2 from the text

Questions on Article 14.1: Irish battered by ERM crisis that Britain escaped

1. Explain the possible link between the 'five-month currency crisis' and the rise in both interest rates and the unemployment rate in Ireland.
2. Why is the exchange rate link with sterling so important to the Irish authorities?
3. In what way could the EC have come to 'Ireland's aid'? What action could the Bundesbank have taken to support the Irish pound?

Questions on Article 14.2: A question of options

1. Explain the difference between a 'fiscal union' and a 'monetary union'. How are these dealt with in the Maastricht treaty?
2. What are the implications arising from the setting up of a European Central Bank? What role, if any, will the Central Bank of Ireland play?
3. What benefits have accrued to Ireland from membership of the EU? How will enlargement of the EU affect Ireland?

[The answers are not included.]

Appendix 14.1: Purchasing power parity

Purchasing power parity (PPP) or the law of one price explains changes in exchange rates in terms of inflation differentials. PPP can be expressed in many different ways.

In its simplest form, the law of one price states that the price of a commodity in different countries, but expressed in a common currency, should be equal. It can be written as follows:

$$\boxed{P_{UK} \times E = P_{US}} \qquad [1]$$

where P_{UK} is the price of the good in the UK, E is the exchange rate (expressed as the number of dollars per one UK pound) and P_{US} is the price of the same good, sold in the US and expressed in US dollars. This is called the strong version of PPP.[35]

For example, we can compare the price of a McDonald's Big Mac in London with a Big Mac in New York by adjusting for the exchange rate.[36] In April 1995, a Big Mac cost UK£1.74 in London and US$2.32 in New York. The actual UK£/US$ exchange rate in April 1995 was UK£1 = US$1.61. We can compare the two prices by converting into a common currency. Consider converting sterling into dollars, as follows,

UK£1.74 x 1.61 = US$2.80

By converting into a common currency, in this case US$, we can compare the price of a Big Mac in New York with the price in London. If these prices are equal we can say that the law of one price holds. In this case they are not equal. In New York, a Big Mac costs US$2.32 whereas according to the law of one price a Big Mac in New York should cost US$2.80. This begs the question – why, in theory at least, should they be equal and why, it seems in practice, are they not equal? In theory, prices should equate across frontiers because of price competition and arbitrage where arbitrage is the buying and selling of goods in different markets in order to exploit price differentials and to make a riskless profit. Suppose, for example, that a personal computer is relatively cheap in the US compared to the UK. By buying them in the US and selling them in the UK, a profit can be made. As a result, US exports will increase. Holding all other things equal, this will give rise to a balance of payments surplus in the US.

Two possible results may emerge. First, the balance of payments surplus will cause an increase in the exchange rate (explained in Section 14.3). Second, the increase in demand for computers will push up the domestic price level. Either way, the differential between the domestic price level and the foreign price level diminishes. Over time, the price differential between the personal computer sold in the US and that sold in the UK disappears.

In the real world, however, factors exist which allow price differentials to persist. These factors include transport costs, tariffs, quotas and indirect taxes. These drive a wedge between prices.

Appendix 14.2: Fixed vs flexible exchange rate systems: the arguments for and against

The arguments in favour of the fixed exchange rate system are outlined below. This is followed by the case for the flexible exchange rate system.

Arguments in favour of the fixed exchange rate system

1. It creates a more stable trading environment. It facilitates international trade with importers and exporters assured of fixed payments in terms of their domestic currency. Governments need not fear the damage caused by market uncertainty or volatile exchange rate movements. International institutions operate more effectively under a fixed exchange rate system.
2. Adherence to a fixed exchange rate system can result in favourable economic conditions at home. For example, low inflation, stable interest rates and a favourable trade balance can all result from a fixed exchange rate policy.
3. The transition to a single currency is easier from a fixed exchange rate system than it is from a flexible exchange rate system. Fewer adjustments and fewer sacrifices are necessary.
4. Fiscal policy is effective under a fixed exchange rate system.
5. By imposing increased discipline on internal economic policy, it can sometimes prevent national governments from adopting irresponsible economic policies for short-term political gain.

Arguments in favour of the flexible exchange rate system
....

1. Adherence to a flexible exchange rate system does not involve any costly inter-ventions by the monetary authorities. Imbalances will be corrected automatically if there are any shocks to the economy. The costs which are normally associated with the depletion of a country's external reserves are eliminated.
2. There is no loss of autonomy with a flexible exchange rate system. There is no balance of payments constraint on domestic policy. Hence, the government is free to pursue whatever policy suits domestic conditions.
3. In times of severe recession the government may allow the currency to depreciate. This would increase the volume of exports and in doing so boost demand. Also, during inflationary times the government may allow the currency to appreciate. In doing so, it may stem the inflationary pressures from abroad. Also, flexible exchange rates can insulate the domestic economy from external shocks.
4. The exchange rate at any given time is the 'true' exchange rate; true in the sense that it is determined by the forces of demand and supply. There is no Central Bank intervention. Currencies are not under- or over-valued or misaligned.
5. Under a flexible exchange rate system, monetary policy is effective.

Appendix 14.3: The effectiveness of monetary and fiscal policy in an open economy: the Mundell-Fleming model

We use the Mundell-Fleming model which was first developed in the early 1960s to assess the effectiveness of fiscal and monetary policy within an open economy framework. We examine both policies under fixed and flexible exchange rate systems with the assumption that capital flows are perfectly mobile.

Monetary policy under a fixed exchange rate regime
....

Consider an increase in the money supply by the Central Bank. As the money supply increases, interest rates fall and national income increases. Because domestic interest rates are lower than world interest rates, an outflow of capital results. A deficit in the current account also emerges as a result of the higher income levels and the subsequent higher import levels. We know from our analysis of the exchange rate market that an overall balance of payments deficit causes a depreciation of the domestic currency against other currencies. Because of its membership in the exchange rate system, the Central Bank is obliged to maintain the value of its currency between certain limits. Hence, the Central Bank intervenes by selling the stock of foreign currency in exchange for domestic currency. By taking these pounds out of circulation the domestic money supply decreases. In doing so, the economy reverts back to its original level of national income. Hence, an independent monetary policy is ineffective.

Fiscal policy under a fixed exchange rate regime

Consider an increase in spending by the government. As government expenditure increases, interest rates and national income levels rise. Because domestic interest rates are now higher than world interest rates, an inflow of capital results, leading to a capital account surplus. This surplus is only partly offset by a deficit in the current account which arises because the higher income level means that more goods are imported. The overall surplus results in an increase in the exchange rate. The Central Bank intervenes in order to maintain the value of the domestic currency between certain limits. It buys foreign currency and sells domestic currency. By injecting more pounds into circulation, the Central Bank increases the domestic money supply. In doing so, it increases income levels further. Hence, fiscal policy is effective.

Monetary policy under a flexible exchange rate regime

Consider an increase in the money supply by the Central Bank. As the money supply increases, interest rates fall. With domestic interest rates now lower than world interest rates, an outflow of capital results. A capital outflow results in a lowering of the domestic currency against other currencies. As the domestic currency depreciates, imports become more expensive and exports become cheaper. We know from the Keynesian income determination model that an increase in exports will increase the level of national income. Under this flexible exchange rate system national income increases, initially out of the increase in the money supply and subsequently from an increase in exports. Hence, monetary policy is effective.

Fiscal policy under a flexible exchange rate regime

Consider an increase in spending by the government. As government expenditure increases, interest rates and income levels rise. The increase in interest rates leads to an inflow of capital, resulting in a capital account surplus. This surplus is partly offset by a deficit in the current account which arises from the higher income levels and the higher import levels. This overall balance of payments surplus results in an increase in the exchange rate. As the exchange rate appreciates, exports become more expensive whereas imports become cheaper. The subsequent decline in exports reduces the income level which in turn reverts to its original position. Hence, fiscal policy is ineffective.

In summary, under a fixed exchange rate system fiscal policy is more effective than monetary policy whereas under a flexible exchange rate system monetary policy is more effective than fiscal policy.

CHAPTER 15

MACROECONOMIC ISSUES

'Inflation occurs when too much money is chasing too few goods.'

Anonymous

'We believe that if men have the talent to invent new machines that put men out of work, they have the talent to put those men back to work.'[1]

John F. Kennedy

'No nation was ever ruined by trade.'[2]

Benjamin Franklin

Chapter objectives

Upon completing this chapter, the student should understand:

- the meaning of inflation;
- the causes, consequences and remedies;
- problems of defining and measuring unemployment;
- the costs and theories of unemployment;
- traditional trade theory, comparative advantage and trade barriers;
- new trade theory and economies of scale.

Outline

15.1 Inflation
15.2 Unemployment
15.3 International trade

Introduction

There are many important and controversial issues in macroeconomics. Throughout the centuries, economists, sociologists and philosophers together with lorry drivers, domestic workers and shopkeepers have argued over the costs of inflation, the evils of unemployment and the merits of free trade. The debate remains lively because problems relating to these issues remain unresolved.

In this chapter, we will begin by discussing the issue of inflation, and then continue with the topics of unemployment and international trade.

15.1 Inflation

15.1.1 Defining and measuring inflation

We will begin by defining the relevant terms.

Definition
● ● ● ● ● ●

Inflation refers to a rise in the general or aggregate price level.

Alternatively, inflation can be defined as a fall in the value of money because it erodes the purchasing power of money. In any discussion on inflation, we generally refer to changes in the inflation rate.

Definition
● ● ● ● ● ●

The inflation rate is the percentage change in the price level from one period to the next period.

Since inflation refers to an increase in the price level, the percentage change is positive.

Definition
● ● ● ● ● ●

Deflation is a fall in the general level of prices.

In this situation, the percentage change in the price level is negative; the price level is falling from one period to the next. This phenomenon has not been observed on a yearly basis in Ireland since the mid-1940s. Often, this term is used loosely, to refer to policies or events which will lead to a slowdown in economic activity. Contractionary monetary and fiscal policies are sometimes labelled as 'deflationary'. A more accurate description is 'disinflationary'.[3]

Definition
● ● ● ● ● ●

Disinflation is defined as a reduction in the rate of inflation.

In this case, the rate of inflation is positive but decreasing from one period to the next. Contractionary policies normally reduce, rather than reverse inflation.

There are different categories of inflation including creeping inflation, hyper-inflation and stagflation. Creeping inflation exists when the rise in the price level is both relatively modest and stable. Hyper-inflation refers to a situation where inflation is escalating and the value of money diminishes so quickly that it ceases to perform its main functions. Table 15.1 shows the unfortunate state of the Hungarian currency between 1938 and 1946. Finally, stagflation refers to the simultaneous existence of both high rates of inflation and stagnant or negative economic growth. Unemployment is often a problem during periods of hyper-inflation or stagflation.

Table 15.1: The Hungarian hyper-inflation 1945–46

	Mid-1938 = 100	% increase at an annual rate
Mid-1939	100	–
Mid-1941	139	18
Mid-1943	217	25
15 July 1945	9,200	527
31 Aug.	17,300	15,000
30 Sept.	38,900	1,700,000
31 Oct.	250,300	5.0×10^{11}
30 Nov.	1,545,700	3.1×10^{11}
31 Dec.	3,778,000	4.5×10^{6}
31 Jan. 1946	7,089,000	1.9×10^{5}
28 Feb.	45,845,300	5.4×10^{11}
31 Mar.	205,060,000	6.4×10^{9}
30 Apr.	3,575,600,000	7.9×10^{16}
31 May	1,076,400,000,000	5.5×10^{31}
30 June	470,300,000,000,000	4.8×10^{33}
31 July	12,572,000,000,000,000,000	1.3×10^{55}

Source: Falush, P. 'The Hungarian Hyper-Inflation of 1945–46', *NatWest Quarterly Review*, August 1976.

Inflation is measured using a price index.

Definition
● ● ● ● ● ●

A price index measures the level of prices in one period as a percentage of the level in another period called the base period.

The price index most frequently discussed by the media in Ireland is the Consumer Price Index.[4]

Definition
● ● ● ● ● ●

The Consumer Price Index (CPI) is designed to measure the average change in the level of the prices paid (inclusive of all indirect taxes) for consumer goods and services by all private households in the country.

A price index is composed of a number of goods and services, each with its own weighting. For the CPI, these weights express the proportion of the household's budget which is spent on each category of good and service.[5] The weights are updated every seven years following the publication of the *Household Budget Survey*.[6] The 'basket of goods' used for the Irish CPI and the respective weightings of each category are shown in Table 15.2.

Table 15.2: Weights used for the CPI in 1996

Food	22.8497
Services and related expenditure	16.7232
Transport	13.9402
Alcoholic drink	12.6298
Housing	8.0385
Clothing and footwear	6.1311
Fuel and light	4.9038
Other goods	6.3810
Household durables	3.5786
Tobacco	4.8242
	100.0000

Source: Central Statistics Office.

We will calculate the Irish rate of inflation for the year 1995 using the CPI. The base year is 1985. The CPI was 129.9 in 1994 and 133.2 in 1995. To find the annual inflation rate for 1995 we use the following formula:

$$\text{1995 Inflation rate} = \frac{\text{CPI 1995} - \text{CPI 1994}}{\text{CPI 1994}} \times 100 \qquad [15.1]$$

Insert values for CPI 1994 and for CPI 1995 to get

$$\frac{133.2 - 129.9}{129.9} \times 100 = \frac{3.3}{129.9} \times 100 = 2.5\%$$

Using the CPI as an index, the inflation rate for 1995 was approximately 2.5%. In other words, the general price level in Ireland rose by 2.5% in 1995.

In Ireland the inflation rate is measured by the Central Statistics Office (CSO) on a quarterly and yearly basis.[7]

The CPI is the most frequently mentioned price index, but there are others. Some indices concentrate on the price of particular types of goods. Examples include the Capital Goods Price Index for Industry and the Import and Export Indices. Others refer to particular sectors of the economy like the Agricultural Output Price Index, the Agricultural Input Price Index and the Building and Construction Index. All of these indices are published monthly by the CSO.

Finally, the GDP deflator is a price index which measures changes in the entire range of goods and services produced in the economy. It is the most comprehensive measure of inflation. We can calculate the GDP deflator by using the following formula:

$$\text{GDP deflator} = \frac{\text{Nominal GDP}}{\text{Real GDP}} \times 100 \qquad [15.2]$$

In 1995, nominal GDP (GDP at current prices) was £38,616m. Real GDP or GDP at constant prices was £34,046m. With a base year of 1990, the GDP price index or deflator is 1.13 approximately. This indicates that prices increased by about 13% between 1990 and 1995.

15.1.2 Consequences of inflation

The consequences of inflation are many and varied. Before we discuss them, we will define some relevant terms.

Definition
● ● ● ● ● ●

The nominal rate of interest is the actual rate of interest which is charged when money is borrowed.

Definition
● ● ● ● ● ●

The real rate of interest is the nominal rate of interest adjusted for the inflation rate.

It is calculated by subtracting the inflation rate from the nominal rate of interest. For example, if the nominal interest rate is 12% and the inflation rate is 5%, the real rate of interest is 7%.

Definition
● ● ● ● ● ●

People are on fixed incomes, if their income is set at a particular nominal amount which is not adjusted for inflation.

Definition
● ● ● ● ● ●

Menu costs refer to the costs which result when prices are adjusted.

For example, wholesalers must publish and mail new catalogues if prices increase. At the retail level, vending machines must be reprogrammed and merchandise must be physically reticketed when prices change. These costs are explicit and are fairly easy to monitor. What is more difficult to calculate is the loss of goodwill which firms encounter if they constantly increase their prices. Also, retailing firms may be slower to reorder if all of their current stock must be repriced.

The following is a comprehensive, although not exhaustive list of the possible effects of inflation.

- Depending on the level of real interest rates, inflation can involve a redistribution of income from lenders to borrowers. For example, suppose Helen borrows £2,000 from her local bank manager at a fixed rate of interest of 6% for one year. Unexpectedly, the annual inflation rate increases to 10%. The real rate of interest paid by Helen is negative, at minus 4%. When repaying the loan, Helen will return pounds to the bank which are worth less in purchasing power terms than the pounds lent to her by the bank. As a result of inflation, the borrower gains at the expense of the lender. In general, borrowers welcome unanticipated inflation. Interestingly, the biggest borrower of all is government.

- Savings are adversely affected by inflation. Since inflation reduces the value of money, any stock of savings over time will lose its purchasing power. The inflation-adjusted interest rate, i.e. the real rate of interest, may be low or even negative. Hence, during inflationary times savings are discouraged and consumption is encouraged.

- Those sections of society that are on fixed money incomes lose. Moreover, it is usually the more vulnerable sections of society, pensioners for example, who are on fixed money incomes. In this instance inflation is a form of 'tax' on money holdings. The adjustment of incomes in line with price changes, called indexation, allows for some protection against inflation.

- Inflation prevents money from fulfilling its functions effectively. The primary function of money is as a medium of exchange. During periods of hyper-inflation, the domestic currency is shunned because of its rapid loss of value. If possible, exchanges are transacted in a reliable, foreign currency. Bartering, which is both time-consuming and inefficient, is often a feature of an economy experiencing hyper-inflation.

- Inflation often changes the pattern of investment. Capital moves out of assets like government bonds or gilts because the real rate of interest is low or negative. Investment in 'real' assets like property, fine art or gold increases because, in general, they appreciate over time. These assets are safe but unproductive. In a period characterised by growing inflation, productive investments, which lead to national economic growth, may be avoided because firms are unable to evaluate the potential for profit. Inflation breeds uncertainty which is generally unfavourable to investment decisions.

- Inflation can also affect the level of government expenditure and revenue. For example, if there is no indexation built into the tax system, tax revenues automatically increase as inflation forces more taxpayers into higher tax brackets. This is commonly known as fiscal drag. In effect, it is a transfer of resources from the taxpayer to the government.

- Inflation has serious implications for international competitiveness. For example, if Ireland's inflation rate is low relative to her trading partners' inflation rate within a fixed exchange rate system, a competitive advantage is gained. Exports increase and contribute to an increase in Irish GDP. In the absence of a fixed exchange rate system, inflation differentials can cause movements in exchange rates. Refer to Section 14.2.

- Inflation can lead to money illusion. Money illusion exists when economic agents confuse changes in money variables with changes in real variables. In times of inflation, workers who receive higher wages might be fooled into thinking that they are better off. In reality, however, the wage increase is offset by the higher prices. These workers are said to be suffering from money illusion.

Finally, the effects of inflation are often different depending on whether inflation is anticipated or unanticipated. In general, anticipated inflation imposes fewer costs on society than unanticipated inflation. The normal costs to anticipated inflation are changes in menu costs and the extra time spent managing the finances. In turn, this may involve more frequent visits to the bank. The cost of these extra trips is called the 'shoe leather' effect.

Unanticipated inflation is not built into wage contracts or tax brackets/bands. The additional costs associated with unexpected inflation include misallocation of resources, income redistribution, tax distortions and the adverse impact on the incentive to save.

15.1.3 Explanations of inflation

Many explanations of inflation have been advanced over the years. In this section, we will look at four: demand pull, the Quantity Theory of Money, cost push, and imported inflation. We will also briefly discuss the role of expectations. Although we will discuss each case separately, in reality they may act simultaneously.

Demand pull inflation

We will begin by defining the concept of demand pull inflation and then we will explain it within the context of the model of income determination.

Definition
● ● ● ● ● ●

Demand pull inflation occurs when the total demand for goods and services is greater than the total supply of goods and services.

There is unsatisfied demand at the existing price level. The excess demand 'pulls up' the price level.

Demand pull inflation is generally but not exclusively associated with the Keynesian school. Although Keynes was primarily concerned with the issue of unemployment, he did consider the implications of inflation in an essay that was published in 1940 entitled *How to Pay for the War*. In this essay, Keynes looked at the problem of an increase in government spending caused by a war, particularly if the economy is at full-employment equilibrium at the outbreak.

We can illustrate this idea by returning to the model of income determination described in Section 10.1. Although the equilibrium can exist at any point along the 45° line, we are specifying that initially equilibrium is at full employment. This is shown as point E in Figure 15.1 where the aggregate expenditure curve AE cuts the 45° line.

Figure 15.1: The inflationary gap caused by demand pull inflation

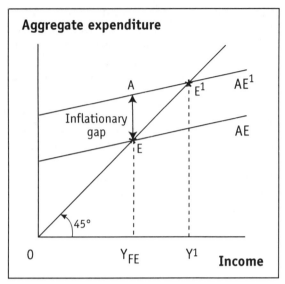

Recall that any increase in autonomous expenditure, of which government spending is one component, causes the AE curve to shift upward. In this case, government spending increases to purchase the arms and supplies needed to fight the war. The AE curve shifts upwards from AE to AE^1. Output at the new equilibrium, E^1, is above full employment. Keynes agreed that in this situation, inflation would logically result (see Appendix 15.1 on the Phillips curve).

Price is not a variable in this model. However, we have labelled the 'inflationary' gap in the diagram.

● Definition
● ● ● ● ● ●

An inflationary gap exists when the equilibrium of the economy is greater than the full-employment level of output.

In Figure 15.1 the inflationary gap is measured by |AE|.

This model demonstrates the essential features of demand pull inflation. Inflation is caused by excess demand which causes the price level to increase. In the first instance, the excess demand may be caused by greater spending or tax cuts or some combination of these factors.

The Quantity Theory of Money

The Quantity Theory of Money (QTM) is the oldest theory of inflation. It is attributed to the classical economists, but it was popularised by Irving Fisher at the beginning of this century (see Information Box 15.1). In the years following World War II, inflation was not a pressing issue and the QTM was considered to be an appropriate topic for a course on the history of economic thought. However, the monetarist Milton Friedman revived the QTM in 1956 with the essay 'The Quantity Theory of Money – A Restatement'.[8] The powerful policy conclusions of this model concerning the ineffectiveness of monetary policy continue to influence the thinking of monetarists in particular, and neoclassical economists in general.

The classical view

In its simplest form the QTM states that there is a relationship between the money supply and the price level. It predicts that the price level will change with changes in the money supply. The more rapid the rate of increase in the money supply, the higher the inflation rate.

The following equation describes the income version of the QTM.

$$M \overline{V} = P \overline{Y}$$

[15.3]

where: M = money supply; V = velocity of money;[9] P = the price level; Y = real income or output or GDP.

Notice that there is a bar over V and Y. This means that these variables are held constant. This is not an arbitrary decision, but reflects the assumptions of the classical economists. We can think of the velocity of money as the number of times a sum of money changes hands in a year. Advocates of this model believe that velocity is determined by institutional factors which change slowly over time. Holding real output as constant reflects the classical belief that the economy is always close to its full-employment output level.

If we hold velocity and output constant, any change in the money supply is reflected by a proportional change in the price level. Continuous increases in the money supply cause inflation. This model implies that monetary policy is ineffective. It causes deflation or inflation, but does not lead to changes in 'real' variables like output or employment.

INFORMATION BOX 15.1

The Quantity Theory of Money

Irving Fisher, the great American economist of the early twentieth century, is credited with popularising the Quantity Theory of Money.[1] In his book The Purchasing Power of Money *(1911) he began with the simple equation of exchange MV = PT where M is the quantity of money, V is the rate of turnover of money or the velocity of money, P is the price level and T is the number of transactions. Since T is difficult to measure it can be replaced by output, Y.*

As it stands, this equation is simply an identity or truism – something which is true by definition. It states that for the aggregate economy, the value of trans-actions, PT, is equal to the value of receipts, MV. A number of assumptions have to be made about the level of transactions and the velocity of money in order for this identity to be converted into a theory of inflation.

Fisher assumed that the level of transactions was fixed because it bore a close relationship with income which in the classical model was fixed at a level consistent with full employment. In addition Fisher argued that the velocity of money was determined by institutional factors which had a stabilising effect in the short term. If velocity and transactions are fixed, these assumptions transform the equation of exchange into a theory of inflation where changes in the money supply determine the price level.

Although the Cambridge version of the Quantity theory is similar, there are some important differences. Whereas Fisher focused solely on the transactions demand for money the approach developed by Marshall and Pigou extended the functions of money to include the store of value function. This cash-balance approach also allowed for some flexibility in terms of how much money was held, with individual choice playing an important role. In the Fisher model, institutional constraints prevented any freedom in terms of the amount of money held. Finally, interest rates were not ruled out of the Cambridge version as a possible factor explaining changes in money demand. It was left to others, however, including Keynes to investigate the possible relationship between interest rates and money demand (see Section 11.2).

1   *Fisher was not the first to develop the theory. It is believed that the first attempts at formulating the Quantity Theory of Money were independently made by David Hume in 1752 and Simon Newcomb in 1885.*

The monetarist view

The monetarist view can be easily understood if we return to the AD/AS model developed in Chapter 13. Recall the downward sloping AD curve which depicts the relationship between the price level and national output, *ceteris paribus*. One variable which was held constant was the money supply.

The AS curve also depicts the relationship between the price level and national output, holding the characteristics of the labour force, technology and expectations constant. The aggregate supply curve is depicted as upward sloping in the short-run as shown in Figure 15.2.

Figure 15.2: The AD/AS model

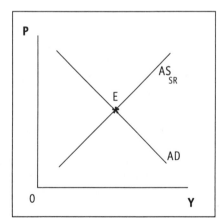

The AS curve is upward sloping, which reflects the assumption that as price rises, the output level also rises. The monetarists agree with the classical economists that the economy returns to full-employment equilibrium, represented by point E in Figure 15.2.

During the period when interest in the QTM resurged, monetarists believed in adaptive expectations (see Appendix 15.2 on expectations). Briefly, adaptive expectations refers to a phenomenon where neither management nor labour accurately interpret the meaning of a change in the price level. In the short run, they may be temporarily fooled into producing at a level of output which is higher than full employment. In the long run, the economy will return to full employment, at a higher price level.

We will demonstrate the model by illustrating an increase in the money supply which shifts the AD curve to AD^1, shown in Figure 15.3.

Figure 15.3: AD/AS model featuring adaptive expectations

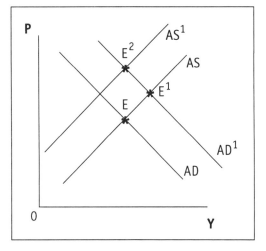

The change in the money supply has caused the price level to increase.

Firms interpret upward pressure on price as a signal to increase production. To do this, they hire more labour. Since the labour supply curve is upward sloping, they must pay a higher nominal wage. A new equilibrium is reached in (P,Y) space at E^1.

Recall that we began at full employment. The wage has increased, but so has the price level. Labour has not correctly understood that the change in the price level is eroding their purchasing power. In other words, although their nominal wage is increasing, their real wage has not increased.[10] When labour 'cops on', they will cut back the amount of labour that they are willing to supply at the new price level. This causes the AS curve to shift to AS^1 as shown in Figure 15.3. At the new equilibrium, E^2, the price level is higher, but the level of output returns to the full-employment level.

This led the monetarists to conclude that changes in the money supply have short-term effects on output, but in the long run, they are inflationary. According to Friedman, 'Inflation is always and everywhere a monetary phenomenon in the sense that it is and can be produced only by a more rapid increase in the quantity of money than in output.'[11] Essentially, he revived the QTM.[12] For more information on Milton Friedman and monetarism, see Information Box 15.2.

INFORMATION BOX 15.2

Monetarism

Monetarism is the economic school of thought which lays special emphasis on the role of money in the economy. It does not, however, confine itself to the topic of money. Monetarists have a view on the role of government, the role of the market, fiscal policy, unemployment, inflation and many other issues.

Just as the classical economists succeeded the Physiocrats, the monetarists are the modern bearers of the classical tradition. Like the classicals, monetarists believe in the efficacy and the efficiency of the market system. They are suspicious of government intervention in the economy. Gaining insights from extended periods of demand management, they cast a jaundiced eye on the efforts of government to change the level of output and employment by altering government expenditure.

It is their view of money, however, which distinguishes monetarism from other economic doctrines. According to monetarists, the rate of money growth is paramount in the determination of short-run output and long-run inflation. In order to combat inflation, money growth must not exceed output growth. A steady rate of money growth ensures low levels of inflation and facilitates long-term economic prosperity.

The emergence of monetarism in the 1970s in the US was largely due to the Nobel Laureate Milton Friedman. His most famous works include A Monetary History of the United States *and the best-seller* Free to Choose *in which he makes a strong defence of free enterprise and the market system. Although he has written widely on many different issues in economics he will be remembered for restoring many of the tenets of the classical doctrine of economics.*

The most famous proponent of monetarism was the British Prime Minister, Mrs Thatcher. With the support of Keith Joseph and Professor Alan Walters, Mrs Thatcher strongly advocated the principles of monetarism. Combating inflation became the ultimate priority for the Tory government. The economic instrument used to achieve this objective was the money supply. Monitoring the money supply growth rate was central to the Medium Term Financial Strategy (MTFS). Fiscal spending was no longer used to increase aggregate demand. Mrs Thatcher was more concerned with how spending was to be financed.

By the late 1980s, the star of monetarism began to fall. Fiscal rectitude and scrupulous adherence to monetary targets did not ensure employment creation. While these goals have not been abandoned, most governments seem to believe that some intervention is necessary to combat the rising rates of unemployment that persist across western Europe. This does not signal a return to Keynesian demand management, but it does suggest a more prominent role for government in the economy than advocated by either the classicals or the monetarists.

Cost push inflation

During the post-war years inflation continued even in times when there was little or no evidence of excess demand in the economy. This prompted economists to examine other explanations and, in particular, possible causes arising from the supply side of the economy.

We begin by defining cost push inflation and then we will explain its application using the AD/AS model.

Definition
● ● ● ● ● ●

> Cost push inflation occurs when the source of upward pressure on prices is the rising costs of the factors of production in the absence of any corresponding increase in productivity.

The most important factor cost is labour. Consider a situation where an important labour union signs an agreement for a significant wage increase which sets off a round of wage increases throughout the economy. This causes the AS curve to shift to the left as shown in Figure 15.4.

Figure 15.4: Demonstrating cost push inflation

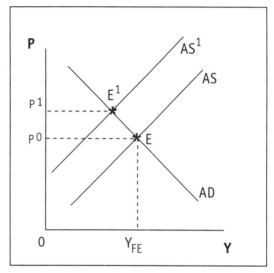

The original equilibrium, E, represents a level of output where all factors of production are fully employed. At the associated price level P^0, aggregate supply is now less than aggregate demand. In response to the wage increase, firms are unwilling to supply the original level of output to the market at that price. Eventually, the economy reaches a new equilibrium at E^1, at a higher price level and a lower level of output. Higher taxes or the imposition of more extensive legislation would result in a similar outcome.

This particular pattern of inflation can lead to a wage-price spiral. Labour unions force a wage increase. To return the economy to full employment the state responds by adopting expansionary monetary and/or fiscal policies. This shifts the AD curve to the right resulting in another increase in the price level. Labour unions look for another wage increase to compensate for higher inflation. The AS curve shifts leftwards. Once started, the spiral is difficult to end.

Imported inflation

This type of inflation is another form of cost push inflation which is particularly relevant to countries, like Ireland, with open economies. Suppose the Irish authorities devalue the Irish currency in the hope that Irish products will be more competitive in foreign markets. Many raw materials and inputs for industry are imported. As a result, Irish-based firms are faced with higher costs which, in turn, are reflected in higher prices for their finished good. This leads to inflation in the domestic market, which again leads to problems with competitiveness in foreign markets.

If policy-makers resort to another devaluation, a devaluation-inflation spiral may result. This is one reason why monetary authorities do not rush to devalue. A devaluation-inflation spiral, once started, is difficult to stop, and seriously damages the prospect for long-term growth in an economy.

Expectations

In an economy where people become accustomed to high rates of inflation, they expect it to persist into the future. Unions incorporate the inflation rate into their contract demands. To compensate for the higher prices, higher wages are sought. This, in turn, causes the price level to increase further. We can see from this that the expectation of inflation is validated by actual increases in the inflation rate. Even after the initial causes of inflation have been removed, people's expectations may cause the inflationary process to continue.

The importance of expectations in explaining the actual rate of inflation (and other related topics) has become increasingly recognised by economists in recent years.[13] As you might expect, there is considerable disagreement, and it is one of the most controversial topics in economics today (see Article 15.1).

15.1.4 Counter-inflationary policies
....

Policies aimed at combating inflation are usually categorised as either demand-side policies or supply-side policies. Although the solutions to inflation should redress the specific source of the rise in the price level, it may be difficult in reality to correctly assess the actual cause. If there is more than one source, a package of measures may be required. It may also be difficult to completely eradicate inflation. In fact it has been argued that a little inflation is not necessarily a bad thing as it may be conducive to economic growth.

Demand-side policies

In the last section, we discussed inflationary pressures placed on an economy due to a country's entry into a war. Theoretically, that increase in autonomous expenditure could be offset by either contractionary monetary or fiscal policy. Contractionary monetary policy causes an increase in the interest rate and leads to a fall in the level of private investment. Contractionary fiscal policy can take the form of a tax increase which would cut disposable income and therefore income-induced consumption. Either alternative will cause the aggregate expenditure curve to shift down towards the full-employment level of output and in doing so eliminate the inflationary gap.

Supply-side policies

There are two objectives of supply-side policies. One is to moderate inflation by increasing the rate of growth of output. The other objective is to reduce the rate of increase of the costs of production. Achieving either of these objectives shifts the AS curve to the right and is therefore deflationary as we can see from Figure 15.5.

Figure 15.5: Deflationary supply-side policies

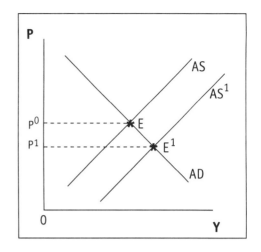

Supply-side policies generally focus on promoting competition, containing labour costs and increasing work incentives. Examples of policies which promote competition include restricting the number of mergers and takeovers. Monopoly powers are curbed to limit the control over price and profits.

Supply-side economists recommend lowering the corporate and personal tax rates which they believe will have beneficial effects on the competitiveness of firms (see Section 13.3). Although Keynes argued that the tax changes work by altering the demand side of the economy, this group of economists believe that this particular type of fiscal policy affects the supply side. The primary focus of these policies is to increase national output.

Containing labour costs can take two forms. Traditionally, supply-side economists advocate restricting the power of labour unions and avoiding legislation which guarantees a minimum wage. In neoclassical models, the economy moves towards full employment, if – and only if – wages are flexible. Unionised labour, it is believed can negotiate a wage rate above the equilibrium wage rate, causing unemployment. They argue that minimum wage legislation has the same effect. Many feel that if labour is unorganised and if contract arrangements are decentralised, wage demands will be lower and more flexible.

A different model has been used in Ireland for the past decade.[14] The social partners negotiated successive national wage agreements beginning with the Programme for National Recovery (1987). This was replaced by the Programme for Economic and Social Progress (1991) and the Programme for Competitiveness and Work (1994). The current agreement is the Partnership 2000 for Inclusion, Employment and Competitiveness. This process allows the economic interests of different sections of society to be considered in an organised way. The wage increases negotiated under these programmes have been modest, influenced by the high rates of unemployment. While many have argued that these agreements promote price stability, some commentators have argued that returning to decentralised agreements would increase labour market flexibility and lower the wage bill.

Finally, attempts at maintaining the domestic currency within a semi-fixed or fixed exchange rate system is anti-inflationary.[15] This policy ensures stable import prices from the country's main trading partners, so inflation is not imported (see Article 15.1). The option of devaluation is shunned on the basis that it will fuel inflationary pressures.

The success of all anti-inflationary policies depends on the credibility of the state. Trade unions, firms and consumers form their expectations based on government actions, rather than government statements. Policies must be both reasonable and consistently applied.

ARTICLE 15.1

Extract from The Irish Times
Red faces in Central Bank as inflation knocks knockers
by Cliff Taylor

So much for an 'over-heating' economy. The latest figures from the Central Statistics Office show that the rate of inflation was running at a moderate 2.4% in mid-August, down from 2.8% the previous quarter and below the estimates of even the most optimistic forecasters. The low inflation rate improves the prospect for interest rates and is a mortal blow for the school of thought which held that rapid economic growth would inevitably knock on to a higher rate of inflation. It adds weight to forecasts that the relationship between growth and inflation is changing fundamentally, as the old inflationary psychology of business and consumers breaks down. Inflation may not be 'dead', but it is certainly resting.

In Ireland, the strength of the pound on the currency markets is one of the key factors behind the impressive inflation performance. By reducing the price of goods imported from Britain and the US it maintains downward pressure on prices and, analysts believe, allows wholesalers and retailers to boost their profit margins without increasing the price to the consumer. Increased competition in some sectors must also be contributing. For example, the latest figures show a 2.1% quarterly fall in clothing and footwear prices, partly related to Dunnes Stores price cuts as it reopened after the strike but also reflecting fierce competition.

The Irish story of surprisingly low inflation is repeated in many other economies. Internationally, one influential theory holds that increased competition as economies integrate and new low-cost production comes on stream in places like Eastern Europe and east Asia is acting to keep a lid on prices. The evidence of the past couple of years is that inflation rates almost everywhere are much lower than would have been expected on the basis of growth rates. We may now be entering a new type of economic cycle, more reminiscent of the 1960s experience of buoyant growth and restrained inflation than anything seen since. A change in the way consumers and businesses in many countries think about inflation – called inflationary expectations in economic jargon – must also be a factor. Moderate international inflation is another key contributor to moderating price pressures in Ireland, both by restraining import costs and by keeping pressure on companies selling in export markets to moderate their own costs.

Source: The Irish Times, *15 September 1995.*

15.1.5 *The Irish experience*
....

Ireland is a small open economy (SOE). On account of its size, it has little or no control over the international price of goods and services. In other words, it is a price taker in an international environment.

In 1995, exports were valued at £30 billion which is approximately 78% of Irish GDP. Imports were valued at over £25 billion which represents approximately 66% of GDP. Both of these figures attest to the extreme openness of the Irish economy.

As a SOE, Irish policy-makers must take the issue of inflation seriously. A high domestic inflation rate erodes the competitiveness of Irish goods on foreign markets. High foreign inflation rates, particularly from Ireland's main trading partners are quickly imported to the Irish economy.

Until 1979 when the fixed exchange rate between Ireland and Britain was finally broken, the Irish inflation rate was largely determined by the UK inflation rate, and the Irish authorities had little control over Irish inflation. The level of trade with the UK, UK interest rates, UK monetary policy and sterling's value on the foreign exchange markets were the primary factors in determining the Irish inflation rate.

Although sterling remains outside the ERM, the British inflation rate continues to influence the Irish rate because of the strong trading links between the two countries. However, Ireland is also influenced by the inflation rate of EU countries participating in the ERM. One attraction to joining the ERM was the belief that the Irish inflation rate would eventually converge to the German rate (see Section 14.6). Participation in the ERM alone, did not guarantee convergence, as we shall see.

CASE STUDY

Extract from The Irish Times
Inflation rate falls to 3.6%
by Cliff Taylor

The rate of inflation fell to 3.6% in the middle of last month, down from February's 3.7% figure, despite budget tax increases which had been expected to increase the rate. The figures show that Ireland remains near the bottom of the EC inflation league, with only three states having lower figures.

The Budget increase in the 12.5% VAT rate to 16% had been expected to push up the annual rate to 3.8% or 3.9%. But despite the tax change, which added about 0.5% to prices during the three months to mid-May, the total quarterly rise was just 0.7%, down from 0.8% in the previous three-month period. The latest figures end a slow upward creep, which has seen the annual rate of inflation rise from 2.6% at the start of last year. Forecasters expect that the rate will continue to ease back in the remaining months and NCB stockbrokers expect it to fall towards 3% by the end of the year. Details of the latest figures will not be published until this evening.

The low rate of inflation relative to our EC partners is an important boost to the competitiveness of exporters. Irish inflation remains below the rate in our biggest overseas market, the UK, which is 4.3% and is also below that of Germany, our second biggest export destination, where it is running at 4.5%. In the EC only Belgium (2.8%), France (3.1%) and Denmark (2.5%) have lower inflation rates. The government wants to see inflation remaining low as the Maastricht Treaty says member states wishing to join the final stage of economic and monetary union after 1996 should have a rate which compares well with the three lowest in the Community, a criterion on which Ireland would now easily qualify.

→

While the good inflation performance is welcome news for the government, it may indicate that economic growth remains subdued, with retailers and wholesalers unable to increase their prices in the face of slack demand. The latest Central Bank figures show that borrowing from banks and building societies remains low, which may be restraining demand.

Source: The Irish Times, *19 June 1992.*

Questions

1. Interpret a 'rate of inflation' of '3.6%'.
2. Explain how inflation affects the 'competitiveness of exporters'.
3. Other than a 'slack demand' what factors may be contributing to the 'good inflation performance'?

Answers

1. The rate of inflation is the percentage change in the price level. An annual inflation rate of 3.6% means that the general price level rose by 3.6% over the calendar year.
2. Inflation affects the competitiveness of firms involved in foreign trade by affecting the foreign price of exports. A low and stable inflation rate in Ireland relative to the inflation rates of our trading partners means that the prices of Irish goods sold abroad are stable. This results in a competitive gain to Irish firms. By keeping costs low and prices stable, domestic firms can maintain high profit margins.
3. A firm exchange rate, moderate wage increases and modest increases in costs are all possible factors contributing to the favourable inflationary environment. The international trend in prices may also be another explanatory factor. Others, such as market expectations may have also played a contributing role.

The Irish inflation rate has varied greatly since the early 1970s. The inflation rates during the period between 1970 and 1995 are illustrated in Figure 15.6.

Figure 15.6: Irish inflation rate 1970–95

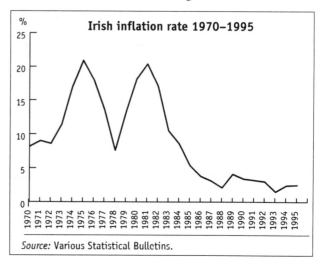

Irish inflation rate 1970–1995

Source: Various Statistical Bulletins.

It is evident from Figure 15.6 that inflation in Ireland was high from 1973 to 1982. Since the early to mid-1980s the inflation rate has declined. By the early 1990s the Irish inflation rate was close to, and often below, the EU average. Ireland has become a low inflation economy.

The inflationary period 1973 to 1980 coincided with an increase in inflationary pressures throughout western Europe. The main sources of Irish inflation were the volatility of sterling and the supply-side shocks of 1973 and 1979 arising from the increase in the price of oil. As a small open economy, Ireland is likely to record similar rates of inflation to its main trading partners. Expansionary fiscal policy practiced by Irish governments after 1973 also contributed to the high inflation rates.

Likewise, the decline in the inflation rate experienced by most EU countries in the mid- to late 1980s was also evident in Ireland. Although the international experience of low and stable inflation was a contributory factor in reducing the Irish inflation rate, it was not the only factor.[16] Domestic policy was largely deflationary in the late 1980s. The combination of tight fiscal policy and moderate pay increases reinforced the international anti-inflationary experience of the time.

The firm exchange rate policy followed by the Irish authorities was also influential in the reduction of Irish inflation. Price stability had become the sole objective of domestic exchange rate and monetary policy. Interest rate levels were set in order to attain low and stable inflation. By the mid-1990s, the Irish inflation rate was one of the lowest in the EU. In addition, by achieving a low inflation rate, Ireland meets the inflation criterion as set down in the Maastricht treaty (see Section 14.5). Given the Irish authorities' determination to participate in the single currency, Ireland's commitment to achieving a low and stable inflation rate is both desirable and necessary.

We leave the last few words on inflation to a former President of the US Gerald Ford: ' . . . our inflation, our public enemy number one, will unless whipped destroy our country, our homes, our liberties, our property, and finally our national pride, as surely as any well-armed wartime enemy.'[17]

15.2 Unemployment

Undoubtedly, the most serious economic problem facing society is unemployment. A section discussing this topic is an exercise in humility for any economist. We have trouble defining it. The number of unemployed depends on the statistic that we use. We cannot come close to measuring the opportunity cost of unemployment. Many of the theories that we cling to may have never been appropriate. The persistently high rates of unemployment observed in western Europe offer no consolation that our policies are effective.

Unfortunately, we cannot offer a solution to the unemployment problem in this section. Hopefully we can explain the issues in such a way that the policy discussions which you hear and read about will make more sense. You are already familiar with many of the definitions and the models. We will refer you to the appropriate section of the book if the concepts have been introduced before.

15.2.1 Defining unemployment
....

Unemployment is surprisingly difficult to define and to measure.[18] We will begin by looking at the Labour Force Survey (LFS) and the Live Register (LR), two measures of Irish unemployment. The two measures have one thing in common. In both, unemployment is a stock concept; they look at the number of unemployed at a point in time.[19] However, each measure defines unemployment differently and, as a result, the number of people which they count as unemployed differs widely.

Labour Force Survey

The LFS is carried out annually by the CSO in accordance with the rules laid down by the International Labour Organisation. Forty-seven thousand households are surveyed every April. The following definitions are used in the compilation of the LFS.

Definition
● ● ● ● ● ●

The population includes everyone who is 15 years or older. It is divided between those who are in the labour force and those who are not in the labour force. Those who are not in the labour force are classified as students, on home duties, retired, unable to work or 'other.'

Definition
● ● ● ● ● ●

The labour force includes those who are employed and those who are unemployed.

Definition
● ● ● ● ● ●

The unemployed include those who are not working and who are actively seeking employment. People are unemployed because they lost or gave up their previous job. Also included are school-leavers and people who are looking for their first regular job.

Definition
● ● ● ● ● ●

The unemployment rate is the number of people unemployed divided by the labour force.

The LFS allows people to classify their own employment status.

Live Register

The LR figures are released on the last Friday of each month and published by the CSO in the *Statistical Bulletin*. The LR defines unemployment in the following way.

Definition
● ● ● ● ● ●

The Live Register counts as unemployed, the people who are registered at local offices of the Department of Social Welfare for either unemployment benefits or unemployment assistance.

The LR excludes the following categories of people who receive unemployment assistance: smallholders; persons on systematic short-time; persons working week-on/week-off like job sharers; and self-employed individuals. Individuals who are involved in industrial disputes are also excluded.[20]

The difference between the LR and the LFS

The difference between the two measures is a matter of current interest in the media (see Article 15.2). There is a huge gap between the two measures which is shown in Table 15.3.

Table 15.3: Difference between those classified as unemployed on the LFS and those receiving social welfare benefits

Year	LR (April)	LFS
1992	281,000	217,000
1993	294,600	230,000
1994	284,500	218,000
1995	276,000	191,000
1996	281,300	190,000

The gap between these two figures was increasing until late 1996. What accounts for the gap? Recall that for the LFS, people classify themselves. Women particularly classify themselves as 'on home duties' if they are not employed. In the LFS, this classifies them as 'not in the labour force'. However, they may also be entitled to social welfare payments and therefore appear on the Live Register. Therefore, on the LR, they are classified as both in the labour force and unemployed. Each measure is defining 'unemployment' differently.

Social welfare fraud appears to be another reason why the two statistics differ. A survey commissioned by the government to compare the LR with the LFS found that for a sample of 2600 cases, 16% of the people claiming unemployment benefits were working and not entitled to those benefits. Promises made by the government to prosecute cases of social welfare fraud led to an immediate drop in the Live Register. In October 1996, over 11,000 'signed off' the dole.

Unravelling the differences between the two statistics is difficult. Deciding which is the 'better' measure is both difficult and politically risky. Parties in power tend to focus on the lower unemployment rates derived from the LFS. These are also the figures which are used for international comparisons. Opposition parties concentrate on the higher LR figures.

The 'best measure' probably depends on the policy issue. One thing is certain. Each measure should be fully understood prior to the policy discussion.

ARTICLE 15.2

Extract from The Irish Independent
At last, the truth about unemployment
by Brendan Keenan

The professional pessimists really have a problem, with the preliminary labour force survey for 1995. The figures are much better than anyone expected, showing a jump of 49,000 in the numbers at work between April 1994 and last April. Most economists estimated a figure of around 35,000. Even better, the numbers unemployed fell by 26,000, to 194,000, bringing the unemployment rate to 13.5%. This may be high, but it is lower than some other EU countries. Nor is it out of line with Ireland's past unemployment rates compared with the rest of Europe. Where does that leave the Live Register figures published on the first Friday of every month, and which have been the subject of much hand-wringing this year? The total number 'signing on' last April stood, not at 194,000 but at 276,000. The number has risen since then.

The difficulty is to define unemployment – not as simple a matter as it might seem. The Live Register simply counts everyone who is signing on. People have to sign on to get benefits to which they are entitled. But are they all 'unemployed?' This is not just a matter of people signing on who already have work of some kind – fiddling the system – although the social welfare authorities should perhaps scrutinise the gap carefully. The question is how many on the Register actively want a job? If they do not – if they are near retirement age and would hate to start working again, or fully engaged in looking after children, or just scared stiff of the idea of a job – they can hardly be classified as unemployed in any real sense. The labour force survey adopts a very straightforward approach to this. It simply asks people to describe their own situation. If they say that they are unemployed, that is how they are counted. If they say they are in work, they join the 1.2 million estimated to be in employment.

There are other ways of counting unemployment, even in surveys. The International Labour Organisation would exclude people who are not actively seeking work, even if they said they were unemployed. But common sense would suggest that how people see themselves is as good a measure as any. If we accept the definition, how accurate is the survey? After all, there has been a lot of debate about the reliability of Irish economic statistics, and significant revisions to estimates for growth and trade. Some data is more prone to error than others. The Central Statistics Office also produced estimates for emigration and immigration yesterday. But the CSO is the first to admit that this figure is subject to a wide margin of error. The survey, on the other hand, is massive, covering 47,000 households and 148,000 people. Considering that a typical national opinion poll would question just 1,000 people, the accuracy of the labour force survey can hardly be doubted.

. . .

Source: Irish Independent, *25 October 1995.*

Unemployment can be classified into a number of different types. These include frictional, seasonal, structural, demand deficient and classical. These classifications correspond broadly with the causes of unemployment.

Frictional. This arises when workers who are 'between jobs' find themselves unemployed for a short period of time although work is available. A job vacancy may remain unfilled for a period of time because of imperfect information in the labour market or because of an immobile work force. This is also called search unemployment. Economists and policy-makers are not overly concerned with frictional unemployment which they see as inevitable in any dynamic economy. Measures that will shorten the job search time are likely to reduce frictional unemployment.

Seasonal. Employment in certain industries is seasonal in nature, requiring a work force for only a particular time of year. Employees are then laid off when the season ends. This is also called 'casual' unemployment. Industries which hire seasonally include tourism, construction and farming.

Structural. Economies sometimes face fundamental or structural changes which lead to unemployment. Technological change and the invention of new products may make old products and even whole industries obsolete. If that industry is important to a region or to a national economy, unemployment may persist until new firms and new industries are developed or until labour can be retrained to work in different industries. Examples include the mining industry in the UK and the linen industry in Northern Ireland.

Demand deficient. This type of unemployment arises from a deficiency in aggregate demand in the economy. It occurs during the downturn of the business cycle. It is caused by too much savings and an insufficient amount of spending (see Section 9.3).

Classical. This is the explanation of unemployment associated with the classical school. It arises from a combination of uncompetitive forces at work in the labour market. Powerful trade unions, costly labour legislation and monopoly influences are all sources of wage inflexibility. This is also called 'real wage' unemployment.

15.2.2 The costs
. . . .

So far, we have stated that unemployment is difficult to define and to measure. We will begin this section by admitting that the costs of unemployment are impossible to calculate. Some of the costs, like the total of social welfare payments, can be determined. Many costs, including the loss of production, of tax revenue and of self-esteem are difficult to quantify. They are felt by all sections of society, but disproportionately by the unemployed and their dependants.

The unemployed do not earn an income. This is only partially offset by the state in the form of unemployment allowances, rental allowances and medical cards. Although a person on the dole may not be literally dying of hunger, their relative standard of living is below that of people who are working. In a world where success is measured by our accumulation of material goods, there is a stigma attached to those who cannot participate in that accumulation. Higher security costs, both public and private, are incurred by societies as the size of the gap between the social classes widens. Length of life can be affected along with the quality of life. The poverty associated with unemployment leads to increased physical and mental breakdowns.

The unemployed tend to be 'ghettoised'. They live in areas where the rates of unemployment are substantially higher than the national average. These neighbour-hoods face high levels of crime and substance abuse. Few students finish with second-level qualifications. Fewer still participate at third level. Not only are their surroundings bleak, their exits are blocked by a lack of access to education.

Society loses if people are unemployed. The unemployed are a resource which is not being utilised. If all of the unemployed were working, an economy would produce more and the national income would increase. If everyone was working, the tax base would be broader; there would be more sources of tax revenue. More public goods could be provided.

The money transferred to the unemployed is taken from the taxpayer. This constitutes a redistribution of resources from one section of society to another. This is not considered to be a cost to society in an economic sense. However, if the unemployment rate is high, the tax base is relatively narrow and individuals who are working must pay high rates of taxes to finance government spending. Some econo-mists suggest that high tax rates act as a disincentive to employment, so the productive capacity of the economy may again be affected (see Information Box 13.1).

This brief discussion shows the difficulty of 'counting the costs'. The costs that we can count are huge. The magnitude of the opportunity cost of unemployment is painful to contemplate. We will now discuss some of the theories developed to explain unemployment.

15.2.3 The theories and policies
....

There are a number of different theories of unemployment. Some of them are conven-tional, others are radical; some are modern whereas others are centuries old; some blame government and the state while others apportion blame to the market system. The one feature common to the different theories is the recognition of the social and economic costs associated with unemployment. We begin with the classical explanation.

The classical theory

The classical model of the labour market was explained in detail in Section 6.1. The downward sloping demand curve for labour is based on the diminishing marginal productivity of labour. In order for firms to hire more labour, the real wage must fall. The upward sloping supply curve of labour is based on the idea that workers trade off the disutility associated with work with the utility associated with consuming goods and services. In order for labour to work additional hours or for more people to enter the labour market, the real wage rate must increase.

Figure 15.7 shows the classical labour market.

Figure 15.7: The classical labour market

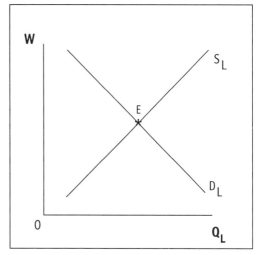

Full employment is shown at point E. The level of output of goods and services is determined by the number of people working. The classicals believed that the labour market moves automatically toward full employment, if wages are flexible. At point E, there is no involuntary unemployment. The supply curve above point E represents people who are voluntarily unemployed. Their utility-maximising decision is to withhold their services, preferring leisure to labour.

If unemployment persisted in the economy, the classicals believed that the source of the unemployment must be in the labour market itself. Since full employment depended on wage flexibility, unemployment meant that wages were not flexible. Rigidities were caused by labour unions, minimum wage legislation or other anti-competitive practices.

The solution to classical unemployment follows directly from their model; the sources of wage rigidity must be eliminated. The labour market will then return to full employment.

The Keynesian theory

The Keynesian theory of unemployment can be explained within the context of the model of income determination (see Section 10.1). Keynes did not think that the source of unemployment was to be found in the labour market. Instead, he believed that the source of unemployment was in the goods market. Labour demand was derived from the demand for goods. There was nothing automatic about full employment. Deficient demand led to persistent unemployment.

Suppose we begin at a point where the level of output corresponds coincidentally with full employment in the labour market. Panel (a) of Figure 15.8 shows the model of income determination. The equilibrium level of output is determined by adding together the different sources of aggregate expenditure including consumption, investment, government spending and net exports. The economy is at equilibrium indicated by point E, which corresponds to full employment in the labour market shown in panel (b).

Figure 15.8: Involuntary unemployment explained using the Keynesian model

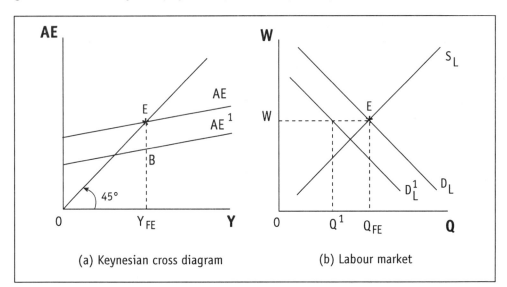

(a) Keynesian cross diagram (b) Labour market

Now, suppose that war breaks out between the states of the former Yugoslavia and the markets are concerned about future economic stability in the Baltic regions. Firms, facing uncertainty, decide to postpone their expansion plans. Investment falls, causing the AE curve to shift downwards to AE^1.

Because labour demand is determined by the demand in the goods market, the decrease in investment means that the demand for labour falls. This is shown by a shift of the demand curve for labour to $D_L{}^1$. An additional feature to the Keynesian model is the assumption that wages are rigid for institutional reasons such as the existence of labour contracts. Therefore, the wage rate does not fall, but remains at W. The gap between Q^1 and Q_{FE} represents involuntary unemployment. In the goods market, the distance |EB| measures the deflationary gap.

Keynes did not argue in favour of flexible wages. He believed that the source of unemployment was demand-determined. A fall in wages would lead to a fall in consumption, another component of aggregate expenditure. Government intervention in the form of expansionary monetary or fiscal policy is the preferred solution. Only government controls a sufficient level of resources to overcome the deficiency in demand.

CASE STUDY

Extract from The Sunday Tribune
The Labour Pains of the West

Unemployment is costly in many ways. Apart from the human suffering, the economy as a whole suffers through loss of output and the costs to taxpayers of welfare payments. Yet despite such waste and despite reams of learned economic articles, governments have failed to solve the problem.

. . .

Economists fall into two camps. In the 1930s, when unemployment soared above 20% in America and Britain, a British economist, John Maynard Keynes, argued that the cure was to stimulate demand by increasing public expenditure or cutting taxes. In the 1950s and 1960s Keynesian demand management seemed to do the trick. Unemployment stayed low. But since the early 1970s, it has ratcheted up in each cycle.

An increasing proportion of unemployment is clearly structural. So the second camp, neoclassical economists, argues that the real problem is that labour markets are over-rigid, over-regulated and over-priced – in other words, that workers have priced themselves out of jobs. Today, most economists accept that both forms of failure exist.

Europe, in particular, is riddled with rigidities that prevent the labour market from clearing. For example, trade unions or minimum wages put an artificial floor under wages. Instead of protecting workers as intended, they actually push some out of a job. Likewise, over-generous benefits discourage the unemployed from seeking work, while high labour taxes deter employers from hiring more workers. It is surely no coincidence that America's more flexible job market – with lower trade-union membership, lower labour taxes and less generous unemployment benefits – delivers a lower unemployment rate than in the EU.

. . .

Source: The Sunday Tribune, *13 March 1994.*

Questions
....

1. The article discusses two camps of economists. In what ways do the neoclassical economists resemble the classicals, rather than the Keynesians?
2. Although the author states that economists believe that unemployment may be caused by labour market rigidities as well as demand-deficiencies, do you think s/he prefers one explanation to the other?
3. The author describes the American job market as one which 'delivers a lower unemployment rate than in the EU'. Are there any aspects of the 'flexible' market which the EU would seek to avoid?

Answers
....

1. Like the classicals, the neoclassicals concentrate on the labour market as the source of unemployment. The neoclassical description of the labour market is 'over-rigid, over-regulated and over-priced'. This resembles the classical argument against wage rigidity and in favour of wage flexibility. This is certainly not Keynesian because

Keynes believed that rigid wages kept consumption from falling. If wages fell, consumption fell, aggregate expenditure fell and more people became unemployed.

2. The author concentrates on the labour market and its imperfections. For that reason, it seems that his/her bias is in favour of the neoclassical model of unemployment. For example, s/he states that trade unions and minimum wages 'put an artificial floor under wages.' These are preventing wages from clearing the market and contribute to the problem of unemployment.

'Over-generous benefits' affect the supply curve for labour. Social welfare legislation probably makes the supply curve inelastic meaning that labour is less responsive to changes in the real wage. Also, the supply curve for labour probably begins at a wage level above the payment for social welfare. In other words, people will only work if their wages are greater than the social welfare payment.

The high labour tax rate affects the demand curve for labour. From the firm's point of view, high taxes on labour increase the cost of labour. At a high cost, firms demand less labour.

On the other hand, the author has not mentioned one example of demand-deficient unemployment.

3. While acknowledging the low unemployment rate in the US, there are many drawbacks to the American job-creation policy. Most of the new jobs created have been in low-paid service industries. Working conditions are often poor, with many employees living on wages that are below the poverty line. There is little protection for employees and competition for jobs is often fierce. The hire-and-fire strategy results in an absence of worker loyalty unlike the Japanese model where the labour/employer relationship is often entered for life. There is less attention paid to skills development compared to Europe. On a wider level, some think that this extreme labour market strategy has directly contributed to many of America's social and political problems. It is argued that the sharp class division in the US is related to the jobs strategy.

The monetarist theory

The monetarist theory essentially agrees with the classical conception of the economy and of the appropriate role of government. Additions to the theory resulted from their observation of what they considered to be inappropriate demand-management policies enacted by the Keynesian economists who influenced policy-makers in the 1960s and the 1970s.

Monetarists believe that the existence of unemployment in the labour market is due to imperfections in the market system and misguided demand-management policies. A flexible labour market without excessive government interference should return to the 'natural rate' of unemployment.[21] Examples of market imperfections include the existence of monopolies, strong labour unions and minimum wage legislation.

The source of employment creation, according to monetarists, is in the private sector. Demand-management policies are not only ineffective in increasing the level of employment, but inflationary. Inflation interferes with the price mechanism, the most important source of information between households and firms. Inflationary policies short-circuit the price mechanism and counteract the ability of the private sector to create jobs.

The supply-side theory

Supply-side economists also begin with the classical conception of the economy. Total output depends on factors such as the level of technology, the training of the labour force and the accumulation of capital. One source of unemployment in the economy is 'supply-side' shocks. The most memorable example of a supply-side shock is the oil crisis. Figure 15.9 shows how a negative supply-side shock moves an economy to a level of output which is less than full employment.

Figure 15.9: A supply-side shock

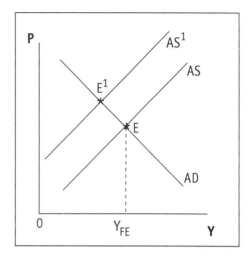

The supply siders also agree with the monetarists that government policy impedes the natural progress of the economy to full-employment. Some of the supply-side economists believe in the validity of the Laffer curve relationship (see Information Box 13.1). Briefly, this economist suggested that tax rates act as a disincentive to work. The more heavily that work is taxed, the greater the disincentive. Onerous tax rates limit the productive output of the economy. For this reason, supply siders advocate a revision of the tax system to limit this disincentive.

The supply-side economists differ from the Keynesians because they believe that tax reform will affect the supply side, rather than the demand side of the economy. Tax reform pushes the aggregate supply curve out and to the right, increasing the economy's output. Supply siders differ from the monetarists because they focus primarily on fiscal policy rather than monetary policy.

The Marxian theory

Marxian unemployment theory is based on the conflicting relationship between labour and the capitalist. Marx believed that labour is productive and the source of all surplus. This surplus is divided between labour and the capitalist, depending on who is the most powerful. If labour is more powerful, wages rise above the subsistence level. If the capitalist is more powerful a larger share of the surplus goes to the capitalist in the form of profit.

Marx agreed with Keynes that the capitalist system is prone to periodic expansions and contractions.[22] Involuntary unemployment of labour is a feature of both models in recessions and depressions. In the Keynesian model, involuntary unemployment is caused by the failure of private investment which occurs because of the 'animal spirits' of investors. In the Keynesian model, the failure of investment is a consequence of instability; in the Marxian model, it is a tactic designed to create instability.

In the Marxian model, high levels of unemployment serve a regulatory purpose. During periods when workers are powerful, profits decline. If profits are falling, capitalists reduce investment. This leads to a recession, which reduces labour power. When unemployment is high, workers are in a weaker bargaining position. The capitalist can force workers to increase productivity and to work for less. Workers realise that there is a 'reserve army of unemployed' waiting to take their place.

We have already observed that differences in modelling the unemployment problem lead to different policy prescriptions. The Marxian model is no exception. Marx believed that government, in protecting the private property rights of the capitalist, was an active participant in the problem of unemployment. Profits, extracted from the workers who produced the surplus, were protected by the police and the legal system. The source of unemployment in the Marxian model is the link between profits and investment. The solution is to break that link. It was in this sense that Marx advocated the abolition of private property. To end the exploitation of labour and to eradicate unemployment, the capitalist system had to be destroyed. For more on the life of Marx, see Information Box 15.3.

INFORMATION BOX 15.3

Karl Marx (1818–1883)

Karl Marx was born in Germany and educated at the University of Bonn where he studied law. He furthered his education at the University of Berlin where he began to take a keen interest in philosophy. His teacher was the radical philosopher Georg Hegel. Marx was influenced by Hegel and began work on a thesis with a view to getting a university lectureship. He received his doctorate in 1841.

Marx's radical views, however, were a major obstacle in his search for an academic position. Instead he worked as a freelance journalist. After marrying his childhood sweetheart, Marx moved to Paris, the centre of radical reformers, where he met Friedrich Engels, the revolutionary socialist. They became lifetime friends and collaborators.

Marx and his family were expelled from France in 1845, and subsequently moved to Brussels where he organised a Communist Correspondence Committee. Three years later, the outline to Marx's theory The Communist Manifesto *was complete. According to Engels it was 'to do for history what Darwin's theory has done for biology'. It concluded with the famous lines 'The workers have nothing to lose in this but their chains. They have the world to gain. Workers of the world, unite!'*

After being expelled from a number of European cities, Marx moved to London where he lived for the rest of his life. Although he contributed regularly to the New

> York Tribune, *he and his family spent many years in poverty. It was during this time that he wrote his most famous work* Capital *wherein he prophesied that capitalism would collapse and would be replaced by an alternative economic system – socialism. Socialism in turn would be replaced by the utopian state of communism.*
>
> *While things on the money side improved vastly in the later years of his life, due to inheritances, his personal life was shattered by the early deaths of his children and his grandchildren. This was followed by the death of his wife in 1881 and his eldest daughter in 1883. He died of bronchitis at the age of 65 in March 1883.*

In recent times, explanations of unemployment focus on specific features of the economic system in general and the labour market in particular. These include the time and effort involved in searching for employment, the insider-outsider composition of the labour market and the effects of long-term wage contracts.[23]

15.2.4 The Irish experience

One of the most unforgettable comments by a senior political figure in Ireland was made in 1978. The Taoiseach and leader of Fianna Fáil, Jack Lynch was interviewed by RTE's 'This Week' programme. In response to a question on unemployment and whether the electorate should put the government out of office if the figures rose to 100,000, Mr Lynch replied, 'Absolutely, I think they would be well justified if there are that many . . . if we don't deliver then the electorate are entitled to put us out of office.'[24]

Since then governments from different political parties have come and gone. Yet the unemployment figure has soared. By January 1993 it was over 300,000. It had become the second highest rate within the EU (second to Spain) and the third highest within the OECD (behind Spain and Finland). One in five of the labour force was unemployed.

High unemployment is not a recent phenomenon in Ireland. In the past there have been periods of high and rising unemployment. Our analysis of unemployment is limited to the period since the early 1970s.

The unemployment rate in Ireland during the period 1970–95 is shown in Figure 15.10.

Figure 15.10: Unemployment rate in Ireland 1970–95

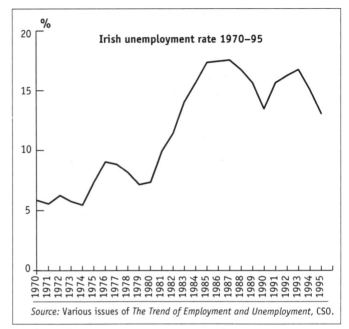

Source: Various issues of *The Trend of Employment and Unemployment*, CSO.

The causes of Irish unemployment are many and diverse. Factors such as the lack of natural resources, peripherality and the absence of entrepreneurial spirit are some of the causes which often get a mention. In reality, their contribution to the high unemployment rate is questionable.

The unemployment problem is complex. In order to gain some understanding of the nature of the problem, we will begin by attempting to group possible causes into four classifications: demographic factors, external factors, inappropriate demand-management policies and other domestic factors. We will end this section by considering possible solutions.

The demographic factor

There is considerable disagreement over the relationship between population changes, changes in the labour force and changes in unemployment in Ireland. As a result of the increase in birth rates and the reversal of the emigration pattern from the 1960s onwards, the Irish labour force began to record significant increases in new entrants. Although many new jobs were created during this period, unemployment numbers also rose. Many experts, however, do not view these demographic changes as a significant factor contributing to the increase in Irish unemployment. In support of their argument, they highlight the following points: Irish birth rates peaked in the early 1980s (21.9 per 1,000), falling close to EU levels thereafter; and other countries, including the US and Japan, recorded similar increases in population without any matching increase in unemployment levels.

The views of many economists in Ireland on this subject are neatly summed up in the words of Brendan Walsh, 'Thus, while unemployment might have risen less if the Irish labour force had been growing more slowly, it is not plausible to attribute the exceptional increase that occurred to an unusually rapid rate of increase in labour supply.'[25]

External

A number of shocks external to the economy contributed to the poor performance of the Irish labour market. These include the two oil crises, the break-up of the Bretton Woods system, the liberalisation of financial markets and high real interest rates, the world recessions of 1980–82 and 1990–91 and the poor performance of the UK economy. The supply-side shocks of the 1970s were price inflationary and demand deflationary. This caused problems for policy-makers throughout the western world, including Ireland. Higher oil prices added to the production costs of many Irish and Irish-based firms. The break-up of the fixed exchange rate system created uncertainty in financial markets both at home and abroad. Exchange rate volatility and greater interest rate fluctuations caused problems for both exporters and importers. World recession and, in particular the sluggish growth recorded in the UK contributed to the already weak domestic demand. The combination of all these events had an adverse effect on Irish economic growth and, likewise, Irish unemployment.[26]

Inappropriate demand-management policies

The fiscal, monetary, incomes and exchange rate policies adopted by different governments may have contributed in different ways to the high unemployment rates of the last two decades. In terms of fiscal policy, a number of mistakes were made. First, the authorities responded to the supply-side shocks of the 1970s with orthodox demand-management policies.[27] Second, the borrowing which subsequent governments undertook was partly to finance day-to-day spending.[28] Third, fiscal policy from the mid-1970s until the mid-1980s was largely pro-cyclical.[29] Fourth, although the Fine Gael/Labour Coalition government was forced by the burgeoning debt to enact contractionary fiscal policy, their policy mix was flawed.[30] Hence, we arrive at the assessment of some commentators that the legacy of Irish fiscal policy is a massive debt.

Fiscal policy was not the only culprit during this period. Job creation was hindered by the combination, at different times, of high interest rates arising from tight monetary policy, a real exchange rate appreciation arising from Ireland's participation in the EMS exchange rate mechanism and excessive increases in wage levels arising from pay agreements between the government and the social partners.[31]

Other domestic factors

There are a large number of other domestic factors which have contributed to high unemployment in Ireland; most of these have affected the supply side. Production was adversely affected because of factors which contributed to high costs. We deal with two: taxation and labour market rigidities.

Taxation

There are many aspects of the tax system which hinder job creation and contribute to high unemployment rates. A number of these are considered below:

- The Irish tax system treats labour and capital differently. Since the early 1960s the cost of capital has been subsidised by the state in order to attract foreign investment. Allowances against corporate tax for capital expenditure in addition to flexible depreciation allowances were offered to multinationals as part of the incentive package. Tax on labour, on the other hand, has been excessive. Labour has been the main source of tax revenue, with the PAYE sector carrying the burden.[32] In particular, marginal tax rates on labour are high and are applicable at low income levels. It has been acknowledged that no other country subsidises capital at the expense of labour to the same degree as Ireland. With a large excess supply of labour, it is surprising to see labour treated in this fashion. In the words of the internationally renowned economist, Rudiger Dornbusch, 'Ireland's taxation is nothing short of oppressive.'[33]
- The lack of integration between the tax and welfare systems in Ireland has been highlighted as a possible contributing factor to the unemployment crisis in Ireland.[34] The non-integration of the tax and welfare systems result in many anomalies. One such anomaly is referred to as the unemployment trap. This occurs when an unemployed person finds that he is financially worse off if he accepts a job offer. One measure of the unemployment trap is the replacement ratio (RR), described in (15.4) below.

$$\text{Replacement ratio} = \frac{\text{unemployment benefits}}{\text{after-tax income}} \times 100 \qquad [15.4]$$

This is the proportion of a worker's after-tax income that is replaced by unemployment benefits. As the replacement ratio approaches 100, the gap narrows between working and remaining unemployed. The higher the ratio, the less financial incentive there is to work. A sample of replacement ratios for a single person (no children) and for a married couple (two children) in Ireland is included in Table 15.4 below.

Table 15.4: Replacement ratios 1995–96

Income (£)	Single person (no children)	Married couple (FIS recipients)	Married couple (Non-recipients of FIS)
5,000	88.33%	88.31%	149.20%
6,000	75.70%	85.15%	125.90%
8,000	58.93%	82.57%	101.40%
9,000	53.07%	82.72%	93.18%
11,000	45.28%	83.98%	83.98%
12,000	41.84%	79.43%	79.43%
14,000	37.65%	70.97%	70.97%
15,000	35.97%	66.93%	66.93%
17,000	33.05%	60.09%	60.09%
18,000	31.76%	57.15%	57.15%

Source: *Expert Working Group Report on the Integration of the Tax and Social Welfare Systems*, June 1996.

For a single person earning £6,000 or less a year, the welfare system will replace over 75% of take-home pay. The disincentive to work is more striking for larger families. As is evident from the table, welfare payments may be up to 1.5 times higher than the after-tax income of a married couple with two children. For a family earning close to the average industrial wage, the replacement ratio is still quite high, at close to 70%.

Replacement ratios increased in Ireland during the period 1977–94. There is both international and domestic evidence to indicate a correlation between rising replacement ratios and the persistence and duration of unemployment.[35]

- Another anomaly within the tax system is the occurrence of a poverty trap. A poverty trap exists when there is no financial incentive for an employed person to take up a better job offer. Given the nature of the tax and welfare systems in Ireland, a poverty trap exists for low-paid workers who are supporting large families. An example follows. Mick is a factory worker. His gross pay is £7,000 (1995–96 figures). Mick lives in a local authority house and supports a wife and two children.

The state will aid Mick with the help of Family Income Supplement, a medical card and some allowances.[36] The only taxes paid by Mick are his PRSI contributions. Taking all these into account, his net income amounts to £153.18 per week. The factory that employs Mick advertises for a new foreman with a salary of £11,000. Before Mick applies for the job, he calculates the benefits that will supposedly accrue from the new post. Earning £11,000 a year, Mick falls into the tax net. He will pay the standard rate of income tax in addition to his PRSI contributions. He will also lose his entitlements to the FIS and the medical card. After all these adjustments are made, his take-home pay will be £149.15, £4 per week less than if he were earning £7,000. At low levels of income, a fall in earnings is a disincentive to accepting a 'better' job. This example highlights the poverty trap as it exists for Mick and his family. This particular example of a poverty trap is shown in Figure 15.11.

Figure 15.11: The poverty trap

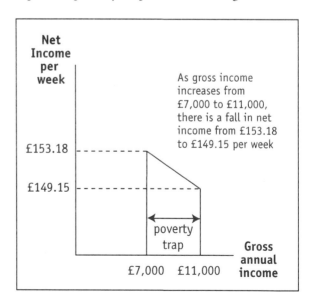

- For there to be low unemployment, employees must have an incentive to accept employment in addition to the employers having an incentive to hire additional workers. Central to this issue is the level of labour costs and the tax applied to wages. The tax wedge, as it is commonly referred to, is the difference between the after-tax earnings of the employee and the gross cost incurred by the employer. A significant tax wedge acts as a dual disincentive. Considering the supply curve for labour, a low take-home pay does not overcome the disutility of labour. The tax-inflated marginal cost of hiring another worker is a disincentive on the demand side of the labour market.[37]

In 1980/81 the tax wedge for a single person earning the average industrial wage amounted to £1,835.93. Ten years later, the tax wedge was £5,004.57. This 173% increase far exceeds the rise in prices over the same period.[38] Arthur Andersen & Co. (1991) estimated that the marginal tax wedge for a single person in Ireland was 61%, the second highest of the countries surveyed.[39] An OECD study in 1991 calculated that the economy-wide tax wedge in Ireland was the fourth highest in the OECD, behind the wealthier nations of Denmark, Holland and Sweden.[40] The tax wedge for a single person in 1994 is shown in Figure 15.12.

Figure 15.12: The tax wedge

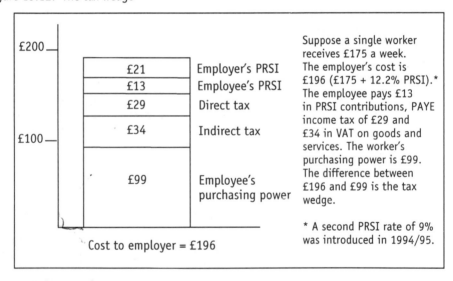

Labour market rigidities

Neoclassical labour market models predict that in a market without rigidities, the wage rate should fall, eliminating involuntary unemployment. Similar to other national labour markets, the Irish labour market is characterised by a number of rigidities.

Obviously, we cannot talk about the elimination of rigidities without acknowledging that this will lead to an erosion of the institutional arrangements, developed over the years to protect labour. It is not easy to strike a balance. In this section, we will describe some of the economic problems which arise because of the rigidities. However, we acknowledge that the resolution of these issues must take place within the context of a wider social debate.

- The wage bargaining process in Ireland has been characterised as an example of the insider-outsider model. Those employed are 'insiders' who negotiate for their own income and job security to the detriment of the 'outsiders' who are the unemployed. The insiders' demands impose a floor on wages which is above the market clearing wage.

Since 1987, centralised wage agreements have been the norm. Until 1996 the negotiations between the government and the social partners excluded the unemployed. Between 1987 and 1993 real earnings in Ireland, as measured by the average hourly earnings index, rose by over 30%. Over the same period unemployment increased by 47,000. In the words of Dermot McAleese 'The insiders did what came naturally – put themselves first, while protesting concern for the unemployed – and the outsiders stayed outside.'[41] Not everyone accepts the validity of Professor McAleese's claim. For a contrasting view, see Information Box 15.4.

INFORMATION BOX 15.4

Do high wages cost jobs?
Two contrasting views

The debate over the relationship between wage rates and unemployment levels dates back to the classical school of economics. Followers of the classical school argued that high unemployment was caused by uncompetitive forces in the labour market. If wages were high, an excess supply of labour can result. The solution to high unemployment levels was a reduction in wages levels. Keynes took a very different view of the labour market. Deficiencies in demand were largely responsible for rising unemployment. Any attempt to pursue the classical policy response of a cut in wages may only make the situation worse; by cutting wage levels, workers' ability to boost demand is reduced. The solution lies with government and active fiscal policy.

Professor Dermot McAleese of TCD says Yes, high wages can cost jobs. He supports this view by examining the increases in the public services pay bill since 1987. If a 2.5% increase had been granted (sufficient to compensate for inflation) rather than the recorded 6% increase, the remaining £600m 'could have been used to generate extra employment'. Such a saving could have financed tax cuts or increased public sector employment, he argues. In relation to public sector pay he concludes by saying 'Many thousands of jobs have been priced out of existence because of public sector unions' success in obtaining high increases in remuneration'. His criticisms are not solely directed at the public sector. He estimates that at least 10,000 extra jobs could have been provided in the private sector if the same pay criteria which he applied to the public sector was applied to the private sector.

Peter Cassells, General Secretary of the ICTU says No, high wages do not cost jobs. He defends his position by outlining the positive aspects of high earnings and by examining Ireland's record against international standards. A summary of his main points is listed below.

1. Lower wages reduce purchasing power which in turn reduces the demand for goods and services. The demand for labour to provide these same goods and services is subsequently lowered.
2. Lower wages result in less tax revenue for the government. Less revenue translates into less expenditure and less social services. Consequently, fewer people are required to provide these services.
3. High wages do not necessarily translate into uncompetitiveness. Wage increases are justified if they are in line with productivity gains.
4. Ireland's wage levels or increases in wage levels are not out of line with other EU countries. The evidence that he provides indicates relatively low wage levels and moderate increases in the period 1987–91.

The views expressed above reflect a much wider debate concerning the different approaches to tackling unemployment.[1] Is the low-wage, low-skilled, hire-and-fire approach followed in the US preferable to the high-wage, high-skilled, heavily protected approach adopted by the EU?[2] The passage of time has not lessened the intensity of this debate.

1 The Irish Times, 18 September 1992.
2 For more on this debate read the Europe Working Supplement to the Sunday Tribune dated 27 November 1994.

- In terms of trade union membership, Ireland is quite similar to many continental European countries. The trade union density which refers to the percentage of all wage and salary earners who are trade union members in Ireland was 49.7% in 1990. This translates to approximately 450,000 workers affiliated to a trade union. In contrast, the union densities for 1990 in the US and the UK were 15.6% and 39.1% respectively. The US has traditionally been a low-union membership country whereas in the UK the trade union movement was badly damaged by Thatcherite policies. Trade unions seek to improve the working conditions of their members. In addition, they negotiate wage increases for the workers. Some commentators have argued that the combination of restrictive practices and industrial strikes gave a bad image of Irish industrial relations to foreign investors.
- In the past twenty years Irish workers have benefited from protective labour legislation. In 1967, the first Redundancy Payments Act was passed. The Protection of Employment and Unfair Dismissals Act was introduced in 1977. In the same year the Employment Equality Act was passed. Since then, notable pieces of legislation include the Maternity Act (1981), the Hours of Work Act (1984) and the Safety, Health and Welfare at Work Act (1989). To quote Dermot McAleese, again, 'Ireland has acquired a labour market regime, in terms of protection of employee rights and trade union privileges, which stands comparison with the best in Europe.'[42] Notwithstanding the importance of protecting workers' rights, the drawback of such extensive legislation is the added cost to the employer. The net effect for many indigenous firms is higher costs, a loss of business and subsequent job losses. When confronted with extensive labour legislation in Ireland, multi-

nationals may be enticed abroad to countries where labour costs are lower (Greece) or to countries where legislation is not as extensive (UK). A study by Emerson in 1988 concluded that workers in Ireland were no worse off in terms of protection than their counterparts in other EU countries.[43]

We now turn our attention to the remedies. As expected, there is much disagreement over the solutions to Irish unemployment. Possible solutions are outlined below.[44]

Favourable economic climate

It is generally agreed that the Irish authorities should maintain an economic climate at home conducive to economic growth and job creation.[45] This environment is characterised by low inflation rates, low interest rates and low public sector borrowing. This is achieved by implementing consistent and credible macroeconomic policies.[46] Achieving a favourable economic environment at home is now considered to be a necessary but not sufficient condition in the search for low unemployment. In other words 'a rising tide will not lift all boats'. Brendan Walsh estimated that an annual 'GDP growth rate of 4.7%' was necessary to stabilise the unemployment rate.[47]

Even with a favourable economic climate at home and abroad, unemployment numbers are unlikely to fall beyond a certain level. A more fundamental readjustment of the economy is required. Given the small, open nature of the Irish economy, there is a view that employment in Ireland, in the long-run, is determined by supply-side factors. Hence, many of these adjustment policies are targeted at aggregate supply. Among others, we discuss a reform of the tax and welfare systems, more competition for the state bodies and for private sector companies, changes in pay determination, a change in education and training policy and a revamping of industrial policy.

Structural adjustments

A radical overhaul of many areas of public policy is now considered to be essential in the fight against unemployment.[48] Necessary structural changes include:

- *A reform of the tax and welfare systems.*[49] Greater integration of the tax and welfare systems is required. A widening of the tax base is considered important as is an elimination of the anomalies that exist in the tax system. The poverty and unemployment traps should be eliminated. In addition, the tax wedge should be lowered.[50] Other forms of tax such as property, wealth and energy should be considered in order to widen the tax base. The level of bureaucracy and red-tape should be minimised. More intervention is required by the state in order to avoid the move from short-term unemployment to long-term unemployment.[51] The evidence concerning the relationship between welfare payments and unemployment numbers is unclear.
- *Increasing the competitiveness of commercial state bodies.* The commercial state bodies face challenging times ahead. They must be prepared for greater competition. This

may require a radical restructuring in many of the semi-state bodies. Restrictive practices, excessive overheads and state subsidisation require examination. Only those companies that are cost competitive will survive in the single European market. This challenge applies equally well to private sector companies.

- *Adjustments in the wage bargaining process.* There is a recognition that the wage bargaining process cannot continue to ignore the large numbers of unemployed. Hence, in future negotiations, the inclusion of the unemployed must be continued. Another issue is whether local wage bargaining should replace the centralised wage agreements which have dominated incomes policy since 1987. Opinions are mixed. Some argue that localised bargaining will lead to lower wage agreements. Others believe that the national agreements have led to modest wage increases and have imposed order on an otherwise chaotic process. What is indisputable is the need to maintain our competitiveness. This objective can be achieved by controlling costs. Wages increases must be based on productivity gains and they must also reflect employment conditions in the labour market.

- *Changes in education and training.* Notwithstanding the past achievements of the Irish educational system, there is a need for a change in education policy. Features of other European educational systems may be useful. These include the focus on vocational and technical training from Germany and Switzerland, the emphasis on languages and oral communications found in central and eastern Europe and, finally, the focus on non-academic skills such as music and art as established in the former Soviet Union. The educational system must help students to develop entrepreneurial skills. Active manpower policies, the upgrading of existing skills and the search for new skills is an area which requires much improvement in Ireland. All members of the labour force, those at work and those out of work require further training to adapt to our knowledge-based society.

- *A reappraisal of industrial policy.* This process began in the early 1980s. Although many reports and countless recommendations have followed, little action has been taken. While acknowledging the success of the multinational sector in Ireland, there is no doubt that the performance of the indigenous sector has been disappointing. More attention needs to be paid to small Irish-owned firms. Within this sector, there needs to be a greater awareness of the importance of ancillary activities such as R&D, marketing, management, product design and development. Most firms suffer from a finance gap which also requires attention. The amount of time spent on paperwork to comply with various government regulations must be reduced. Resources should be focused on the sectors of food, tourism and leisure where Ireland appears to have a competitive advantage over other nations.[52]

Labour supply changes

Finally, there are a number of policies available which reduce the labour supply. These include a shorter working week, job-sharing, and early retirement. These specific policies raise many doubts and questions, including the following: Will they work in practice? Are they difficult to implement? Are they too costly to implement? Are they a violation of workers' rights? Should they be introduced at the EU level? Many of these proposals are likely to form part of the next decade's attempt at solving the unemployment problem. Given Europe's commitment to some of these policies, Ireland is unlikely to escape from such measures.[53]

From our analysis of unemployment it is clear that there is little consensus as to the cause of or remedy to Irish unemployment. What is evident is the fact that unemployment is likely to remain a problem which domestic policy-makers and others will find difficult to solve. If we are to learn anything from the countries with low rates of unemployment, we must embrace the same 'long-standing social consensus to treat unemployment as an unacceptable feature of the economy'.[54]

15.3 International trade

by Eithne Murphy

15.3.1 Traditional trade theory
....

Mercantilism

Mercantilism was the principal economic doctrine of the seventeenth and eighteenth centuries. As a doctrine it probably reflected as well as influenced the prevailing commercial practices of the period. According to mercantilists, countries get wealthy through the accumulation of precious metals; in that instance, gold and silver. Since gold and silver were the means of payment for goods and services, a country could accumulate such wealth if it ran continuous balance of payments surpluses; that is to say, if it exported more than it imported. Hence policies designed to achieve this end were those that limited imports (especially imports of high valued added products) and encouraged exports.

This philosophy, although subsequently discredited intellectually, has continued to influence international trade practice. The few exceptions were the UK in the nineteenth century and contemporary Hong Kong. Most policy-makers consider a balance of payments surplus to be a positive economic sign. Most policy-makers consider the removal of trade barriers in their national markets to be a concession on their part and one that has to be paid for by reciprocal trade barrier dismantlement on the part of other countries. This is simply mercantilist philosophy in modern guise.

Absolute advantage

Adam Smith is generally considered to be the founding father of economics.[55] For the purposes of the history of international trade theory, two aspects of his philosophy will be highlighted. Firstly, he considered that the objective of all economic activities was consumption. Here, we have the first blow against mercantilism. Gold and silver do not contribute directly to our individual welfare, the consumption of goods and services do. Metals are only useful to the extent that they aid consumption. A country that runs a continuous balance of payments surplus is akin to the miser who will not spend his money.

Secondly, individual self-sufficiency is never efficient, in the sense of representing an optimum use of an individual's energies and talents. Most individuals specialise in their choice of work which still allows them to consume a wide variety of goods and services if they trade with one another.

Laissez-faire, which is a policy of non-interference in the economic affairs of individuals, will ensure that the goods produced in the economy will be those that consumers want, while competition will ensure that the consumer gets these goods at the cheapest possible price. What holds for the individual also holds for the nation state. If self-sufficiency is inefficient for an individual, it must also be inefficient for a country. A country should specialise in production, producing what it does best and import other products; this will ensure global efficiency, and it will also allow a country to enjoy a higher overall level of consumption.

Table 15.5: Production per person per working day

	Ireland	France
Beef	20 kg	5 kg
Grain	2 kg	10 kg

If one person fewer engages in grain production in Ireland and instead devotes his energies to beef production, then grain output will fall by 2 kilos per day and beef output will increase by 20 kilos per day. Do the opposite in France and beef output will fall by 5 kilos while grain production will rise by 10 kilos. The net effect is that overall beef production rises by 15 kilos per day and overall grain production rises by 8 kilos per day. If both countries trade with each other then both can enjoy the benefits of higher overall production.

Comparative advantage

The problem with the theory of absolute advantage is that it assumes that countries and the world can gain from specialisation and trade if they are absolutely more efficient than other countries in some line of production. David Ricardo however showed that a country and the world can gain from specialisation and trade even if one country is better at producing all goods. He called this the theory of comparative advantage.[56]

Table 15.6: Production per person per working day

	Ireland	France
Beef	6 kg	10 kg
Grain	2 kg	10 kg

Workers in France are more productive in both beef and grain production. How then can Ireland and France gainfully trade? According to David Ricardo, if each country specialises in what it does 'relatively' best, both can gain from trade. We can see that in grain production, France is five times more productive than Ireland, whereas in beef production it is less than twice as productive. Accordingly, Ireland should specialise where its absolute disadvantage is least, i.e. in beef production, and France should specialise where its absolute advantage is greatest, i.e. in grain production.

In Ireland the true cost of a kilo of grain is 3 kilos of beef. Taking a person away from beef production and employing them in the grain sector means sacrificing 3 kilos of beef daily in order to have 1 kilo of grain. In France the cost of a kilo of grain is 1 kilo of beef. True cost is opportunity cost. Alternatively the cost of 1 kilo of beef in France is 1 kilo of grain. If France can import beef and pay less than 1 kilo of grain for it then France is better off than it was before. If Ireland can import grain and pay less than 3 kilos of beef for 1 kilo of grain then Ireland is better off than it was before.

So an exchange of beef for grain at a price somewhere between 1:1 and 1:3 will benefit both countries. In other words, if international terms of trade (the cost of a unit of imported goods in terms of the amount of exports required to purchase them) are different to a country's opportunity cost of production, then the country can gain from specialising and trading. If, for example, the international terms of trade were 2 kilos of beef for 1 kilo of grain, then the gains to Ireland and France from specialising in beef and grain respectively would be the following:

Ireland

Take a person away from grain production and put them working in the beef sector. Output of beef would rise by 6 kilos a day while output of grain would fall by 2 kilos a day. But 6 kilos of beef buys 3 kilos of grain on the international market. So Ireland can actually enjoy a higher level of grain consumption than before.

France

As an exercise, see how France can also gain and enjoy a higher level of beef consumption than it did before, by specialising out of beef and into grain.

We can represent graphically the production and consumption possibilities of both countries both before and after trade. The only additional information that we need are the number of workers in an economy. For simplicity let us assume that both countries have 1 million workers.

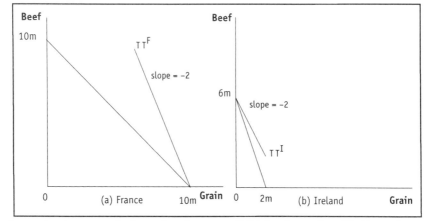

Figure 15.13: Production possibilities for Ireland and France

Figure 15.13 shows both countries' production possibilities for a day. If all workers are fully employed in France in the beef sector only, it can product 10 million kilos of beef daily. Alternatively, if all workers are employed in the grain sector, it can produce 10 million kilos of grain daily. Or if some workers are employed in the beef sector and others in the grain sector it can produce less than 10 million kilos of both goods daily. For example, if 70% of the labour force were employed in the beef sector and 30% in the grain sector, it could produce 7 million kilos of beef and 3 million kilos of grain daily. The production possibility frontier (PPF) shows all the different combinations of beef and grain that are feasible, given the resource base and given the productivity of the resource base in both sectors (see An Introduction to Economics). The slope of the PPF shows the cost of a kilo of grain in terms of beef which is -1. Before trade, France is forced to consume exactly what it produces.

Similarly Ireland can produce either 6 million kilos of beef daily or 2 million kilos of grain daily or some combination thereof. The slope of the PPF is -3 indicating the cost of a kilo of grain. Again before trade Ireland can only consume what it produces.

With trade Ireland produces only beef and France only grain. The international terms of trade are 2 kilos of beef for 1 kilo of grain. Both countries are now no longer obliged to consume exactly what they produce: they are merely obliged to ensure that the value of domestic production equals the value of domestic consumption, where prices are determined internationally. The line TT^I for Ireland shows us Ireland's potential consumption. We can see that potential consumption with trade is greater than it was without trade. Similarly for France, the line TT^F shows us France's potential consumption post-trade and we can see that it dominates pre-trade consumption possibilities. The rate at which goods exchange internationally is determined by international demand and supply.

What we can conclude from David Ricardo's analysis of trade is that all countries, even the most inefficient, can gain from trade, provided that they specialise in what they do relatively best and provided that the international terms of trade differ from the domestic opportunity cost of production.

Revealed comparative advantage and competitiveness

How do we know where a country's comparative advantage lies? One way is to look at the unit cost of producing different goods; another is to look at the prices of these goods before trade, assuming, of course, that prices equal unit costs. If the only factor of production is labour and all labour gets paid the same wage, then the price of grain in Ireland will be three times the price of beef since workers in the grain sector are only one-third as productive as workers in the beef sector. In France the price of a kilo of grain will be the same as the price of a kilo of beef since workers are equally productive in both sectors and get paid the same amount.

	Ireland	France
Pbeef	1	1
Pgrain	3	1

Since one-third is less than 1, indicating that Ireland's relative price of beef is less than that of France, it follows that Ireland has a comparative advantage in beef production.

	Ireland	**France**
Pgrain	3	1
Pbeef	1	1

Since 1 is less than 3, indicating that France's relative price of grain is less than that of Ireland, it follows that France has a comparative advantage in grain production. It is interesting and important to note that in our stylised two-good, two-country world, as long as the domestic opportunity cost of production is different in both countries, then it is impossible for one country to have a comparative advantage in the production of both goods.

Many individuals still find the theory of comparative advantage counter-intuitive. It is all very well to say that what matters for trade purposes is domestic opportunity, cost of production or domestic relative prices, but in the real world what matters are absolute prices. How then in the real world can an Ireland of the above example compete with France if it is less productive in all lines of production?

The answer to this puzzle is to realise that prices are determined by two elements, the productivity of factors of production and the cost of employing factors of production. Since workers in Ireland are less productive than workers in France, they will earn less, even after trade. For example, if Irish workers were paid £10 a day and French workers 70Frf a day and the Irish pound-French franc exchange rate was £1 = 7Frf, then we can see the Irish and French workers get the same return. In this situation Ireland would not be able to export anything to France; it would be uncompetitive as its prices would be too high.

If on the other hand, Irish wages were £3 a day to France's 70Frf and the exchange rate was still £1 = 7Frf, then Ireland would be able to successfully export beef at a lower price than the French. This is because although the Irish worker in the beef sector has a productivity of only 60% of his French counterparts, his wages are only 30% of French wages. They would still, however, not be able to export grain as the price of grain in Ireland would still be higher than in France. This is because an Irish worker has a productivity in the grain sector which is only 20% of that of a French worker in grain production but his wages are 30% of French wages.

So lower wages in the less productive country allow it to compete successfully against the more productive country. This does not mean that the less productive country does not gain from trade. If the imported good costs less than it did before trade, then the country has gained.

Another means by which a less productive country pays its workers less than the more productive country is through a depreciation of its currency. Let us return to the example where Irish workers were paid £10 a day to France's 70Frf. At the £1 = 7Frf exchange rate, Ireland would want to import both grain and beef from France, and France would not want to import anything from Ireland. The excess demand for French francs and the excess supply of Irish pounds would cause a depreciation of the Irish pound against the French franc. This depreciation would continue until such time as the excess demand for French francs and the corresponding excess supply of Irish pounds had been eliminated. If the exchange rates were for example £1 to 2Frf then Ireland would be able to successfully export beef at that exchange rate.

It should be noted that an exchange rate depreciation is analogous to a reduction in the return to domestic factors of production. In this example, the exchange rate depreciation is the same as a cut in the domestic wage rate.

The sources of comparative advantage

In the previous section we have seen that all countries can engage in mutually beneficial trade, provided that the relative prices of their goods prior to trade differ. This naturally begs the question, what determines pre-trade relative prices? The answer is straightforward. Prices of goods in a country are determined by the interaction of supply and demand. If pre-trade relative prices differ among countries, this is indicative of inter-country differences in domestic conditions of supply and demand. All other things being equal (*ceteris paribus*), the greater the supply of a good, the lower its price; and the greater the demand for a good, the higher its price. There are two principal theories as to why supply conditions differ among countries. These are, firstly, technological and climatic differences; and secondly, resource differences.

David Ricardo's explanation of international trade, which was based on differences in the levels of productivity per person per day in various industries, could be an example of technological or climatic differences among countries. In the example of France and Ireland, the French worker has a higher productivity in all sectors compared to the Irish worker. This could be due to a climate that is more conducive to higher yields or, alternatively, it could be due to superior French technology.

Ricardo's model is essentially based on a labour theory of value, since labour is the only factor of production that he considers and it is the productivity of labour that determines the domestic opportunity cost of production. There are no distribution effects in Ricardo's model because labour is considered to be the only factor of production. Hence, if free trade benefits a country, then it must be benefiting all of its workers, since all income earned accrues to workers.

At the beginning of this century two Swedish economists, Eli Heckscher and Bertil Ohlin offered a new explanation as to why supply conditions and hence relative prices differ among countries; countries differ in terms of natural endowments.[57] These endowments (for example land, labour and capital) are inputs that are used in the production of goods and services. So differences in endowments get reflected in differences in the cost of producing various goods. For example, one would expect that a country with an abundance of good farmland would be an efficient producer of agricultural products. The reasoning is simple: an abundance of good farmland means low rental values for land and hence low prices for agricultural products, since agricultural products are intensive users of land.

The Heckscher-Ohlin model of trade (as it is popularly known) differs from the Ricardian model in another respect: the distribution consequences of free trade. In this model, notwithstanding the fact that the country as a whole gains from trade, there are income redistribution effects within a country. Putting it more starkly, there are winners and losers when a country opens its borders and engages in free trade. This is a consequence of the fact that there is more than one factor of production. Free trade will not only change the production structure of a country (more specialisation) it will also change the demand for factors of production.

Take the example of a country that, as a result of free trade, now specialises in the production of land-intensive agricultural products, whereas before free trade, it was also producing capital-intensive industrial products. The change in the country's production structure would have increased the demand for land and reduced the demand for capital. This would have resulted in increased returns for landowners and decreased returns for the owners of capital. Landowners gain and capitalists lose as a result of free trade.

These two principal theories of comparative advantage are similar, to the extent that they conclude that a country will have a comparative advantage in products which they produce in relative abundance, regardless of whether that abundance is determined by climate, technology or resource availability.

Demand conditions can also help determine a country's comparative advantage. If, for example, two countries had identical supply conditions but different tastes, pre-trade relative prices would differ. If the Irish consumer displayed a relatively stronger preference for grain than her French counterpart, this would lead to higher pre-trade prices for grain in Ireland compared to France (assuming identical supply conditions) thus indicating comparative disadvantage in Ireland in grain production. So in trade between Ireland and France, we would expect Ireland to be an importer of grain.

Although demand differences across countries can help explain comparative advantage, it is little more than a theoretical curiosity since it is unlikely that it is the principal determinant of comparative advantage.

Policy implications of traditional trade theory

The common feature of traditional trade theories (be they of the Ricardian or Heckscher-Ohlin variety) is that economic agents are assumed to be operating in perfectly competitive markets. In other words increasing returns to scale or spillover effects do not exist and no individual or firm can influence prices. Countries trade because they are different and the greater the differences between countries the greater the gains from trade. We also expect trade between countries to be of an 'inter-industry' variety. In other words countries will not have two-way trade in the same product: they will either be an exporter or importer of that product.

In an earlier section we saw how a country can enjoy a higher level of consumption in the aggregate if it removes its trade barriers. If all countries remove barriers to trade, all countries will enjoy a higher level of aggregate consumption and income. But even if some countries continue to pursue protectionist policies, the countries that unilaterally remove their trade barriers increase their level of national income. This is an incredibly strong result: it implies that all policy-makers can increase real national income simply by removing trade barriers. Moreover, it also means that policy-makers can increase national welfare through trade barrier dismantlement and a proper redistribution of the gains from trade.

Of course in practice, liberalisation will hurt some sections of society, but if the national cake has grown, a taxation and transfer policy that taxes the beneficiaries of trade liberalisation and transfers the proceeds of this tax to those whom trade liberalisation has made worse off, could ensure that everybody gains. This does of course presuppose that there are no inefficiencies associated with a tax and transfer policy. If we ignore the possibility of a tax and transfer system, then we can assert that the principal beneficiary of free trade is the consumer, who is now able to enjoy cheaper imported goods than was previously the case.

If trade liberalisation is so beneficial we must ask why the world is not characterised by free trade? What causes governments to interfere with trade? A whole literature has developed designed to answer this question and we will address it in a later section. For the moment the most important thing to remember is that the gains from trade outlined so far all depend on the assumption that markets are perfectly competitive. Remove this assumption (as we will do later) and the whole edifice of unilaterally realisable gains from trade becomes much more fragile.

Trade barriers

Governments interfere with the international movement of goods and services for a variety of economic, political and fiscal reasons. In this section we will identify the principal instruments which governments use which impede free trade. A good overview of the effects of trade policy is provided by Corden (1971).[58]

Tariffs

A tariff is a tax on imports and is usually *ad valorem*; a percentage of the price of the imported goods. It is inherently discriminatory, since it does not apply to domestic goods that compete with imports. It results in a redistribution of income away from consumers in favour of domestic producers and the government. Governments have a new source of revenue while domestic producers can now charge a higher price thanks to the protective effect of the tariff. The real income of consumers is reduced as they must now pay more for those goods that are subject to tariffs.

Quotas

Tariffs operate by taxing imports and allowing demand and supply to adjust to the new domestic price. Quotas operate by restricting the volume of imports and allowing the domestic price to adjust in such a way that the domestic market clears, i.e. domestic demand equals domestic and foreign supply. If a quota is to be effective in restricting imports it will inevitably result in higher domestic prices for the product subject to such a restriction. This is because the restriction of foreign supply will result in excess demand for the product which will increase its price.

Again, as with the tariff, the consumer will suffer a loss in real income due to higher domestic prices for the good subject to quantitative import restrictions. Domestic producers of competing products will gain due to higher prices for their output but there will be no fiscal gain for the government. Those fortunate enough to hold import licences (or quotas) will gain as they now hold a valuable asset: the right to import good(s) at world prices and sell them at inflated domestic prices.

Voluntary restraint on exports

This is very similar to a quota except in this instance it is the exporting country that agrees to limit the quantity of its exports to the importing country, thus increasing the price of such goods in the countries that import them. The only difference in the income redistribution effect of this measure compared to quotas is that it is the foreign exporter, as opposed to the holder of import quotas, who enjoys the rent (the difference between the domestic price of the good in the importing countries and its world price) associated with this form of trade restriction. It is also a very popular means of restricting trade, as it is not very visible and it allows countries to contravene international trade laws in a way that would be impossible with tariffs or import quotas.

Administrative barriers

The governments of many countries make it difficult for foreign exporters to penetrate their domestic markets by putting in place a whole series of rules and regulations with which the foreign exporter must comply, at some cost. These rules often come in the guise of health and safety standards or measures designed to give consumers protection.

Frontier delays and the paperwork associated with crossing national borders add to the cost of trying to penetrate certain markets and hence is akin to a tax on imports.

Governments are important players in an economy, not just as the overseer who determines the rules of the game, but also as a player in the market. In a free international market, governments would purchase goods from the supplier who offers the product(s) that they desire at the best price, regardless of the nationality of the supplier. In reality, public procurement tends to have a decidedly nationalistic bent; in other words public contracts invariably go to domestic firms.

Export subsidies and export taxes

Giving domestic producers a subsidy when they export encourages them to produce more for foreign markets at the expense of the domestic market. The cost of this policy is borne by the taxpayer and the domestic consumer, since the diversion of supply away from the domestic market raises domestic prices. Export taxes have the opposite effect of penalising producers who serve foreign markets, with positive fiscal consequences for the government and lower prices for the domestic consumer.

All the above measures, be they designed to protect producers who serve the domestic market or aid producers who serve foreign markets, are an interference with free trade. In a perfectly competitive world, such measures reduce national and global income through their interference with the market mechanism. They distort the allocation of resources between different sectors of the economy, promoting some sectors at the expense of others.

Justifying trade restrictions

Non-economic reasons

The government of a country may restrict the importation of certain goods in order to be self-sufficient in those products. Self-sufficiency, although it entails an economic cost, may be desired to achieve some political goal. This goal could be national security, it could form part of a country's international strategic objectives or merely be designed to protect a country from foreign influences that are considered dangerous and pernicious. For example, self-sufficiency in agriculture and armaments could be justified as a precautionary measure in case imports of these products are cut off in times of war. One means of settling scores, when countries' governments disagree politically with one another, is to impose a trade embargo. The importation of animals into rabies-free countries is restricted for obvious national health reasons; the same goes for drugs. All these restrictions are costly, but that is not to say that the realisation of such objectives does not merit such a cost.

Economic reasons

A good survey of economic arguments for and against protectionism is provided by Corden (1974).[59]

The principal economic reasons given for interfering with free trade are the protection of infant industries and the maintenance of employment. The infant industry argument is associated with the German economist Friedrich List (1789–1846), who advocated the protection of industries from foreign competition in order to allow them to develop. Without such protectionism, such industries would not be able to withstand foreign competition. Once these industries had developed sufficiently so as to be in a position to compete with foreign producers, such protection could be removed.

There are two principal criticisms of this theory: the first criticism questions the *a priori* assumption that there are market factors which prevent the spontaneous emergence of these industries in an unrestricted market, and the second criticism asserts that overprotected infants never mature.

Recall that traditional trade theory operates within the neoclassical framework of perfect competition. Perfect competition implies, *inter-alia*, perfect knowledge, no barriers to entry and no spillover effects or externalities. In such a world, if there are potentially profitable industries that are as yet undeveloped, then entrepreneurs, driven by a desire to make profit, will enter these industries. If those industries are potentially profitable, even if that profit is not immediately realisable, then there is no need for government-inspired protection to help them develop. The second criticism makes the point that protectionism, instead of aiding the development of industries, can often inhibit their development by shielding them from the forces of international competition.

Protectionism allows workers in protected industries to retain jobs that would otherwise have been lost. However, in a perfectly competitive world, removing trade restrictions would cause the import competing sector to shrink but the export sector would expand, so workers and resources would move from the import competing sector to the export sector. Unemployment should only be a temporary phenomenon, lasting as long as it takes displaced workers to find new jobs. If it persists, then according to economists there must be some reason (other than the removal of trade barriers) that is causing its persistence, such as inflexible labour markets and minimum wages. Removal of these institutionally imposed rigidities will solve the problem of unemployment. Protectionism is a more costly way of achieving the same objective.

Distributional reasons

As mentioned earlier, the removal of trade barriers, like any other form of structural adjustment, involves winners and losers. Losers are those who witness a reduction in their real income as a result of trade liberalisation. Governments are very susceptible to political pressure and those sections of society that are threatened with a reduction in income, as a result of trade liberalisation, have every incentive to organise in order to lobby the government against such measures.

Many political economists argue that the protectionist bias of most governments reflects the political power of interest groups associated with protected industries. But just as some sections of society are adversely affected by free trade, others are adversely affected by protectionism; namely consumers. If commercial policy has a protectionist bias, it must mean that the political power of pro-protectionist groups is greater than the political power of free-trade groups.

How can this be? Olson (1965) discusses the logic of collective action and the impact of interest groups on the political process.[60] Consumers, who are the main beneficiaries of free trade policies, are a large dispersed group. So the benefits of free trade are spread over a large body of people. Hence, even though in the aggregate the gains to consumers outweigh the losses to those associated with protected sectors, their *per capita* gains must be much less than the *per capita* losses of the losers.

Moreover, these gains, since they come in the form of lower prices, are not very visible whereas the losses (which usually take the form of a fall in earnings) are highly visible. Thus there exists an asymmetry in the incentive to organise and lobby among consumers and protectionist interests; the latter having a much greater incentive than the former to defend their position. It is also much easier to organise a lobby group when the number is smaller and geographically and sectorally concentrated, which is usually the case with protected industries.

Concluding remarks on traditional trade theory

All of the preceding analysis takes as its starting point the assumption of perfectly competitive markets. As a consequence, we see that protectionism unambiguously reduces national income and that there is no economic or even distributional justification for its existence. In the next section we will look at new theories of trade and specialisation that assume that markets are imperfect. We will see that in the context of imperfect markets, trade restrictions may not necessarily be welfare reducing. However, we will also see that trade restrictions are a second-best means of achieving certain economic and distributional objectives. In other words, free trade combined with other policies can realise the same objectives at a lower social cost.

15.3.2 New trade theory
....

Traditional trade theory dominated intellectual thinking for more than a hundred years. However, increasingly, academics, students and general observers began to notice the disparity between theory and reality. Most world trade in the post-war period was not trade between very different nations but trade between developed countries with similar resource bases, similar technology and similar tastes. Moreover, most trade between these nations was not of an inter-industry variety but rather of an intra-industry type; that is the simultaneous import and export of similar products.

In the 1980s, economists put forward new theories to explain this phenomenon. Foremost among them has been Paul Krugman; in fact his name has become almost synonomous with new trade theory.[61] Firstly, they claimed that consumers desire diversity. Some Germans drive BMWs and some drive Peugeots: likewise in France. If diverse consumer tastes cannot be satisfied by domestic supply, we will witness a two-way flow of trade in similar products, in this instance a two-way flow in car trade.

What makes intra-industry trade in identifiable branded products more probable and profitable is the existence of economies of scale. When technology exhibits economies of scale, it tends to result in high levels of output, since the more a firm produces the lower the unit cost of production. So it does not make sense for French or German manufacturers of cars to try and produce all varieties themselves, since this would lead to much shorter production runs, and much higher costs and prices as a result. Therefore, the combination of diverse consumer tastes and economies of scale are sufficient to ensure trade of an intra-industry variety.

It should also be noted that the market structure in which such trade takes place is necessarily imperfect, since goods are distinguishable by brand (which is never the case under perfect competition) and economies of scale tend to promote large firms who dominate an industry. The industrial structure may be monopolistic or oligopolistic, depending on the degree of competition that exists in an industry.

According to traditional trade theory, if two countries had identical demand and supply conditions and hence identical pre-trade prices, there would be no basis for mutually beneficial trade. When, however, economies of scale exist, two identical countries can engage in mutually beneficial trade by specialising and realising the lower unit cost that specialisation brings. Unlike trade based on comparative advantage, trade based on increasing returns to scale is hard to predict in advance of its occurrence. We cannot with confidence predict what country is likely to produce what product. All we know is that the country with the largest domestic market is probably more likely to be competitive in industries exhibiting increasing returns to scale.

Other forms of market imperfections that have important implications for trade policy are externalities or spillover effects. In many instances the private and social cost of an action differs. An individual entrepreneur thinking about setting up a plant in a certain region will weigh up the private costs and benefits of such a decision. He will reject the option if, *ex-ante*, it appears to be unprofitable. Yet if many firms take this decision, what appeared initially as a non-viable option could become viable due to positive spillover effects. Without being exhaustive, these spillover effects (or externalities) could be: the availability of cheaper and more varied services (which are greater the greater the concentration of industry); greater access to skilled labour (which tends to be attracted to regions with a high firm density); and easier access to vital information, which is so crucial to the success of business in a competitive environment.

The policy implications of new trade theory or the policy implications of imperfect markets

When markets exhibit imperfections there is always a justification for government intervention to correct the market imperfection; this does not mean that intervention always improves upon the market outcome. Efficiency improving intervention requires appropriate information in order to know where market imperfections exist and their extent. It also requires the choice of the correct instrument of intervention.

All the aforementioned is relevant to new trade theory, since the latter is firmly rooted within an imperfect market context. For example, in a world characterised by diverse industries, some of which exhibit increasing returns to scale, while others exhibit decreasing, or constant returns to scale, the effect of trade liberalisation is much less clear. The beauty of traditional trade theory was that it showed that trade liberalisation benefited all countries, even the most technologically backward. New trade theory, on the other hand, can make a case for free trade based on global efficiency or even the need for good international relations between countries, but it cannot unambiguously claim to benefit all countries.

Free trade brings about a restructuring of an economy. If a country witnesses a decline in its increasing returns industries and growth in its decreasing or constant returns industries, due to trade liberalisation, then the average productivity of resources will have declined. This does not mean that the country is necessarily worse off as a result, since this loss in terms of the productivity of its resources has to be weighed against the gain to consumers from cheaper imports.

The situation is no longer clear-cut. Such a result is not as startling as it may first appear, since we are all familiar with the phenomena of declining or economically backward regions within what is often a prosperous country. Since free trade exists between regions within a country, it is not obvious all have benefited from free inter-regional trade.[62]

The policy implications of new trade theory is that it creates a 'case' (that is to say a necessary but not sufficient condition) for intervention. Intervention could take the form of import barriers or export subsidies or even production subsidies in those industries where economies of scale exist. The objective is clear: to try and ensure that a country has a high percentage of increasing returns or high value-added industries. The decline of the traditionally high wage manufacturing sector in the UK and its replacement by low wage services should not be a matter of policy indifference. Of course the negative side of the intervention argument is that it is a zero sum game. Not all countries can have a monopoly on increasing returns industries. If all try, then all will suffer as a consequence. Also, certain kinds of intervention such as export subsidies only serve to antagonise international competitors and can easily degenerate into a trade war from which no one emerges as victor.

Externalities are in essence the core of the infant industry argument. Social and private benefits and costs differ, so governments protect certain industries, where they consider that the social benefits of that industry's existence outweigh the private benefits to the industry's proprietors. Often, however, there are more effective and direct means of tackling market imperfections. If, for example, private entrepreneurs are unable to exploit a sector where a country may have a potential comparative or competitive advantage, due to lack of availability of finance, the correct response by policy-makers is to improve the nature of financial institutions, to overcome this imperfection. Barring this strategy, capital or loan subsidies may be appropriate. Protectionism, according to economists, is down this list of appropriate policy measures to combat market imperfections.

Even though theoretically there is a strong case to be made against unlimited free trade, very few of the new trade theorists actually advocate protectionism or other forms of interference with the market mechanism. Their failure to breach the gap between theory and policy could be due to an innate conservatism or to their fear of what can be broadly termed political failures. The market is not the only social system riddled with imperfections. The informational requirements necessary to intervene correctly are enormous and, at a more serious level, there is always the fear that governments will become hostages to vested interests if they make it standard politics to intervene in trade policy.

For these reasons, notwithstanding the less rosy picture presented by new trade theory (especially for poorer and smaller countries), new trade theorists still advocate free trade as the best option in an imperfect world.

15.3.3 The Irish experience

Irish trade policy

It is difficult to find real-world examples of the polar extremes of trade policy as defined in theory; that is to say self-sufficiency and complete free trade. The reality is that nearly all countries engage to some extent in the international exchange of goods and services and nearly all countries have rules and regulations in place, that interfere to some extent with the volume and direction of international trade. However, along the spectrum from self-sufficiency to free trade, we can judge the bias of a country's trade policy over time and also make comparisons between countries.

It is in this context that we can say that Ireland's trade policy was relatively liberal (free-trade oriented) in the 1920s, highly protectionist from the 1930s to the end of the 1950s, and progressively liberal ever since. The global environment during the period of protectionism varied considerably. The 1930s witnessed a worldwide global depression, followed by a world war, followed by a period of reconstruction and very rapid growth in the post-war period.

Despite the varying fortunes of the world economy in this period, the contemporaneous Irish economic experience singularly failed to live up to expectations. The disillusionment with protectionism as a strategy for economic development led to a reversal in the direction of commercial policy. This shift in policy direction was reflected in a unilateral cut in tariffs in 1963 and 1964, followed by the Anglo-Irish Free Trade Agreement in 1965 and culminating in our admission to what was then the European Economic Community in 1973.

The principal aim of the European Economic Community (EEC), which was set up by the Treaty of Rome in 1957, was to foster free trade among its member states and to pursue a common trade policy with regard to non-member states. Hence since 1973, Ireland has essentially waived its right to an autonomous trade policy, by agreeing to abide by the rules and regulations of the EEC. The European Economic Community has itself evolved since its original inception. It now has many more member states (and potential applicants knocking on the door) and has renewed itself and its commitment to freer internal trade through the Single European Act, which came into force in July 1987, and more recently the Treaty on European Union which was finalised at Maastricht in December 1991.

The European Union (as it is now known) has also participated in international agreements and signed treaties designed to foster freer trade at a more global level. Some of these arrangements are bilateral, such as its free trade agreement with EFTA (European Free Trade Association), while others are more global and non-discriminatory such as its participation in the GATT (General Agreement on Tariffs and Trade), which was itself replaced by the WTO (World Trade Organisation) in 1995.

GATT has been the most important organisation governing world trade in the post-war period. It has been committed to global free trade as enshrined in its principles of National Treatment and Non-Discrimination. 'National Treatment' is a commitment to give equal treatment to national and international transactions, while 'Non-Discrimination' is a commitment to not distinguish between countries on the grounds of origin. It has also overseen successive rounds of multilateral trade barrier reductions, whereby all member countries agreed to reduce trade barriers by some agreed amount. The latest round of multilateral trade negotiations, known as the Uruguay Round, was concluded in 1994.

What should be clear is that Ireland's trade policy has to be looked at within the international institutional framework, firstly as a member of the EU and secondly within the context of the EU's membership of the WTO. The fact that Ireland and all the other member countries of the EU and WTO have agreed to bind themselves to rules that increasingly curtail these countries' rights to interfere with international trade, is testament to the general faith that global prosperity requires the unfettered movement of goods and services between countries.

Summary

1. Inflation is a rise in the general price level. There are many different causes of inflation. The Quantity Theory of Money is the earliest model of inflation. It suggests that the price level increases with the money supply and that monetary policy is ineffective in changing an economy's level of output. Demand pull inflation is caused by increases in aggregate demand. Cost push inflation results from a rise in costs in general, and of wages in particular. A depreciating currency, unless checked, results in imported inflation. Expectations also play an important role. During inflationary periods, debtors gain at the expense of creditors, individuals on fixed incomes lose, consumption is encouraged, and fixed-income assets and productive assets become less attractive.

2. Policies to combat inflation concentrate on either the demand side or the supply side of the economy. Tighter control over the money supply, increases in tax rates and reductions in public expenditure are all examples of demand-side measures. Increasing competition and cutting labour costs are examples of supply-side measures. Imported inflation requires a firm exchange rate policy.

3. Unemployment is a stock concept: it measures the number of people who are out of work at a particular point in time. There are different types of unemployment. They include frictional, seasonal, structural, demand deficient and classical. The

costs of unemployment are both private and social. They accrue to the unemployed, to the taxpayer and to society at large. Whereas it is possible to measure the economic costs arising from unemployment, it is very difficult to estimate the social costs.

4. There are many different explanations of unemployment. With the assumption of freely flexible wages, unemployment in the classical world is temporary and voluntary. For Keynes, unemployment could be long-term and involuntary. It is caused by insufficient aggregate demand and requires government action. Fiscal policy is the preferred option. The monetarist and the supply-side theories of unemployment are similar to the classical explanation. Government intervention is seen as part of the problem rather than the solution. A large number of unemployed is a cyclical characteristic of the capitalist system, according to Marx: unemployment is the result of the inevitable class struggle between capitalists and workers.

5. Trade theories attempt to explain the causes and consequences of the international exchange of goods and services. The multiplicity of theories can be broadly categorised into two schools of thought: traditional trade theory and new trade theory. The essential difference between the two approaches is that traditional trade theory assumes that markets are perfectly competitive, while new trade theory assumes that markets are imperfectly competitive to a greater or lesser extent.

6. The key concept in traditional trade theory is 'comparative advantage'. It says that all countries can engage in mutually beneficial trade by specialising in what they do 'relatively' best. Countries trade because they are different and this difference reflects itself in their domestic relative costs. The greater the differences between countries, the greater the gains from trade. Such trade will be inter-industry in type. The optimal trade strategy in a perfectly competitive environment is unilateral trade barrier dismantlement. The bases for new trade theory are economies of scale and consumer demand for product diversity. Such trade tends to be intra-industry in type and to take place between relatively similar countries. It results in global production efficiency but all countries may not necessarily gain from such trade. The optimal trade strategy in this context may be interventionist in order to maximise a country's share of the gains from trade.

Key terms

Inflation	*Unemployment*	*International trade*
Inflation	Labour force survey	Mercantilism
Inflation rate	Live register	Absolute advantage
Deflation	Labour force	Comparative advantage
Disinflation	Unemployment rate	International terms of trade
Creeping inflation	Frictional unemployment	Opportunity cost of
Hyper-inflation	Seasonal unemployment	production
Stagflation	Structural unemployment	Production possibility frontier
Price index	Demand-deficient	Pre-trade relative prices
	unemployment	Revealed comparative
		advantage

Consumer Price Index
GDP deflator
Nominal interest rate
Real interest rate
Menu costs
Indexation
Fiscal drag
Shoe leather effect
Unanticipated inflation
Anticipated inflation
Demand pull inflation
Inflationary gap
Quantity Theory of Money
Money Velocity
Monetarism
Adaptive expectations
Cost push inflation
Imported inflation
Rational expectations

Classical unemployment
Voluntary unemployment
Involuntary unemployment
Natural Rate of
  Unemployment
Reserve army of
  unemployed
Unemployment trap
Replacement ratio
Poverty trap
Tax wedge
Labour market rigidities
Wage bargaining process
Insider-outsider model
Labour legislation

Factor endowments
Inter-industry trade
Tariffs
Quotas
Voluntary export
  restraints
Export subsidies/taxes
Infant industries
Imperfect markets
Economies of scale
Externalities
Intra-industry trade

Review questions

1. Explain the term 'inflation'. Why is inflation undesirable? Who benefits from inflation?
2. Explain the causes of inflation. Suggest how each cause can be tackled.
3. What are the costs of unemployment?
4. Explain the theories of unemployment. How do they relate to the Irish experience of unemployment?
5. Explain the theory of comparative advantage. How does it differ from absolute advantage? According to the theory of comparative advantage, what countries are most likely to engage in mutually beneficial trade?
6. By what mechanism is comparative advantage translated into absolute competitiveness?

Working problems

1. The figures in Table 15.7 were taken from the annual report entitled *National Income and Expenditure*, published by the CSO. It shows GDP at current market prices and GDP at constant market prices.

Table 15.7: GDP at constant and current market prices (1987–94)

Year	Current GDP (£ million)	Constant GDP (£ million)
1987	21,074.8	22,792.9
1988	22,717.9	23,765.3
1989	25,418.3	25,218.7
1990	27,187.6	27,187.6
1991	28,263.4	27,792.2
1992	29,971.8	28,889.5
1993	32,174.0	29,781.0
1994	34,741.0	31,787.0

(a) What is the base year? On a diagram with £ on the vertical axis and the year on the horizontal axis, graph the two series.

(b) Calculate the GDP deflator for each year. What is the general trend? What year deviates from that trend?

(c) Calculate the inflation rate for 1992.

2. The working population of the home country is two million. The working population of the foreign country is ten million. Both countries can only produce two goods: beer and grain. The average productivity of labour in the production of both goods is shown in Table 15.8.

Table 15.8

	Home	Foreign
Beer (litre per person per day)	4	16
Grain (kg per person per day)	8	8

Describe and explain the pattern of trade between the home country and the foreign country.

Multi-choice questions

1. The inflation rate for 1989 was 4%. The CPI for 1988 was 109.4. What was the CPI for 1989?

   (a) 104.6;
   (b) 105.2;
   (c) 113.8;
   (d) 112.7;
   (e) none of the above.

2. Anticipated inflation:

   (a) imposes no costs on society;
   (b) can result in menu costs and the shoe leather effect;

    (c) imposes more costs on society than unanticipated inflation;
    (d) both (b) and (c) above;
    (e) none of the above.

3. For monetarists, unemployment:
    (a) is largely involuntary;
    (b) is caused by a deficiency in demand;
    (c) often results from inappropriate demand-management policies;
    (d) can be cured by active demand-management policies;
    (e) both (b) and (d) above.

4. Involuntary unemployment:
    (a) is caused by a deficient demand for goods;
    (b) is closely associated with Keynesian unemployment;
    (c) is difficult to measure accurately;
    (d) is a measure of those who are willing to work but who cannot find a job at the market wage rate;
    (e) all of the above.

5. In working problem 2, what is the domestic opportunity cost of grain production in the home country?
    (a) 2 litres of beer per 1 kg of grain;
    (b) 1 litre of beer per 1 kg of grain;
    (c) 5 litres of beer per 1 kg of grain;
    (d) $\frac{1}{2}$ litre of beer per 1 kg of grain;
    (e) there is no opportunity cost.

6. Refer again to working problem 2. If wages are identical in both countries then the 'competitive' position of home and foreign will be as follows:
    (a) Home is competitive in grain only and foreign in beer only.
    (b) Home is competitive in beer only and foreign in grain only.
    (c) Home is competitive in grain and foreign is competitive in both grain and beer.
    (d) Home is not competitive in either grain or beer and foreign is competitive in both grain and beer.
    (e) None of the above.

True or false

1. Disinflation is defined as a continuous decline in the price level. _____
2. In combating inflation, monetarists advocate a steady rate of growth of the money supply. _____
3. The total cost of unemployment can be measured by summing the amount of money spent on social welfare benefits. _____
4. The poverty trap is the estimated number of citizens below the poverty line. ____
5. A country can have a 'comparative advantage' in the production of 'all goods' if it is more efficient at producing all goods than its competitors. _____

6. The infant industry argument for protection is only valid if some market imperfection has prevented thus far the emergence of that industry. _____

Fill in the blanks

Inflation is a rise in the general level of _____ . It is measured by a price _____ . The CPI and the GDP _____ are examples of price indices. Causes of inflation include _____ pull, cost push, a _____ of the exchange rate, excessive wage increases and expectations. Creditors, exporters and those sections of society on _____ money incomes suffer from inflation. Beneficiaries of inflation can include the government and _____ . Counter-inflationary policies include _____ fiscal and monetary policies, wage restraint and _____-_____ policies targeted at reducing production _____ . The factors influencing the Irish inflation rate include domestic economic policy, the international trend in prices and the strength of the Irish pound against other currencies of the _____ .

Unemployment is a _____ concept. It measures the number of people who are willing and _____ to work but who cannot find a job. The different types of unemployment include _____ , seasonal, structural, demand-deficient and classical. _____-_____ unemployment is caused by insufficient spending in the economy. Involuntary unemployment is possible in the _____ theory whereas the classical theory assumes unemployment is of a _____ nature. Market _____ and _____ flexibility are central in explaining the differences between the classical and the Keynesian theories of unemployment. _____ explains unemployment in the context of the struggle between the capitalists and the working class. The _____ and social costs to unemployment accrue to the unemployed, the _____ and to the economy.

Traditional trade theory assumes that markets are _____ _____ . The key concept is the law of _____ advantage which is a more sophisticated concept than the law of _____ advantage. It says that countries should specialise in what they do _____ best. Comparative advantage reveals itself in lower pre-trade relative _____ . Trade based on comparative advantage tends to be _____-industry in type. _____ countries can gain from such trade and the greater the difference between international terms of trade and domestic _____ _____ , the greater the gains from trade. New trade theory by contrast assumes that markets are _____ _____ . Such trade takes place between _____ countries and the bases for such trade are _____ of _____ and product _____ .

CASE STUDY A: INFLATION

Extract from **The Irish Times**
Vigilant central banker guards restless inflation
by Cliff Taylor

'I never relax about inflation, that is the one thing that you never do as a central banker, you are never complacent.' So says Mr Maurice O'Connell after eighteen months in the governor's chair on the top floor of the Central Bank building on Dame Street.

For the moment, the governor says he is 'optimistic about the inflation outlook'. The last figures for mid-August showed a surprisingly low 2.5% inflation rate, while the rate of increase of borrowing from the financial institutions has been moving back closer to the Central Bank's target increase level.

The bank is watching the housing market closely, after recent figures showing strong price increases in some areas.

Mr O'Connell will not speculate on the future trend of interest rates.

. . .

Looking at budgetary policy, Mr O'Connell welcomed the government's commitment to a 2% limit for the increase in real spending next year. The key thing was to remain on course for EMU, he said.

Source: The Irish Times, *6 October 1995.*

Questions
. . . .

1. Why would, in particular, a Central Bank governor be concerned with inflation?
2. Why is there concern expressed over 'the rate of increase of borrowing from the financial institutions'? What type of inflation does this suggest? Can you show this in terms of a model?
3. What monetary and fiscal policies are mentioned or inferred in the article? What effect might they have on inflation?

Additional case study questions based on Article 15.1 from the text

Questions on Article 15.1: Red faces in Central Bank as inflation knocks knockers

1. According to the author, what factors have contributed to Ireland's inflation rate of 2.4%?
2. Is this 'moderate' inflation rate surprising? Explain your answer.
3. How would a lower US dollar or a weak sterling affect the Irish inflation rate?

[The answers are not included.]

CASE STUDY B: UNEMPLOYMENT

Extract from the Irish Independent
241,600 An Economy not Working
by Dermot McAleese

Ireland's unemployment rate has been the highest in the EC for the past decade. Contrary to popular belief, this high unemployment has nothing necessarily to do with either our peripheral location or with our comparative lack of development.

One obvious factor in explaining the rise in Irish unemployment is the recession in the UK and the US. During the last twelve months, the number out of work has escalated by 2.4 percentage points in Britain, 1.8 in the US, 2.6 in Australia and 3.0 in Canada. These increases help to put Ireland's increase of 2.8 percentage points in perspective. Given the close ties between the Irish labour market and these countries, some increase in the Irish unemployment rate is inevitable.

Another factor – this one of our own making – is the rise in Irish welfare payments during the past decade. During the 1980s, social welfare spending increased threefold compared with doubling of prices. The real value of social assistance for the unemployed and provision of social services from housing to health and education have risen appreciably in real terms. The level of overall state support is now at least as high, and in many respects higher, in Ireland than in the UK and the US. The propensity to return home rather than stay abroad awaiting the recovery is thus more enhanced.

The major problem of Irish unemployment is the number of long-term unemployed. We've had a particularly bad record in getting people back into the labour market once they have left it for any period of time. About half of our unemployed are long-term, compared with 6% in the US. A temporary increase in numbers out of work is always to be regretted, and can represent real hardship for the individuals affected. But when the world economy recovers, and recover it certainly will, they can anticipate a return to the workforce. It is a different matter when unemployment feeds on itself, as happens in too many Irish families with as much as three generations without jobs. Hard to believe, the Irish tax and social welfare system still strongly discourage many long-term unemployed from taking up jobs when they are offered.

There is no quick-fix solution to the unemployment problem. However, things could be much improved if a really concentrated effort were made to make Irish labour cheaper and administratively easier to hire.

Source: The Irish Independent, *9 August 1991.*

Questions
....

1. From your knowledge of the Irish economy, why would Ireland be more susceptible to world recessions than other EU countries?
2. What problems might the granting of a threefold increase in social welfare payments during the 1980s create?

3. Explain how the Irish tax and welfare systems discourage the long-term unemployed from accepting employment.

Additional case study questions based on Article 15.2 from the text

Questions on Article 15.2: At last, the truth about unemployment

1. How is unemployment defined according to the labour force survey? How does this differ from the Live Register?
2. What factors might account for the difference between the two unemployment figures?
3. How can the labour force survey, as a means of measuring unemployment, be improved?

[The answers are not included.]

CASE STUDY C: INTERNATIONAL TRADE

Extract from the Guardian Weekly
Putting Trade in its Proper Place
by Larry Elliott

Fauchon's, in the Place de la Madelaine in Paris, is a gastronomic paradise. In the section devoted to fruit and veg. there are dainties to whet the appetite of Parisian foodies – mangoes from Mali, maracujas from Colombia and kiwanos from Portugal. This is the way supporters of global liberalisation would have us believe it could be everywhere from Kuala Lumpur to Knightsbridge. It is taking as read that the meshing of free trade and unfettered capital flows lead to rising world prosperity and a way out of poverty for the developing world.

Last week the Organisation for Economic Co-operation and Development summed up current thinking when it said globalisation 'gives all countries the possibility of participating in world development and all consumers the assurance of benefit from increasingly vigorous competition between producers'.

The theory is that liberalisation and deregulated capital flows allow countries to specialise in what they are good (or least bad) at, and this international division of labour raises global income.

. . . the developing countries that do best are those with the least state intervention and the freest trade and those new 'tiger economies' pose a massive competitive threat to living standards in the developed world.

Source: Guardian Weekly, *2 June 1996.*

Questions
············
1. Why does the OECD think that freer trade can be beneficial to all countries?
2. If workers in developing countries are not as productive as workers in developed countries (due to the superior technology that is to be found in developed countries), how will such countries be able to compete in an era of globalisation?
3. Who gains and who could possibly lose in the so-called developed countries from freer world trade?

Appendix 15.1: The Phillips curve

The Phillips curve was named after A. W. Phillips, a professor at the London School of Economics. In 1958, he published a paper based on an empirical study. He stated that in the UK, during the period between 1861 and 1957, there was a stable, inverse relationship between the rate of change in money wages and the unemployment rate.[63] In other words, a high rate of money wage inflation was associated with a low rate of unemployment.

In 1960, Samuelson and Solow redefined the variables to look at the relationship between the inflation rate and the unemployment rate. This adaptation, shown in Figure 15.14 is called the Phillips curve.

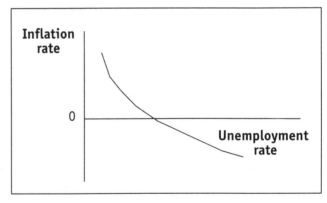

Figure 15.14: The Phillips curve

Keynesian economists accepted the Phillips curve relationship into their theoretical framework. The omission of a price variable was one of the main weaknesses of the Keynesian model.

The Phillips curve appeared to offer a 'menu of choice'. Economists could choose between different rates of inflation and unemployment. Unfortunately, when the relationship was exploited, it broke down. To combat the high rate of unemployment in the 1970s, many western governments followed policies which were inflationary. Unfortunately, the unemployment rates did not fall.

Friedman (1968) and Phelps (1967) tried to explain the breakdown of the Phillips curve relationship in terms of price expectations. Friedman argued that there is a natural rate of unemployment associated with variables like the skills of the labour force, the size of the capital stock and the level of technology. Figure 15.15 depicts the natural rate of unemployment (U^*), at 5%.

Figure 15.15: The long-run Phillips curve and the natural rate of unemployment

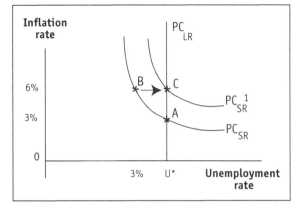

Initially, the economy is at equilibrium at point A. The inflation rate is stable at 3% and unemployment is at the natural rate. Suppose the government decides to reduce the unemployment rate by adopting expansionary policies. On the initial short-term Phillips curve PC_{SR}, the economy moves from point A to point B. The inflation rate rises from 3% to 6% and the unemployment rate falls below the natural rate, U^*, to 3%.

According to Friedman, workers do not realise that increasing inflation means that the real wage is falling. However, they are not fooled for long. A change in expectations shifts the Phillips curve upwards, from PC_{SR} to PC_{SR}^1. The economy returns to equilibrium at point C. Unemployment is again at the natural rate, but inflation is higher.

The inverse relationship between inflation and unemployment is temporary, according to Friedman. Unemployment returns to the natural rate as soon as expectations adjust. A continuation of expansionary policies leads inevitably to accelerating inflation.

In the long run, Friedman argued that the Phillips curve is vertical, at the natural rate of unemployment, U^*. For Friedman, inflation has no long-run effect on the unemployment rate. The long-run expectations-augmented Phillips curve is labelled PC_{LR} in Figure 15.15.

The policy implications differ from the simple case. In attempting to reduce unemployment below its natural rate, the government only succeeds in accelerating domestic inflation. Unemployment can be reduced below the natural rate only if inflation is unexpected. In the long term the natural rate of unemployment can only be reduced by supply-side measures. These changes result in a shift of the aggregate supply curve.

Incidentally, the Phillips curve is simply another way of depicting the AS curve. Consider the different types of AS curves. The conventional AS curve depicts a positive relationship between prices and output levels. Unemployment fluctuates inversely with output. Hence, the rate of change in the price level and unemployment are inversely related. This is depicted in the downward sloping Phillips curve.

The classical AS curve is vertical. Output is independent of the price level; a price rise has no effect on the level of output. Unemployment remains constant. This is depicted by the vertical Phillips curve where the inflation rate and the unemployment rate are unrelated.

From this brief analysis we can see that the Phillips curve is another way of expressing and explaining aggregate supply.

Appendix 15.2 Expectations

Because of Keynes, expectations are an important feature of all modern macro-economic models. Recall that Keynes believed that investors' expectations about the future were the main cause of instability in the national economy. He discussed the 'animal spirits' of investors, which is very different from the careful, cost-benefit analysis which many believe underlie any profit-maximising investment decision.

The volatility of expectations, so colourfully described by Keynes, was very difficult to model and too unpredictable to be accepted by the neoclassical economists. Until the 1970s, the neoclassicals believed that adaptive expectations could be used to explain the behaviour of economic agents. According to this theory, expectations for the current period are based on what actually happened in the past. If we use this concept in a model, the success of that model depends on how accurately the past explains the present and can be extrapolated into the future.

For example, we can develop a model incorporating adaptive expectations to predict the inflation rate. The most basic model is described by Equation [1]

$$\Pi^*_t = \Pi_{t-1}$$ [1]

which states that the predicted inflation rate (Π^*_t) for period t is the same as the actual inflation rate for the previous period (Π_{t-1}).

We can expand this model to take account of errors which we made in our previous prediction. In other words, we are adapting our predictions based on our previous mistakes. One such model is described by Equation [2]

$$\Pi^*_t = \Pi^*_{t-1} + \emptyset\,(\Pi_{t-1} - \Pi^*_{t-1}) \quad 0 < \emptyset < 1$$ [2]

where:

Π^*_t = inflation forecast for the present period.
Π^*_{t-1} = inflation forecast for the previous period.
$\emptyset$ = weight attached to last period's forecasting error.
Π_{t-1} = actual inflation rate for the previous period.

The expression inside the parenthesis represents the forecasting error. It shows the discrepancy between the actual inflation rate in period $t-1$ and the predicted inflation rate. $\emptyset$ represents the importance which we attach to that discrepancy. If we think that the discrepancy will persist into the future, $\emptyset$ will have a value close to one. Then our new inflation rate will equal our old inflation rate plus last period's mistake. If we think that the discrepancy will not persist, we will assign to $\emptyset$ a number which is close to zero. This means that we expect the inflation rate in period t to equal the predicted inflation rate in the previous period.

The importance of this model is that it allows us to incorporate our previous errors into our predictions. Our predictions for the future are based on the mistakes that we made in the past. Unfortunately, if we made consistent errors in the past, they will persist into the future. The adaptive expectations models were criticised for this and also because they limit the information which economic agents utilise.

The concept of adaptive expectations was replaced by rational expectations. Rational expectations assumes that economic agents will use all relevant past and current information when making decisions. In the inflation example, agents consider the past inflation rate but also changes in government monetary and fiscal policy, pressures in the labour market and international problems. Models based on rational expectations assume that all agents have 'perfect information'. They are fully informed of all relevant information which they need to make their forecast.

This simple concept has surprising implications for the effectiveness of economic policy and, in the broader sense, of government intervention in the economy. An important assumption of this model is that wages are fully flexible and that labour, as rational economic agents, will increase their wage demands in line with any inflationary pressures. Under these circumstances, the aggregate supply curve is vertical in the short run.

Under the rational expectations hypothesis, governments cannot 'fool' the people. People will anticipate the government's behaviour and act accordingly. Hence, any demand-management policies of the state will lead only to a change in the price level. Fiscal and monetary policies are ineffective in the short run and in the long run. Proponents of the rational expectations hypothesis were also concerned with policy issues of credibility and sustainability.

The leading proponents of rational expectations were Robert Lucas of Chicago, Thomas Sargent of Stanford and Robert Barro of Harvard.[64]

The New Keynesians responded to this with another modification to the expectations story. While acknowledging the possibility of rational expectations in the long run, new Keynesians were primarily concerned with the short run; a period of time when full adjustments in the labour market were unlikely. This allowed for the existence of high unemployment and as a policy response, active demand-management policies. As for the long run, ' . . . we are all dead'.[65]

Regardless of which doctrine you support, expectations are considered to be a crucial feature of modern macroeconomics.

ANSWERS TO QUESTIONS

Chapter 1

Working problems
••••••••••••••••••••

1. (a) Qd = Qs

    79 – 3P = 2P + 4

    79 – 4 = 2P + 3P

    75 = 5P

    15 = P. Insert P = 15 into Qd or Qs to get Qe.

    Qe = Qd = 79 – 3(15)

    Qe = 79 – 45

    Qe = 34. This can be confirmed by inserting P = 15 into the supply equation.

    (b) *Figure 1.24*

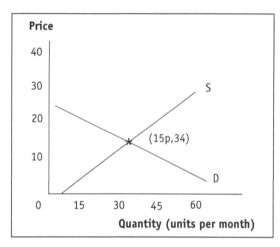

    (c) A price ceiling is a maximum price. A maximum price imposed at 13p would result in the following:

    Qd = 79 – 3(13) = 79 – 39 = 40.

    Qs = 2(13) + 4 = 26 + 4 = 30.

    Qd – Qs = 40 – 30 = 10 units of excess demand.

    (d) Excess supply would result.

    Qs = 2(16) + 4 = 32 + 4 = 36.

    Qd = 79 –3(16) = 79 – 48 = 31.

    Qs – Qd = 36 – 31 = 5 units of excess supply.

2. (a) Set Qd = Qs and solve for P.

    150 – P = –50 + P

    150 + 50 = P + P

    200 = 2P

    100 = P

(b) Insert P = 100 into either of the two equations.

Qe = Qd = 150 – P

Qe = 150 – 100

Qe = 50. This can be confirmed by inserting P = 100 into the supply equation.

(c) A minimum price of P* = 125 would be imposed above the equilibrium price. The excess can be estimated as follows:

Qs = –50 + (125) = 75.

Qd = 150 – (125) = 25.

Qs – Qd = 75 – 25 = 50.

An excess supply, equal to 50, would result.

Multi-choice questions
....

1. (c)   2. (d)   3. (c)   4. (c)   5. (d)   6. (a)

True or false
....

1. False   2. False   3. True   4. False   5. True   6. True

Fill in the blanks
....

Consumers and their actions are represented by a negatively sloped demand curve. It shows the quantity of the good demanded at each price. All other factors which influence demand are held constant. Producers and their actions are reflected in an upwardly sloped supply curve. This shows the positive relationship between price and quantity supplied, holding all other factors equal. It is the intersection of the demand curve and the supply curve which determines the equilibrium price and equilibrium quantity. In a market economy it is the price mechanism rather than the government which allocates scarce resources. Excess demand is choked off by a price rise whereas excess supply is eliminated by a price fall. In both planned economies and market economies, governments sometimes impose price controls. They can be in the form of price ceilings or price floors. Unintended and sometimes unfavourable results such as the need for rationing, in the case of a price ceiling, can follow. Butter mountains, which is an excess supply of butter, resulted from price floors set through the CAP.

Case study
....

1. The 'Troubles' in Derry negatively affected its image as a tourist destination. The cessation of violence was widely broadcast across Ireland, Britain and the United States. This caused the preferences of tourists to change, making Derry an attractive holiday destination. As a result, a record-breaking number of tourists visited Derry in 1995 (Jan–Aug).

2. The market for bed and breakfast accommodation is shown in Figure 1.25. Price is on the vertical axis and the number of beds is on the horizontal axis.

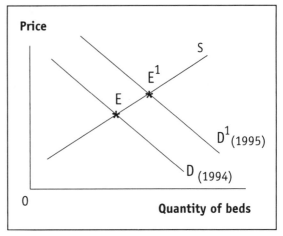

The change in preferences, caused by the peace process, caused the demand curve to shift to the right from D to D^1. If there are no price controls, we expect the equilibrium price and quantity for this type of accommodation to increase. This change is shown by the change from the original equilibrium of E to a new equilibrium of E^1.

3. If price is held constant by agreement, the result will be the same as with a price ceiling. Price will not adjust to equate supply with demand. The change in demand could lead to a shortage for this type of accommodation. This is shown in Figure 1.26 by the distance between point A and point B.

Figure 1.26: The bed and breakfast market for Derry (with price constraint) 1994–95

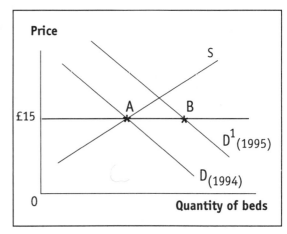

Chapter 2

Working problems
....

1. (a) *Figure 2.15*

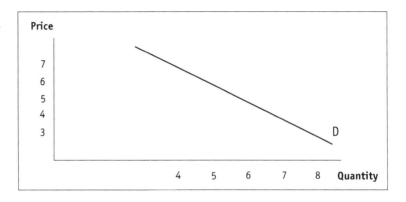

(b)
$P_1 = 3, Q_1 = 8$
$P_2 = 4, Q_2 = 7$

$$\frac{\dfrac{Q_2 - Q_1}{Q_1}}{\dfrac{P_2 - P_1}{P_1}} = \frac{\dfrac{7-8}{8}}{\dfrac{4-3}{3}} = \frac{\dfrac{-1}{8}}{\dfrac{1}{3}} = -.375$$

$P_1 = 4, Q_1 = 7$
$P_2 = 5, Q_2 = 6$

$$\frac{\dfrac{Q_2 - Q_1}{Q_1}}{\dfrac{P_2 - P_1}{P_1}} = \frac{\dfrac{6-7}{7}}{\dfrac{5-4}{4}} = \frac{\dfrac{-1}{7}}{\dfrac{1}{4}} = -.571$$

$P_1 = 5, Q_1 = 6$
$P_2 = 6, Q_2 = 5$

$$\frac{\dfrac{Q_2 - Q_1}{Q_1}}{\dfrac{P_2 - P_1}{P_1}} = \frac{\dfrac{5-6}{6}}{\dfrac{6-5}{5}} = \frac{\dfrac{-1}{6}}{\dfrac{1}{5}} = -.833$$

$P_1 = 6, Q_1 = 5$
$P_2 = 7, Q_2 = 4$

$$\frac{\dfrac{Q_2 - Q_1}{Q_1}}{\dfrac{P_2 - P_1}{P_1}} = \frac{\dfrac{4-5}{5}}{\dfrac{7-6}{6}} = \frac{\dfrac{-1}{5}}{\dfrac{1}{6}} = -1.2$$

(c) The absolute value of the elasticity coefficients declines as the demand curve slopes down from left to right. On the top part of the demand curve, near the vertical axis, the percentage change in quantity is large relative to the percentage change in price. On the bottom part of the demand curve, near the horizontal axis, the percentage change in quantity is small relative to the percentage change in price. Thus, as we move down the demand curve the fractional measure of price elasticity declines.

2. (a) The price elasticity of demand for A is the percentage change in quantity demanded of good A divided by the percentage change in its respective price, holding all other factors constant. In this case the other factors are family income and the price of B. These are constant in year 2 and year 4. Thus,

$$P_1 = £60; Q_1 = 75 \qquad \dfrac{\dfrac{Q_2 - Q_1}{Q_1}}{\dfrac{P_2 - P_1}{P_1}} = \dfrac{\dfrac{70 - 75}{75}}{\dfrac{66 - 60}{60}} = \dfrac{\dfrac{-5}{75}}{\dfrac{6}{60}} = \dfrac{\dfrac{-1}{15}}{\dfrac{1}{10}} = -.67$$
$$P_2 = £66; Q_2 = 70$$

The demand for good A, between these prices, is price inelastic.

(b) The price elasticity of demand for B is defined as the percentage change in quantity demanded of good B divided by the percentage change in its respective price, holding all other factors constant. In this case the other factors are family income and the price of A. These are constant in year 2 and year 3. Thus,

$$P_1 = £28; Q_1 = 150 \qquad \dfrac{\dfrac{Q_2 - Q_1}{Q_1}}{\dfrac{P_2 - P_1}{P_1}} = \dfrac{\dfrac{180 - 150}{150}}{\dfrac{22 - 28}{28}} = \dfrac{\dfrac{30}{150}}{\dfrac{-6}{28}} = -.93$$
$$P_2 = £22; Q_2 = 180$$

The demand for good B, between these prices, is close to unit elastic.

(c) The income elasticity of demand for A is defined as the percentage change in quantity demanded of good A divided by the percentage change in income, holding all other factors constant. In this case the other factors are the price of A and the price of B. These are constant in year 1 and year 5. Thus,

$$\begin{aligned} Y_1 &= £170,000; \\ Q_1 &= 60 \\ Y_2 &= £265,000; \\ Q_2 &= 65 \end{aligned} \qquad \dfrac{\dfrac{Q_2 - Q_1}{Q_1}}{\dfrac{Y_2 - Y_1}{Y_1}} = \dfrac{\dfrac{65 - 60}{60}}{\dfrac{265,000 - 170,000}{170,000}} = \dfrac{\dfrac{5}{60}}{\dfrac{95,000}{170,000}} = \dfrac{\dfrac{1}{12}}{\dfrac{19}{34}} = .15$$

Good A is normal and a necessity.

(d) The cross-price elasticity of demand for B is defined as the percentage change in quantity demanded of good B divided by the percentage change in the price of good A, holding all other factors constant. In this case the other factors are family income and the price of B. These are constant in year 2 and year 4.

Thus,

$P1 = £60; Q1 = 150$
$P2 = £66; Q2 = 170$

$$\frac{\dfrac{Q_2 - Q_1}{Q_1}}{\dfrac{P_2 - P_1}{P_1}} = \frac{\dfrac{170 - 150}{150}}{\dfrac{66 - 60}{60}} = \frac{\dfrac{20}{150}}{\dfrac{6}{60}} = \frac{\dfrac{2}{15}}{\dfrac{1}{10}} = 1.33$$

Goods A and B are substitutes for each other.

Multi-choice questions

1. (c)   2. (c)   3. (d)   4. (b)   5. (e)   6. (e)

True or false

1. False   2. False   3. True   4. True   5. True   6. True

Fill in the blanks

In economic terms elasticity measures the <u>sensitivity</u> of one variable to changes in another variable. Economists are interested in both the elasticity of <u>demand</u> and the elasticity of <u>supply</u>. There are <u>three</u> different elasticities of demand. <u>Own</u> price elasticity measures the sensitivity of quantity <u>demanded</u> to changes in the <u>price</u> of the good. It is usually <u>negative</u> which confirms the <u>law</u> of demand, *ceteris paribus*. Furthermore, there are three categories of price elasticity of demand: elastic, <u>inelastic</u> and <u>unit</u> elastic. <u>Cross</u>-price elasticity measures the sensitivity between the price of one good and the quantity of <u>another</u> good. The relevant elasticity coefficient can be <u>positive</u> or <u>negative</u>. The third is income elasticity of demand where the <u>independent</u> variable is <u>income</u>. Normal goods have a <u>positive</u> income coefficient, <u>inferior</u> goods have a negative income <u>coefficient</u>. The elasticity coefficient for price elasticity of supply is usually <u>positive</u> reflecting the conventional <u>upward</u> sloping <u>supply</u> curve.

Case study

1. Detaining dealers could lead to a disruption in the distribution of drugs. It could also cause an increase in the 'labour costs' of the drug manufacturers who will need to either replace dealers or pay for their legal costs. Both of these would increase the cost per unit of drugs and can be shown by a leftward shift of the supply curve.
2. Since drugs are addictive, the demand curve is probably inelastic. We can see from Figure 2.16 that the inelastic demand curve means that the shift in supply leads to a substantial increase in price; the market price rises from P to P^1.

Figure 2.16: The Irish drug market

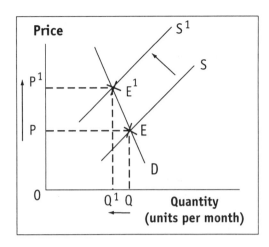

3. As can be seen from the diagram above, because the demand for drugs is inelastic, even if the supply is disrupted, the total amount paid to dealers increases. The rectangle [OPEQ] represents the revenue paid to dealers before the seizures. The larger rectangle, [OP^{1}E^{1}Q^1] represents the revenue accruing to dealers after the seizures. Since a large amount of the money which is for drugs is illegally gained, this supports the claim that curtailing the supply of drugs through seizures actually leads to increased crime.

4. Mr Geoghegan suggests that more attention and resources should be devoted to the 'demand' side of the problem, the drug users. Prevention programmes would limit the demand for drugs in the future. Drug treatment facilities would help users to break their addiction. Both of these measures would, in his opinion, help to shift the demand curve for drugs to the left. The problem that he will face in tackling the demand side, aside from financial, is finding locations for drug treatment facilities.

Chapter 3

Working problems
....

1. Table 3.7 (completed) depicts the MUs per pound spent for all cases.

Table 3.7 (completed): Maximising utility by equalising MUs per pound spent

	Mineral water				Ice cream				Soft drinks		
Q	MU	P	MU/P	Q	MU	P	MU/P	Q	MU	P	MU/P
1	36	4	9	1	30	2	15	1	32	1	32
2	24	4	6	2	22	2	11	2	28	1	28
3	20	4	5	3	16	2	8	3	20	1	20
4	18	4	4.5	4	12	2	6	4	14	1	14
5	16	4	4	5	10	2	5	5	8	1	8
6	10	4	2.5	6	4	2	2	6	6	1	6
7	6	4	1.5	7	2	2	1	7	4	1	4

The consumer who seeks the combination of goods which maximises utility, with the given level of income, must ensure that the following equation holds:

$$\frac{MU_X}{P_X} = \frac{MU_Y}{P_Y} = \frac{MU_Z}{P_Z}$$

The combination which ensures that this equation is met is 2 mineral waters, 4 ice creams and 6 soft drinks. The calculation (2 x £4) + (4 x £2) + (6 x £1) = £22 confirms that all the income is utilised, given the set of prices for the goods. It is impossible to distribute this income in any other way and at the same time achieve a higher level of utility. This is the basis of the equi-marginal principle.

2. *Figure 3.27: The indifference curves for Tom and Gerry*

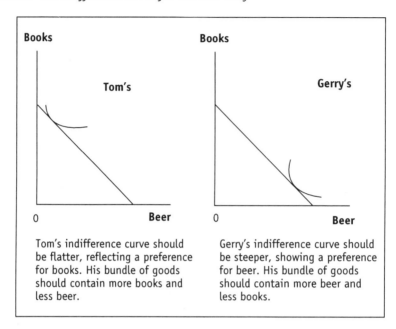

Tom's indifference curve should be flatter, reflecting a preference for books. His bundle of goods should contain more books and less beer.

Gerry's indifference curve should be steeper, showing a preference for beer. His bundle of goods should contain more beer and less books.

Multi-choice questions
....
1. (c)   2. (d)   3. (e)   4. (b)   5. (d)   6. (a)

True or false
....
1. False   2. True   3. False   4. False   5. False   6. False

Fill in the blanks
....
The theory of demand is concerned with consumer <u>behaviour</u> in the face of income and price constraints. The <u>marginal</u> utility approach assumes that utility is <u>measurable</u> whereas the indifference-preference approach requires only the <u>ranking</u> of different combinations. According to the former, the consumer maximises utility where the utility for the last <u>pound</u> spent on each good is the <u>same</u>. In the latter case the <u>optimal consumption</u> bundle is where the <u>budget line</u>, which reflects the income and <u>price</u> constraints, cuts the highest possible <u>indifference curve</u> at a point of <u>tangency</u>. A change in income <u>shifts</u> the budget line, out to the right for an <u>increase</u> in income and in to the <u>left</u> for a decrease in income. The <u>position</u> of the new consumer equilibrium point will depend on the type of good – normal or <u>inferior</u>. A change in price causes a <u>rotation</u> of the budget line and with the help of the <u>substitution</u> and <u>income</u> effect analysis we can derive the downward sloping demand curve for a <u>normal</u> good. A similar exercise results in a <u>downward</u> sloping demand curve for an inferior good but, in contrast, an upward sloping demand curve for a <u>Giffen</u> good.

Case study
··············

1. Carlsberg is a lager. The company hoped that the campaign would cause lager drinkers to switch from their current brand to Carlsberg. In economic terminology, they were hoping that consumer preferences would change in favour of Carlsberg.

2. *Figure 3.28: Changing preference of the consumer as a result of the Carlsberg advertising campaign*

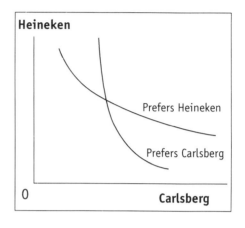

Heineken is depicted on the vertical axis and Carlsberg is depicted on the horizontal axis. The indifference curve of the individual who initially prefers Heineken to Carlsberg must be relatively flat – indicating a consumer who is willing to trade off several units of Carlsberg in order to gain only one extra unit of Heineken (see Figure 3.3 in text). The Carlsberg campaign is successful in altering the preferences of the consumer. This consumer now prefers Carlsberg to Heineken. This preference is reflected in a relatively steep indifference curve. To gain an additional unit of Carlsberg, the consumer is willing to give up several units of Heineken.

3. By drawing two 'intersecting' indifference curves, we have violated the property that indifference curves do not intersect. This should alert us to the fact that the particular model of consumer theory that we have presented in this chapter is based on a number of very restrictive assumptions. We assume that consumers are rational and that their preferences are transitive. However, the consumer above has obviously changed his preferences as a result of advertising. Initially Heineken was preferred to Carlsberg, now Carlsberg is preferred to Heineken. Some economists would argue that tastes change very slowly over time. Therefore, the assumptions are valid over the 'relevant' time period. The massive amount of money spent on advertising campaigns challenges the validity of this argument, and consequently, raises questions about the usefulness of consumer theory.

Chapter 4

Working problems

1. *Table 4.6 completed*

Land	Labour	Output	Average	Marginal
20	0	0	–	
				1
20	1	1	1	
				2
20	2	3	1.5	
				3
20	3	6	2	
				4
20	4	10	2.5	
				6
20	5	16	3.2	
				4
20	6	20	3.3	
				1
20	7	21	3	
				–1
20	8	20	2.5	
				–2
20	9	18	2	

(a) Land and labour.
(b) One of the inputs, land, is fixed. Short-run production implies at least one fixed factor of production. Land is the fixed input whereas labour is the variable input.

(c) *Figure 4.14: The total product curve*

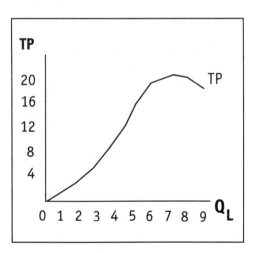

(d) Completed as above.
(e) Production is limited in the short run because of the fixed amount of land. Adding more and more farm labourers may increase output but the pace at which it increases will slow. The extra output generated by an additional labourer will eventually be less than the previous labourer's contribution. Thus, the MP of labour curve declines.
(f) The MP of labour curve cuts the AP of labour curve at its maximum point. If the MP is greater than the AP then the AP will be forced upwards. This will be reflected in an upward sloping AP curve. If the MP is less than the AP then the AP will be forced downwards. This will be reflected in a downward sloping AP curve. By implication, the MP curve must cut the AP curve at the point where the AP curve changes from being upward sloping to downward sloping. This is the maximum point of the AP curve.

2. *Table 4.7 completed*

Land	Labour	Q	SFC	SVC	STC	SMC	SAFC	SAVC	SATC
2	0	0	100	0	100				
						100			
2	1	1	100	100	200		100	100	200
						50			
2	2	3	100	200	300		33.33	66.67	100
						33.33			
2	3	6	100	300	400		16.67	50	66.67
						25			
2	4	10	100	400	500		10	40	50
						16.67			
2	5	16	100	500	600		6.25	31.25	37.5
						25			
2	6	20	100	600	700		5	30	35
						33.33			
2	7	23	100	700	800		4.35	30.43	34.78
						50			
2	8	25	100	800	900		4	32	36
						100			
2	9	26	100	900	1000		3.85	34.61	38.46
						—			
2	10	24	—	—	—				

The cost of land is £50 per acre and the cost of labour is £100 per worker per week.

(a) Completed as above.

(b) *Figure 4.15: Short-run cost curves*

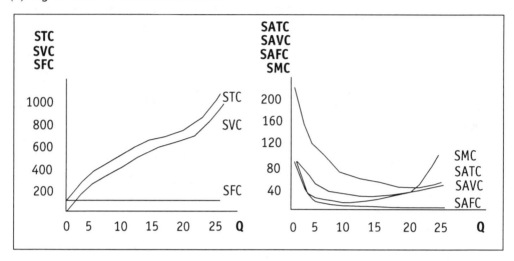

(c) No. The difference between total cost and variable cost is a value for fixed cost. Likewise, the difference between SATC and SAVC is SAFC. Thus, the gap between the SATC curve and the SAVC curve is accounted for by SAFC.

(d) The SMC curve cuts the SAVC and the SATC curves at their respective minimum points. This can be explained by examining the relationship between the marginal and average, in the context of costs. If SMC is below the SAVC and SATC it drags down both curves. Likewise, if SMC is above the SAVC and SATC it drags up both curves. By implication, the SMC must cut both the SAVC and the SATC curves at their respective minimum points.

Multi-choice questions
....
1. (e)   2. (e)   3. (e)   4. (b)   5. (b)   6. (d)

True or false
....
1. True   2. False   3. True   4. True   5. False   6. False

Fill in the blanks
....
Production involves the process of transforming <u>inputs</u> into output. Short-run production assumes that at least one input is <u>fixed</u>. <u>Long-run</u> production involves a time period where all factors of production are variable. The relation between inputs and outputs is reflected in the short run by the <u>law of diminishing returns</u> and in the long run by <u>returns to scale</u>. This latter concept is closely linked to economies and <u>diseconomies</u> of scale. Any production involves the use of inputs which in turn involves <u>costs</u>. Short-run costs are associated with the inputs used in <u>short-run</u> production and can be either <u>fixed</u> or variable. In contrast, all long-run costs are variable. A firm

will produce in the short run as long as it can cover its <u>variable</u> costs and make some progress in covering its fixed costs. In the long run <u>all</u> costs must be covered. The above analysis is based on the traditional <u>neoclassical</u> model of the firm which assumes <u>profit</u> maximisation. Economists are concerned primarily with <u>opportunity</u> <u>cost</u> which is a measure of the best <u>alternative</u> forgone. Any difference between total revenue and total <u>economic</u> <u>cost</u>, which incorporates opportunity cost, is termed pure or <u>supernormal</u> profit.

Case study

1. Most legislation is enacted to protect the rights of labour. This protection can take several forms. Legislation sometimes concerns labour relations so that a labourer has some recourse if she feels that she has been treated unfairly or fired without provocation. Laws cover areas like the age at which people can be employed, the number of continuous hours that they are permitted to work and the procedures for dismissal.

   Also, some legislated regulations impact on the labour market but are actually enacted to protect both labour and the public. Firms that dispose of toxic waste must protect their workers with clothing and machinery. The procedures must minimise public risk. Workers in restaurants must dress in a certain way and follow procedures to ensure that the facilities are sanitary.

   Politicians attempt to protect the rights of workers and at the same time maintain a suitable environment for job creation. At times these goals conflict. Mr Madden accuses politicians of concentrating on the 'worst possible scenario'. They are legislating for situations which seldom occur. He points out that this imposes high costs on the firms, and this could discourage employment, particularly for small firms. Therefore, Mr Madden suggests that the opportunity cost of legislation is employment creation.

2. Madden states that legislation should be examined in terms of the cost of implementation for the firm. He states that 'it should not have a disproportionate effect on different firms because of their size'. This sounds as if the cost of compliance is a fixed cost. A high fixed costs affects a small firm disproportionately because it spreads those costs over fewer units.

3. Employers pay PRSI as a percentage of the wage bill. In the 1997 budget, the PRSI rate was 8.5% for incomes below £13,500 per year and 12.0% for incomes above that threshold. From the point of view of the firm, this tax must be added to the cost of labour. Since labour is a variable input, PRSI increases a variable cost.

Chapter 5

Working problems
....

1. *Figure 5.22 and Table 5.7 completed*

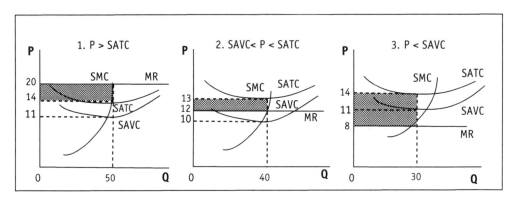

TR = £1000	TR = £480	TR = £240
TVC = £550	TVC = £400	TVC = £330
TFC = £150	TFC = £120	TFC = £90
TC = £700	TC = £520	TC = £420
Profit = £300	Profit = –£40	Profit = –£90
Production	Production	Production
Decision: produce	Decision: produce	Decision: shut down

2. (P_1,Q_1) is the equilibrium point for the monopolistic competitor. (P_2, Q_2) is the optimal price/output combination for the perfectly competitive firm. The long-run equilibrium condition for the monopolistically competitive firm is MR = MC and AR = AC. The perfectly competitive firm produces in the long run where AC = AR = MR = MC. This corresponds to the minimum point of the LAC curve.

It is evident from the diagram that the price charged by the monopolistic competitor is higher than the price charged by the perfectly competitive firm. In terms of production, the quantity produced by the monopolistically competitive firm is less than that produced by the perfectly competitive firm. Also, the perfectly competitive firm generates economic efficiency by producing on the minimum point of the LAC curve and by charging a price equal to MC. The monopolistic competitor does not yield economic efficiency. In terms of the similarities, both aim to maximise profits, produce where MR = MC and make normal profits only in the long run.

Multi-choice questions
....

1. (e)   2. (d)   3. (c)   4. (b)   5. (d)   6. (d)

True or false
··············
1. True   2. True   3. False   4. False   5. False   6. False

Fill in the blanks
··················
An important factor in determining a firm's <u>behaviour</u> is the market structure to which it belongs. There are four main types of market structures: perfect competition, oligopoly, <u>monopolistic</u> competition and monopoly. The difference between all four categories hinges on the degree of market <u>power</u> and the extent of <u>competition</u> facing the respective firm. <u>Perfect</u> competition, although not very representative of the real world today, is a useful theoretical model. With the perfectly competitive firm facing a <u>horizontal</u> demand curve for its product, its market power is zero. In the long run, perfectly competitive firms are <u>efficient</u> in the sense that they produce at the point of <u>minimum</u> average cost and they charge a price equal to the <u>marginal</u> cost of production. Any market structure which consists of firms that hold some degree of market power is defined as <u>imperfect</u> <u>competition</u>. The extreme case is monopoly where the monopolist can earn <u>supernormal</u> profits in the long run. In this case a <u>unique</u> product is sold and the demand curve is downward sloping and <u>inelastic</u>. Most firms and industries do not subscribe to these extreme cases and are normally examples of either monopolistic competition or <u>oligopoly</u>. Of vital importance to the monopolistic competitor is her ability to influence price because of product <u>differentiation</u>. This may take the form of branding, <u>advertising</u> or the use of promotional gimmicks. <u>Interdependency</u> between firms is a characteristic of an oligopoly. Oligopolists may or may not <u>collude</u>. This collusion may be formal or informal. If collusion takes place, there is an incentive to <u>cheat</u>.

Case study
·············
1. Oligopoly. The market for oil is one of the best examples of an oligopoly. It comprises a small number of mutually dependent producers with each having some ability to affect the price of oil. This is evident in different parts of the article, for example 'by keeping a lid on the price of crude' and also 'While others want to cut output and raise prices'. Finally, cartels are quite common in oligopolistic markets with OPEC being a prime example.
2. The price leadership model. The price leadership model usually comprises a dominant firm and a number of smaller producers. Since its inception in 1960, OPEC has been dominated on many separate occasions by Saudi Arabia. In accounting for 8% of production and approximately 25% of reserves (Source: Oxford Institute for Energy Studies, OECD figures), Saudi Arabia fulfils the role of a dominant firm.
3. A monopoly. A monopolist charges a higher price for a lower output compared to other market structures. Since it is protected by entry barriers, a monopolist can earn supernormal profits, resulting in a transfer of purchasing power from the consumer to the monopolistic seller. It charges a price in excess of its marginal cost

of production and in doing so it is inefficient in resource allocation. A monopolist that practises price discrimination removes the consumer surplus from the buying public. Finally, monopolies sometimes engage in price-fixing, erecting artificial barriers to entry and predatory pricing. These all involve a cost to the consumer and society at large.

The article mentions that Saudi Arabia's plans differ from the OPEC secretariat. We know that cartel arrangements are fragile. Additionally, a number of oil-exporting countries are not members of OPEC. Therefore, it is unlikely that Saudi Arabia could ever run the oil market as a monopoly.

Chapter 6

Working problems

....

1. (a) *Table 6.2 completed*

Labour (wkrs)	TP (units)	MP (units)	P (£)	MRP (£)	Wage (£)
0	0				
		12	5	60	40
1	12				
		15	5	75	40
2	27				
		13	5	65	40
3	40				
		10	5	50	40
4	50				
		9	5	45	40
5	59				
		6	5	30	40
6	65				

(b) A firm will hire labour where MRP = W. In this example with a wage rate equal to £40, five workers will be employed. The sixth worker has a MRP less than the marginal cost of its employment.

(c) If the wage rate rises, the number of workers employed falls. The MRP of the fourth worker is equal to £50. Hence, the firm will employ up to and including the fourth worker. If the wage rate rise to £50, four workers will be employed.

2. (a) Total earnings is given by the area [WEY0].
   (b) Transfer earnings is given by the area [AEY0].
   (c) Economic rent is given by the area [WEA].
   (d) Transfer earnings for worker X is equal to OW^1.
   (e) Economic rent for worker X is equal to WW^1.

Multi-choice questions
....
1. (e)   2. (d)   3. (c)   4. (c)   5. (b)   6. (d)

True or false
....
1. True   2. False   3. True   4. True   5. True   6. True

Fill in the blanks
....
Labour, capital, <u>land</u> and entrepreneurship are the four factors of production. The wage rate is the return on labour; <u>interest</u> is the reward to capital; rent is the reward to land; profit is the return on <u>entrepreneurship</u>. The demand for a factor input is a <u>derived</u> demand. It can be explained using the <u>marginal</u> productivity theory which states that a factor input depends on its <u>productivity</u>. For labour and land, the MRP curve is equal to the <u>demand</u> curve. The supply curve of the respective factors varies; <u>labour</u> supply is influenced by the trade-off between work and <u>leisure</u>; the supply of capital is affected by the consumption-<u>savings</u> trade-off; the supply of land is <u>fixed</u>. A fixed resource results in the payment of <u>economic</u> rent. The <u>equilibrium</u> factor price clears the respective resource market; quantity demanded equals quantity <u>supplied</u>. The fourth resource is entrepreneurship and its return is called <u>profit</u>. It is a <u>residual</u>. Risk, <u>innovation</u> and monopolies are the sources of profit.

Case study
....
1. Ireland has the same proportion of graduates as Germany, but a smaller percentage of the labour force is trained as skilled craftsmen. This skills deficiency is increasing because a larger percentage of the German labour force is trained annually as apprentices when compared to the Irish labour force.
2. The article suggests that training workers in the crafts makes the labour force more productive. As productivity increases, so does the marginal revenue product of the worker. Since the employment decision is based on the relationship between the marginal revenue product and the real wage, as the MRP increases, the wage which firms are willing to pay workers also increases.

     The article suggests that the discrepancies between the GDP per capita in different European countries results from the differences in training.
3. The article states that the small proportion of craft workers reflects 'undervaluing within business of the making function as opposed to the financing or the selling functions'. In general, most commentators believe that the 'best' Irish students are attracted to academic courses because Irish society values the professions more highly than craft or trade occupations. This raises the issue that changing the educational system is only one part of the problem of increasing the skills of the labour force. Students must value the courses and recognise the important contribution the trades make in an economy.

Chapter 8

Working problems

....

1. *Table 8.18*

(a) Income method	
Compensation of employees	4,200
Rent	450
Interest	300
Profits	300
NDP at factor cost	5,250
Net income from abroad	–250
NNP at factor cost = National income	5,000
(b) Output method	
Agriculture	100
Industry	3,000
Public administration	650
Transport and communication	1,500
NDP at factor cost	5,250
Net income from abroad	–250
NNP at factor cost = National income	5,000
(c) Expenditure method	
Personal consumption	4,000
Investment	600
Government expenditure	700
Exports	3,050
Imports	–2,400
GDP at market prices	5,950
Net income from abroad	–250
GNP at market prices	5,700
Depreciation	–300
NNP at market prices	5,400
Indirect taxes	–800
Subsidies	400
NNP at factor cost = National income	5,000

2. (a) GDP = C + I + G + (X – M) = 250 + 150 + 500 + (360 – 340) = £920bn
   (b) disposable income = GDP + TR – TA = 920 + 200 – 350 = £770bn
   (c) savings = disposable income – C = 770 – 250 = £520bn
   (d) net exports = X – M = 360 – 340 = £20bn.
   (e) injections = G + I + TR + X = 500 + 150 + 200 + 360 = £1,210bn
   leakages = S + TX + M = 520 + 350 + 340 = £1,210bn
   So, total injections = total leakages in this model.

Multi-choice questions
....
1. (d)   2. (b)   3. (c)   4. (b)   5. (d)   6. (c)

True or false
....
1. False   2. False   3. True   4. False   5. False   6. True

Fill in the blanks
....
The simple <u>circular</u> <u>flow</u> model shows the transactions between <u>households</u> and <u>firms</u>. All flows are either <u>real</u> or <u>monetary</u>. A more detailed version includes the <u>government</u>, the <u>banking</u> system and the <u>foreign</u> sector. Savings, taxes and imports are all described as <u>leakages</u> whereas <u>investment</u>, <u>government</u> <u>expenditure</u>, <u>transfer</u> <u>payments</u> and <u>exports</u> are defined as injections. <u>Equilibrium</u> is achieved in the economy if these leakages and injections are equal. Such economic activity can be measured by three methods: <u>expenditure</u>, <u>income</u> and <u>output</u>. The most common measure used in the national income accounts is <u>GDP</u> or <u>GNP</u>, the difference being a value of net income from abroad. In Ireland <u>GDP</u> exceeds <u>GNP</u>. GDP or any of its variations is not a <u>perfect</u> measure of economic activity. It <u>omits</u> a large number of substantial activities for one reason or another. These include, among others, transactions within the <u>shadow</u> economy, externalities and non-<u>monetary</u> activities. In addition, it does not account for changes in economic <u>welfare</u>, a country's <u>competitiveness</u> or the distribution of <u>wealth</u>. Possible alternatives include the United Nations' <u>HDI</u> or Tobin's <u>NEW</u>. Notwithstanding these problems, GDP still remains the most universal measure of economic prosperity.

Case study
....
1. The expenditure approach. Consumer spending, government spending, investment and exports are all mentioned in the article. These are the components of GDP using the expenditure method. The other two methods are the income and the output approaches. Profit, interest, wages and rent are the components of the income approach. The output approach measures the value added in each sector. The designated sectors are agriculture, industry, distribution, transport and communication, public administration and others.
2. Higher incomes, lower prices, lower interest rates and lower taxes or the prospects of these some time in the near future are all possible explanations for the increase

in consumer expenditure. Higher incomes abroad, a favourable exchange rate and improved competitiveness are possible factors behind the buoyancy in exports.

3. Increases in government expenditure need to be financed by the Exchequer either by higher taxes or borrowing. In turn, higher taxes may result in lower consumer spending whereas higher borrowing may result in increases in domestic interest rates. Both these results, in terms of potential increases in economic activity, are undesirable.

Chapter 10

Working problems

....

1. (a) $Y = \bar{A} \times \dfrac{1}{1 - b + m}$

   where $\bar{A} = \bar{C} + \bar{I} + \bar{G} + \bar{X} = 110 + 300 + 150 + 250 = £810$

   and $\dfrac{1}{1 - b + m} = \dfrac{1}{1 - .8 + .2} = \dfrac{1}{.4} = 2.5$

   $Y = 810 \times 2.5 = £2,025.$

(b) Government expenditure is doubled from £150 to £300.

   $\Delta Y = \Delta \bar{G} \times \dfrac{1}{1 - b + m} = 150 \times 2.5 = £375.$

   The change (increase) in Y is equal to £375. Thus, the new and higher level of equilibrium income is £2,025 + £375 = £2,400. This can be confirmed by using the equilibrium level of income equation with $\bar{G} = 300$, as follows;

   $Y = \bar{A} \times \dfrac{1}{1 - b + m} = 960 \times 2.5 = £2,400.$

(c) The multiplier formula for this particular example is $\dfrac{1}{1 - b + m}$ where b = MPC = .8 and m = MPM = .2. The value for the multiplier works out to be 2.5. This means that any change in autonomous spending will result in a 2.5 times change in the equilibrium level of income. For example, a £100 increase in autonomous government spending will result in a 100 x 2.5 = £250 increase in the equilibrium level of income.

2. $$Y_d \equiv C + S$$

   $$\Delta Y_d \equiv \Delta C + \Delta S$$

Divide by Y_d to get

$$\frac{\Delta Y_d}{Y_d} \equiv \frac{\Delta C}{Y_d} + \frac{\Delta S}{Y_d}$$

If the above holds, what follows is also true, i.e.:

$$\frac{\Delta Y_d}{\Delta Y_d} \equiv \frac{\Delta C}{\Delta Y_d} + \frac{\Delta S}{\Delta Y_d}$$

$$1 \equiv MPC + MPS.$$

Multi-choice questions
....
1. (d)   2. (e)   3. (d)   4. (b)   5. (b)   6. (a)

True or false
....
1. True   2. False   3. True   4. False   5. True   6. True

Fill in the blanks
....
The pre-Keynesian or <u>classical</u> school of economics believed that markets were inherently <u>stable</u> and they tended <u>automatically</u> towards a full-employment equilibrium level. The mechanisms which guaranteed this were the <u>flexibility</u> of wages, prices and <u>interest</u> <u>rates</u>. The latter was responsible for equating <u>savings</u> and investment. There was little role for <u>state</u> intervention. Keynesian economics viewed the market and its operations very differently. <u>Keynes</u> believed that the economy could be at an equilibrium which was <u>below</u> the full-employment level. The level of output in the economy was determined largely by the level of <u>demand</u>. Wages were <u>sticky</u> which prevented a clearing of the <u>labour</u> market. Hence, <u>unemployment</u>, of an involuntary and long-term nature, was possible. In order to tackle the problem of unemployment government intervention in the form of higher <u>spending</u> was required. Furthermore, a <u>multiplier</u> effect was likely which would result in a <u>greater</u> increase in income than the initial injection in autonomous spending. However, this multiplier is <u>reduced</u> by <u>leakages</u> such as high taxes and a high propensity to import. The simple Keynesian model, as described, is <u>incomplete</u> and requires adjustments to include such variables as money and interest rates, wages, prices and <u>foreign</u> levels of GDP and interest rates.

Case study
....
1. Fiscal policy. An expansionary fiscal policy (increasing expenditure, cutting taxes or some combination of the two) creates an additional demand for goods and

services. This additional demand causes unplanned falls in inventories. Firms respond to this by increasing output. This additional production may require extra labour, resulting in the creation of jobs.

Keynes, the person primarily responsible for bringing this to the forefront of economic thinking, advocated the active use of fiscal policy and in particular high government spending on public works projects in order to generate additional employment.

2. There is a variety of 'dangers', the number and the extent depending largely on the position of the economy with respect to the business cycle and, secondly, on the openness of the economy. Here are a number of possible 'dangers'. First, higher government expenditure can crowd out private sector spending. Second, expansionary fiscal policy normally results in budget deficits. The financing of these deficits can lead to higher interest rates (see Chapter 11) which are not conducive to economic growth. Third, successive budget deficits contribute to a public debt which, in effect, is a liability for the next and future generations. Fourth, the debt can be viewed simply as deferred taxation. Fifth, higher public spending or lower taxes stimulate demand which may fuel inflationary pressures (see Chapter 15). Sixth, the increase in demand may only result in higher imports. This last possibility applies particularly to open economies which have a relatively high MPM. Ireland is one such example.

It is a matter of opinion whether the attitudes of some commentators is 'paranoiac'. Although the state can play a vital role in stimulating demand during a recession, it is evident from the above that there can be some adverse effects. This may limit the effectiveness of the government's intervention. Without knowing the economic climate of the time, the importance of external trade, the flexibility of its currency, the mobility of capital, the nation's tendency to save and other factors, it is difficult to arrive at a definite conclusion.

3. Counter-cyclical fiscal policy. The difference between this and the classical position is as follows. The classical doctrine was one of balanced budgets. This was to be applied from year to year regardless of the economic climate of the time. The Keynesian school also supported a balanced budget but over the lifetime of the cycle and not necessarily from year to year. In fact, budget deficits were advocated in times of recession; budget surpluses in times of boom. In effect they would be counter-cyclical, thus avoiding the adverse effects of each stage of the business cycle – unemployment during the recessionary times and inflationary pressures during the boom period.

Chapter 11

Working problems
....

1. (a) $\dfrac{1}{r} = \dfrac{1}{.2} = 5$

(b) The increase in the money supply can be calculated from the following equation:

$$\Delta M = \frac{1}{r} \Delta R$$

£25,000 = 5 x £5,000

Money supply will increase by £25,000.

(c) *Table 11.7 completed*

Stages	Deposits (£)	Reserves (£)	Loans (£)
1	5,000	1,000	4,000
2	4,000	800	3,200
3	3,200	640	2,560
4	2,560	512	2,048
5			
6 . . .			
etc . . .			
Total	£ 25,000	£ 5,000	£ 20,000

2. The minimum increase in the money supply is £400. If Maria decides to hold all of it in the form of cash, the currency component of the money supply increases by £400. There is no increase in deposits.

   The maximum increase in the money supply is £8,000. Suppose Maria decides to deposit the £400 in her local, student-friendly college bank. The bank manager knows from experience that the student population is unlikely to cause a 'run' on the branch. Consequently, the bank manager decides to meet the required reserve ratio of 5% but lends out the other 95%. In doing so, the bank manager creates a multiplier effect. With a reserve ratio of 5%, the money multiplier is equal to 20. The maximum increase in deposits arising from this process is £8,000. It is comprised of the original £400 and a further £7,600 in deposit accounts created when new loans were extended to other students in college.

Multi-choice questions
. . . .
1. (b)   2. (a)   3. (e)   4. (d)   5. (d)   6. (a)

True or false
. . . .
1. True   2. False   3. False   4. True   5. True   6. False

Fill in the blanks
. . . .
Money is anything that is generally accepted as a means of payment. Its other functions are as a unit of measurement, as a store of value and as a standard of deferred payment.

Money is created within the <u>banking</u> system. It is the <u>reserves</u> of the commercial banks which support the creation of <u>deposits</u>. In the <u>classical</u> model of interest rate determination, the demand for capital funds depends solely on the <u>interest rate</u>. In contrast, the demand for money in Keynes' <u>liquidity preference</u> theory depends on the interest rate and the level of <u>income</u>. The <u>supply</u> of loanable funds is determined from the level of household savings. Keynes' supply of money is interest rate <u>inelastic</u>; it is controlled by the <u>monetary authorities</u>. It can be changed by an <u>open market</u> operation, a change in the <u>reserve</u> ratio or a change in the <u>discount</u> rate. In a <u>SOE</u>, the Central Bank has less control over monetary policy and interest rates. <u>External</u> factors are more influential. The Central Bank does attempt to control <u>liquidity</u> in the domestic <u>money</u> market. Nevertheless, monetary policy is an important policy option available to the authorities in achieving <u>macroeconomic</u> objectives.

Case study
....

1. Building societies are generally more vulnerable to interest rate changes. Until recently, building societies were limited in terms of the products which they could offer their customers. Their business consisted of mortgages and restricted forms of savings accounts. Banks, on the other hand, were involved in other activities such as life assurance, leasing and foreign exchange transactions. Hence, any change in market interest rates has an almost immediate impact on the building societies with a lesser impact on the banks. For example, if interest rates increase, banks can rely on their ancillary services/activities to partly compensate for the increase in costs arising out of the increase in interest rates.

2. The STF rate is the interest rate charged by Central Bank on its lending to financial institutions that are short reserves. The one-month interbank rate is the interest rate that is determined in the money market, where financial institutions borrow and lend from one another. Causation is normally only one way. The one-month rate is determined in the market by demand and supply forces. Normally, the Central Bank sets its STF rate in line with the interbank rate. Changes in market conditions result in a change in the interbank rate. In turn, the Central Bank changes its STF rate unless it perceives the market changes as temporary.

3. Currency markets and, in particular, the performance of the Irish pound relative to other currencies play an important role in the determination of Irish interest rates. This arises from Ireland's membership of a semi-fixed exchange rate system. Ireland's commitment to the ERM has implications for Irish interest rates. For example, suppose market expectations are for a fall in the value or a devaluation of the Irish pound. In order to support the currency and in order to avoid large external reserve losses, the monetary authorities may tighten monetary policy, i.e. increase interest rates. In general, the more volatile the currency markets, the more uncertain the money markets. Subsequently, the extent of interest rate uncertainty increases and interest rate movements become more frequent and increasingly more difficult to predict.

Chapter 12

Working problems
....

1. (a) The IS curve is given by the equation

   $$Y = k\,(\overline{A} - di)$$

   where, in this particular example,

   $$k = \frac{1}{1-b} = \frac{1}{1-.85} = \frac{1}{.15} = 6.67$$

   $$\overline{A} = \overline{I} + \overline{G} = 700 + 540 = 1240$$
   $$d = 25$$
   Insert into IS equation, to get
   $$Y = 6.67\,(1240 - 25i)$$
   $$Y = 8270.8 - 166.75i$$

   (b) The LM curve is given by the equation

   $$Y = \frac{1}{j}\left(hi + \frac{\overline{M}}{P}\right)$$

   where, in this particular example,
   $$j = .5$$
   $$h = 70$$

   $$\frac{\overline{M}}{P} = 400$$

   Insert into LM equation, to get

   $$Y = \frac{1}{.5}(70i + 400)$$

   $$Y = 140i + 800$$

   (c) Using IS and LM equations, solve for i
   $$Y = 8270.8 - 166.75i = 140i + 800 = Y$$
   $$8270.8 - 800 = (140 + 166.75)i$$
   $$7470.8 = 306.75i$$
   $$i = 24.35\%$$

   If $i = 24.35\%$ then $Y = ?$
   Substitute $i = 24.35$ into either IS or LM equation
   $$Y = 140i + 800$$
   $$Y = 140(24.35) + 800$$
   $$Y = 4{,}209.$$

(d) *Figure 12.10: The equilibrium position*

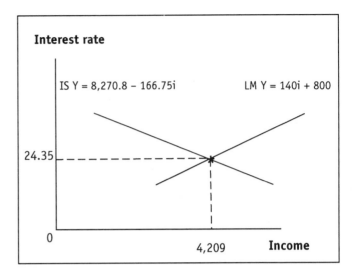

2. If investment is not responding to changes in the interest rate, then d is small and the IS curve is steep. This is the Keynesian case where investors are not responding to changes in the interest rate. With a vertical IS curve, we will examine the effectiveness of both expansionary fiscal policy and expansionary monetary policy.

We will begin with fiscal policy. The government decides to increase spending. The IS curve shifts to the right. This is shown in panel (a) of Figure 12.11. Interest rates increase, but the government is not concerned about crowding out because firms are not responding to changes in the interest rate. National income increases as a result of this change in fiscal policy. Fiscal policy is effective.

Figure 12.11: Fiscal and monetary policy with a vertical IS curve

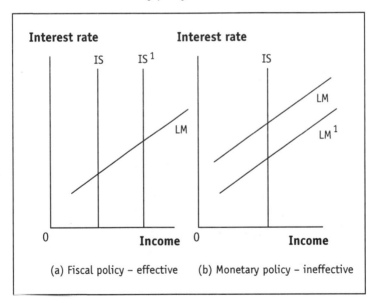

Now, we will consider monetary policy. If the Central Bank increases the money supply, the LM curve shifts to the right. This causes interest rates to fall. Because investors are not reacting to changes in the interest rate, the transmission mechanism is weak. In the extreme case, where the IS curve is vertical, the fall in interest rates does not lead to an increase in investment. Interest rates fall but investment and national income remain unchanged. This is shown in panel (b) of Figure 12.11. In this case, monetary policy is ineffective.

In this set of circumstances, fiscal policy is clearly more effective than monetary policy.

Multi-choice questions
....
1. (d)   2. (e)   3. (b)   4. (d)   5. (e)   6. (c)

True or false
....
1. True   2. False   3. True   4. True   5. False   6. True

Fill in the blanks
....
The IS/LM model is a Keynesian, <u>demand</u>-side, closed economy model where <u>prices</u> are assumed to be held constant. It is comprised of <u>two</u> markets, each with their respective curves. Equilibrium in the <u>goods</u> market, where expenditure equals <u>income</u> is represented by the IS curve. The <u>LM</u> curve reflects equilibrium between the <u>demand</u> for and the stock of money. <u>Autonomous</u> spending is constant along the IS curve whereas the real <u>money</u> <u>supply</u> is constant along the LM curve. The <u>multiplier</u> and different <u>elasticity</u> measures are the factors which determine the <u>slopes</u> of both curves. The model is useful in many different ways. Firstly, it can be used to determine the equilibrium level of <u>national</u> <u>income</u> and <u>interest</u> <u>rates</u>. Secondly, the effects of fiscal and <u>monetary</u> policy can be determined. Thirdly, the Keynesian-<u>monetarist</u> debate, with both crowding out and the <u>liquidity</u> <u>trap</u> explained, can be analysed using such a model. However, it does have its limitations. It is a static model where prices are assumed to be <u>fixed</u>. <u>External</u> variables such as foreign interest rates and income levels are excluded. The <u>supply</u>-side of the economy is absent.

Case study
....
1. An increase in indirect tax combined with a reduction in public spending is an example of contractionary fiscal policy. The policy and its effects on the economy are shown in Figure 12.12.

Figure 12.12: Doubling of VAT and a slashing of public spending

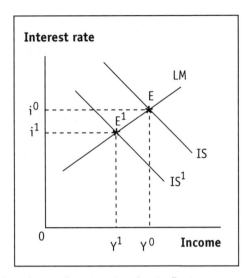

Contractionary fiscal policy results in a leftward shift of the IS curve. All other things equal, interest rates and national income fall. In this particular case national output fell 'by over 2% in 1980 and by 1.5% in 1981'.

2. One possible motivating factor would be the reduction in the inflation rate. Unfortunately, the simple IS/LM model is based on a fixed-price assumption. Therefore, analysing possible price changes is outside the scope of this model.

3. Figure 12.13 illustrates the effect of a 'loosening of monetary policy' combined with 'tax cuts'.

Figure 12.13: A loosening of monetary policy combined with tax cuts

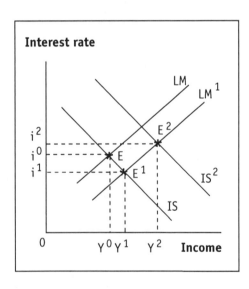

Loose (expansionary) monetary policy (an increase in money supply, for example) shifts the LM to the right. A reduction in tax rates is an example of an expansionary fiscal policy. This causes a rightward shift of the IS curve. The net effect of these policies is an increase in national income. This leads to an 'expansion' of the economy. In regard to interest rate changes, it is difficult to predict the net result since loose monetary policy tends to reduce interest rates whereas expansionary fiscal policy tends to increase interest rates. In the diagram, the interest rate reduction (i^0 to i^1) that arises from the change in monetary policy (LM to LM^1) is outweighed by the interest rate rise (i^1 to i^2) that results from the fiscal policy change (IS to IS^2).

Chapter 13

Working problems
....

1. (a) *Figure 13.18*

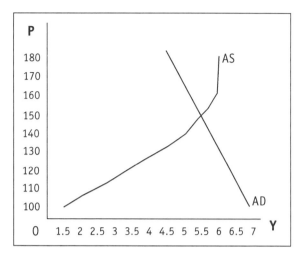

(b) The AS curve is upward sloping. At low output levels where spare capacity exists alongside wage rigidity, a price increase will elicit a large increase in output. At the intermediate range of output levels, some firms are approaching full capacity. Hence, as price increases the output response is limited. The AS curve is much steeper over this range of production. The final portion of the AS curve describes the economy's full-employment output level. Output does not respond to price changes. The AS curve is vertical.

2. *Figure 13.19*

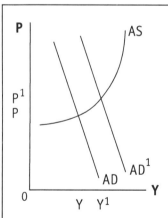 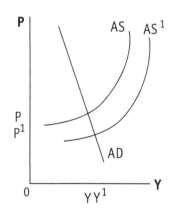

(a) the expansionary fiscal policy of the 1970s. The boost in demand is reflected in a rightward shift of the AD curve. Higher prices and a rise in output results.

(b) the reduction in oil prices since the early 1980s is reflected in a rightward shift of the AS curve. A reduction in prices and an increase in output results.

Multi-choice questions

1. (d) 2. (e) 3. (b) 4. (a) 5. (d) 6. (d)

True or false

1. False 2. False 3. True 4. True 5. True 6. True

Fill in the blanks

<u>Macroeconomic</u> equilibrium occurs at the intersection of the AD and AS curves; the point at which the output which households and firms <u>demand</u> is equal to the output which <u>firms</u> are willing to supply. The aggregate demand curve shows the quantity of output demanded at different <u>price</u> levels. The aggregate <u>supply</u> curve depicts the output produced by firms at different price levels. The AD curve is <u>downward</u> sloping; as prices rise, fewer goods and services are demanded. The <u>slope</u> of the AS curve varies. In the <u>short run</u>, the AS curve is <u>upward</u> sloping; reflecting higher output levels at higher prices. In the <u>long run</u> when resource costs move in tandem with prices, the AS curve is <u>vertical</u> at the full-employment output level. If output is demand-determined, the AS curve is <u>horizontal</u>; if output is <u>cost</u> or supply-determined, the AS curve is vertical. The former requires demand-management policies and receives support from <u>Keynesians</u>. The latter requires <u>supply</u>-<u>side</u> policies which find favour with those who support the non-interventionist, <u>market</u> system doctrine.

Case study

1. Fianna Fail and Labour. Both parties, as part of their manifestos, advocate an increase in 'capital spending . . . in an attempt to boost the economy'. By increasing exchequer capital investment, additional demand is injected into the economy. Both parties' support of tax 'reforms to benefit lower-paid workers' is a further indication of the desire to inject greater demand into the economy. There are some other references to Keynesian-style policies. Labour's desire for 'extra equity for state industry' and their 'interventionist role in building up Irish industry' are the types of policies which would broadly find favour with supporters of Keynesian economics.

2. It is generally agreed that the Irish tax system in its present form acts as a disincentive to work and risk-taking and hinders job creation. All-party support for tax reform, however does not imply that there is an absence of ideological differences. Democratic Left, Labour and, to a lesser extent, Fianna Fail would support tax reform as a way of redistributing wealth in the economy in favour of the less well-off. Whereas all three would support 'reforms to benefit lower-paid workers', there would be differences in the way they would deal with the top rate of tax (see article). In macro terms, their tax changes would be targeted at boosting aggregate demand. The PDs and to a lesser extent Fine Gael would support tax reform as a way of tackling the 'jobs crisis'. Fine Gael's proposal to cut employers'

PRSI is supply-side in nature and would not find favour with Labour. In macro terms, their tax changes would be targeted primarily at increasing aggregate supply.
3. Of all the political parties in Ireland, the PDs is the only party that comes close to supporting the policies advocated by supply siders. Some of these policies are referred to directly in the article. For example, the author writes that the PDs would oppose 'pushing up exchequer borrowing to boost public capital spending'. Curtailing public expenditure is a central plank of supply-side economics. The PDs support tax reform and specifically a cut in the top rate of tax 'to 40%'. According to supply siders, a cut in taxes increases incentives, work effort and output. The article refers to the PDs' desire 'to create the right climate for business'. Again, this proposal can be interpreted as supply-side in nature. The right environment for business would involve lower business tax rates, less state interference and greater control over government expenditure. The PDs would be likely to support such policies.

Chapter 14

Working problems
....
1. *Table 14.7* completed.

   The balance of payments

   Current account

Merchandise trade	2,244
Imports	−12,114
Exports	14,358
International freight	77
Other transportation	265
Tourism and travel	53
Other services	−863
Remuneration of employees	16
Trading and investment income	−3,249
Gross profits, dividends, royalties outflows	−2,564
National debt interest	−973
Gross other interest outflows	−1,041
Gross inflows	1,329
International transfers	1,108
Net balance on current account	−348

   Capital account

Private capital	−1,870
Semi-state companies	83
Other private capital	−1,953

<u>Official capital</u>	964
Exchequer foreign borrowing	−50
Government securities	1,320
Other public transactions	−307
<u>Banking transactions</u>	−186
Associated banks	−493
Other licensed banks	146
Other financial institutions	115
Counterpart to valuation changes	46
External reserves	640
Net balance on capital account	−453
Net residual	801

2. I propose the following groups (as of January 1996):

Tier 1 Germany, Austria, Holland, Belgium and Luxembourg.
Tier 2 France, Denmark, Ireland, Sweden and Finland.
Tier 3 Italy, Spain, Portugal and Greece.

The UK, given their strong opposition to a single currency, is omitted from the list.

The first tier consists of the core member states of the ERM and/or those countries whose currency is fixed to the German mark. A separate case can be made for each country.

- The German mark and the Dutch guilder are the only two currencies of the old system that trade (post-August 1993) within the old fluctuation band of 2.25% either way.
- The case for the Austrian schilling arises because of the close economic links between Germany and Austria.
- Luxembourg is one of the few countries that continues to meet the convergence criteria.
- The Belgian authorities have tried to fix the Belgian franc to the German mark. In the days when the fluctuation bands within the ERM were 2.25% and 6%, the Belgian authorities adopted an 'unofficial' 1% band for the DM/BFr. The only stumbling block for the Belgian authorities is their poor financial position, reflected in a high budget deficit and an equally high debt/GDP ratio.

The second tier consists of the countries whose economies are financially sound but doubts remain about certain aspects of their willingness or fitness to commit to a single currency. Again, a separate case is made for each country.

- The Danes' fear of Germany is one stumbling block. This was the main reason behind their rejection of the Maastricht treaty in June 1992. Their opt-out clause on the single currency is another obstacle. Like the French franc, the Danish krone came under a lot of pressure from the speculators in Autumn 1992 and again in Summer 1993.

- The French, although one of the founding members of the EU and still a key member of the ERM, have had their problems in the recent past. During the currency crisis of 1992–93 the French franc came under enormous pressure. In 1995, their deficit/ GDP ratio was 5%. The 3% reference value is unlikely to be met by 1997 unless substantial cuts in expenditure are implemented.[+]
- Although Ireland manages to meet four out of five convergence criteria (see endnote 29), doubts persist about Ireland's achievements to date and, moreover, their commitment to a single currency if the UK decides to opt out. The devaluation of the Irish pound in January 1993 is another example of how the market perceives Ireland's ability to adopt a single currency.[*]
- Sweden and Finland have only recently joined the EU. Both countries were badly affected by the currency crisis of 1992 when the link between the krona, the markka and the ECU was broken. Internally, the Finnish economy is still struggling with the after-effects of the break-up of the old Russian empire. Sweden has also many internal problems.

The third tier consists of countries whose economies are in difficulty. Serious doubts remain about their capacity to adopt a single currency before the end of the century. A separate case is made for each country.

- Italy, although one of the G-7 nations, has many internal problems, both political and economic. Subsequently, the market perceives the Italian lira as one of the weaker currencies. Continuous pressure by the market forced the Italian authorities to, first devalue the lira and, second, suspend its membership of the ERM in September 1992. Although the lira rejoined the ERM in late 1996, their membership of the 'first-tier' group of countries is likely to be opposed.
- The Spanish and the Portuguese are usually grouped together although they experience many different problems. They are two of the 'Group of Four' weak nations of the EU. Although substantial transfers of funds have managed to close the wealth gap, financial markets are still not convinced. During the currency crisis of 1992–93 the peseta and the escudo were devalued on a number of occasions.
- The Greek economy is the weakest in the EU. Inflation is relatively high and its financial position is poor. It is also a country whose currency was never a member of the ERM. Structural adjustments on a large scale are necessary before the Greek economy can be considered a serious contender for EMU entry.

I suspect that the Irish delegation will oppose my proposal for a three tier system on the basis that Ireland is omitted from the first tier. There is little doubt that Ireland has progressed from the days of high taxes, high expenditure and high borrowing. Notwithstanding these admirable achievements, problems still remain

---

[+] For political reasons, EMU without France is a non-starter.

[*] Since the writing of this analysis in January 1996, the outlook for Ireland has improved. With a low inflation rate, historically low interest rates, a deficit/GDP ratio below the 3% reference value, a declining debt/GDP ratio and a stable currency, Ireland is likely to be one of the first-tier countries.

with Ireland's adaptability to a single currency. Problems such as high unemployment, a high debt/GDP ratio and an overdependence on the UK market have to be addressed before Ireland can consider itself a likely candidate for the first tier.

Multi-choice questions
....
1. (d)   2. (c)   3. (a)   4. (d)   5. (e)   6. (c)

True or false
....
1. True   2. True   3. False   4. False   5. False   6. False

Fill in the blanks
....
The balance of <u>payments</u> is a record of all transactions between one country and the rest of the world. It is divided into a <u>current</u> account and a capital account. It is closely related to the exchange rate which is simply the <u>price</u> of one currency in terms of another. Under a flexible exchange rate regime, the exchange rate between the two currencies is determined in the <u>foreign</u> <u>exchange</u> market by the demand for and <u>supply</u> of the respective currencies. In turn, these are determined by the level of <u>exports</u> and imports and also by the level of <u>capital</u> flows. The Irish pound belongs to a <u>semi</u>-<u>fixed</u> exchange rate system, called the <u>EMS</u>. A member of the EMS exchange rate mechanism is committed to a <u>central</u> <u>rate</u> against other member states' currencies and a <u>band</u> <u>of</u> <u>fluctuation</u>. In keeping the currency within the limits, the Central Bank has three options available; foreign exchange <u>intervention</u> which involves the use of <u>external</u> <u>reserves</u>, a change of interest rates or a <u>realignment</u> of the currency. The Irish pound has been devalued twice since it joined in <u>1979</u>; by <u>8%</u> in 1986 and by 10% in <u>1993</u>. The latter came at the end of the currency crisis of 1992/93 when the <u>lira</u> and sterling left the system, the peseta, the <u>escudo</u> and the Irish pound were all devalued and the unofficial link which the <u>Scandinavian</u> currencies had with the ECU was broken. The weakening of the <u>ERM</u> is a setback to EMU. The <u>Maastricht</u> treaty aims for a <u>single</u> currency by 1999 at the latest. Ireland is fully committed to EMU and, by meeting the <u>convergence</u> <u>criteria</u>, hopes to be in the 'fast track' to EMU.

Case study
....
1. In August 1993 the ERM bands of fluctuation were changed from 2.25% and 6% to 2.25% and 15%. The German mark and the Dutch guilder were the only currencies to retain the narrow band of 2.25%. A Central Bank has a number of options available to it in order to ensure that its currency stays inside the intervention limits. A short-term measure is the use of external reserves for the purposes of foreign exchange intervention. A medium-term measure is a change in interest rates. A long-term measure is a realignment of the currency within the ERM.
2. London is one of the world's top financial centres, along with New York and Tokyo. In terms of volume of daily trading it easily surpasses all other financial centres in

Europe. Hence, on the basis of status and tradition, London would be the ideal location for the EMI. Other considerations, however, took precedent. The Germans were adamant that the new European Central Bank had to be similar to the Bundesbank, particularly in terms of its anti-inflationary policy. The first step to this was the establishment of the EMI in Frankfurt, it was argued. Also, given that the British government had an opt-out clause on the single currency, it was felt that it would be inappropriate to set up the EMI in the country which was most sceptical and least supportive of EMU.

3. The Maastricht treaty which set out the timetable for a single currency by 1999 was signed in December 1991. A number of unforeseen events have taken place since then which make the move to a single currency as set out in the treaty 'unachievable'. For one, there was the currency crisis of 1992–93. Between September 1992 and August 1993 four currencies of the ERM were devalued and, in addition, two currencies' membership of the ERM was suspended. The UK has still not rejoined (at the time of writing this book).

Then, in August 1993 the ERM bands of fluctuation were widened considerably. This raises doubts about the validity of the exchange rate criterion.

Also, some countries have experienced grave financial problems since the early 1990s. For example, the Greek financial position has worsened, the UK and German budget deficits have increased significantly whereas the Italian and the Portuguese debt/GDP ratios have also increased. Doubts have begun to emerge over the timetable for the move towards full EMU and the capacity of certain member states to adopt to a single currency.

Chapter 15

Working problems
....

1. (a) The base year of this index is 1990. We know this because it is the one year that both series have in common. The row of figures showing GDP at constant prices, is using the value of the pound in 1990 as the base.

Figure 15.16 shows both the constant and current GDP series.

Figure 15.16: GDP at constant and current prices (1987–94)

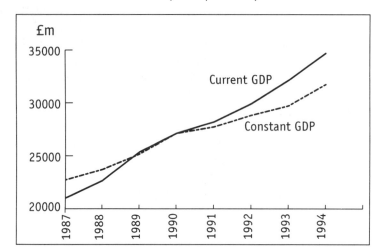

(b) The GDP deflator is calculated below.

Table 15.7 completed

Year	Current GDP (£ million)	Constant GDP (£ million)	GDP Deflator
1987	21,074.8	22,792.9	92.5
1988	22,717.9	23,765.3	95.6
1989	25,418.3	25,218.7	100.8
1990	27,187.6	27,187.6	100.0
1991	28,263.4	27,792.2	101.7
1992	29,971.8	28,889.5	103.7
1993	32,174.0	29,781.0	108.0
1994	34,741.0	31,787.0	109.3

The deflator for the base year is 100. Generally, the deflator prior to the base year is less than 100. The deflator after the base year is greater than 100. The year 1989 deviates from that trend. It appears that the price level in 1990 was actually lower than in 1989. Deflation is so rarely observed, that this is probably due to some unusual feature of the national accounts between 1989 and 1990. It would take considerable research to explain that result. It shows, however, that you have to be careful when you work with data.

(c) For 1992, we compare 1992 with 1991 to find the change in the price level for 1992.

$$\frac{1992 \text{ deflator} - 1991 \text{ deflator}}{1991 \text{ deflator}} \times 100 = \text{inflation rate}$$

$$\frac{103.7 - 101.7}{101.7} \times 100 = 1.97\%$$

2. The home country will export grain and the foreign country will export beer. Foreign is four times as productive as home in the production of beer, whereas in grain production, both countries are equally productive.

So home's absolute disadvantage *vis-à-vis* foreign is at a minimum in grain production, while foreign's absolute advantage is at a maximum in beer production. Hence home's comparative advantage is in grain while foreign's comparative advantage is in beer.

Multi-choice questions
....
1. (c)   2. (b)   3. (c)   4. (e)   5. (d)   6. (c)

True or false
....
1. False   2. True   3. False   4. False   5. False   6. True

Fill in the blanks
....
Inflation is a rise in the general level of prices. It is measured by a price index. The CPI and the GDP deflator are examples of price indices. The causes of inflation are demand pull, cost push, a weakening of the exchange rate, excessive wage increases and expectations. Creditors, exporters and those sections of society on fixed money incomes suffer from inflation. Beneficiaries of inflation can include the government and borrowers. Counter-inflationary policies include contractionary fiscal and monetary policies, wage restraint and supply-side policies targeted at reducing production costs. The factors influencing the Irish inflation rate include domestic economic policy, the international trend in prices and the strength of the Irish pound against other currencies of the ERM.

Unemployment is a stock concept. It measures the number of people who are willing and able to work but who cannot find a job. The different types of unemployment include frictional, seasonal, structural, demand-deficient and classical. Demand-deficient unemployment is caused by insufficient spending in the economy. Involuntary unemployment is possible in the Keynesian theory whereas the classical theory assumes unemployment is of a voluntary nature. Market stability and wage flexibility are central in explaining the differences between the classical and the Keynesian theories of unemployment. Marx explains unemployment in the context of the struggle between the capitalists and the working class. The economic and social costs to unemployment accrue to the unemployed, the government and to the economy.

Traditional trade theory assumes that markets are perfectly competitive. The key concept is the law of comparative advantage which is a more sophisticated concept than the law of absolute advantage. It says that countries should specialise in what they do relatively best. Comparative advantage reveals itself in lower pre-trade relative prices. Trade based on comparative advantage tends to be inter-industry in type. All countries can gain from such trade and the greater the difference between international terms of trade and domestic relative prices, the greater the gains from trade.

New trade theory by contrast assumes that markets are <u>imperfectly</u> <u>competitive</u>. Such trade takes place between <u>similar</u> countries and the bases for such trade are <u>economies</u> of <u>scale</u> and product <u>differentiation</u>.

Case studies
....

A. Inflation

1. Most institutions and economic agents are concerned with high inflation. A Central Bank governor is particularly concerned with inflation because price stability is one of the objectives of a Central Bank. Among its many roles, it is responsible for maintaining price stability. Whereas the Department of Finance is responsible for the formulation and implementation of fiscal policy and also for the formulation of exchange rate policy, it is the Central Bank which has sole responsibility for monetary policy.

2. Private borrowing is used to finance either consumption or investment. Both of these are components of demand. If borrowing increases and an economy is at or near the full-employment level of output, there may be an inflationary gap. Consider Figure 15.17.

Figure 15.17: Inflationary gap caused by excess demand

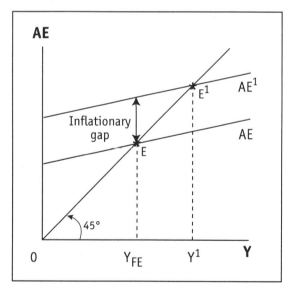

The economy begins at full-employment equilibrium, which is shown by point E. Increased borrowing is used for investment. This shifts the AE curve up to AE^1. The new equilibrium, E^1, indicates that the level of output is above the full-employment level. The inflationary gap is indicated on the diagram.

3. Mr O'Connell mentions that government spending will increase. This fiscal policy change is only a small increase, but technically, it should be shown as an upward shift to AE^2 as shown in Figure 15.18.

Figure 15.18: Expansionary fiscal and contractionary monetary policy

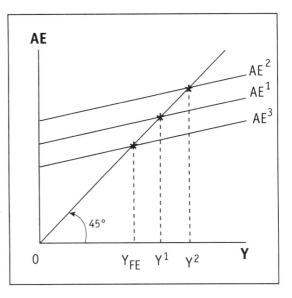

He mentions but does not speculate on interest rates. In the light of inflationary pressures, we would expect the Central Bank to enact contractionary monetary policy which will cause interest rates to increase. This acts as a disincentive to investment. We will show this decrease in investment by lowering the AE curve to AE^3. Hopefully, if this action is taken, the economy will return to the full-employment level of output, and eliminate the inflationary gap.

B. Unemployment

1. There are a number of reasons for Ireland's susceptibility to world recession and, in particular a recession in the UK and the US. Ireland is a small economy which takes the price of commodities and raw materials as given, determined by world factors. It is also an open economy, exporting over 70% of its production of goods and services. The US and the UK are two of Ireland's most important markets. This vulnerability to the international environment is heightened by the fact that multinationals account for a large proportion of Ireland's output. Finally, fewer job opportunities abroad combined with relatively generous welfare payments in Ireland attracts migrants 'to return home', creating more pressures in the domestic labour market.

2. Modern societies have accepted the responsibility of assisting all sections of society, including the unemployed. The state redistributes resources through the social welfare system. The unemployed receive unemployment benefits in addition to other allowances. Increases in unemployment benefits in line with inflation allow the unemployed to maintain their purchasing power from year to year.

   There are, however, problems associated with real increases in welfare payments. For one, it increases public expenditure which leads to higher taxes and/or higher borrowing. Two, depending on the relationship between the welfare system and the tax system, there may be little incentive to seek employment. This applies particularly to the long-term unemployed who are effectively outside the labour market. Large increases in welfare payments, however well intentioned may act as a disincentive to return to the job market. Three, social welfare payments may create a dependency culture where the unemployed rely heavily on the state.

3. The non-integration of the tax and the welfare system contributes to the unemployment problem in Ireland. Changes to the Irish tax system have been made

largely on an *ad hoc*, piecemeal, reactive, short-term basis. The welfare system supports the unemployed through benefits of an indefinite nature. There are two features of the tax system, in particular, which discourage the unemployed from seeking out and taking up employment. The first is the unemployment trap which results largely in the absence of any incentive to take up a low-paid job. The welfare system replaces a large proportion of after-tax income. This is reflected in high replacement ratios. The second is the tax wedge. Although the cost (wage + PRSI contributions) to the employer of hiring labour may be quite high, the income accruing to the employee after adjusting for taxes may be quite low. Indeed, the after-tax income, when compared to welfare payments, may not be high enough to entice the unemployed back into the labour market.

C. *International trade*

1. The OECD implicitly assumes that the law of comparative advantage holds. That is to say, if all countries specialise where their relative advantage *vis-à-vis* the rest of the world is greatest, their earning power will be enhanced. Additional benefits are cheaper imported products and a greater variety of such goods.
2. Comparative advantage translates into absolute competitiveness via the returns paid to national factors of production. A less productive country will pay its workers lower wages. The country as a whole, however is better off as a result of free trade. National income valued at world prices should increase as a result of free trade.
3. According to the Heckscher-Ohlin theory of trade, the abundant national factor of production gains, while the scarce national factor of production loses. If we accept that countries in the developed world are more capital abundant (or less labour abundant) than countries in the developing world, then capital stands to gain and labour stands to lose as a result of freer global trade.

ENDNOTES

An Introduction to Economics

1 John E. Maher, *What is Economics?*, John Wiley & Sons, 1969. In this book the author attempts to explain what economics is about (and what it is not about!).

2 Barbara Wootton, *Lament for Economics*, Allen, 1938. For a more up-to-date attack on economics, read Paul Ormerod's *The Death of Economics*, Faber and Faber, 1994. A less critical though nonetheless useful attempt to get over the deliberate 'jargon and mystique' common to practitioners of economics is given by Peter Donaldson in *Economics of the Real World*, 3rd ed., Penguin, 1984. Finally, no reader of economics who is disillusioned with the 'Man serving Capital' approach to society should miss E. F. Schumacher's *Small is Beautiful. A Study of Economics as if People Mattered*, Abacus, 1974.

3 George Bernard Shaw. Attributed.

4 J. M. Keynes, 'The Dilemma of Modern Socialism', *Political Quarterly*, 3, 1932.

5 Keynes' work coincided with the independent work of Richard Stone and Simon Kuznets on national income measurements. The birth of macroeconomics is traced back to these specific developments.

6 Loosely translated, 'micro' is the Greek word for small; 'macro' is the Greek word for large.

7 Sir Arthur Conan Doyle, 'A Scandal in Bohemia', in *The Annotated Sherlock Holmes*, Wings Books, 1992. (Originally published in 1887.)

8 Joan Robinson, *Marx, Marshall and Keynes*, Delphi School of Economics (Occasional Paper No. 9), 1955.

9 Alfred Marshall. Quoted in J. M. Keynes, *Essays in Biography*, Royal Economic Society, 1933.

Chapter 1

1 George Bernard Shaw, 'Socialism and Superior Brains', *The Fortnightly Review*, April 1894.

2 J. R. Hicks, *The Social Framework: An Introduction to Economics*, Clarendon Press, 1942.

3 Alfred Marshall, *Principles of Economics*, 8th edition, Macmillan, 1920.

4 The law of demand only holds when we qualify it with the '*ceteris paribus*' clause. This will be clarified in Chapter 3 when the substitution and income effects are introduced. In Chapter 3 we will discover that the law of demand refers only to the substitution effect and not to the total price change. Any reference to the law of demand in Chapters 1 to 3 is made with this same qualification.

5 It appears that Giffen did not make any such 'observation'. It was Alfred Marshall who attributed this 'observation' to Giffen. See Marshall, *Principles of Economics*.

6 Chapter 5 provides us with a rigorous and detailed proof of this observation under perfectly competitive conditions. See Endnote 8.

7 Traditional microeconomic theory assumes that the objective of the firm is profit-maximisation. This and other objectives are discussed in Chapter 4.

8 We assume that we are dealing with a competitive market (what economists call 'perfect competition'). Such a market is comprised of a large number of sellers. The commodity produced is homogeneous. Consumers and producers have perfect knowledge of the

market. This assumption of a perfectly competitive market is crucial in the derivation of the supply curve. Market structures, including perfect competition, are discussed in Chapter 5.

9 'We might as reasonably dispute whether it is the upper or the under blade of a pair of scissors that cuts a piece of paper, as whether value is governed by utility or cost of production.' Marshall, *Principles of Economics*.

10 J. FitzGerald, and D. O'Connor, 'Economic Consequences of CAP Reform' in J. Bradley, J. FitzGerald and D. McCoy, *Medium-Term Review: 1991–96*, ESRI, 1991.

Chapter 2

1 *The Random House Dictionary of the English Language*, the unabridged edition, Random House, 1967.

2 Marshall, *Principles of Economics*.

3 W. Stanley Jevons, *The Theory of Political Economy*, 5th edition, A. M. Kelley, 1957.

4 The Greek letter eeta (η) is the symbol commonly used for price elasticity of demand.

5 This can be written in a number of different ways. For example,

$$\eta = \frac{\dfrac{\Delta Q}{Q}}{\dfrac{\Delta P}{P}} = \frac{\Delta Q}{Q} \times \frac{P}{\Delta P} = \frac{\Delta Q}{\Delta P} \times \frac{P}{Q}$$

All three can be used when calculating the elasticity coefficient. The same answer results.

6 The elasticity coefficient does not vary with direction. We get the same coefficient regardless of the direction of the price change. For example, if price falls from £9 to £6 and with the respective quantity changes, the coefficient is equal to –1.5. Likewise, if price rises from £9 to £12 the coefficient is equal to –1.5. Why? Because the percentage price change and the percentage quantity change are equal for the two examples. The size of the elasticity coefficient depends on the magnitude of the price and quantity changes and not on the direction of the change.

7 The geometry of total revenue is straightforward. Total revenue is P (price) multiplied by Q (quantity). The area of a rectangle is H (height) multiplied by L (length). In (P,Q) space with dimensions of price and quantity, the rectangular area represents total revenue.

8 We are assuming, at this point, that the firm is attempting to maximise total revenue. This is not the same as maximising profits. The latter implies cost considerations whereas the former does not take into account costs. The objectives of the firm are considered in Chapter 4.

9 We acknowledge the comments offered by one of the reviewers on the appropriateness of VAT in the case study. He is correct when he makes the case for excise tax in preference to VAT. However, since the author of the article writes exclusively in terms of VAT, we have done likewise.

10 Apply the laws of mathematics and in particular the laws of division: like-signs in the numerator and the denominator result in an overall positive value for the quotient; unlike-signs result in an overall negative value for the quotient.

11 This finding applies not only across countries but within countries. Different social classes exist in an economy. A good which may be a luxury for low-income families may be a necessity or possibly even an inferior good for families of high incomes.

12 These are all economic definitions and may not coincide with an individual's ideas about what is a luxury good, a necessity, an inferior good etc.

13 Time, from the perspective of the economics profession, is divided into two periods. The short run is the period of time in which the firm cannot adjust all of its inputs in response to a change in conditions. The long run is a period of time which allows the firm to make total adjustments, if necessary, to its inputs. The actual length of these periods varies from market to market. The time factor is discussed in greater detail in Chapter 4.

14 The word 'secular' is derived from the Latin word *saecula* which means a generation.

Chapter 3

1 See Bonar's Preface to *Letters of Ricardo to Malthus*, Clarendon Press, 1887.

2 Jevons, *The Theory of Political Economy*.

3 H. H. Gossen, *Entwicklung der Gesetze des menschlichen Verkehrs*, 3rd edition, Prager, 1927.

4 He went on to say 'Nothing is more useful than water: but it will purchase scarce any thing; . . . A diamond, on the contrary, has scarce any value in use; but a very great quantity of other goods may frequently be had in exchange for it.' Adam Smith, *An Inquiry into the Nature and Causes of The Wealth of Nations*, edited Edwin Cannon, reprint ed., Methuen and Co. Ltd, 1961. (Originally printed in 1776.)

5 Jevons' *The Theory of Political Economy* was published in English in 1871. In the same year Menger's *Grundsätze der Volkswirtschaftslehre (Principles of Economics)* was published in German. Walras' *Éléments d'économie politique pure (Elements of Pure Economics)* was published in 1874, in French. It is interesting to note that none of the three actually used the term marginal utility and, in some cases, not even the term utility. Furthermore, only Jevons explicitly referred to the cardinal nature of the analysis. At the time he was writing the book he accepted that utility was immeasurable but he was hopeful that it would become measurable with the help of further developments some time in the future.

6 The basic demand and supply analysis which we described in Chapter 1 was not universally accepted in the 1870s. It was Alfred Marshall in his monumental book *Principles of Economics* who was primarily responsible for bringing the demand and supply framework to the core of economic theory. Until then, different theories were used to explain price and value. The classical theory of value focused on the supply side of the market. Price was determined by the costs of the factors of production. The marginal utility theory was a demand-side explanation for the determination of price. This is true although the example which both Jevons and Menger use implies some consideration of demand and supply in the determination of value and price. Any full explanation of value must take into account both demand and supply. Despite this oversight, the marginal utility approach did provide the first, albeit partial, explanation to the water-diamond dilemma.

7 'A Reconsideration of the Theory of Value' by Hicks & Allen was published in *Economica*, 1934. Hick's ideas were popularised in his famous book *Value and Capital* (1939).

8 Marginal analysis is an application of the branch of mathematics known as differential calculus. Students of economics and mathematics know that the concept of change is common both to differentiation and to marginal analysis. It is this concept of change which links both topics.

9 Marshall, *Principles of Economics*.

10 This is sometimes referred to as Gossen's Second Law. Hermann H. Gossen's main work entitled *Development of the Laws of Human Relationships and of Rules to be Derived Therefrom for Human Action*, published in 1854, preceded the writings of Jevons, Walras and Menger. It did not have the same effect on the economics profession as the later works and, as a result, his work was and still is largely unrecognised. Gossen was so disappointed with

the public's response to his book that he recalled all of the unsold copies and proceeded to destroy them.

11 There is a distinction to be made between a real variable and a nominal variable. A nominal variable is one that is not adjusted for changes in the price level. In contrast, a real variable has been corrected to account for changes in the price level. This distinction is important and reappears in many different sections of the textbook. If we do not account for changes in the price level, we cannot accurately compare economic data for different years. For example, if income per head of the population increases from £10,000 to £10,300 between 1995 and 1996, it appears that income has increased by 3%. If, however, the general level of prices has also increased by 3%, income adjusted for the change in the price level has not changed. In this case, nominal income increased by 3%, but real income has remained unchanged.

12 Researchers now believe that Giffen never made this claim. It appears that Paul Samuelson was responsible for accrediting Giffen with this observation. In addition, there is no evidence to suggest that the consumption of potatoes increased during the famine years. Indeed, with the potato blight damaging the crop, it is hard to imagine how the consumption of potatoes could have increased. This adds credence to the argument made in Chapter 1 that a Giffen good, although theoretically possible, is seldom observed in reality.

13 Marshall, *Principles of Economics*.

Chapter 4

1 Augustin Cournot, *Researches into the Mathematical Principles of the Theory of Wealth*, trans. Nathan T. Bacon, Macmillan, 1897. (Originally published in 1838.)

2 H. J. Davenport, 'The Formula of Sacrifice', *Journal of Political Economy*, 1893–94.

3 Joan Robinson, 'What is Perfect Competition?', *Quarterly Journal of Economics*, Nov. 1934.

4 John Stuart Mill, *Principles of Political Economy*, edited Sir W. J. Ashley, A. M. Kelley, 1961. (Originally published in 1848.)

5 Students who have studied calculus will recognise that the slope of the total product curve is changing as labour is added. The slope of the total product can be derived by calculating the first derivative at any point. The economic concept described by the first derivative of the total product curve is the marginal product of labour.

6 Technically, the term 'returns to scale' refers to the relationship between changes in inputs and subsequent changes in output. Moreover, 'returns to scale' is a long-run concept describing what happens when all inputs are changed, whereas the 'law of diminishing returns' is a short-run concept describing what happens to output when the variable input is changed and the fixed inputs are constant.

7 We can show this by referring to Equation 4.4:

$$STC = SFC + SVC$$

Furthermore,

$$SATC = \frac{STC}{Q} \; ; \; SAVC = \frac{SVC}{Q} \; ; \; SAFC = \frac{SFC}{Q}$$

Thus,

$$\frac{STC}{Q} = \frac{SVC}{Q} + \frac{SFC}{Q}$$

$$SATC = SAFC + SAVC$$

8 This highlights the link between production and costs. Production theory and, in particular, the total product and marginal product are the sources of the cost curves which have been described in this chapter. The cost curves are grounded in the production techniques employed by the firm, the amount of inputs used, and also the prices that the firm pays for the inputs.

9 The economist who first developed the envelope curve was Jacob Viner in 1931. In the drafting of the envelope curve he and his draftsman, a brilliant mathematician at the University of Chicago, made what has become a famous error. He drew the LAC curve from the minimum points of the SATC curves. He acknowledged his mistake in a supplementary note written in 1950 where he wrote 'future teachers and students may share the pleasure of many of their predecessors of pointing out that if I had known what an "envelope" was I would not have given my excellent draftsman the technically impossible and economically inappropriate assignment of drawing an AC curve which would pass through the lowest cost points of all the ac curves and yet not rise above any ac curve at any point.' However, this error does not, in any way, take from Viner's contribution to the theory of costs. The name of the article, regarded as a classic, is 'Cost Curves and Supply Curves', *Zeitschrift fur Nationalokonomie*, 3, 1931. Finally, the explanation of the envelope curve which is to be found in the text is rather brief. A fuller explanation is left to authors of intermediate textbooks.

10 The average revenue received is simply the price of the product. This can be confirmed as follows:

$$TR = P \times Q$$

Divide both sides by Q:

$$\frac{TR}{Q} = \frac{P.Q}{Q}$$

The left-hand side is equal to AR. The right-hand side simplifies to P with the cancellation of Q above and below the line. Thus AR = P.

11 Commission of the European Communities, *Completing the Internal Market; Cockfield White Paper, Brussels/Luxembourg*, June 1985.

Chapter 5

1 Joan Robinson, 'What is Perfect Competition?'.

2 Smith, *An Enquiry into the Nature and Causes of the Wealth of Nations*.

3 The use of the terms 'perfect' and 'competition' is both unfortunate and misleading. Perfect does not suggest best or desirable. It simply means that there are no restrictions on competition. Competition is used in the sense that no single firm can gain any advantage over its 'competitors' because any advantage will be 'competed' away.

4 We noted in Chapter 2 that the elasticity of demand for a good is determined by the number of available substitutes. The greater the number of readily available and close substitutes, the more elastic is demand. Under conditions of perfect competition, there are many close substitutes for the firm's product. The result is an elastic demand curve. It is important to recognise that this feature does not apply to the market demand curve. The market as an entity can only sell a greater amount of goods if it lowers its price. There exists a negatively sloped market demand curve.

5 The word 'monopolist' is derived from the Greek words 'mono' meaning 'one' and 'polist' meaning 'seller'.

6 This does not occur when the monopolist can engage in price discrimination, which is why he is willing to increase output up to Q_2.

7 Edward Chamberlin, *The Theory of Monopolistic Competition*, 1933, Joan Robinson, *The Economics of Imperfect Competition*, 1933, Piero Sraffa, *The Law of Return under Competitive Conditions*, 1926.

8 The word 'oligopolist' is derived from the Greek words 'oligos' meaning 'few' and 'polist' meaning 'seller'.

9 See P. M. Sweezy, 'Demand under Conditions of Oligopoly,' *Journal of Political Economy*, 47, August 1939 and R. L. Hall and C. J. Hitch, 'Price Theory and Business Behaviour', *Oxford Economic Papers*, No. 2, May 1939. Sweezy was interested in the downward stickiness of prices which was evident during the Great Depression.

Chapter 6

1 Karl Marx, 'First Manuscript' in *Early Writings, (of) Karl Marx*, trans. Rodney Livingstone and Gregor Bentan, introduced by Lucio Colletti, Penguin, 1975.

2 D. Ricardo, *The Principles of Political Economy and Taxation*, Dent & Sons Ltd, 1965. (Reprint of 3rd edition, originally published in 1821.)

3 Frederick B. Hawley, *Enterprise and the Productive Process*, G. P. Putnam and Sons, 1907.

4 Refer to the circular flow of economic activity in Chapter 8 to see how this flow of factor resources is only one of many transactions in the macroeconomy. Refer also to Figure 8.7 column 6 to see the distribution of income.

5 The demand for other factor inputs is also a derived demand. It is derived from the consumer demand for final goods and services that the factors produce.

6 The American economist J. Bates Clark is accredited with writing the most comprehensive book on marginal productivity theory. The book entitled *The Distribution of Wealth: A Theory of Wages, Interest and Profits* (1899) became the basis for the theory of income distribution. The idea for the book came from issues raised by his fellow American Henry George (see endnote 17). The marginal productivity theory has a number of shortcomings. First, it is extremely difficult to calculate the marginal productivity of labour. Second, it assumes that all other factor inputs are constant. This is unlikely in reality. Third, it fails to account for wage differentials. Fourth, it ignores imperfections in the market. Fifth, it is difficult to separate out the marginal products of the various factor inputs. Notwithstanding these limitations, the marginal productivity theory makes a significant contribution to factor markets and the theory of income distribution.

7 We know that:

$$MRP = \frac{\Delta TR}{\Delta Q_L} \qquad [6.1]$$

and

$$MRP = MP \times MR \qquad [6.2]$$

We will prove that in perfectly competitive markets

$$\frac{\Delta TR}{\Delta Q_L} = MRP = MP \times MR$$

Begin with Equation 6.2.

$$MRP = MP \times MR$$

Recall from Chapter 4 that $MP = \dfrac{\Delta TP}{\Delta Q_L}$. Substitute this expression into the right-hand side of Equation 6.2.

$$MRP = \frac{\Delta TP}{\Delta Q_L} \times MR$$

TP is nothing more than the total output of the firm. Therefore, TP = Q. Substitute Q into the equation above.

$$MRP = \frac{\Delta Q}{\Delta Q_L} \times MR$$

From Chapter 4 we know that $MR = \dfrac{\Delta TR}{\Delta Q}$. Substituting this expression for MR into the equation above, we get

$$MRP = \frac{\Delta Q}{\Delta Q_L} \times \frac{\Delta TR}{\Delta Q}$$

When we cancel ΔQ from both variables on the right-hand side, the remainder is Equation 6.1.

$$MRP = \frac{\Delta TR}{\Delta Q_L}$$

Therefore, Equations 6.1 and 6.2 are two ways to define marginal revenue product (MRP) in a perfectly competitive market.

8 We are assuming that all labourers can be hired at the same wage.

9 The rationale of the optimal condition MRP = W is similar in principle to the condition MR = MC which was explained in Chapter 4. The only difference is that in Chapter 4 we were concerned with the marginal revenue and marginal cost of producing an additional unit of output whereas in this chapter we are interested in the marginal revenue and marginal cost of employing an extra unit of labour. The optimal condition in Chapter 4 implies that the firm will produce where MR = MC. The optimal condition in this chapter implies that the same firm will hire until the MRP of labour = W.

10 In our example, the MRP curve of labour declines with each addition of labour. In other words, diminishing marginal returns begins with the addition of the second worker, since the second worker produces less than the first. We know from the discussion in Chapter 4, that marginal returns may increase with the addition of labour initially and then decrease. This means that in a perfectly competitive goods market (a market where a firm can sell all of its product at a single price), the marginal revenue product curve will initially increase and then fall.

On the upward sloping portion of the marginal revenue product curve, wage increases are matched by productivity increases. A firm which decides to produce in the short run, will always hire additional employees if their marginal revenue product is increasing. The demand curve for labour, therefore, is the downward sloping portion of the marginal revenue product curve.

11 There is an important distinction between capital goods (plant, equipment, machinery etc.) and human capital (the education, training and skills of the labour force). In recent times, the economics profession has rediscovered an interest in human capital theory. Adam Smith, David Ricardo and David Hume all at one time or another wrote about the importance of education and of investing in 'human capital'. It was Alfred Marshall who wrote 'The most valuable of all capital is that invested in human beings.' It wasn't, however, until the 1960s that an American economist by the name of Gary Becker once again restored human capital theory to its rightful place in the economics literature. For that and other work, Becker was to receive the Nobel prize in economics in 1992.

12 A more intuitive explanation of the demand curve for capital is considered here. Interest rates represent the cost of borrowing money. A firm may purchase assets from retained earnings or it may borrow money to acquire a capital good. If interest rates are high, only assets with the highest rates of return are considered. As interest rates fall, less productive assets with lower rates of return are considered. In both cases, as interest rates fall, the demand for capital goods increases.

13 Like the individual labour supply curve, the individual supply curve for capital is also thought to be influenced by substitution and income effects. First, consider the substitution effect. As the interest rate rises, each individual has the choice of whether to consume or to save. Higher interest rates increase the opportunity cost of present consumption. The individual who chooses to save is substituting future consumption for present consumption. The relationship between interest rates and savings is positive. The income effect differs, depending on whether an individual is a borrower or a lender. For the borrower, a person with a variable mortgage, for instance, the income which remains for consumption or savings, falls as interest rates rise. For the borrower, the income effect moves in the opposite direction as the substitution effect. Higher interest rates may result in lower savings.

    For the lender, an increase in interest rates adds to income. This person will save more income for two reasons. First, the high interest rate encourages her to forgo present consumption. Second, she has more to save because her income is higher. For the lender, the substitution effect and the income effect move in the same direction. This person will save more as interest rates increase. Even though the increasing interest rates affect the two groups differently, the market supply curve of capital is considered to be upward sloping. The substitution effect overwhelms the income effect. As interest rates rise, people put more money into savings, which in turn is the source of funds for capital.

14 Rent was defined by Ricardo as ' . . . that portion of the produce of the earth which is paid to the landlord for the use of the original and indestructible powers of the soil'. See Ricardo, *The Principles of Political Economy and Taxation*.

15 Economic rent is to factor markets what consumer surplus is to product markets. In Chapter 3 we defined consumer surplus as the difference between the price the consumer pays for the good and the maximum price he is willing to pay for the good. Economic rent can be defined in the same terms: it is the difference between the actual factor price that the owner receives and the minimum factor price at which the owner is willing to supply the factor input.

16 In reality, the supply of land is not necessarily fixed and there are alternative uses. Irrigation, other forms of reclamation and fertilisers allow for the existing parcels of land to be extended or improved. For the sake of simplicity, however, we assume a fixed supply of land with no alternative uses.

17 As land is in fixed supply and has zero supply cost, all its earnings are economic rent. Any change in demand, small or large, will have no effect on the supply. It is unearned income and it is for this reason that a tax on land is often proposed. Rent could be subject to tax in the knowledge that the supply of land will remain unchanged. Those who argue against a land tax maintain that with all the alternative uses, land is not fixed in reality. In addition, they would argue that there are many other factors which earn economic rent and are viable sources of tax, e.g. movie actors or professional sports stars. For a definitive analysis on the reasons for why landowners should be subject to tax, read Henry George's (of the single tax movement) classic *Progress and Poverty* (1879).

18 Classical economic theory divided factor income into three rather than four categories – wages (the return on labour), rents (the return on land) and profits (the return on capital). For classical economists, profit and interest were indistinguishable. This reflected the structure of the corporate sector in the nineteenth century when the role of the capitalist and the entrepreneur were combined.

19 F. Knight, *Risk, Uncertainty and Profit*, Houghton Mifflin Co., 1921.

20 Schumpeter was only one of many central European economists who were interested in the theory of profit. Nineteenth-century German economists (Roscher, von Thunen and Von Mangoldt) had developed a theory of profit and entrepreneurship long before Schumpeter.

21 Ricardo, *The Principles of Political Economy and Taxation*.

Chapter 7

1 George Bernard Shaw, *John Bull's Other Island*, Penguin Books, 1984. (First published 1907.)

2 Thomas Fuller, *Gnomologia: adages and proverbs; wise sayings and witty sentences, ancient and modern*, 1932. (Originally published in 1732.)

3 A. C. Pigou, *The Economics of Welfare*, Macmillan, 1962. (Reprint of 1952 edition.)

4 If producers produce goods that consumers do not want, then they will go out of business. In addition, if producers do not sell at the lowest conceivable price, then the forces of competition will drive them out of business.

5 B. Mandeville, *The Fable of the Bees*, edit P. Harth, Penguin Books, 1970. (First published in 1714.)

6 Pigou, *The Economics of Welfare*.

7 R. H. Coase, 'The Problem of Social Cost', *Journal of Law and Economics*, 3, 1960.

8 P. A. Samuelson, 'The Pure Theory of Public Expenditure', *Review of Economics and Statistics*, 36, 1954. Also, 'A Diagrammatic Exposition of a Theory of Public Expenditure', *Review of Economics and Statistics*, 37, 1955.

Chapter 8

1 Simon Kuznets, *Economic Growth and Structure: Selected Essays*, Heinemann, 1966.

2 Paul Ormerod, *The Death of Economics*, Faber and Faber, 1995.

3 Richard Douthwaite, *The Growth Illusion*, The Lilliput Press, 1992. *The Growth Illusion* is an attack on the belief that economic growth is beneficial. Douthwaite, a former

professional economist who now works in the West of Ireland, argues that the benefits accruing from economic growth do not outweigh the substantial costs involved. Among others, these include environmental costs and the damage done to community life.

4   Quesnay was one of the leading physiocrats (see Chapter 9 for an explanation on the physiocrats) of the eighteenth century. His main work *Tableau Économique (Economic Table)* was published in 1758. This table analysed the circulation of wealth in the economy and it is believed that it was one of the first models to describe the macroeconomy in a circular flow fashion.

5   Taxes are usually divided into two categories: direct and indirect. The former is a tax charged on income. Examples include personal income tax and corporate tax. Indirect tax is a charge on expenditure. Excise duties and Value Added Tax (VAT) are examples.

6   For a more detailed description of the Irish National Income Accounts read *Irish Economic Statistics* by F. Kirwan and J. McGilvray, Institute of Public Administration, 1983. Another source of reference for these sets of accounts is the *Economic Review and Outlook* report published every year by the Department of Finance.

7   'It consists of what remains after deducting from the income-based estimate of Gross Domestic Output the amounts accounted for by certain figures such as our excess of exports over imports of goods and services and certain other figures that can be determined reasonably accurately – although not precisely – such as fixed investment, stock-building and public consumption.' Garret FitzGerald, 'National Accounts adjustment permits revisionist economics', *The Irish Times*, September 1993.

8   Explanatory note 55 in *National Income and Expenditure 1995*, Central Statistics Office, 1996.

9   In the report *National Income and Expenditure*, each item is defined in the explanatory notes found in Appendix 2.

10 Kuznets' contribution to macroeconomics was recognised by the profession in 1971 when he was awarded the Nobel prize in economics for his work on accounting and measurement techniques. Many economists regard Kuznets, in preference to Keynes, as the founding father of modern macroeconomics. His pioneering works include *National Income and Capital Formation 1919–1935*, NBER, 32, 1937 and 'National Income: A New Version', *Review of Economics And Statistics*, 30, August 1948. At the same time, work was been carried out in the UK on the construction of the national accounts by Richard Stone and James Meade. Today, their book entitled *National Income and Expenditure*, Oxford University Press, 1944 is regarded as a classic. In recognition of this and other related works, Stone received the 1984 Nobel prize in economics.

11 Consumer goods are usually divided into two groups: those which are consumed almost immediately and those which last much longer. The former is known as non-durables and examples include food, drink and transport. The latter is called durables and includes toasters, washing machines and other electrical appliances.

12 United Nations Development Programme, *Human Development Report 1995*, Oxford University Press, 1995.

13 In each of the first three components of Identity 8.1 (consumer, investment and government expenditure), expenditure on imported goods and services is included whereas the export of domestic output is not included. In order to estimate a value of gross domestic product (by the expenditure method), we need to add a value of exports and subtract a value of imports.

14 Many commentators believe that Irish GDP is artificially inflated because of 'transfer pricing'. Transfer pricing refers to a practice of foreign multinationals in countries with a low rate of taxation. Partially manufactured inputs, manufactured by a subsidiary in another country, are imported into Ireland. Some processing occurs in this country and the intermediate or final good is exported. The 'value added' by the manufacturing process which

takes place in Ireland is inflated to take advantage of the low Irish corporate tax rate. In doing so, the multinationals minimise their tax bill. The Irish measure of GDP is overvalued as a result of this practice. For more on this topic, read A. Murphy's *The Irish Economy: Celtic Tiger or Tortoise?*, Money Markets International, 1994 and Central Statistics Office's *Proceedings of Conference on Measuring Economic Growth*, November 1995.

15 For information on how the CSO estimate a 'provision for depreciation', read explanatory note 24 in Appendix 2 of *National Income and Expenditure*.

16 Economists and sociologists have attempted to develop satisfactory measures of economic and social well-being. A review of the international research is included in S. Scott, B. Nolan and T. Fahey, *Formulating Environmental and Social Indicators for Sustainable Development*, Economic and Social Research Institute, 1996. In the Irish context, recent work has been done on developing an index which measures Ireland's 'social progress over time'. The Social Progress Index (SPI), as it is called, is similar to other social progress indices (the Index of Social Health and the Genuine Progress Indicator) that were developed for the US economy. For a critique on GDP and an explanation of the SPI read C. Clarke and C. Kavanagh, 'Progress, Values and Economic Indicators', *Progress, Values and Public Policy*, Conference of Religious of Ireland, September 1996.

17 Direct income is defined as 'All market income of a recurring nature earned by members of a household, including wages, salaries, income from self-employment, investments, rental income, pensions from previous employments and the value in cash of any free good or service regularly obtained through employment'. R. Breen, D. Hannan, D. Rottman, C. Whelan, *Understanding Contemporary Ireland*, Gill & Macmillan, 1990.

18 Ibid.

19 *The Economist*, in an article published in November 1994, stated that the Gini coefficient for both the US and Britain had increased over the past two decades. In the US it rose from 0.35 in 1969 to 0.40 in 1992 while in Britain it increased from 0.23 in 1977 to 0.34 in 1991. An increase in the Gini coefficient reflects greater income inequality. 'For Richer, For Poorer', *The Economist*, 5 November 1994.

20 United Nations Development Programme, *Human Development Report 1995*.

21 James Tobin was a member of President Kennedy's Council of Economic Advisers and a winner of the Nobel prize in economics in 1981. William Nordhaus served as a member of President's Carter Council of Economic Advisers from 1977 to 1979.

22 For an excellent account of the Irish economy and its recent performance as measured by GDP and other indicators read 'What We Have Achieved', Ch. 1 in Forfás, *Shaping Our Future*, 1996. For a broader view of Ireland's progress to date, read C. Guiomard, *The Irish Disease, And How to Cure It*, Oak Tree Press, 1995. Broader still, J. J. Lee's, *Ireland 1912–1985: Politics and Society*, Cambridge University Press, 1989 is an excellent read.

23 To calculate net factor income from abroad, using 1995 as an example:

7. Remuneration of employees	Cr	230
	Db	–49
8. Investment income	Cr	2,950

Components of debit item

Direct investment income	–5,435
National debt interest	–1,015
Other	–1,496
62. Net factor income from abroad	–4,815

24 It is unusual for an entire country to qualify as an Objective 1 region. Greece, Ireland and Portugal qualified according to the 1988 regulations. However, parts of Spain, France, Italy and the UK also qualified. Structural funds awarded to those countries were directed to the Objective 1 regions.

25 NESC No. 94, *The Association between Economic Growth and Employment Growth in Ireland*, National Economic and Social Council, December 1992.

26 Ibid.

27 You may wonder why the unemployment rate did not fall by as much. We will discuss the difference between employment and unemployment in Chapter 15.

Chapter 9

1 J. B. Say, *A Treatise on Political Economy*, trans. C. R. Prinsep, A. M. Kelley, 1971. (Originally published in 1803.)

2 J. R. Hicks, 'Mr. Keynes and the "Classics"; A Suggested Interpretation', *Econometrica*, 5, April 1937.

3 Quoted by Benjamin Higgins, *What do Economists Know?*, Melbourne University Press, 1951.

4 Smith's contribution to economics is captured brilliantly in the words of Kenneth Boulding, 'It is always depressing to go back to Adam Smith, especially on economic development, as one realises how little we have learned in nearly two hundred years.' 'The Economics of Knowledge and the Knowledge of Economics', *American Economic Review*, May 1966.

5 His example of a pin-manufacturing company is famous and is still to be found in textbooks today, over two hundred years after the publication of *The Wealth of Nations*.

6 Although some of Smith's contemporaries had different views on many topics, history has labelled them as belonging to the one school of economic thought. One thing, however, which they all had in common was their mistrust of government. They saw little justification for government intervention except in the areas of justice, defence and other activities which commanded a large public interest.

7 It is generally believed that Keynes got his inspiration for the title of *The General Theory* from Einstein's general theory of relativity. The classical doctrine was a special case in economics that held under specific conditions with Keynes' analysis being described as the general case just as Sir Isaac Newton's (also a Professor at Cambridge University) classical Newtonian mechanics was a special case of Einstein's General Theory. This general/special case relationship and his criticism of the special case are evident from the opening words of *The General Theory*: 'I shall argue that the postulates of the classical theory are applicable to a special case only and not to the general case, the situation which it assumes being a limited point of the possible positions of equilibrium. Moreover, the characteristics of the special case assumed by the classical theory happen not to be those of the economic society in which we actually live, with the result that its teaching is misleading and disastrous if we attempt to apply it to the facts of experience.' *The General Theory of Employment, Interest and Money*, Macmillan, 1936.

8 Quoted in R. F. Harrod, *The Life of John Maynard Keynes*, Macmillan, 1951.

9 J. M. Keynes, *The General Theory of Employment, Interest and Money*.

10 Letter to George Bernard Shaw, 1 January 1935.

11 This may be explained by the fact that *The General Theory*, as was the case with the *Treatise*, was 'chiefly addressed to . . . fellow economists'. Yet it is not widely known that many of

the ideas which were to be found in *The General Theory* and which were accredited to Keynes were partly developed by other less well-known scholars. A number of examples are included here. The Russian economist Michel Tugan-Baranowsky, who died sixteen years before *The General Theory* was published, espoused the heterogeneous nature of savings and investment and, in addition, wrote about the possibility of a domino effect which might arise from an initial change in investment spending. Both Richard Kahn and the Polish economist Michael Kalechi developed this idea further. The eccentric Swedish economist Knut Wicksell argued that equilibrium could only be achieved by changes in the level of economic activity and not by changes in interest rates as followers of the classical doctrine argued. Dennis Robertson, a colleague of Keynes at Cambridge, explained the relationship between savings, investment and equilibrium, arguing that the latter was not necessarily an automatic process. These specific ideas of Robertson were published in a short book in 1926, ten years before the publication of *The General Theory*. However, it was Keynes, an economist who was known both inside and outside of academic circles, who provided the theoretical foundation for all of these previously diverse and unrelated ideas.

12 Others see it as a book which primarily revolutionises monetary theory. Keynes, for most of his academic and professional career, was concerned with money and monetary theory. To him money was more than just a simple medium for exchange. It could serve as an asset.

13 The 1944 UK White Paper on *Employment Policy* was also heavily influenced by the Beveridge Report of 1942. The welfare state as we know it today has its origins in the writings of Lord Beveridge.

14 A similar crash occurred on Monday, 19 October 1987 when the Dow Jones Industrial average on Wall Street fell 508 points and in the process wiped over 22% off share values. This collapse on Black Monday was almost double the drop on the worst day of the 1929 crash. In London £50 billion, or 10%, was wiped off the value of publicly-quoted companies. The major difference between the 1929 crash and the 1987 crash was not the extent of the collapse on any one day but the economic decline that followed. The first crash was followed by the Great Depression whereas a similar downturn in economic activity was avoided after the second crash of 1987. This was due to the deliberate actions taken by the authorities after October 1987.

15 'The Past', *Business Week*, 3 September 1979.

16 The actual responses from the US and the UK administrations varied. In Washington President Hoover requested extra funds from Congress for a federal programme to create jobs. Yet in the depths of the depression, he also increased taxes, justifying it by the need to balance the federal budget. In fact, Hoover was criticised by his opponent, Franklin Roosevelt, in the election of 1932 for not cutting government expenditure and for failing to balance the budget (Roosevelt himself was to oversee some 'Keynesian-style' policies in the second period of the New Deal). In London the Labour government announced a public works programme. Opposition parties were critical of the government's response and called for urgent action on the jobs front. In particular the Liberals, led by Lloyd George, proposed an increase in the amount of public works programmes. He was advised by a young radical economist by the name of John Maynard Keynes. The advice given was based on the model of income determination (see Section 10.1).

17 Say's Law can be explained in broad macro terms. It implies that the production of goods and services will generate enough income to ensure that these goods and services are sold (see endnote 1). The emphasis is on the supply or production side of the economy. For Keynes, it was the level of demand or spending which determined the level of output in the economy. In addition, Keynes argued that the main factor behind short-term fluctuations in national output was changes in the level of demand.

18 Keynes, *The General Theory of Employment, Interest and Money*.

19 Keynes, *The General Theory of Employment, Interest and Money*. Although it is generally agreed that these were the policy recommendations which Keynes supported, it would be difficult to arrive at these from one reading of *The General Theory*. For a book which literally revolutionised the use of fiscal policy it has surprisingly few explicit references to such policy recommendations. This absence of explicit policy implications, combined with the esoteric language and unfamiliar terminology used, made *The General Theory*, in the words of Mark Blaug an 'exceedingly difficult book', *John Maynard Keynes: Life, Ideas, Legacy*, Macmillan, 1990.

20 J. M. Keynes, *A Tract on Monetary Reform*, Macmillan, 1932.

Chapter 10

1 L. Tarshis, 'Keynesian Revolution' in *The New Palgrave: A Dictionary of Economics*, edited by J. Eatwell, M. Milgate, P. Newman, 3, Macmillan, 1987.

2 Keynes, *The General Theory of Employment, Interest and Money*.

3 Keynes, 'National Self-Sufficiency', *Studies*, 22, 1933.

4 Keynes, *The General Theory of Employment, Interest and Money*.

5 This diagram can be drawn by substituting values for disposable income (Y_d) and solving for consumption (C). Alternatively, the points can be plotted directly from Table 10.1.

6 Many studies of the Irish consumption function have been carried out. The earliest work was by Kennedy and Dowling in 1970. Since then important contributions have been made by Kelleher (1977), Honohan (1979 and 1982), McCarthy (1979), Bradley (1979), Boyle (1982), Moore (1987), Walsh (1988) and Whelan (1991). These studies attribute various degrees of importance to different determinants of consumption. They also differ on the size of the marginal propensity to consume. The explanatory variables tested included liquid assets, inflation, unemployment and the rate of income growth as well as current disposable income. The size of the MPC varied from Moore's 0.67 to Walsh's upper value of 0.855. However, we know from Chapter 8 that consumer expenditure in Ireland is estimated as a residual. Hence, the data used in some studies of the Irish consumption function may be unreliable.

7 Refer to endnote 18 of Chapter 9.

8 In Chapter 12 we assume investment is determined by the rate of interest. This assumption is essential in the derivation of the IS curve.

9 We draw your attention to two points. First, the terms 'aggregate demand' and 'total expenditure' are also used to describe the aggregate expenditure function. We use aggregate expenditure rather than aggregate demand in order to avoid confusion with the aggregate demand curve which is derived and explained in Chapter 13. Secondly, disposable income was the explanatory variable used in the text up to this point. From now on, we 'proxy' Y_d with Y, national income.

10 The term 'income' can be interchanged with both output and GDP. The term 'expenditure' can be interchanged with both demand and spending.

11 Notice that Y = AE is the equation for the 45° line. We are simply using simultaneous equations to find the 'Keynesian cross' which is the intersection of the aggregate expenditure line and the 45° line.

12 In order to keep our model simple we assume that taxes are zero (T = 0). A more complex analysis would incorporate taxes as autonomous (T = $\overline{T}$) or as a function of income (T = tY).

13 Keynes, *The General Theory of Employment, Interest and Money*.
14 For more information read R. F. Kahn, 'Home Investment and Unemployment', *Economic Journal*, June 1931.
15 The equation

$$£1,000 + £750 + £562.50 + £421.875 + £316.40625 + \ldots$$

can be written as

$$£1,000 + (£1,000 \times .75) + (£1,000 \times <.75^2>) + (£1,000 \times <.75^3>) + (£1,000 \times <.75^4>) + \ldots$$
$$= £1,000 (1 + <.75> + <.75^2> + <.75^3> + <.75^4> + \ldots)$$

See endnote 16.
16 Infinite geometric progressions can be summed if the absolute value of the multiplying coefficient is less than 1. In this case the sum of the infinite series $1 + r + r^2 + r^3 + r^4 \ldots$ is equal to $\frac{1}{1-r}$. From our description of the MPC we know it to be less than 1. Our series can be summed and in this particular case it adds to 4. Appendix 10.3 contains the formal derivation of the Keynesian multiplier.
17 The new equilibrium level of income can be calculated by using the formula as derived in the text. In this case:

$$\overline{A} = \overline{C} + \overline{I} + \overline{G} = 50 + 100 + 90 = £240$$
$$b = .75$$

Thus,

$$Y = \overline{A} \times \frac{1}{1-b} = 240 \times \frac{1}{1-.75} = 240 \times 4 = £960.$$

18 This contrasts sharply with those economists who argue that inappropriate monetary policy by the Fed was the significant factor in explaining the Great Depression of the 1930s. A good account of this view is given by Milton and Rose Friedman in *Free to Choose*, Penguin, 1980.
19 If consumer expenditure is determined by gross income and by taxation, the multiplier is equal to $\frac{1}{\text{MPS} + \text{MPM} + \text{MPT}}$.
20 These values are taken from Norton's *Economics for an Open Economy: Ireland*. Walsh & Leddin's estimates are slightly different. For more, read B. Walsh and A. Leddin, *The Macroeconomy of Ireland*, 3rd edition, Gill & Macmillan, 1995; and D. Norton, *Economics for an Open Economy: Ireland*, Oak Tree Press and Graduate School of Business UCD, 1994.
21 The relatively small size of the Keynesian multiplier for small open economies was noted as far back as 1956 by T. K. Whitaker when he wrote 'In the real world, however, there are few, if any, completely isolated economies and the effects of the creation of new incomes are, therefore, not wholly retained within the system', 'Capital Formation, Saving and Economic Progress', reprinted in *Interests*, Institute of Public Administration, 1983. O. Katsiaouni came to the same conclusion in his paper 'Planning in a Small Economy: The Republic of Ireland' read to the Statistical and Social Inquiry Society of Ireland in May 1978. He explicitly referred to the Irish situation when he wrote 'demand management, thus is rendered ineffectual . . .' Des Norton emphasises the point in his open economy textbook *Economics for an Open Economy: Ireland*. He writes 'The tax leakage aside, Ireland's high marginal propensity to import explains why national income multipliers for the small open economy of Ireland are quite low.' Finally, on account of a high MPM, a domestic fiscal boost may only succeed in aggravating the trade balance between Ireland and the rest of the world (see Chapter 14).

22 The word 'fiscal' comes from the Latin word 'fiscus' which means a money purse or a state's treasury/exchequer.

23 Budgets are to be distinguished from plans or programmes. In Ireland the relationship between the annual budget and government plans has been, at times, rather loose and ambiguous. Another component of fiscal policy is the Book of Estimates. The expenditure estimates are published in advance of the Budget. It shows predicted current government spending for the fiscal year. With so much information available prior to the publication of the Budget, Budget day itself has declined in importance. In recognition of this, the Treasury of the UK present the Estimates and the budget to Parliament on the same day.

24 The first capital budget was introduced by Patrick McGilligan, the Finance Minister, in 1950. Some economic commentators view this as the first evidence of Keynes' influence on the Irish budgetary process. In terms of personalities, Patrick Lynch (Professor of Political Economy at UCD) was one of the first Irish academics to espouse Keynesian economics. On a political level, it was Sean Lemass (former Taoiseach) who enthusiastically embraced the economics of Keynes (see endnote 35). T. K. Whitaker, the person primarily responsible for the First Programme for Economic Expansion, devoted a section to the Keynesian multiplier in his seminal paper 'Capital Formation, Saving and Economic Progress' of 1956. Interestingly, two of the people who were involved in a debate on 'full-employment' back in April 1945 at the Statistical and Social Inquiry Society of Ireland were Patrick Lynch and T. K. Whitaker. It is also far from coincidental that the public speech given by the then Taoiseach, John A. Costello in 1949 on the need for a sufficient level of demand in the economy was drafted by Patrick Lynch, his adviser.

25 We use budget deficits, rather than budget surpluses, in the definition of the EBR because we are more familiar with them.

26 The responsibility for managing the National Debt has changed hands from the Department of Finance to the National Treasury Management Agency (NTMA) or otherwise known as 'Auntie Mae'. Through the use of prudent risk management, it made savings of over £500m during the period 1993–96.

27 The 'business cycle' is the term used to explain fluctuations in the level of national income. Terms such as troughs, peaks, booms, slumps, recession, depression and recovery relate specifically to different phases of the business cycle. The business cycle is a well-established economic phenomenon, observed since the industrial revolution. However, there is little consensus among economists and academics on the causes of such fluctuations. The one economic factor, however, which is constantly referred to in the literature on business cycles is investment expenditure and its inherent volatility. This suggests a role for government policy, which is aimed at stabilising the economy close to its potential output level. This is referred to as stabilisation policy. This is simply a collective term to describe various short-term demand-side policies such as fiscal, monetary, incomes and exchange rate policy which attempt to smooth out fluctuations in output and keep the actual level of output close to its potential level, i.e. the output level that results in the full employment of resources.

28 Another controversy regarding counter-cyclical policy is whether it had the support of J. M. Keynes. Most textbooks today accredit Keynes with counter-cyclical policy. Yet there is little or no mention of such a policy in *The General Theory*. The problem is compounded by the obscure language used in the book. It is one of the many issues which remain unresolved sixty years after the publication of *The General Theory*.

29 See Chapter 11 for a discussion on the money market and how interest rates are determined.

30 This does not suggest that Keynes, a former member of the Apostles and the Bloomsbury group which advocated personal freedom and liberty, approved of Hitler's authoritarian methods. Solving unemployment at the expense of freedom was not to be tolerated, according to Keynes.

31 Tobin, Okun and Heller were all, at one stage or another, members of the Council of Economic Advisers. Samuelson was an adviser to President Kennedy.

32 The Phillips curve depicts the relationship between the unemployment rate and the inflation rate. Supporters of Keynesian economics who were disenchanted with the simple fixed-price Keynesian model used this concept to develop a more sophisticated theory of inflation and explain how price changes were related to the changes in demand, output and unemployment. The Phillips curve is explained in Appendix 15.1.

33 Whereas the Labour party in Ireland has been constrained in its use of fiscal policy by the Maastricht criteria, President Clinton has disappointed some of his supporters by adopting more 'conservative-style' policies. This may change during his second term of office.

34 A good example of this was the advice given by Keynes at the first Finlay lecture in UCD in 1933. In his address 'National Self-Sufficiency' he congratulated the De Valera government in its commitment to maintaining protectionism in order to support indigenous industry. Over sixty years later, the same advice would be rejected by the vast majority of the economics profession, even if given by Keynes. This article can be found in *Studies*, 22, 1933.

35 This is not to suggest that Keynesian ideas lacked support in Ireland before the 1970s (refer back to endnote 24). In fact, Keynes had many followers in Ireland, including Sean Lemass, Taoiseach from 1959 to 1966. Lemass had a keen interest in economics. Before he ever entered politics he had read many books on Keynes and his policies. However, Lemass was more interested in adopting Keynesian policies to enhance the long-term development of the country. It wasn't until the early 1970s that short-term Keynesian policies were adopted in Ireland. To find out more about Lemass and his interest in economics in general and Keynes in particular read M. O'Sullivan, *Sean Lemass: A Biography*, Blackwater Press, 1995.

36 *Budget 1972*, Government Publications Office, 1972.

37 *Budget 1976*, Government Publications Office, 1976.

38 One prosperous country which did request financial aid from the IMF was the UK. The reason for such intervention was the sterling crisis of 1967. The crisis culminated in the devaluation of sterling by 14% on 18 November. This followed massive speculation on the foreign exchange markets. On the day before the British pound was finally devalued it is estimated the Bank of England purchased over $1 billion of sterling to support the currency. This was an enormous loss in exchange rate terms even compared to the amount lost in the more recent currency crisis of 1992–93.

39 The Tallaght Strategy, of supporting the government's austere fiscal measures, receives its name because it began with a speech given by the then leader of the main opposition party, Mr Alan Dukes, in Tallaght, Dublin.

40 The phrase 'Expansionary Fiscal Contraction' originated from work done by F. Giavazzi and M. Pagano at the University of Bologna in 1990.

41 D. McAleese, 'Ireland's Economic Recovery', *Irish Banking Review*, Summer 1990.

42 The consumption function in the form $C = bY_d$ is a functional relationship whereas $S \equiv Y_d - C$ is simply a definition, i.e. savings is defined as the difference between disposable income and consumption.

Chapter 11

1 George Bernard Shaw, *John Bull's Other Island: and Major Barbara, Also How He Lied to Her Husband*, Constable, 1911.

2 J. R. Hicks, *Critical Essays in Monetary Theory*, Clarendon Press, 1967.

3 The complete definitions for M1 and M3 are included in any Central Bank bulletin. There is also a M3E which is M3 plus deposits at building societies, state-sponsored financial institutions and the Post Office. On a lighter note, in attempting to highlight people's awareness of these monetary aggregates, a certain US Senator William Proxmire once said 'Most people think that M_1 is a gun used in World War II.'

4 This assumption is rather restrictive. In reality, a portion of the loan may not find its way back into the banking system but instead end up in the form of cash. This implies that the subsequent increase in the money supply will not be as large as originally suggested. This curtailment in the money creation process may also happen if the bank decides to keep reserves over and above the minimum amount that is required by law. See Appendix 11.1 on the money multiplier.

5 All credit institutions in Ireland are required to maintain a reserve ratio, called the 'liquidity' ratio. The primary liquidity ratio is the ratio of required holdings of primary liquid assets to relevant resources. Its purpose when introduced in 1972 was to avoid a 'run' on the banking system and also to control the amount of lending. Although they are an essential part of monetary policy today, they should also be seen as prudential protection for depositors. As of July 1996 the liquidity ratio is 3%. The terms 'primary liquid assets' and 'relevant resources' are explained in any Central Bank bulletin.

   Credit institutions are continually faced with the conflict between profitability and liquidity where liquidity is the ease with which an asset can be converted into cash without financial loss. In order for financial institutions to make a profit, they must engage in the act of lending. On the other hand, credit institutions must always be ready to meet the daily demands of their clients, both personal and corporate. Maintenance of a reserve ratio helps to resolve this conflict and in doing so, contributes to a relatively secure banking system.

6 Its derivation is similar to the derivation of the expenditure multiplier. The sum of the created deposits forms a geometric series. It can be proven that this sum is equal to the reciprocal of the reserve ratio. This is called the deposit multiplier. With 10% kept in reserves, reserves increase by £1,000. Hence, bank deposits increase by £10,000. In practice, the multiplier will be much smaller than the above example suggests. This is because the public is likely to hold some of their borrowings in the form of cash. Also, some banks may decide to hold a greater amount of their deposits on reserve than is generally required. These 'leakages' will result in a lower multiplier.

7 This analysis applies to the fractional reserve banking system, i.e. the system where the institutions (banks) only keep a fraction of their deposits as reserves. This system dates back to the Middle Ages when people deposited gold with goldsmiths. Over time, goldsmiths noticed that it was unlikely that all depositors would withdraw their gold all at once. On recognising this, they kept some gold in reserve to meet the immediate demands of their depositors. The remainder was lent out to new clients. This is the way in which the early banking system developed.

8 Firms can also finance capital goods from retained earnings. However, their decision will still be determined by the interest rate. We can think of the interest rate as the opportunity cost. The opportunity cost of purchasing capital goods is the best opportunity forgone. If the interest rate is high, the firm could earn the market rate of interest. If the firm earns more by lending than investing, we must assume that at higher rates of interest, their demand for capital goods is low.

9 The relationship between interest rates and savings is quite complex. See endnote 13 in Chapter 6.

10 More recent money demand models have been independently developed by William Baumol and James Tobin. For more information read William J. Baumol 'The Transactions Demand for Cash: An Inventory Theoretic Approach', *Quarterly Journal of Economics*, November 1952 and James Tobin 'The Interest-Elasticity of the Transaction Demand for Cash', *Review of Economics and Statistics*, August 1956.

11 A bond or a fixed-interest security is a government IOU. It is an instrument in which one party (the debtor/borrower) promises to repay the other party (lender/investor) the amount borrowed plus interest. They can be bought or sold on the equity (capital) market. Bonds are known as gilts in the UK and Ireland.

12 Keynes, *The General Theory of Employment, Interest and Money*.

13 The negative relationship that exists between the price of a bond and the interest rate can be explained by defining the price of a bond as the present value of a set of future cash flows. The lower the interest rate that is earned on any sum invested today, the greater is the amount that needs to be invested (today) in order to realise a specified value (in the future). Hence, for a given future value at some specified time in the future, the lower the interest rate, the higher the present value. By now applying the definition as above, we observe the negative relationship that exists between interest rates and the price of a bond. For more material on this see F. Mishkin, *The Economics of Money, Banking and Financial Markets*, HarperCollins Publishers, 3rd edition, 1992.

14 For more on Irish yield curves see B. Walsh and A. Leddin, *The Macroeconomy of Ireland*, 2nd edition, Gill & Macmillan, 1992.

15 The Swedish Central Bank is the oldest, dating back to 1668. The Bank of England was established shortly afterwards in 1694. In contrast, the US Federal Reserve System ('Fed' for short) was set up in 1913. The Central Bank of Ireland was established as recently as 1943.

16 The Irish pound has a chequered history. We begin in 1689 when an exchange rate of 13:12 was set for the Irish pound/British pound. In 1826 the two currencies were amalgamated. Over a century later, the Banking Commission of 1927 established the Saorstat pound, which was set at parity with sterling. Parity was maintained until 1979 when the Irish pound became a member, unlike the British pound, of the Exchange Rate Mechanism (ERM) in the European Monetary System. With this the 153-year, one-for-one, fixed link with sterling ended. Approaching the turn of the century, the prospect is for currencies of the ERM, including the Irish pound, to be replaced by a single European currency, called the Euro. That will put an end to the Irish pound as we know it today.

17 For more on the evolution of the Central Bank of Ireland read Padraig McGowan, *Money and Banking in Ireland*, Institute of Public Administration, 1990; and Joseph Doherty, 'The Evolution of Central Banking in Ireland', *Central Bank Annual Report 1992*, Summer 1993.

18 The more important functions of the Central Bank are neatly captured in the words of Padraig McGowan, 'The national monetary authority [is] responsible for the formulation and implementation of monetary policy, management of the exchange rate and official external reserves, provision of notes and coins, and supervision of banks, building societies, other financial institutions and the financial and capital markets.' See reference in endnote 17.

19 In recent times concern has been registered over the lack of transparency and account-ability in Irish central banking. A change in Governor coupled with some media criticisms

has led to some recent changes. The Central Bank Governor is now obliged to attend a Dail Committee, at which he is required to answer questions on the activities of the Central Bank and, more interestingly, on monetary and exchange rate policy.

20 We know from the discussion on money creation that the amount of money which the banking system can create is a multiple of the amount of reserves that they hold. Hence, if the monetary authorities can control the amount of reserves which the banks hold, they can then regulate the amount of money which they can create. For example, by simply creating more reserves, it provides the banks with the opportunity to make more loans and consequently more deposits. As a result, money supply increases. The three tools of monetary policy which are described in the chapter are, in effect, ways of controlling the supply of reserves rather than the supply of money, *per se*.

21 It is obvious from this discussion that the degree of sensitivity between interest rates and investment expenditure is an important factor in determining the effectiveness of monetary policy. This particular elasticity measure is important in explaining the difference between the Keynesian and the monetarist view of monetary policy. This and other sensitivity measures are discussed in Chapter 12.

22 The Keynesian cross diagram which we used in the previous chapter was based on the assumption that investment is exogenous. In this analysis investment is dependent on the rate of interest. Panel (b) depicts this relationship between interest rates and investment. Consequently, there is an adjustment to the AE function. There is more material on this in the next chapter.

23 Monetarism and supply-side economics are discussed in greater detail in Chapter 13. The quantity theory of money which is central to both monetarism and the theory of inflation is discussed in Chapter 15.

24 See Milton Friedman, 'The Role of Monetary Policy,' *American Economic Review*, 58, March 1968.

25 D. Romer, 'Comment on Bosworth', *The Brookings Papers on Economic Activity*, no. 1, 1989.

26 The terms 'fixed', 'semi-fixed exchange rate system' and 'free mobility of capital' are explained in Chapter 14.

27 Some of the material used to describe the ineffectiveness of monetary policy for a SOE is unfamiliar. A more detailed explanation of this and other material is contained in Chapter 14.

28 The inability to control the domestic money supply was recognised by the monetary authorities in the late 1970s. In a 1979 Central Bank bulletin there was the following admission: 'In an open economy such as Ireland's, it is generally accepted that the supply of money responds to the demand for it, so that monetary authorities cannot exercise a significant degree of control on the increase in money holdings;' C. H. Murray, 'Monetary Policy', *Central Bank Report*, Winter 1979. The same recognition was reached in relation to interest rate determination. Dr T. K. Whitaker, as Governor of the Central Bank, wrote in 1975 'In our circumstances of fixed parity of exchange rates and free movement of funds between Ireland and the UK, autonomous interest rate changes have virtually to be ruled out as specific national instruments of monetary policy.' T. K. Whitaker, 'Monetary Policy', *Central Bank Report*, Winter 1975.

29 Monetary authorities increase interest rates for a number of different reasons. In this particular case, high interest rates benefit the domestic currency. All other things equal, an increase in domestic interest rates will increase the value of the domestic currency against other currencies. High interest rates are also anti-inflationary. By increasing interest rates, the Central Bank increases the cost of borrowing. Higher borrowing costs lower consumer and investment spending. All other things equal, as demand falls (or the growth

in demand falls), the rate of inflation falls. Also, high interest rates benefit savers who receive a greater return on their investment. Unfortunately, high interest rates can also lead to lower economic growth, higher mortgage rates and higher debt-service repayments.

30 For a good and concise description of Irish monetary policy, read Maurice Doyle 'Interest Rates – Preserving a Balance', *Central Bank Report*, Spring 1990. For a more detailed examination of monetary policy and its operation read Padraig McGowan, 'The Operation of Monetary Policy in Ireland', Presidential Address to the Statistical and Social Inquiry Society of Ireland, 29 October 1992. For a more recent commentary on monetary policy (post-currency crisis and changes in the ERM) read Maurice Doyle, 'Monetary Policy After the Narrow Band', *Central Bank Report*, Spring 1994.

31 Credit policy was also used by the Central Bank of Ireland, in the years between 1965 and 1984. It involved the imposition of credit guidelines in order to influence the level of bank lending. It was not very successful for a number of reasons. For one, the penalties imposed on the commercial banks for breaking the credit guidelines were, in many cases, not severe enough. Also, the theoretical foundations underlying the credit guidelines were inappropriate. In 1984, the Central Bank suspended its use of formal credit guidelines.

32 One party to the contract agrees to the spot purchase (sale) of one currency for another. This is one part of the swap. The other part of the swap is the forward sale (purchase).

33 Kevin Barry, a senior economist with the Central Bank, put it succinctly when he wrote '. . . the Bank's role is essentially that of smoothing short-term fluctuations or distortions – it does not seek to resist the market's view in the determination of interest rates'. K. Barry, 'The Central Bank's Management of the Aggregate Liquidity of Licensed Banks', *Central Bank Annual Report 1982*, Spring 1983. For more detail on liquidity management read P. Bourke and R. P. Kinsella, *The Financial Services Revolution. An Irish Perspective*, Gill & Macmillan, 1988.

34 The Central Bank issues a monetary policy statement in the spring of every year. This usually entails a brief statement on the objective of monetary policy, the out-turn for the previous year and the outlook for the coming year. Predictions for money supply and credit growth are also normally included.

35 Paul Tansey, 'Money Matters', *Magill*, August 1989.

36 Maurice Doyle, 'Monetary Policy – The Hidden Stabiliser', *Central Bank Annual Report 1988*, Spring 1989.

37 The objective of monetary policy in Ireland is price stability. There is no commitment to other goals. In other countries, the US for example, central banks are committed to achieving a number of objectives, including low inflation, low unemployment and high growth rates.

38 This does not apply to currencies which are not members of fixed exchange rate systems, but instead float freely on the foreign exchange market. A good example of this is the US dollar. Changes in the value of the dollar against other currencies do not necessarily result in a change in US interest rates.

39 'Monetary Policy Statement 1992', *Central Bank Report*, Spring 1992.

40 Since the widening of the fluctuation bands in the ERM the Irish monetary authorities have gained a greater degree of control over Irish interest rates. For example, by allowing greater movements in the Irish pound within the 15% fluctuation bands (and particularly against the DM), the Irish monetary authorities have been able to avoid unnecessary increases in domestic interest rates arising from a weakness in sterling. More recently, the rise in sterling since Autumn 1996 has been partly offset by a strengthening of the Irish pound against other currencies of the ERM. The ERM and its fluctuation bands will be explained in Chapter 14.

41 Maurice Doyle, 'Monetary Policy – The Hidden Stabiliser', *Central Bank Annual Report 1988*, Spring 1989.

42 The 'associated banks' are the commercial banks of Allied Irish Bank, Bank of Ireland, Ulster Bank and National Irish Bank. They derive their name from the special status which was granted to them by the Central Bank Act of 1942. The non-associated banks comprise of other commercial banks, industrial banks, merchant banks and others.

Chapter 12

1 Christopher Bliss, 'John R. Hicks' in *The New Palgrave: A Dictionary of Economics*.

2 J. R. Hicks in 'IS-LM: An Explanation', *Modern Macroeconomic Theory*, edited by J-P. Fitoussi, Basil Blackwell, 1983.

3 Jordi Gali, 'How Well Does the IS-LM Model Fit Postwar U.S. Data?', *Quarterly Journal of Economics*, 67, May 1992.

4 Hicks has received most of the credit for the development of the IS/LM framework and, as a result, for spreading the Keynesian doctrine among his contemporaries and to the general public. Although Alvin Hansen did not receive the same acknowledgments his contribution was of no lesser importance. His book succeeded in spreading Keynes' ideas to countless academic institutions and universities throughout the US. A. Hansen, *A Guide to Keynes*, McGraw-Hill, 1953.

5 Prices are incorporated into the macro model in Chapter 13, and again in Chapter 15.

6 We know from Chapter 10 that equilibrium in the goods market (without the government sector) can be expressed in terms of investment and savings. It is this view of equilibrium (investment, I = savings, S) which gives us the name the IS curve. This simple injections-leakages approach is useful in explaining the negative relationship that exists between interest rates and income levels in the goods market. The lower interest rate level induces lower savings and higher investment. This increase in investment causes a multiplier effect which will result in higher income levels. Hence, with an initial reduction in interest rates, equilibrium is maintained in the goods market (I = S) through a subsequent increase in national income.

7 Keynes called this the marginal efficiency of capital. According to Keynes, the expected rate of return on each project had to be compared with the opportunity cost of capital investment. A project which was expected to yield a return more than the opportunity cost would be undertaken by the entrepreneur. Projects not meeting this criterion would be deferred.

8 With interest rates as an explanatory variable, the resulting AE function is different from that presented in Chapter 10. In Chapter 10, the AE function was of the form $AE = \overline{A} + bY$. In this chapter the AE function is of the form $AE = \overline{A} - di + bY$ (see Figure 12.2). The algebraic derivation of this function is contained in Appendix 12.1.

9 This textbook is limited in terms of the coverage of the IS and LM curves. In particular, the position and the slope of the respective curves are only briefly discussed. Extensive detail on these and other aspects of the IS/LM model are left to intermediate macro-economic textbooks.

10 We distinguished between real income and nominal income in Chapter 3 (endnote 11). Nominal income is not adjusted for changes in the price level whereas real income has been corrected to account for changes in the price level. In the analysis of the money market, we are concerned with the supply of real balances. Hence, our discussion is limited to the real money stock and the real money supply curve.

11 Since L refers to liquidity and M refers to the money supply, L = M along the LM curve. The demand for real balances (liquidity) equals the supply of money at every point along the curve.

12 Since prices are fixed, a change in $\overline{\frac{M}{P}}$ can arise only from a change in the nominal money stock.

13 This can be explained by reference to the upper panel (the Keynesian cross diagram) of Figure 12.2. Point A would coincide with a point corresponding to income level Y^0 and interest rate level i^1. This point lies on a higher aggregate expenditure curve than AE^0. This means that the demand for goods exceeds the level of output, i.e. there is an excess demand for goods.

14 This can be explained by reference to the right-hand panel (the money market diagram) of Figure 12.3. Point A would coincide with a point corresponding to interest rate, i^1 and an income level, Y^0. This point lies on a lower money demand curve than $L(Y^1)$. With the demand for money less than the supply of money, an excess supply of money will result.

15 An important aspect of expansionary fiscal policy is the method of financing. Two methods exist. First, the government can finance the additional spending through an expansion of the money supply. This method is called monetary financing. Second, additional spending can be financed by issuing government bonds or gilts to the non-bank public. This method is commonly known as bond financing. The effectiveness of expansionary fiscal policy may depend on whether the additional spending is monetary or bond financed. For example, additional spending financed from monetary sources tends to be accompanied by increases in the money supply. With no subsequent rise in interest rates, the risk of crowding out is reduced. Alternatively, additional spending financed by the sale of bonds to the non-bank public may increase the demand for funds in the money market and, subsequently, push interest rates higher. Under a fixed exchange rate, however, the rise in interest rates may lead to capital inflows rather than any 'crowding out' of private investment (see Chapter 14). Again, crowding out fails to occur.

   On a related issue, there is disagreement within the economics profession on the degree of crowding out that results from an expansionary phase of fiscal policy. One view was espoused by David Ricardo and it is known as the Ricardian Equivalence. It states that government deficits have no effect on real interest rates and, thus, crowding out does not occur. This assertion is based on the argument that the public's expectations of future tax increases will result in a rise in savings. This increase in savings offsets any upward pressure on interest rates that may arise from higher government borrowing.

16 The presentation of expansionary fiscal policy in this format is helpful. For example, the effectiveness of fiscal policy depends largely on the strength of each link in the chain and, in particular, between [increases Y → increases L] and [increases i → reduces I]. As an exercise the student should change the slope of the LM curve to see the impact on interest rates and national income.

17 This may appear confusing, particularly the last link where an increase in interest rates occurs as it does not appear to be consistent with the diagram. This 'problem' arises where more than one change in a variable occurs. It was said in the main part of the text that the 'initial easing of interest rates may be partly offset by this subsequent increase'. Figure 12.6 illustrates the equilibrium interest rate at the end of the adjustment process. What it fails to show is that the initial decrease in interest rates has outweighed the subsequent increase in interest rates.

18 In Chapter 13 we will see that fiscal expansion can lead to higher inflation. This possibility is not considered here because the IS/LM is a fixed-price model.

Chapter 13

1 Ralph Harris, 'Everyman's Guide to Contemporary Economic Jargon', *Growth*, *Advertising and the Consumer*, Institute of Economic Affairs, 1964.

2 Alan S. Blinder, *Hard Heads, Soft Hearts. Tough-Minded Economics for a Just Society*, Addison-Wesley, 1987.

3 Mark Brownrigg, *Understanding the Economy*, Addison-Wesley, 1990. A good description of supply-side economics is given in Chapter 10 of this textbook.

4 This assumption may be apt for the short run but it is unrealistic for describing long-run economic prosperity. The conventional belief is that long-run economic well-being is determined by supply-side factors such as the quality of resources and the level of technology.

5 The real balance effect owes its prominence in the economic literature to A. C. Pigou and Donald Patinkin who independently worked on the existence of such an effect.

6 We know from Chapter 12 that the goods market is in equilibrium at each point along the IS curve. Similarly, the money market is in equilibrium at each point along the LM curve. In Appendix 13.1, we derive the AD curve from the IS/LM model. We will see that at every point along the AD curve, both the goods market and the money market are in equilibrium.

7 The various AS curves can be derived graphically by examining the labour market and the production function. This form of derivation is particularly useful when explaining the difference between the classical and the Keynesian AS curves. It is, however, quite complex and we will leave the graphical derivation to intermediate macroeconomic textbooks. For more on this, see B. Walsh and A. Leddin, *The Macroeconomy of Ireland*, 3rd edition.

8 At the full-employment output level, unemployment is at its natural rate, i.e. some unemployment such as frictional unemployment exists. For more on this refer to the text in Chapter 15 and endnote 21 of Chapter 15.

9 We generally discuss the negative aspects of government policy when we discuss the 'supply side'. For example, according to economists who focus on the supply side, demand-management policy is ineffective and inflationary. However, there are some government policies which are advocated by these economists. 'Positive' supply-side policies promote the research and adoption of new technologies and programmes to provide relevant training opportunities for labour. These measures actually push the AS curve out and to the right, increasing the potential output of the economy.

10 Privatisation refers to the transfer of public sector companies to the private sector. Deregulation involves the removal of restrictions on competition. It is commonly argued, although fiercely disputed, that both processes lead to greater efficiency, greater competition and more accountability.

11 Many commentators regard the disinflationary aspect of tax cuts as the central plank of supply-side economics. Whereas Keynesians emphasised the demand-side effects of a tax cut, supply siders focused in on the supply-side effect. They argue that lower taxes increase incentives and, in turn, stimulate work, savings, risk-taking and investment. For Keynesians, a tax cut shifts the aggregate demand curve to the right, while for supply siders, a tax cut shifts the aggregate supply curve to the right. Although this seems to be a relatively minor point, the implications are not. For the Keynesians, government action is leading to an increase in output. For the supply siders, the reduction of government involvement is improving the incentive system which promotes expansion in the private sector. The key to long-term growth for supply siders is to unleash the productive capacity of the private sector.

12 The buzz-word 'supply-side economics' means different things to different people. For some, it is an antithesis to Keynesian economics. To others, it is closer to Keynesian economics than it is to 'monetarism'. While for some, it dates back to pre-Keynesian times and is simply a modern-day version of the old classical school of economics. For example, consider the interventionist aspect of supply-side economics. Many view supply siders as supporters of the market system and critics of interventionist style policies. Others, in contrast, view supply siders as interventionists; critics of demand-management intervention but supporters of supply-side intervention. A rigorous definition is given by Niskanen. He states that supply-side economics is 'the application of microeconomic theory to the effects of fiscal policy on the incentives to work, save and invest and on the allocation of resources in the economy'. For a detailed insider's account of Reaganomics, read W. Niskanen, *Reaganomics: an insider's account of the policies and the people*, Oxford University Press, 1988. Niskanen (a self-confessed Reaganaut or Reaganite) served on Reagan's Council of Economic Advisers from April 1981 to March 1985. Contrary to Reagan's beliefs, Niskanen wrote that 'there was no "supply-side revolution" in economic theory'.

13 The term 'Reaganomics' apparently originated from the title that a copy-editor put on an article which was written by Paul Craig Roberts and submitted to the *New York Times* for publication in November 1980 (see endnote 16).

14 It is reported that Laffer drew the now famous Laffer curve on one of the restaurant's cocktail napkins. Years later, when asked about the accuracy of the story, both Laffer and Cheney denied it. Many people put the story down to the journalistic style of Wanniski.

15 The theoretical core of supply-side economics can be reduced to four basic assertions, according to F. Juster. They are as follows:

   (i)   Entitlement programmes erode work incentives.
  (ii)   The tax system can be biased against effort, savings and investment.
 (iii)   Regulations designed to protect consumer and employee groups can impede economic progress.
 (iv)   Expectations arising out of expansionary fiscal and monetary policies cause inflation; modifying expectations can reduce inflation.

For more detail, read F. Thomas Juster, 'The Economics and Politics of the Supply-Side View', reprinted in *Introduction to Macroeconomics*, edited by Peter D. McClelland, McGraw-Hill, 1986.

16 To describe Reaganomics and the associated tax cuts as a 'second revolution' is somewhat of an exaggeration. In the words of Paul Craig Roberts (a supply sider and member of Reagan's Council of Economic Advisers) 'Reaganomics was a compromise from the beginning, a conglomerate if you will, of three points of view: supply-side economics, monetarism, and traditional Republican budget balancing.' For another insider's view of the Reagan administration read Paul Craig Roberts, *The Supply-Side Revolution: an insider's account of policymaking in Washington*, Harvard University Press, 1984. It is a very interesting account of the enormous difficulties that the supply siders faced both from the traditional Keynesians outside the administration and those inside the administration who were less than enthusiastic about the change in policy. The persistent conflict between politics and policy is also examined.

17 Laffer and his colleagues belonged to the extreme wing of the supply siders. The mainstream group was represented in later administrations: Martin Feldstein, president of the National Bureau of Economic Research and chairman of the Council of Economic Advisers from 1982 to 1984 and Michael Boskin, chairman of President Bush's Council of Economic Advisers from 1989 to 1993. Their claims were less sensational than those

who belonged to the more extreme wing. The differences between the two groups are outlined in M. Feldstein,'Supply Side Economics: Old Truths and New Claims', *American Economic Review*, 76, May 1986.

18 Other derogatory descriptions include 'a riverboat gamble' (Senator Howard Baker, former White House chief of staff) and 'trickle-down economics' (Paul Simon, the Democrat from Illinois).

19 When judging Mrs Thatcher's time in office, most commentators focus on her mistrust of active fiscal policy and fixed exchange rate systems (as exemplified by the ERM) and her adherence to 'monetarism'. The use of supply-side policies was just as important in her attempt 'to roll back the frontiers of the state'.

20 M. Feldstein, 'Supply Side Economics: Old Truths and New Claims'.

21 Over time, the increase in unemployment arising out of the fall in output will dampen wage demands. As wages fall, the economy returns to output level, Y^0. Changes in wages and other inputs costs are central to any long-run analysis of macroeconomic policies and disturbances. This is considered in the next section.

22 At full employment, the economy is at a point on its production possibility frontier (refer back to An Introduction to Economics). Supply-side policies attempt to push out the boundaries of the nation's production possibility frontier. In other words, a rightward shift of the long-run AS curve is equivalent to an outward shift of the production possibility frontier.

23 Notwithstanding the usefulness of the AD/AS macroeconomic model, it has a number of shortcomings. A brief account of some deficiencies are to be found in R. Barro and V. Grilli, *European Macroeconomics*, Macmillan, 1994. Given the open nature of the Irish economy, its failure to incorporate open macroeconomics is a particular drawback. The AD/AS model in the context of an open economy (and building on the new macro-economics of rational expectations, intertemporal choice and microeconomic under-pinnings) is examined in M. Burda and C. Wyplosz, *Macroeconomics: A European Text*, Oxford University Press, 1993. From an Irish perspective read D. Norton, *Economics for an Open Economy: Ireland*.

24 A. Protopapadakis, 'Supply-Side Economics: What Chance For Success?' in *The Supply-Side Solution* edited by B. Bartlett and T. P. Roth, Macmillan, 1983.

25 Given the open nature of the economy, Ireland's ability to use monetary policy was limited. This was further diminished by the relaxation of exchange controls and by the fixed exchange rate system within which the Irish pound operated.

26 At the time of writing this book, there had been only limited success in reducing public expenditure increases.

27 The Business Expansion Scheme was set up in 1984 in order to attract investment capital for small Irish firms. Investors can invest up to £25,000 per annum into a BES fund. This amount can then be written off against taxable income. Since its inception, a number of BES funds have been established.

28 In response to the lacklustre performance of Irish industry during the 1980s, the then Minister of Industry and Commerce, Des O'Malley, established the Industrial Policy Review Group. Its role was to assess the performance of Irish industry and, in particular, Irish-owned companies and to recommend appropriate policy changes. The report entitled *A Time for Change: Industrial Policy for the 1990s* was published in January 1992 (Government Publications Office). It is commonly referred to as the *Culliton report*. The creation of an 'enterprise culture', which is one of Culliton's key recommendations and encouraged by supply siders, has resurfaced in a number of other reports recently. These include

Employment through Enterprise, Government Publications Office, 1993 and *Shaping Our Future*, Forfás, 1996. For more, see endnote 52 in Chapter 15.

29 D. Ó Cearbhaill, 'The same, and more', *Fortnight*, February 1992.

30 In the Central Bank Autumn 1996 bulletin there is an article on the evolution of potential output in Ireland from the early 1970s. The conclusions relating to measurement, the output gap and the correlation with inflation are interesting. For more, read G. Kenny 'Economic Growth in Ireland: Sources, Potential and Inflation', *Central Bank Report*, Autumn 1996.

31 Industrial Policy Review Group, *A Time for Change: Industrial Policy for the 1990s*.

Chapter 14

1 Margaret Thatcher, *The Downing Street Years*, HarperCollins Publishers, 1993.

2 Jean Monnet, *Memoirs*, Doubleday, 1978.

3 Bernard Connolly, *The Rotten Heart Of Europe*, Faber and Faber, 1995.

4 When commentators are talking about a country's balance of payments deficit or surplus, they are generally referring to the current account balance unless otherwise stated. Remember, although the balance of payments statement should balance, each subsection may not. Hence, economists and journalists are explicitly talking about this particular component of the balance of payments.

5 The trade balance must be distinguished from the terms of trade which is simply the ratio of export prices to import prices, i.e. it reflects relative prices P_x/P_y. An improvement in the terms of trade implies that the prices of exports have risen relative to the prices of imports. In other words, we need to export less in order to secure a given quantity of imports. The terms of trade index can be found in any Central Bank quarterly bulletin.

6 The openness of the Irish economy has already been recognised in previous chapters (Chapters 8, 10 and 11). External trade as a percentage of national income is used as a benchmark to measure the openness of an economy. Ireland's ratio is over 100%. Belgium (114.5%) and Holland (86.8%) are two other examples of open economies. These compare to a figure of 41.3% for the UK and 17% for the US (Eurostat, *Basics Statistics of the European Community*, 32nd edition, April 1995).

7 In particular, we make no explicit reference in the text to the role that the price elasticity of demand for imports plays in determining the supply of the base currency (see endnote 8). The supply curve will only appear as a 'normal' upward sloping curve if the demand for imports is elastic, i.e. a lower exchange rate (higher import prices) leads to less imports and hence a lower quantity of pounds supplied. This assumption is implicit in the text when we discuss the supply of Irish pounds. In the case of inelastic demand, the supply curve will have a negative slope. Norton in his book *Economics for an Open Economy: Ireland* points out that this possibility could arise if the 'Home' country were ' . . . a large country relative to the rest of the world'. A discussion on the price elasticity of demand for imports (and exports) usually leads to some debate on the related topics of the J-curve effect and the Marshall-Lerner condition. A good description of both is included in Sloman's *Economics*, 2nd edition, Harvester Wheatsheaf, 1994.

8 With two currencies involved, there are two ways to express the exchange rate. We can express it as the number of Irish pounds per one dollar or as the number of dollars per one Irish pound. In the domestic (Dublin) foreign exchange market, it is customary to express the IR£/US$ exchange rate as the number of dollars per one Irish pound. The Irish pound is called the base currency and the US dollar is called the counter currency.

9 Explaining the exchange rate in terms of simple demand and supply analysis is the traditional approach to exchange rate determination. The other theoretical approaches are the Purchasing Power Parity theory (see Appendix 14.1), the monetary approach and the portfolio-balance approach.

10 Market participants, in the belief that the value of the Irish pound will be lower, sell the Irish pound today (known as selling short) with the intention of buying it back some time in the future at a lower rate. If this happens, the traders are left with a tidy profit from this Irish pound trade.

11 The deficits and surpluses recorded in the balance of payments are an indicator of whether a country is a net borrower from or a lender to the rest of the world. For example, under a flexible exchange rate system a current account deficit is matched by a surplus in the capital account. The deficit in the current account is financed by either running down its assets or borrowing from abroad. The latter is done by the sale of bonds and other financial assets, recorded in the capital account as a surplus. This signals that the country is a net borrower from the rest of the world. A country is defined as a net debtor when it owes more to the rest of the world than it is owed; a net creditor is owed more from the rest of the world than it owes.

12 The two great fixed exchange rate systems were the Gold Standard (1815–1914) and the Bretton Woods system (1945–71). The Gold Standard fixed the value of each participating currency in terms of gold. The Bretton Woods system, set up at the end of World War II, fixed all currencies in terms of the dollar. Not surprisingly, it was also called the Dollar Exchange Standard. An interesting feature of the Bretton Woods system was the adjustable peg, i.e. although currencies were pegged to each other, adjustments were permitted in the event of persistent imbalances.

13 The term used by journalists and the public to describe these hidden flows is the 'black hole'. It was a topic which caused controversy and much heated debate in Ireland during the early 1980s. In 1986, for example, a record net residual of –£908m (the minus sign reflecting unaccounted outflows) was recorded. Since then, the net residual has declined and in recent years the net residual has been positive. This improvement brought an abrupt end to the debate on the 'black hole'.

14 The US dollar is an example of a managed float. The value of the dollar was the main topic for consideration at both the Plaza Accord (1985) and the Louvre Agreement (1987). The former acknowledged that the dollar was overvalued and set as its aim a reduction in the value of the US dollar. The Louvre Agreement, although less concerned with the dollar's value, acknowledged the danger of volatile foreign exchange markets and called for greater co-ordination of monetary policy in order to provide a more stable economic environment.

15 Its predecessor was the Snake. The Snake was similar to the Bretton Woods system in that the currencies were fixed in relation to each other but with a fluctuation band of 1.125% either way. There was an additional 2.25% band allowable against the dollar.

16 'The Exchange-Rate Mechanism of the European Monetary System', *Central Bank Annual Report 1978*, Spring 1979. This article includes a detailed discussion on how the ERM operates.

17 From 1979 to 1987 the ERM operated as an adjustable peg system. Realignments were quite common in these early years. The convergence of many economic indicators such as interest rates, government borrowing and inflation rates among member states was partly responsible for the change in the system to a semi-fixed exchange rate system by the late 1980s. Until the autumn of 1992, member states were reluctant to realign their currencies. By August 1993, the bands of fluctuation were widened to 15% either way for all but two member states. The ERM had become more of a managed floating system rather than a semi-fixed exchange rate system.

18 In 1979 when the ERM was set up, the 6% band was perceived to be a temporary measure. In 1996, at the time of writing, the 6% band no longer existed and was replaced with an even wider band of 15%.

19 Divergent indicators also operate within the ERM. These act as early warning systems. When a currency reaches 75% of its 'theoretical maximum divergence' the Central Banks of the respective currencies are obliged to intervene. In practice, these divergence indicators have not played an important role in the day-to-day operation of the ERM.

20 The German mark is taken as an example because in practice it plays the same central role within the ERM as the dollar played in the Bretton Woods system. Over the years the German mark has assumed the role of an anchor currency.

21 This exchange rate is expressed in the same way as the IR£/US$ rate was expressed in an earlier section. With the Irish pound as the base currency and the German mark as the counter currency, we express it as the number of German marks per one Irish pound.

22 For more material on the currency crisis from an Irish perspective read Brendan Walsh's article 'Irish Exchange Rate Policy in the Aftermath of the Currency Crisis', *Irish Banking Review*, Autumn 1993.

23 The Irish pound was unilaterally devalued once before, in August 1986 when the currency was devalued by 8%. Although the 1986 and the 1993 devaluations were expressed in terms of changing the central rate within the ERM parity grid, the source for both devaluations was similar – a rising Irish pound against a weak pound sterling.

24 There were some benefits accruing to Irish industry from the currency crisis. For example, firms that were importing from the UK were benefiting from the change in the exchange rate. In addition, some Irish firms gained a short-term competitive advantage over their trading partners in Germany and other countries because of the fall in the value of the Irish pound against these currencies.

25 'Hedging' is practised by importers and exporters in order to reduce possible losses arising from fluctuations in the exchange rate. For example, suppose the Galway dealership for Volvo contracts for DM 1m of automobiles and has to pay for them in 30 days. If the Irish pound depreciates against the German mark during these 30 days, the cost of the automobiles in Irish pounds will increase. To ensure against an exchange rate loss the automobile dealer contracts to buy DM 1m at the forward exchange rate. This protects the dealer against loss due to depreciation. Unfortunately, the automobile dealer will not benefit from an appreciation of the Irish pound *vis-à-vis* the German mark. He is locked into an agreement at a specified rate. The practice of hedging involves a transaction cost. It is generally not used by small firms.

26 There are several different institutions within the EU. There is the Parliament, the Council and the Commission. The European Parliament has many functions. It is involved in legislation, in the budgetary process and has also a supervisory role. The Council acts as supreme decision-maker. It is the institution that makes the major policy decisions of the Community. However, the Commission is the initiator and the executive. The Commission implements Community decisions.

27 An excellent article outlining the timetable for the changeover is 'The Path to Economic and Monetary Union', *Central Bank Annual Report 1995*, Summer 1996.

28 The Council and Commission of the European Communities, 'The Treaty on European Union', Office for Official Publications of the European Communities, 1992.

29 This is of particular interest to Ireland. The reference value for the national debt/GDP ratio is 60%. In 1995 Ireland's national debt/GDP ratio was 85.9%. If applied strictly, Ireland does not meet this criterion. This would be the view of the German authorities. However, there is another viewpoint. It was written into the Maastricht Treaty that if a

member state's 'ratio of government debt to gross domestic product' is 'sufficiently diminishing and approaching the reference value at a satisfactory pace' then this is sufficient. This is a loose interpretation of the national debt/GDP criterion. The Irish authorities argue that if the above interpretation is applied, the reduction in the Irish national debt/GDP ratio from over 110% in 1987 to 85.9% in 1995 is sufficient to meet the criterion. The debate over how the currency criterion should be applied is yet another example of the many different ways in which the convergence criteria can be interpreted. It is written into the Maastricht treaty that each member state should observe the 'normal fluctuation margins provided for by the exchange-rate mechanism of the European Monetary System, for at least two years, without devaluing against the currency of any other Member State'. During the currency crisis of 1992–93 three currencies, some on more than one occasion, were devalued and the membership of two others was suspended. In addition, the fluctuation bands were widened from 2.25% and 6% to 2.25% and 15%. Those who support the move towards a single currency argue that the 15% fluctuation bands are now 'normal'. Hence, although the ERM has changed fundamentally since the days of the Maastricht treaty, the currency criterion can still be met through a loose interpretation of the rules.

30 The objections raised in the UK and in Germany are for very different reasons. The notion of 'rule from Brussels' and the move towards a federal state have little support in the UK. In Germany, the disquiet is over the loss of the mark which is inevitable on the changeover to the single currency. The Germans support a new European Central Bank similar to the Bundesbank which focuses primarily on controlling inflation.

31 On joining the EMS exchange controls became an issue. Prior to 1978 there were no restrictions on capital movements between Ireland and the UK. Furthermore, the exchange controls which Ireland imposed on the rest of the world were similar to those operated by the UK authorities. When Ireland joined the ERM, it extended her exchange controls to the UK. While all this was happening, the UK was dismantling its controls.

32 This division, incidentally, is similar to the split in the fortunes of the ERM itself. In the first few years realignments were quite common, exchange rates were volatile and little or no convergence between the member states took place. By the late 1980s things had changed. Realignments were fewer, exchange rates were stable and greater convergence was evident between member states. In fact, many commentators viewed the ERM by the turn of the decade as a *de facto* fixed exchange rate system.

33 From a theoretical perspective, a review of the literature on Optimum Currency Areas might be useful. Chapter 17 of Walsh and Leddin's *The Macroeconomy of Ireland* provides a brief insight into the theory of currency unions. A comprehensive analysis of the costs and benefits to Ireland of membership in the EMU was carried out by the Economic and Social Research Institute. For more, read *Economic Implications for Ireland of EMU*, edited by T. Baker, J. FitzGerald and P. Honohan, Economic and Social Research Institute, no. 28, July 1996.

34 The existence of a gap between the richest nations and the poorest member states of the EU has always been a lively issue. The structural funds and the EU commitment to 'economic and social cohesion' arose out of the debate on the 'wealth gap'. The progress of the peripheral countries, as a group, has been at best slow and at worst poor. Ireland has probably achieved most of the four (the others being Spain, Portugal and Greece) in the past twenty years. In 1975 Ireland's GDP per capita was 62.7% of the EU average. In 1996 it is approaching 85%. Indeed, some commentators argue that any further improvement may put Ireland's next tranche of EU funds in jeopardy. How's that for progress! For an interesting account of Ireland's progress within the EU read Kieran Kennedy, 'Real Convergence, the European Community and Ireland', Presidential Address to the Statistical and Social Inquiry Society of Ireland, 14 May 1992.

35 The weak version of PPP is written as follows:

$$\Delta E = \Delta P_{US} - \Delta P_{UK}$$

where

ΔE = the change in the exchange rate

ΔP_{US} = change in the US price level, i.e. US inflation rate

ΔP_{UK} = change in the UK price level, i.e. UK inflation rate.

The weak version states that changes in the exchange rate arise out of inflation rate differentials.

36 'Big MacCurrencies', *The Economist*, 15 April 1995. Ireland was not included in their survey. Ideally, an internationally traded good should be used in any discussion of PPP.

Chapter 15

1 John F. Kennedy. Speech, 1962.

2 Benjamin Franklin, *Thoughts on Commercial Subjects*.

3 See Rudiger Dornbusch's article on the Irish economy entitled 'Ireland's disinflation', *Economic Policy*, April 1989.

4 Central Statistics Office, *Statistical Bulletin*, CSO, June 1990.

5 Although used in both the US and Ireland, the CPI has a number of weaknesses. Its shortcomings include the use of a constant market basket despite frequent changes in consumption patterns, the difficulty in capturing changes in quality and the inclusion of mortgage costs which may explain why inflation is sometimes overstated. The 'core' or 'underlying' rate of inflation which some commentators prefer to use excludes mortgage rates.

6 The Household Budget Survey is conducted by the CSO. Between 7,000 and 8,000 rural and urban households complete the survey which is designed to provide details concerning the allocation of their income.

7 In Ireland, as from January 1997 the CPI is compiled monthly.

8 M. Friedman, 'The Quantity Theory of Money – A Restatement', in *Studies in the Quantity Theory of Money*, Chicago University Press, 1956.

9 It is possible for a given stock of money to finance a level of transactions many times greater than the value of the money stock itself. For example, suppose I spend £10 on an article. In turn, the seller then spends it on another article. Over a period of time, the same £10 has financed a number of transactions. This is the velocity of money.

10 Remember that the supply curve of labour is based on the assumption that work causes disutility. An increase in the real wage compensates for the disutility caused by work. For this reason, the relationship between the number of hours worked or the number of people working and the real wage is positive. Workers should be interested in their real wage, rather than their nominal wage because they are concerned about the quantity of goods and services which they can purchase.

11 Wincott Memorial lecture, London, 16 September 1970.

12 Replacing adaptive expectations with the rational expectations hypothesis (see Appendix 15.2) means that the AS curve is vertical in the short run. Any increase in the money supply immediately increases the price level and the level of output remains unaffected. This completely validates the QTM. Acceptance of the rational expectations hypothesis means that monetary policy is ineffective in the short run and the long run.

13 The 1995 Nobel prize in economics was awarded to Robert Lucas, a leading figure in the field of expectations.

14 The Programme for National Recovery (PNR) was largely responsible for the moderate increases in wages during the period 1987–90. According to the agreement, wages were to increase by no more than 2.5% per annum during the period of the programme. Subsequent wage agreements were less successful in limiting the wage increases of the public sector. The Programme for Economic and Social Progress (PESP) provided for wage increases of 4% in 1991, 3% in 1992 and 3.75% in 1993. Its successor, the Programme for Competitiveness and Work (PCW) awarded wage increases of 8% for the private sector over the lifetime of the programme as well as an 11% rise for the public sector over the same four-year period. All these programmes involved agreement by the social partners. Although centralised wage bargaining has brought many benefits to the Irish economy, there have being many criticisms of this period of corporatism in Ireland. In the words of one economist, 'The PESP and its predecessor agreements are at the core of our failure to translate GNP growth into jobs. There should not be another.' (Sean Barrett, in an article entitled 'Let's learn from the US on creating jobs' written for the *Sunday Independent*, 2 May 1993). For a more detailed review of wage determination in Ireland read James O'Brien, 'Pay Determination in Ireland', *Industrial Relations in Ireland. Contemporary Issues and Developments*, University College Dublin, 1989; and also William K. Roche 'Pay Determination, the State and the Politics of Industrial Relations', *Irish Industrial Relations in Practice*, edited by Thomas V. Murphy and William K. Roche, Oak Tree Press and Graduate School of Business UCD, 1994. For a background on the successor to the PCW (called Partnership 2000 for Inclusion, Employment and Competitiveness – its main commitment is a 9.25% increase over 39 months for public and private sector workers), read NESC No. 99 *Strategy into the 21st Century*, National Economic and Social Council, November 1996.

15 Exchange-rate policy has both demand-side and supply-side effects.

16 During the 1980s inflation had become 'public enemy number one' in the UK. Although there were considerable inflationary pressures in Ireland during this time, there was less attention paid to inflation. For one, the Irish authorities were more concerned with the state of the public finances than with inflation. Also, monetarists had less support for their policies in Ireland than they had in the UK. Although the inflation rate did fall during the 1980s it had little to do with the monetarist ideology. For an account of Irish inflation in recent times, see G. Kenny and D. McGettigan, 'The Inflationary Process in Ireland – An Overview', *Central Bank Report*, Winter 1996. An international perspective on current inflationary trends is given by R. Bootle in his 'thought-provoking' book *Death of Inflation – Surviving and Thriving in the Zero Era*, Nicholas Brealy Publishing, 1996.

17 US President Gerald Ford, *Weekly Compilation of Presidential Documents*, 10, no. 41.

18 Read 'Counting the jobless', *The Economist*, 22 July 1995.

19 If the number of unemployed decreases by 5,000 between 1995 and 1996, the number of people counted at the end of 1996 is 5,000 less than the number of people counted at the end of 1995. However, 15,000 new people may have become unemployed because they lost their jobs, finished school or returned home from abroad and could not find employment. On the other hand, 20,000 people must have found jobs, retired from the labour force or emigrated. In other words, a small change in the stock of the unemployed may mask larger flows of people into and out of employment.

20 People can receive unemployment benefits for a maximum of fifteen months after which they are paid unemployment allowance. This is means-tested and lasts indefinitely. It is commonly referred to as 'the dole'.

21 The natural rate of unemployment is a term used by monetarists and new classical economists. When the economy is at full employment, frictional unemployment is

inevitable. The rate of unemployment associated with full employment is called the natural rate of unemployment. It is also the unemployment rate which is consistent with a stable rate of inflation, hence the name 'the non-accelerating inflationary rate of unemployment' or simply NAIRU. There is evidence to suggest that the natural rate of unemployment in the US for example, has increased over time, from an estimated 4% in the 1950s to an estimated 6.5% in the mid-1980s. However, there is still considerable disagreement over what is the natural rate of unemployment and the extent to which it has changed. Estimates should be treated with caution! An interesting aspect on Ireland's NAIRU can be read in 'Hysteresis: a new concept in Irish unemployment' by George Lee, *Labour Market Review*, Summer 1991.

22 Marx and Keynes had very different views on the long-term prospects for the capitalist system. Whereas Keynes was largely optimistic about the future, Marx predicted a total collapse of the capitalist system. To date, Marx is wrong.

23 The insider-outsider theory is a relatively new way of looking at the behaviour of participants in the labour market. The insiders are those who already have jobs whereas the outsiders are those who are unemployed. Given the conservative nature of the labour market which confers advantages on the insiders at the expense of the outsiders, this model predicts no great change in the unemployment structure.

24 *The Jobs Crisis*, edited by Colm Keane, Mercier Press, 1993.

25 Brendan Walsh, 'Why is Unemployment so High in Ireland Today?', *Perspectives on Economic Policy*, Centre for Economic Research, UCD, 1987.

26 For a comprehensive examination of the unemployment problem in Europe, the proceedings of a conference with European unemployment as its topic were published in *Economica*, 53, 1986.

 On a broader level, the job creation record of the EU since the late 1970s has been easily surpassed by both the US and Japan. The reasons given for such a poor EU performance include the absence of full economic and monetary integration, adverse movements in the terms of trade, the rigidity of the labour market in the EU and its poor record on science and technology, research and development, innovation and entrepreneurship. In addition, it is significant that, according to flows in and out of the labour market, the high unemployment rates in the EU appear to be associated with a reduction in the probability of finding a job rather than an increased likelihood of losing one. This compares sharply with the US experience, see Charles Bean, 'European Unemployment: A Survey'. *The Journal of Economic Literature*, 32, 1994.

27 The increase in the price of oil was both price inflationary and demand deflationary for oil-importing countries, including Ireland. Expansionary fiscal policy only fuels inflation whereas contractionary fiscal policy slows down economic activity further. Policy-makers were faced with a dilemma. The Irish authorities opted for an expansion of fiscal policy. Yet, unemployment numbers increased, inflation rose, the budget deficit soared and the balance of payments deteriorated.

28 Although there are valid economic arguments in favour of borrowing to finance productive investment (capital borrowing), there is less justification for borrowing to finance current spending. Current spending is usually financed out of tax revenue.

29 It is argued that for fiscal policy to be effective, it must be counter-cyclical (see Section 10.2). During the mid-1970s the Irish economy was experiencing strong growth. The domestic economy was benefiting from an increase in world trade. Hence, restrictive fiscal policy was required. The incumbent government, however, opted for an expansionary phase. In the early 1980s economic activity was sluggish. The international background was unfavourable. Yet, driven by the urgent need to restore order to the public finances,

a highly contractionary fiscal policy was implemented. In both these periods Irish fiscal policy was pro-cyclical. Although the contractionary policy of the early 1980s was inappropriate on theoretical grounds, the Irish authorities were forced to practise fiscal rectitude because of the poor state of the public finances. In retrospect, the decision taken seems to have been the correct one. The same cannot be said for the experience of the mid-1970s. With the economy growing at a satisfactory rate, there was little or no need for a fiscal stimulus by the state. The long-term costs of such a policy outweighed the short-term gains.

30 The Coalition government of the early 1980s began to tackle the problem of the public finances. Both capital spending and taxation were targeted. Increases in capital spending were to be curtailed while at the same time tax rates were increased in order to boost revenue. Current spending was left largely intact. This policy mix, however, was flawed. Capital expenditure, assuming it is productive, is essential for the long-term prosperity of the economy. Moreover, capital expenditure was not the problem. The primary source of the high budget deficits was the growth in current expenditure. Yet the increases in current spending went largely unchecked. The increase in the tax rates was also considered as unhelpful. Tax rates were already penal. The revenue raised from the hike in the tax rates was not enough to compensate for the damage done to both the demand side and the supply side of the labour market.

31 There is considerable debate over each of these issues and their contribution to Irish unemployment. For example, the Irish authorities had little control over the level of interest rates. Hence, should blame be apportioned to our counterparts in Europe rather than to the monetary authorities in Ireland? The same argument applies to the value of the Irish pound. Membership of the ERM and the link with the German mark were helpful in achieving price stability. Was this achieved, however, at the cost of thousands of job losses? Finally, did the employed benefit, in terms of pay increases, at the expense of the unemployed? Were the centralised pay agreements successful or was there a need for local wage bargaining given the high unemployment numbers? For more material on these and other issues relating to Irish unemployment see A. Newell and J. Symons, 'The Causes of Ireland's Unemployment', *The Economic and Social Review*, 21, no. 4, 1990; F. Barry and J. Bradley, 'On the Causes of Ireland's Unemployment', *The Economic and Social Review*, 22, no. 4, 1991; and F. Browne and D. McGettigan, 'The Evolution of Irish Unemployment: Some Explanations and Lessons', *Labour Market Review*, 4, no. 2, 1993.

32 The existing tax system is recognised as being heavily biased against labour, the PAYE sector, low-paid earners and single persons.

33 'Ireland's disinflation' by Rudiger Dornbusch, *Economic Policy*, April 1989.

34 A feature of the Irish welfare system is the indefinite nature of unemployment assistance. This contrasts sharply with the welfare system in other countries where welfare payments are conditional on looking for work, retraining or participating in community service projects. This partly explains the differences between the numbers of long-term unemployed (over one year without a job) in Ireland as opposed to other countries. For example, it is estimated that the long-term unemployment rate in Ireland in 1993 was 8.9%. The equivalent figures in Sweden and the US (two countries where entitlements are 'limited') were 0.9% and 0.8% respectively (*Employment Outlook*, OECD, July 1994).

It is widely accepted in Ireland that the most serious issue confronting policy-makers is how to tackle the long-term unemployment problem. Some commentators argue for less state intervention. By making welfare payments conditional on a job search and by withdrawing them after a certain time period, the unemployed become less dependent on the state and more willing to seek out employment. Others argue that the solution lies in greater state intervention. The long-term unemployed, it is argued, are for all intents and purposes outside the labour market. In many cases their skills are obsolete. A job search is a futile exercise. More services should be provided to the unemployed, including training, counselling and interviewing techniques. The debate continues.

35 The evidence of a link between replacement ratios and unemployment rates is not conclusive. For a synopsis of the international and Irish studies, read 'Implications of Incentives for Employment. A review of the Economic Evidence', in *Expert Working Group Report on the Integration of the Tax and Social Welfare Systems*, Government Publications Office, June 1996.

36 The Family Income Supplement was introduced to provide financial assistance to low-income families. In our example, for a couple with two children and with gross earnings of £7,000, the FIS in 1995/96 amounted to £43 per week. This is a graded system. Mick's family would have received only £8 per week if his gross income had increased to £10,000.

37 It was estimated that the cost to the employer of providing a single employee on average industrial earnings an increase of £1 in net income rose from £1.82 in 1980–81 to £2.54 in 1990–91: a period when tax reform was supposed to be an important element of government policy. See Paul Tansey, *Making the Irish Labour Market Work*, Gill & Macmillan, 1991.

38 Ibid.

39 Arthur Andersen & Co., 'Reform of the Irish Tax System from an Industrial Point of View', a report to the Industrial Policy Review Group. A table of the tax wedge for the different countries is reprinted in NESC No. 96, *A Strategy for Competitiveness, Growth and Employment*, National Economic and Social Council, November 1993.

40 *OECD Economic Surveys: Ireland, 1990/91*, Organisation for Economic Co-operation and Development, 1991. Also, in Browne and McGettigan paper (see endnote 31).

41 Dermot McAleese, 'Solutions and Political Implications' in *The Dark Shadow of Unemployment in the Republic and Northern Ireland*. Studies, 82, no. 325, Spring 1993.

42 Dermot McAleese, 'Unemployment: The Macroeconomic Framework'. Published in Alan Gray's book *Responses to Irish Unemployment*, Indecon, 1993.

43 See M. Emerson, 'Regulation or Deregulation of the Labour Market', *European Economic Review*, 32, no. 4, 1988. Contrary to the opinion expressed by McAleese and others, there is evidence to suggest that Irish workers are not as protected as many of their EU counterparts. Ireland and the UK are the two EU countries (pre-January 1995) without a national minimum wage. Also, temporary and part-time workers in Ireland have been largely excluded from much of the labour legislation enacted in the 1980s. Goodhart claims that Ireland, along with the UK and Denmark, were the 'three most *laissez-faire* countries when it comes to closures and sackings'. See D. Goodhart, 'Ground Rules for the Firing Squad', *Financial Times*, 15 February 1993. This view was endorsed by the OECD in their 1994 *Jobs Study* report.

44 This package is similar in composition to the proposals outlined by NESC No. 89, *A Strategy for the Nineties*, National Economic and Social Council, October 1990. An alternative approach is given by Kieran Kennedy. He outlines four broad models which policy-makers in Ireland could pursue. For more on these options read K. Kennedy, 'Facing The Unemployment Crisis in Ireland', *Undercurrents*, Cork University Press, 1993.

45 The need for greater economic growth as a precondition for low unemployment is the conventional view which is largely endorsed by the economics profession. There are, however, a small number of dissenting voices. One such dissenter is Richard Douthwaite who argued that economic growth destroys rather than creates jobs. For Douthwaite, the

record speaks for itself: 'Economic growth has enriched the few, impoverished the many, and endangered the planet.' See *The Growth Illusion*, The Lilliput Press, 1992.

46 Adherence to the convergence criteria as outlined in the Maastricht treaty would result in a favourable economic environment. These convergence criteria relate to monetary variables such as interest rates, exchange rates, inflation rates, budget deficits and the national debt.

47 Brendan Walsh, 'Unemployment and Economic Performance in Ireland: The Background', *Labour Market Review*, 4, no. 2, 1993.

48 This view was endorsed by the EU Commission in their response to the unemployment crisis across Europe. In the *White Paper on Growth, Competitiveness and Employment* the Commission recommended more investment in 'lifelong' education and training, an overhaul of employment schemes and services, reductions in the cost of labour and greater flexibility at work. The OECD's *Jobs Study* of 1994 also called for radical job market reform. Their proposals included more flexible wages, an assessment of labour legislation, reforms of welfare systems and more relevant education and training programmes. These would ensure greater flexibility in labour markets and would help to underpin economic growth.

49 Read 'Employment and Unemployment' by J. O'Hagan in *The Economy of Ireland*, Gill & Macmillan, 1995.

50 The evidence relating to the cause and effect relationship between tax wedges and unemployment rates in Ireland is reasonably strong. Browne and McGettigan estimated that over 40% of the increase in unemployment in the first half of the 1980s was accounted for by the growth in the combined tax and real exchange rate wedge. See endnote 31.

51 A report on how to tackle the long-term unemployment problem in Ireland was published by the National Economic and Social Forum (NESF) in June 1994. Their conclusions include appropriate macroeconomic policies, early intervention in the education sector, the establishment of an Employment Service and specific policies directed at both the demand and supply dimensions of long-term unemployment. For more material on this read *Ending Long-term Unemployment*, National Economic and Social Forum, no. 4, 1994.

52 For more material on these and other recommendations read the report of the Industrial Policy Review Group, *A Time for Change: Industrial Policy for the 1990s*. For an analysis of the *Culliton report* read 'The Culliton Report – Three Years On' by Sean Barrett, *Irish Banking Review*, Spring 1995.

53 The popular view that shorter working hours and early retirement can reduce unemployment has been questioned by three eminent economists from the London School of Economics. In their fascinating book *Unemployment – Macroeconomic Performance and the Labour Market*, Oxford University Press, 1991, the authors R. Layard, S. Nickell and R. Jackman conclude that such policies are more likely to reduce a nation's wealth rather than reduce its unemployment. They are less empathic about the damages of protective legislation. In their own words 'They require review but not abolition'. A case is made for a reform of the wage-bargaining process along the lines of centralised wage agreements, in addition to an incomes policy. While advocating the use of active manpower policies in order to enhance the employability of the unemployed, they also conclude that unemployment will fall if benefits 'are of limited duration and subject to stronger job-search tests'.

54 Kieran Kennedy, 'Facing The Unemployment Crisis in Ireland', *Undercurrents*, Cork University Press, 1993.

55 Adam Smith, *An Inquiry into the Nature and Causes of the Wealth of Nations*.

56 David Ricardo, *The Principles of Political Economy and Taxation*.

57 Eli Heckscher, *The Effect of Foreign Trade on the Distribution of Income*, Ekonomisk Tidskerift, 21, 1919. Bertil Ohlin, *Interregional and International Trade*, Harvard University Press, 1933.

58 W. M. Corden, *The Theory of Protection*, Clarendon Press, 1971.

59 W. M. Corden, *Trade Policy and Economic Welfare*, Clarendon Press, 1974.

60 Mancur Olson, *The Logic of Collective Action*, Harvard University Press, 1965.

61 Paul Krugman, 'Increasing Returns, Monopolistic Competition and International Trade', *Journal of International Economics*, 9, 1979. Also, 'Scale Economies, Product Differentiation and the Pattern of Trade', *American Economic Review*, 1980.

62 Of course it could be argued that these regions would have remained poor even if they were not engaged in free inter-regional trade. But if this were true, it merely serves to highlight that free trade will not necessarily bring great economic advancement to a region with poor resources.

63 A. W. Phillips, 'The Relation between Unemployment and the Rate of Change of Money Wages in the United Kingdom 1861–1957', *Economica*, 25, November 1958.

64 The theory of rational expectations dates from the early 1960s and to a seminal paper, written by John Muth and entitled 'Rational Expectations and the Theory of Price Movements', *Econometrica*, 29, 1960.

65 See endnote 20 in Chapter 9.

GLOSSARY OF TERMS

Absolute advantage A country has an absolute advantage if it can produce more of a commodity than any other country with the same amount of resources.

Aggregate demand is the total output which is demanded at each price level holding all other variables constant.

Aggregate demand curve This shows the level of national output demanded at different price levels.

Aggregate expenditure is total planned spending on goods and services.

Aggregate supply describes the total quantity of national output supplied by all producers at each level of price.

Aggregate supply curve shows the output of GDP produced at different price levels.

Arbitrage refers to the buying and selling of goods in different markets in order to exploit price differentials and to make a riskless profit.

Arc elasticity measures the elasticity of demand over a price range using the midpoint or average price as the base.

Average product is the total output divided by the number of units of the variable input employed.

Average revenue is a firm's total revenue divided by the quantity sold.

Average total cost is total cost divided by the number of units produced.

Balance of payments It is a set of accounts showing all economic transactions between residents of the home country and the rest of the world in any one year.

Balance of payments capital account This is a record of a country's inflows and outflows of capital or assets.

Balance of payments current account This records all visible and invisible trade.

Broad money supply is defined as notes and coins in circulation plus current account and deposit account balances.

Budget line It illustrates the maximum combination of two goods that the consumer can purchase, given her level of income and prices.

Capital goods are durable assets used during the production process.

Capital stock All of the capital goods controlled by a firm.

Cartel A group of firms in a particular market who collude on price and output decisions in an effort to earn monopoly profits.

Ceteris paribus means that all other variables are held constant.

Comparative advantage A country has a comparative advantage in producing a commodity if it can produce that commodity at a lower opportunity cost than any other country.

Complements are goods that are bought and consumed together. This implies that if the price of one good falls, demand for the other good increases and vice versa.

Constant returns to scale exist when a change in inputs results in an equal change in output.

Consumer price index This index is designed to measure the average change in the level of the prices paid for consumer goods and services by all private households in the country.

Consumer surplus is the excess of what a person is prepared to pay for a good over what the person actually pays.

Consumption function It shows consumer expenditure at different levels of income.

Cost push inflation occurs when the source of upward pressure on prices is the rising costs of the factors of production in the absence of any corresponding increase in productivity.

Cross-price elasticity measures the sensitivity of quantity demanded of one good to a change in the price of another good.

Deflation A fall in the general level of prices.

Demand curve It shows the quantity of a good demanded at each price, *ceteris paribus.*

Demand, law of It refers to the inverse or negative relationship between price and quantity demanded, *ceteris paribus.*

Demand management is the collective term used to explain various government policies which influence the level of aggregate expenditure in the economy.

Demand pull inflation occurs when the total demand for goods and services is greater than the total supply of goods and services.

Demand schedule A table which indicates the quantity of a particular good which consumers are willing to purchase at various prices during a specified time period.

Deposit multiplier The multiple by which deposits will increase for every pound increase in reserves.

Depreciation is the value of capital which has been used up during the production process.

Derived demand for an input means that it is not demanded for its own sake but for its use in the production of goods and services.

Devaluation refers to a reduction in the value of a currency *vis-à-vis* other currencies in a fixed or semi-fixed exchange rate regime.

Diminishing marginal utility, principle of It states that the more of a commodity we consume, the less extra satisfaction we gain.

Diminishing returns, law of This describes the phenomenon of extra units of the variable factor added to constant levels of the fixed factor leading to a decline in marginal output.

Discount rate The rate which the Central Bank charges financial institutions that borrow from it for purposes of maintaining the reserve requirement.

Discounting is the process of reducing the future value of a sum of money or a flow of revenues to the present value.

Discretionary fiscal policy refers to deliberate, as opposed to automatic, changes in government expenditure or tax rates in order to influence national income.

Diseconomies of scale exist where an increase in the scale of production leads to higher costs per unit produced.

Disinflation is a reduction in the rate of inflation.

Double counting occurs if the expenditure on intermediate goods is included in the calculation of national output.

Economic profit is the difference between revenue and economic costs.

Economic rent is a payment in excess of the opportunity cost.

Economies of scale exist where an increase in the scale of production leads to lower costs per unit produced.

Elasticity measures the change in one variable in response to a change in another variable.

Equi-marginal principle This states that utility is maximised when the utility for the last pound spent on each good is the same.

Equilibrium implies a state of balance, a position from which there is no tendency to change.

Exchange rate The exchange rate between two currencies is the price of one currency in terms of another.

Exchequer Borrowing Requirement This is the total amount of money that the central government must borrow in any one fiscal year in order to match revenue with expenditure.

Expenditure multiplier It is the ratio of the change in income to the change in autonomous spending.

External reserves refer to the stock of foreign currency held by the Central Bank for the purpose of intervention in the foreign exchange market.

Externalities These are positive or negative by-products of production or consumption decisions.

First degree price discrimination occurs when every buyer is charged the maximum price that he is willing to pay.

Fiscal policy refers to the use of government expenditure and taxation in order to influence aggregate expenditure and, in turn, national output.

Fixed exchange rate system A system where member states' currencies are pegged to each other at rates which are usually agreed by their respective Central Banks.

Flexible exchange rate system This operates on the basis of market forces whereby the exchange rate between two currencies is determined by demand and supply.

GDP at constant prices measures economic activity in the prices of a fixed or base year.

GDP at current prices is a measure of economic activity based on the current prices of the goods and services produced.

GDP deflator This is the ratio of nominal GDP to real GDP expressed as an index.

Giffen good A very inferior good with an upward sloping demand curve.

Gross domestic product is the value of all goods and services produced domestically in the economy, regardless of the nationality of the owners of the factors of production.

Gross national product is the value of all goods and services produced by a country's citizens regardless of their geographical location.

High-powered money is equal to currency plus reserves held by the Central Bank.

Income effect It is the adjustment of demand to a change in real income.

Income elasticity of demand measures the responsiveness of the quantity demanded for a good to a change in income.

Increasing marginal returns means that over a range of production, each additional worker adds more to total product than the previous worker.

Indifference curve It shows all the bundles of two goods that give the same level of utility to the consumer.

Inferior good A good is classified as inferior, if demand for that good falls when income increases and vice versa.

Inflation A rise in the general or aggregate price level.

Inflation rate The percentage change in the price level from one period to the next period.

Inflationary gap An inflationary gap exists when the equilibrium of the economy is greater than the full-employment level of output.

Interest is the amount that is paid on a loan or the amount that is received on a deposit.

Interest rate This is the interest amount expressed as a percentage of the sum borrowed or lent.

Investment expenditure is the corporate or business expenditure on machinery, fixtures and fittings, vehicles and buildings. It also includes inventory build-ups of raw materials, semi-finished and finished goods.

IS curve It depicts the combination of interest rates and income levels that is consistent with equilibrium in the goods market.

Isocost line It shows all the combinations of two inputs that can be employed for a certain amount of money.

Isoquant It is a locus of points, showing the various combinations of two inputs that can be used to produce a given level of output.

Liquidity preference is the desire by households to hold assets in liquid form.

LM curve It depicts the combination of interest rates and income levels that is consistent with equilibrium in the money market.

Long run This is a period of time when all the factors of production can be varied in quantity.

Macroeconomics is concerned with the operation of the economy as a whole.

Managed floating exchange rate system A system characterised by an exchange rate which changes with the market forces of demand and supply. However, the Central Bank intervenes periodically, particularly when the currency is very weak or very strong.

Marginal cost is the extra cost incurred from producing an additional unit of output.

Marginal product is the change in total output obtained from an additional unit of a variable input, holding other inputs constant.

Marginal propensity to consume is the fraction of each additional pound of disposable income that is spent on consumer goods and services.

Marginal propensity to import is the fraction of an increase in income that is spent on imports.

Marginal propensity to save is the proportion of a change in disposable income that is saved.

Marginal propensity to tax is the proportion of any increment in income paid in taxes.

Marginal rate of substitution indicates the willingness of the consumer to give up a certain amount of one good in order to obtain one unit of the other good without changing utility.

Marginal rate of technical substitution is the amount of an input that can be replaced by one unit of another input without changing the level of output.

Marginal revenue is the change in total revenue resulting from a one unit change in output.

Marginal revenue product is the addition to revenue from the employment of an extra unit of an input.

Marginal social cost is the total cost to society from producing an additional unit of output.

Marginal utility is the extra or additional satisfaction that the consumer gains from consuming one extra unit of the good.

Market It is any arrangement whereby consumers and suppliers of goods and services exchange goods for goods or goods for money.

Menu costs refer to costs which are associated with adjustments in prices. Examples include the printing of price lists and the reticketing of merchandise.

Merchandise trade balance This is a record of transactions of merchandise exports and imports during a year.

Microeconomics studies individual decision-making units.

Monetary policy refers to the use of money supply, credit and interest rates to achieve economic objectives.

Monetary transmission mechanism is the process where a change in monetary policy affects aggregate expenditure and national output.

Narrow money supply is defined as the notes and coins in circulation plus current account balances.

Net factor income from the rest of the world is the outflows of income earned by foreigners operating in Ireland minus the inflows of income earned by Irish companies with foreign subsidiaries.

Nominal rate of interest The actual rate of interest which is charged when money is borrowed.

Normal good Demand for a normal good increases with income. If income falls, demand for the normal good falls.

Normal profit is the level of profit, below which the entrepreneur will not supply his expertise.

Opportunity cost The opportunity cost of an activity is measured in terms of the highest valued alternative foregone.

Potential output represents the maximum level of output that can be produced given a country's productive capacity.

Present value is the estimate of what the revenue stream of a capital asset is worth today.

Price can be defined as that which is given in exchange for a good or service.

Price ceiling is a form of price control. To help consumers, the government legislates that the selling price cannot exceed this maximum price.

Price controls are government regulations which limit the ability of the market to determine price.

Price discriminating monopolist is a monopolist who charges different prices to different customers for the same product for reasons other than differences in costs.

Price elastic The demand for a good is price elastic if the percentage change in quantity demanded is greater than the percentage change in price.

Price elasticity of demand measures the responsiveness of quantity demanded to changes in the price of the same good or service.

Price elasticity of supply measures the responsiveness of quantity supplied to changes in price.

Price floor is a form of price control designed to help producers. The selling price is not allowed to fall below a minimum price legislated by government.

Price index A price index measures the level of prices in one period as a percentage of the level in another period called the base period.

Price inelastic The demand for a good is price inelastic if the percentage change in quantity demanded is less than the percentage change in price.

Product differentiation means that the good produced by one firm is different from the good produced by the firm's competitor.

Production function This shows the relationship between the amounts of inputs used and the subsequent maximum amount of output generated.

Production possibility frontier shows all possible combinations of two goods that can be produced using the available technology and all available resources.

Public goods must be consumed by everyone in the same amount and no one can be excluded from consumption.

Rate of return on capital is a measure of the productivity of a particular capital asset.

Real rate of interest is the nominal rate of interest adjusted for the inflation rate.

Reserve requirement This is the percentage of deposits which banks are legally obligated to lodge at the Central Bank.

Returns to scale refers to the long-run relationship between changes in inputs and subsequent changes in output.

Revaluation is an increase in the value of one currency *vis-à-vis* other currencies in a fixed or semi-fixed exchange rate regime.

Savings function It shows the relationship between savings and disposable income.

Semi-fixed exchange rate system is a system where member states set the value of their currencies in relation to other participating currencies. However, currencies are permitted to fluctuate above and below these rates.

Short run This is a period of time where there is at least one factor of production which is said to be 'fixed'.

Shutdown price is less than the short-run average variable cost of producing a unit of output.

Small open economy refers to an economy that is so small relative to the world economy that domestic economic events have no effect on the rest of the world. The domestic economy is a price taker: it accepts world prices. Also, external trade (exports and imports) represents a high proportion of the country's GDP.

Substitutes Two goods are substitutes if consumers consider one good as an alternative for the other good. If the price of one good falls, demand for the other good falls and vice versa.

Substitution effect It is the change in consumption that is caused by the change in the relative prices of the two goods.

Supply curve It maps the relationship between price and quantity supplied over a particular period of time.

Supply schedule A table which indicates the quantity of a particular good which producers are willing to supply at various prices, over a particular period of time.

Supply-side policies are targeted at increasing the productive capacity of the economy.

Supply-side shock This refers to changes in the conditions of productivity or costs which in turn impacts on aggregate supply.

Tariffs A tariff is a tax on imports and is usually *ad valorem* which means that a percentage of the price is added to the price of the imported good.

Third degree price discrimination occurs when a market is divided into a number of submarkets.

Total utility is the total satisfaction that a consumer gains from the consumption of a given quantity of a good.

Transfer earnings is what a resource could earn in its best alternative use.

Transfer payments redistribute wealth. They include pensions, unemployment benefits, disability allowances and other payments.

Unemployment rate The number of people unemployed divided by the labour force.

Unit elastic The demand for a good is unit elastic if the percentage change in quantity demanded is equal to the percentage change in price.

Utility is the economist's term for the satisfaction or pleasure that we derive from consuming a good or service.

Yield curve This shows the way in which the yield on a security varies according to its maturity or expiry date.

INDEX